KV-393-815
SUPREME COURTS LIBRARY
LIBRARY COPY
Acc 2020/016

The Modern Law of Insurance

Second Edition

The Modern Law of Insurance

Second Edition

Professor Andrew McGee
MA, BCL (Oxon), Barrister
Professor of Business Law, Manchester University
Barrister, Kings Chambers, Leeds and Manchester

Members of the LexisNexis Group worldwide

United Kingdom	LexisNexis Butterworths, a Division of Reed Elsevier (UK) Ltd, Halsbury House, 35 Chancery Lane, London, WC2A 1EL, and RSH, 1–3 Baxter's Place, Leith Walk Edinburgh EH1 3AF
Argentina	LexisNexis Argentina, Buenos Aires
Australia	LexisNexis Butterworths, Chatswood, New South Wales
Austria	LexisNexis Verlag ARD Orac GmbH & Co KG, Vienna
Benelux	LexisNexis Benelux, Amsterdam
Canada	LexisNexis Canada, Markham, Ontario
Chile	LexisNexis Chile Ltda, Santiago
China	LexisNexis China, Beijing and Shanghai
France	LexisNexis SA, Paris
Germany	LexisNexis Deutschland GmbH, Munster
Hong Kong	LexisNexis Hong Kong, Hong Kong
India	LexisNexis India, New Delhi
Italy	Giuffrè Editore, Milan
Japan	LexisNexis Japan, Tokyo
Malaysia	Malayan Law Journal Sdn Bhd, Kuala Lumpur
Mexico	LexisNexis Mexico, Mexico
New Zealand	LexisNexis NZ Ltd, Wellington
Poland	Wydawnictwo Prawnicze LexisNexis Sp, Warsaw
Singapore	LexisNexis Singapore, Singapore
South Africa	LexisNexis Butterworths, Durban
USA	LexisNexis, Dayton, Ohio

Published by LexisNexis Butterworths

A CIP Catalogue record for this book is available from the British Library.

ISBN 10: 0406972974
ISBN 13: 9780406972972

Typeset by Kerrypress Ltd, Luton, Beds, http://www.kerrypress.co.uk

Printed and bound in Great Britain by CPI Bath Press, Bath

Visit LexisNexis Butterworths at www.lexisnexis.co.uk

Preface

It is five years since the first edition of this book was published. In that time there have been major developments in the law and practice of insurance. Most importantly the Financial Services and Markets Act 2000 has at last come fully into force, with its comprehensive scheme of regulation for insurance intermediaries in both general and long-term insurance. The FSA Handbook is a daunting document, but its remains essential reading for all those involved in this area of law. Although it is too soon to say with any certainty how well this scheme will work, the early signs are that intermediaries have done an enormous amount of work to be ready to comply with the rules.

The FSMA has also brought about the repeal of the Policyholders Protection Acts and their replacement with a new scheme.

Meanwhile, the courts too have been busy. There are important new cases in a number of areas, notably insurable interest, non-disclosure, third parties rights, continuing duty of utmost good faith (including fraudulent claims) and alteration of risk.

As in the first edition I have tried to focus on those areas which are of practical importance, and I have where appropriate drawn on the experience of my practice as a barrister to illustrate those areas. I have also again paid attention to the work of the Financial Ombudsman Service, which has now settled into a fairly well-honed rhythm in its work. Having been involved with its predecessor schemes for a number of years, I watch with interest and admiration the continued development of FOS.

As ever, I have many people to whom thanks are due. My students have over the years proved adept at asking the kinds of question which unexpectedly illuminate areas of the subject. Many of them are from other jurisdictions, and their knowledge of other insurance law systems has been very helpful to me. Clients, who have to remain nameless, have managed to stretch my knowledge of insurance law in unexpected ways – though some of them wish they had not had to do so!

The Editorial Staff of Butterworths have been very patient when the many demands on my time meant that the delivery of the manuscript was delayed. They have also done an impressively rapid job of turning that manuscript into the finished product you are about to read.

Finally, but above all, I have to thank my wife and daughter, who have now had many years' practice at smiling patiently when I am hidden behind the word processor and a mountain of case reports trying to get the latest opus finished. They make it all worthwhile.

The law is stated as at 1 February 2006.

Andrew McGee
Leeds
June 2006

Contents

Chapter 16 – Construction of policies (including fairness of terms)

Chapter 17 – Warranties and Conditions

PART D – THE INSURER'S LIABILITY

Chapter 18 – Causation

Chapter 19 – The claims process and indemnity

Part H – Particular types of policy

Chapter 34 – Life assurance

Chapter 35 – Personal accident policies

Chapter 36 – Permanent health insurance and critical illness cover

Chapter 37 – Motor policies

Chapter 38 – Household contents policies

Chapter 39 – Household buildings policies

Table of Statutes

Those paragraph numbers in **bold** indicate where the Statute is set out in part or in full

Table of Statutory Instruments

Those paragraph numbers in **bold** indicate where the Statutory Instrument is set out in part or in full

Table of European and International Legislation

Those paragraph numbers in **bold** indicate where the Legislation is set out in part or in full

Secondary Legislation

Directives

Regulations

Table of Cases

A

B

C

PARA

E

I

J

K

L

O

P

PARA

Q

R

Y

Z

List of abbreviations

AA 1996	=	Arbitration Act 1996
ABI	=	Association of British Insurers
ARF	=	Appointed Representative Firms
AVCs	=	Additional Voluntary Contributions
BDS	=	Business Development Services
C(AL)A 1990	=	Contracts (Applicable Law) Act 1990
CCA 1974	=	Consumer Credit Act 1974
CICB	=	Criminal Injuries Compensation Board
CIF	=	Carriage Insurance and Freight
CPR 1998	=	Civil Procedure Rules 1998
CPS	=	Crown Prosecution Service
C(RTP)A 1999	=	Contracts (Rights of Third Parties) Act 1999
DTI	=	Department of Trade and Industry
ECJ	=	European Courts of Justice
EL(CI)A 1969	=	Employer's Liability (Compulsory Insurance) Act 1969
EL(CI)R 1998	=	Employer's Liability (Compulsory Insurance) Regulations 1998
E&O insurance	=	Errors & Omissions insurance
FoA 1982	=	Forfeiture Act 1982
FSA	=	Financial Services Authority
FSA 1986	=	Financial Services Act 1986
FSAVCs	=	Free-Standing Additional Voluntary Contributions
FSMA 2000	=	Financial Services and Markets Act 2000
FSO	=	Financial Services Ombudsman
FSOS	=	Financial Services Ombudsman Scheme
GISC	=	General Insurance Standards Council
GMC	=	General Medical Council
HIPs	=	Home Income Plans
IA 1986	=	Insolvency Act 1986
ICA 1982	=	Insurance Companies Act 1982
ICS	=	Investors Compensation Scheme
ICTA 1988	=	Income and Corporation Taxes Act 1988
IFAs	=	Independent Financial Advisors
IOB	=	Insurance Ombudsman Bureau
IVAs	=	Individual Voluntary Arrangements
JCT	=	Joint Contracts Tribunal
LAA 1774	=	Life Assurance Act 1774
LAPR	=	Life Assurance Premium Relief
LAUTRO	=	Life Assurance and Unit Trust Regulatory Organisation
LOC	=	Letters of Credit
LPA 1925	=	Law of Property Act 1925
MDU	=	Medical Reference Union
MIA 1906	=	Marine Insurance Act 1906

MIB	=	Motor Insurers' Bureau
MIG	=	Mortgage Indemnity Guarantee
NDC	=	No Claims Discount
NHBC	=	National House Builders' Council
NU	=	Norwich Union
OBO	=	Office of the Banking Ombudsman
OFT	=	Office of Fair Trading
OPS	=	Occupational Pension Scheme
P & I club	=	Protection and Indemnity club
PAA 1867	=	Policies of Assurance Act 1867
PHI	=	Permanent Health Insurance
PIA	=	Personal Investment Authority
PIAOB	=	Personal Investment Authority Ombudsman Bureau
PPA 1975/1997	=	Policyholders Protection Acts 1975/1997
PPB	=	Policyholders Protection Board
PPI	=	Payment Protection Insurance
PTSD	=	Post-traumatic stress disorder
REA 1964	=	Riding Establishments Act 1964
ROA 1974	=	Rehabilitation of Offenders Act 1974
RTA 1988	=	Road Traffic Act 1988
RTRA 1984	=	Road Traffic Regulation Act 1984
SCA 1981	=	Supreme Court Act 1981
SGIP	=	Statement of General Insurance Practice
SIB	=	Securities Investment Board
SIF	=	Solicitors Indemnity Fund
SLIP	=	Statement of Long-Term Insurance Practice
TBA clause	=	To Be Arranged clause
TEU	=	Treaty on European Union
UCTA 1977	=	Unfair Contract Terms Act 1977
UTCCR 1994/1999	=	Unfair Terms in Consumer Contracts Regulations 1994/1999

Part A

Definition and regulation

Chapter 1

What is insurance?

1.1 The law of insurance is commonly recognised as a distinct branch of the law. The law regulating insurance may conveniently be divided into three parts. The first, *insurance contract law*, regulates the contractual relationships between policyholders and insurers. The second, *the law of intermediaries*, regulates the conduct of and liability for those intermediaries who are commonly found in the process of creating insurance contracts. The third, *insurance company law*, regulates the financial soundness and probity of insurance companies. This book is primarily concerned with the first of these three categories, to a lesser extent with the second and only to a minimal extent[1] with the third.

1 See Chapter 2.

The definition of insurance

1.2 There are various reasons why it is important to have some definition of what amounts to insurance or to a contract of insurance. First, there are common law rules, such as the duty of disclosure and the rules on insurable interest, which are relevant only to contracts of insurance. Secondly, there are statutory provisions which govern the carrying on of insurance business[1] and which regulate insurance contracts (or in some cases exempt insurance contracts from regulation[2]. In other cases the holding of an appropriate insurance policy is required by law[3]. The Statements of Insurance Practice, issued by the Association of British Insurers ('ABI')[4], apply only to contracts of insurance.

1 Insurance Companies Act 1982; special rules apply to insurance placed at Lloyd's. See Chapter 52.
2 Unfair Contract Terms Act 1977.
3 Road Traffic Act 1988, s 143; Employers' Liability (Compulsory Insurance) Act 1969.
4 See principally Chapters 5 and 6.

1.3 In these circumstances it is perhaps surprising that there is no proper statutory definition of 'insurance' or 'insurance contract', though some limited guidance may perhaps be gleaned from the provisions of the Insurance Companies Act 1982 ('ICA 1982'), which is the major statute regulating the authorisation and monitoring of insurance companies. It must be borne in mind that the definitions given in that Act are incomplete and that they are intended solely for regulatory purposes. Moreover, they are definitions of insurance and insurance business, rather than of insurance contract. Caution must therefore be exercised when trying to apply those definitions to the broader question of what is and is not a contract of insurance.

Insurance Companies Act 1982, s 95

1.4 This section reads:

> 'For the purposes of this Act "insurance business" includes:
> (a) the effecting and carrying out, by a person not carrying on a banking business, of contracts for fidelity bonds, performance bonds, administration bonds, bail bonds or customs bonds or similar contracts of guarantee, being contracts effected by way of business (and not merely incidentally to some other business carried on by the person effecting them) in return for the payment of one or more premiums;
> (b) the effecting and carrying out of tontines[1];
> (c) the effecting and carrying out, by a body (not being a body carrying on a banking business) that carries on business which is insurance business apart from this paragraph, of
>   (i) capital redemption contracts;
>   (ii) contracts to manage the investments of pension funds (other than funds solely for the benefit of its own officers or employees and their dependants or, in the case of a company, partly for the benefit of those persons and partly for the benefit of officers and employees and their dependants of its subsidiary or holding company or a subsidiary of its holding company);
> (d) the effecting and carrying out of contracts to pay annuities on human life'.

[1] A form of insurance arrangement under which all participants pay premiums, and the resulting pool is paid to the last survivor.

1.5 It is obvious from a reading of this provision that the definition is not intended to be exhaustive. Rather, it deals with some cases which might otherwise be considered doubtful[1]. The fact that this definition is relevant primarily if not exclusively for regulatory purposes is emphasised in s 95(a) and again in s 95(c) where the status of particular business as insurance business depends on the fact that the party carrying on that business is not also engaged in banking business. The reason for this is that parties carrying on banking business would fall for regulatory purposes within the ambit of the regulatory scheme applicable to banking[2].

Given the obviously incomplete nature of the s 95 definition, it is necessary to turn to the case law for guidance on the meaning of the term 'insurance' or 'insurance contract'. Here again some caution is necessary. As will become apparent in the following discussion, all the most important cases in this area have arisen in the context of regulatory issues or of apparently unrelated issues such as taxation. There are obvious dangers in trying to use such specific cases to induce a general rule for the definition of the concept.

[1] *Encyclopaedia of Insurance Law* (1992, Sweet and Maxwell), annotations to s 95.
[2] Now the FSMA 2000.

Modern case law

1.6 The modern law is normally considered to start with the case of *Prudential Insurance Co v IRC*[1]. This was a stamp duty case, where the question was whether the document which had been executed was a 'policy of insurance on a contingency depending upon a life'. The facts were that the contract required the purchaser to pay 6d per week until death or his 65th birthday. If he died before the age of 65, his estate would get £30. If he survived to that date, he would get £95. The difficulty in the case lies in the possibility of the payment of a sum of money if the purchaser survives, since there could presumably have been no argument about the proper outcome of the case if the document had simply provided for the payment of a sum of money on death[2]. Channell J dealt with the case by considering the essential requirements of a contract of insurance. He held that they were as follows:

- The payment of one or more sums of money, commonly called premiums, by one party ('the policyholder'). In return for these payments the other party ('the insurer') undertakes to pay a sum of money on the happening of a specified event.
- The event must be one which is adverse to the interests of the policyholder.

[1] [1904] 2 KB 658, Channell J.
[2] Ie a 'pure term' assurance policy.

1.7 It is this third requirement which was most contentious in *Prudential*, since the contract there was not one of pure term assurance, but rather what would now be recognised as a straightforward endowment policy, with a sum payable on death or a different sum payable if the policyholder lived to the age of 65. Whilst it is easy to see that death must be regarded as an event adverse to the policyholder, it is less easy to see how the same can be said of living to an advanced age. Channell J dealt with this problem by the rather artificial technique of saying that in the case of a relatively poor man, such as would have been likely to take out a policy for the sums involved in this case, living to 65 would be adverse to his interests because he would by then be less able to earn his living (this was of course in the days before the State Retirement Pension). A few years later, in *Gould v Curtis*[1] the point was considered again by the Court of Appeal, which adopted the somewhat more realistic approach of distinguishing between two types of policy. In indemnity policies the intention is that the insured shall receive no more than an indemnity for the loss which he has actually suffered. In policies of this type it is relevant to look for the prospect of loss when considering the validity of the policy. Property, liability and financial loss policies are normally of this type. In contingency policies, by contrast, the intention is simply that the insured shall receive a specified sum of money on the happening of the insured event. Life policies and personal accident policies are normally of this type. It must be recognised that there is nothing in any legislative provision which compels or even supports this conclusion. One important effect of the distinction is to increase the importance of the concept of insurable interest in relation to contingency policies, since it is insurable interest alone which effectively decides who may take out a contingency policy in relation to any given risk. The drawing of the distinction is nevertheless a practical recognition of the way in which the insurance market works. It would certainly have been absurd to hold that policies such as this were not contracts of insurance.

[1] [1913] 3 KB 84, CA.

1.8 Since then a number of cases have developed the concept of insurance. In *Hampton v Toxteth Co-operative Provident Society Ltd*[1] and again in *Hall D'Ath v British Provident Association*[2] It was held that there could be no carrying on of insurance business where no written policies were issued. However, these cases appear to turn on the fact that the relevant legislation[3] referred to the carrying on of business 'under policies of insurance'. The cases should therefore not be regarded as authoritative on the need for a written policy under the modern legislation, which makes no reference to this point. Indeed, it is obvious that the regulatory purposes of the modern legislation apply equally whether or not there is a written policy.

1 [1915] 1 Ch 721, CA.
2 (1932) 48 TLR 240.
3 Assurance Companies Act 1909.

Profit motive

1.9 Another point which arose in *Hall D'Ath v British Provident Association* was whether it was necessary for the insurance to be carried on with a profit motive. It was held that such a motive was essential. On the one hand it may be said that the regulatory purposes of the statute are relevant without regard to the profit motive. On the other hand, the statute referred to the carrying on of 'business', and it is normally understood that business must be done with a view of profit. This point is of course still relevant under the modern legislation. It is submitted, in the absence of authority, that at present the importance of regulating any kind of insurance should and probably would prevail over the technical point of construction based upon the meaning of 'business'.

Benefits in kind

1.10 In *Department of Trade and Industry v St Christopher Motorists' Association*[1] the Association operated a scheme for the benefit of its members under which they would receive the services of a chauffeur if they were prevented from driving for any lengthy period. In practice it appears to have been contemplated that the most likely reason for this would be disqualification resulting from an accident or from driving with excess alcohol. However, under no circumstances were they to receive benefits in cash. The Association was not authorised to carry on insurance business. Templeman J held that the arrangement in this case amounted to the provision of insurance. Although Channell J had included among his essential elements of a contract of insurance the payment of a sum of money on the happening of the insured event, this formulation could be seen, in the light of more sophisticated modern schemes, to be unduly narrow. The short-term consequence of this decision was that the Insurance Companies Regulations 1981[2] exempted motor vehicle breakdown services from the scope of the regulatory scheme. Later, however, the regulatory authorities became concerned at the way in which these schemes appeared to offer drivers a degree of protection against the consequences of reckless or drunken driving. It was therefore intimated that such arrangements would be prohibited if they were not voluntarily discontinued. They have now disappeared, though of course this does not affect the general point that benefits in kind are capable of falling within the regulatory scheme.

[1] [1974] 1 WLR 99.
[2] SI 1981/1654 now replaced by the Insurance Companies Regulations 1994, SI 1994/1516. On this particular point see reg 3 of those Regulations.

Statutory fund

1.11 One unusual situation which is worthy of mention here is that of the Solicitors Indemnity Fund ('SIF'). SIF was set up to allow the solicitors' profession to provide a degree of self-insurance, after it became difficult to obtain adequate cover in the market. SIF has never had an authorisation to carry on insurance business. It has sought to justify this state of affairs on the basis that it is in fact a statutory fund which does not carry on insurance business. In order to achieve this state of affairs the rules of the scheme (which are made under powers contained in the Solicitors Act 1974, s 37) seek to create obligations to make payments into the fund and rights to recover from that fund are established even though there is never a contract between those responsible for the management of the fund and those seeking indemnity out of the fund. Because of this lack of a contract, it is said that SIF never carried on insurance business. This was accepted by the Department of Trade and Industry ('DTI'), which agreed that SIF was not carrying on insurance business. The point is one of fine distinction. Clause 9 of the SIF Rules says:

> 'The following persons ... shall be provided with indemnity out of the Fund ...
> That is a rule that certain persons have a *right* to indemnity. That right exists as against the Fund, and it is therefore necessary to consider what is the nature of that right. If it is contractual, then there surely is a contract, and it would seem to follow more or less automatically that SIF is carrying on insurance business. The alternative must be that the right is one given by statute and that there is no contract. This is perhaps a way of formulating the essential difference between a mutual insurer and a statutory fund. In applying that distinction to the present case the following points may be worth considering.'

1.12 First, it is true that the SIF Rules persistently refer to indemnity, rather than to insurance, though that seems to be largely a matter of terminology.

Secondly, it is true that members of SIF acquire potentially unlimited liability for the debts of the Fund. This is relevant in the sense that it is incompatible with the idea that SIF is acting as a conventional insurer. However, it is not inconsistent with the possibility that SIF is a mutual insurer.

Thirdly, it is true that SIF does not seek to make a profit. It might therefore be thought that it was not carrying on any kind of 'business'. However, this is equally true of most mutual insurers. An interesting and striking comparison may be drawn between SIF and the Bar Mutual Indemnity Fund. The latter is, as its name implies, a mutual insurer, but it is authorised by the DTI, and it accordingly complies with the various rules in the ICA 1982, including the maintenance of an adequate solvency margin.

1.13 On balance it is submitted that SIF ought to be regarded as having carried on insurance business, though the obvious inconvenience of this conclusion may well make a court disinclined to accept it. Although SIF is now in run-off, the question is still of some practical importance in relation to a number of outstanding issues between SIF and solicitors who have previously been members of it, as well as being of general interest in relation to the limits of the notion of insurance business under the ICA 1982.

Discretionary benefits

1.14 In *Medical Defence Union Ltd v Department of Trade*[1] the defendants were a professional association of doctors and dentists. In return for their subscription members received, among other things, the possibility of financial and other assistance if they became defendants in proceedings alleging professional negligence. They could apply to the Committee of the Union for such assistance, but it was in the discretion of the Committee whether or not to grant it. The Union ('MDU') sought a declaration that it was not carrying on insurance business, whilst the Department sought a contrary declaration. On the face of it the only distinction between this case and the *St Christopher's* case was that here the granting of the benefits was a matter of discretion. Megarry V-C, after a lengthy analysis of the authorities, held that this was a vital distinction, so that the Union was not carrying on insurance business. The justification given for regarding this distinction as crucial was that the discretionary element in the conferring of benefits prevented the member's rights from being classed as 'money or money's worth'. A number of obvious criticisms of this view may be advanced. The first is that the possible benefit was obviously something which at least some members of the MDU valued – had they not done so, it is unlikely that it would have continued to be offered. The second is that there is no obvious good reason why a technical test such as whether something amounts to money or money's worth should be the crucial one for deciding whether what is offered amounts to insurance. It is true that Channell J's definition talked in terms of the payment of money, as well as of the insurer being under an obligation to pay, but general principles laid down in case law are not to be treated as if they were statutory provisions. Channell J would no doubt not have contemplated a scheme of this kind, and there was no reason to place heavy reliance on his form of words[2]. The third, which follows on from the second, is that this case is in effect a case about regulation. The reason why the parties were litigating this point is that it would decide whether or not the scheme in question fell within the ambit of the Insurance Companies Legislation[3]. Consequently, the proper approach would have been to ask whether the essential features of the scheme were such that for the protection of members and of the public generally it needed to be regulated in the same way as insurance companies. It is submitted that this question ought then to have been answered in the affirmative. The scheme has all the essential elements which make insurance a fit subject for regulation – it involves taking money in advance and then providing benefits at a later stage based on an assessment of the risks which have materialised. Thus, the same dangers of dishonest or incompetent underwriting arise as in any other scheme of insurance. It has been suggested that Megarry V-C might have been influenced by the fact that an insurance company is not allowed to carry on any other business, so that the MDU's scheme could not have continued in that form if it had been held to be a scheme of insurance. Such concern is misplaced for two reasons. First, if this really was insurance, then the policy reasons which require the ring-fencing of insurance business would have applied to it. Secondly, it would have been a simple enough matter for the MDU to set up an associated or subsidiary company, within which the insurance part of its operations could have been safely ring-fenced and properly regulated.

The decision has of course only the authority of the High Court, and it is submitted that it ought to be regarded as wrong and should not be followed.

1 [1980] Ch 82, Megarry V-C.
2 This is especially so, given that the *Prudential* case was about stamp duty, not about insurance regulation.
3 At that time the Insurance Companies Act 1974, but now the ICA 1982.

1.15 Insurance practice has naturally developed significantly since 1904, and at the present day there is a greater overlap between insurance-based products and those which are intended primarily as saving and/or investment vehicles. Some of this development has been fuelled by favourable tax treatment over the years for life assurance premiums[1] and for the proceeds of endowment policies. The most recent case on the meaning of insurance may be said to stem from these developments.

In *Fuji Finance Inc v Aetna Life Assurance Co Ltd*[2] the defendant insurers had entered into a contract with the claimant company. The documentation variously described the arrangement as a life assurance policy or a capital investment bond. The essential feature of the contract for present purposes was that the amount payable on the surrender of the policy was exactly the same as that payable on the death of the person named in the policy. It was accepted that the claimant company had no insurable interest in the life of that person. Thus, if the policy was one of life assurance, it was rendered void by s 1 of the Life Assurance Act 1774 ('LAA 1774')[3]. For the claimant company it was argued that the contract could not be a policy of insurance because the amount to be paid out was fixed and did not depend on the life or death (or date of death) of the life. It was also suggested that the appropriate way to tell whether a particular contract amounts to a policy of insurance is to ask what is the primary purpose of the policyholder in entering into the arrangement. The Court of Appeal rejected both arguments. As to the fixed amount argument, reliance was placed on a number of Commonwealth authorities[4], which had held that it was sufficient that the date of payment was uncertain, either because the date of death could not be predicted in advance or because the policyholder had the choice of surrender date. On the question of the primary purpose, it was observed that in many cases it might be difficult to tell with any confidence what had been the policyholder's primary purpose. Moreover, it is increasingly the case that life policies are taken out with investment as at least a significant part of their purpose (for example this is so in those pension plans which are also life policies) and it would be unrealistic to suggest that such arrangements should be excluded from the definition of life assurance. Insurance and investment are at the present day closely intertwined, and the most sensible approach is to say that there is no obstacle to a contract being regarded as both an investment contract and a policy of life assurance.

1 Abolished in 1984, though not retrospectively. There may still be a few 25-year policies benefiting from this relief, though the number must by now be small and steadily declining.
2 [1997] Ch 173, CA.
3 For the insurable interest issues arising in this case see Chapter 4.
4 *Marac Life Assurance Ltd v IRC* [1986] 1 NZLR 694; *NM Superannuation Pty Ltd v Young* (1993) 113 ALR 39; *Jones v AMP Perpetual Trustee Co NZ Ltd* [1994] 1 NZLR 690.

Contract made abroad

1.16 The fact that a contract of insurance is made abroad does not mean that it cannot constitute the carrying on of insurance business within the UK: *Re a Company (No 007816 of 1994)*[1]. This decision raises the difficult question of where business is considered to be 'carried on' in cases where the business supplies only a service[2]. The carrying on of a business of insurance involves a number of different elements, such as advertising, pre-contractual negotiation[3], underwriting, claims handling etc. The process of forming the contract, although clearly vital, is in fact only a relatively small part of that process, and some of the other parts of it must have happened before the contract can be formed. Even if the contract is formed outside the UK, it may very well happen that some of the other parts of the process take place in the UK, so that insurance business is in fact carried on here[4].

1 [1997] 2 BCLC 685, CA.
2 Ie not goods.
3 See para 1.17.
4 See also *Re Sentinel Securities plc* [1996] 1 WLR 316.

Negotiation and other pre-contractual activities

1.17 In *R v Wilson*[1] the defendant purported to offer insurance cover on behalf of a company, of which he claimed to be a senior employee. Neither he nor the company was authorised to carry on insurance business in the UK. Part of his defence was to argue that he had not carried on business because it did not appear that any contracts of insurance had been entered into. It was held by the Court of Appeal that 'carry on any insurance business' includes the processes of negotiation prior to the formation of a contract of insurance. Thus, carrying on business is a broader concept than effecting contracts of insurance.

1 [1997] 1 All ER 119, CA.

Reinsurance

1.18 In *Re NRG Victory Reinsurance Ltd*[1] it was held that reinsurance business is 'insurance business' for the purposes of the ICA 1982, s 49(1), and long term reinsurance business is therefore 'long term business' for the purposes of the Act. It would have been extraordinary had any other conclusion been reached.

1 [1995] 1 WLR 239.

Mutual insurance

1.19 Mutual insurance, most commonly encountered in the marine context, is an arrangement under which a number of parties agree to insure each other's losses[1]. It is common in such cases not to pay a premium (or to pay a greatly reduced premium at the outset), but instead to offer a guarantee of contributing to losses as required[2]. The best-known marine examples of mutual insurance are the Protection and Indemnity clubs ('P & I clubs'), which offer extensive protection against marine risks. Mutual insurance offers the advantages of not having to pay full premiums in advance, though it is usual to have a limited advance call at the start of the premium year, and of not having to contribute to the profit of any insurance company. On the other hand the insureds (also commonly referred to as the 'members') are also in effect the insurers and are therefore at risk if there is a sudden deterioration in the claims experience[3]. Consequently, a scheme of mutual insurance can only work if there are enough members to spread the risks acceptably. Another risk for insureds is of course that other members will prove unable to meet any calls on their guarantees.

Mutual insurance is also occasionally encountered elsewhere, one of the prominent examples being the scheme operated by the Bar, under which its members provide insurance against the risks of liability for professional negligence.

The fact that insurance is provided on a mutual basis does not exempt the arrangement from the normal regulatory requirements[4].

[1] Marine Insurance Act 1906, s 85(1).
[2] Such an arrangement is authorised by Marine Insurance Act 1906, s 85(2).
[3] Though this risk may of course be offset by suitable reinsurance arrangements.
[4] See Chapter 2.

Friendly societies

1.20 These societies are now regulated under the Friendly Societies Act 1992. Many of their activities do clearly amount to carrying on insurance business, even though they are in effect mutual organisations which do not have the classic profit motive.

Conclusion

1.21 It is perhaps a typically English phenomenon that after several centuries of leading the world in the provision of insurance English law still has no proper definition of the underlying concept. A common lawyer would no doubt point to the fact that the present arrangement appears to work perfectly well in practice, though a civil lawyer would be horrified by the lack of conceptual clarity in the present position. It is submitted that a proper analysis of the problem of definition reveals two important things, from which certain conclusions may reasonably be deduced. The first is the pre-eminence of regulatory issues in cases in this area. Given the importance currently attached to insurance as part of the financial planning of individuals, the proper conclusion to be drawn from this is that anyone seeking to provide a service which may reasonably be described as being of an insurance character is likely to find that activity drawn within the regulatory net. It is unlikely that a court will be sympathetic to artificial attempts to take such activity outside the definition of insurance business. The second conclusion is that the problem of identifying an insurance contract has proved much less problematic. *Fuji v Aetna* is apparently the only case of any significance where the issue has arisen in this form. That case is very important because it confirms that the modern developments in insurance and investment contracts are still to be regarded as falling within the definition of insurance contract, and the conclusion to be drawn from the case is that there will rarely, if ever, be any contract which has a discernible element of insurance but which is held not to be a contract of insurance.

Chapter 2

The regulation of insurance

2.1 There are various good reasons why the conduct of insurance business needs to be regulated more strictly than many other forms of business. Policyholders have to be able to rely on the competence and probity of those providing insurance so that the insurer will be able to meet any claims which may arise. The importance of insurance in modern life can scarcely be overstated, since it is used for financial planning (including pensions) as well as for the more traditional role of protecting against loss.

The regulation of insurance business ('insurance company law' to use the terminology adopted in Chapter 1[1]) in the UK takes a number of different forms, as will become apparent in the following paragraphs.

[1] See para 1.1.

Regulation of freedom to carry on business

2.2 This aspect of regulation is conducted primarily through the FSMA 2000 and delegated legislation thereunder. Much of the present regulatory structure is derived from and dictated by the EU Directives on the subject of insurance business[1]. It may be divided into:

(1) initial authorisation;
(2) capital adequacy requirements;
(3) fit and proper person requirements;
(4) ongoing monitoring.

The earliest legislation imposing control on the freedom to carry on business was the Life Assurance Companies Act 1870, which was succeeded by the Assurance Companies Act 1909. Both required the payment of deposits to the regulatory agency as a pre-condition of starting business, but did not create the kind of prior authorisation system which is in use today, since there was no attempt to assess the suitability of applicants – once the money was paid, permission was given. The development of EU law in the area of freedom to provide services[2] led to the Insurance Companies Act 1974, which was in turn replaced by the ICA 1982.

FSMA 2000 has collected together the regulation of all financial services activity in the UK under the control of the FSA, which operates under the auspices of the Treasury. For insurance business this represents a change from the previous arrangements, which were under the ultimate control of the DTI.

FSMA imposes a regulatory system under which prior authorisation from the FSA is required before carrying on insurance business[3]. That authorisation will not be given unless the FSA is satisfied that the managers of the business are fit and proper persons for the purpose[4]. Insurance business is divided into a number of classes, and separate authorisation is required for each class. It is possible and common to be authorised for only some classes of business.

The Act imposes requirements of financial solvency[5] on insurance companies. There are also ongoing accounting and supervisory arrangements[6], which may lead to the restricting or withdrawal of authorisation[7]. It is a criminal offence to carry on business without authorisation[8]. Each year the FSA removes a small number of authorisations, either in relation to specific classes of business or for all classes of business. For the purposes of this legislation a person carries on insurance business by engaging in pre-contractual negotiations or by issuing invitations to treat (which may be in the form of advertisements) as well as by entering into purported contracts of insurance[9].

It is also a requirement that those concerned in the management of an insurance company must appear to the FSA to be fit and proper persons. This rule does not affect those lower down the hierarchy of the company and therefore has nothing to do with the authorisation or monitoring of individual salespersons within the company.

These rules are clearly intended to address one part of the information deficit problems addressed above, namely the need for the purchaser to pay for the product in advance and then to trust that the insurer will still be available and solvent if a claim arises.

Permission to carry on regulated activities may be in respect of one or more regulated activities[10]. This appears to be a departure from the former rule in ICA 1982, s 16 that an entity carrying out insurance activities could not carry on any other activity. However, FSMA 2000 allows the FSA to impose conditions on the giving of permission[11], and it is still the practice to require different regulated activities to be separated. The purpose of this rule is to prevent insurance companies from putting policyholders' capital at risk by entering into other forms of business. The rule extends to a prohibition on mixing life and non-life business within the same company. In practice the rule is effectively circumvented by insurance groups which form a number of different subsidiaries, each conducting a different aspect of financial services business.

In *Secretary of State for Trade and Industry v Great Western Assurance Co; Secretary of State for Trade and Industry v Loxley House (London) Ltd; D&L Underwriting Agencies Ltd*[12] it was alleged that insurance business carried on in the UK by offshore companies had, in reality, been conducted on their behalf by UK brokers in a way calculated to mislead the regulatory authorities.

It was held that the ICA 1982 did not prohibit UK risks being placed with unauthorised insurers, merely the effecting or carrying out of such business within the UK – *Scher v Policyholders Protection Board (No 2)*[13]. Where a contract of insurance is made outside the UK, there may still be the carrying on of insurance business within the UK. However, insurance business requires a degree of continuity or regularity as an integral part of the way the insurer's affairs are conducted, so isolated, non-recurrent activities within a particular jurisdiction may not amount to carrying on insurance business there – this is a matter of fact and degree. Although the use of agents cannot circumvent s 2(1) of the ICA 1982[14] that does not apply to those acting as brokers. A distinction was drawn between brokers who act as agents for insured and those who act as agents for the insurer. On the facts there was no evidence to show that the parties had appreciated the need for authorisation on the part of the offshore companies and given the state of the law they could not be criticised for this omission. It was not therefore just or equitable to wind up the offshore companies for breach of s 2(1) due to the adverse effect this would have on their legitimate non-UK business and the lack of evidence to show that UK policyholders had been prejudiced by the manner in which their policies had been managed. It appears that these cases are not affected by the introduction of the FSMA 2000.

Sections 141 and 142 of the Financial Services and Markets Act 2000 ('FSMA 2000') give the Financial Services Authority ('FSA') additional powers to restrict the activities carried on by authorised insurers. The activities which the FSA can forbid such insurers to carry on include but are not limited to activities regulated under the FSMA 2000.

[1] For a fuller account of the European aspects of the subject see Part G of this book and McGee *EC Insurance Law* (1998, Ashworth).
[2] For a fuller account of this aspect of the subject see McGee *EC Insurance Law* (1998, Ashworth).
[3] The general prohibition on carrying on insurance business without authority is now found in FSMA 2000, s 19, whilst s 40 provides for the making of applications for permission. The scheme of prior authorisation is more or less laid down by the first generation of Insurance Directives (First non-Life Directive-Directive 73/239; First Life Directive-Directive 79/267, so that it would not be possible for the UK to make significant relaxations in the requirements, even if it were thought desirable to do so.
[4] FSMA 2000, s 41, imposing the conditions set out in Sch 6 to the Act; see also the FIT section of the FSA Handbook.
[5] FSMA 2000, Sch 6, para 5.
[6] FSMA 2000, Sch 6, para 4.
[7] FSMA 2000, Sch 6, para 4.
[8] FSMA 2000, s 19.
[9] *R v Wilson* [1997] 1 All ER 119, CA.
[10] FSMA 2000, s 40.
[11] FSMA 2000, s 43.
[12] [1997] 6 Re LR 197.
[13] [1994] 2 AC 57.
[14] *Stewart v Oriental Fire and Marine Insurance Co Ltd* [1984] 3 All ER 777, Leggatt J.

Effect of not being authorised

2.3 In addition to the criminal sanctions for conducting business without authorisation, an important question arises as to the validity of purported insurance contracts entered into by an insurer acting without the necessary authorisation. In the worst cases the question is of no practical importance, for a rogue unauthorised insurer will not have the funds to meet claims anyway. The point is of more importance in those cases where the offence is committed by accident, for example in the sense that an insurer writes a policy which falls within a class for which it has no authorisation, being at the time under the impression that the policy fell within a different class of insurance business, for which it *did* have authorisation.

In a series of cases in the 1980's it was held that the provisions of the ICA 1982 rendered unenforceable contracts written by insurers who lacked the necessary authorisation[1]. The position is now governed by FSMA 2000, ss 26–28.

[1] *Bedford Insurance Co Ltd v Istituto de Ressaguros do Brasil* [1984] 3 All ER 766, Parker J; *Stewart v Oriental Fire and Marine Insurance Co Ltd* [1984] 3 All ER 777, Leggatt J; *Phoenix General Insurance Co of Greece SA v Halvanon Insurance Co Ltd* [1986] 1 All ER 908, Hobhouse J, appealed to the Court of Appeal as *Phoenix General Insurance of Greece v Administratia Asigurarilor de Stat* [1987] 2 All ER 152 which had concluded that the original provisions of the ICA 1982 precluded the court from allowing policyholders to enforce such contracts because the Act forbade, among other things, the 'carrying out' of policies of insurance where there was no authorisation.

2.4 FSMA 2000, s 26 provides that an agreement made by a person in the course of carrying on a regulated activity in contravention of the general prohibition is unenforceable against the other party[1]. The other party is entitled to recover any money or other property paid or transferred by him under the agreement; and compensation for any loss sustained by him as a result of having parted with it[2]. The section is not retrospective[3].

[1] Section 26(1).
[2] Section 26(2).
[3] Section 26(3).

2.5 An agreement made by an authorised person in the course of carrying on a regulated activity (not in contravention of the general prohibition), but in consequence of something said or done by another person ('the third party') in the course of a regulated activity carried on by the third party in contravention of the general prohibition, is unenforceable against the other party[1]. The other party is entitled to recover any money or other property paid or transferred by him under the agreement; and compensation for any loss sustained by him as a result of having parted with it[2]. The section is not retrospective[3].

[1] Section 27(1).
[2] Section 27(2).
[3] Section 27(3).

2.6 However, both section 26 and section 27 are subject to section 28, which provides as follows:

> '... The amount of compensation recoverable under either section is–
> (a) the amount agreed by the parties; or
> (b) on the application of either party, the amount determined by the court[1].'

(However, If the court is satisfied that it is just and equitable in the circumstances of the case, it may allow the agreement to be enforced; or money and property paid or transferred under the agreement to be retained[2]. This sub-section resolves doubts which had arisen under the predecessors to this legislation[3] about the possibly absolute character of the retain to avoid the policy and recover back money paid. The following sub-sections of section 28 also deal with possible consequences of avoidance.)

In considering whether to allow the agreement to be enforced or (as the case may be) the money or property paid or transferred under the agreement to be retained the court must, if the case arises as a result of section 26, have regard to whether the person carrying on the regulated activity concerned reasonably believed that he was not contravening the general prohibition by making the agreement. If the case arises as a result of section 27, the court must have regard to whether the provider knew that the third party was (in carrying on the regulated activity) contravening the general prohibition[4].

[1] Section 28(2).
[2] Section 28(3).
[3] FSA 1985, ss 5 and 132.
[4] Section 28(4)–(6).

2.7 If the person against whom the agreement is unenforceable elects not to perform the agreement, or as a result of this section, recovers money paid or other property transferred by him under the agreement, he must repay any money and return any other property received by him under the agreement[1].

[1] Section 28(7).

Transfer of long-term business

2.8 Where it is proposed to carry out a scheme under which the whole or part of the long-term business carried on by an insurance company is to be transferred to another body, whether incorporated or not, the transferor company or the transferee company may apply to the court, by petition, for an order sanctioning the scheme[1]. In *Re Hill Samuel Life Assurance Ltd; Re Ambassador Life Co Ltd*[2] the principles to be applied when considering whether to sanction a scheme for the transfer of long-term insurance business were considered. Rimer J held that the vital question is whether the scheme which is proposed is fair as between the different classes of affected persons. This may be regarded as a short way of stating the principles laid down by Hoffmann J in *Re London Life Association Ltd*[3], namely that account must be taken of the fact that the board of the proposing transferors must have concluded that the scheme is in the best interests of the transferors. At the same time it is necessary to see whether any policyholders, employees or other persons will be adversely affected by the scheme. However, even if there are adverse effects on some or all of these groups, it does not automatically follow that the scheme must be rejected. In deciding this question it is necessary to have regard primarily to the actuarial report which is required to accompany the scheme.

It may well be observed that the criteria mentioned here are very general, though that is perhaps an inevitable feature of a discretion which by its nature will fall to be exercised in many different situations. A more pertinent point is whether there is ever any real likelihood that an application made by an authorised insurer will fail. It may be assumed that the actuarial report accompanying the application will invariably be favourable-an insurer which cannot obtain such a report is unlikely to proceed with the application. This report will carry great weight. Often, the application will not be opposed. Relatively few policyholders will have the resources to oppose, so the only likely opponent is the Secretary of State. It is suggested that the only situation in which a real battle over the transfer is at all likely is where the Secretary of State for some reason chooses to oppose the transfer. Otherwise, a well-prepared application is likely to be little more than a formality.

The FSMA 2000 introduces further requirements in the case of a cross-border transfer[4]. Section 111 provides that the court must be satisfied firstly that the appropriate certificates have been obtained. These are (in all cases) a certificate to the effect that, taking the proposed transfer into account) the transferee possesses, or will possess before the scheme takes effect, the necessary margin of solvency, or that there is no necessary margin of solvency applicable to the transferee.

If the authorised person concerned is a UK authorised person who has received authorisation under Article 6 of the first life insurance directive or of the first non-life insurance directive from the Authority, and the establishment from which the business is to be transferred under the proposed insurance business transfer scheme is in an EEA State other than the UK, then the necessary certificate is one given by the FSA. This certificate declares that the host State regulator has been notified of the proposed scheme and that that regulator has responded to the notification, or that it has not responded but the period of three months beginning with the notification has elapsed.

If the authorised person concerned has received authorisation under Article 6 of the first life insurance directive from the Authority, the proposed transfer relates to business which consists of the effecting or carrying out of contracts of long-term insurance, and as regards any policy which is included in the proposed transfer and which evidences a contract of insurance (other than reinsurance), an EEA State other than the UK is the State of the commitment, then the necessary certificate is one given by the FSA. This certificate declares that the authority responsible for supervising persons who effect or carry out contracts of insurance in the State of the commitment has been notified of the proposed scheme and that that authority has consented to the proposed scheme, or the period of three months beginning with the notification has elapsed and that authority has not refused its consent.

If the authorised person concerned has received authorisation under Article 6 of the first non-life insurance directive from the FSA, the business to which the proposed insurance business transfer scheme relates is business which consists of the effecting or carrying out of contracts of general insurance, and as regards any policy which is included in the proposed transfer and which evidences a contract of insurance (other than reinsurance), the risk is situated in an EEA State other than the UK, then the necessary certificate is one given by the FSA. This certificate declares that the authority responsible for supervising persons who effect or carry out contracts of insurance in the EEA State in which the risk is situated has been notified of the proposed scheme and that that authority has consented to the proposed scheme or the period of three months beginning with the notification has elapsed and that authority has not refused its consent.

The court must then be satisfied that the transferee has the authorisation required (if any) to enable the business, or part of the business, which is to be transferred to be carried on in the place to which it is to be transferred (or will have it before the scheme takes effect). Finally, the court must consider that, in all the circumstances of the case, it is appropriate to sanction the scheme.

1 FSMA 2000, s 111 and Sch 12.
2 [1998] 3 All ER 176.
3 21 February 1989, unreported.
4 For the cross-border aspects of the subject generally see Chapters 30–33.

THE FSA Handbook

2.9 The FSA Handbook consists of delegated legislation made by the FSA by virtue of its powers under FSMA 2000. The Handbook is now a document of fundamental importance in understanding the regulation of insurance business, because many of the detailed provisions are found in it. The FSA has extensive powers to amend the Handbook, and the best place to find an up-to-date version is online[1]. Many of its provisions are considered in detail elsewhere in this book[2]. Sections which are of particular relevance in the present Chapter are PRIN, dealing with the fundamental obligations of all firms under the regulatory system, COND, the minimum standards for becoming and remaining authorised, APER, the fundamental obligations of approved persons and FIT, the minimum standards for becoming and remaining an approved person.

1 At www.fsa.gov.uk/pages/handbook.
2 Notably Chapter 6 dealing with intermediaries and Chapter 27 dealing with the Financial Services Compensation Scheme.

Fundamental obligations of all firms

2.10 These are as follows[1]:

(1) **Integrity** – A firm must conduct its business with integrity.
(2) **Skill, care and diligence** – A firm must conduct its business with due skill, care and diligence.
(3) **Management and control** – A firm must take reasonable care to organise and control its affairs responsibly and effectively, with adequate risk management systems.
(4) **Financial prudence** – A firm must maintain adequate financial resources.
(5) **Market conduct** – A firm must observe proper standards of market conduct.
(6) **Customers' interests** – A firm must pay due regard to the interests of its customers and treat them fairly.
(7) **Communications with clients** – A firm must pay due regard to the information needs of its clients, and communicate information to them in a way which is clear, fair and not misleading.
(8) **Conflicts of interest** – A firm must manage conflicts of interest fairly, both between itself and its customers and between a customer and another client.
(9) **Customers: relationships of trust** – A firm must take reasonable care to ensure the suitability of its advice and discretionary decisions for any customer who is entitled to rely upon its judgment.

(10) **Clients' assets** – A firm must arrange adequate protection for clients' assets when it is responsible for them.
(11) **Relations with regulators** – A firm must deal with its regulators in an open and cooperative way, and must disclose to the FSA appropriately anything relating to the firm of which the FSA would reasonably expect notice.

It can be seen that these principles are couched in the most general and aspirational of terms. Whilst they form a useful framework for the detailed rules, they do not by themselves give rise to specific obligations.

1 FSA Handbook PRIN.

Fit and Proper Person Requirements

2.11 These are contained in the FIT section of the FSA Handbook. The criteria may be divided into three principal issues-honesty, integrity and reputation, competence and capability, financial soundness[1].

1 FIT 2.

2.12 As to honesty integrity and reputation the issues which the FSA will consider include the following[1]:

(1) whether the person has been convicted of any criminal offence; this must include, where relevant, any spent convictions excepted under the Rehabilitation of Offenders Act 1974 (Exceptions) Order 1975 (see Articles 3 and 4 of the Order); particular consideration will be given to offences of dishonesty, fraud, financial crime or an offence whether or not in the United Kingdom or other offences under legislation relating to companies, building societies, industrial and provident societies, credit unions, friendly societies, banking and or other financial services, insolvency, consumer credit companies, insurance, and consumer protection, money laundering, market manipulation or insider dealing;
(2) whether the person has been the subject of any adverse finding or any settlement in civil proceedings, particularly in connection with investment or other financial business, misconduct, fraud or the formation or management of a body corporate;
(3) whether the person has been the subject of, or interviewed in the course of, any existing or previous investigation or disciplinary proceedings, by the FSA, by other regulatory authorities (including a previous regulator), clearing houses and exchanges, professional bodies, or government bodies or agencies;
(4) whether the person is or has been the subject of any proceedings of a disciplinary or criminal nature, or has been notified of any potential proceedings or of any investigation which might lead to those proceedings;
(5) whether the person has contravened any of the requirements and standards of the regulatory system or the equivalent standards or requirements of other regulatory authorities (including a previous regulator), clearing houses and exchanges, professional bodies, or government bodies or agencies;
(6) whether the person has been the subject of any justified complaint relating to regulated activities;

(7) whether the person has been involved with a company, partnership or other organisation that has been refused registration, authorisation, membership or a licence to carry out a trade, business or profession, or has had that registration, authorisation, membership or licence revoked, withdrawn or terminated, or has been expelled by a regulatory or government body;
(8) whether, as a result of the removal of the relevant licence, registration or other authority, the person has been refused the right to carry on a trade, business or profession requiring a licence, registration or other authority;
(9) whether the person has been a director, partner, or concerned in the management, of a business that has gone into insolvency, liquidation or administration while the person has been connected with that organisation or within one year of that connection;
(10) whether the person, or any business with which the person has been involved, has been investigated, disciplined, censured or suspended or criticised by a regulatory or professional body, a court or Tribunal, whether publicly or privately;
(11) whether the person has been dismissed, or asked to resign and resigned, from employment or from a position of trust, fiduciary appointment or similar;
(12) whether the person has ever been disqualified from acting as a director or disqualified from acting in any managerial capacity;
(13) whether, in the past, the person has been candid and truthful in all his dealings with any regulatory body and whether the person demonstrates a readiness and willingness to comply with the requirements and standards of the regulatory system and with other legal, regulatory and professional requirements and standards.

[1] FIT 2.1.

2.13 As to competence and capability the listed criteria are[1]:

(1) whether the person satisfies the relevant requirements of the FSA's Training and Competence sourcebook (TC) in relation to the controlled function the person performs or is intended to perform;
(2) whether the person has demonstrated by experience and training that the person is able, or will be able if approved, to perform the controlled function.

[1] FIT 2.2.

2.14 As to financial soundness the listed criteria are[1]:

(1) whether the person has been the subject of any judgment debt or award, in the United Kingdom or elsewhere, that remains outstanding or was not satisfied within a reasonable period;
(2) whether, in the United Kingdom or elsewhere, the person has made any arrangements with his creditors, filed for bankruptcy, had a bankruptcy petition served on him, been adjudged bankrupt, been the subject of a bankruptcy restrictions order (including an interim bankruptcy restrictions order), offered a bankruptcy restrictions undertaking, had assets sequestrated, or been involved in proceedings relating to any of these.

[1] FIT 2.3.

Conduct of business rules

2.15 These are now found in the COB (for general insurance) and ICOB (for investment policies) sections of the FSA Handbook. The most important parts of these in the context of insurance contracts are those dealing with product disclosure and the role of intermediaries. There are examined in detail in Chapter 7. However, it is also appropriate at this point to note the APER section of the handbook, which deals with the obligations of approved persons. APER 2.1 is a statement of principle issued under FSMA 2000, s 64, and its terms are as follows:

> '**Statement of Principle 1**: An approved person must act with integrity in carrying out his controlled function.'

The guidance in APER 4 indicates conduct which is likely to be regarded as not complying with this principle, as follows[1]:

- deliberately misleading (or attempting to mislead) by act or omission: a client; or his firm (or its auditors or an actuary appointed by his firm under SUP 4 (Actuaries)); or the FSA;
- falsifying documents;
- misleading a client about the risks of an investment;
- misleading a client about the charges or surrender penalties of investment products;
- misleading a client about the likely performance of investment products by providing inappropriate projections of future investment returns;
- misleading a client by informing him that products require only a single payment when that is not the case;
- deliberately recommending an investment to a customer, or carrying out a discretionary transaction for a customer where the approved person knows that he is unable to justify its suitability for that customer.

> '**Statement of Principle 2:** An approved person must act with due skill, care and diligence in carrying out his controlled function.'

The relevant APER 4 guidance on this is as follows:

- failing to inform: a customer; or his firm (or its auditors or an actuary appointed by his firm under SUP 4 Actuaries)); of material information in circumstances where he was aware, or ought to have been aware, of such information, and of the fact that he should provide it;
- failing to explain the risks of an investment to a customer;
- failing to disclose to a customer details of the charges or surrender penalties of investment products;
- recommending an investment to a customer, or carrying out a discretionary transaction for a customer, where he does not have reasonable grounds to believe that it is suitable for that customer;
- failing without good reason to disclose the existence of a conflict of interest in connection with dealings with a client.

> '**Statement of Principle 3:** An approved person must observe proper standards of market conduct in carrying out his controlled function.'

This is primarily relevant in securities markets and does not call for further comment here.

> '**Statement of Principle 4:** An approved person must deal with the FSA and with other regulators in an open and cooperative way and must disclose appropriately any information of which the FSA would reasonably expect notice.'

This is of relevance to the general standard of conduct of an approved person, but has no specific relevant to insurance business.

> '**Statement of Principle 5:** An approved person performing a significant influence function must take reasonable steps to ensure that the business of the firm for which he is responsible in his controlled function is organised so that it can be controlled effectively.
> **Statement of Principle 6:** An approved person performing a significant influence function must exercise due skill, care and diligence in managing the business of the firm for which he is responsible in his controlled function.
> **Statement of Principle 7:** An approved person performing a significant influence function must take reasonable steps to ensure that the business of the firm for which he is responsible in his controlled function complies with the relevant requirements and standards of the regulatory system.'

These relate to the exercise of managerial functions and are not specifically related to insurance business.

Like the PRIN section of the Handbook, this may be regarded as primarily aspirational. However, APER 4, whose provisions are inserted at the appropriate placcs above, gives more specific guidance as to conduct which the FSA is likely to regard as not complying with the principles.

[1] These extracts are limited to those matters which are particularly relevant to insurance business.

Complaints-handling schemes

2.16 It is open to debate whether complaints-handling mechanisms such as Ombudsman schemes should be regarded as part of the regulatory apparatus. These schemes are clearly distinguishable from other bodies considered here in that they act only *ex post facto* and deal with specific cases rather than addressing general principles. It is not a formal part of their agenda to be involved in setting and maintaining general standards. On the other hand this formalistic account of the rules of these schemes may justly be regarded as somewhat unrealistic. First, it is clear that more traditional regulatory agencies may also have a disciplinary function which is exercised in relation to particular cases, even if that is not their primary function. Secondly, there can be no doubt that the pronouncements of the various Ombudsmen active in this sector do in practice have the effect of laying down standards which are of general importance-the industries concerned take note of what the Ombudsman says and adjust their complaints-handling procedures accordingly. For these reasons the Ombudsman schemes will be treated in the present context as forming part of the regulatory apparatus, though account will obviously be taken of the limitations of their regulatory role.

The FSMA 2000 has created a new Ombudsman scheme, the Financial Services Ombudsman ('FSO'), which has absorbed both the IOB and the PIAOB, as well as other Ombudsman schemes previously existing in financial services. Membership of the new scheme is compulsory for all regulated organisations, decisions are binding on the member but not on the complainant, and the Ombudsman is required to make a fair and reasonable decision. There has been considerable continuity of personnel between the old schemes and the new scheme[1], so it is not surprising to find that the ethos of the previous schemes has been very largely continued. Throughout the present work the decisions of the various Ombudsman schemes are noted and discussed when they impact on the various issues considered. Although the Ombudsman schemes make binding decisions only in relation to personal lines policies[2] and small businesses[3], their decisions often illuminate difficult questions of insurance law generally. Even where it seems clear that an Ombudsman has made a decision which does not follow the strict law, that very fact frequently helps to clarify thinking about what the law is.

1 The Chief Ombudsman is Walter Merricks, who was previously Insurance Ombudsman.
2 Ie the policyholder does not act in the course of any business of his.
3 Ie businesses with a turnover of not more than £1million per annum.

Conclusion

2.17 The above sketch does no more than explain the general outlines of the regulatory system for insurance in the UK. Clearly the system is fragmented. Some of it depends on EC legislation, some depends on purely domestic legislation, other parts reflect the traditional UK preference for some form of self-regulation. It could not be claimed that there is any overall coherent pattern of regulation. This is no doubt partly explained by the *ad hoc* way in which the system has grown up, but it may also be relevant to observe that different parts of the regulatory structure address quite different objectives. The creation of the FSA will, it is hoped, bring some greater degree of coherence to the regulation of the marketing and selling of policies, but beyond that the fragmentation is likely to continue.

Part B

Contractual formation

Chapter 3

Offer and acceptance

The importance of the question

3.1 The question when the contract of insurance is formed is important for various reasons. It marks the point at which both parties are bound and the earliest point at which the insurer can possibly be on risk, so that a loss occurring before this time will not be covered (except in the case of a marine policy which is written 'lost or not lost'[1]). It is also normally understood to mark the point at which the duty of disclosure ceases to operate, subject to any contrary provision in the policy and to questions arising from subsequent alterations of the risk[2]. It is therefore important to be able to identify accurately the moment when the contract is formed. It is a curious but undeniable fact that many of the important points of law in this area are not clearly resolved by any judicial decision. The following discussion therefore seeks mainly to apply general contractual principles to the problem, modified by such statutory provision and case law as appears to be in point.

In principle the moment of formation ought to be when there is an acceptance of an offer and acceptance[3], together with a consideration recognised by the law. If, as is usual, the offer takes the form of a proposal submitted by the prospective policy-holder, the acceptance will have to come from the insurer. The general principle is that acceptance is not effective until communicated to the offeror, though of course in the case of a postal acceptance, the acceptance is deemed complete upon posting[4]. It is submitted that it is not normally possible to construe an acceptance from a purely administrative decision by an insurer to issue a policy, nor even from the preparation and sealing of documents within the company's office. There is no reason to depart from the general principle requiring actual or deemed communication. There is apparently no case which contradicts this contention, though equally there is none which unequivocally supports it.

1 Marine Insurance Act 1906, s 6.
2 As to these see Chapter 11.
3 Or, it might be said, an offer which has been accepted.
4 *Adams v Linsell* (1818) 1 B & Ald 681.

3.2 Coupon insurance provides an example of a situation where the application of the normal principles of offer and acceptance in insurance policies may need to be modified. The term 'coupon insurance' is used here to mean insurance which is sold 'off-the-page' so that acceptance by the insurer is guaranteed provided that the proposer meets certain criteria which are announced in advance by the insurer. Indeed, in practice this guaranteed acceptance is a feature which is heavily stressed in the advertising material for many such policies. The significance of this guarantee is of course that the advertisement itself may properly be treated as an offer of insurance (provided of course that the terms are sufficiently described in the advertisement), which is accepted by anyone who completes the form in the correct way and tenders the necessary premium. On the basis of this reasoning it would follow that the contract is complete as soon as the coupon is posted by the proposer. This rule would of course be subject to any contrary indication contained in the offer, though it is submitted that an option for the policyholder to examine the policy for a limited period to be satisfied that it is suitable would not amount to a contrary indication for these purposes.

The argument that there is a policy immediately on submission of the proposal form applies even more strongly in relation to insurances such as the life and accident policies which are sometimes sold at airports and commonly dispensed by machine. Here the insurer has in effect abdicated any control over the suitability of the policyholder beyond the very limited questions contained on the form. The need to hold the contract immediately binding is of course even more pressing in these situations, since the policies usually provide protection only against the risks of the impending journey. If offer and acceptance had to await the normal course of the post, the journey would be over and the insurer could simply decline the risk in the case of anyone who suffered injury or death during it[1].

[1] Of course, it may be observed that in many cases no claim is made on policies of this kind, since the only person who knows that it has been taken out is the dead policyholder and the only documentary evidence of its existence is likely to have been on the policyholder's person at the time of the loss.

Offer and acceptance and inception

3.3 The moment when the contract is formed may also mark the point at which cover commences, although in practice it is probably more common at the present day for this to be delayed until the first premium is paid[1]. Where the policy contains a provision of this kind problems may occur when there is a material change of circumstances between the formation of the contract and the payment of the first premium. In this area there appears to be a conflict between principle and certain leading authorities. As a matter of principle the answer would appear to be that a bilateral executory contract comes into existence once the proposer has submitted an offer in the form of a proposal and the insurer has indicated an intention to accept. Even where cover is expressed to commence only on payment of the first premium, both sides ought to be bound immediately. This can be tested by asking whether the insurer is in principle entitled to sue for the premium should the proposer refuse to pay. It is submitted that such an action should succeed[2]. On this basis, the duty of disclosure ought to come to an end once acceptance has been signified.

The cases in this area are mostly fairly old, and it may justly be said that the reports of them which have come down to us fall short of resolving the various problems.

In *British Equitable Insurance Co v Great Western Rly Co*[3] the proposer correctly stated on the proposal form that he had always been in good health. After medical examination he was accepted for insurance at ordinary rates. Before the first premium was paid he consulted another doctor and was told that he was dangerously ill. He tendered the first premium without disclosing any of this and, after a few months' premiums had been paid, he died. The receipt for the first premium stated that the policy would be void if there had been any material alteration in his health since the proposal form. It was held that there had been fraudulent non-disclosure and that the policy was void. The case is unsatisfactory in certain respects. First, it is not clear why the policy had not already been concluded, as discussed in the previous paragraph. Secondly, the relevance of the statement is obscure. If the proposal form or the policy document had contained such a statement (and it does not appear from the report that either did so) then this could well have been effective; but in that event the statement on the receipt – seen by the policyholder only after the contract was formed and the premium paid – would be irrelevant. If there was no such statement on the proposal form or in the policy, then the later attempt to insert this clause would be ineffective.

[1] In some cases, especially liability insurance, it may alternatively be retroactive, though usually only by a short period, and with appropriate warranties to protect the insurer against the risk of claims arising between the notional commencement date and the date at which the formalities are completed.
[2] The difficulties arising where the policy has been effected through a broker are considered below.
[3] (1869) 38 LJ Ch 314.

3.4 One of the most often quoted cases in this area is *Looker v Law Union and Rock Insurance Co Ltd*[1]. The proposer stated on the proposal form that he was in good health. The statement was apparently true at the time when it was written, but before he could post it, the proposer fell ill, and it was posted on his behalf by someone else (who, it may be assumed, had no realisation of the significance of the form). The insurers accepted the application and issued the policy, but the policyholder died the following day. Acton J upheld the insurers' refusal to pay out on the policy. The case requires to be treated with caution. It is clear that the statements on the proposal form were inaccurate by the time it was posted, and the insurers clearly were misled by this. The case does not establish what would have happened if the proposer had fallen ill after posting the form, still less what would have happened if he had fallen ill after the insurers had read the form and determined to accept the proposal. It would appear that in the first case the policy would still have been voidable, though in the second case it is quite possible that the insurers would have been bound.

In *Canning v Farquhar*[2] a proposal for life assurance was accepted subject to payment of the first premium. The proposal form contained a Basis of the Contract clause. Before the premium was tendered, the life suffered an accident, of which he soon died. The premium was then tendered but was refused. It was held that the company was entitled to refuse the premium because the circumstances had altered. Where there is a Basis of the Contract clause the representations must remain true up to the time of contract, and in this case that meant the tender of premium, since cover was expressly stated not to commence until that time. The court suggested, *obiter*, that the position might be different if there had been no change in material circumstances – it might be that in such a case the company would be bound to accept the premium when tendered.

In *Harrington v Pearl Life Assurance Co Ltd*[3] P proposed for policies on his own life, but by the time the premium was paid he was very ill, and died shortly thereafter. Although there was no Basis of the Contract clause, it was held that there could be no recovery on the life policy. It is not clear from the report whether cover was stated to commence only on receipt of first premium. The premium was actually paid, unlike in *Canning*.

1 [1928] 1 KB 554.
2 (1886) 16 QBD 727, CA.
3 (1914) 30 TLR 613, CA.

3.5 It is not easy to derive general principles from these cases, but it is suggested that the following propositions should be accepted as representing the law:

(1) the proposal form must be accurate when it is submitted to the insurers (this surely cannot be doubted);
(2) the proposal form must remain accurate up until the time when the insurers make an underwriting decision to accept the risk as presented to them (again this appears uncontentious);
(3) acceptance is not effective until communicated to the offeror (such communication may be made in accordance with the postal acceptance rule). Accordingly the duty of disclosure continues until the offer has been accepted. It is not sufficient that an underwriting decision has been made, nor that the policy documentation has been prepared. This is the most contentious of the propositions, but it is submitted that the ordinary principles of contract law allow of no other result,
(4) in the absence of an express statement on the proposal form or in the acceptance documentation, the duty of disclosure comes to an end on acceptance, even if the risk is not to commence until some later event such as the payment of the first premium. This is of course without prejudice to the continuing duty of utmost good faith.

Revocability of offer

3.6 This is largely a question of ordinary common law principles. A contractual offer may be revoked at any time before its acceptance. It is essential that the fact of revocation be communicated to the offeree[1], and that the communication reaches him before the offer has been accepted[2]. It is therefore important to know when the offer is deemed to have been accepted. It must be said first that in many cases the offer will come not from the insurance company but from the proposer. However, in those cases where the offer does come from the insurer and the proposer's acceptance is made by post, the postal rule for the acceptance of contractual offers will apply. This principle, derived from the case of *Adams v Lindsell*[3], states that where acceptance is made by post, it is complete as soon as the letter of acceptance is posted.

1 *Dickinson v Dodds* (1876) 2 Ch D 463.
2 *Byrne & Co v van Tienhoven* (1880) 5 CPD 344.
3 (1818) 1 B & Ald 681.

Cover notes

3.7 These are extensively used in motor insurance, where it is essential for the proposer to have effective insurance in place before driving a motor vehicle on a public road. The question of inception of risk in such cases is dealt with in Chapter 8. For present purposes it is sufficient to note that the issue of a cover note does not amount to an acceptance of the proposal made by the proposer. The insurer remains free, after examining the proposal in full, to decline the risk, though the effect of the cover note is to provide the proposer with cover which is effective for the purposes of the Road Traffic Act 1988 ('RTA 1988') until the insurer decides to decline the risk. In other types of insurance the term 'cover note' is apparently used to refer to a document issued by a broker confirming the placing of effective insurance and setting out the major terms of the policy.

Terms to be arranged

3.8 In some areas of insurance it is common practice to leave certain terms (generally the premium) to be arranged at a later stage. This is particularly so in marine insurance, and in this area the position is settled by s 31(1) of the Marine Insurance Act 1906 ('MIA 1906'), which provides that where no agreement as to premium can be reached, the insured must pay a reasonable premium. In effect this throws the decision back on to the court, which will be required to decide what is, in the circumstances, a reasonable premium. The MIA 1906 is by its terms applicable only to marine insurance, which leaves open the question whether such arrangements are enforceable outside marine insurance and, if they are, what is to happen in the absence of agreement. There is authority supporting the enforceability of TBA clauses (ie To Be Arranged)[1] in a marine context before the passing of the MIA 1906, and it might be thought that this also points to their more general validity. In more modern cases, however, whilst judges have been prepared to say that these clauses are in principle valid[2], there appears to be no case in which a TBA clause has been upheld on the facts. The practical difficulty is, of course, that a court may be quite unable to decide what would be a reasonable premium, and in some cases it may be apparent that the risk was effectively uninsurable or insurable only at prohibitive rates. The problem is likely to be even more acute where the terms left as TBA go beyond the premium, as happened in *American Airlines Inc v Hope*[3], where even the geographical limits of a war risks extension had been left TBA, and it was held on this ground amongst others that there was no cover. Whilst it may be accepted that TBA clauses are in principle capable of being enforced, it is suggested that in practice it will be only in the clearest of cases that a clause will be found to be enforceable.

A special point arises in relation to TBA clauses at Lloyd's, where it is common to find TBA L/U, where the L/U stands for 'leading underwriter' (ie the first underwriter to have initialled the slip). In this situation the practice of the market is quite clearly that subsequent underwriters are bound by the terms agreed by the leading underwriter, even though they have no control over them[4].

1 *Greenock Steamship Co v Maritime Insurance Co* [1903] 1 KB 367, Bigham J.
2 *Liberian Insurance Agency Inc v Mosse* [1977] 2 Lloyd's Rep 560. Donaldson J; *American Airlines Inc v Hope* [1972] 1 Lloyd's Rep 253, Mocatta J.
3 [1972] 1 Lloyd's Rep 253, Mocatta J.
4 This practice is also found to some extent in the company market.

Formation at Lloyd's[1]

3.9 It should be noted that the practice of contract formation at Lloyd's differs significantly from the general pattern described above. The broker will offer the risk successively to a number of underwriters. Any who wish to accept it will initial the paper on which details are written (the 'slip' in Lloyd's terminology) to indicate the percentage of the risk they wish to take. After the risk has been fully subscribed, it is usual for a standard form Lloyd's policy to be issued by the Policy Signing Office, though this is a matter of record rather than a pre-condition of the existence of the risk. It is understood within the market that each underwriter concludes his share of the contract on signing the slip. It is also clear that each underwriter enters into a separate contract with the insured, there being no joint liability among the subscribers of the slip. This logic is carried to its full extent in that where a risk (or part of a risk) is placed with a Lloyd's syndicate, the risk is in fact borne by each individual member of that syndicate in proportion to his share of the syndicate – even within a syndicate there is no joint liability.

This simple account of the practice does not account adequately for a number of difficulties which may arise. The broker may cause the slip to be subscribed for more than 100% of the risk[2], in which case the practice is that the share held by each underwriter abates proportionately[3]. Although there is no doubt some considerable conceptual difficulty in allowing a retrospective variation of the contracts in this way, the market practice is clear, and it is submitted that this is one of those areas where commercial practice must be allowed to make law.

[1] For the effect of a signing-down indication by the broker, see Chapter 6.
[2] Though some underwriters adopt the practice of marking the slip 'not to sign less than [x%]'.
[3] The difficulties in this area have been considered in a number of cases, which are worthy of careful reading. The principal authorities are *Fennia Patria* [1983] QB 856; *Jaglom v Excess Insurance Co Ltd* [1972] 2 QB 250; *The Zephyr* [1984] 1 Lloyd's Rep 58, Hobhouse J; [1985] 2 Lloyd's Rep 529, CA.

3.10 Where the broker is not able to obtain cover for the whole of the risk on identical terms or at all, other problems arise. There is no practice of increasing the share held by each underwriter. It may be suggested that in this event the risk does not attach, but that is inconsistent with the principle that each underwriter has a binding contract as soon as he initials the slip. The idea that the insured can have a unilateral right of rescission of pre-existing contracts if the slip is not fully subscribed has been cogently criticised[1], but is nevertheless probably preferable to the alternative, which appears to be that underwriters are entitled to insist on retaining their proportion of the risk even if the risk is not fully subscribed. Of course, as has been pointed out judicially[2], in practice underwriters will normally be prepared to make a commercial decision to set aside the contracts already made.

[1] Clarke *The Law of Insurance Contracts* (1999, LLP), section 11–3.
[2] *Fennia Patria* [1983] QB 856, Slade LJ.

Telephone Selling

3.11 An important feature of the past ten years has been the development of the direct selling of insurance by telephone. The usual practice is that proposers are taken through the proposal form, before being given an insurance quotation, which they can accept or reject. If they accept it, payment is made over the telephone. The details are then confirmed in writing. The unresolved question is when the policy comes into existence, whether in the telephone conversation or at some later stage. The point is important if a loss occurs after the conversation but before the documentation has been sent out and/or received. It is also important in the context of compulsory insurance such as motor insurance, where it may be vital to know whether a person was insured at a given time. In principle the answer to the question must be that it depends on the intentions of the parties. In practice the proposer may not have given much thought to the point, and it is not obvious what the insurer's intention is. It is submitted that the usual answer ought to be that cover is immediately effective. In order to refute this proposition, the insurer should be required to make clear to the proposer at the time of the telephone conversation that there will be no cover until later. However, even this solution is not entirely satisfactory, for the proposer will not at that stage have seen full details of the cover provided. There ought therefore to be an option for the proposer to cancel the contract and get the premium back (so long as no claim has been made) within say seven days of receiving the details. The latter regime would probably have to be imposed by statute. It must be stressed that in the absence of authority there can be no certainty as to what view a court would take[1].

[1] The point does not appear to have come before the Insurance Ombudsman for consideration.

Renewal

3.12 The point at which an insurance contract is 'renewed' marks the creation of a new contract rather than merely the continuance of an existing one. Issues of offer and acceptance are therefore applicable to this process. The questions arising at renewal are more exhaustively dealt with in Chapter 14.

Chapter 4

Insurable interest

History and rationale

4.1 The law of insurance has long sought to distinguish between legitimate insurance on the one hand and gambling on the other. Although in the seventeenth century English law was apparently happy to enforce gaming contracts, the attitude of the courts changed in the eighteenth century, and this change may in part be attributed to some celebrated cases of purported insurance policies which were in effect merely wagers on the happening of specified events, sometimes including the lifespan of famous men[1] with whom the parties had no blood relationship. Apart from the undesirability of wasting the time of the court with such matters, it was also perceived that a wager on the life of an individual could give one of the parties an incentive to murder[2]. It was in these circumstances that legislation was passed in 1774 to address the question of which matters might legitimately be insured[3].

1 Napoleon seems to have been especially popular in this role.
2 *Merkin* (1980) 4 Anglo-American LR 345.
3 LAA 1774.

The concept

4.2 There is of course no general statutory definition of what amounts to an insurable interest[1]. On the basis of *Lucena v Craufurd*[2] it is commonly said that in the case of tangible property the policyholder must stand in some legal or equitable relationship to the property insured. This is no doubt a worthy statement of principle, but, as appears from the cases discussed below, it is of little use in deciding exactly what legal or equitable relationship is to be accepted as founding insurable interest. It is also of no relevance to the very important and quite difficult question of who has an insurable interest in a human life. The most recent authority on the point supports the idea that a complete definition may be impossible, and that formulations which are helpful in relation to life assurance may be unhelpful in relation to other forms of insurance[3].

It is settled that the court should lean in favour of finding insurable interest where possible, though of course without going beyond the facts of the case or stretching the law to breaking point. It is an unattractive position for insurers to take the premium and then deny the existence of an insurable interest when faced with an otherwise legitimate claim, and the court is understandably reluctant to countenance such conduct[4].

[1] For a partial definition of insurable interest in a marine context, see the MIA 1906, s 6, discussed below.
[2] (1806) 2 Bos & PNR 269; (1806) 1 Taunt 325, HL, expanding on the definition first given in *Barclay v Cousins* 2 East 544.
[3] *Feasey v Sun Life Assurance Corporation of Canada* [2003] Lloyd's Rep IR 637, CA at para 66.
[4] *Stock v Inglis* (1884) 12 QBD 564 at 571 per Brett MR, cited with approval by Waller LJ in *Feasey v Sun Life,* above.

The Life Assurance Act 1774

4.3 The LAA 1774 was introduced to prevent the practice of gambling on lives, ie seeking to make a profit by insuring the life of a person with whom one had no legitimate connection. Section 1 of the Act provides:

> 'From and after the passing of this Act no insurance shall be made by any person or persons, bodies politick or corporate, on the life or lives of any person or persons or on any other event or events whatsoever, wherein the person or persons for whose use, benefit, or on whose account such policy or policies shall be made shall have no interest, or by way of gaming or wagering; and that every assurance made contrary to the true intent and meaning hereof shall be null and void to all intents and purposes whatsoever'.

From this it can be seen that any purported policy in which the insured has no proper interest in the subject matter is void. By its express terms the Act applies to all policies, except those expressly excluded by s 4 of the Act, namely policies on 'goods, ships and merchandises'. The name of the Act is to that extent misleading. As appears below, the courts have not always been prepared to give full effect to the broad application of the Act. Exactly what is recognised as sufficient insurable interest in particular types of insurance is considered at length below.

Consequences of lack of insurable interest

4.4 Section 1 of the LAA 1774 declares that policies effected without interest are 'null and void'. It follows that no claim can be made on any such policy. It is to be noted also that it is not possible to contract out of the statute, which was enacted for the protection of the public at large rather than for the protection of either of the parties to the purported contract. There is, however, nothing to prevent an insurance company from granting a policy in the absence of interest, nor from paying on it when a claim arises, and it is generally understood that at the present day many such policies are effected and carried out, especially in life assurance. Despite the legal position, it does seem somewhat unconscionable for an insurance company to take the premiums and then refuse to pay on the policy because of lack of interest, and it might be thought that the regulatory authorities would be unhappy with a company which was issuing large numbers of void policies then refusing to pay on them, since a purported policy which is in reality void would surely not be in the policyholder's best interests. However, in an action on a void policy, it is the duty of the court to raise the question of illegality even if the insurer does not do so and seeks to defend the action on some other ground[1]. This follows from the principle that the illegality is a matter of public policy and cannot be waived by agreement between the parties. On the other hand an insurer who purports to effect a void policy does not necessarily commit any criminal offence (though questions of obtaining by deception contrary to the Theft Act 1968 might arise if the insurer or its agents knew that the policy was void). Moreover, it is not a criminal offence to pay out on a void policy[2]. Thus, the parties can in practice enter into and carry through a void policy – the effect of the Act is merely that the court will not assist either side in relation to the transaction.

1 *Gedge v Royal Exchange Insurance Corpn* [1900] 2 QB 214, Kennedy J.
2 The policy is *illegal* but not *criminal*.

4.5 Curious results may follow where an insurer makes a payment under a void policy. Such a payment will not normally be recoverable, even if made under a mistake of fact, and it appears that the payee will be entitled to keep the money as against anyone else, since no one else will have a better title to it than he does[1]. This may be regarded as following from the general rule in illegal[2] contracts that money paid or property transferred is not recoverable where the parties are equally guilty. The position might therefore be different if the contract had been induced by the fraud of the policyholder in leading the insurer to believe that insurable interest existed. The principle that a payment under a void policy is effective is taken to considerable lengths. In one old case[3] a father insured his son's life and assigned the benefit of the policy to the trustees of his son's marriage settlement. After the death of the son the insurers paid the policy proceeds to the trustees of the settlement, notwithstanding that the policy was obviously void. In an action by the Attorney-General, it was held that the payment was liable to estate duty. The same result would appear to arise at the present day in relation to inheritance tax. In both cases, the point, for tax purposes, is that the money has been received and is liable to tax accordingly.

1 *Worthington v Curtis* (1875) 1 Ch D 419, CA.
2 For the principle that such contracts are illegal as well as void see the next paragraph.
3 *A-G v Murray* [1904] 1 KB 165, CA.

4.6 A second, and less obvious, consequence of the voidness of the policy is that the policyholder may not reclaim the premiums which he has paid. This is not a general rule in contracts which are merely void, but the position under the LAA 1774 was considered in *Harse v Pearl Assurance*[1]. In that case it was held that policies effected without insurable interest are not merely void, but also illegal, and that the general principle of not allowing any action on an illegal contract must apply to the situation[2], so that premiums paid under a void policy cannot be recovered by the policyholder[3]. The rule is of course applicable only in those cases where the parties are equally guilty in relation to the illegality. The effect of this principle may be seen by comparing the result in *Harse* with that in *Hughes v Liverpool Victoria Legal Friendly Society*[4]. In the former case, the claimant[5] effected a policy of insurance on his mother's life for the purpose of covering the funeral expenses. Unfortunately, the claimant had no insurable interest in his mother's life, and the policy was therefore void. The question was whether he could recover back the premiums which he had paid. It was held that the insurance agent who had led the policyholder to believe that the policy would be valid had acted negligently but not fraudulently. Consequently the parties were treated as being equally guilty, and the premiums were not recoverable. By contrast, in the latter case, valid policies of life assurance had been taken out, but had been allowed to lapse for non-payment of premium. The agent of the defendant society represented to the claimant that she could take over these policies, though they had lapsed and though she had in any event no interest in the lives assured. It was held that the agent was fraudulent in his representations to the policyholder. The parties were therefore not equally guilty, and the premiums were recoverable. It is clear that distinctions of this kind depend entirely upon the court's findings as to the state of knowledge of the parties. It may be suggested, however, that today a court would be reluctant to accept that a life assurance salesperson, probably[6] accredited by the FSO and having passed the necessary tests of competence, was ignorant of the basic rules as to insurable interest.

[1] [1904] 1 KB 558, CA.
[2] See also *Howard v Refuge Friendly Society* (1886) 54 LT 644, DC.
[3] *Howard v Refuge Friendly Society* (1886) 54 LT 644, DC.
[4] [1916] 2 KB 482.
[5] As this is the first appearance in the present work of the term 'claimant' it is appropriate to explain the approach adopted to the question whether those who bring civil actions are 'claimants' or 'plaintiffs'. Before 26 April 1999 they had for many centuries been plaintiffs. Those starting actions after that date are claimants. Strictly speaking the term 'plaintiff' remains appropriate for all actions begun before that date. However, the use of dual terminology in one text is all too likely to cause confusion. Consequently, and with some reluctance, the text follows the practice of making them all 'claimants'.
[6] A salesperson who was authorised only to sell whole of life and term life policies would not need such authorisation since he would not be involved in Relevant Investment Business within the meaning of the Financial Services Authority Rules. Although it is apparently common practice to authorise new salespersons only to sell whole of life policies, it appears that this authorisation would normally be accompanied by a Financial Services Ombudsman registration.

Policies in trust

4.7 Where it is desired to effect an insurance for the benefit of a person who has no insurable interest in the subject matter assured, a possible solution is for the policy to be written in trust, ie for it to be effected by a person who *does* have interest but for the policy to state that it is held in trust for the intended beneficiary. This practice is extensively followed in cases of life assurance, where it may confer certain tax advantages, but there appears to be little reason to adopt it in other areas of insurance.

Assignment of policies

4.8 Another possible solution to the absence of an appropriate insurable interest is for the policy to be effected by someone with an interest and then assigned to the intended beneficiary. Although assignments of life policies are possible, this approach is somewhat more problematic, since it may in some cases be held that the policy was in reality always that of the assignee and that it is accordingly void for lack of insurable interest[1]. An alternative argument which may be encountered here is that the policy is void because it contravenes s 2 of the LAA 1774 by failing to state the name of the person for whose benefit it was made. This argument may be raised even where that person *does* have an insurable interest in the life, since the s 2 requirement is additional to the requirement of interest. The response to such an argument depends upon whether the policy was in fact always intended to benefit the third party. If so, then the argument is in principle correct, and the policy should be regarded as contravening s 2. However, cases of this sort should be carefully distinguished from cases where the policy was in fact intended for the benefit of the original policyholder, who subsequently chooses to assign the policy. The distinction is not always easy to draw, for it all depends upon the intention of the policyholder at the time when the policy was taken out, and this will not always be easy to ascertain. Sometimes there may be extrinsic evidence of intention, such as letters written by the policyholder at or about the relevant time, but more often the only evidence will be that of the policyholder himself, who clearly has an incentive to say that he originally intended the policy for himself. It is suggested that, except in a clear case, the court will be slow to conclude that the policy is void on this ground.

1 *Shilling v Accidental Death Insurance Co* (1857) 2 H & N 42, 157 ER 18.

Timing of interest

4.9 The LAA 1774 does not state when interest is required. It is implicit in the wording of s 1 that the requirement applies at the time when the policy is taken out, since that section prohibits the *making* of policies without interest. It might be thought that the requirement ought also to apply at the time when the life assured dies, since the lapsing of interest in the life of another deprives the insured of any legitimate reason for keeping the policy on foot, and might even be said to turn it in effect into a gaming policy. In *Dalby v India and London Life Assurance Co*[1] the claimant was the primary insurer in respect of a policy on the life of the Duke of Cambridge, and had reinsured that risk with the defendant. There was no doubt that at the time when both the primary policy and the policy of reinsurance were effected all parties had the necessary insurable interests. The primary policy was allowed to lapse through non-payment of the premiums, so that the claimant no longer had any interest in the risk, but the claimant maintained the policy of reinsurance. On the Duke's death the reinsurers refused to pay on this policy, alleging lack of interest, and the claimant brought this action. It was held that he could recover on the policy. The requirement of insurable interest applies only at the time when the policy is taken out. This decision appears to negate a significant part of the purpose of the 1774 Act, and it has been much criticised[2], but it remains law at the present day. Thus, for example, employers may maintain Keyman policies (under which the life of a particular employee of a business is insured) on employees who are no longer with the firm and ex-spouses[3] may maintain policies on each others' lives effected during the marriage. Another oddity about this decision may be noted. The argument and decision proceed upon the basis that the claimant had reinsured the Duke's life. This is not the normal way of effecting reinsurance. It would be more usual to reinsure the risk of becoming liable on the primary policy. The requirement of insurable interest would still apply to such a policy, but there would be other important consequences. First, such a policy would apparently not be a life policy, but a liability policy, and it would be necessary to consider whether the rules on timing of interest applied in the same way outside life situations[4] or indeed whether the requirement of interest applies at all in such a case[5]. Secondly, such a policy would be a policy of indemnity, not a contingency[6] policy, and whatever the rules as to insurable interest the principle of indemnity would prevent the claimant from recovering in respect of a loss which he had not suffered. Despite this, the case remains good authority for the proposition that in life policies insurable interest is required only when the policy is taken out.

Another curious decision in this area is *Dodson v Peter H Dodson Insurance Services (a firm)*[7], where it was held that a motor policy did not lapse when the insured vehicle was sold. The most recent authority[8] confirms that the *Dalby* rule remains good for life assurance, but that for all other classes of insurance the date of loss is relevant.

1 (1854) 15 CB 365; see also *Law v London Indisputable Life Policy Co* (1855) 1 K & J 223 for a very similar principle.
2 *Merkin* (1980) 4 Anglo-American LR 345.
3 It seems that for virtually all practical legal purposes the term 'spouse' now needs to be understood as including a registered Civil Partner, the Civil Partnerships Act 2004 having given Civil Partners the status of married couples in all but name.
4 MIA 1906, s 6(1) requires interest only at the time of loss in the case of marine policies, and this may perhaps be regarded as symptomatic of the general common law approach.
5 See para 4.3 above.
6 Ie policies to pay a specified amount rather than policies to indemnify against actual loss. See also Chapter 1, where this distinction is more fully explored.
7 [2001] Lloyd's Rep IR 278, CA.
8 *Feasey v Sun Life Assurance Corporation of Canada* [2003] Lloyd's Rep IR 637, CA at para 68.

Naming those interested

4.10 Section 2 of the LAA 1774 provides:

> 'It shall not be lawful to make any policy or policies on the life or lives of any person or persons, or other event or events, without inserting in such policy or policies the person or persons name or names interested therein, or for whose use, benefit, or on whose account such policy is so made or underwrote'.

Section 2 has given rise to certain difficulties. It was for a time uncertain whether group policies, ie policies which insured the lives of the current members of a group whose membership changed from time to time, could be valid in the light of s 2. The point was resolved beyond doubt by s 50 of the Insurance Companies Amendment Act 1973, which provides that s 2 shall not invalidate a policy so long as the description of the group of persons intended to benefit is stated with sufficient particularity to make it possible to ascertain at any time the identity of those individuals currently entitled to benefit. This requirement is satisfied even if the identities of those interested cannot be ascertained at the outset of the policy, perhaps because the class is likely to change in ways which cannot be predicted. It is sufficient that membership of the class can be sufficiently ascertained at any given time[1]. Section 2 was apparently enacted as an anti-avoidance device in the wake of s 1, to prevent life of another policies being apparently written as own life policies or as life of another policies for someone who had no insurable interest but whose identity was concealed. It may be questioned whether the section serves much useful purpose today.

In other cases, however, policies may be invalidated for failure to comply with s 2. This is particularly the case with life of another policies, where an accidental omission to indicate the name of the insured can have this effect. Perhaps the most difficult situation arises where it is alleged that a policy taken out by one person (whether on an own life or life of another basis) is really intended to benefit someone else. In many such cases the use of the trust device may alleviate this problem, but there are occasional cases where this is not done and where it appears that the premiums are to be paid by someone other than the insured. This is likely to give rise to a presumption that the policy was really intended for the benefit of that person, and unless this presumption can be rebutted, it must follow that the policy fails for want of interest.

1 *Feasey v Sun Life Assurance Corporation of Canada* [2003] Lloyd's Rep IR 637, CA.

4.11 An important and difficult case in this area is *Shilling v Accidental Death Insurance Co*[1]. This was a policy on a father's life expressed as an own life policy. There was evidence that the son was going to pay the premiums in return for father's promise to bequeath him the proceeds of the policy. The insurers pleaded that there was a breach of s 2 because the policy was really made for the son's benefit. The court held that this intention, *if established*, would give the insurers a good defence. However, it is important to understand the nature of the proceedings which were reported here. The insurers had demurred to the claimant's declaration, and the claimant had joined issue on the demurrer. Under the procedural rules then in force, the result of this hearing had to be determined on the assumption that the defendants' version of the facts was the correct one, though it would of course still have been open to the claimant at the substantive trial to prove that the policy was not really made for the son's benefit. Indeed, the judges expressed the view that the claimant would most probably succeed on this ground. Consequently, the case does no more than emphasise the simple and obvious point that it is always essential to identify accurately for whose benefit the policy is in reality made.

It should be noted that there is no legal requirement to state in the policy the nature of the insured's interest in the subject matter insured. As a matter of practice, proposal forms very commonly ask for this information, but this is merely a matter of commercial convenience. The omission of any statement of the nature of the interest from the policy does not invalidate the policy[2].

1 (1857) 2 H & N 42, 157 ER 18.
2 Though obviously a mis-statement of that interest in the proposal form would render the policy voidable for a breach of the duty of pre-contractual disclosure.

Amount of recovery

4.12 Section 3 of the LAA 1774 provides:

> 'In all cases where the insured hath interest in such life or lives, event or events, no greater sum shall be recovered or received from the insurer or insurers than the amount of value of the interest of the insured in such life or lives, event or events'.

This section is of no practical importance in own life policies or in policies on the life of a spouse, since, as was explained above, the interest in these cases is presumed to be unlimited. It is, however, of importance in all other cases of life assurance. The operation of this section reveals something of an anomaly in relation to life assurance. It is commonly said that life policies are *contingency* policies rather than *indemnity* policies[1]. It is for this reason that the principle of indemnity and the doctrine of subrogation do not apply to them. This distinction between indemnity policies and contingency policies was adopted when the courts were struggling to formulate a definition of insurance for the purposes of stamp duty, and was intended to deal with the problem that there is no obvious loss to the policyholder in surviving to the maturity date[2]. This distinction was considered to provide a better rationale for recognising such policies as life policies than did Channell J's observation in *Prudential Insurance Co v IRC*[3] that there was loss in reaching that date because it was to be expected that by the maturity date the policyholder would be less able to earn his own living. Unfortunately, the categorisation adopted in *Gould v Curtis*[4] has tended to obscure the fact that s 3 of the LAA 1774 does not make any sense unless there is some way of valuing interests in lives, and that some life policies, ie those where there is no automatic interest, have to be regarded as indemnity policies. Despite the observations of the Court of Appeal in *Gould*, life policies in which there is no automatic insurable interest have to be treated as indemnity policies in the sense that the amount which can be recovered is limited to the amount of the policyholder's interest.

However, it appears that the rule in *Dalby v India and London Life Assurance Co*[5] applies to this situation as well, so that not only the existence, but also the value of the interest must be determined at the time when the policy is taken out. This can obviously produce absurd results. A creditor's policy on a debtor may insure the full amount of the original loan, which may be recovered even if the debtor dies after paying off part (or even all) of the loan. This rule is of course subject to contrary provision in the policy, and in commercial debt protection policies it is quite common to provide that only the outstanding debt may be recovered.

It might be thought that the point would be of more importance in indemnity policies, where it is obviously inappropriate for the policyholder to receive more than his loss. In reality, though, even here the section operates only to cause injustice. The principle of indemnity in any event prevents the policyholder from recovering more than his actual loss. The only possible additional effect of s 3 is further to restrict recovery to the value of the interest at the time when the policy is taken out, even if that is less than the value of the interest when the loss occurs.

1 *Gould v Curtis* [1913] 3 KB 84, CA.
2 See n 1 above.
3 [1904] 2 KB 658.
4 [1913] 3 KB 84, CA.
5 (1854) 15 CB 365.

4.13 In practice s 3 of the LAA 1774 does not seem to be treated very seriously by courts or insurance companies. There are no modern reported cases where recovery has been restricted on the basis of s 3, and the practice is apparently to pay out the sum mentioned in the policy unless it is so obviously excessive as to give rise to a suspicion that the policy contains an element of wagering or to raise suspicions about the validity of the claim. It is in any event objectionable that the insurer should receive a premium calculated on the basis of one insured sum and then claim to pay out only a much smaller sum.

The Life Assurance Act 1774 and general insurance

4.14 The LAA 1774 gives rise to at least one obvious and major conundrum. Given that the Act is called the Life Assurance Act, and that the preamble refers to the undesirability of gambling on lives, it might naturally be supposed that it applied only to life assurance. On the other hand, as has been pointed out, the Act by its terms applies to all policies other than those excluded by s 4[1]. However, judicial decision-making in this area has been both inconsistent and problematic. In *Macaura v Northern Assurance Co Ltd*[2] the claimant held a controlling interest in a company which owned some cut timber. He effected a policy in his own name insuring the timber against loss or damage. When the timber was later destroyed by fire the insurers refused to pay on the policy, alleging lack of insurable interest. This defence was upheld on the basis that shareholders in a company do not own the property of the company. The premise is of course perfectly correct, but what is almost impossible to understand is why it was supposed that the LAA 1774 applied to the case at all. The cut timber surely fell within the term 'goods' in s 4 of that Act, so that the Act did not apply[3]. It is interesting to contrast the decision of AD Colman QC in *The Moonacre*[4], where the plaintiff was held to have an insurable interest in a boat owned by a company of which he was a 100% shareholder. The two decisions are in theory distinguishable on the basis that in the latter case the company (acting of course through the plaintiff) had given the plaintiff very wide powers of attorney to deal with the boat. Although the correctness of the decision was the subject of some disagreement between the members of the Court of Appeal in *Glengate KG Properties Ltd v Norwich Union Fire Insurance Society Ltd*[5], it is submitted that the decision is in fact a sensible one.

By contrast, in *Prudential Staff Union v Hall*[6] Morris J said, *obiter*, that money collected by insurance agents as part of industrial assurance business was goods within the meaning of s 4. Although money will not always be goods for these purposes, it will be so when it is in a form which is capable of being burned or asported. In effect this observation would make all notes and coins goods for these purposes. The remarks do not form part of the *ratio* of the case, which was decided on the basis that the claim was fraudulent, and there appears to be no other authority supporting this rather surprising conclusion.

1 Section 4 reads: 'Provided, always, that nothing herein contained shall extend or be construed to extend to insurances bona fide made by any person or persons on ships, goods, or merchandises, but every such insurance shall be as valid and effectual in the law as if this Act had not been made.'
2 [1925] AC 619.
3 One of the very unsatisfactory features of the judgments in this case is that the possible application of s 4 is completely ignored.
4 [1992] 2 Lloyd's Reports 501.
5 [1996] 1 Lloyd's Rep 614; Neill LJ considered the judgment 'valuable' but Auld LJ expressed greater scepticism.
6 (1947) 80 Lloyd's Rep 410, Morris J.

4.15 The law in relation to insurable interest was thrown into some confusion by observations made by the Court of Appeal in *Mark Rowlands Ltd v Berni Inns Ltd*[1] to the effect that s 2 of the LAA 1774 does not apply to indemnity policies, but only to contingency policies. This view was of course inconsistent with the *obiter dicta* of Lord Denning MR in *Re King, Robinson v Gray*[2] to the effect that s 2 applied to fire insurance. The matter was further considered by the Privy Council in *Siu Yin Kwan v Eastern Insurance Co Ltd*[3]. This time the point arose squarely for decision, s 2 having been pleaded by the defendant insurers as an essential part of their defence. The Privy Council chose to follow the decision in the *Mark Rowlands* case. Lord Lloyd of Berwick, delivering the advice of the Privy Council, relied on two points, one of which is of general interest, whilst the other relates more specifically to the facts of the case. The general point is that the interpretation of s 2 of the LAA 1774 should bear in mind the overall purposes of the Act, which are stated in the preamble as being the elimination of a 'mischievous kind of gaming' arising from the practice of insuring lives. Self-evidently, indemnity insurance cannot be described as any kind of gaming. The more specific point is that s 2 refers to insurances on 'any event or events'. Lord Lloyd considered that this form of words was not appropriate to describe the arising of liability to pay workman's compensation under statute, which was the subject-matter of the present case. The two points give rise to different problems. The premise underlying the more general point is obviously correct, and it has often been observed that one oddity of the LAA 1774 is its apparent application beyond the scope suggested by its title and its preamble. It is a matter of legitimate disagreement whether this point can properly justify the disregard of the apparently clear words of the Act. The narrower point would lead to other undesirable anomalies, since it would seem to exclude from the scope of s 2 liability policies, but not policies on real or personal property. As well as being anomalous, this result is different from that indicated by the broader argument.

1 [1985] 3 All ER 473, CA.
2 [1963] 1 All ER 781 at 790, CA.
3 [1994] 1 All ER 213, PC.

4.16 A point of more fundamental importance is whether all these arguments are restricted to s 2 of the LAA 1774, or whether they apply to all the provisions of that Act. It seems fairly clear that the latter is the only possible solution. It cannot seriously be argued that s 1 of the Act applies to indemnity policies but s 2 does not – both Lord Lloyd's arguments are equally forceful in relation to both sections. Thus, the proper conclusion to be drawn from this decision is apparently that English law is moving towards the position of saying that there is no requirement at all of insurable interest in indemnity policies. If that is so, then the most important effect will be to put much greater weight on the principle of indemnity and on the notion of gaming and wagering contracts under s 18 of the Gaming Act 1845. It would, however, be wrong to assume that the notion of insurable interest will disappear entirely from cases of indemnity insurance. In *Glengate-KG Properties Ltd v Norwich Union Fire Insurance Society Ltd*[1] the claimants, who were property developers, insured against possible loss of rent on a building which they were proposing to redevelop where such loss was caused by damage to the building. It was a condition of the insurer's liability that at the time of the damage there must be insurance in force covering the interest of the insured in the property. The redevelopment was delayed because of a fire which destroyed the architects work-in-progress drawings, which had to be reconstructed. These drawings were not insured. When the claimant tried to claim on the loss of rent policy, the insurers declined the claim on the ground that the drawings had not been insured. The Court of Appeal held that this defence could not succeed. The drawings had clearly been the property of the architects rather than of the claimants, so that the claimants had had no insurable interest in them. They were therefore not required under the loss of rent policy to have insurance in force relating to them. The case illustrates the tendency of insurers to continue to think in terms of insurable interest even in relation to indemnity policies. It seems likely that some insurers, wishing to restrict the scope of cover, will continue to insist that policyholders have an insurable interest before they will enter into an indemnity policy. The discussion of insurable interest in the context of indemnity policies which appears later in this Chapter should therefore be read subject to the points made here about the possible limitations on the doctrine in the modern law.

It should be noted that there are no criminal sanctions for contravening the LAA 1774, whether this is done deliberately or by oversight – the voidness of the policy is the only sanction. However, a policyholder who fraudulently misrepresents the nature of his interest in the life assured in order to induce the insurers to grant a policy and subsequently to pay on it might well be guilty of attempting to obtain property by deception contrary to s 15 of the Theft Act 1968. If the insurers did in fact pay this money, then the completed offence of obtaining property by deception will have been committed.

[1] [1996] 2 All ER 487, CA.

Insurable interest and the principle of indemnity

4.17 Most insurance policies are indemnity[1] policies, that is to say they are intended to do no more than indemnify the policyholder against losses which he may suffer as a result of the operation of an insured peril[2]. As a matter of construction, such policies will not allow the policyholder to recover more than his actual loss. This principle operates in addition to any requirement of insurable interest which may apply to a policy. The point is important because it shows that, at any rate in indemnity policies, it is not necessary to rely on the doctrine of insurable interest to prevent the use of insurance as what the LAA 1774 called 'a mischievous kind of gaming'. The principle is properly regarded as a presumption rather than as a rule of law. Thus it may be displaced by appropriate wording in the policy, though a policy which obviously afforded the prospect of more than an indemnity might be in some danger of being regarded as a wagering policy. A nice point in this area concerns policies such as household contents policies which allow the policyholder to claim on a 'new for old' basis, ie to recover the cost of replacing lost items as new, rather than merely paying the value of these items immediately before the loss. It might well be argued that this affords more than a true indemnity and therefore amounts to a wagering contract. Despite this the practice is well established and does not appear to have been challenged. It is also possible – and more or less universal in marine insurance[3] – to have policies where the value of the insured property is agreed. This value may in practice be greater than the actual value, but in the absence of fraud the policy is considered valid.

The principle of indemnity has of course no application to contingency policies, and it is in relation to these policies that the doctrine of insurable interest remains relevant and useful.

[1] On the distinction between indemnity policies and contingency policies see also Chapter 1.
[2] Policy provisions such as an excess or a limit of cover may reduce the protection to less than a full indemnity.
[3] See Chapter 43.

The Gaming Act 1845

4.18 Section 18 of this statute declares all policies by way of gaming or wagering to be void. No action can be brought on such policies, nor can money paid under them normally be recovered. In theory the prohibition on gaming policies is additional to the requirement of insurable interest under s 1 of the LAA 1774, but in practice it appears that, at least in life assurance, there is no case where interest is held to exist but the policy will nevertheless be held to be one of gaming or wagering[1]. It also seems unlikely that this section can be used to defeat claims in those cases where interest has lapsed, since it the question whether the policy is one of gaming or wagering under the 1845 Act must presumably be determined at the time when the policy is effected. In truth, s 18 was not intended to deal with insurance policies at all, but merely to reverse the common law rule that blatant wagering policies were enforceable by the courts.

[1] Though in *Feasey v Sun Life Assurance Corporation of Canada* [2003] Lloyd's Rep IR 637, CA the Court of Appeal was at pains to point out that the two things are not logically the same, and that the possibility of such overlap remains.

Insurable interest in particular types of insurance

Life

4.19 A person always has an insurable interest in his own life[1], and the amount of this interest is unlimited[2]. Thus, he may insure his own life for any amount he chooses, the only constraint being his ability to pay the premiums. This was established in *Wainewright v Bland*[3]. In principle this would seem to act as an effective check on gross over-insurance, since a relatively poor person is not likely to be able to afford the premiums for a very high level of cover. However, it may be suggested that a proposal for an own life policy where the sum insured is obviously greatly excessive should not necessarily be accepted without question. There may well be some particular reason why the policy is being taken out for that amount at that time. and that reason may itself be a material factor in determining whether and on what terms to accept the risk[4].

[1] *Wainewright v Bland* (1835) 1 Mood & R; *Wainwright v Bland* 481 (1836) 1 M & W 32.
[2] See n 1 above.
[3] (1835) 1 Mood & R 481.
[4] *Pan Atlantic Insurance Co Ltd v Pine Top Insurance Co Ltd* [1994] 3 All ER 581, HL.

Life of another

4.20 The rules on policies insuring the life of another person are more complex. In a strictly limited class of case there is automatic insurable interest, that is to say that the interest exists without the need to prove any financial loss in the event of the death of the life assured. The only situation in which it has been held that there is automatic insurable interest is that of husband and wife. *Reed v Royal Exchange Assurance Co*[1] is usually treated as establishing that a wife has an automatic interest in the life of her husband[2], and in *Griffith v Fleming*[3] it was held that the converse also applied. Registered civil partners have automatic unlimited insurance interest in each other's lives[4]. However, parents do not have an automatic interest in the lives of their children[5], nor *vice versa*, and siblings do not have automatic interest in each others' lives – *Harse v Pearl Assurance*[6]. These principles apply even in cases where it might appear that the assured has a reasonable moral (but not legal) expectation of being supported by the life assured and therefore stands to lose from the death of the life assured[7]. Perhaps the most contentious case at present is that of the couple who are engaged to be married, or who are living together without any agreement to marry. It has never been held that they have automatic interest, but nor has it been held that they do not, and it is obvious that they fall on the borderline. The Insurance Ombudsman's practice was generally to treat engaged couples as having insurable interest in each others' lives[8], and the FSO's duty to make a fair and reasonable decision may well lead him to take the same view. The principle as applied by the Insurance Ombudsman does not appear to apply in the absence of an agreement to marry, even if the couple are to a greater or lesser extent financially dependant on each other. Of course, in such a case there might well be an actual interest based upon financial dependency.

Even where there is no automatic interest, there may still be a recognised interest in the life of another, but this will depend upon showing the expectation of loss in the event that the life assured dies. A number of common cases will be discussed in the following paragraphs.

1 (1795) Peake Add Cas 70.
2 In fact, the judge, Lord Kenyon CJ, made a remark to this effect during the argument, but it never formed part of any *ratio decidendi* in the case, for the claimant consented to a nonsuit after counsel for the insurers read out a number of letters which the claimant had written to a young man of her acquaintance. The content of these letters may perhaps be deduced from the further information that the claimant was subsequently tried at Gloucester Assizes for the murder of her husband. She was acquitted.
3 [1909] 1 KB 805.
4 Civil Partnerships Act 2004, s 253.
5 *Halford v Kymer* [1830] 10 B & C 724, 109 ER 619.
6 [1904] 1 KB 558.
7 *Halford v Kymer*, n 5 above.
8 Annual Report 1991.

Debtor-creditor

4.21 It is common for creditors to insure against the death of their debtors. This practice appears to have originated in the nineteenth century, when the action in respect of the debt died with the debtor. That rule was abolished in 1934[1], so that at the present day the action can be maintained against the estate of the deceased debtor. Despite this, the death of the debtor is likely in many cases to weaken the creditor's position, since he will be left to claim against the assets of the estate, which may not be sufficient; often, the original intention will have been for the debtor to repay the loan out of his continuing earnings, but these will naturally cease on his death. Consequently, the practice of insuring against the death of a debtor remains commonplace. A good early example of this rule is to be found in *Von Lindenau v Desbrugh*[2], where The Duke of Saxe Gotha entered into an agreement with his predecessor's creditors under which the debts would be paid off over five years. It was held, that the creditors had an insurable interest in his life during that period. A practical problem arises in relation to the amount of the insurance. As is explained below, the LAA 1774 forbids the insured to recover more than the amount of his interest. As this is not a case of unlimited interest, it is necessary to value the interest, and it would appear that such value cannot exceed the amount currently outstanding on the loan. Where, as is usual, the loan is to be repaid in instalments, the amount outstanding will diminish steadily over the lifetime of the loan. Although the original policy will be for the full amount of the loan, some of this may have been paid off by the date of death. However, it appears that the full sum insured can still be recovered[3].

1 Law Reform (Miscellaneous Provisions Act) 1934, s 1.
2 (1828) 3 C & P 353.
3 See para 4.27 below.

4.22 A more unusual case occurs where the debtor seeks to insure the life of his creditor. The classic example of this was seen in *Hebdon v West*[1], where the claimant was indebted to a third party, who was the manager of a bank (though it appears from the report that he was indebted to the third party in the latter's personal capacity, rather than being indebted to the bank). The third party had promised that he would not call in the loan during his lifetime. The claimant was also employed by the third party under a contract for a fixed term of six years at £700 per annum. The claimant effected two policies on the life of the third party, one for £5,000, the other for £2,500. When the third party died, the insurers under the £5,000 policy paid out, but the insurers under the £2,500 policy refused payment, and the claimant sued. This is a somewhat confusing case in which the claimant arguably had interest in the third party's life in two distinct capacities; first as debtor and secondly as potential creditor under the contract of employment. It was held that the claimant as debtor had no such interest, because the third party's promise not to call in the debt during his lifetime was unenforceable in the absence of consideration. As creditor, the claimant *did* have an interest, but this was limited to the value of the possible wages under the contract, a total of £4,200. The payment of the £5,000 more than exhausted this interest, and the claimant was therefore not entitled to recover any further sum.

Various points of interest may be derived from this case. First, the case should not be treated as establishing that a debtor may never have an interest in the life of his creditor. There may be cases where the agreement not to enforce the debt during lifetime is legally enforceable, either because it is a term of a contract between the parties or by means of the doctrine of promissory estoppel. Indeed, it may be suggested that were *Hebdon* to reoccur today, the result could possibly be different, since promissory estoppel would arguably prevent the third party from resiling from his promise not to enforce the debt[2]. Secondly, the rule that the insured may recover only the total value of his interest applies in cases where there are multiple policies as well as where there is only a single policy. Thirdly, it appears that the insurers under the £5,000 policy would have been justified in refusing to pay the full amount under that policy. Clearly, this depends upon the order in which claims are made – the insurers on the first policy found themselves fully liable because no previous claim had been made.

[1] (1863) 3 B & S 579.
[2] *Central London Property Trust Ltd v High Trees House Ltd* [1947] KB 130.

Employer-employee

4.23 Another common practice is that of effecting what are sometimes called Keyman policies. As the name of the policy implies, this is normally done in cases where the employee's contribution to the business is so vital that the business cannot afford to lose him[1]. Given that there is an obvious financial risk involved, it is accepted that the employer can have an insurable interest. Indeed, there is no reason of principle why there should not be such interest in every employee, though in the majority of cases, where the employee can be fairly readily replaced, the amount of the loss (and therefore the amount of the interest) is likely to be relatively small. Although Keyman policies ought in principle to be treated as indemnity policies, it appears that in practice they are treated as contingency policies, the full sum insured being paid out on death without enquiry as to the actual loss.

[1] Policies of this kind may also be effected in personal accident insurance to guard against the risk that the employee's services are lost through a non-fatal cause.

Partners

4.24 It is generally understood that persons who are partners within the meaning of the Partnership Act 1890 are to be treated as having insurable interest in each other's lives. There is no authority to support the idea that there is automatic interest in these cases, but it is likely that there will normally be actual interest, especially in the common situation where the partnership agreement requires the survivors to buy out the share of a deceased partner.

Family relationships

4.25 Although there is no authority for an automatic interest outside the husband-wife relationship, it is possible for family relationships to give rise to insurable interest where there is discernible risk of financial loss. The usual objection to the recognition of insurable interest in these cases has been that there is no legal obligation to support even where there is a moral obligation. This objection would of course not apply in the case of a child in whose favour there was a maintenance order against one parent. In any case, it seems that this objection is rather outdated, and that at the present day mere moral obligations may be recognised. Thus, it may be possible for a dependent child to insure against the financial loss resulting from the death of one or more parents, and a parent who, perhaps because of age, is now financially dependent on his/her children ought to be able to insure the lives of one or more of those children. In appropriate cases there is no reason why interest should not exist between siblings or other more distant relations. On a similar principle, unmarried couples ought to be able to insure each other's lives (whether or not they are engaged to be married). This is most clearly seen in cases where one partner is entirely financially dependent on the other, but ought to apply even in cases where both partners are working, since the death of either will in such circumstances certainly lead to a reduction in the living standards of the other. Although there is no authority on the point, it is submitted that these principles apply to homosexual couples as much as to heterosexual couples. At one time it would have been inconceivable that courts would have been prepared to accord such recognition to homosexual couples, but it is submitted that the welcome changes in social attitudes in recent years now afford some ground for thinking that such interests will be recognised.

It seems unlikely that any other family relationships will regularly give rise to insurable interest, though it cannot be denied that social and demographic changes over the last 50 years have led to a much greater variety of family relationships, so that the possibility of identifying new situations containing the necessary element of dependence should not be ruled out. In particular, step-children and step-parents might well have insurable interest in each others' lives, and in cases where a couple live together outside marriage but with the children of one or other of them, those children might be allowed an insurable interest in the adult on whom they are dependent, even though the law recognises no family relationship between them. Attention is, however, drawn to a number of statutory provisions which deal expressly with certain situations. A person who maintains a foster child for reward has no insurable interest in the life of that child[1] and a person who maintains a protected child within the meaning of s 32 of the Adoption Act 1976 has no insurable interest in the life of that child[2].

[1] Foster Children Act 1980, s 19.
[2] Adoption Act 1976, s 31.

Joint mortgagors

4.26 Many joint mortgagors will be married to each other, or at least engaged to be married, and the position with regard to insurable interest in such cases may be dealt with under the principles applicable to those groups. However, some will not fall into this category. If a joint life policy is taken out, as will usually happen since this is cheaper than having two or more separate own life policies, then a question of insurable interest may arise, since each is in effect insuring the life of the other. Although there is no authority on the point, it is suggested that in this situation there is insurable interest, since each stands to lose financially by the death of the other. If there is a joint mortgage, each is in principle fully liable to the mortgagee for the debt, and is in fact relying on the other party to pay his/her share. This financial interest in the continued survival of the joint mortgagor ought to be enough to constitute a recognised insurable interest. This principle would apply with equal force to siblings who had a joint mortgage.

Valuing the interest in own life policies

4.27 A curious decision in relation to the valuing of an interest in an own life policy is *Lynne v Gordon Doctors and Walton*[1]. The deceased had instructed the defendants to procure for him an endowment policy to back a mortgage, but they failed to do so. The question was, assuming that the defendants had been negligent, how much could the estate recover? Phillips J held that there was no loss in this case, since the interest in question is not capable of pecuniary valuation. It is submitted that this is a wholly erroneous application of the notion that interests in an own life policy are not capable of valuation. The deceased needed this policy for a very practical reason, namely to ensure that his mortgage would be paid if he died prematurely. The loss to him during his lifetime was the absence of the cover which such a policy would have provided (and the possibility of selling the policy on the open market[2]), and on his death the loss was the irretrievable loss of the opportunity to obtain such a policy, even on worse terms because of a deterioration in his condition.

[1] (1991) 135 Sol Jo LB 29.
[2] *Insurance Law Monthly*, October 1991.

Friendly societies

4.28 Under the Friendly Societies Act 1974 Friendly Societies enjoyed limited immunity from the LAA 1774, being permitted to issue policies for events including deaths of relatives in whom there would not otherwise have been insurable interest, as well as marriage and the birth of a child. The full list of exemptions was contained in s 7 of the 1974 Act. However, this section was repealed by the Friendly Societies Act 1992[1], and even societies which remain registered under the 1974 Act can no longer issue such policies. However, this does not affect the validity of pre-existing policies of this type, some of which will no doubt continue to be found for many years to come.

[1] Section 120.

Property

4.29 So far as real property is concerned, s 1 of the LAA 1774 apparently applies, so that insurable interest is required. Although there is little authority specifically on what amounts to insurable interest in real property, it is surely clear that any legal or equitable interest in land will suffice. The borderline cases in this area are such as tenancies at will, those holding over after the expiry of a tenancy, other squatters and possibly licensees. As a general proposition it is submitted that a broad view of insurable interest should be taken, so that anyone who may suffer loss as a result of damage to real property is enabled to insure. Appropriate use of the principle of indemnity will prevent policyholders making adventitious gains.

In the case of personal property, the position is complicated by s 4 of the LAA 1774, which removes the requirement of insurable interest in the case of policies on goods. Although the LAA 1774 has no application to such policies, it does not follow that the absence of interest is irrelevant. It may be relevant in two ways. First, there is the question of the amount which the policyholder can recover when a loss happens. Since goods policies are always indemnity policies, it follows that they must be construed so as to provide the policyholder with no more than an indemnity for his actual loss. It is possible, as *Macaura v Northern Assur-*

ance Co Ltd[1] demonstrates, to suffer a loss through the destruction of property in which one has no insurable interest, but in practice that loss is likely to be somewhat limited in the great majority of cases. The claimant in *Macaura* presumably suffered a depreciation in the value of his shares in the company as a result of the destruction of the timber, though that depreciation may well have been less than the value of the timber. A proper application of the principle of indemnity would have led to the conclusion that he could recover that loss only. The second possible relevance of lack of insurable interest arises from the operation of s 18 of the Gaming Act 1845. That section provides that any contract entered into by way of gaming or wagering is void. This is a mandatory rule, not subject to the contrary agreement of the parties. The absence of insurable interest does not by itself prove that the policy is a gaming contract. Both *Macaura and Prudential Staff Union v Hall*[2] may be regarded as cases where there was no insurable interest, but where the policy could not properly have been described as a wagering contract. On the other hand the absence of insurable interest will almost always cause a court to ask the question why the policyholder has sought to insure these goods, and there will inevitably be some cases where there is no proper answer to that question, so that the policy must be held to be a gaming transaction.

Despite the points made above, there is case law on what is recognised as a sufficient interest to support insurance in particular property cases.

1 [1925] AC 619.
2 (1947) 80 Ll L 410, Morris J.

Mortgagor and mortgagee

4.30 This situation is one which normally will require insurable interest, since mortgages of goods are not normally found[1]. The mortgagor has an insurable interest in the full value of the property insured[2], even though it is mortgaged to its full value, because in case of loss he would not only be deprived of the property but would also remain liable for the mortgage debt – *Bank of Nova Scotia v Hellenic Mutual War Risks Association (Bermuda) Ltd, The Good Luck*[3] (insurers who failed to inform mortgagees that insurance had been avoided by the assured's causing vessels to enter prohibited zone, were in breach of an undertaking so to inform and liable upon that breach). There is Commonwealth authority that a mortgagee also has insurable interest[4]. This accords with principle and should be followed in England.

1 The only common exception to this is a mortgage on a ship or an aircraft.
2 Though it is normal to require the mortgagee to assign his own insurance policy to the mortgagee.
3 [1992] 1 AC 233, [1991] 3 All ER 1, HL.
4 *Walker v Rural & General Insurance Ltd* [1997] 6 Re LR 253 Sup, CT NSW.

Bailee and bailor

4.31 Where goods are entrusted to a bailee, he can insure them for their full value, even though his interest in them is limited to the value of the bailee's special property in goods[1]. The case is of course not subject to the LAA 1774, being a policy on goods. It is generally assumed that in such a case the bailee will hold the balance of the value of the goods on trust for the bailor. *Hepburn v Tomlinson (Hauliers) Ltd*[2] is commonly cited as the authority for this proposition, though it is to be noted that in that case the bailor was not a party to the action, and the only point which the House of Lords had to decide was whether the bailee could lawfully effect the policy at all. Despite this uncertainty, the conclusion reached is without doubt just and convenient, and it may be expected that it will continue to be followed.

1 *Hepburn v Tomlinson (Hauliers) Ltd* [1966] AC 451.
2 [1966] AC 451.

Economic interest

4.32 Intangible property rights such as intellectual property should fall within the LAA 1774, but again a broad view of insurable interest can be taken. It is submitted, in the absence of authority, that ownership of the right must be sufficient to found an insurable interest, but that a mere expectation of indirect profit from exploitation of a right held by another does not confer insurable interest. Such policies are of course widespread at the present day – the category includes all professional indemnity policies, as well as all business interruption policies. No one is likely to seek to insure where there is no prospect of loss, and the policy will in any event not pay out more than an indemnity. Consequently, in such cases the principle of indemnity by itself can operate to regulate perfectly satisfactorily the taking out of policies.

Marine

4.33 Sections 4, 5 and 6 of the MIA 1906 deal with the requirement of insurable interest in marine policies[1]. Section 4(1) provides that every marine policy by way of gaming or wagering is void. Section 4(2) goes on to say that a marine policy is deemed to be a gaming or wagering contract if the assured has no insurable interest and the contract is entered into with no expectation of acquiring such an interest, or where the policy is expressed to be made 'interest or no interest' or 'without further proof of interest than the policy itself' or 'without benefit of salvage to the insurer' (save where there is no possibility of salvage) or contains any other like term. These terms are not commonly found in modern policies, though there was a time when their use posed something of a problem. Accordingly, today the use of s 4 is more or less confined to those cases where there is in fact no insurable interest.

Section 5(1) of the MIA 1906 provides that every person has an insurable interest who is interested in a marine adventure. This is a rather unhelpful and self-referential definition, which is somewhat supplemented by s 5(2). This says that in particular a person is interested in a marine adventure where he stands in any legal or equitable relation to the adventure or to any insurable property at risk therein, in consequence of which he may benefit by the safety or due arrival of insurable property, or may be prejudiced by its loss, or by damage thereto, or by the detention thereof, or may incur liability in respect thereof. It might well be thought that this definition provides a good summary of the general principles of insurable interest in all forms of property, notwithstanding that s 5 is strictly applicable only to marine policies.

Section 6 of the MIA 1906 provides that the interest must attach at the time of the loss, though it need not attach at the time when the policy is taken out. However, if there is no interest at the time when the policy is taken out, there must at least be a reasonable expectation of acquiring one, since otherwise the policy is by way of gaming or wagering[2].

It is to be observed that the rule here is the opposite of that applying in life assurance[3]. It is suggested that the marine rule works satisfactorily – better indeed than the life assurance rule, which can produce anomalous consequences, as shown by the cases discussed in the section on life assurance above.

In the case of a policy written 'lost or not lost' it is permissible for the insured to have acquired his interest after the time of the loss, provided that at the time of taking out the policy he must not have known of the loss[4].

These provisions must be understood in the light of ss 16 and 27 of the MIA 1906. Section 16 creates some presumptions as to the insurable value of the subject matter insured in the cases of insurances on ship, goods, freight and other subject matters respectively. However, these presumptions are said to be subject to any express provision or valuation in the policy, and s 27 allows the use of valued policies, ie policies which specify the agreed value of the subject matter insured[5]. In the absence of fraud this valuation is conclusive as between assured and insurer. In the modern practice marine policies are always written as valued policies. Clearly this practice is capable of a certain degree of abuse, since it is possible for the parties to collude in overvaluing the subject matter of the insurance.

An important recent case on insurable interest in a marine context is *Cepheus Shipping Corpn v Guardian Royal Exchange Assurance plc*[6]. The vessel in that case was a refrigerated cargo vessel, and as such was likely to be laid up for at least part of the year. The relevant clause of the policy described the insured risk as 'loss of earnings and/or expense and/or hire' and provided for cover for up to 60 days' loss. In the event the ship was out of commission at a time when it would probably have been laid up anyway. Mance J was able to hold as a matter of the construction of the policy that this phrase referred only to loss of income which would in fact otherwise have been earned. However, his Lordship went on to consider the phrase from the point of view of insurable interest. The difficulty is of course that on one construction the drafting appears to give cover for loss not actually suffered and not foreseeably likely to be suffered. It was suggested that the insured value could be regarded as falling within s 27, so that the insurer would be liable for 60 days' hire, even where the vessel would have been laid up anyway. Mance J observed that it might be possible to draft a valuation clause in this way, but that it was most unlikely in practice that the parties would choose to do so. Certainly in this case they had not done so.

[1] It will be recalled that the LAA 1774 does not apply to marine policies.

[2] Section 4(2).

[3] *Dalby v India and London Life Assurance Co* (1854) 15 CB (NS) 365.

[4] This summary way of expressing the effect of s 6 appears to derive, albeit somewhat indirectly, from the wording, which allows recovery on a lost or not lost policy 'unless at the time of effecting

the contract ... the assured was aware of the loss and the insurer was not'. Taken literally, the words do not appear to prevent recovery in a case where both parties are aware of the loss, but it is submitted that in such a case the policy is clearly by way of gaming or wagering under s 4, with the result that the assured cannot recover. The consequence of this reasoning is that the assured cannot recover where he knows of the loss at the time of the policy, whatever the insurer's state of knowledge.

[5] Section 27(2).

[6] [1995] 1 Lloyd's Rep 622, Mance J.

Conclusion

4.34 The difficulties explored in the preceding paragraphs point quite strongly towards the conclusion that the LAA 1774 has outlived its usefulness. There does not at the present day appear to be any noticeable social problem in relation to 'wagering on lives', and life of another policies are generally effected for legitimate reasons even in those cases where the law does not recognise any insurable interest. It would surely be preferable either to abolish the statute completely and to rely instead upon the Gaming Act 1845, or to enact a sensible and broad definition of the cases where interest exists.

Chapter 5

Utmost good faith and the duty of disclosure

Introduction

5.1 The general rule of English law is that in pre-contractual negotiations there is no positive duty on either party to disclose material facts to the other party. The only duty is the negative one not to engage in misrepresentations. As is shown below, contracts of insurance form an important exception to this principle in that there are onerous duties of disclosure. However, misrepresentation remains important in insurance law.

Misrepresentation

5.2 Section 20 of the MIA 1906 deals with misrepresentation in the context of marine insurance, though these rules are commonly understood to apply to non-marine insurance as well.

Section 20(1) provides:

> 'Every material representation made by the assured or his agent to the insurer during the negotiations for the contract, and before the contract is concluded, must be true. If it be untrue the insurer may avoid the contract.'

Any misrepresentation which induces the other party to enter into the contract renders the contract voidable at the option of the other party. This applies even where the misrepresentation is entirely innocent, ie the misrepresentor has neither actual nor constructive knowledge of the falsity of the statement[1]. However, there must be a positive misrepresentation – mere silence is not enough. The telling of a half truth, which conceals the full truth or gives a misleading impression as to the full truth can amount to misrepresentation for these purposes[2]. These situations are occasionally of importance in insurance law. In the majority of cases, though, it is open to the insurer to rely on the much stricter rules relating to non-disclosure of material facts, which are discussed below. As will become apparent from that discussion, there are many cases where no misrepresentation can be identified, but the insurer is nevertheless able to rely on a non-disclosure. This significantly reduces the practical importance of misrepresentation in the insurance law context.

Where the misrepresentation is made fraudulently or negligently, the common law and statutory[3] rule is that the innocent victim may also recover damages. The application of this principle in an insurance law context is unclear. In the overwhelming majority of cases the misrepresentation will be made by the proposer. Once the insurer has avoided the policy, it is hard to see what further loss he has suffered[4], so that no damages could be awarded. The same point appears to apply in the relatively rare situation where the misrepresentation is perpetrated by the insurer. Certainly, it will not normally be possible for the policyholder to enforce the policy as if the representation were true. The only case where such an approach could have any prospect of success at all would be where the insurer's misrepresentation had somehow become a term of the contract, in which event the policyholder would be entitled to damages to put him in a position as if the representation had been true. It is thought that the only possible relevance of this in an insurance contract is where there is a misrepresentation by the insurer[5] as to the cover and other benefits[6] provided by the policy. Even here it will be very difficult to argue that the representation has become a term of the policy, since it is usual to have a written policy document which is expressed to contain all the terms of the agreement between the parties. Similarly, rectification will not be available because it will be impossible to show that the insurance company intended these representations to be terms of the contract[7]. It might be thought that an estoppel argument could be made, but it is not clear which form of estoppel would allow the policyholder to found a cause of action which he would not otherwise have – promissory estoppel does not normally have this effect.

Attention should also be drawn to *Economides v Commercial Union Assurance Co plc*[8] where it was held that a household contents policy could not be avoided where the proposer made honest, but erroneous, representations as to value of property insured. Although the law is formally the same in household contents policies as it is in marine policies, it is suggested that the approach of the court in that case can be at least partly explained by the fact that this was a personal lines policy.

Section 20(2) adds:

> 'A representation is material which would influence the judgment of a prudent insurer in fixing the premium, or determining whether he will take the risk.'

The notion of materiality is considered at length in relation to non-disclosure, below.

Section 20(3),(4) and (5) amplify these rules by providing that a representation may be either a representation as to a matter of fact, or as to a matter of expectation or belief and that a representation as to matter of fact is true, if it be substantially correct, that is to say, if the difference between what is represented and what is actually correct would not be considered material by a prudent insurer. A representation as to a matter of expectation or belief is true if it be made in good faith.

[1] *Urquhart v MacPherson* (1878) 3 App Cas 831.

[2] *With v O'Flanagan* [1936] Ch 575; *Nottingham Patent Brick and Tile Co v Butler* (1886) 16 QBD 778.
[3] Misrepresentation Act 1967.
[4] The costs of investigating the claim are caused by the claim and not by the misrepresentation, so they would not be recoverable.
[5] Or, more likely, an agent acting on the insurer's behalf.
[6] Such as the likely return in the case of an investment policy.
[7] Though in some cases the Insurance Ombudsman may be more sympathetic to arguments of this kind- as to the approach of the various Ombudsmen see Chapter 21.
[8] [1997] 3 All ER 636, CA, discussed further in Chapter 38; the point that valuation is ultimately a matter of opinion was reiterated in *Eagle Star Insurance Co Ltd v Games Video Co* [2004] EWHC 15 (Comm), [2004] Lloyd's Rep IR 867, Simon J.

Utmost good faith

5.3 It is perhaps the most important single rule of insurance law that insurance is a contract of utmost good faith[1]. The principle derives from the well-known case of *Carter v Boehm*[2], where Lord Mansfield CJ said:

> 'Insurance is a contract upon speculation. The special facts, upon which the contingent chance is to be computed, lie most commonly in the knowledge of the insured only; the underwriter trusts to his representation, and proceeds upon confidence that he does not keep back any circumstance in his knowledge, to mislead the underwriter into a belief that the circumstance does not exist, and to induce him to estimate the risque as if it did not exist.'

Some preliminary points should be made about that case, before the modern rules are explored in detail. First, Lord Mansfield speaks only in terms of the duty of the proposer, since that is all that was in issue in the case. More modern authority, considered below, has also looked at the duties of the insurer. Secondly, although the duty of disclosure is certainly the most important part of the doctrine of utmost good faith, it is not the only part. Again, later sections of this Chapter will consider other aspects of utmost good faith[3]. Thirdly, the duty of disclosure exists in addition to and independently of the general legal duty not to induce contracts by misrepresentations. Logically, there is a difference between a misrepresentation, which involves something which can properly be characterised as an active representation, and a non-disclosure, which requires only a failure to disclose, even where this takes the form of silence. In practice, however, insurance lawyers tend to conflate the two notions, with blatant misrepresentations being treated as if they were non-disclosures[4]. From one point of view this practice may be treated as justified, since the consequences of either seem to be more or less identical in the modern law.

[1] Or *uberrimae fidei*. The present text reluctantly adopts the modern practice of avoiding the traditional Latin phrases as far as possible. For the history of the doctrine, see Bennett [1999] LMCL 165.
[2] (1766) 3 Burr 1905.
[3] And Chapter 13 will consider post-contractual good faith.
[4] The best modern example is to be found in the case of *Pan Atlantic Insurance Co Ltd v Pine Top Insurance Co Ltd* [1994] 3 All ER 581, which concerns a number of misrepresentations, but where the House of Lords took the opportunity to restate the law on non-disclosure.

The duty of pre-contractual disclosure

5.4 From the point of view of the proposer the law is reasonably clear and very onerous. It is the duty of the proposer to disclose before the contract is entered into all material facts of which he is or ought to be aware. Constructive knowledge of the relevant facts is sufficient[1], and material facts are defined as those which would be likely to influence the judgment of a hypothetical prudent insurer in deciding whether and on what terms to accept the risk. This test is derived from the decision of the Court of Appeal in *Lambert v Co-operative Insurance Society Ltd*[2]. Although this was a case of household assurance, the judgment proceeds expressly on the basis that the relevant rules and tests should not differ between one class of insurance and another[3].

1 *Joel v Law Union and Crown Insurance* [1908] 2 KB 863.
2 [1975] 2 Lloyd's Rep 485, CA.
3 Although the comparison drawn in that case was between marine and non-marine cases, it is thought that the same principle should apply to all classes of life assurance.

Eliciting the information

5.5 In practice insurers naturally do not simply leave it to the proposer to disclose all material facts. It is usual, at least in personal lines policies, for insurers to provide the proposer with a form ('the proposal form') which asks a number of specific questions about matters relevant to the class of insurance in question. The role of the proposal form in insurance contract law requires careful consideration. First, it is apparent that giving a false answer to any question on the proposal form will amount not merely to non-disclosure but to active misrepresentation. Consequently, the most difficult issues in relation to the proposal form are the extent to which the questions on the form should be regarded as exhausting the duty of disclosure and the construction of particular questions.

It is important to understand, however, that as a matter of law the proposer's duties in relation to disclosure of material facts to the insurer do not depend on the existence of a proposal form[1]. The duty to disclose material facts exists independently of the proposal form, though the proposal form may well extend that duty by asking specific questions about matters which would not otherwise be considered material. The effect and status of such additional questions are less clear than they once were, in the light of the case of *Pan Atlantic Insurance Co Ltd v Pine Top Insurance Co Ltd*[2], which is considered below at para 5.10.

1 *Godfrey v Britannic Assurance Co Ltd* [1963] 2 Lloyd's Rep 515, Roskill J.
2 [1994] 3 All ER 581.

Where there is no proposal form

5.6 The use of proposal forms is widespread, but not universal – there are some types of insurance which are commonly sold without a proposal form. In personal lines policies perhaps the best example is travel insurance[1], where the policy is sold incidentally to the sale of the travel package. In commercial insurance it is increasingly common to find that proposal forms are not used. It is also sometimes possible to get 'over the counter' insurance sold on the spot and without detailed enquiries as to material facts[2]. This practice gives rise to some difficulties. It is inevitable that in the absence of a proposal form the proposer will give very little information to the insurer – whatever the strict legal rule, proposers rarely volunteer information, probably because they trust the insurer to ask about all matters which are material. Although the absence of questions from the proposal form, or indeed the absence of a form at all, does not in theory affect the scope of the duty of disclosure, courts are understandably reluctant to penalise policyholders for not answering questions which are not asked. In addition, the Insurance Ombudsman has adopted the general principle that insurers should ask for information which they want to know and should not be allowed to rely on failure to disclose additional information voluntarily.

A further point arising from the absence of a proposal form is the tendency of some insurers to deal with the problem of limited information through the drafting of the policy. Thus, in travel policies it will usually be found that no pre-contract questions are asked about the proposer's medical circumstances, even though the policy provides cover for costs of medical treatment etc. It may be found, on closer examination, that the policy also contains an exclusion for medical treatment resulting from pre-existing conditions. In this way it becomes unnecessary for the insurer to ask questions about these matters, since they are no longer material to the risk run by the insurer. This technique, although on the face of it lawful, may legitimately be thought objectionable, since they amount in effect to the conduct of the underwriting process at the claims stage. Naturally, very little is done to bring these exclusions to the policyholder's attention before the contract is entered into[3].

1 Considered in detail in Chapter 46.

2 See *Aro Road and Land Vehicles Ltd v Insurance Corpn of Ireland Ltd* [1986] IR 403, noted at (1988) 9 Co Lawyer 226.

3 Where the policy is sold through intermediaries the General Insurance Standards Council Code of Practice may also be relevant. As to the effects of this, see Chapter 6.

Telephone selling of insurance

5.7 The increasingly common practice of selling insurance over the telephone provides another important example of a situation where there is no proposal form. Prudent insurers using this method of selling provide proposers with written copies of the information held in the insurer's records as a means of reducing the incidence of disputes about what was said[1]. From a strict legal point of view the nature and extent of the duty of disclosure are of course unaffected by the fact of telephone selling, though the Ombudsman, in deciding what is fair and reasonable in any given case, might well want to take account of the absence of a proposal form and the fact that the proposer had no opportunity to reduce his answers to writing.

1 IOB 10.27.

Adequacy of disclosure

5.8 There must be sufficient disclosure to put the insurer properly on notice of the material facts. The status of the insurance contract as a contract of utmost good faith means that a presentation of the facts which, although not strictly inaccurate, tends to mislead the insurer is not an adequate disclosure[1]. The disclosure must be made to a part of the insurance company's operation which is equipped to understand the significance of what is disclosed. In *Malhi v Abbey Life Assurance Co Ltd*[2] P applied for an endowment policy, which was refused on the basis of a medical report. He already had a term policy, in respect of which he had committed two non-disclosures. The first was pre-contractual, whilst the second occurred in a Declaration of Continuing Good Health when reinstating the policy after it had lapsed for non-payment of premiums. If the underwriters considering the endowment application had cross-referenced it with the earlier term policy documentation, they would have spotted the non-disclosure, but the earlier documentation was not readily to hand, and they did not do so. Further premiums were subsequently paid, and it was argued on behalf of the policyholder that the acceptance of these premiums with knowledge of the non-disclosure amounted to a waiver of the right to avoid[3]. It was held, by a majority, that knowledge of the earlier non-disclosure could not be imputed to the company, because the information had not been given to a person authorised and able to appreciate its significance. The case is of some importance for it may be regarded as establishing the principle that the duty is not complied with by absolutely any communication to any arm of the insurer, which cannot for these purposes be treated simply as a monolithic organisation.

1 *Pan Atlantic* itself may be regarded as an example of such a case.
2 [1996] LRLR 237, CA.
3 See below.

Meaning of 'material fact'

5.9 The MIA 1906 has a definition of materiality:

> 'Every circumstance is material which would influence the judgment of a prudent insurer in fixing the premium or determining whether he will take the risk[1].'

Although there is an enormous body of case law on the meaning of materiality, only a small part of it will be considered here, for many of the cases are effectively overtaken by the decision of the House of Lords in *Pan Atlantic Insurance Co Ltd v Pine Top Insurance Co Ltd*[2].

In *Lambert v Co-operative Insurance Society*[3], the Court of Appeal rejected suggestions that the test for materiality in the context of domestic household insurance should be couched in terms which related to the expectations of the proposer or to the views of the particular insurer. The test is thus objective by reference to the views of a hypothetical reasonable insurer. For the purpose of determining whether this hypothetical reasonable insurer would consider a particular fact material the court may take expert evidence from actual insurers as to their practice, but like all expert evidence this testimony assists the court but does not bind it[4].

A further important point concerns the meaning of the words 'facts which would *influence the judgment* of a prudent insurer'. At first sight it might be thought that the italicised words imply that the fact must be one which would cause the insurer to make a different decision, either about whether to accept the risks or about the terms as to premium or otherwise which should be offered. However, in *Berger and Light Diffusers Pty Ltd v Pollock*[5] the Court of Appeal held that a fact may influence the judgment of an insurer even though it does not cause him to change his decision. Thus, in a banker's blanket bond and professional indemnity policy it was a material fact that allegations of dishonesty had been made against the president of the bank, even if those allegations were unfounded[6]. It is sufficient that the fact is one which the insurer would wish to know and consider when making his decision, even though in the end the decision would in all respects be the same. The judgments proceed on the assumption that the same principles are applicable to all classes of insurance, and it is obviously sensible that this should be so. However, the position is apparently different if the allegations are unfounded and the assured is able to prove this at trial[7]. It is submitted, however, that this must go to inducement rather than to materiality – insurers are still entitled to the information, even if, with full disclosure of the evidence for the untruth of the allegations they would make the same decision.

Container Transport International Inc v Oceanus Mutual Underwriting Association (Bermuda) Ltd[8] perhaps marks one extreme of the development of the law of non-disclosure, moving as far as it is possible to do in the direction of requiring disclosure.

1 MIA 1906, s 18(2).
2 [1994] 3 All ER 581, HL.
3 [1975] 2 Lloyd's Rep 485, CA.
4 For an example of the operation of this principle see *Roselodge Ltd v Castle* [1966] 2 Lloyd's Rep 105, CA, a case of jewellery insurance, where the trial judge refused to accept expert evidence as to the materiality of certain facts.
5 [1973] 2 Lloyd's Rep 42.
6 [2003] Lloyd's Rep IR 746, CA.
7 *Strive Shipping Corp v Hellenic Mutual War Risks Association (Bermuda) Ltd* [2002] 2 All ER (Comm) 213, Colman J.
8 [1984] 1 Lloyd's Rep 476, CA.

The modern law – Pan Atlantic Insurance Co Ltd v Pine Top Insurance Co Ltd

5.10 The modern law on the duty of disclosure must now be regarded as being centred on the decision of the House of Lords in this case[1]. The relevant facts of the case may be briefly stated. The claimants wished to re-insure long-tail environmental liability business, and the broker acting on their behalf presented the risk to the re-insurer in such a way as to distract attention from the more mature years of the loss record (which of course give a better indication of the true position in long-tail cases) and, three weeks after the initial meeting between the parties told the re-insurer that the losses for later years had not significantly increased since that meeting, when in fact the total of claims had doubled in that time. Not surprisingly, the latter misrepresentation was held to render the policy voidable, though the earlier misleading of the re-insurer was held irrelevant on the ground that a competent underwriter should have known that the earlier years were more reliable and should not have allowed himself to be distracted from them. Although their Lordships were unanimous in reaching this conclusion, the approaches which they adopted to the general questions of law are of such fundamental importance to the law of non-disclosure that the speeches require to be analysed at some length.

The House of Lords took this opportunity to review at length the general principles applicable to the law of non-disclosure. Indeed, it is noticeable that the facts of the case itself received only cursory treatment. It was agreed by all members of the Appellate Committee[2] that the case resolved itself into two issues, namely whether a fact is material only if it would exercise a decisive influence on the hypothetical reasonable underwriter's decision whether and at what premium to accept the risk or whether it is sufficient that it would have been one of the facts which the hypothetical reasonable underwriter would have wanted to know in making that decision and, secondly, whether the insurer is entitled to avoid the policy for non-disclosure of a material fact even though the non-disclosure did not induce the actual insurer to enter into the contract.

It is convenient to begin by identifying some important but peripheral points which are involved in the decision in this case. First, it was clearly stated that the law on non-disclosure is the same in marine and non-marine cases. It is noticeable that the discussion of the issues was centred on ss 18 and 20 of the MIA 1906 notwithstanding that this is not a case of marine insurance. Although it is obviously desirable that the law should be the same in all types of insurance, this concentration on the words of the statute did, as will appear below, lead to some difficulties arising from what are arguable omissions from the sections in question. Secondly, although the question of non-disclosure arises only in relation to contracts of utmost good faith, that of misrepresentation arises in all contracts, including insurance contracts. It is obviously desirable that the law on misrepresentation should be the same in all types of contract. Moreover, it seems undesirable that the status of an insurance contract should differ according to whether the behaviour of the proposer is classified as misrepresentation or as non-disclosure, since there is a fine line between the two and it is often a matter of chance which designation is adopted.

[1] It is for this reason that this Chapter deliberately omits many of the older authorities, whose relevance must now be at best questionable.

[2] Lord Templeman, Lord Goff, Lord Mustill, Lord Slynn and Lord Lloyd.

The definition of materiality

5.11 As indicated above, many of the criticisms of *CTI v Oceanus* were aimed at showing that materiality should require some impact on the decision made by either the actual insurer or the hypothetical reasonable insurer. As Lord Mustill points out in his speech, this anxiety to narrow the concept of materiality was a natural consequence of the long-held belief that materiality was the only question in relation to non-disclosure, ie that any non-disclosure of a material fact must always make the contract voidable. This view is of course derived largely from the wording of s 18 of the MIA 1906, which declares contracts voidable for non-disclosure (s 20 does the same in respect of misrepresentations). However, if it were possible to treat what might be called the causation question, ie the question whether the non-disclosure induced the *actual* insurer to enter into the contract, separately from the question whether the fact would, if disclosed, have influenced the judgment of the *hypothetical reasonable* insurer, this pressure to recast the definition of materiality would greatly diminish. The drawing of such a distinction forms the basis of the speech of Lord Mustill, with whom Lord Goff and Lord Slynn agreed. After an extensive review of authorities and academic writings pre-dating the MIA 1906, Lord Mustill held that the Court of Appeal in *CTI v Oceanus* had been right to decide that a fact is material once it is shown that it is one which the hypothetical reasonable insurer would have wanted to know. It is not necessary to show that knowledge of the fact would have exerted a decisive influence on his decision. His Lordship suggests the decisive influence test is unworkable because it offers too great an opportunity for dispute between underwriters about what they would have done if the fact had been disclosed. It is interesting to contrast the alternative view taken by Lord Templeman and Lord Lloyd, which is that identifying what the hypothetical reasonable underwriter would have done is much easier than identifying what he would have wanted to know, the latter being a much more nebulous question. There appears to be much good sense in this view. Lord Mustill's view is, however, the one which must now be regarded as being good law.

The causation question

5.12 Prior to this decision it had appeared that the causation question did not really exist in this context since any material non-disclosure would allow the insurers to avoid the contract. The radical change which the decision of the House of Lords in this case makes is that it recognises the central importance of the causation question. On this point all five members of the Appellate Committee were in agreement. The insurer is not entitled to avoid the policy unless he demonstrates that the non-disclosure actually induced him to enter into the policy. It must be observed that this test focuses on the actual insurer rather than on a hypothetical prudent insurer. Although there is no mention of the need for inducement in the MIA 1906, the House of Lords was prepared to hold that such a requirement must be implied on the basis that the Act was intended only to codify the common law, which, in their Lordships view had included such a requirement, and that the absence of any specific reference to inducement could be explained on the basis that the Act was dealing with materiality not with inducement. The importance of this decision for the law of non-disclosure can scarcely be overestimated. Insurers now face a much greater burden in seeking to avoid a policy for non-disclosure or misrepresentation that they previously did, and it appears that this is so even where the policyholder has been guilty of fraud, since the principles upon which the observations of the House of Lords in *Pan Atlantic* are based do not depend on the absence of fraud. However, the court does not look for the decisive cause or main reason – underwriters can rely on any factor which is an (not *the*) effective or real cause of the decision to enter into the contract[1]. This test clearly waters down the standard which insurers have to meet in order to avoid non-disclosure of a material fact.

[1] *Assicurazioni Generali SpA v Arab Insurance Group (BSC)* [2002] EWCA Civ 1642, [2003] 1 All ER (Comm) 140.

Pan Atlantic – Some unresolved questions

5.13 So far as materiality is concerned, it seems that expert evidence will still be required, and that it is not relevant to know what the actual insurer would have done. Where there is conflicting expert evidence, the court will have to choose which it prefers. The more difficult questions seem, however, to arise in relation to inducement. Where only one material fact has not been disclosed, it will probably be easy enough to decide whether its disclosure would have led the insurer to act differently, but the position is more complex where more than one fact has been concealed, Here it may happen that no one undisclosed fact would by itself have been sufficient to alter the insurer's behaviour, but that the facts (or some one or more combinations of them taken together) would have done so. Presumably the test must be whether the insurer would have acted differently had full disclosure been made.

Another oddity arising from the decision concerns the ways in which the insurer's behaviour might have been changed. The MIA 1906, dealing with materiality, refers only to the decision whether to accept the risk, but the judgments in this case assume that this must be treated as including accepting the risk at a higher premium. The Act does not of course deal expressly with the ways in which the actual insurer might have behaved differently, but the judgments again assume that the change will be of one of the two kinds already described. In fact there are other ways in which an insurer might react to the information, including in the context of life assurance, reducing the cover or altering the policy wording by excluding death arising from specified causes. It is not clear from the judgments whether a potential change of this kind is sufficient to allow avoidance of the policy. In principle it is suggested that any alteration which goes beyond the purely trivial ought to be sufficient.

Actual and constructive knowledge of the proposer

5.14 The proposer must disclose every material circumstance of which he is or ought to be aware[1]. It is no excuse for him to say that he was not in fact aware of the relevant circumstance. An assured is deemed to know every circumstance which, in the ordinary course of business, ought to be known by him – *PCW Syndicates v PCW Reinsurers*[2] (the dishonesty of an underwriting agent was not a circumstance which 'in the ordinary course of business, ought to be known' to an assured). Clearly the proposer must disclose every material fact of which he is actually aware. Moreover, he must disclose facts of which he ought to have been aware. Thus, in *Joel v Law Union*[3] it was said that a proposer could not escape the duty to disclose facts relating to his health by closing his eyes to the significance of medical symptoms. That was a personal lines case, and more recently the same point was considered in the reinsurance case of *Simner v New India Assurance Co Ltd*[4], where it was held that the proposer must disclose every fact known to him or which in the ordinary course of business ought to be known to him, but is under no positive duty to make enquiries to discover facts which go beyond that scope. It must remain a question of fact whether in any given case a particular matter ought to have been known to the proposer. In *Keating v New Ireland Assurance Co plc*[5] there was a Basis of the Contract clause cast in absolute terms. The insurers sought to rely on a failure to disclose angina in a proposal for life assurance. The evidence was that the proposer had had a medical examination which had detected the condition, but he had never been informed of it. Despite the Basis of the Contract clause it was held that the proposer could not be expected to disclose something of which he had neither actual nor constructive knowledge.

Because the case is based on Irish law the Statements of Insurance Practice are not relevant[6], and it is interesting to observe the Irish Supreme Court in effect refusing to implement the strict words of the proposal form on the ground that they are wholly unreasonable. It is unclear whether the same approach would have prevailed in a case of commercial insurance.

1 *Joel v Law Union* [1908] 2 KB 863, CA.
2 [1996] 1 All ER 774, CA.
3 [1908] 2 KB 863, CA.
4 [1995] LRLR 240, Judge Diamond QC.
5 [1990] 2 IR 383 Sup Ct.
6 They would of course not be directly relevant before a court of law in the UK.

5.15 Where an insurance is effected for the assured by an *agent*, the agent must, subject to certain exceptions, disclose to the insurer every material circumstance which is known to himself, and an agent to insure is deemed to know every circumstance which in the ordinary course of business ought to be known by, or to have been communicated to, him. The words 'agent to insure' apply only to those who actually deal with the insurers and make the contract in question, intermediate agents are not included within the ambit of s 19(a): *PCW Syndicates v PCW Reinsurers*[1]. Where the proposer is a private individual and the insurance sought is other than in the ordinary course of business, the duty is one of honesty to disclose facts actually known; provided the proposer does not wilfully shut his eyes to the truth, there is no duty to inquire further into the facts: *Economides v Commercial Union Assurance Co plc*[2]. It was held in that case that an honest representation of belief in an insurance context must have some basis, but there is no implied representation that there exist reasonable grounds for making it. If insurers wish their clients to obtain independent valuations of their goods then that must be made a term of the contract. *Crédit Lyonnais Bank Nederland (NV) v Export Credits Guarantee Department*[3] was distinguished because the asserted opinion had been contrary to the representor's own knowledge. It was also held that the test for non-disclosure is that of honesty. An individual purchasing private household insurance cannot be burdened with deemed or constructive knowledge: *Group Josi, Re v Walbrook Insurance Co Ltd*[4].

In *Manifest Shipping & Co Ltd v Uni Polaris Shipping Co Ltd, The Star Sea*[5] it was alleged that there had been a breach of the duty of utmost good faith in failing to disclose reports of previous losses of other ships sooner and fraud in misleading the underwriters by concealing evidence. Although the MIA 1906, s 17 does not say that underwriters are not liable for fraudulent claims, there is less agreement as to the content of the duty of utmost good faith or remedies for breach of the duty. When a claim is made, the duty rests on both assured and insurer but the duty of disclosure is not co-extensive with the pre-contractual duty. The House of Lords approved the view of Malcolm Clarke[6] that the duty of disclosure continues throughout the contract but at a level appropriate to the circumstances. There is a duty not to make fraudulent claims, but the very onerous pre-contractual duty of care does not apply to the making of claims. One reason for coming to this conclusion was that in many cases there will be ongoing or imminent litigation between the insured and the insurer. To impose the full duty of disclosure in such circumstances would in effect require the insured to provide the insurer with ammunition with which to defend the claim. The Court of Appeal considered that such a duty would not be justified. Instead, the obligation to disclose material facts is limited to that imposed on litigants generally by the Civil Procedure Rules 1998

('CPR 1998'). One effect of the decision is likely to be that claim forms will tend to become longer and more detailed, since insurers must have a better chance of rejecting a claim if they can show that they asked specific questions about matters material to the claim and that they received false answers. In turn, insureds are likely to be found arguing that any inaccurate statement on the claim form occurred as a result of simple negligence rather than of fraud.

1 [1996] 1 All ER 774, CA.
2 [1997] 3 All ER 636, CA.
3 [1996] 1 Lloyd's Rep 200.
4 [1996] 1 WLR 1152.
5 [2001] UKHL 1, [2001] 1 Lloyd's Rep IR 247. See also Chapter 13.
6 Clarke *The Law of Insurance Contracts* (2nd edn, LPP), p 708; see now the 4th edn (2002).

Composite/joint insurance – misrepresentation/non-disclosure by one party

5.16 In *Glicksman v Lancashire & General Assurance Co Ltd*[1] the policyholders were two individuals carrying on business in partnership. The proposal form which they completed asked whether 'your proposal' for insurance had ever been declined. They answered in the negative. In fact one of them when proposing for insurance alone, had had a proposal declined, and the insurers sought to repudiate liability for an insured loss on this basis. The House of Lords held that the previous declinature was obviously material, so that the insurers were entitled to succeed. It is unfortunate that the question was ambiguously worded; at the present day such a question, if included in a personal lines policy, would probably fall foul of the Statements of Practice and thus of the Insurance Ombudsman. However, in a commercial policy such as this, the insurers would still be entitled to rely on the strict law, which, among other things, continues to require disclosure of all material facts, even where these are not the subject of an express question. More recently, in *DSG Retail Ltd v QBE International Insurance Ltd*[2] the subject matter of the insurance was the potential loss suffered by Dixons (electrical equipment) and JSI (travel agents) arising out of a promotion similar to the infamous Hoover deal in that customers purchasing certain items from Dixons were offered free flights. JSI hoped to make money out of extras – eg car hire and accommodation.

When JSI went into liquidation and Dixons sought to claim under the policy, the insurers refused to pay on the grounds of misrepresentation, non-disclosure and/or breach of warranty in the proposal form and the accompanying placing documentation presented to them. There was no dispute that all these 'misdemeanours' were on the part of JSI, not Dixons, and the question was what effect they had on Dixons insurance.

Here, Dixons argued that the insurance was composite – ie the parties had different interests, and were separately insured albeit that the separate insurances were embodied in one composite insurance. They therefore submitted that a breach of the duty of utmost good faith by JSI did not entitle the insurers to avoid their contract with Dixons. In contrast, where there is joint insurance, each insured is affected by the misconduct or breach of the duty of utmost good faith of any of them[3]. It was held that the insurance was neither joint nor composite – there was only one risk, namely whether the promotion would result in a net loss, and this would be calculated in the same way whether the claimant was JSI or Dixons. The judge considered the wording of the slip and was particularly influenced by the fact that the slip did not state that JSI and Dixons were insured for their respective interests. The slip provided that Dixons could *'only take over the insured's rights under the policy should JSI be unable to continue to run the promotion'* and this was construed as recognising that the interests of JSI and Dixons were the same. This meant that Dixons, in taking over the claim from JSI, obtained no better rights than JSI had so the insurers were entitled to rely on the same defences against Dixons as they would have been able to against JSI.

Although he did not need to deal with them, the judge also commented on two other issues as follows:

- He held that JSI and Dixons, by making their declarations on the proposal forms, had each taken responsibility for the accuracy of the proposal forms and each was making a representation about what they both expected.
- He held that as no policy wording was ever agreed, a term in the proposal forms and the slip making the statements contained in the forms 'the basis of the' insurance, did not become a term of the contract.

[1] [1927] AC 139, HL.
[2] [1999] Lloyd's Rep IR 283.
[3] See *First National Commercial Bank plc v Barnet Devanney (Harrow) Ltd* [1999] Lloyd's Rep IR 459, CA on the distinction between composite and joint insurance.

Adequacy of disclosure

5.17 In *Hill v Citadel Insurance Co Ltd and Citadel Reinsurance Co Ltd*[1] the question was whether the defendant could avoid its obligations under subscribed quota share treaties reinsuring two Lloyd's syndicates on the grounds of material misrepresentation and non disclosure contained in the information provided by the syndicates' brokers. It was suggested that the fact that the information given was vague should have put the defendant on enquiry as to whether other information should be disclosed. It was held that the information fell far short of being capable of putting the Defendant on enquiry as to whether other material matters had been disclosed.

[1] [1997] LRLR 167.

Facts which are commonly found to be material

5.18 In dealing with material facts for the purposes of the duty of disclosure it is customary to distinguish between facts which are relevant to the physical hazard, and facts which are relevant to the moral hazard.

Facts relevant to the physical hazard

5.19 These may be defined as those facts which make it more likely that the insured peril will materialise. These naturally vary from one class of insurance to another. The following paragraphs give a number of examples of matters which have been held to be material in particular classes of insurance. It should be borne in mind that no list can be exhaustive, and that it is always essential to look at the context of the individual proposal. It is therefore dangerous to rely unquestioningly on any previously decided case.

Property assurance

5.20 In this context material matters include the age, condition and location of the property. Location is obviously crucial for real property. In the case of personal property the place of storage (parking in the case of a vehicle) is also likely to be relevant. The use made or to be made of the property will be also be vital. Where there is to be theft cover, security precautions will be of importance. In a combined hotel, catering and leisure insurance in respect of a motel, the fact that a discotheque was operated on the premises should have been disclosed[1]. The claimant insured his hotel, which included a discotheque. The proposal form did not mention the existence of the discotheque. When the premises were damaged by fire the insurers refused indemnity on the basis of this non-disclosure. Two issues were argued. The first was whether the existence of the discotheque was material at all, and the second was whether (assuming it to be material) the claimant had complied with the duty of disclosure in respect of it. The Court of Appeal held that the fact was material, since the existence of a discotheque contributed to the risk of loss or damage, but that there had been no breach of the duty of disclosure. On this point two arguments were used. The first was that the running of a discotheque as part of a hotel is now such a common practice that the insurers ought to have been aware of it, and that it was therefore implicitly disclosed when the claimant stated on the proposal form that the premises were used as a hotel. The second was that the wording of the questions on the proposal form was such as to waive the duty of disclosure in this respect. The Court of Appeal accepted both arguments. The first is essentially a question of fact, but the second raises more difficult issues as to waiver of duty of disclosure. The proposal form was imprecisely worded, and it was held as a matter of construction that it did not ask about the possibility of a discotheque. However, this seems to be a departure from the general principle that material facts have to be disclosed even if not asked about, and there is no general principle that asking about certain matters waives the need to disclose other matters. The first ground of decision seems much more convincing than the second. The price paid for the property has also been held by the Insurance Ombudsman to be material, at least in a case where the proposal form expressly seeks this information[2].

1 *Roberts v Plaisted* [1989] 2 Lloyd's Rep 341, CA.
2 IOB 3.21.

Insurance of the person

5.21 In relation to life and permanent health insurance ('PHI') policies they obviously include such things as the physical characteristics of the proposer – age, height, weight for example, facts about the proposer's medical history and condition and facts about the proposer's occupation and hobbies. All these matters will normally be the subject of specific questions on the proposal form, and the answers are obviously material in the sense explained above.

Two rather contentious issues at the present day in this context are AIDS and genetic testing. So far as AIDS is concerned, the position is certainly less serious than it was a few years ago, largely as a result of the welcome decline in the incidence of cases of the disease, at any rate in Europe. Despite this, some insurers still ask questions about the 'lifestyle' (a euphemism for the sexual and drug-taking habits) of proposers identified as being in the high-risk groups for AIDS, ie homosexual men, bi-sexual men[1], intravenous drug-users and sexual partners of any of these[2]. Although this practice has caused considerable controversy and has been condemned in some quarters as an invasion of privacy, it cannot be denied that these facts are highly relevant to the risk which the insurer is taking. Insurers have also become more sensitive in recognising the difference between the number of sexual partners a person has had and that person's sexual orientation. The former is probably more relevant to the risk of AIDS than the latter. Another welcome development of recent years has been the abandonment of the practice of loading premiums for those who have taken who have taken an AIDS test, which has proved negative. In accordance with a 1994 ABI recommendation, the practice now is not to require disclosure of negative AIDS tests.

The provision of the Statement of Long-Term Insurance Practice ('SLIP')[3] that a proposer need only answer questions to the best of his knowledge and belief is also relevant since a proposer could conceivably have been a sexual partner of someone in a high-risk group without being aware of the fact.

Genetic testing raises somewhat different problems which are by no means entirely solved. The development of these tests in the past 20 years has led to a situation in which testing can give individuals a very good idea of the diseases to which they are most prone and even of their life expectancy. The tests are accurate enough that this kind of prognosis is possible at a fairly young age. The insurance industry still appears to be in a state of some confusion about how to react to this. On the one hand it might be said that the information is crucial since it allows for much more accurate premium rating. Certainly the initial response of the industry has been to embrace genetic testing with every sign of enthusiasm. The alternative view would be that widespread genetic testing has the potential to undermine the life assurance industry. At present the industry works on the basis that those who live long will by their premiums pay for those who die young, all parties taking a gamble on their life expectancy when the policy is taken out. If the element of gamble is significantly reduced, then it may be that those with a long life expectancy will be less inclined to insure, leaving only a pool of poorer risks, whose premiums will have to increase to a point where the insurance may be too expensive for them. On this theory the industry would do well to discourage the practice of genetic testing. For the moment the solution adopted is not to require testing, but to require disclosure of the results of any tests which the proposer may have taken. Some proposers would therefore do well not to have the test.

1 Whether these terms are to be regarded as referring to inclination or only to activity is still unresolved.
2 The virtual elimination of the risk of infection through contaminated blood transfusions has removed haemophiliacs from the high-risk category.
3 See Appendix 3.

Pending claims

5.22 In liability policies it is common to require disclosure of events which have already happened and which are thought likely to give rise to a claim. In this context, 'likely', means a chance greater than 50%[1].

[1] *Jacobs v Coster* [2000] Lloyd's Rep IR 506, CA: *Layher Ltd v Lowe* [2000] Lloyd's Rep IR 510, CA.

Facts which are relevant to the moral hazard

5.23 The moral hazard in insurance may be defined as the risk that the proposer will in some way act dishonestly in relation to the insurance policy, in particular the risk that he will make false claims. This definition is admittedly imperfect, for it is customary in general insurance to regard the proposer's claims history as part of the moral hazard, notwithstanding that all previous claims may have been genuine and that this evidence may then go only to show that the proposer is particularly prone to incurring genuine losses. It is appropriate to discuss separately life policies and other types of insurance.

In non-life insurance three particular areas of importance may be identified, namely claims history, insurance history and criminal records

Claims history

5.24 Proposal forms commonly ask for disclosure of previous insurance claims. Where the question is expressly asked, materiality can scarcely be in doubt; Even where it is not asked, there can be little scope to deny that at least some criminal convictions are material. Sometimes the history is limited to a particular period of time eg the last five years, but in other cases a complete history may be required. Ambiguities can arise in relation to claims, however, since proposal forms do not always make clear whether they are restricted to claims for the same type of loss as that which is to be insured. Thus, for example, where a motor proposal form asks for all claims within the past five years, it is not obvious whether this includes claims on household insurance policies during that time. As a general principle it is suggested that only claims of the same type of insurance ought to be included, though it might be thought that a long history of claims for any type of insurance would be relevant as giving rise to a suspicion about the policyholder's honesty or carefulness or proneness to ill-fortune. In one IOB case[1] the proposal form in a case of household insurance asked about 'accidents or losses' within the past three years. The proposer did not disclose two attempted break-ins where nothing had been stolen. The Insurance Ombudsman held that the proposal form was not sufficiently explicit to require disclosure of events which had not led to any losses. From a strict legal point of view the failure to ask about attempted break-ins does not excuse non-disclosure of them, and it seems hard to deny that they are material facts. However, in the context of a personal lines policy the decision is correct because of the provision of the Statement of General Insurance Practice ('SGIP') that material matters should be the subject of clear questions on the proposal form.

[1] IOB 14.2.

Insurance history

5.25 This is a matter which goes beyond claims history. Specifically the proposal form usually asks whether the proposer has ever had a proposal for insurance rejected or accepted only on special terms. Insurers are prone to regard a positive answer to this question as a very bad sign. Full details of the incident will be required, but the outcome will often be that the subsequent proposal is rejected. The Insurance Ombudsman has rightly commented[1] that these practices are objectionable. Insurers ought not simply to rely on a former refusal, but should make their own independent judgments of the circumstances. It seems that the question about previous refusals can be objectively justified only if and to the extent that its purpose is to discover relevant circumstances and then apply a proper judgment to them.

[1] Annual Report 1988.

Behaviour in other claims

5.26 In *Insurance Corpn of the Channel Islands, Royal Insurance (UK) Ltd v Royal Hotel Ltd*[1] it was held to be material that the insured had behaved fraudulently in relation to an outstanding claim on the policy which was being renewed.

[1] [1998] Lloyd's Rep IR 151, CA. For the effect of fraudulent claims generally, see Chapter 19.

Criminal record

5.27 This is another matter which is frequently the subject of questions on proposal forms, and which is obviously relevant to the moral hazard even where not expressly asked about. Motor proposal forms now commonly allow non-disclosure of up to two speeding convictions, which may be regarded as a sad commentary on the prevalence of such convictions[1]. Underwriting guides usually provide for all convictions to be taken into account in the rating exercise, so that any conviction will be material, even if it is for a matter not directly connected with the class of insurance in question. This is especially so in the case of convictions for offences of dishonesty, since dishonesty may always properly be regarded as going to moral hazard. An extreme example of this was seen in *Wollacott v Sun Alliance and London Insurance Ltd*[2], where the proposer had served a sentence of imprisonment for armed robbery. After his release he bought a house and took out buildings insurance for it. He failed to disclose the conviction, and it was held that this non-disclosure rendered the policy voidable. It could not seriously be said that the conviction went to the physical hazard, but it was considered to go to the moral hazard. In the past the courts have been prepared to hold previous convictions material even when they were very old, though in *Roselodge Ltd v Castle*[3] the insurers unsuccessfully attempted to argue that a single instance of stealing apples at the age of 17 would be material on an insurance proposal 50 years later. The Insurance Ombudsman has been prepared to look at what underwriters would have done if the conviction had been disclosed. Thus, in one case[4] an applicant for household insurance failed to disclose a pending prosecution for being drunk and disorderly. The Ombudsman rejected the insurer's attempt to avoid the policy because the Underwriting Guide said only that the matter should be referred to the underwriters; it was not clear that cover would have been refused. This seems a somewhat generous approach, given that the non-disclosure can scarcely have been thought to be inadvertent.

The requirement to disclose previous convictions on a proposal form is materially affected by the Rehabilitation of Offenders Act 1974 ('ROA 1974'), which allows for convictions to become spent after a certain period has elapsed. Once a conviction is spent, it need not be disclosed, and it is perfectly legitimate for a person with no unspent convictions to say on a proposal form[5] that he has no convictions at all. It is therefore important to know the ROA 1974 rules as to when convictions become spent. The length of time required depends on the sentence imposed for the offence (not on the maximum possible sentence, nor on the length of any term of imprisonment actually served[6]). Time runs from the date of conviction (not from the date of sentence, if that is later[7]). The periods are[8]:

Sentence	**Rehabilitation period**
Non-custodial	5 years
Custodial not exceeding six months	7 years
Custodial exceeding six months, but not exceeding 30 months	10 years
Custodial exceeding 30 months	Never spent

1 An alternative view would be that insurers recognise that it is possible to break the speed limit without driving dangerously or becoming more likely to have an accident.
2 [1978] 1 WLR 493.
3 [1966] 2 Lloyd's Rep 113.
4 IOB 21.2.
5 Or anywhere else, unless the situation is one which is the subject of an Order exempting it from the provisions of the ROA 1974. There are no such orders in relation to policies of insurance.
6 Section 5(2).
7 Each individual section dealing with a rehabilitation period provides this.
8 Different rules apply where a person is convicted while still a juvenile: see s 5(2); generally the rehabilitation period is cut in half.

Other matters

5.28 In *Sharp and Roarer Investments Ltd v Sphere Drake Insurance plc, Minster Insurance Co Ltd and EC Parker & Co Ltd, The 'Moonacre'*[1] the proposer's signature had been forged on the proposal form by the brokers, though it appeared that the proposer was aware of and agreed with the answers given. It was held that this information would have caused the prudent underwriter to refuse to insure until the insured had confirmed the proposal in writing. it made no difference that the proposer would have confirmed the truth of the answers appearing in the form above the bogus signature and would have been prepared to sign; there was non-disclosure of material facts by the broker's concealment that the signature was bogus and that non-disclosure entitled the insurers to avoid the policy[2]. The insured's occupation is a material fact[3], and in this context any occupation is relevant, even if the insured does not (or not yet) engage in it for gain[4].

1 [1992] 2 Lloyd's Rep 501.
2 The case pre-dates *Pan Atlantic*, so inducement was not relevant, but it appears that the result would be the same at the present day, since the court believed that the prudent underwriter (and perhaps the actual underwriter?) would have behaved differently if the truth had been known.

[3] *McNealy v Pennine Insurance Co Ltd* [1978] RTR 285.
[4] *Hazel for Lloyd's Syndicate 260 v Whitlam* [2004] EWCA Civ 1600, [2005] Lloyd's Rep IR 168.

Life assurance

5.29 Moral hazard is of much less importance in life assurance than in general insurance, for there are relatively few people who will consent to their own death in order to see someone else reap the rewards. However, it is not unknown for those in desperate financial straits to effect a life policy and then commit suicide with a view to benefiting their dependants, though quite apart from any question of non-disclosure it is suggested that a claim on the policy could properly be rejected in these circumstances[1]. Alternatively, there have been cases of policyholders staging their own disappearance and 'death' with the intention of benefiting later from a claim on the policy. However, cases of this kind tend to be relatively rare, and in practice, life proposal forms do not ask any questions relating to the moral hazard.

[1] See also Chapter 20 on illegality.

'Life of another' policies

5.30 A particular difficulty arises in life of another policies when the non-disclosure or misrepresentation is perpetrated by the life assured rather than by the proposer. In *Wheelton v Hardisty*[1] it was held that in the absence of collusion such misconduct is not to be attributed to the assured and therefore does not render the policy voidable.

[1] (1857) 8 E & B 232, 120 ER 86.

Race and nationality

5.31 It may be helpful at this point to say something about the relevance of race and nationality in an insurance context. There are some cases[1] which have held that the nationality or ethnic origin of the proposer can be a material fact for the purposes of insurance. These cases cannot be regarded as good law at the present day. Section 20 of the Race Relations Act 1976 prohibits discrimination by the provider of a service on the basis of race, nationality or ethnic origin. It is therefore not permissible to argue, as was done in *Horne v Poland*[1], that the information may be relevant because some races are known to be more honest than others. Nor can it said that certain races have a history of making proportionately more claims than others[2].

[1] *Horne v Poland* [1922] 2 KB 364 is perhaps the most vivid example. These cases may fairly be regarded as dating from an earlier era, when attitudes to these matters were very different from those which prevail today.
[2] On the other hand it is still standard practice for household insurance to be rated partly by reference to postcodes, even though this may have discriminatory effects on certain immigrant and ethnic minority communities.

Reinsurance

5.32 Insurers who are reinsuring part of a risk do not need to disclose to the reinsurers that they have a reasonable level of excess of loss cover in respect of the retained part, even where it is a term of the insurance that they will retain that part[1].

[1] *Kingscroft Insurance Co Ltd v Nissan Fire and Marine Insurance Co Ltd* [2000] 1 All ER (Comm) 272, Moore-Bick J.

Facts which do not need to be disclosed

5.33 In *Carter v Boehm*[1] Lord Mansfield also gave guidance as to facts which do not need to be disclosed:

> 'The insured need not mention what the underwriter ought to know; what he takes upon himself the knowledge of; or what he waives being informed of.'

At the present day the facts which do not require disclosure are commonly grouped under the four heads which follow, based on s 18 of the MIA 1906.

[1] (1766) 3 Burr 1905.

Facts which the underwriter ought to know

5.34 This is a difficult area of law. There is much conflicting authority on the question of which facts the underwriter ought to know[1]. In the end, however, it is submitted that little is to be gained from minute analysis of these cases. It is ultimately a question of fact whether the information is such as the underwriter might be expected to know, and every case will naturally turn on its own specific circumstances. The following observations can provide no more than the most general of guides.

[1] See following paragraphs.

Property insurance

5.35 Insurers are deemed to have a knowledge of claims history, according to location and to type of building (whether classified by method of construction or by usage).

Insurance of the person

5.36 There are few reported cases in this area, and it is difficult to extract from them any general principle which will be helpful in dealing with life cases. However, the following propositions are suggested as being good law and in accordance with principle:

(1) The underwriter is assumed to have access to actuarial tables of mortality.

(2) The underwriter is deemed to have some level of knowledge as to the risks inherent in common activities, even where these are within the class of activities generally regarded as extra-hazardous.
(3) The underwriter is not normally deemed to have any special knowledge about the particular life, even where the life is a well-known person, the scope of whose activities is in the public eye.

Insurance of intangible interests

5.37 Insurers are deemed to have knowledge of claims history.

Information in the proposal form

5.38 It may also happen that the underwriter effectively has knowledge because of something contained in the proposal form. in *Keeling v Pearl Assurance Co Ltd*[1] the proposal form included questions about the assured's date of birth and age next birthday. The answers given to these two questions were mutually contradictory, but the policy was nevertheless issued without further enquiry. It was held that the company should have realised that at least one of the answers was wrong, and that they could not rely on the misrepresentation since they had chosen not to question it. It is submitted that this principle can apply only in the fairly narrow range of cases where it is obvious even in the absence of specialised knowledge that the proposal form must be incorrect.

[1] (1923) 129 LT 573, Bailhache J.

Facts which diminish the risk

5.39 Clearly, there is no need for the proposer to disclose facts which diminish the risk, since the insurer cannot be prejudiced by their non-disclosure. That this is so, at least in the absence of enquiry, is confirmed by *St Paul Fire and Marine Insurance Co (UK) Ltd v McConnell Dowell Constructors Ltd*[1]. (a circumstance which diminishes the risk may be a 'material circumstance' within the definition of s 18(2), and may have to be disclosed under s 18(1). As a matter of law any fact can effectively be converted into a material one merely by requiring the proposer to warrant that it is true, but the Statements of Insurance Practice, discussed below, place restrictions on insurers' freedom to require warranties in relation to life policies.

[1] [1995] 2 Lloyd's Rep 116, CA.

Facts whose disclosure is waived

5.40 It is always open to the insurer to waive the disclosure of any fact. However, it should be understood that the courts have been reluctant to hold that there has been a waiver in the absence of unequivocal evidence. Thus, disclosure of a fact is not waived merely because there is no question about it on the proposal form, nor where the insured fails to answer a specific question on the form and the insurer does not query this omission. In the latter event it will be assumed that the insured is representing that there is nothing to disclose[1]. Similarly, it is not usually open to the policyholder to claim that a question asking about certain specific things implicitly waives disclosure of other things which might otherwise have been material. In *Godfrey v Britannic Assurance Co Ltd*[2] a question on the proposal form asked:

> 'Have you suffered from any illness or accident or received medical advice or treatment, with or without an operation?'

The proposer had recently suffered a serious loss of weight, but had not been diagnosed as suffering from any illness, nor had he taken medical advice on the subject. He did not disclose the weight loss. Roskill J held that the question on the form could not be construed as cutting down the duty of disclosure, and that the weight loss was obviously material and therefore ought to have been disclosed. At the same time an underwriter who knows that certain material information is being made available to him but who declines to look at it is likely to be held to have waived disclosure. The point arose in a commercial context in *Pan Atlantic Insurance Co Ltd v Pine Top Insurance Co Ltd*[3], where the broker took a detailed loss record to his meeting with the underwriter, and offered to him for examination. The issue is unlikely to arise in quite this way in a life policy, but it is clear that if, for example, a proposer submits a medical report on his condition with the proposal form, and the insurers do not bother to read it, they cannot later be heard to say that there has been a non-disclosure of the information contained in the report. On the other hand, a proposer who is asked whether he has suffered previous losses and merely replies 'Yes' without giving further details, does not thereby discharge his duty of disclosure, and no question of waiver arises when the insurer issues the policy without seeking further details[4].

[1] *Roberts v Avon Insurance Co Ltd* [1956] 2 Lloyd's Rep 240; see also *New Hampshire Insurance Co v Oil Refineries Ltd* [2003] Lloyd's Rep IR 386, Chambers J where the presentation of the risk dealt with the claims history over a five-year period, but ignored claims from earlier dates. Although the insurer was fully aware of the limitated nature of the presentation, it was held that there had been non-disclosure – by failing to mention the earlier period the proposer had impliedly represented that there was nothing relevant to disclose.
[2] [1963] 2 Lloyd's Rep 515, Roskill J.
[3] [1994] 3 All ER 581.
[4] *Stowers v G A Bonus plc* [2003] Lloyd's Rep IR 402, Knight J. But see also para 5.44 below.

5.41 Disclosure can be waived by express clause, but the courts are reluctant to accept that this has been done in the absence of very clear wording[1]. In addition, public policy precludes a party from excluding liability for his own personal fraudulent misrepresentation which induces a contract[2].

[1] *HIH Casualty and General Insurance Ltd v Chase Manhattan Bank* [2001] Lloyd's Rep IR 191, Aikens J affirmed [2003] Lloyd's Rep IR 230, HL.
[2] See n 1 above at para 35.

Subsequent waiver

5.42 Where the non-disclosure comes to light after the policy has commenced, it may be waived by the insurer. In the absence of express waiver the court may be prepared to find that there is implicit waiver if premiums are accepted after the insurer has knowledge of the non-disclosure[1]. This may be especially important in those classes of insurance where retrospective declarations of turnover are made – a subsequent declaration showing a very large increase in turnover may be sufficient to put underwriters on notice that previously declared limits are being exceeded. If they continue to accept premiums thereafter, they risk being held to have waived the right to avoid[2]. Further, a notice of cancellation (as distinct from avoidance) served at a time when the underwriter is aware of his right to avoid may be held to amount to an affirmation, since it is explicable only on the basis that the policy is still in force and is not being avoided[3].

[1] *Keeling v Pearl Assurance Co Ltd* (1923) 129 LT 573, Bailhache J.
[2] *Moore Large & Co Ltd v Hermes Credit & Guarantee plc* [2003] EWHC 26 (Comm), [2003] Lloyd's Rep IR 315, Colman J.
[3] *Wise Underwriting Agency Ltd v Grupo Nacional Provincial SA* [2004] Lloyd's Rep IR 764, CA; see also *Mint Security Ltd v Blair* [1982] 1 Lloyd's Rep 188.

Facts which it is superfluous to disclose by reason of an express or implied warranty

5.43 This exception is chiefly of importance in marine insurance[1], and can rarely arise in life assurance at all in view of the restrictions imposed by the SLIP[2] on requiring warranties.

[1] See Chapter 17 on Warranties.
[2] Clause 2.

The need for a fair presentation of the risk and the concept of waiver

5.44 There are authorities which support the idea that once there has been a fair presentation of the risk to the underwriter, it is incumbent on him to seek more information if he wants it. This is akin to a doctrine of constructive notice in that the fair presentation may be regarded as giving the underwriter constructive knowledge of the matters which reasonable further enquiry would have revealed. The majority of the Court of Appeal took this view in *CTI v Oceanus*[1] and the matter was considered further by the Court of Appeal in *Wise Underwriting Agency Ltd v Grupo Nacional Provincial SA*[2], where the view was expressed that an underwriter who failed to ask an obvious question arising from a fair presentation of the risk would be held to have waived disclosure of the answer to that question[3]. However, this formulation inevitably throws great stress on the question whether there has been a 'fair' presentation of the risk and this necessarily involves taking into account the factors mentioned in s 18(3) of the MIA 1906 and discussed above. Ultimately the court has to decide whether it is 'fair' to allow the insurer to avoid on the basis of a fact as to which he was put on enquiry and ought to have satisfied himself. This might involve balancing the elements of unfairness to both sides and considering to what extent both parties could be considered to have acted in utmost good faith.

[1] [1984] 1 Lloyd's Rep 476.
[2] [2004] Lloyd's Rep IR 764, CA.
[3] Referring also to *Asfar & Co v Blundell* [1896] 1 QB 123; *Cantieré Meccanico Brindisino v Janson* [1912] 3 KB 452; *Mann McNeal & Steeves Ltd v Capital & Counties Insurance Co Ltd* [1921] 2 KB 300.

Consequences of non-disclosure

5.45 The law is equally clear about the consequences of failure to disclose a material fact. Such failure makes the policy voidable at the instance of the insurer provided that the non-disclosure induced the insurer to enter into the contract[1]. Before *Pan Atlantic* it had been assumed for at least two centuries that the question of inducement was irrelevant once materiality had been established. However, it is now clear that actual inducement must be shown. In *Drake Insurance plc v Provident Insurance plc*[2] it was said that the question was whether the insurer had been induced by the non-disclosure, not whether he would have imposed the same terms if other information which diminished the risk has also been available to him. It is submitted that the unusual case of non-disclosure of information reducing the risk is the only situation where this analysis can be sustained. Otherwise the question must be whether the insurer in fact made a different decision than he otherwise would have done must be the crucial question.

[1] *Pan Atlantic Insurance Co Ltd v Pine Top Insurance Co Ltd* [1994] 3 All ER 581.
[2] [2003] Lloyd's Rep IR 781, Moore-Bick J.

Proof of inducement

5.46 In *Pan Atlantic* the House of Lords appears to have assumed that, once materiality is established, there is a presumption that the non-disclosure has induced the underwriter to enter into the policy, and that it is for the policyholder to bring evidence to rebut this presumption. The point has been further considered in two subsequent cases.

In *Fraser Shipping Ltd v Colton*[1] a vessel was insured against actual total loss only while being towed to the breakers' yard. The vessel's destination was changed en route, but underwriters were not notified of this until after its arrival at the new destination, when they were asked to agree to the change. This change was scratched on the policy, but underwriters later sought to avoid for non-disclosure of the change at the time it happened. It was held that they had succeeded in discharging the burden of showing that the non-disclosure had induced them to agree to the change. For present purposes the interest of the case lies in the fact that it was assumed that the burden of proof in relation to inducement was on the underwriters, an assumption which appears to contradict that made in *Winter v Irish Life Assurance plc.*

The question of inducement was further considered by Astill J in *Aldridge Estates Investments Co Ltd v McCarthy*[2], a case of landlords' insurance of mostly residential properties. A claim for liability to a tenant for personal injury was rejected on the ground of non-disclosure of two matters, the issue of a Notice under the Housing Act 1985[3] by the local authority concerning part of the property where the accident happened and the claimants' knowledge of the presence of squatters in May 1987 in that property. It was clear that these matters had not been disclosed, though the claimants argued that the defendants should have been aware of the Housing Act 1985 notice from other matters.

On the question of inducement, the claimants argued that in the context of the overall portfolio of insured properties (valued at in excess of £27m) these matters were trivial and could not be regarded as having induced the insurers to enter into the policy. They said that on previous occasions matters of this sort had been disclosed and the insurers had made little or no response. Astill J rejected this argument. He said:

> 'If the Insurer does very little in response that does not indicate that the information has not affected his thought processes. The Insurer may do very little out of commercial considerations. He may wish to be generous or lenient or not overburden the Insured. He may feel loyalty to a long standing account; he may wish to ensure that the Insured retained him as the Insurer. In order for him to consider any of those matters he must first know of the information. His lack of significant action cannot relieve the Insured of the duty to disclose. It cannot be used as an argument to demonstrate that the Insurer considered and that the information was trivial and therefore not material. If that information was not disclosed then the Insurer was presented with a distorted picture of the risk.'

This may be regarded as establishing that the facts were material in the sense of s 18 of the MIA 1906. It does not of course establish that they induced the insurers to enter into the contract.

The claimants' argument that the defendants were deemed to know of these matters appears to rest on the long history of dealing between the parties in relation to the insurance of these properties. It was argued that because of this the insurer should in the ordinary course of business have known that there were likely to be matters of this kind and should have made enquiries about them. Astill J said:

> 'I am unable to accept [counsel's] contention as correct in law. The fact that a contract of insurance is a contract made in good faith places a heavy primary burden on the Insured who has all the knowledge. All authorities reflect that proposition. [Counsel] places a burden upon Insurers that does not initially exist. They must first be presented with a substantially fair and accurate picture of the risk; they then have a duty to ask for more information if that is required. [Counsel's] opinion assumes that the Slip was a fair and accurate picture. I have found that it was not. What would have been a fair and accurate picture was a disclosure of squatting; the Housing Act Notice and the condition of 37 Belgrave Gardens and the unoccupancy rates. It would then have been for the underwriter to enquire further so as to assess the risk if he thought it was necessary. This information was not given to Insurers as part of the 1987 presentation.'

On the question of inducement it was argued for the claimants that the insurers must show that the material facts not disclosed would, if they had been disclosed, have caused them: (a) To refuse cover. (b) To cover only with an increased premium or (c) to offer cover on *substantially* different terms. Astill J said:

> 'The evidence here shows that when information such as that complained of was given to Insurers they reacted. If they reacted in a lenient way … it is not clear why. It might

> well have been that they were justified in loading the policy more yet did not for commercial reasons or reasons of loyalty to a long standing account. I do not know the answer and I do not believe that the Law says that I should speculate. The test seems to me to be whether the policy would have been written on the same terms as it was in 1987 had these matters been disclosed. That I believe is a matter of fact and not of degree. That view is consistent with that expressed by Lord Mustill that the act or omission complained of had no effect on the decision of the actual underwriter. The actual underwriter was these Defendants and these Defendants did respond.'

Consequently, the claimants had not succeeded in showing absence of inducement and their claim failed.

In *St Paul Fire and Marine insurance Co (UK) Ltd v McConnell Dowell Constructors Ltd*[4] the insured were building contractors engaged in a major building project. In effecting insurance of the project they told the insurers that the plan was to erect the building on piled foundations. The information was true at the time, but, prior to the issue of the policy the insured decided to change the method of construction to spread foundations, a somewhat cheaper method, but arguably one which involves greater risks. They did not tell the insurers that the information on the proposal form was now out of date, and the policy was duly issued. Later, substantial subsidence damage happened to the building while it was still in the course of construction. The insurers denied liability and sought a declaration that they were entitled to avoid the policy because of the non-disclosure of the method of foundation. This was the first reported case in which lower courts had had to take on the task of attempting to discern and apply the principles laid down in *Pan Atlantic*. The case is also reminiscent of *Pan Atlantic* in the sense that the outcome of the case seems very obvious – it is hard to imagine that any court could possibly have held that this change in the method of foundation was not material. Consequently, the reader is left with the suspicion, as in *Pan Atlantic*, that the parties took the opportunity to ask the Court of Appeal to clarify the decision in *Pan Atlantic* for the benefit of the insurance market generally. In the event it was held that avoidance of the contract for non-disclosure of a material fact was available only where the prudent underwriter would have taken that fact into account when assessing the risk and where the non-disclosure had induced the actual underwriter to enter into the contract.

The Court of Appeal added that a fact can be material within the meaning of s 18 of the MIA 1906 even though it diminishes the risk, since such a fact will be likely to affect the insurer's assessment of that risk. The point appears, however, to be of no more than theoretical interest, since s 18(3)(a) of the Act expressly provides that such a fact need not be disclosed.

However, the real interest of the case lies in the valiant efforts of Evans LJ to explain the *Pan Atlantic* judgments. Lord Mustill in *Pan Atlantic* had expressed the question of law in that case in the following way:

> 'must it be shown that full and accurate disclosure would have led the prudent underwriter to a different decision on accepting or rating the risk; or is a lesser standard of impact on the mind of the prudent underwriter sufficient; and if so, what is that lesser standard?[5]'

The question to be addressed in this case was whether it was possible to extract from the judgments in *Pan Atlantic* a binding answer to the second part of that question, namely, what is the lesser standard?

Evans LJ went on to hold that Lord Mustill's own answer, namely that a circumstance may be material even if a proper consideration of it would not have led the prudent underwriter to make a different decision about accepting or rating the risk was implicitly accepted at least by Lord Goff. He added that this test does not appear to be significantly different from that advanced by Steyn LJ in the Court of Appeal in *Pan Atlantic*, namely that the fact is material if its disclosure would have led the underwriter to perceive what was being presented to him as a different risk from the risk without disclosure of the fact. However, Evans LJ added that, contrary to Steyn LJ's view, the different risk need not be a greater one – it is sufficient if the risk is *different*, so that even a fact which diminishes the risk is likely to be material[6].

1 [1997] 1 Lloyd's Rep 586, Queen's Bench Division (Commercial Court), Potter J.
2 [1996] EGCS 167, Astill J, unreported.
3 Ie a notice requiring the defective condition of the premises to be remedied.
4 [1996] 1 All ER 96, CA.
5 [1994] 3 All ER 581 at 591.
6 Obviously, the non-disclosure of such a fact is unlikely ever to induce the insurer to accept the risk.

Excluding the right to avoid

5.47 In *Toomey v Eagle Star Insurance Co Ltd (No 2)*[1] Lloyd's underwriters had effected reinsurance to close in accordance with the Lloyd's practice. The policy contained a clause which provided:

> 'This contract is neither cancellable nor voidable by either party.'

Coleman J held that it is possible to exclude by contractual term the right to rely upon non-disclosure. However, as a matter of construction this clause excludes the right to rely upon innocent non-disclosure or misrepresentation, but did not exclude the right to rely upon negligent or fraudulent non-disclosure or misrepresentation. The right to claim damages for misrepresentation was not affected by the clause.

The decision is in some respects puzzling, though this may in part reflect the fact that the clause is of a somewhat unusual character. It is easy to understand why Lloyd's underwriters need to have an absolute assurance that their reinsurance to close is effective and why they would therefore want a clause of this type[2]. On the other hand the clause, if interpreted literally, appears to allow scope for any amount of non-disclosure and/or misrepresentation. It is perhaps for this reason that Coleman J sought to limit the scope of the clause. On the question of the right to damages, it is of course true that the clause says nothing about this. However, it must be asked whether there is any relevant right to damages in the first place. It is settled law, after *The Good Luck*[3] that a breach of the duty of utmost good faith by the insurer does not give rise to a right to damages, and it will be remembered that this decision was reached at least partly on the basis that there should be parity between the parties in this matter. It would appear that the position must logically be the same in relation to pre-contractual misrepresentations as in relation to non-disclosures. On this basis the conclusion must be that the wording of the policy leaves no room for insurers to reclaim sums paid in settlement of claims on the basis of misrepresentation. Certainly, the opposite conclusion would deprive the clause of much of its practical effect.

1 [1995] 2 Lloyd's Rep 88, Coleman J.
2 Though there is also a certain irony in watching professional underwriters seeking to circumvent the normal effects of the duty of disclosure, on which they are more than happy to rely against their own policyholders.
3 [1991] 3 All ER 1, HL. See also *HIH Casualty and General Insurance Ltd v Chase Manhattan Bank* [2003] Lloyd's Rep IR 230, HL.

Statements of insurance practice

5.48 The common law rules on disclosure are frequently perceived as being unduly harsh to the proposer, as are the rules relating to warranties discussed later in this Chapter. When the Unfair Contract Terms Act 1977 ('UCTA 1977') was still a Bill it was suggested that its scope might be widened to include insurance policies. In the event the Act does not cover policies of insurance, but the price that the insurance industry had to pay for this exclusion was the original version of the Statements of Insurance Practice, which were issued in 1976. The current version of the Statements dates from 1986, and in view of the immense practical importance of these documents it is necessary to discuss them here in some detail. It may be added that the decision in *Pan Atlantic* has possibly reduced the importance of those parts of the Statements dealing with non-disclosure, though even this is unclear in view of the uncertain ambit of the *Pan Atlantic* principle.

There are two Statements, one relating to general insurance, the other to long-term insurance. The Statement is not legally binding, being merely, as its name implies, a statement of the practice which is proposed to be adopted by those who are party to it. It is issued by the ABI and it is therefore to be expected that it will be adhered to by all insurers who are members of that Association. However, as it is not legally binding, it is not open to the policyholder to rely upon it in legal proceedings. The unfortunate effect of this rule is largely mitigated by the fact that the Insurance Ombudsman takes account of the Statements of Insurance Practice in deciding cases which come before him. He will insist that insurers comply with the Statements, and has been known, for example, to refuse to allow insurers to rely upon non-disclosures in proposal forms which do not correspond with the requirements of the Statements. Although the ABI website[1] indicates that the SGIP was replaced by FSA Regulation with effect from 14 January 2005, it appears that the Ombudsman continues to treat its provisions – as well as the provisions of SLIP – as relevant to the exercise of his discretion.

1 www.abi.org.uk It is not there suggested that SLIP has been replaced.

The Statement of General Insurance Practice[1]

5.49 Clause 1(a) provides that the declaration at the foot of the proposal form is to be restricted to completion according to the proposer's knowledge and belief. This prevents insurers from requiring the proposer to warrant the truth of every statement on the proposal form. Thus, for example, a clause making the *entire* proposal form the basis of the contract would contravene this clause. It does not follow that no warranties can be included, as appears from cl 1(b). This forbids the use, in proposal form or policy of provisions converting statements on the proposal form as to past or present fact, into warranties. The clause goes on to say that insurers may nevertheless require specific warranties about matters which are material to the risk. The relationship between the two parts of this clause is not altogether clear. On one reading the specific warranties would have to be promissory in nature, since they cannot relate to past or present fact. On an alternative reading a specific warranty about a material matter can relate to past or present fact. The difference of interpretation depends on whether the first part of the clause is considered to have priority over the second, or *vice versa*. It is suggested that the better interpretation is that specific warranties as to past or present fact are permitted, though of course only where it can be shown that they are directly relevant to the risk. The clause should be understood as prohibiting only the practice of making all statements on the proposal form into warranties.

Clause 1(c) deals with the question of informing proposers of the consequences of non-disclosure. The proposal form must contain, either in the declaration or elsewhere, a prominent statement drawing attention to the consequences of failure to disclose all material facts. It must be made clear that 'material facts' for these purposes are those which an insurer would regard as likely to influence the acceptance and assessment of the proposal. The statement must also advise the proposer that if he is in any doubt about the materiality of any given fact, he should disclose it. The role and significance of this clause may be considered to have changed somewhat since it was originally drafted. In 1986 it was still assumed that non-disclosure of any material fact was sufficient to render the policy voidable; only in 1994 did it become apparent that the non-disclosure must also induce the insurer to enter into the contract[2]. It is therefore suggested that the wordings which have commonly been adopted by insurers over the years need to be modified in the light of the decision in *Pan Atlantic*.

Clause 1(d) provides that those matters which insurers have generally found to be material will be the subject of clear questions in proposal forms. This is intended to address the problem created by the fact that the duty of disclosure extends to all material facts, rather than being limited to matters which are asked about in the proposal form. Although the SGIP cannot abrogate that rule of law, it does offer proposers some protection in that they can expect all the most important matters in the particular class of insurance to be specifically asked about on the form. The protection is not of course complete, since in any given case there may be some matter which is material to the particular case and which is unique to that case. The importance of wording the questions clearly is shown by an IOB case[3] where the policyholder was asked whether the flat for which he was seeking insurance was 'in any way associated with a business'. He replied in the negative, and the insurer subsequently sought to avoid the policy when it became clear that the flat was above a shop and had no separate entrance. The Ombudsman held that this did not mean that the flat and the business were 'associated', so that the proposer had been justified in answering the question in the negative. The question had not been asked with sufficient clarity.

Clause 1(e) enjoins insurers to refrain, so far as possible, from asking questions which would require expert knowledge beyond that which the proposer could reasonably be expected to possess or which would require a value judgment on the part of the proposer. In the context of general insurance this clause is important in a number of situations. Examples include the following: questions about subsidence in household buildings policies, where proposers should not be asked whether other houses in the area have been subject to subsidence (unless the question is clearly limited to the proposer's knowledge and belief). Questions about the value of particular items of property where such valuations are a matter of expert opinion. Generally, matters relating to the activities or opinions of third parties which are not within the proposer's knowledge.

Clause 1(f) requires the proposal form to include a prominent statement that a specimen copy of the policy form is available on request, unless either the prospectus or the proposal form contains full details of the standard cover (an outline is not sufficient). This clause goes some way towards addressing the familiar problem of the policyholder who is insured under a contract which he has never read and may indeed never have seen. At the same time it must be acknowledged that many proposers do not exercise their right to request a copy of the policy before entering into the contract.

Clause 1(g) requires a further warning on proposal forms to the effect that the proposer should keep a record (including copies of letters) of all information supplied to the insurer for the purpose of entering into the contract. This is an obviously sensible warning, but there is little doubt that in practice it is frequently disregarded. It might be suggested that there ought to be no technological difficulty about automatically providing the proposer with a photocopy of the proposal form and that the SGIP is out of date in this respect. This point may be taken further when considering cl 1(h), which requires the form to state that a copy of the completed form is either automatically provided for retention at the time of completion or will be supplied as part of the insurer's normal practice or will be supplied on request within a period of three months after its completion. Again, it is suggested that modern technology should enable the first option to be the invariable practice.

Finally, cl 1(i) forbids an insurer to raise an issue under the proposal form without providing the policyholder with a copy of the completed form. This obviously sensible proposal compels insurers to keep copies of proposal forms and ensures that policyholders whose form is subsequently called into question at least have the chance to see the original document.

[1] See Appendix 3.
[2] *Pan Atlantic Insurance Co Ltd v Pine Top Insurance Co Ltd* [1994] 3 All ER 581.
[3] IOB 14.1.

The Statement of Long-Term Insurance Practice[1]

5.50 In its present form this Statement deals with matters relating to proposal forms, to warranties and to claims. Only items falling under the first two heads will be dealt with here.

[1] See Appendix 3.

Clause 1(a)

5.51 This clause provides as follows:

> 'If the proposal form calls for the disclosure of material facts a statement should be included in the declaration, or prominently displayed elsewhere on the form or in the document of which it forms part:
> (i) drawing attention to the consequences of failure to disclose all material facts and explaining that these are facts that an insurer would regard as likely to influence the assessment and acceptance of a proposal;
> (ii) warning that if the signatory is in any doubt about whether certain facts are material, these facts should be disclosed.'

In practice the proposal form will almost always require disclosure of material facts – that is after all the major purpose of a proposal form, so this clause will apply in virtually every case. The usual practice appears to be to reproduce the definition of material facts given in this clause more or less verbatim. It may be noted that this definition closely follows that given in *Container Transport International Inc v Mutual Underwriting Association (Bermuda) Ltd*[1] by extending material facts to those 'influencing' the assessment and acceptance, so that a fact may be material even though it does not lead the insurer to make a different decision. Cases do still occasionally arise where the proposal form does not comply with this clause, and the Insurance Ombudsman has held that an insurer should not rely upon a non-disclosure in a form which lacks the necessary warning.

1 [1984] 1 Lloyd's Rep 476, CA.

Clause 1(b)

5.52 This clause provides:

> 'Neither the proposal nor the policy shall contain any provision converting the statements as to past or present fact in the proposal form into warranties except where the warranty relates to a statement of fact concerning the life to be assured under a life of another policy. Insurers may, however, require specific warranties about matters which are material to the risk.'

This provision deals with the question of warranties rather than with that of non-disclosure. It aims to restrict the use of what are sometimes called 'Basis of the Contract' clauses, ie clauses which require the proposer to warrant the truth of the statements in the proposal form. The effect of such a warranty is to render the policy voidable in the event of an untrue answer[1], even where the question does not relate to a material fact[2] or where the inaccuracy overstates the risk[3]. These clauses have often been considered objectionable since they will often allow the insurer to avoid the policy even though it has not in any way been prejudiced. The present clause imposes some restrictions on the use of Basis of the Contract clauses, but does not prohibit them entirely. In own life policies, statements as to past or present fact may not be converted into warranties. Statements as to these matters may still be required to be true to the best of the proposer's knowledge and belief, however[4]. Difficulties sometimes arise in relation to medical history or as to cause of death of ancestors – often the subject of an express question on the form – where proposers may legitimately be unsure of the exact details. In these circumstances cl 1(b) may come to their aid. It is important, though, to note the restrictions on the protection given to proposers by this clause. First, it has no application where the proposer commits a deliberate or negligent non-disclosure. Secondly, it applies only to statements as to *past or present fact*. There is no prohibition on requiring warranties as to the future. Thus, where a policy gives a discount on premiums to non-smokers there is under this clause no reason why the proposer should not be required to warrant that he will not at any stage in the future smoke a cigarette[5]. Thirdly, the rules operate rather differently in relation to life of another policies, where warranties of fact (past or present) relating to the life to be assured are permitted. The exact scope of this part of the clause is far from clear. On the face of it, the effect is to disapply completely the provision contained in the earlier part of the clause, and it is hard to see what other interpretation can possibly be given to it. On the other hand, there is no obvious reason why such warranties should be allowed in life of another policies when they are forbidden in own life policies. The final point in relation to this clause concerns its last sentence. Interpreted literally, this would seem to mean that specific warranties about material matters are permitted, even when, for example, they are warranties of past or present fact under own life policies. It is submitted that this interpretation is incorrect. This sentence means only that specific warranties are permitted in relation to material facts *which do not fall within the general prohibition of the clause*; Thus, there may be warranties as to material future facts (but not as to immaterial facts of any kind).

1 *Anderson v Fitzgerald* (1853) 4 HL Cas 484.
2 *Duckett v Williams* (1834) 2 Cr & M 348.
3 *Dawsons Ltd v Bonnin* [1922] 2 AC 413.
4 The SLIP contains no provision expressly limiting the declaration on the form to accuracy according to proposer's knowledge and belief – unlike the SGIP, where cl 1(a) expressly does this – but cl 1(b) has a somewhat similar effect in most cases.
5 Though it may be doubted whether the Ombudsman would accept such a warranty as a fair one.

Clause 1(c)

5.53 This clause provides:

> 'Those matters which insurers have commonly found to be material should be the subject of clear questions in proposal forms.'

On the face of it this clause merely expresses an undeniably good intention. In particular, it provides no sanction for any failure to ask clear questions about material matters. It is of course clear that in law the failure to ask a question about a material fact does not relieve the proposer of the duty to disclose that fact, but this clause is obviously intended to reduce the number of cases where the fact is not disclosed because its significance is not brought to the proposer's mind. In practice the effective sanction for the absence of appropriate questions lies, as so often, in the hands of the Insurance Ombudsman, who will not normally allow insurers to rely on failure to disclose a fact which has not been clearly asked for, at least in the absence of fraud or some evidence of bad faith on the part of the proposer (and an insurer alleging this will be expected to produce some evidence to support the allegation). Cases of failure to comply with this provision are now rare, and most of the difficulties which arise in relation to unasked questions occur because the fact in question is an unusual one which is not commonly found to be material. Even in these cases, though, the Insurance Ombudsman is reluctant to allow reliance on the non-disclosure.

Clause 1(d)

5.54 This clause provides:

> 'Insurers should avoid asking questions which would require knowledge beyond that which the signatory could reasonably be expected to possess.'

In relation to life policies this provision is important mainly when dealing with questions as to health and medical history. A proposer who has at some stage consulted a doctor will of course be aware of the consultation, but may not know exactly what the diagnosis was, since patients are not always told the exact details of their condition. When these details are of a somewhat technical medical character and were given some time ago, a proposer may also be excused for having forgotten them (or indeed for not having fully understood them in the first place). For these reasons, a disclosure of the date of the consultation with the doctor, accompanied by an explanation in layman's terms of the reason for the consultation, ought to be regarded as sufficient. It is to be assumed that a Private Medical Attendant's Report will be obtained in any case where the proposal form gives rise to any doubts, and the full details can no doubt be obtained in this way. Another variant of this problem arises where the proposer has had some symptoms which might or might not indicate some serious condition. The clause should be regarded as making clear that in such circumstances non-disclosure of the underlying condition is not required where the symptoms are sufficiently ambiguous that the proposer might excusably have failed to realise what they indicated. It may be noted in passing that in this respect at least the clause probably does no more than reproduce the strict legal rule, since it was established in *Joel v Law Union Assurance*[1] that there is no legal duty to disclose a fact of which the proposer has neither actual nor constructive knowledge.

1 [1908] 2 KB 863.

Clauses 1(e) and 1(f)

5.55 These clauses provide:

> '1(e) The proposal form or a supporting document should include a statement that a copy of the policy form or of the policy conditions is available on request.
>
> 1(f) The proposal form or a supporting document should include a statement that a copy of the completed proposal form is available on request.'

These two clauses are obviously related to each other and may therefore conveniently be treated together. Jointly, they aim to ensure that the proposer is provided with all necessary information in relation to the policy. The availability of the policy conditions is obviously essential in order to inform the policyholder of the terms of the contract. The availability of the proposal form is usually relevant where a claim is made and is resisted on the basis of non-disclosure, misrepresentation or breach of warranty. In such a case it is obviously fair that the policyholder (or his personal representatives in the case of an own life policy) should have access to the form on which the insurer is relying. Although the clause only requires a statement to the effect that these documents are available on request, it is implicit in this that they should in fact be available on request. It is most unlikely that the Insurance Ombudsman would allow an insurer to rely on a policy term or on an error on the proposal form if copies were not provided to the proposer.

Consequences of avoidance

5.56 The avoidance of an insurance policy operates in the same way as the avoidance of any other contract. In other words it is as if the contract had never existed and the insurer cannot be liable for any claim, even if the facts which would otherwise have given rise to a claim have already occurred. The rule is that upon avoidance of the contract the insurer must make *restitutio in integrum*, ie the insured must be restored to the position in which he was before the contract was entered into. This naturally involves returning all premiums which have been paid. Where the policy has been in existence only a short time this may not give rise to any great difficulty, but if the policy has been in force for some years two related but contrasting questions may be posed. First, is the insured entitled to interest on the money which the insurer has had for the duration of the policy? Secondly, is the insurer entitled to deduct anything for the life cover which has been provided during the policy. The second question is more easily answered than the first. The avoidance of the policy is retrospective, and the matter is to be considered as if the policy had never existed at all. It is therefore clear that nothing can be retained for the cover, since the effect of the avoidance is that the cover never existed, even though at the time the parties thought that it did. The first question is more difficult because it is not now clear on what basis the insurer was ever entitled to hold the insured's money at all, unless perhaps it was paid under a mistake of fact, namely the mistaken impression that the policy was fully valid. However, the general principle appears to be that on the avoidance of a contract (whether a contract of insurance or some other type of contract) money received under the contract is repaid but without interest. This is certainly the practice within the industry, and it is submitted that it does accord with the legal position, though of course if proceedings are issued, it will be open to the court to award interest under s 35A of the Supreme Court Act 1981 ('SCA 1981') (in the case of High Court Proceedings) or s 69 of the County Courts Act 1984 (in the case of county court proceedings).

The bilateral nature of the duty

5.57 The duty of good faith is incumbent on insurers just as much as on the proposer – *Banque Keyser Ullman SA v Skandia (UK) Insurance Co Ltd*[1], sub nom *Banque Financière de la Cité SA v Westgate Insurance Co Ltd*[2]. The present discussion will concentrate only on the insurer's pre-contractual duty of good faith, the post-contractual position being examined at length in Chapter 13.

The major difficulty in relation to the insurer's pre-contractual duty is to know what it requires the insurer to do. It is obvious that for the most part pre-contractual disclosure will be made by the proposer. All that the proposer really needs to know from the insurer is the premium and the cover being offered, both of which are likely to be readily available. A rare example of a reported case on the insurer's duty of pre-contractual disclosure is *Norwich Union Life Insurance Society v Afzal Hameed Qureshi*[3]. The question was whether certain Lloyd's Names had a right of action against Norwich Union ('NU') in respect of alleged dishonest concealment of material facts in relation to endowment policies entered into by the Names with NU. The actions arose out of plans marketed by NU, under which NU gave guarantees on behalf of the Names to Lloyds to meet losses incurred by the Names. Under the plans the Names charged real property or investments to NU to secure the liabilities of NU under the guarantees. The Names also took out endowment policies with NU and assigned them to NU by way of further security. Any sums paid by NU under the guarantees were to be treated as sums advanced under the charge. Provided that the Names paid interest on those sums and premiums under the policy, they were not required to repay to NU the principal sum unless and until the policy matured. NU had honoured calls under the guarantees, but the Names claimed to be entitled to be relieved of their obligations to make repayment on the ground of dishonest concealment of material facts by NU. In particular, they alleged that at the time that they were considering entering into the policies NU owed them a duty of utmost good faith to disclose that subsidiary or associated companies of NU were already affected by the kind of adverse losses which were later to escalate with catastrophic effects for the syndicates of which the Names were members. The Court of Appeal, affirming separate decisions of Rix J and Rimer J held that the issue was whether the risk of losses by the Names at Lloyds, and the facts which were known to NU in relation to the potential for such losses, were facts or matters material to the risk covered by the endowment policies. The only matter material to the risk covered by each policy was the life of the Name to which it related, and the duty of disclosure was therefore limited to matters material to that risk. The duty of disclosure did not therefore operate to require disclosure of any fact which would or might induce a person to enter into the policy or into a composite transaction of which the policy formed part. Section 47 of the FSA 1986 (as to which see below) did not create a duty wider than that existing at common law. There was no evidence of fraud on the part of NU. The position might well have been different if the premiums under the policy had not been assessed by reference to the risk of death alone, but by reference also to the risk of the guarantees being called in.

Although it is not spelled out in this case the defendant here appears to have been an outside Name. He made an arrangement with the NU under which NU provided a guarantee to Lloyd's in the sum of £400,000 in respect of the defendant's liabilities as a Name against the security of a mortgage on the defendant's home and an endowment policy on his life.

When the defendant's syndicates got caught up in the Lloyd's troubles involving catastrophic losses, Lloyd's made calls upon the guarantee provided by NU until it was exhausted. The defendant was unable or unwilling to maintain both the premiums payable upon his life policy and the interest payable upon the sums which NU debited to the mortgage on his home so NU commenced possession proceedings against him.

NU issued a summons to strike out the defendant's amended defence and counterclaim and for final judgment against the defendant in the money claim against him. It is relevant that the group of which NU was a part included two companies which conducted insurance and reinsurance business within the Lloyd's market. Essentially, the defendant's defence was that, by reason of these companies, NU was well aware at the time that he entered into the arrangement with them that substantial losses were about to be incurred by several underwriting syndicates operating in the Lloyd's market including those in which the defendant had a line. He asserted that because of this knowledge NU had a duty of disclosure which they failed to observe. He claimed that if he had been aware of the information regarding impending losses he would have stopped his underwriting activities or at least changed the syndicates with which he was involved and would not have entered into the plan with NU.

It was held that:

(1) As regards the allegation that NU owed the defendant a duty to disclose to him what they know about the Lloyd's market, it was held that the question of the extent of NU's knowledge was not suitable for determination by the summons – as it raised issues of fact and law. However, the judge held that the scope of the NU's duty of disclosure in good faith was an entirely different question – he held that NU's obligation of good faith did not extend to information material to a prospective plan customer's decision whether to underwrite as a name at Lloyd's. Reference was made to the case of *Banque Financiere de la Cite SA (formerly Banque Keyser Ullmann SA) v Westgate Insurance Co Ltd*[4] in which it was held that the fact that it could be contemplated by the insurer that the insured would not have entered into a business transaction if disclosure had been made was not enough in itself to make the withheld information material, even though that business transaction was the subject matter of the insurance.
It was held that the defendant's underwriting at Lloyd's was not material to the risk on his life nor to his ability to recover a claim from NU under his policy and so the information regarding impending losses was not material to the insurance transaction – with the result that the defendant's claim of breach of the duty of good faith must fail.

(2) The court also considered whether NU had been guilty of unconscionable conduct in entering into the arrangement with the defendant. The relevant principles are set out in, inter alia, *Boustany v Pigott*[5], but the defendant had none of the characteristics of a classic unconscionable conduct victim – he was not young, poor, ignorant or bereft of advice and that defence was also rejected.

(3) It was also alleged by the defendant that NU were in breach of their statutory duty under s 47(1) of the FSA 1986 in that they dishonestly concealed the information about the impending Lloyd's losses. It was held that there is no right of action for damages arising out of a contravention of s 47(1) of the FSA 1986. This was largely irrelevant, in any event, as the court had already held that there was no duty of disclosure.

(4) Finally, the defendant had alleged that NU had been notified of clear fraud at Lloyd's before payment under the guarantee. It was held that the heavy burden of showing clear fraud had not even arguably been met.

It was therefore held that the defendant's defence and counterclaim would have to be struck out even if leave to serve it was given.

Therefore, whilst having every sympathy for the defendant's losses arising out of his Lloyd's underwriting, the judge held that NU were entitled to final judgment on their monetary claim.

The case is of course unusual in that it involves insurers on both sides, and each side is taking out policies of insurance with the other. For this reason, interesting though the case is, it may be doubted whether the case is of great general importance.

1 [1991] 2 AC 249.
2 [1990] 2 All ER 947, HL.
3 [1999] Lloyd's Rep IR 263, CA.
4 [1991] 2 AC 249.
5 (1993) 69 P & CR 298.

Consequences of insurer's breach of duty

5.58 *Banque Keyser Ullman SA v Skandia (UK) Insurance Co Ltd*[1] is authority for the point that although an insurer's breach of the obligation to deal with the proposer with the utmost good faith does not give rise to a remedy in damages, the proposer is entitled to a return of the premium. This conclusion is based on the wording of s 18 of the MIA 1906, which says that in the absence of utmost good faith by one party , the other party may avoid the contract. Although the section does not expressly state that such avoidance is the only remedy, the House of Lords took the view that this was the proper conclusion to draw. On the one hand it may fairly be said that it would be odd if the remedies for insurer's breach of duty were different from those for insured's breach of duty. On the other hand it must be admitted that the option of avoiding the contract is rarely of any practical value to an insured, whereas it is often of value to the insurer. From the point of view of the insured a right to damages would frequently be far more useful, but the House of Lords expressly rejected this as a possibility.

1 [1991] 2 AC 249, *sub nom Banque Financière de la Cité SA v Westgate Insurance Co Ltd* [1990] 2 All ER 947 HL.

Regulatory Requirements

5.59 The FSA Handbook[1] now sets out pre-contractual disclosure requirements which are imposed on the insurer. These are expressed in formalistic terms, and are not to be regarded as a substitute for the general legal duty to disclose material facts. However, it seems likely that in the great majority of cases compliance with these rules will also achieve compliance with the insurer's pre-contractual duty of utmost good faith.

1 Available at www.fsa.gov.uk.

5.60 The relevant rules are in the ICOB section of the Handbook and are summarised below. There is as yet no relevant authority on the interpretation of these rules. The rules distinguish between retail customers (ICOB 5.3) and commercial customers (ICOB 5.4).

Provision of information to retail customers

5.61 If a non-investment insurance contract is not a distance contract, an insurance intermediary must, in good time before the conclusion of the contract: (1) provide a retail customer with the following information in a durable medium:

(a) a policy summary;
(b) a statement of price;
(c) the relevant directive-required information set out in ICOB 5.5.20 R;

and (2) must draw the attention of the retail customer orally to the importance of reading the policy summary, and in particular the section of the policy summary on significant and unusual exclusions or limitations[1].

[1] ICOB 5.3.1.

On conclusion of a contract which is not a distance contract

5.62 Where the retail customer does not have the opportunity to read the information provided in accordance with ICOB 5.3.1 R(1) before conclusion of the contract, for example, because it is provided in a sealed pack, the insurance intermediary should provide a specimen copy of all the information in such a way that the retail customer is able to read it before conclusion of the contract. For example, a stand with sealed packs could be accompanied by a copy of the policy summary and other required information, with a notice that they contain important information the retail customer should read before buying the policy. Oral disclosure at the point of sale must still be given[1].

[1] ICOB 5.3.2.

Before the conclusion of a distance contract

5.63 If a non-investment insurance contract is a distance contract, an insurance intermediary must provide a retail customer, in good time before the conclusion of the contract, with the following information in a durable medium, unless the contract is made by telephone or some other means which does not allow the provision of the information in a durable medium:

(a) a policy summary;
(b) a statement of price;
(c) the relevant directive-required information set out in ICOB 5.5.20 R;
(d) the policy document;
(e) information about the claims handling process;
(f) information, where applicable, about cancellation rights;
(g) information, where applicable, about the extent and level of compensation cover and how further information can be obtained about compensation arrangements, if not already included in (a)[1].

[1] ICOB 5.3.6.

5.64 Where the contract is made by telephone or some other means which does not allow the provision of the information in a durable medium, the insurance intermediary must provide the following information by other means before the conclusion of the contract:

(i) name of the insurance undertaking;
(ii) type of insurance and cover;
(iii) significant features and benefits;
(iv) significant and unusual exclusions or limitations;
(v) the total price to be paid by the retail customer for the non-investment insurance contract (or, if an exact price cannot be indicated, the basis for calculation of the price enabling the retail customer to verify it);
(vi) notice of the possibility that other taxes or costs may exist in respect of the non-investment insurance contract that are not payable via the insurance intermediary or imposed by him;
(vii) the existence or absence of the right of cancellation and, where applicable, the duration of the cancellation period and the conditions for exercising the right to cancel, including information on the amount which the retail customer may be required to pay; and
(viii) a telephone number or address to which a claim may be notified[1].

[1] ICOB 5.3.6.

On conclusion of a contract which is a distance contract

5.65 When a non-investment insurance contract which is a distance contract is concluded in accordance with ICOB 5.3.6 R(2)(a) or (b), an insurance intermediary must provide a retail customer with the information in ICOB 5.3.6 R(1) in a durable medium immediately after conclusion of the contract.

[1] ICOB 5.3.8.

ICOB 5.4 – Provision of information to commercial customers

5.66 Before the conclusion of a non-investment insurance contract, an insurance intermediary must provide a commercial customer with:

(1) sufficient information to enable the commercial customer to make an informed decision about the contract being proposed;
(2) the directive-required information in ICOB 5.5.20 R(1) to (3) or ICOB 5.5.20 R(4) to (15) in writing (subject to ICOB 5.5.17 G to ICOB 5.5.19 R), unless the contract is being concluded by telephone; and
(3) the premium and any fees relating to the non-investment insurance contract[1].

[1] ICOB 5.4.1.

5.67 If the information referred to in ICOB 5.4.1 R(2) and (3) was not provided in writing before the non-investment insurance contract was concluded, it must be provided in writing immediately afterwards[1]. An insurance intermediary must provide a commercial customer with a policy document promptly after the conclusion of the non-investment insurance contract[2].

[1] ICOB 5.4.4.
[2] ICOB 5.4.5.

Group policies sold to commercial customers

5.68 When an insurance intermediary sells a group policy to a commercial customer the terms of which provide for persons, other than the commercial customer who concludes the non-investment insurance contract, to become policyholders, the insurance intermediary must, promptly after the conclusion of the contract:

(1) provide a policy document and a policy summary containing the information in ICOB 5.5.5 R except ICOB 5.5.5 R(6) (cross-references to the policy document) to the commercial customer (but a policy summary need not be supplied if there is no policyholder who would be a retail customer);
(2) inform the commercial customer that he should:
  (a) where a policy summary is supplied, provide the policy summary containing the information in (1) to each policyholder who is capable of being a retail customer; and
  (b) inform each policyholder that a copy of the policy document is available on request; and
(3) where a policy summary is provided, if the policy replaces a previous group policy, inform the commercial customer that he should inform each policyholder who is capable of being a retail customer of any changes to the information in the policy summary[1].

[1] ICOB 5.4.8.

Information form and content

5.69 A policy summary must contain only:

(1) the information specified in ICOB 5.5.5 R[1] in relation to a non-investment insurance contract; and
(2) at the option of the insurer or insurance intermediary:
  (a) all or part of the information in ICOB 5.5.14 R (Statement of price);
  (b) for any applicable compensation scheme mentioned in ICOB 5.5.5 R(12), the extent and level of cover and how further information can be obtained; and
  (c) the information on cancellation in ICOB 5.3.12 R[2].

A policy summary, if not set out in a separate document, must be:

(1) in a prominent place within the other document and clearly identifiable as key information that the retail customer should read; and
(2) separate from the other content of the document in which it is included.

[1] See para 5.71 below.
[2] ICOB 5.5.1.

Key features as an alternative to a policy summary

5.70 A firm may provide key features instead of a policy summary. The key features must include the information required in ICOB 5.5.5 R(6), (10) and (13) (cross-references from significant or unusual exclusions or limitations to related sections of the policy document, a telephone number or address for notification of claims and the key facts logo)[1].

[1] ICOB 5.5.4.

Policy summary content

5.71

Policy summary content

(1) a statement that the policy summary does not contain the full terms and conditions of the non-investment insurance contract, which can be found in the policy document;

(2) name of the insurance undertaking;

(3) type of insurance and cover;

(4) significant features and benefits;

(5) significant or unusual exclusions or limitations;

(6) cross-references from (5) to the related sections of the policy document;

(7) the duration of the non-investment insurance contract;

(8) (for policies of more than one year), a statement, where relevant, that the retail customer may need to review and update his cover periodically to ensure it remains adequate;

(9) the existence or absence of the right of cancellation and, where applicable, the duration of the cancellation period;

(10) a telephone number or address to which a claim may be notified;

(11) how to complain to the insurance undertaking and that complaints may subsequently be referred to the Financial Ombudsman Service or any other applicable named complaints scheme;

(12) that, should the insurance undertaking be unable to meet its liabilities, the retail customer may be entitled to compensation from the compensation scheme, or from any other applicable named compensation scheme, or that there is no compensation scheme.

Chapter 6

Intermediaries

General points

6.1 Many insurance contracts are made through one or more intermediaries, and it is therefore important to understand the legal rules relating to such persons. It is necessary to distinguish first between intermediaries who act for the insurer and those who act for the proposer/policyholder. It is also necessary to be aware that the common law duties of intermediaries, derived from the general law of agency, are now extensively modified in an insurance context by the scheme of statutory regulation under the FSMA 2000, a scheme which applied both to general insurance business and to life and investment business[1].

[1] Details of the statutory scheme appear later in this Chapter. Readers should note that this scheme is very significantly different from that which obtained under the FSA 1986.

Whose agent?

6.2 In all cases of insurance intermediaries it is necessary to ask first the fundamental question, whom does this intermediary represent? An insurance intermediary may represent either the insurer or the insured (often at the vital time the proposer), since many of the difficulties in this area relate to the period leading up to the formation of the policy). An intermediary should not represent both parties to that transaction, since as an agent he is in a fiduciary position, and will inevitably commit a breach of his fiduciary duties if he represents both parties simultaneously[1]. So far as the selling of insurance is concerned there are at common law two classes of intermediary, namely the insurance salesperson, who works for the insurer, sometimes as an employee but more often as a self-employed independent contractor and the broker, who acts as the agent of the proposer in seeking out the most suitable policy for his needs.

[1] *Fullwood v Hurley* [1928] 1 KB 498; in an insurance context see *Anglo-African Merchants Ltd v Bayley* [1970] 1 QB 311; and *North and South Trust Co v Berkeley* [1971] 1 WLR 470.

Insurance salespersons

General insurance

Individuals

6.3 Those who work for insurance companies may do so under a variety of different arrangements. Some are individuals who are self-employed and work on a freelance basis, whilst others are employed by the insurer. Under either system there can be no doubt that the individuals concerned act as agents of the insurer when endeavouring to sell policies. The only material difference which may be identified between the two categories is that it is virtually impossible for the insurer to deny responsibility for the actions of those directly employed (because of the rules as to vicarious responsibility for employees) whereas the rules as to actual and apparent authority discussed below may offer some prospect of escaping responsibility for the actions of self-employed agents.

Businesses

6.4 In other cases firms or limited companies with their own employees are appointed to be agents of an insurance company. In such cases it is the business which is the insurance company's agents, the employees of that business being its agents but not directly the agents of the insurance company. Despite this, such employees will in practice have the power to act on behalf of (and in such a way as to bind) the insurance company, for their employer will have vicarious responsibility for their actions and will itself have the power to bind the insurance company.

Agent's rights and duties at common law

Commission

6.5 For virtually all sellers of insurance, payment is by commission, based upon the value of policies sold. This applies to both salespersons and brokers, despite the obvious conflict of interest which the practice may create for the latter group. In effect, the commission charge is borne by the policyholder, since the need to pay it merely results in an increased premium. It is unfortunate that the price is not directly paid by policyholders.

The agent's rights to remuneration

6.6 An agent may have two possible rights to remuneration: a right to commission and a right to be indemnified for expenditure incurred. The right to commission, how much the agent is entitled to, and what he must do in order to earn it, will naturally fall to be assessed in the light of the relevant terms of his contract with his principal.

The normal principle of commission is that it follows the event. In other words the agent is entitled to commission only when he has sold the policy. This system rewards only success in selling, not endeavour in selling. The agent's commission is due as soon as the contract has been placed. It is irrelevant that the insurance is later cancelled[1].

[1] *Velos Group Ltd v Harbour Insurance Services Ltd* [1997] 2 Lloyd's Rep 461.

Unauthorised contracts

6.7 Occasionally an agent may purport to sell a contract which the insurance company has not authorised him to sell. In theory, no commission will be payable in respect of an unauthorised contract concluded by the agent, for he will not have done what he was supposed to do to earn it. This situation might arise where a agent purports to sell a policy which his company has not authorised him to sell. In such a case the company may choose to decline the proposal. In this event, the agent is clearly not entitled to commission. If the company choose to accept the proposal, the agent will be entitled to the commission. The agent will have no claim if the contract is unenforceable, for example, because of a misrepresentation made by the agent. Although the company's Commission Rules are likely to refer to business 'introduced' by the agent this must be taken to be limited to those contracts which are fully enforceable. If commission has been paid before it becomes apparent that the policyholder can avoid the contract, the right to indemnity contained in the contract will apply, so that the commission can be reclaimed.

Even if the contract with the client is fully enforceable, the agent will still be unable to claim his commission if he has committed a serious breach of one of his duties. This may be the case if, for example, the agent accepts a premium cheque from the proposer.

Payment of expenses

6.8 The company's contracts should deal expressly with the right to payment of expenses: subject to limited exceptions with the prior approval of the company, agents are not normally entitled to expenses.

The agent's duties at common law

6.9 This too depends essentially upon the contract between the agent and the principal. The question of the agent's duties is important as between agent and principal, since a breach of those duties may well give rise to a right to damages or to terminate the agency relationship. It is not appropriate to include in the contract other financial penalties for breach. However, in dealing with third parties the agent's apparent authority is usually at least as important as his actual authority, since the principal will be bound by any act within the scope of the agent's actual or apparent authority. The question of apparent authority is dealt with below.

The insurance salesperson is the agent of the insurer. Thus the insurer must accept responsibility for this agent's actions. Communication to this agent is effective communication to the insurer. This is a point which gives rise to many disputes in non-disclosure cases, the insured alleging that the facts were fully disclosed, notwithstanding that they do not appear on the proposal form. The law has generally been reluctant to accept the validity of this argument, since there is normally a clause in the proposal form where the proposer declares that he has read the form and that he warrants the truth of the statements contained in it (see especially *Newsholme Bros v Road Transport and General Insurance Co Ltd (1937) Ltd*[1]). The Insurance Ombudsman has been somewhat more sympathetic, if it can be established that there was in fact disclosure to the agent. In any event, it has been suggested that some of the old authorities may no longer be legally valid. *Customs and Excise Commrs v Pools Finance (1937) Ltd*[2] suggests an alternative approach based upon looking at the reality of the situation rather than at what is written on the form; *Stone v Reliance Mutual Insurance Society Ltd*[3] suggested that the agent who took away the completed form could be taken to represent that he has filled it in correctly and that the insurer was therefore estopped from challenging the accuracy of the form. Both approaches must be regarded as questionable, though it is easy to sympathise with the court's hostility to clauses of this type. More modern judicial consideration of the question came in *Roberts v Plaisted*[4] where the Court of Appeal suggested, obiter, that it is unsatisfactory to treat a broker as the agent of the proposer if the broker is in fact remunerated by the insurer. Legislative reform was suggested, but there is no reason to believe that it is imminent. In commercial policies it is probably still safe to say that proposers are assumed to know that brokers act for them (whatever the remuneration arrangements) but the position is perhaps less clear in relation to personal lines policies, at any rate if a complaint is brought before the Ombudsman.

It may be noted in passing that there is some remote possibility that a client who is unable to sue in contract will attempt to sue in tort, basing his claim upon negligent selection of an agent or negligent failure to supervise an agent. It is submitted, however, that such an action is bound to fail, for at common law there will normally be no evidence that the company has assumed any degree of responsibility to the policyholder for the supervision of the agent, and in the absence of such assumption it is unlikely that the modern law of tort would find a duty of care[5].

1 [1929] 2 KB 356.
2 [1952] 1 All ER 775.
3 [1972] 1 Lloyd's Rep 469, CA.
4 [1989] 2 Lloyd's Rep 341.
5 *Caparo Industries plc v Dickman* [1990] 1 All ER 568, HL; *Murphy v Brentwood District Council* [1990] 2 All ER 908, HL.

Actual authority

6.10 In deciding whether an agent has authority, the courts will look first to the express instructions given to him; in particular, this will entail an examination of the terms of the contract under which the agent is employed. If an act has not been expressly authorised, the courts will then consider whether authority can be implied. Authority can be implied in a number of ways. To start with, it has to be seen what can be deduced from what has been expressly authorised. All the contracts between companies and their agents confer some degree of discretion (as is inevitable) but this discretion is carefully limited in those areas where problems are thought likely to arise. No implication can be made which contradicts the express instructions under which the agent operates: the principal can, therefore, restrict his agent's implied authority, for example, by forbidding him to do something that is usually done by someone in his position. The agent in ignoring such instructions will be in breach of contract and may forfeit his commission. Care must be taken in the drafting of the contracts because it is possible that a court will imply terms which may have the effect of extending the agent's express authority.

Apparent authority

6.11 Even where there is neither express nor implied authority, the principal will be liable for the acts of the agent if the agent has acted within his apparent authority. If a person in the agent's position would normally have authority to perform acts of the type in question, he will be held to have apparent authority because the client is reasonably entitled to assume that authority exists. It is therefore necessary to look at two fundamental questions – when apparent authority arises, and what steps can be taken to avoid it.

Apparent authority arises when the agent appears to have actual authority to act. This appearance of authority may arise either because it is usual for such an agent to have the particular authority ('usual authority'), or because the principal has held him out as having that authority ('ostensible authority').

So far as usual authority is concerned, the real problems arise in relation to proposal forms and premium cheques. It is common practice for agents to complete the former and accept the latter. Both these practices are legally problematic, though no doubt practically convenient. A pragmatic view might be that they are almost impossible to eradicate, so that it is more sensible to acknowledge them and try to regulate them.

So far as ostensible authority is concerned, an appearance of authority could arise simply by virtue of the agent falsely stating to a client that he has been empowered to act; but this is clearly not enough to make the principal liable. The law requires conduct on the part of the principal which creates the impression of authority: there must be a representation by the principal to the client that the agent has actual authority. In determining whether the principal has been guilty of misleading conduct, a sharp distinction has to be drawn between situations where the agent performs an authorised type of act in an unauthorised way (for example, explaining the meaning of a policy incorrectly) and situations where he performs an unauthorised type of act (for example, where an agent authorised for relevant investment business gives a client stockbroking advice).

Unauthorised manner of performing an authorised type of act

6.12 In this situation, apparent authority will be easily established. The standard case is where the principal forbids the agent to do something which agents in his position usually do (such as the example of filling in the proposal form, discussed earlier). Here the principal will be bound if the agent ignores this prohibition:

apparent authority arises because the principal has consented to the agent occupying a position from which clients would conclude that he has actual authority, ie there has been the requisite representation by conduct. The same applies where the prohibition is implicit rather than express: it is on this basis that a principal will be liable where an agent whose job includes the giving of advice gives it negligently or even fraudulently.

Unauthorised type of transaction

6.13 In this situation, the principal will seldom be bound by his agent's acts. Simply by authorising the agent to do one thing, he does not hold him out as being empowered to do something different. This would include the case of the agent authorised to sell relevant investment business who sells other types of insurance contract. Furthermore, the principal will not be held bound on the ground that he has negligently failed to warn the client that the agent is not authorised to act on his behalf. As a matter of prudence the giving of such a warning may nevertheless be recommended. A negligent omission in theory could constitute a representation by conduct, but that requires the principal to be under a duty of care to the client, and, except in rare circumstances not relevant to most insurers' operations, such a duty will not arise. This has been the traditional standpoint of the law, and given that the duty in question would be a duty of care to prevent pure economic loss, it is much reinforced by decisions of the House of Lords such as *Caparo Industries plc v Dickman*[1] denying such a duty in the tort of negligence.

This leaves the possibility that misleading information about the agent's authority may be given to the client by or on behalf of the company, in which case the company will be bound. A simple case is where the client telephones one of the company's offices and is erroneously told that the agent is empowered to perform the unauthorised act, though even here the case of *British Bank of the Middle East v Sun Life Assurance Co of Canada*[2] shows that there is room for differences of interpretation, since in that case it was held that there was no actual or apparent authority, despite the fact that the case concerned an employee.

More problematic is the situation where, for example, the company gives the agent headed notepaper (as is likely to happen with many insurance agents) indicating his status as agent or the agent has such notepaper printed with the company's consent (as is likely to happen in some cases) and the agent uses this in the context of an unauthorised type of work. Consider specifically the case of an agent who also practices as an estate agent using company notepaper for estate agency work, perhaps giving negligent advice for which the client is seeking to make the company liable. There are cases which indicate that there can be a representation by conduct if an agent is put in a position where a third party would reasonably conclude that he had authority to carry out a particular type of transaction[3], and it is suggested that this principle would extend to cases where the agent is equipped by the principal with documents giving a misleading impression of his authority. Certain requirements have to be satisfied, however. The first is that the wording on the notepaper must be such as to indicate to a reasonable client that the unauthorised work is something the agent is empowered to do on behalf of the principal. Assume that the notepaper simply indicates that the agent is an authorised agent: a reasonable client would understand that as relating to the sorts of transactions that the company is known to engage in. If, therefore, the work in question falls outside the scope of those known transactions, there is no representation by conduct at all. There is a practical problem here in relation to any appointed representatives who also act as brokers for general insurance business. The life company will not of course transact such business, but this may well not be obvious to an unsophisticated client. There is some danger that a client may assume that the general business is also sold on behalf of the life company[4].

[1] [1990] 1 All ER 568, HL.
[2] [1983] 2 Lloyd's Rep 9. Although that case concerned an employee rather than an agent, it is thought that the result ought to be the same in the case of a self-employed agent.
[3] *Summers v Solomon* (1857) 7 E & B 879.
[4] For the FSMA 2000 consequences of this see below.

Preventing reliance on apparent authority

6.14 Several methods are available for preventing clients from being able to rely upon an agent's apparent authority. The first is to avoid the conduct that gives rise to the authority. This is clearly the appropriate course, for example, in the case of notepaper being used in the context of unauthorised work: the company should make it clear on the notepaper to what transactions the agency relates. In very many cases, however, the initial representation cannot be avoided: it may arise simply by virtue of engaging the agent, and covers many aspects of dealings with current and potential clients.

A further possibility is to disclaim liability for unauthorised acts of the agent: this could be done simply by inserting an exclusion clause in clients' contracts. However, depending upon the nature of the liability in question and the type of contract, the use of such disclaimers might be prevented by the Misrepresentation Act 1967. Section 3 of the 1967 Act provides that a disclaimer of liability for misrepresentation must satisfy the requirement of reasonableness, and the onus will be on the company to demonstrate that the disclaimer is reasonable. It is suggested that such a clause would fail the test of reasonableness. It is also most unlikely that the FSO would allow the company to rely upon such a clause.

A third technique available is to give the client notice that the agent is acting without authority: The client will then not be entitled to rely upon the agent's appearance of authority. The only practical method of achieving this end would be to give all prospective investors a written notice declaring the limits on the agent's authority. It is unclear whether this would be legally effective. At the very least it may be said that such a document would be subjected to close scrutiny by a court, which would be very ready to construe any ambiguities in it in favour of the client and which would require strong evidence that the client had received the document in the first place. It is surely extremely unlikely that the FSO would allow the company to rely on such a notice.

Authority to make representations

6.15 To prevent the client from having a remedy against the company for misrepresentation (whether a right to damages or a right to rescind his contract), notice may be given that the agent has no authority to make representations on behalf of the principal. In practice the major problems which arise here are oral statements by the agent as to likely investment returns, or as to the terms on which payments may be discontinued or the circumstances in which policies will lapse or become paid up. Wherever information on these matters appears in the literature given to investors (in practice this will mean the projection tables and the brochure for the policy) it should include a statement to the effect that no agent of the company has any authority to vary these terms or to make any representations which are in any way inconsistent with them[1]. Although s 3 of the Misrepresentation Act 1967 applies, it is submitted that a notice of this kind will satisfy any relevant reasonableness requirement, since the statement is clearly true.

A word of warning is called for, however. The agent will have given the client a statement of his position, which invites the client to consult the agent and, impliedly, to rely upon what he says. For the company then to declare that the client is not entitled so to rely may be considered inconsistent with this statement. The fact that the client is being given conflicting information about the agent's authority may make the notice ineffective.

[1] In the case of the projection tables it would be appropriate to explain that such oral representations are in any event forbidden by FSA Rules. As to this see further below.

Authority to vary the terms of the contract

6.16 The agent may purport to change the terms of a standard contract or to make a collateral contract modifying their effect. Usually, agents have no actual authority to do this, and it is submitted that they do not have even apparent authority. In any event some policies have express terms rendering such purported alteration invalid. It is submitted that it would be prudent to incorporate such terms in all policies, if this is not already done. However, there must be some doubt as to the effectiveness of these terms in respect of pre-contractual variations, either at law or before the FSO, since it will be only very rarely that the policyholder sees the policy document before the contract is concluded. It is therefore necessary to consider pre-contractual notices on this point. If there is apparent authority to vary, a notice denying that authority will not be subject to the Misrepresentation Act 1967 or UCTA 1977[1]. One possibility would be to rely on the Unfair Terms in Consumer Contracts Regulations 1999 ('UTCCR 1999')[2], though it would first be necessary to establish that the notice amounted to a contractual term, since the regulations (unlike UCTA 1977) do not apply to non-contractual notices.

The standard statement referred to above would not appear to have any bearing on variations of the contract promised by the agent: it merely invites the client to seek information and advice from the agent.

[1] Although the Act does not apply to contracts of insurance, the point may still be of relevance before the Insurance Ombudsman, who seeks to apply the spirit of the Act to such policies.
[2] See Chapter 17.

Authority to explain the contract

6.17 Although most agents do not have authority to alter the terms of the company's standard contracts, they have express authority to explain their terms.

They may therefore bind the company by misrepresenting their effect. In addition to the remedies for misrepresentation outlined above, the client can insist on the contract being performed as it was (wrongly) explained to him. A notice making it clear that the agent has no authority to explain the effect of the contract will escape control under s 3 of the Misrepresentation Act 1967, as explained earlier. However, as with authority to make representations, the standard statement referred to above is incompatible with such a notice, with the consequences outlined earlier.

Money and cheques received by representatives

6.18 It is obviously in the company's interests to minimise the risk of misappropriation by representatives of payments received by them, since payment to the company's agent will be payment to the company (though it will not necessarily follow that the company is bound by the policy, since this may state that there is to be no liability until the policy itself is issued, which may not happen until the money is actually received by the company). Insurance companies are increasingly reluctant to allow agents to accept cash, and even the practice of paying by cheque given to the agent is somewhat discouraged in favour of electronic means of payment which obviate the risks of misappropriation. Where cheques are used, they should of course always be made payable to the company, never to the agent.

Termination of agency

6.19 Terminating an agent's contract will merely bring his actual authority to an end. The possibility remains of the principal being held bound by the agent's post-termination acts on the basis of apparent authority. Such authority will arise simply by virtue of the agent's earlier employment as agent, at least as far as clients are concerned who had contact with the agent before his contract was terminated: at that time, the client would have been given the authorised impression that the agent had actual authority to act for the principal. The client is entitled to continue to rely on that representation of authority in later transactions. New clients, however, will not be able to plead apparent authority: *Jerome v Bentley & Co*[1]; and this may be so even if the agent sends them, for example, notepaper issued by the principal, for the agent would no longer have permission to send it to anyone.

The apparent authority that arises on termination may be counteracted if the principal notifies existing clients without delay that the agent no longer has authority to act on the principal's behalf. This, in effect, means writing to them all: newspaper advertisements or the like will only prevent those who read them from relying on apparent authority.

[1] [1952] 2 TLR 58.

Acting for both sides

6.20 It was mentioned above that an agent may not properly act for both sides in the same transaction. It must nevertheless be admitted that there are a number of cases where insurance intermediaries at least give the impression of acting for both sides. It is appropriate to begin by considering some of the older authorities before looking at some more recent cases.

Transferred agency clauses

6.21 Where a person is employed as the representative of the insurance company, he will of course normally be considered to be that company's representative, and thus not to be the agent of the proposer. In earlier times it was the practice of some companies to include on their proposal forms a statement to the effect that where the agent fills in the proposal form on behalf of the proposer he is to be treated for that purpose as being the agent of the proposer and not the agent of the company. The purpose of such a clause was to fix on the proposer the responsibility for any errors which may be found in the proposal form – were the agent still the agent of the insurance company, it would be possible to argue that the errors were the fault of the company, which was therefore precluded from relying on them. Although the validity of such clauses was unambiguously upheld by the Court of Appeal in *Newsholme Bros v Road Transport and General Insurance Co Ltd*[1], the subsequent cases of *Customs and Excise Comrs v Pools Finance (1937) Ltd*[2] and *Stone v Reliance Mutual*[3] have tended to undermine the effect of that decision. Much effort might be spent on analysing and reconciling these cases[4], but it is submitted that at the present day the effort is probably largely misplaced. The truth is that the differences between the cases, both in result and in reasoning, reflect significant philosophical differences between judges such as Scrutton LJ, who believed strongly in sanctity of contract and not at all in the protection of consumers, and Lord Denning MR, who might fairly be characterised as being at the opposite end of the spectrum from Scrutton LJ. At the present day it is fair to say that Lord Denning's views have somewhat the upper hand, though the reasoning which he adopts in these cases is by no means above criticism. Transferred agency clauses are rarely found at today (perhaps because insurance companies recognise the extreme unlikelihood that the Ombudsman would accept them) but if such a clause is encountered, perhaps in a commercial policy, it is submitted that the proper approach would be to argue that the clause cannot be allowed to divert the court from examining the reality of the situation. This approach may fairly be regarded as being in accordance with the judicial attitudes shown in the most recent authority. In *Winter v Irish Life Assurance Ltd*[5] it was said that the broker is normally to be treated as being the agent of the assured, though this presumption may be rebutted by appropriate evidence. The question to which this gives rise if of course, how much evidence will be required before the presumption can be rebutted. In *Re Great Western Assurance Co SA*[6] brokers were authorised to filter risks and settle claims on behalf of insurers. It was held that to this extent they were acting as the agents of the insurer. This view seems uncontentious, but more difficulty is perhaps caused by the observations of the Court of Appeal in *JA Chapman & Co Ltd v Kadirga Denizcilik Ve Ticaret*[7] to the effect that a broker may become a common agent acting for both parties. The term 'common agent' is in this context unfortunate, since it is normally assumed that an agent cannot act for both parties. The Court of Appeal's alternative suggestion that the broker might be an independent intermediary acting for himself as a sort of market-maker is more interesting, though it must be admitted that it involves the adoption of an approach which has not traditionally been seen in the context of insurance.

Despite these interesting new developments the most common situation will still be that the agent will be found still to be acting for the company, though it must be admitted that there will be cases where the agent simply writes the answers on the form at the proposer's direction and is to that extent to be regarded as the proposer's agent. This attention to substance rather than form is, it is submitted, in keeping with modern judicial attitudes, as well as being more likely to produce a more just result than would either a strict attention to the words of the clause (as in *Newsholme*) or a somewhat artificial reliance on notions of estoppel (as in *Stone*).

1 [1929] 2 KB 356, CA.
2 [1952] 1 All ER 775, CA.
3 [1972] 1 Lloyd's Rep 469, CA.
4 See McGee *The Law of Life Assurance Contracts* (2006, Cavendish).
5 [1995] 2 Lloyd's Rep 274.
6 [1999] Lloyd's Rep IR 377, CA.
7 [1998] Lloyd's Rep IR 377.

Maturity cheques

6.22 Maturity cheques for endowment policies should always be sent by post direct to the policyholder. They should never be entrusted to representatives. As an additional precaution the cheques should be made payable to the policyholder, and should be marked 'Not Transferable' and 'a/c payee only'. Cheques for this purpose should not include the words 'or order' after the payee's name. This appears to deprive the representative of the opportunity to call on the policyholder to solicit more business. This can be circumvented by informing the representative of the despatch of the maturity cheque.

Authority to qualify annual statements

6.23 The agent may mislead the client after the contract has been made, for example, by representing that his policy is performing better than the annual statement indicates. Agents clearly have no actual authority to make any such representations. It is a matter of some doubt whether the agent will have apparent authority to make such representations; though it must be said that the practice of sending annual statements to agents rather than to clients strengthens the agent's appearance of authority. It is recommended that a warning be placed on annual statements, advising the client that the agent has no authority to qualify the information contained therein. Such a notice will be unaffected by the statutory controls, being simply a statement that the agent has no authority to make representations (see above). The standard statement referred to above would appear to have no relevance in this context.

In order to weaken the agent's appearance of authority and also to reduce the opportunities for misrepresentations by the agent, it is recommended in addition that annual statements should always be sent direct to the client.

Brokers

The duties of a broker

6.24 Although there is no formal list of the duties of a broker, it is suggested that analysis of the case law allows the division of these duties into the following categories:

A Choosing the policy;
B Completing the proposal;
C Paying the premium;
D Post contractual duties;
E Lapse of policy,
F Renewal.

A general point which should first be made is that the broker's duties normally extend only to his client. Thus, a broker acting for a company owes a contractual duty to that company, but does not owe any tortious duty to the directors of the company[1].

[1] *Verderame v Commercial Union Assurance Co plc* [1992] BCLC 793, CA.

Choosing the policy

6.25 In general insurance the broker is likely to have available to him a wide range of policies, all more or less similar. Which of these is the best for his client will depend upon which aspects of the policy the client values most highly. In personal lines policies it is probably fair to say that most proposers focus on price above anything else. Certainly those high street brokers who use computer software to identify the 'best' policy have their systems programmed to produce the cheapest policy without regard to precise details of the cover provided. In commercial insurance the priorities are often somewhat different, and a broker who fails to attend carefully to the details of the cover may incur liability. In *Tudor Jones v Crowley Colosso*[1] brokers placing a contractors' all risks policy obtained cover which had an exclusion for any part of the works in respect of which a Certificate of Practical Completion had been granted. In many cases this would not cause a problem, but it happened that the particular project was being carried out in a way which meant that some parts of the works would receive separate Certificates of Practical Completion at a relatively early stage. Damage was suffered by parts of the works which had been certified, and the insurers were accordingly not liable. It was held that the brokers had been negligent in allowing the cover to be drafted in these terms. This is of course an example of a bespoke policy, where the broker's duty is likely to be considerably more onerous than in the case of a standard form policy.

In life assurance the matter is perhaps somewhat more complicated. Simple term assurance is often straightforward enough, depending largely upon a simple cost comparison. On the other hand, once any element of investment enters the equation, a wide variety of complex policies becomes available, and the broker's task becomes correspondingly more difficult.

A number of specific elements of the broker's duty were considered in *JW Bollom & Co Ltd v Byas Moseley & Co Ltd*[2], where it was held that brokers are required to ensure that the proposer is aware of the nature and terms of the insurance. This extends in particular to identifying and, if necessary, explaining any terms the breach of which might lead to the proposer becoming uninsured. It is suggested that a duty as onerous as this is appropriate in a commercial insurance case (which this was) but that the standard might need to be modified considerably in the case of personal lines business done on a volume basis. Where the policy is of a new or unusual type, there may be a particular onus on the broker to check the policy wording to ensure that it meets the needs of the policyholder[3]. This situation is clearly more likely to arise in highly specialised commercial insurance than in standard personal lines policies.

1 [1996] 2 Lloyd's Rep 619, Langley J.
2 [2000] Lloyd's Rep IR 136, Moore-Bick J.
3 *GE Reinsurance Corpn v New Hampshire Insurance Co and Willis Ltd* [2003] EWHC 302 (Comm), [2004] Lloyd's Rep IR 404, Langley J.

Completing the proposal

6.26 The law requires that the proposal form be completed correctly and that all material facts be properly disclosed[1]. It is not uncommon for the proposer to seek advice from the insurance broker on filling in the form. He may also ask the broker to verify that the proposal has been completed correctly. Given that the brokers' power here is limited to detecting obvious errors or a complete failure to answer a question, his responsibility in this respect is also limited. It would be an overstatement to suggest that the broker has a responsibility to ensure that the form is correctly filled in[2]. It may be observed, however, that a broker should be readily able to identify those questions on a proposal form which are most likely to give rise to difficulties and to recognise also the kinds of ambiguous answers which are prone to cause problems in the event of a claim. The value and importance of the broker's experience of similar types of form should not be underestimated. At the same time the proposer must retain a duty to check the proposal form before signing it. If the form contains obvious errors, he cannot cast liability for that onto the broker by saying that the latter filled it in for him[3].

1 As to this, see further Chapter B3.
2 This matter was canvassed though not fully decided in *Stowers v GA Bonus plc* [2003] Lloyd's Rep IR 402, Knight J.
3 *Kapur v JW Francis & Co and Hinkson* [2000] Lloyd's Rep IR 361, CA; see also *Pacific and General Insurance Co Ltd v Hazell* [1997] Lloyd's Rep IR 65.

Paying the premium

6.27 In general insurance the premium for the policy is commonly paid through the broker, either as a lump sum or by means of instalments. Payment to the broker is not by itself a valid payment to the insurer, and the broker remains responsible for making this payment[1]. However, unless the broker is authorised to issue and does issue a cover note providing temporary cover, the completion of the proposal form and the payment of the premium to the broker will not by themselves bring into existence a contract of insurance, and there will at that point be no insurance cover in place.

In life assurance it is not normally the duty of the broker to arrange for payment of the premium. Where premiums are paid by instalments (as is usual) arrangements are normally made for payment by standing order or direct debit through the policyholder's bank account.

Marine insurance has special statutory rules in relation to the payment of the premium[2]. The broker is directly responsible to the insurer for payment of the premium. In a Lloyd's policy there is a recital that the premium has been paid, and the assured can take advantage of this, even if the broker has not in fact paid the premium. In other marine policies, s 53 of the MIA 1906 creates a statutory fiction that the premium has been paid[3].

[1] For the special rules applicable in marine insurance, see Chapter 40.
[2] MIA 1906, s 53.
[3] *Universo Insurance Co of Milan v Merchants' Marine Insurance Co* [1897] 1 QB 205; [1897] 2 QB 93, CA; although this case predates the MIA 1906, s 53 appears to restate the principle which it lays down.

Post-contractual duties

6.28 In general insurance the major post-contractual duty of the broker is in relation to claims[1]. In general insurance it is common (though nowadays not a universal practice) to require claims to be made through the broker who placed the policy. Brokers who take it upon themselves to give policyholders advice in relation to the making of claims are likely to incur a duty to give reasonably competent advice, and may therefore be liable if their failure to handle this aspect of the case properly prejudices the policyholder's recovery under the policy. A broker handling claims for the policyholder owes duties going beyond those of a postbox. The broker needs to get a grip on a proposed notification and appraise it. There must be a strategy for handling claims. Thus, where a the policyholder had two policies, only one of which covered the loss in question, it was negligent of the broker to give notice under the wrong policy, with the result that the eventual notification under the correct policy was out of time[2]. A Lloyd's broker must retain the policy documentation for as long as a claim is to be regarded as possible[3]. It is thought that this principle is of general application, being merely an example of the rule that the broker must take reasonable care to protect the interests of his client. In that case the documentation in question was the slip, but any other documentation necessary in order to support a claim ought to be regarded in the same way.

[1] Though it is probably correct to say that this is a matter separate from the policy, ie merely by placing the policy the broker does not take on the duty of handling the claim. Indeed, some brokers make a separate charge for doing so.
[2] *Alexander Forbes Europe Ltd v SBJ Ltd* [2003] Lloyd's Rep IR 432, Mackie J.
[3] *Grace v Leslie & Godwin Financial Services Ltd* [1995] Lloyd's Rep IR 472, Clarke J.

Renewal

6.29 The major points for a broker to consider at renewal are complying with the duty of disclosure (or at least making sure than the insured is aware of the duty) and dealing with changes in cover. It is particularly important that any significant changes in the cover should be properly brought to the attention of the insured. In *Harvest Trucking Co Ltd v Davis*[1] the brokers were dealing with the renewal of a fleet motor policy. The insurers wanted to insert a clause removing theft cover from certain vehicles unless they were individually attended. Later a loss occurred in exactly those circumstances. The insured succeeded in recovering damages from the brokers for their failure to warn the insured of this clause.

In life assurance the most important situations which are likely to arise are lapse, maturity and insolvency of insurer (since renewal is not normally relevant, and claims on life policies are not normally handled through brokers).

[1] [1991] 2 Lloyd's Rep 638, Judge Diamond QC.

Lapse of policy

6.30 If premiums are not paid, the policy will eventually lapse[1]. In personal lines policies it is not in principle the duty of the broker to monitor this – indeed he will normally have no means of doing so, since he will not be handling the payments. In most commercial insurance the practice is for premiums to be paid through brokers. Occasionally the fact of lapse may be notified to the broker who arranged the policy, but even then it is not clear that he has any ongoing duty to alert the policyholder as to the position.

[1] As to this, see Chapter 14.

Maturity

6.31 When an endowment policy reaches maturity, notice of this fact may be sent to the broker, who in such a case acts merely as a messenger to transmit the information to the policyholder. The same applies if the maturity cheque is sent to the policyholder. It appears that the broker has no duties in this regard beyond the transmission of documents.

Insolvency of insurer

6.32 This is happily a rare situation, but it may occasionally happen that the broker becomes aware that a particular insurer is in some degree of financial difficulty[1]. Cases about this have mostly concerned motor insurance[2] where the issue is made most immediate by the statutory requirement for such insurance. However, the problem may for different reasons be significant in cases of life assurance. Where the policyholder has a simple term assurance, the insurer's insolvency threatens to leave him without cover. It is suggested that the broker has a duty to bring this point to the policyholder's attention without delay. In the case of an investment policy the position is rather different. Although insurance cover will not normally be the primary motive for having such a policy, the policyholder will need to be aware of the situation so that he can consider withdrawing his investment and switching it to another insurer. The broker is therefore under a similar duty to advise him of the situation.

[1] Larger brokers naturally monitor carefully the financial health of insurers. Both the Policyholders Protection Acts, discussed in Chapter 27, may also be relevant in cases of insurer insolvency.
[2] The best-known example is *Osman J Ralph v Moss Ltd* [1970] 1 Lloyd's Rep 313, CA.

Brokers and insurers

6.33 The general principle is that insurers are not responsible to the client for the activities of brokers, since they act as agents of the client, not as agents of the insurer[1]. A possible exception to this principle arises where the broker is in possession of a policy document issued to him by the company. Presumably this will have been sent to him for transmission to the client (or to the mortgagee in the case of a mortgage policy). The danger is that the broker may misappropriate the policy and may attempt to assign it, or to use it as the basis for a forged policy which is then sold to a third party. It is submitted that the company is unlikely to be held liable to the third party in such a case, but the matter is far from clear. The problem can be avoided if policy documents are not entrusted to brokers, but are sent direct to clients.

[1] For the difficulties arising from the involvement of brokers in claims handling, see Chapter 19.

Remuneration of brokers

6.34 Brokers are normally paid commission by the company whose policies they recommend, though there are a small number of insurance companies which do not pay commission to brokers. On the face of it this situation appears to give rise to obvious possibilities for conflicts of interests, and it does seem hard to deny that a broker who is faced with the question whether a client should invest, for example, in a building society savings account (on which the broker will receive no commission) or an insurance policy on which commission will be paid faces a difficult task in acting solely in the best interests of the client. It is hardly surprising if some brokers occasionally succumb to the temptation to lean towards recommending the insurance policy, even though this is a clear breach of duty unless it happens to coincide with the client's interests. The point has been judicially recognised, at least in the context of general insurance. In *Roberts v Plaisted*[1] the Court of Appeal commented on the unsatisfactory nature of the present arrangement, and observed that it would seem preferable for the broker to be remunerated directly by the client. At present the broker is of course indirectly remunerated by the client, since the commission is charged to the surrender value of the policy in the same way as if the policy had been sold by a salesperson. It has for a long time been assumed that clients would be unwilling to pay a fee direct to the broker, preferring instead the indirect recovery of the cost, though it should be added that this assumption has never been directly tested. One interesting effect of the introduction of the commission disclosure rules has been to encourage insurance companies to move away from rewarding their staff by means of commission in the direction of a structure which is at least partly salary-based. This has had the desirable effect of reducing the temptation to mis-sell products. It does not, however, directly address the problem of the ways in which brokers are remunerated, and for the present the commission system continues unabated in this area. In this connection it is also interesting to note *Eagle Star Life Assurance Co Ltd v Griggs and Miles*[2]. In that case, the defendants were two men trading as Business Development Services ('BDS'). BDS entered into an agreement with the claimant whereby it was appointed as an Appointed Representative of the claimant. Clause 9 of the agreement provided for the remuneration to be paid to BDS and also incorporated certain Life Assurance and Unit Trust Regulatory Organisation ('LAUTRO')[3] terms re payment of commission on an indemnity basis.

BDS introduced a couple who took out insurance with the claimant. The first monthly premium was paid. Under the terms of the agreement between BDS and the claimant the former's commission was due on the inception of the policy. No commission was paid at any time. The second monthly premium was not paid. There were negotiations between the parties concerning the policy and the first premium was returned.

The claimant brought proceedings against BDS to recover monies paid to BDS under the agreement which had now been terminated. BDS counterclaimed, inter alia, in respect of the commission.

It was held that it was clear that the claimant never intended to pay the commission and there was a clear breach of contract. It was held that the non-payment of the second premium entitled the claimant to treat the policy as lapsed so that the assured could not object to the cancellation of the policy. However, it was also found that there was an agreement between the claimant and the defendants that the first premium would be returned and the policy cancelled. It was therefore held that on the cancellation of the policy the parties reverted to their positions before the commencement of the policy and the right to commission disappeared.

The case emphasises the need to consider the payment of commission in circumstances where there are problems with the policy and to ensure that, if commission has been earned, provision for it to be paid is included in any agreement reached concerning the policy itself.

1 [1989] 2 Lloyd's Rep 341, CA.
2 [1998] 1 Lloyd's Rep 256, CA.
3 At the date of the events, LAUTRO was still the relevant regulator.

6.35 Other problems occur where intermediaries change their status. A former salesperson may be regarded by the client as still being an agent of his former company, and this impression may be reinforced if he is still in possession of any written material of the company. It appears that some former salespersons adopt the practice of selling only the products of the company for which they formerly worked. This is surely a breach of the broker's duty to secure the best policy he can for his client, since it is unlikely that one company's policies will always be the most suitable, but there is the further danger that the company may become aware of this and may fail to take sufficiently prompt action to put a stop to it. In this event, there seems to be an argument that the company will again become liable for the agent as if he were still tied. This is another very unclear area, but the risk of liability can be minimised by insisting on the return of all material which might suggest that the broker remained the company's agent. In practice this means headed notepaper, promotional literature and any policies which may be in his possession. Existing clients should also be notified by the company of his change of status (from a marketing point of view this can also be used to introduce the new representative). In addition, if the company ever discover that a former agent is selling only its policies, it is suggested that drastic action is required. That broker's authority to sell the company's products should certainly be withdrawn. Moreover, a case of this kind will usually involve FSA 1986 implications, with the result that it will be necessary to notify the appropriate regulatory authorities.

Changes from being a broker to being a salesperson do also happen, but these are less likely to give rise to problems, since it is clear that after the change the person concerned may only sell the policies of his new principal.

Extent of broker's duty

6.36 In *Duncan Stevenson MacMillan v AW Knott Becker Scott*[1] Lloyd's brokers were alleged to have been negligent in placing certain risks. They were in liquidation, so the clients who has suffered loss sought to claim on the brokers' Errors & Omissions ('E & O') insurance. The latter denied liability, alleging that the policies were voidable. So the clients next sought to sue the brokers who had placed the E & O insurance (the defendants). Evans J held that the loss was within the reasonable foresight of the defendant brokers and that the necessary proximity to found a tort claim existed because the E & O insurance (which is compulsory for Lloyd's brokers) was meant to protect the claimants. However, the defendants had not made any voluntary assumption of responsibility to the claimants, their only duty being towards their own clients. Consequently, the claim must fail.

1 [1990] 1 Lloyd's Rep 98, Evans J.

Consequences of breach of broker's duty

6.37 A breach of duty by the broker is in principle capable of giving rise to an action for damages by the client. Such damages are of course compensatory in nature, and it follows that the client must be able to identify loss caused to him directly by the breach. Where the failure consists in a failure to arrange insurance at all there may be no identifiable loss. There will obviously be loss if the client dies without life insurance which he would otherwise have had or if his health deteriorates to the point where he can no longer get insurance at the same premium or at all. Where the failure consists in recommending the wrong policy, compensation is a matter of calculating how much better off the policyholder would have been with the right policy. It should be observed in this context that a person buying an investment policy is not automatically entitled to the best possible investment performance – such contracts are necessarily speculative and the investor's entitlement is only to the exercise of reasonable diligence in recommending a suitable contract. Similar principles apply in relation to post-contractual failure, where the nature and extent of the loss will again depend heavily on the circumstances. Some of the cases cited above illustrate the ways in which brokers may become liable for failure to perform their duties correctly.

In *Aneco Reinsurance Underwriting Ltd (In Liquidation) v Johnson & Higgins Ltd*[1] the defendant reinsurance brokers obtained reinsurance cover for the claimant which the underwriters of the reinsurance later avoided on grounds of the defendant's failure to disclose material facts. The defendant admitted negligence and breach of duty. The cover which was avoided was in the sum of $US10m, and the defendant contended that that sum represented the correct measure of damages.

The claimant contended that if the defendant had made full disclosure to the underwriters, then the defendant would have discovered that reinsurance cover of the kind required by the claimant was not available, either at all or on terms acceptable to the claimant, and the defendant would have had to report this outcome to the claimant. This, as the defendant knew, would have caused the claimant to decline to enter into the transaction for which the reinsurance cover was required, and as a result of which the claimant suffered the losses of $US30m. The claimant therefore argued that the entirety of its losses was caused by the defendant's breach of duty. The Court of Appeal held that the case raised two issues: (a) whether reinsurance cover of the kind required by the claimant was available, and if so whether on terms which would have been acceptable to the claimant; and (b) what was the proper measure of the claimant's losses? On the balance of probabilities reinsurance cover of the kind required by the claimant could not have been obtained, and the defendant should have so reported to the claimant. The proper measure of damages was the full extent of the claimant's losses, since the defendant knew that the claimant would not have exposed itself to any risk without an assurance that sufficient cover was in place, and it was therefore unreasonable to require the claimant to bear liabilities which it had expressly told the defendant that it was not prepared to accept. It would be dangerous to attempt to draw very broad conclusions from this case. It appears that the decision depends upon the view of the Court of Appeal as to what would have happened if the defendants had performed their duty properly. On the facts of the case it was held that the claimants would not have exposed themselves to the risks in question. The outcome would presumably have been different if the court had concluded that the claimants would have accepted the risks anyway.

1 [2000] Lloyd's Rep 1R 12, CA.

6.38 The question of the broker's possible liability to the insurer for misrepresentation has been considered in two recent cases. In *Avon Insurance plc v Swire Fraser Ltd*[1] the claim failed because no misrepresentation could be established, but the judge assumed that liability under the Misrepresentation Act 1967 was at least a possibility. In *HIH Casualty and General Insurance Ltd v Chase Manhattan Bank*[2], Aikens J re-asserted the rule that avoidance of the contract is the only remedy for non-disclosure/misrepresentation. He held that it was not open to the court to create an additional remedy against the agent to insure. It is submitted that the decision is to be welcomed. To hold otherwise would put brokers in an impossible conflict of interest.

1 [2000] Lloyd's Rep IR 535, Rix J.
2 [2001] Lloyd's Rep IR 191, Aikens J.

Record keeping

6.39 In *Aneco Reinsurance Underwriting Ltd (in liquidation) v Johnson and Higgins*[1] it was held that it would be highly desirable to find a means of recording, in a form to avoid later disputes, what was said between brokers and underwriters at the time of presentation of risk. At the level of principle the wisdom of this statement cannot be doubted. On the other hand it must also be observed that for a busy broker and underwriter the prospect of having to record, whether in writing or on tape the content of every piece of broking is extremely daunting. The likelihood is that both sides will prefer to continue the present practice, accepting the occasional dispute as an occupational hazard.

1 [2000] Lloyd's Rep IR 12, CA.

Procedure

6.40 In the same case the judge also said that it was highly desirable that, whenever practicable, claims against brokers be heard at the same time and by the same tribunal that determines whether underwriters have validly avoided the contract. This is because the claim against the broker is intimately linked with the avoidance of the policy. If the policy is held to provide valid cover for the necessary risks then the broker may be said to have achieved the necessary result for the policyholder (whatever questions may arise about the way in which he went about the task). It is only if the policyholder's claim is wholly or partly unsuccessful, that the question of a right of recourse against the broker becomes a real issue.

6.41 In *Total Graphics Ltd v AGF Insurance Ltd*[1] the brokers had failed to obtain the required insurance (in the sense of the right insurer and full disclosure) which resulted in the insured having to compromise its claim against its insurers. The insured then claimed against the brokers' professional indemnity insurers under the TP(RAI)A 1930. It was held that the broker was in all probability aware of the full facts of the insurance required but did not pass them on to the insurers. The reason for the insured's shortfall in insurance was the broker's misstatement. The true cause of the insured's loss was found to be that the broker placed the insurance with the syndicate it did. It was held that the broker's liability to the insured fell outside the professional indemnity policy because the failure to place insurance with the insurers requested was not proved to be a negligent act error or omission in terms of the policy.

[1] [1997] 1 Lloyd's Rep 599.

6.42 The question in all these cases is whether the act or omission complained of is inconsistent with that reasonable degree of care and skill which persons of ordinary prudence and ability might be expected to show in the agent's situation and profession – *Seavision Investment Norman Thomas SA v Evennett and Clarkson Puckle Ltd, The Tiburon*[1] (broker's failure to make proper declaration under open cover).

In *Pacific & General Insurance Co Ltd v Hazell; Pacific & General Insurance Co Ltd v Home & Overseas Insurance Co Ltd*[2] consideration was given to a broker's duty to advance premiums to reinsurers when the insurer is in liquidation and to fund the insurer's liabilities. The essence of the decision is that brokers are not in any contractual relationship with reinsurers. Consequently, they do not have any obligation to advance premiums to them. The appointment of a provisional liquidator to the reinsured perminated the broker's authority to act on its behalf. Thus, payment of premium by the broker is not effective to discharge the reinsured's liability unless it is explicitly made on behalf of the reinsured and is subsequently ratified by them. This outcome depends entirely on the particular consequences of various types of insolvency proceeding. The principles on which it is based should therefore not be thought to be of application outside the insolvency context.

[1] [1990] 2 Lloyd's Rep 418.
[2] [1997] 6 Re LR 157, Moore-Bick J.

6.43 An assured who places cover expressly on behalf both of himself and of other interests does not subject his co-assureds to a general lien in respect of his indebtedness to the brokers under a running insurance account: *Eide UK Ltd v Lowndes Lambert Group Ltd*[1].

A broker owes a duty of care to a specific person who to his knowledge is to become an assignee of the policy, at any rate if to the broker's knowledge that person has participated in giving instructions for the insurance[2].

It may happen that a policy which is defective by reason of the broker's breach of duty is also affected by some other defect. For example, it may be that the policyholder has committed some other breach of condition which would, at least arguably, prevent him from recovering for a particular loss or which would even allow the insurers to avoid the policy entirely. In such circumstances the brokers are likely to take the point that their breach has caused no loss, since the policyholder could not have recovered under the policy anyway. This was the situation in *O & R Jewellers Ltd v Michael John Terry*[3], where the policyholders were said to have committed various breaches of the security conditions in a jewellers' policy. It was held that the court had to take account of the likelihood that insurers would in fact have taken the various points and would have succeeded on them. In other words, the proper approach in such cases is to treat them as involving the loss of a chance[4] and to award an appropriate proportion of the total recoverable loss. It is of course for the court to assess the likelihood of the various possible events – insurers taking points, insureds agreeing settlements etc – and from that to derive a figure for the relevant percentage of the loss[5].

1 [1998] 1 All ER 946, [1999] QB 199, CA.
2 *Punjab National Bank v de Boinville* [1992] 1 Lloyd's Rep 7.
3 [1999] Lloyd's Rep IR 436, Le Quesne QC.
4 Based on the approach of the Court of Appeal in *Allied Maples Group Ltd v Simmons & Simmons* [1995] 4 All ER 907, CA.
5 *J W Bollom & Co Ltd v Byas Moseley & Co Ltd* [2000] Lloyd's Rep IR 136, Moore-Bick J.

6.44 When may the insurer be bound by the acts of brokers? Obviously the major issue here is that of responsibility for the acts of Appointed agents and Company agents, but the possibility of being bound by the acts of brokers also needs to be considered. If an agent purports to make a contract on behalf of his principal or to vary a contract being concluded between his principal and a client, or if he misleads the client as to what the contract he is about to conclude means or gives other incorrect advice, the key question is whether the agent has authority so to act.

Independent Financial Advisers

6.45 Independent Financial Advisers ('IFAs') act as agents of the proposer, and have a duty to give their client best advice, which implies making a survey of the entire range of products to see what is most suited to the client's needs. Included in this is an obligation to consider whether an insurance policy is the appropriate method of protecting the client's interests. The role of the IFA is in this respect fundamentally different from that of the Company Representative, and the concept of best advice differs as between the two categories of intermediary.

The question of contractual liability depends upon the ordinary principles of agency. There is a distinct possibility that a client of the agent may be able to hold the insurance company liable in respect of business which lies quite outside the scope of the authority granted by the insurance company, simply because the distinction between insurance company business and other business may well be quite unclear to an outsider. This is particularly so where insurance companies have bought chains of estate agents, who sell houses and offer mortgage advice and possibly other financial services. Some of these insurance companies have their name prominently displayed on the fascia boards and the notepaper of the estate agent. These companies are likely to have some difficulty in denying responsibility for any of the business done by the estate agents. The position will be somewhat alleviated by the FSA requirement that the ARFs indicate the limit of their authority on their notepaper, but there will inevitably be cases where clients have never seen the notepaper, though they have seen the insurance company's name and logo prominently displayed. If the ARF and the company have taken reasonable steps to draw the situation to the attention of clients, then FSA may be satisfied, but the attitude of the Insurance Ombudsman is less clear, as is the strict contractual position. Presumably the question would have to be decided according to the ordinary principles of agency as set out above.

The Statutory Framework under FSMA 2000

6.46 The duties of insurance intermediaries are extensively regulated by the FSMA 2000 and legislation under that Act. In particular the FSA Handbook has two relevant sections – COB, which deals with the conduct of investment insurance business, and ICOB, which deals with the conduct of general insurance business. The following paragraphs provide a summary of the relevant rules.

General insurance contracts

Status disclosure

6.47 For both retail and commercial customers certain information must be provided by the intermediary before or immediately after conclusion of an insurance contract. The requisite information is as follows[1]:

(1) The name and address of the insurance intermediary.
(2) The insurance intermediary's statutory status (in accordance with GEN 4 Annex 1 (Statutory status disclosure)).
(3) That items 1 and 2 can be checked on the FSA's Register by visiting the FSA's website http://www.fsa.gov.uk/register or by contacting the FSA on 0845-606-1234.
(4) Unless the insurance intermediary is an insurer, details of any holding, direct or indirect, that an insurance intermediary has that represents more than 10% of the voting rights or of the capital in an insurance undertaking.
(5) Unless the insurance intermediary is an insurer, details of any holding, direct or indirect, that an insurance undertaking or parent of an insurance undertaking has that represents more than 10% of the voting rights or of the capital in the insurance intermediary.
(6) In relation to the non-investment insurance contract provided, whether the insurance intermediary has provided, or will provide, advice or information:
    (a) on the basis of a fair analysis of the market; or
    (b) from a limited number of insurance undertakings; or
    (c) from a single insurance undertaking.

    If (b) or (c) applies, the FSA must also disclose whether it is contractually obliged to conduct insurance mediation activity in this way.

(7) If the contract provided has not been selected on the basis of a fair analysis of the market, that the customer can request a copy of the list of the insurance undertakings the insurance intermediary selects from or deals with in relation to the contract provided.
(8) How to complain to the insurance intermediary and that complaints may subsequently be referred to the Financial Ombudsman Service or any other applicable named complaints scheme.
(9) The compensation arrangements should the insurance intermediary be unable to meet its liabilities.

1 ICOB 4.2.

6.48 Point (6) in the above list is of fundamental importance, for it marks a departure from the very unpopular system of 'polarisation' which operated under FSA 1986 and which required all intermediaries to choose between acting for a single product provider (a 'company representative' or, in common parlance a 'tied agent') and being entirely independent with a duty to survey the market as a whole (an 'independent financial adviser'). The FSMA 2000 allows intermediaries to occupy a third category, that of advising on products from a limited range of providers.

6.49 In addition a firm (ie a product provider as distinct from an intermediary) must comply with GEN 4, dealing with information to be given in all correspondence. So far as an appointed representative of an insurer is concerned, GEN 4 provides that every communication to a retail client (including therefore the first such communication to any particular client) must include a statement in the following form[1]:

> '[Name of *appointed representative*] is an appointed representative of [name of *firm*] which is [then continue with the required disclosure of the *firm*]'.

1 GEN 4 ANNEX 1.

6.50 The above rules give the latest time by which status disclosure information must be given to the customer. The insurance intermediary may provide information to the customer earlier than the time specified in the rules. For example, an insurance intermediary who is also providing services in connection with packaged products or regulated mortgage contracts may wish to combine the information required by ICOB 4.2 with the status disclosure requirements in COB or MCOB[1], and provide the information to the customer on initial contact, using the combined initial disclosure document in ICOB 4 Annex 2. But the rules do not specify the format in which information must be provided to the customer. An insurance intermediary may use the initial disclosure document in ICOB 4 Annex 1, the combined initial disclosure document in ICOB 4 Annex 2, a terms of business letter, or another document to provide information to the customer.

1 MCOB is the section of the Handbook which deals with the conduct of mortgage business, which is now regulated by the FSA.

Medium of disclosure[1]

6.51 The general rule is that an insurance intermediary must provide the information in ICOB 4.2.8 R to the customer in a durable medium[2] at any time before conclusion of a non-investment insurance contract. This is subject to limited exemptions. The information may be provided orally before the conclusion of the contract if:

(a) the customer requests this; or
(b) the customer requires immediate cover.

[1] ICOB 4.2.2
[2] Ie in hard copy. Although electronic communication is treated as 'in writing' for the purposes of those rules which specify information in writing, it is not regarded as a 'durable medium' for the purposes of those rules which specify a durable medium.

6.52 Moreover, if the service is being provided on the telephone and the customer wishes to enter into a non-investment insurance contract, then:

(c) Provided the customer gives his explicit consent to receiving only limited information, the insurance intermediary may proceed on the basis of at least the following information[1]:
   (i) the name of the insurance intermediary;
   (ii) (if the call is initiated by the insurance intermediary) the commercial purpose of the call;
   (iii) the identity of the person in contact with the customer and his link with the insurance intermediary; and
   (iv) that other information is available on request, and the nature of the information.

[1] ICOB 4.2.2.

6.53 Where either of the above exemptions applies, the customer must be provided with the full information set out in para 6.51 in a durable medium immediately after the conclusion of the contract.

6.54 The insurance intermediary may tell the customer that he is able to receive the information orally, or (in the case of telephone communications) that the more limited information requirements in para 6.52 may apply. In addition, if the customer requires immediate cover and the non-investment insurance contract is concluded over the telephone, the insurance intermediary may take advantage of either of the exemptions set out above, subject to the customer giving his explicit consent[1].

[1] ICOB 4.2.3.

6.55 The disclosure requirement may be met by use of the initial disclosure document set out in ICOB 4 Annex 1. Alternatively, in circumstances where the insurance intermediary has reasonable grounds to be satisfied that the services which it is likely to provide will, in addition to relating to non-investment insurance contracts, also relate to regulated mortgage contracts, regulated lifetime mortgage contracts or packaged products, the insurance intermediary may use the combined initial disclosure document set out in ICOB 4 Annex 2. However, the use of these documents is not mandatory – the intermediary may choose to provide the information in any form, so long as the necessary information is in fact included.

6.56 If an insurance intermediary chooses to use the initial disclosure document at ICOB 4 Annex 1, it must not include the key facts logo and the heading and text in Section 1 unless it uses the document in full and makes no changes to the text other than changes allowed by the notes to the document[1]. Thus, if the intermediary wants to depart to any significant extent from the standard text, it would be well-advised to abandon the standard form document entirely and produce its own document.

1 ICOB 4.2.5.

6.57 Similarly, If an insurance intermediary chooses to use the combined initial disclosure document at ICOB 4 Annex 2, it must use the document in full and make no change to the text other than changes allowed by the notes to the document[1].

1 ICOB 4.2.7.

Suitability[1]

6.58 An insurance intermediary must take reasonable steps to ensure that, if in the course of insurance mediation activities it makes any personal recommendation to a customer to buy or sell a non-investment insurance contract, the personal recommendation is suitable for the customer's demands and needs at the time the personal recommendation is made. This recommendation must be based on the scope of the service disclosed in accordance with para 6.47. This is the fundamental rule which now governs the duty of an insurance intermediary in selling a non-investment insurance contract. The reference to 'scope of service' alludes to point (6) of the items which must be disclosed. The intermediary must say into which of the three categories of intermediary he falls.

1 ICOB 4.3.

6.59 Despite the above general rule an insurance intermediary may make a personal recommendation of a non-investment insurance contract that does not meet all of the customer's demands and needs, provided that there is no non-investment insurance contract within the insurance intermediary's scope, that meets all of the customer's demands and needs and the insurance intermediary identifies to the customer, at the point at which the personal recommendation is made, the demands and needs that are not met by the contract that it personally recommends[1].

1 ICOB 4.2.9.

6.60 This rule is the equivalent of the old 'Best Advice' rule. The substance of it is that the intermediary must recommend the most suitable product of those which he is authorised to sell. However, the new rule departs from the old one in some important respects. Under the old law it was said that even a tied agent could not recommend a product unless it was 'suitable', as well as being the most suitable product which he was authorised to sell. Thus there were cases where a tied agent could not properly recommend any product, because none of his products was suitable. However, it was never clear what was the minimum level of 'suitability' required. The new law appears to remove this difficulty by allowing the recommendation of even a wholly unsuitable product, so long as the details of how and why it is unsuitable are fully disclosed. It is to be hoped that intermediaries who find themselves unable to recommend a product which even comes close to meeting the customer's demands and needs will take the ethical course of declining to make a recommendation at all.

Information about the customer's demands and needs[1]

6.61 In assessing the customer's demands and needs, the insurance intermediary must seek such information about the customer's circumstances and objectives as might reasonably be expected to be relevant in enabling the insurance intermediary to identify the customer's requirements. This must include any facts that would affect the type of insurance recommended, such as any relevant existing insurance. He must have regard to any relevant details about the customer that are readily available and accessible to the insurance intermediary, for example, in respect of other contracts of insurance on which the insurance intermediary has provided advice or information, and he must explain to the customer his duty to disclose all circumstances material to the insurance and the consequences of any failure to make such a disclosure, both before the non-investment insurance contract commences and throughout the duration of the contract; and take account of the information that the customer discloses.

1 ICOB 4.3.2.

6.62 This rule is the modern equivalent of the old 'know your customer' requirement. It does no more than state the obvious, since it is apparent that no proper advice can be given without the information here referred to.

Assessing the suitability of a contract against the customer's demands and needs[1]

6.63 In assessing whether a non-investment insurance contract is suitable to meet a customer's demands and needs, an insurance intermediary must take into account at least whether the level of cover is sufficient for the risks that the customer wishes to insure, the cost of the contract, where this is relevant to the customer's demands and needs and the relevance of any exclusions, excesses, limitations or conditions in the contract. This may be regarded as another statement of the obvious, but again it gives a clear minimum benchmark against which to measure any advice given.

1 ICOB 4.3.6.

6.64 As a further method of monitoring an intermediary's compliance with the rules ICOB 4.4 provides that where an insurance intermediary arranges for a customer to enter into a non-investment insurance contract (including at renewal), it must, before the conclusion of that contract, provide the customer with a statement that:

(a) sets out the customer's demands and needs;
(b) confirms whether or not the insurance intermediary has personally recommended that contract; and
(c) where a personal recommendation has been made, explains the reasons for personally recommending that contract.

6.65 The general rule is that the statement of demands and needs must be provided in a durable medium, though, as with the status disclosure information, to provide it orally if the customer requests it or the customer requires immediate cover; but in both cases the insurance intermediary must provide the information immediately after the conclusion of the contract, in a durable medium.

Exemptions[1]

6.66 The requirement for a statement of demands and needs does not apply to an insurance intermediary that is an insurer when dealing with a commercial customer, unless the insurer makes a personal recommendation to that commercial customer[2]. If an insurance intermediary that is an insurer makes a personal recommendation to a commercial customer, it need not provide the commercial customer with a statement of demands and needs, provided that it has obtained the consent of the commercial customer not to receive the statement of demands and needs and it has explained to the commercial customer the consequences of giving that consent before it is given.

[1] ICOB 4.4.2.

[2] An insurer which sells direct to a customer is treated as an 'intermediary' for the purposes of these rules in order to ensure that in such cases customers will not have less protection as a result of the absence of an actual intermediary. Sales of life policies to commercial customers do happen, as for example Keyman policies, discussed in Chapter 5.

Telephone sales

6.67 Where a contract is concluded by telephone with a customer (whether retail or commercial) the statement of demands and needs must be provided immediately after the conclusion of the contract in a durable medium and may also be provided orally before the contract is concluded.

Excessive charges to retail customers[1]

6.68 An insurance intermediary must ensure that its charges to a retail customer are not excessive. When determining whether a charge is excessive, an insurance intermediary should consider the amount of its charges for the services or product in question, compared with charges for similar services or products in the market whether the charges are an abuse of the trust that the retail customer has placed in the insurance intermediary; and the nature and extent of the disclosure of the charges to the retail customer. This is in principle a desirable provision (and one which does not appear to have existed as a rule in its own right under the previous law), but the practical difficulties of applying it are readily apparent. It may be suggested that price is likely to be the most important consideration, since it is the only one which comes close to being susceptible to reasonably objective quantification. Provided that an intermediary's charges are not out of line with those charged by other intermediaries for a similar service, it seems unlikely that they will be found to be excessive.

[1] ICOB 4.5.

Investment Insurance Contracts

6.69 The intermediary's duties in relation to these are regulated by COB 5. This applies[1], so far as presently relevant, to a firm that: gives a personal recommendation concerning a designated investment to a private customer; or is not an insurer and makes a personal recommendation to take out a life policy to an intermediate customer or a market counterparty; or is not an insurer and is arranging (but not merely by introducing) a life policy or is an insurer and is arranging a life policy for a private customer. Care is therefore needed in applying the rules of this section in an insurance context.

[1] COB 5.2.1.

6.70 A firm that arranges an execution-only transaction for a private customer is not generally required to obtain any personal or financial information about that customer, except when the Money Laundering sourcebook applies. However, the Insurance Mediation Directive requires that a statement of the demands and needs of a client is provided to the client, whether advice is given or not. This is required whatever the status of the client. Accordingly the demands and needs provisions discussed below apply to all circumstances relating to life policies.

Purpose

6.71 Principle 9 (Customers: relationships of trust) requires a firm to take reasonable care to ensure the suitability of its advice and discretionary decisions. To comply with this, a firm should obtain sufficient information about its private customer to enable it to meet its responsibility to give suitable advice.

Requirement to know your customer

6.72 Before a firm gives a personal recommendation concerning a designated investment to a private customer, or acts as an investment manager for a private customer, it must take reasonable steps to ensure that it is in possession of sufficient personal and financial information about that customer relevant to the services that the firm has agreed to provide[1]. This closely mirrors the provision in relation to pure protection contracts, and the comments made in that connection apply equally here.

[1] COB 5.2.5.

6.73 If a private customer declines to provide relevant personal and financial information, a firm should not proceed to provide the services described above without promptly advising that customer that the lack of such information may affect adversely the quality of the services which it can provide[1]. This is another statement of the obvious. It is expressed as Guidance rather than a Rule, but it is easy to see that ignoring it is very likely to be held to be a breach of duty.

[1] COB 5.2.7.

Statement of demands and needs[1]

6.74 Again these rules closely mirror those applying to pure protection contracts. The general rule is that a firm must provide the client with a statement of his demands and needs if it makes a personal recommendation of a life policy to a client or it arranges (whether through issuing a direct offer financial promotion or otherwise) for the client to enter into a life policy. Normally, the statement must be provided as soon as practicable, and in any event before the conclusion of the contract for the life policy and in a durable medium.

[1] COB 5.2.12.

6.75 However, by way of exception to the normal rule, a firm may provide the statement of demands and needs orally if the client requests it or immediate cover is necessary, but in either case the firm must provide the information immediately after the conclusion of the contract, in a durable medium.

6.76 If the only contact between the firm and the client before conclusion of the contract is by telephone, the statement of demands and needs must be provided immediately after the conclusion of the contract, in a durable medium[1].

[1] COB 5.2.13.

Conclusions

6.77 The old rules under FSA 1986 were, so far as insurance is concerned, more detailed that the rules now contained in COB and ICOB. The FSMA approach to suitability is to rely heavily on the Principles and to supplement this with Rules and Guidance which add little to the Principles. What remains to be seen as the new rules are applied in practice is the extent to which courts and/or the FSA will be prepared to place a strict interpretation on the requirement to take proper steps to ensure suitability. The temptation to earn commission by recommending products which are not truly suitable cannot entirely be removed, and it may be questioned whether the system of merely requiring disclosure of unsuitability is going to provide adequate protection for consumers. Mis-sales commonly occur where the customer does not really understand his own needs and does not have enough sophistication or education to evaluate properly the product which is being offered to him. It seems unlikely that such customers will be adequately protected by being told that the product recommended is not really suitable for them. In this context it is important to bear in mind FSMA s150, which provides:

> '(1) A contravention by an authorised person of a rule is actionable at the suit of a private person who suffers loss as a result of the contravention, subject to the defences and other incidents applying to actions for breach of statutory duty.'

6.78 Section 150 applies to FSA Rules, but not to matters which are solely Guidance, even where contained in the Handbook. However, as explained in Chapter 1[1], compliance or non-compliance with Guidance may be relied upon as tending to show compliance or non-compliance with Rules. Consequently, in the inevitable actions under section 150 against intermediaries for mis-selling policies or otherwise giving bad advice, courts are going to have to consider the matters discussed in this Chapter.

[1] Para 1.2.

Part C

The insurance contract

Chapter 7

Form, commencement and duration of insurance policies

Form

7.1 Outside marine insurance there are no statutory rules as to the form and content of insurance policies. In the case of marine policies, ss 22–24 and 26 of the MIA 1906 require that a contract of insurance must be embodied in a policy of insurance 'in accordance with this Act'[1], which must specify the name of the insured or of some person who effects the policy on his behalf[2] and which must be signed on behalf of the insurer(s)[3]. The subject matter of policy must also be designated with reasonable certainty[4]. The penalty for failing to comply with these requirements is that the policy is inadmissible in evidence[5], which would in effect make it unenforceable. However, this rule apparently applies only to marine insurance, since the marine form is obviously unsuitable for other types of policy, and there is no statutory authority for any form of policy in other classes of insurance.

There is not even a rule that non-marine contracts of insurance must be in writing, though given the complexity of most policies it is hard to imagine that they could ever be effectively expressed purely orally[6]. On the other hand, it is possible to form a contract orally, provided that there is sufficient evidence of the terms, as for example where it is clear that the parties intended the terms to be those of a commonly-used standard form contract[7].

Where the policy is reduced to writing, the question may arise whether the terms written down are an exhaustive account of what has been agreed, or whether other material may be introduced. Where the other material consists of other documents, it is a matter of construction whether they are incorporated into the contract[8]. In a Lloyd's policy it may happen that the provisions of the policy differ slightly from those of the slip. It is a difficult and unresolved question whether in these circumstances the slip forms part of the factual matrix of the policy, and can therefore be referred to, or whether it is to be regarded as superseded by the policy and therefore inadmissible[9]. It is submitted that the better view is that the slip should be admissible (but not automatically decisive), since in normal circumstances the policy should be drawn up on the basis of the slip.

Where the other material consists of alleged oral agreements, the matter must be dealt with under the heading of rectification[10]. In either case, it is fair to say that the courts will be reluctant to accept that notice should be taken of anything beyond the policy documents themselves.

1 Section 22.
2 Section 23.
3 Section 24.
4 Section 26.
5 Section 22.
6 For this point in the context of renewal (though the principle must be generally applicable) see *Great North Eastern Railway Ltd v Avon Insurance plc* [2001] EWCA Civ 780, [2001] 2 All ER (Comm) 526.
7 As in the legendary Lloyd's example of the underwriter who orally agreed to insure the SS Titanic *after* hearing that she had struck an iceberg. The full story emerged before the contract could be reduced to writing, but no one ever doubted that the contract was binding.
8 *Ikerigi Cia Naviera SA v Palmer, The Wondrous* [1992] 2 Lloyd's Rep 566.
9 For conflicting views on this in the Court of Appeal see *Youell v Bland Welch & Co Ltd* [1990] 2 Lloyd's Rep 423, CA.
10 See Chapter 11.

Requirement of signature

7.2 In one IOB case in 1990[1] a policyholder complained because the policies issued to him by a well-known insurance company were not signed by the directors of the company personally. He alleged that in view of this he could have no confidence that the policies would be honoured. The Ombudsman ruled that there was sufficient evidence (company name and logo etc) on the policies to make it clear whose policies they were, and that the company concerned (a very large, well-known and reputable insurer) could be trusted not to attempt to hide behind the lack of signature. He also took the view that there was no legal requirement that insurance policies be signed on behalf of the insurer. It is submitted that this conclusion is clearly right as a matter of general law.

In relation to life policies another necessary formality is that of issuing the statutory cancellation notice, so that the policyholder has the chance to consider whether or not to proceed with the contract[2].

In addition, a life policy must contain the names of those for whose benefit it is made[3].

1 Handled by the author personally.
2 ICA 1982, ss 75–77. For a detailed account of cancellation rights and procedures, see Chapter 9.
3 LAA 1774, s 2. For the details of this and the controversy over whether this section applies to non-life policies, see Chapter 4.

Commencement

7.3 Clearly it a matter of some importance to know when a particular policy comes into force, since that is when the cover will take effect. Many policies contain an express term defining this moment, either by reference to a given date or by reference to the payment of the first premium. The former solution is more commonly found in general personal lines policies, whereas the latter is often encountered in life policies. The starting point must be that a contract of insurance, like any other contract, is created where there has been an unqualified acceptance by one party of an offer made by the other[1]. However, this marks the moment when the contract is formed, rather than the moment when the risk begins to run.

[1] *Lark v Outhwaite* [1991] 2 Lloyd's Rep 132 (reinsurance); and see Chapter 3 on offer and acceptance.

Payment of premium

7.4 Where payment of the premium is specified as a condition precedent of the running of the risk, it is normally a matter of fact whether the payment has been made or not. In marine insurance the position is altered by s 53 of the MIA 1906 under which, unless otherwise agreed, where a marine policy is effected on behalf of the assured by a broker, the broker is directly responsible to the insurer for the premium, and the insurer is directly responsible to the assured for the amount which may be payable in respect of losses or in respect of returnable premium[1]. The section says nothing about the assured's liability to the insurer. However, by the custom of the market the broker is deemed to have paid the insurer, whether or not he has in fact done so. Where there has been no actual payment, the convenient fiction is that the broker has paid and has borrowed the money from the insurer. This has the important consequence that once the policy has been entered into[2] cover can commence even though the premium has not in fact been paid.

Although the practice works well enough in most cases, one situation which tests it to its limits is that of the insolvent broker. The Court of Appeal considered some issues arising out of such a case in *JA Chapman & Co Ltd v Kadirga Denizcilik Ve Ticaret*[3]. The policies in this case had some interesting features. One was a clause by which the policyholder warranted that each instalment of premium would be paid to underwriters within 60 days of the due date. The second was a clause which allowed payment of premium by instalments at three-monthly intervals. The brokers were insolvent, and there was no prospect that they would ever pay outstanding premiums to the insurers. They nevertheless sought to recover the premiums from the assureds, relying upon s 53 of the MIA 1906 as establishing that they were deemed to have paid the premium. The central question before the Court of Appeal was whether the s 53 presumption was effectively displaced by the clauses already described. The court said firstly that the s 53 rule must now be understood as a freestanding statutory rule, divorced from any consideration of the circumstances which led to its original development as a market practice[4]. It is only to be displaced by clear words[5]. The payment of premiums warranty proved somewhat troublesome in this regard. The warranty was of course given by the assureds to the insurer and might therefore have been regarded as a direct assumption of liability by the assureds. The seriousness of the obligation is emphasised by the fact that it was expressed as a warranty, so that a breach would automatically void the policy. Despite this it was held that the policy read as a whole did not support the idea that s 53 had been excluded[6]. In particular, it was noted that the cover note expressly said that the premiums were to be payable by the assureds to the brokers.

As to the payment of premiums by instalments, it had been held at first instance that this created a series of discrete insurance contracts, one for each period for which premiums were to be paid. The Court of Appeal reversed this decision, observing that the policy referred to payment of 'the premium' by instalments, which was a clear indication that there was only one premium and one policy, albeit that the premium was to be paid by instalments.

The apparently odd consequence of this is that the insurers had been released from liability by the breach of warranty in not paying the instalments of premiums in good time, but the assureds remained liable to pay those instalments to the brokers, who would of course be able to retain them. In fact, this outcome does accord with principle – once cover had incepted, the assureds were liable to pay the whole of the premiums, just as the brokers were liable to pay it on their behalf. Only the insolvency of the brokers prevented that arrangement from being properly carried through in the present case.

It appears that there is no general usage to this effect outside marine insurance. It is interesting to note here the decision of Moore-Bick J in *Pacific and General Insurance Company v Hazell*[7], where an attempt to make brokers in such a case personally liable for premiums failed. However, close reading of that case shows that the judge was not able to hold conclusively that no such custom existed. The decision is based upon the rather more limited ground that no proper evidence to that effect had been put before the court[8]. The case does, nevertheless, provide at least a limited indication that the custom is confined to marine insurance[9].

In the rather different context of personal lines policies, it is interesting to note that some major brokers offer facilities for payment by instalments under which they in fact pay the premium to the insurers, offering credit facilities (at a charge) to the policyholder. The legal effect of these arrangements seems to depend upon the exact arrangements between broker and insurer, which in practice are often not disclosed to the policyholder. The practice of charging for credit suggests that the broker is paying the premiums in full at the outset and is in effect lending all or part of it to the policyholder. However, there is no absolute reason why this must be so. If the broker does not pay the premiums in full at the outset, then it is not clear whether the insurer is strictly bound as against the policyholder to accept liability. In practice the answer is no doubt first that insurers are unlikely to take the point and secondly that the Insurance Ombudsman would give short shrift to any insurer who tried to escape liability in this way.

As a general rule, where the broker does pay the premiums the assured is liable to the broker for premiums as money paid on his behalf, whether or not they have been paid over by the broker to the insurer – *Bain Clarkson v Owners of Sea Friends*[10] – where the failure to pay premiums did not entitle the brokers to arrest the ship.

[1] See also *Prentis Donegan & Partners Ltd v Leeds & Leeds Co Inc* [1998] 2 Lloyd's Rep 326.
[2] The standard Lloyd's marine policy contains a recital that the premium has been paid.
[3] [1998] Lloyd's Rep IR 377, CA.

[4] The rule predates the MIA 1906, being, like most of that Act, merely a codification of the common law.
[5] This rule too predates the MIA 1906: see *Universo Marine Insurance Co of Milan v Merchants Marine Insurance Co* [1897] 2 QB 93.
[6] Cf *The Litsion Pride* [1985] 1 Lloyd's Rep 437, Hirst J, where on the facts the opposite conclusion was reached.
[7] [1997] 6 Re LR 157.
[8] [1997] 6 Re LR 157 at 169.
[9] The case also has an interesting account of the payment mechanisms operating at Lloyd's, as a result of which premiums were automatically debited at a time when the provisional liquidation of the claimant reinsured made it very doubtful whether the brokers were authorised to pay. It is also relevant to consider Lloyds Insurance Brokers Committee Circular No 69 of 1997 (dated 27 October 1997) which limited the class of marine cases in which Lloyds Brokers will be personally liable for the premium. See also *Heath Lambert Ltd v Sociedad de Corretaje de Seguros* [2004] EWCA Civ 792, [2004] Lloyd's Rep IR 905, considered in more detail at para 40.15.
[10] [1991] 2 Lloyd's Rep 322, CA.

Inception of risk

7.5 This is again a matter for agreement between the parties. As a general rule it does not appear to give rise to any issues of insurable interest, since the rules on insurable interest apply, if at all[1], at the time when the contract is made, not at the time when risk begins to run.

[1] See Chapter 4.

Commencement of risk on goods

Although goods which do not exist cannot be appropriated to a contract of insurance, there is no reason why parties should not agree that goods appropriated to the contract should be covered by the policy from an earlier date[1].

[1] *Wünsche Handelsgesellschaft International mbH v Tai Ping Insurance Co Ltd* [1998] 2 Lloyd's Rep 8, CA.

Duration

7.6 The vast majority of policies last for no longer than one year and may be for shorter periods. This is simply a matter of market practice and convenience. The exceptions are to be found in those classes of business which are long-term business for the purposes of the ICA 1982. These are insurances on:

(1) life and annuity, marriage and birth;
(2) linked long-term insurance;
(3) permanent health insurance;
(4) tontines and capital redemption contracts;
(5) pension fund management;
(6) collective and social insurance[1].

Policies may have a shorter duration than one year, according to the wishes of the parties. The practice of having policies of no longer than one year is of importance when the question of renewal of policies is considered. As to this, see below. The fact that a policy is long-term business is also of practical importance, since it means that the insurer is not, in the absence of express policy provisions, entitled to cancel the cover or change the premiums merely because of changes in the policyholder's circumstances.

The policy itself frequently defines the period for which the insurance is to be current and, where it does so, normally the precise day, and sometimes the precise hour, at which it respectively begins and ends are specified – *Commercial Union Assurance Co plc v Sun Alliance Insurance Group plc*[2]. This point can be of special significance is those cases where insurance cover is required as a matter of law[3], since care must be taken to ensure that the cover is unbroken.

The policy may contain an extension clause giving the assured an option to extend its duration – eg *Touche Ross & Co v Baker*[4], where the assured under a policy of professional indemnity insurance had the option, in the event of the insurers' refusing to renew, to extend the policy for 36 months after the date of termination in respect of acts committed before the date of termination.

1 List taken from Sch 1 to the ICA 1982.
2 [1992] 1 Lloyd's Rep 475.
3 Chapter 29.
4 [1992] 2 Lloyd's Rep 207, HL. See also below, for discussion of the consequences of exercising the right against only some of the underwriters.

Termination of policy by death of the assured

7.7 Where an insurance is effected on property of the assured, or is in itself a form of investment so as to be property in itself, his death will not affect its duration in the absence of specific provision to that effect. Appropriate premiums having been paid, the value secured will normally pass as property to the personal representatives. However, see *Smith v Clerical Medical Life and General Life Assurance Society*[1] where the claimant, as cohabitee of the deceased, was entitled, rather than his personal representatives, to the proceeds of a joint life assurance which was charged to a mortgagee and designed to be used as the fund for repayment of the mortgage.

1 [1992] 1 FCR 262, CA.

Other termination

7.8 Some policies have clauses providing for their automatic termination when, for example, the policyholder reaches a certain age. In one IOB case[1] about a payment protection policy where there was a clause of this type the insurer by oversight collected five premiums by direct debit after the policyholder's 65th birthday. It was held that this was inconsistent with the purported termination of the policy, and that the insurer should meet the claim for disability benefit. It seems unlikely that a court could have reached the same decision, given the automatic termination clause in the policy, which had been adequately brought to the policyholder's attention. Legally, the answer would seem to be that the policyholder would have been entitled only to the return of premiums, with interest.

1 IOB 11.1.

Renewal

7.9 As a general principle the 'renewal' of an insurance contract is properly regarded as the creation of an entirely new contract, albeit that the terms are often very similar to those of the previous contract. Thus, all the issues about offer and acceptance, consideration, duty of disclosure and insurable interest arise at renewal as if there were no previous contract. In consumer insurance this can give rise to difficulties where policyholders fail to recognise this legal analysis. It is accordingly good practice for insurers and brokers to take steps to bring the position to the attention of the policyholder when soliciting renewal[1]. In particular, a failure to warn of the duty of disclosure may be regarded as a breach of the Statements of Practice[2] and may therefore prevent the insurer from relying on non-disclosure.

Where a policy is set up on terms that renewal is to be automatic unless the policyholder cancels (sometimes a useful practice in commercial motor insurance, where the policyholder is required to maintain effective insurance) a policyholder who wishes to cancel must take care to do so before the renewal date. Otherwise the automatic renewal will take effect, and a cancellation shortly thereafter will leave the policyholder liable to pay for cover at the rates applied for short-term cover, which are generally much less favourable than those applying for longer term cover[3].

In commercial insurance *Touche Ross & Co v Baker*[4] illustrates a point which can arise at renewal when a policy is subscribed by a number of Lloyd's underwriters. The policy in this case[5] had a clause giving the insured the option to renew the policy subject to certain conditions. It was held that the insured could choose to exercise this right against some of the underwriters without having to exercise it against all of them. The decision turns on the fact that at Lloyd's the liability of an underwriting member is several not joint, ie underwriters write their lines on the policy 'each for himself, not one for another'.

1 The FSA Handbook says surprisingly little about renewal, perhaps because it treats it simply as the creation of a new contract, though there are some special rules about information provision in ICOB 5.316 to 5.3.23, and ICOB 6.1 specified that cancellation rights apply on renewal as they do on the original contract.
2 For Lloyd's generally, see Chapter 52.
3 A professional indemnity policy, though nothing appears to turn on this fact.
4 [1992] 2 Lloyd's Rep 207, HL.
5 See IOB 9.16.

Chapter 8

Cancellation

8.1 Cancellation rights are now governed by the FSA Handbook[1]. The COB section contains the rules applicable to general insurance business, whilst the ICOB section contains the rules applicable to investment business.

[1] Available at www.fsa.gov.uk

ICOB Provisions

8.2 These provisions apply to an insurer and a managing agent[1]. A managing agent must give effect to the policy in ICOB 6 that a retail customer must be offered cancellation rights[2].

[1] ICOB 6.1.1.
[2] ICOB 6.1.2.

8.3 These provisions apply to all non-investment insurance contracts[1] except:

(1) a travel and baggage insurance policy or similar short-term insurance policy[2] of less than one month's duration;
(2) a non-investment insurance contract, the performance of which has been fully completed by both parties at the retail customer's express request before the retail customer exercises his right to cancel;
(3) a non-investment insurance contract that is a pure protection contract of six months' duration or less that is not a distance contract;
(4) a pure protection contract effected by the trustees of an occupational pension scheme, an employer or a partnership to secure benefits for the employees or the partners in the partnership;
(5) a general insurance contract that is not a distance contract sold by an intermediary who is an unauthorised person (except where the intermediary is an appointed representative); and
(6) a connected contract that is not a distance contract[3].

[1] ICOB 6.1.4.
[2] Ie any contract of insurance where the event or activity being insured is less than one month's duration. The reference to 'duration' is to the period of the cover rather than the period of the contract. So the exemption will cover travel insurance for a fortnight's holiday, even if the

insurance was taken out two months before the holiday began. However, if the period of cover includes cancellation of the holiday from the point at which the contract is taken out, the policy will not benefit from the exemption: ICOB 6.1.6.
[3] ICOB 6.1.5.

8.4 These provisions are intended to reinforce Principle 6 (Customers' interests) which requires a firm to pay due regard to the interests of its customers and treat them fairly. In certain circumstances, retail customers who have entered into a non-investment insurance contract will be entitled to a period of reflection during which they can decide whether to proceed with their purchase. They also implement, where relevant, elements of the DMD and the Consolidated Life Directive relating to the cancellation of distance contracts and non-investment insurance contracts that are pure protection contracts[1].

[1] ICOB 6.1.11.

Cancellation rights and period

8.5 A retail customer has a right to cancel a non-investment insurance contract in accordance with ICOB 6.2, ICOB 6.3 and ICOB 6.4, explained below[1].

[1] ICOB 6.2.1.

8.6 The period of cancellation is:

(1) 30 days for a non-investment insurance contract that is a pure protection contract; and
(2) 14 days for a general insurance contract[1].

Where the terms of an insurer's contract give a retail customer a longer period to cancel (that is, in excess of the 14 or 30 days specified), the insurer must disclose in the information about the right to cancel the differences between the retail customer's right under ICOB 6.2.1 R and the terms of the contract, which operate independently[2]. Where a contract is a mixed contract, that is, it has elements of both a general insurance contract and a pure protection contract, a 30 day cancellation period must apply[3]. The cancellation period must begin on the later of:

(1) (for a non-investment insurance contract that is a pure protection contract) the day the retail customer is informed that the contract has been concluded; or
(2) (for a general insurance contract) the day of the conclusion of the contract; or
(3) the day on which the retail customer receives the contractual terms and conditions and information in accordance with ICOB 5.3.4 R, ICOB 5.3.6 R(1) or ICOB 5.3.8 R in a durable medium[4].

[1] ICOB 6.2.2.
[2] ICOB 6.2.3.
[3] ICOB 6.2.4.
[4] ICOB 6.2.5.

8.7 If an insurer has provided information about cancellation rights in a durable medium, it need not accept a notice of cancellation if it is served later than the period specified for that contract[1]. But if a firm does not give a retail customer information about his cancellation rights in a durable medium the contract is cancellable, apparently without limit of time[2].

[1] ICOB 6.2.8.
[2] ICOB 6.2.9.

Notification of cancellation by the retail customer

8.8 A retail customer who has a right to cancel under ICOB 6.2.1 R may, without giving any reason, cancel the contract by serving notice upon the insurer, its appointed representative or any agent of the insurer with authority to accept notice on the insurer's behalf before expiry of the relevant cancellation period, in accordance with the practical instructions given to him by the insurer[1]. Where the notice of cancellation is in a durable medium and served in accordance with ICOB 6.3.1 R, it must be treated as being served on the insurer on the date it is despatched by the retail customer[2].

[1] ICOB 6.3.1.
[2] ICOB 6.3.2.

Effects of cancellation

8.9 By exercising his right to cancel under ICOB 6.2.1 R, a retail customer withdraws from the contract[1]. Where a retail customer exercises a right to cancel under ICOB 6.2.1 R:

(1) the insurer must pay to the retail customer without delay, and no later than 30 days after the date on which the insurer received notice of cancellation from the retail customer, any sums which the retail customer has paid to, or for, the benefit of the insurer in connection with the contract (including sums paid by the retail customer to agents of the insurer) except for the amount referred to in (2);

(2) where the contract is a general insurance contract, subject to (3), the insurer is permitted to require the retail customer to pay for the services it has actually provided in connection with the contract. The amount payable, however, must not:
  (a) exceed an amount which is in proportion to the extent of the service already provided to the retail customer by the insurer in comparison with the full coverage of the contract; and
  (b) be such that it could be construed as a penalty;

(3) sub-paragraph (2) applies only:
  (a) where performance of the contract has commenced before expiry of the cancellation period and this was requested by the retail customer; and
  (b) where the insurer can demonstrate that the retail customer was provided with details of the amount which he may be required to pay if exercising his right to cancel in accordance with ICOB 6.2.1 R;

(4) the insurer is entitled to receive without delay, and no later than 30 days after the date on which the retail customer posted or otherwise sent notice of cancellation to the insurer any sums and property that became the retail customer's under the contract[2].

[1] ICOB 6.4.1.
[2] ICOB 6.4.3.

COB provisions

The Policyholder's Right to Cancel

8.10 For a limited period after the commencement of the policy the policyholder has a statutory right of cancellation. The relevant rules are now to be found in the FSA Handbook, which has the force of law by virtue of the FSA's delegated powers under FSMA 2000. In the case of investment insurance contracts the rules are in COB 6.7, whereas for pure protection contracts they are in ICOB 6. It should be noted that in relation to all insurance contracts protection is given by means of a post-contract right to cancel, rather than by the pre-contract right to withdraw which is used for some other investment products. However, as appears from the rules set out below, this distinction does not appear to make any practical difference.

Investment Insurance Contracts

8.11 This is inevitably the more complex part of the cancellation rules, because it applies to investment products generally, not just to investment insurance products. The following account will focus on investment insurance, and in so doing will omit or gloss over those parts of COB 6.7 which relate to other forms of investment.

8.12 COB 6.7 applies to:

(1) a product provider except when providing a non-investment insurance contract;
(2) an insurer which provides pure protection contracts which are long-term care insurance contracts (this is a rare example of a pure protection contract coming within COB rather than ICOB).

8.13 All investment life policies have a right for a retail customer to cancel after sale within a period of up to 30 days[1] except a life policy that relates to or is associated with securing benefits under a defined benefits pension scheme and a life policy for a term of six months or less (but a purchaser of a single premium pension policy has a right to cancel where the designated retirement date is within six months of the date of the policy[2].

[1] COB 6.7.4G.
[2] COB 6.7.16.

Cancellation Period

8.14 When a retail customer has a right to cancel a life policy under COB 6.7.7 R (1), that right must be exercised within 30 days[1], and the cancellation period begins on the date the customer receives the reminder notice of his right to cancel in accordance with COB 6.7.30, except in relation to distance contracts, where it begins on the later of the day the retail customer is informed that the contract has been concluded; or the day on which the retail customer receives the contractual terms and conditions and other information required by other provisions of COB[2]. The provider's terms may allow a longer cancellation period, but may not reduce the three-day period, and any greater period must be specifically drawn to the customer's attention[3].

[1] COB 6.7.10.
[2] COB 3.9, COB 4.2 or COB 6, as applicable.
[3] COB 6.7.11.

8.15 The rules in COB 6.7 permit the firm to issue information about a right to cancel and other communications, and to accept notice from customers who are exercising the right to cancel or withdraw, by electronic means. However, a firm should be able to demonstrate that the customer wishes to communicate electronically[1].

[1] See also the Guidance in COB 1.8.

8.16 Where there is a right to cancel, the firm which enters into the contract with the customer must send the customer, in writing, a clear and prominent reminder notice of this right no later than the end of the fourteenth day after the contract is concluded[1].

[1] COB 6.7.30.

8.17 When the customer is a trustee who is reasonably believed by the firm to be expected to act on the instructions of the individual beneficiary or purchaser of the policy or contract, the firm must send the notice of the right to cancel in COB 6.7.30 to:

(1) the trustee; and
(2) the beneficiary or purchaser;

and must inform the beneficiary or purchaser of the need to give instructions, within the specified cancellation period, to the trustee where the right to cancel is to be exercised[1].

[1] COB 6.7.31.

8.18 If a firm does not give a retail customer information about his cancellation rights in accordance with the COB rules, the contract remains cancellable and the retail customer will not be liable for any shortfall[1] (see COB 6.7.56 (3)).

[1] COB 6.7.41

Exercising the right to cancel

8.19 A retail customer who has a right to cancel under COB 6.7.7 R may, without giving any reason, cancel the contract by serving notice upon the firm, before expiry of the cancellation period either:

(1) by post to the firm's last known address; or
(2) in accordance with any other practical instructions for exercising that right provided to the customer by the firm[1] in accordance with the COB rules.

[1] COB 6.7.42.

8.20 Where the notice of cancellation is in a durable medium and served in accordance with COB 6.7.42, it must be treated as being served on the firm on the date it is despatched by the retail customer[1]. Thus the cancellation is effective as soon as despatched.

[1] COB 6.7.44.

8.21 In the event of any dispute, unless there is clear written evidence to the contrary, the firm should treat the date cited by the customer as being the date when the notice was given, posted or otherwise sent.

8.22 If a firm has provided information on cancellation rights in accordance with the COB rules, it need not (unless COB 6.7.11 R applies) accept a notice of cancellation if it is served later than the period specified for that contract[1] in those rules. This gives a degree of protection to firms which comply with the cancellation rules by ensuring that they can rely on the time periods laid down in the rules.

[1] COB 6.7.48.

Effects of cancellation

8.23 By exercising a right to cancel under COB 6.7.7 R (1), (2) or (4), the customer withdraws from the contract and the entire contract is terminated[1].

[1] COB 6.7.49.

8.24 When a retail customer exercises a right to cancel the firm must pay to the retail customer without delay, and no later than 30 days after the date on which the firm received notice of cancellation from the retail customer, any sums which the customer has paid to or for the benefit of the firm in connection with the contract (including sums paid by the retail customer to agents of the firm). There are provisions for firms to charge customers for services received in connection with the contract, but these do not apply to insurance contracts.

The firm is entitled to receive without delay, and no later than 30 days after the date on which the customer posted or otherwise sent notice of cancellation to the firm:

(a) any sums or property or both that became the customer's under the contract; and
(b) payment of any shortfall due under COB 6.7.54.

Chapter 9

Cover and exclusions

9.1 The question of what the policy does and does not cover is obviously of fundamental importance. It is also a question of interpreting the policy as a contractual document.

Although the matter may thus be viewed as simply a question of construction[1], the law of insurance contracts has a number of very important rules in relation to coverage and exclusions[2].

[1] As to which, see Chapter 16.
[2] See also the discussion of conditions precedent in Chapter 17.

Cover

9.2 First, the policy covers only those risks which are included within the insurance cover by express statement or necessary implication. The policyholder bears the burden of proof in showing that the loss which has happened falls within these risks[1].

Secondly, once the policyholder has established this, it is for the insurer to show that the loss falls within an exception contained in the policy[2].

Thirdly, in the case where there is an exception to an exception, it will be for the policyholder to show that the loss, although covered by the exception, is also covered by the exception to the exception.

It should, however, be remembered that in the case of an 'all risks' policy, the insured need only show that a loss has happened as a result of an accident or casualty. He is not required to specify exactly the nature of the accident or casualty[3]. It is then for the insurers to demonstrate that it falls within one of the exclusions[4].

[1] This is partly a matter of construction but also partly a matter of causation, as to which, see Chapter 20.
[2] As to the construction of individual clauses, see Chapter 16. As to the problems of discharging the burden of proof, see Chapter 19 and *The Popi M* [1985] 2 All ER 712, HL.

[3] *British and Foreign Marine Insurance Co v Gaunt* [1921] 2 AC 41, HL.
[4] See also *British and Foreign Marine Insurance Co v Gaunt* [1921] 2 AC 41.

Exceptions

9.3 These three statements appear simple enough, yet it is also easy to show that the relationship between them is a matter of some difficulty. According to how the policy is worded the same matter may be part of the insured perils or may be the subject of an exception. Thus, a policy might provide cover for the death of the life assured, subject to an exception if the death is not accidental. On this wording it would appear that the claimant need only prove the death, after which the insurer will need to prove that the death is not accidental in order to escape liability. In the alternative the policy might be expressed to provide cover against accidental death. On this wording it would appear that the claimant must prove both the fact of death and its accidental character. The difference in wording is therefore capable of being decisive in those cases where the evidence is ambiguous. It follows also that an insurer can significantly restrict the range of cases in which it will in fact incur liability by careful drafting of these clauses. It may be observed in passing that even in personal lines policies it appears that such choices of wording will not be subject to review under the UTCCR 1999[1], since the clauses defining the cover and the exceptions must surely be considered to be the major terms of the contract. In personal lines cases the fairness of the drafting may of course be considered by the FSO.

It is also useful to consider a number of other risks and causes which are commonly the subject of express exclusions.

[1] SI 1999/2083; see Chapter 16.

Exceptions void for Repugnance

9.4 It is in theory possible for an exception clause to be so widely drafted that it reduces the contract to a mere declaration of intent by effectively removing the whole of the cover. In such circumstances the exclusion may be held to be void for repugnancy[1]. However, this is a doctrine of narrow scope, applicable only in the most extreme cases[2]. At the same time it may be possible for the court to engage in fairly bold construction of a clause so as to confine its meaning within sensible bounds. This approach was adopted in *Blackburn Rovers Football and Athletic Club plc v Avon Insurance plc*[3], where an accident policy for a professional footballer covered total disablement but purported to exclude total disablement if 'attributable directly or indirectly to … degenerative conditions in joints, bones, muscles, tendons or ligaments'. There was evidence that most men of the claimant's age suffered to some extent from such degeneration, and that the proportion was higher among professional sportsmen. Moore-Bick J held that the reference to such conditions was to be construed as applying only to those which were sufficiently serious to be regarded as an illness in their own right and did not extend to conditions which were merely part of the normal process of aging. In this way he was able to avoid holding that the clause was void for repugnancy, but was also able to hold that it did not apply when the claimant injured his back during a practice match and was unable to play again[4].

[1] *Tor Line AB v Alltrans Group of Canada Ltd* [1984] 1 All ER 103.
[2] *Great North Eastern Railway Ltd v Avon Insurance plc* [2001] 2 All ER (Comm) 526, CA.
[3] [2005] Lloyd's Rep IR 239, Moore-Bick J.
[4] Reliance was also placed on *Fraser v Furman* [1967] 1 WLR 898, CA; and *Cornish v Accident Insurance Co* (1889) 23 QBD 453

Inherent vice

9.5 This is a concept which is encountered in all types of cargo insurance, though it is perhaps best known in the marine insurance context. As regards an inherent vice or nature of the subject matter, unless the policy otherwise provides, the insurer is not liable for loss or damage that is not the consequence of some casualty which can properly be considered a peril of the seas[1]. He is, therefore, not liable for loss or damage arising solely from decay or deterioration of the subject matter insured, as when fruit becomes rotten or flour heats, not from external causes, but from internal decomposition; nor is he liable for spontaneous combustion generated by some chemical change in the thing insured, arising from its being put on board in a wet or otherwise damaged condition – *T M Noten BV v Harding*[2]. In truth the notion of inherent vice may be regarded as no more than an illustration of the principle that the insurer is liable only if the loss arises from one of the insured perils.

[1] MIA 1906, s 55(2)(c) specifically excludes inherent vice. This is so even though by the MIA 1906, s 40 there is no implied warranty that goods insured are seaworthy.
[2] [1990] 2 Lloyd's Rep 283, CA.

Wilful misconduct of assured

9.6 The insurer is not liable for any loss attributable to wilful misconduct on the part of the assured, but unless the policy otherwise provides, he is liable for any loss proximately caused by a peril insured against, and is liable even though the loss would not have happened but for the misconduct or negligence of the master or crew. Again, this may be regarded as being at least partly a question of causation, though the exclusion of loss which is in fact caused by the wilful misconduct of the assured is also a matter of public policy. The same result follows when the negligence of any other person (including the assured himself) contributes to the loss[1].

[1] *State of the Netherlands (Represented by the Minister of Defence) v Youell and Hayward* [1997] 2 Lloyd's Rep 440.

Recklessness

9.7 It is common to exclude loss caused by the recklessness of the insured[1]. In *Gunns v Par Insurance Brokers*[2] the claimant took out insurance through the defendant brokers. The insurance was repudiated for non disclosure. It was held on the facts that the brokers had read out the clear questions and answers on the proposal form with the claimant and then passed the information on to the insurer and need do no more. In addition the claimant's conduct in relation to the insured property (it was home contents insurance) was reckless in that he recognised that a danger (of burglary) existed and had not cared whether it was averted (he did not turn on the burglar alarm or use the locks at the back of his property)[3]. Thus, the loss fell within the policy exclusion. Although the point is not altogether clear, it seems reasonable to assume that a policy provision excluding liability in the event of recklessness has much the same effect as a clause requiring the insured to take reasonable care to avoid loss[4].

The test would appear to be substantially identical in both cases, and in both cases the insurer will bear the burden of proof.

1 See also Chapter 12 on the general duty to take reasonable care.
2 [1997] 1 Lloyd's Rep 173.
3 *Sofi v Prudential Insurance Co* [1993] 2 Lloyd's Rep 559 applied.
4 This results from the very restrictive view which the courts have taken of reasonable care clauses: see Chapter 12.

War risks and allied perils

9.8 Standard policies exclude losses arising from risks associated with war. In order to deal with the problems arising from this practice it is possible to obtain specific war risks cover. War Risks policies represent an important but highly specialised class of insurance, of which no more than the most important features can be mentioned here. These policies protect specifically against the risks incidental to exposure to warlike events, which are normally the subject of express exclusions from standard policies, in particular marine and aviation policies, though there is also some interaction between war risks polices and some types of policy covering real property.

The cover normally given by war risks policies deliberately matches the exclusion found in standard form policies, and it is therefore common for insureds to have separate policies for non-war risks and war risks respectively. For example, the current form of the Institute Clauses excludes:

(1) war, civil war, revolution, rebellion, insurrection, or civil strife arising therefrom, or any hostile act by or against a belligerent power;
(2) capture, seizure, arrest or detention (barratry and piracy excepted) and the consequences thereof or any attempt thereat;
(3) derelict mines, torpedoes, bombs or other derelict weapons of war.

But the Institute War and Strike Clauses reinstate this cover. The Institute War Clauses (Cargo) cover, subject to specified exceptions, insurrection. 'Insurrection' means, for insurance purposes, an organised and violent internal revolt within a country, the main object of which is to overthrow the country's government[1].

1 *National Oil Co of Zimbabwe (Pte) Ltd v Sturge* [1991] 2 Lloyd's Rep 281.

Nuclear risks

9.9 As a general principle, risks of loss caused by nuclear incidents are considered uninsurable, presumably because the prospective damage is so enormous.

Thus, such loss is routinely excluded from household, buildings and contents policies. It is also excluded from commercial policies, and, unlike other war-related risks, it is not reinstated by the purchase of a war risks policy. Indeed, standard war risks policies contain an exclusion for losses happening as a result of the outbreak of war between any two or more of the powers possessing nuclear weapons. The policy terminates automatically upon the happening of such an event. Happily, the risk of this peril materialising may be regarded as having diminished substantially in recent years.

Terrorist risks

9.10 In 1992, UK insurers of buildings and other real property decided to withdraw from providing cover for damage caused by terrorist risks. This decision was taken as a result of a number of large-scale and very costly terrorist attacks on the mainland of Great Britain. This threatened to cause an unsatisfactory gap in the provision of insurance cover. The problem was dealt with through the Reinsurance (Acts of Terrorism) Act 1993, which provided for the establishment of a suitable scheme. The scheme which has been created uses a reinsurance company called Pool Re, which is owned and funded by the major UK insurers jointly, and which takes on by way of reinsurance the risks of terrorist damage. This risk is now available as an optional extra in appropriate UK property policies. Pool Re's liabilities are retroceded to the UK government, which thus acts as an insurer of last resort. Premiums for both the primary insurance and the various layers of reinsurance are calculated at commercial rates.

Chapter 10

Rectification of insurance policies

General principles

10.1 This subject may be regarded as part of the general law on rectification of contracts, though it does also have a specific insurance law dimension.

The general principle of contractual construction is that a document must be taken at face value. The apparent meaning of the words used (determined objectively rather than subjectively[1]) is the basis for the interpretation of the contract, and in general it is not open to either party to say that the contract should be re-written because of the omission of a term which he would have wished to include.

The one important exception to this general principle occurs where it can be demonstrated that the contract as written omits a term which *both* parties intended to include. This very stringent test gives rise to the obvious difficulty that the party against whom rectification is sought is likely to deny that the proposed rectification accords with his intention at the time of the contract. In the absence of extrinsic evidence as to what that intention was (which may be very difficult to come by) it will be almost impossible for the court to be satisfied that that party's intention was to agree to anything other than what appears in the contractual documentation.

The mistake which is used as the basis for claiming rectification may be either a common mistake or a unilateral mistake (ie the situation where one party knows that the other is mistaken), though most of the cases in which rectification has been granted have in fact been cases of common mistake.

1 *Smith v Hughes* (1871) LR 6 QB 597.

Case law

10.2 The leading case on rectification in an insurance context is *A Gagniere & Co Ltd v Eastern Company of Warehouses Insurance and Transport of Goods with Advances Ltd*[1] where Bankes LJ laid down the general principles in the following terms:

> 'It seems to me … that if you prove the parties have come to a definite parol agreement, and you then afterwards find in the document which was intended to carry out that definite agreement something other than that definite agreement has been inserted, then it is right to rectify the document in order that it may carry out the real agreement between the parties. But in order to bring that doctrine into play it is necessary to establish beyond doubt that the real agreement between these parties as that which it is sought to insert in the document instead of the agreement which appears there.'

Although on the facts it was held that rectification of the policy was not available, the statement of general principle given here appears impeccable. Particular attention should be directed to the observation that the fact of error in the policy must be proved to a very high standard. For obvious and sound practical reasons the courts are reluctant to accept that properly executed commercial documents do not accurately reflect the deal which the parties have done[2]. It has been said that the case for rectification must be established by 'very strong, clear and convincing evidence'[3], though it appears that the standard remains the ordinary civil standard of proof – it is merely that, as with allegations of fraud, the court is reluctant to find that the burden of proving the matter on the balance of probabilities has been discharged[4].

1 (1921) 8 Ll L Rep 365, CA.
2 *The Olympic Pride* [1980] 2 Lloyd's Rep 67, Mustill J.
3 *Amercian Employers Ins Co v St Paul Fire & Marine Ins Co Ltd* [1978] 1 Lloyd's Rep 417.
4 *Earl v Hector Whaling Ltd* [1961] 1 Lloyd's Rep 459; for a more modern example where the claim again failed because of lack of evidence of a common intention, see *Cape plc v Iron Trades Employers Insurance Association Ltd* [2004] Lloyd's Rep IR 75, Rix J.

10.3 It is perhaps worth distinguishing between those cases where the policy is in standard form and those where there has been rather more negotiation and variation of the terms. In the former case the obvious and serious impediment to rectification is that the insurers are likely to say that they would only ever have issued a policy of this type upon their standard terms, this being their invariable practice and no one in their organisation having any power to depart from those terms. This powerful argument is likely in most cases to defeat entirely the suggestion that both parties intended something other than that which is stated in the contract. Perhaps one of the few possibilities of rectification in this area occurs where it is suggested that the premium or the duration of the policy has been incorrectly recorded.

An example of a case where rectification was granted is *Glen's Trustees v Lancashire and Yorkshire Accident Insurance Co*[1]. In a personal accident policy it was provided that the policyholder's right of action on a claim was to become barred unless within a certain time a settlement had been reached or proceedings had not been commenced. The word 'not' was an obvious error, and the only question argued appears to have been as to the manner of rectification. The policyholder wanted the clause deleted entirely, whereas the insurers sought to have the contract rectified simply by deleting the word 'not'. The Court of Session held that the latter was the correct course of action. This is clearly right as a matter of principle, since the purpose of rectification is to enable the contract to reflect accurately the intentions of the parties, which in the present case had been to have the clause but without the intrusive negative.

The position is more difficult where the policy is of a more bespoke character. Even here it is likely in practice that a standard form will have been used as the basis of the contract, with some additions and/or deletions having been made. The argument is therefore likely to centre on whether the changes made to the standard form accurately reproduce what was agreed in the discussions between the parties. Given the courts' reluctance to grant rectification, and given that the only evidence in many cases will be the oral testimony, some time after the event, of parties who may negotiate many insurance contracts in the course of their work, it is apparent that the party seeking rectification will in such cases face serious obstacles.

Another, related problem which may be found in commercial insurance is the relationship between the policy and the slip. Where both say the same thing and it is alleged that the contract is something different from what they say, rectification becomes very difficult[2]. There may be slightly more prospect of success where the two are different from each other, but even here the substantial difficulty is that it will often not be clear that *both* parties intended to contract to conform exactly with the abbreviated version of the cover which is described on the slip[3]. The problem is well illustrated by the decision in *Pindos Shipping Corpn v Frederick Charles Raven, The Mati Hari*[4]. In that case the insured yacht had become a total loss. The underwriters refused to pay, alleging breach of a class maintained warranty. The claimant argued that this warranty was not part of the original contract and sought rectification. This attempt failed, Bingham J holding that the terms as written down recorded accurately the intention of the underwriters, which was to insist on the warranty.

In any of these events it must be remembered that the remedy of rectification is an exceptional one. The point has been reinforced more recently, when it was held that in cases of insurance rectification will only be granted on the strongest evidence of common mistake[5].

1 (1906) 8 F 915, Ct of Sess.
2 Though it may fairly be observed that an error in the slip is likely to be repeated in the policy, which will have been based upon what appeared in the slip.
3 *Youell v Bland Welch & Co Ltd* [1992] 2 Lloyd's Rep 127, which also casts some doubt on the previously accepted proposition that at Lloyd's the policy is decisive, even when it appears to say something different from the slip: *Eagle Star Insurance Co Ltd v Spratt* [1971] 2 Lloyd's Rep 116.
4 [1983] 2 Lloyd's Rep 449, Bingham J.
5 *Commercial Union Assurance Co plc v Sun Alliance Insurance Group plc* [1992] 1 Lloyd's Rep 475.

The role of intermediaries[1]

10.4 In the context of rectification the involvement of intermediaries in negotiating insurance contracts gives rise to special problems. Where it is alleged that an intermediary has in negotiations agreed to a change in the policy terms, particularly a change from the standard form terms used by the insurer, the question must arise whether he had actual or apparent authority to do so. If not, then no variation agreed at that time can be binding on the agent's principal[2], though of course in such a case the agent might well find himself liable for breach of warranty of authority.

1 See generally Chapter 6.
2 Though presumably the question of breach of warranty of authority might then arise.

Unilateral mistake

10.5 Where unilateral mistake is relied upon as the basis for claiming rectification, the decision of the Court of Appeal in *Bates (Thomas) & Son Ltd v Wyndham's (Lingerie) Ltd*[1] establishes that the claimant must prove the following four things:

(a) one party must have made a mistake about the terms of the policy – that it did or did not contain an agreed term;
(b) the other party must have been aware of the mistake; it is apparently sufficient that he has constructive knowledge through his agent. If the other party is not aware of the mistake, it may be that there is a case of mutual mistake. In this event the theory of contract law would suggest that there is no contract at all, at least if the term is sufficiently important to go to the root of the contract;
(c) the other party must have omitted to draw the mistake to the notice of the party mistaken. It does not appear to matter whether this omission is fraudulent or merely negligent;
(d) the mistake must have been calculated to benefit the party who was aware of it (or perhaps merely to be to the detriment of the party affected by it).

The juridical basis of rectification in cases of unilateral mistake is by no means clear. In cases of common mistake it is clear that the aim is to give effect to the intentions of the parties, but where the mistake is unilateral this explanation clearly cannot stand. It has been suggested[2] that the matter can be put on the basis of estoppel, but this appears simply to use estoppel as a catch-all technique for righting perceived wrongs in those cases where no more rigorous legal doctrine is available.

1 [1981] 1 All ER 1077,CA.
2 Clarke *The Law of Insurance Contracts* (1999, LLP), section 14–3.

Rectification and the Ombudsman

10.6 In a personal lines context it occasionally happens that a policyholder complains to the Insurance Ombudsman or the PIAOB that a policy has been issued which fails to reflect the agreement he has made with the insurers. The Insurance Ombudsman, in particular, is of course not bound by legal rules, but may in appropriate cases be prepared to insist that insurers honour the contract as promised to the policyholder. A rather more unusual application of the principle of rectification occurred in a 1990 Insurance Ombudsman case[1] in which a policyholder had taken out a savings contract at the age of 58. At one place the contract was expressed to be for ten years, but at another place it was expressed to mature on his 65th birthday. He sought to enforce the latter clause, but the Ombudsman ruled that he would treat the contract as rectified by the omission of that clause, since the clear intention, evidenced by pre-contractual correspondence, was that this was to be a ten-year policy.

1 Handled by the author.

Nature of remedy

10.7 Rectification is an equitable remedy, and it therefore follows that it is subject to the same limitations and bars as any other equitable remedy. Thus the remedy may be lost if the party seeking rectification has affirmed the contract, or has not sought rectification promptly on discovering the mistake[1], or has been guilty of unconscionable conduct, or if it is for some reason no longer possible to restore the parties to their pre-contractual position. Although there is relatively little authority on the application of these general principles in an insurance context, there is no reason to doubt that they will be applied in full.

1 Although there appears to be no authority establishing specifically that time for these purposes runs from the discovery of the error rather than from the date it was made, it is submitted that this statement does no more than apply to rectification the ordinary principles of equitable remedies.

Conclusion

10.8 Rectification is a well-established doctrine in the English law of contract, extensively discussed in academic texts. In an insurance context, however, it appears to be discussed much more often that it is encountered. It is suggested that there can be very few cases where an application for rectification of an insurance contract can have any significant prospect of success.

Chapter 11

Alteration of risk

General principles

11.1 The question of alteration of risk in insurance policies is a very difficult one, about which the law is by no means clear. Indeed, not all writers even acknowledge the concept of increase of risk as having any place in the law of insurance[1]. Despite this there is some modest body of case law, from which it appears possible to conclude that in some cases an alteration in the risk undertaken by the insurers, occurring after the inception of the policy, may have some effect on the status of the policy, though in other cases it appears to be treated as irrelevant.

A distinction must be drawn between those cases where the alteration of risk has some effect on the policy as a matter of general principle, and those cases where there is an express policy provision dealing with the matter. In this regard the principles appear to be the same in all types of insurance.

[1] Both *Colinvaux's Law of Insurance* (7th edn, 1997, Sweet and Maxwell) and Clarke *The Law of Insurance Contracts* ignore the subject completely, though it is briefly treated in Merkin *Insurance Contract Law* (1988, Kroner).

Types of alteration of risk clauses

11.2 It is commonly said[1] that alterations of the risk are of three types:

(1) alteration in the subject matter of insurance[2];
(2) changes of locality;
(3) changes of circumstances.

The first of these is obviously relevant only to general insurance. The second is relevant primarily in general insurance, where for example, the property insured is moved from one place to another. It may, however, be of some relevance in life cases, since some policies impose restrictions (or even absolute prohibitions) on the places to which the life insured may go without affecting the validity of the policy. It is clear, however, that this category can be relevant only where there is an express policy provision. The third category is open-ended, and can arise in both general and long-term insurance.

[1] *Mozley and Whiteley's Law Directory* (11th edn, Butterworths), edited by Hardy Ivamy.
[2] *Rogerson v Scottish Automobile Ltd* [1931] All ER Rep 606; *Law, Guarantee, Trust and Accident Society v Munich Reinsurance Co* [1912] 1 Ch 138, Warrington J.

General principle

11.3 There are relatively few reported cases dealing with the possibility of the suspension or termination of cover for increase of risk in the absence of an express policy provision. This is an important point which is often ignored in standard textbooks, many of which treat cases about alteration of risk under policy provisions as if they were about alteration of risk under general common law principles.

Change of circumstances taking risk outside that insured

11.4 There may be an alteration of the risk not affecting the identity of the subject matter which amounts to an alteration of the risk where the alteration is such that the risk no longer corresponds with that defined in the policy. Thus in *Maritime Insurance Co v Stearns*[1] a voyage policy was effected on 2 August, but the ship did not sail until 25 September and was lost on 2 October. It was held that this delayed sailing, which clearly increased the risk of loss due to adverse weather, took the voyage outside that insured by the policy, with the result that the insurers were not liable[2].

There is also authority to the effect that where the definition of the risk includes a description of locality, or of circumstances such as the purpose for which the subject matter is used, the subject matter must, at the time of its loss, be in the locality or be used for the purpose described; the insurers are not responsible if its loss takes place whilst it is in a different locality or is being used for a different purpose. In this case, however, unless the policy expressly so provides, the alteration of the risk does not avoid the policy but merely suspends its operation during the continuance of the alteration[3].

[1] [1901] 2 KB 912, Matthew J.
[2] For a case which on its particular facts went the other way, see *Law, Guarantee, Trust and Accident Society v Munich Re-insurance Co* [1912] 1 Ch 138, Warrington J.
[3] *CTN Cash and Carry Ltd v General Accident Fire and Life Assurance Corpn plc* [1989] 1 Lloyd's Rep 299 (burglary insurance).

Policy provision

11.5 An important early case in this area is *Shaw v Robberds*[1]. The claimant had insured his premises against fire, and had stated on the proposal form that they would be used for 'drying corn'. There was a basis of the contract clause, as well as a clause prohibiting increase of risk unless notified to the insurers and permitted by means of an endorsement on the policy. On one occasion only the claimant used the premises for drying bark, a different activity from drying corn, and much more hazardous. On that occasion the premises burned down. The insurers resisted the claimant's claim on the policy, relying on the increase of risk clause, but the court held them liable. The decision is at first sight surprising, but can be explained in this way. The use to dry bark was a one-off event, and did not change the fact that the normal use was for drying corn. If the question on the proposal form is understood to refer only to the normal use of the premises, then there is no breach of the requirements of the policy, and no material increase of risk, since the normal use has not changed. It may be observed, however, that this involves adopting a somewhat strained construction of the policy. It might reasonably be supposed that the events which happened were of exactly the type against which the insurers were seeking to protect themselves.

A more recent case is *Exchange Theatre Ltd v Iron Trades Mutual Insurance Co Ltd*[2]. This was another case of buildings insurance, in which there was a clause avoiding the policy:

> 'With respect to any item thereof in regard to which there is any alteration ... whereby the risk of destructional damage is increased.'

It was held that there was no breach of this clause where the insured brought onto the premises a quantity of petrol. Although this was an added hazard, it was not an alteration with regard to the premises. This is another example of the adoption of a surprisingly narrow construction of the relevant clause, though it must be admitted that the drafting of the clause in this case left much to be desired. An interesting contrast is to be found in the case of *Farnham v Royal Insurance Co Ltd*[3] where a clause in very similar terms was held to have been breached by allowing welding to take place on the premises.

Kausar v Eagle Star[4] was a case of a shop policy where the insurers repudiated liability for a claim for malicious damage. One of the grounds of the repudiation arose out of a clause in the policy which provided:

> 'You must tell us of any change of circumstances after the start of the insurance which increases the risk of injury or damage. You will not be insured under the policy until we have agreed in writing to accept the increased risk.'

The Court of Appeal held that this clause merely restated the common law position, namely that the insurer would not be on risk if the circumstances had changed to the extent that the risk had become something which the insurers, on the true construction of the policy, had not agreed to cover. However, there is a distinction between cases where the risk changes in degree and cases where it changes in nature. In the former case the policy is not affected, but in the latter case the new risk will be outside the cover afforded by the policy. This is a difference of degree rather than of kind, and it is suggested that it will greatly reduce the range of cases in which the alteration will be held to have any effect on the policy[5].

It may be doubted whether this construction quite accords with what the insurers had in mind when they drafted the clause in question. However, the approach adopted by the Court of Appeal does offer some attempt at a coherent approach to dealing with increase of risk.

During the currency of any policy there may be minor changes which affect the risk; it is not desirable that these should automatically allow the insurers to escape liability. As the Court of Appeal pointed out in *Kausar*, insurers effectively price for such risks when setting the premium. On the other hand, fundamental changes ought to affect the risk.

A final point is that *Kausar* is to some extent a case which depends on the drafting of the clause. It would presumably be possible to draft a clause which did remove the risk in relation to even minor changes. However, it may be supposed that courts would be reluctant to accept the validity of such a clause[6] and would do their best to construe it in such a way as to preserve the distinction explained in *Kausar*.

It can perhaps be said that the borderline between what is and is not an increase of risk for these purposes is very much a matter of impression, with the result that the outcome depends largely on the way in which the matter strikes the judge of first instance.

[1] (1837) 6 Ad & El 75, 112 ER 29. See also *Mitchell Conveyor and Transport Co Ltd v Pullbrook* (1933) 45 Ll L Rep 239.
[2] [1984] 1 Lloyd's Rep 149, CA.
[3] [1976] 2 Lloyd's Rep 437, Ackner J. See also *Forrest & Sons Ltd v CGU Insurance plc* [2006] Lloyd's Rep IR 113, Kershaw J.
[4] [2000] Lloyd's Rep IR 154, CA.
[5] Recent examples in the author's experience where insurers have – apparently wrongly – tried to rely on a clause similar to that in *Kausar* include commercial premises insurance where workmen erected scaffolding to work on the premises and burglars gained access via that scaffolding and another commercial premises insurance case where the tenant of the building abandoned the premises leaving them unsecured.
[6] Given that the definition of the risk is a main term of the contract, it appears that the Unfair Terms in Consumer Contracts Regulations 1999 would not be applicable.

11.6 It is clear, however, that the courts are reluctant to accept that express policy wording can be sufficient to allow the insurer to rely upon increase of risk as a ground for avoiding liability in any given case. It might be thought that the duty not to increase the risk, either without notifying the insurer or, possibly, without the insurer's permission, could be regarded as an incident of the continuing duty of utmost good faith owed by the policyholder[1]. In practice, this argument does not seem to have been pursued in any reported case, and it is suggested that the proposition is unsustainable without the exercise of considerable judicial energy in developing and defining the limits of the doctrine. It clearly cannot be right that any change in the risk affects the status of the policy, having regard to the many minor changes in the habits of policyholders, and, more especially for present purposes, in the lifestyles of assured lives, and it is suggested that the law would do better to leave the defining of the relevant risks in any given policy to the terms of that policy, being at the same time alert to prevent the undue extension of such clauses, which are obviously capable of bearing very harshly on the assured.

[1] As to which see the recent authoritative decision of the House of Lords in *The Star Sea* [2001] Lloyd's Rep IR 247. See also Chapter 13.

Suspension of cover

11.7 Where the change in risk can be regarded as affecting one of the warranties descriptive of the risk, the result of the alteration will be that cover will be suspended so long as the warranty is not being complied with, but the policy will not become voidable. This is a principle well established in general insurance law[1], which ought also to apply in life cases, though there appears to be no reported authority dealing with the point. A possible example would arise where the policy forbids the life to go beyond the boundaries of Europe. Although it would be possible to construe this as a promissory warranty, so that any breach will render the policy voidable, it is submitted that this construction is to be avoided if possible. The purpose of the clause is to protect against the greater risk of death from disease, accident or violence which is perceived to exist in some other parts of the world. Since this risk largely disappears once the life returns to Europe (there is of course some risk that a disease contracted elsewhere will be fatal after the life returns) it is appropriate to regard this requirement as being merely descriptive of the risk, so that cover is suspended while the life is out of Europe, but resumes upon his return. This analysis does involve accepting that the insurer is liable if the life does die in Europe from a disease contracted elsewhere. It would also follow that this interpretation could be displaced by appropriate drafting.

Where cover is suspended in this way, it is suggested that the duty to pay premiums is not suspended. It is not true in such a case that the policyholder receives nothing in return for these premiums. What he receives is the prospect of the revival of the policy on his return to Europe.

[1] The leading cases are *Provincial Insurance Co Ltd v Morgan* [1933] AC 240, HL; *Farr v Motor Traders' Mutual* [1920] 3 KB 669, CA. These are more fully treated in Chapter 17.

11.8 It is of course possible to make a clause of the kind described above (or of any other kind) a promissory warranty merely by declaring it to be so, or by declaring that any breach of the requirement will render the policy void at the insurer's option. A clause may be interpreted as a promissory warranty even though not expressly declared to be so[1]. As a general point, though, it must be remembered that so far as personal lines policies are concerned the SLIP forbids the making of statements about the past or future into promissory warranties (SGIP has no corresponding provision). It should also be remembered that a clause of this kind may legitimately be regarded as a clause excluding or restricting the insurer's liability, with the result that the FSO will want to consider whether it satisfies the test of reasonableness in s 11 of UCTA 1977. Of course both these points apply only to personal lines policies, but the vast majority of life policies will fall into this category, the principal exception being employers' Keyman policies.

[1] *Hales v Reliance Fire* [1960] 2 Lloyd's Rep 391, Mocatta J, though that decision does to some extent turn on the special circumstances of fire insurance.

Voidability of policy

11.9 In cases where there is a duty to disclose the alteration of risk, it becomes necessary to ask what consequences follow from a failure to make that disclosure.

One possibility is that the policy becomes voidable at the option of the insurers. A distinction must be drawn between two types of case. The first is where the policy provides that the insured must obtain the insurer's consent before allowing the increase of risk to occur. Here, it might be thought that the policy is clearly at least voidable at the instance of the insurer, but this may be a dangerous conclusion to draw. It is unsupported by authority (though at the same time not rebutted by any authority) and as a general principle the court should be slow to allow the avoidance of a policy without a properly drafted policy provision. On the other hand, it is hard to see what other sanction can properly be imposed. The only serious possibility would appear to be an appropriate increase in the premium (or proportionate decrease in the sum assured, at least in the case of life assurance), but this is subject to the objections that it gives the policyholder no incentive to disclose the increase in advance, since he may get away with a non-disclosure and is no worse off if he is detected and, in the case of the proportionate decrease in the sum assured, that the doctrine of proportionality is unknown to English insurance law[1]. If the duty to seek approval were construed as part of the duty of utmost good faith, then voidability would seem to be the only possible sanction. In the absence of an express policy provision there is no possible ground for suggesting that the policy is automatically void if the risk is increased without obtaining the necessary consent. The second is where the policy merely provides for subsequent notification. Here the position is less clear. It may be that upon receiving the notification the insurers are entitled to avoid (or perhaps merely to terminate) the policy, but it is suggested that a court is unlikely to accept this conclusion in the absence of a clearly drafted provision to that effect. On the other hand, it is hard to see what is the point of the provision unless it confers some power upon the insurers. A possible compromise would be to say that additional premium terms can be imposed, but there are obvious difficulties about allowing a court to come to this conclusion, since it seems to amount to a re-writing of the bargain which the parties have made. Nor is it clear upon what principle the court could determine what extra premiums are to be allowed – presumably it would be necessary to adopt the rule from the MIA 1906, s 31 that where additional premiums become payable and there is no agreement as to the amount, the assured must pay a reasonable sum. Consideration of these difficulties may go some way towards explaining why English courts have been so reluctant to become involved in dealing with problems of increase of risk.

1 Though the Insurance Ombudsman has been prepared to apply it in appropriate cases: Annual Report 1989.

Increase of risk in life assurance – special considerations

11.10 As indicated above there is no reported life assurance case where the question of increase of risk has been considered. This may reflect the fact that insureds are naturally reluctant to take unnecessary risks with their own lives, but there can be no doubt that assureds do sometimes change the occupations, place of residence or lifestyle in a way which increases the risk. The particular feature of life policies which makes them special in relation to increase of risk is that they are intended to last for many years, whereas general policies do not normally last for more than one year. It seems more likely that insurers do not regard such changes as grounds for resisting a claim under the policy in the absence of express provision. Moreover, such provision appears to be relatively rare.

Life of another policies

11.11 These are capable of producing problems even where there is an express clause, since the life assured is not the policyholder and is not normally a party to the contract. Although the SLIP does allow warranties about matters material to the risk in life of another policies, it would seem impracticable to require the policyholder to prevent the life assured from allowing an increase of risk.

Increase of risk and misrepresentation

11.12 A common problem arises where the life insured, having truthfully stated on the proposal form that he does not engage in some hazardous activity (which may be anything from smoking tobacco to hang-gliding) then subsequently takes up that activity. Inevitably, the premium will originally have been calculated on the basis of the information given on the proposal form, and there is, from the insurer's point of view, a noticeable change in the risk undertaken. The first question is whether the insured has been entirely honest on the proposal form. Where the hazardous activity is commenced shortly after the inception of the policy, this inevitably gives rise to the suspicion that this was always the insured's intention. If so, that is a material fact which should have been declared, and the failure to declare it renders the policy voidable. However, insurers should not be too ready to assume that any change in the risk is one which was always contemplated. They should also remember that the burden of proving a non-disclosure or a material increase of risk rests upon them[1].

It is suggested that it is possible to approach this question from the point of view of principle. In a life policy the insurers must be aware that the exact detail of the risk will not necessarily stay the same. Apart from the inherent additional mortality risk arising with age, it is always to be expected that the life insured will at some point engage in some activity which materially increases the risk, though it will rarely be possible at the outset to predict what those activities will be. In addition, some of them will be of a purely temporary nature, such as crossing the street in an imprudent way, whilst others will be of more lasting effect, such as taking up a dangerous hobby or beginning to smoke tobacco. At some point a line has to be drawn between those activities which might reasonably be regarded as incidental to the main activity of the life insured and those which represent so fundamental a departure from that activity as to be outside it altogether. The former ought not to be regarded as an alteration of risk for these purposes, whereas the latter ought to be.

[1] *Baxendale v Harvey* (1859) 4 H & N 445.

11.13 In the last few years especially difficult and sensitive issues have arisen in connection with the life's sexual habits. This is a matter which is frequently the subject of questions on proposal forms[1], and the question of alteration of risk may arise where the life's sexual habits change after the inception of the policy. Although the principles applicable appear to be no different here than elsewhere, there is likely to be the suggestion that sexual proclivities at least do not change greatly. This may be of some evidential value in relation to the questions about the life's own sexual behaviour (though as a matter of medicine and psychology it is suggested that the proposition is open to some question) but the argument clearly cannot apply to those parts of the lifestyle questionnaire which deal with drug-taking (a habit which can be acquired at any age) or with the habits of the life's sexual partners. There is a danger that insurers will seek to use increase of risk as a way of dealing with those cases where they suspect, but cannot adequately prove, that there has been misrepresentation or non-disclosure on the proposal form in that the risk existed at the time of the policy. It is obviously undesirable that they should be allowed to do this – cases of non-disclosure or misrepresentation should be acknowledged and treated as such.

[1] See Chapter 5.

11.14 A further point which follows on from that above is that it is equally objectionable for insurers to make increase of risk in itself a ground for avoiding or varying the policy cover by means of an express term. If it is desired to limit the cover to a specified geographical area for example, this can be done by a policy term, but the Statements of Practice do not permit warranties as to the future in own life policies, and insurers ought not to be allowed to go beyond asking proposers for a declaration as to their present conduct and present intentions. Thus, for example, the case of the non-smoker who subsequently takes up smoking should be (and often is) dealt with by requiring a declaration on the proposal form that the life does not smoke and has no intention of smoking in the future. This is sufficient to exclude those who know that they are likely to smoke again at some time, but does not exclude those who can honestly make the declaration. The difficulties of proving a false declaration of intention are not alleviated by this solution, however.

Conclusion

11.15 The subject of increase of risk causes great difficulty in English insurance law, largely because the law has never clearly decided whether it wants to adopt a general doctrine of increase of risk, and partly also because the courts have been reluctant to give effect even to express increase of risk clauses. Many cases which might be considered to fall under increase of risk are either better dealt with under some other doctrine or cases where the insurers cannot rely upon the changed circumstances as a defence to a claim on the policy. Until some decision of principle can be made about identifying those increases which affect the cover and those which do not, it will remain unwise to rely upon increase of risk as a defence.

Chapter 12

The duty to take reasonable care

Introduction

12.1 The question of the policyholder's ongoing duty to take reasonable care to avoid the occurrence of insured losses is a vexed one. Section 78 of the MIA 1906 contains a brief reference to the matter:

> '(4) It is the duty of the assured and his agents, in all cases, to take such measures as may be reasonable for the purpose of averting or minimising a loss.'

This provision, however, gives rise to various difficulties. First, it appears in a section which otherwise deals entirely with suing and labouring clauses[1]. Secondly, the subsection gives no indication of the consequence of breach of the duty. In *Irvin v Hine*[2] insurers argued that they were not liable on a claim because of a breach of this duty, namely a failure to have a ship surveyed to see whether she was worth repairing. On the facts it was held that there was no breach of the duty (and the case went mostly on the question of whether there had been a total loss or a partial loss), but it is not at all clear that the claim could have been entirely rejected even if a breach had been found. Although this is one of the earliest reported considerations of the section, it does not resolve any of the difficult questions arising from that section, in particular the question of the effect of a breach.

In the light of the wording of s 78(4) it is submitted that compliance with the duty is a condition (in the insurance law sense[3]) but not a condition precedent to recovery. It follows that the insurer can disclaim liability only to the extent that the loss can be shown to have been caused or increased by the failure to comply. The third problem about s 78(4) is to understand what the duty actually requires. Section 55(2) of the Act clearly says that a marine policy can insure against negligence, so that failure to take reasonable care must presumably involve something more than negligence. This is a point which is by no means confined to marine insurance, as the cases discussed in the rest of this Chapter show. It is submitted that the meaning given to 'lack of reasonable care' by those cases should properly be read back into the interpretation of s 78(4).

In relation to non-marine insurance there is no statutory provision which supports the existence of such a duty, nor does there appear to be any reported case in which a court has said unequivocally that such a duty exists as a matter of general law, rather than in consequence of an express policy provision.

Even where there is an express policy provision, there is considerable disagreement about what 'reasonable care' amounts to in the context of an insurance policy. The dilemma may be simply stated: those who insure do so partly in order to protect against the need to take excessive security precautions. It might reasonably be thought that this aim would be undermined if, having insured, they were still required to take those precautions. On the other hand, insurers have for many years argued that the duty of the insured is to take the same care to avoid loss as he would do in the absence of insurance. It is no doubt for this reason that some reasonable care clauses expressly require the insured to take care 'as if uninsured'.

1 See Chapter 40.
2 [1950] 1 KB 555, Devlin J.
3 See Chapter 17.

General principles

12.2 The starting point of the modern law in this area is *Fraser v Furman*[1], where the policy under consideration was an employer's liability policy including the condition that:

> 'The insured shall take reasonable precautions to prevent accidents and disease.'

The question was whether there was a breach of that condition where an employee was injured by a machine which had not been securely fenced and whose design had been altered by a senior employee of the company in a way which made the accident more likely. Diplock LJ laid down what has come to be regarded as the classic test:

> 'It is not enough that the … omission should be negligent; it must at least be reckless, that is to say made with actual recognition by the insured himself that a danger exists not caring whether or not it is averted. The purpose of the condition is to ensure that the insured will not refrain from taking precautions which he knows ought to be taken because he is covered against loss by the policy[2].'

The Court of Appeal held that in that case there had been no breach of the condition. It was observed that in the nature of a liability policy claims will be made in circumstances where the policyholder has been at least negligent. Clearly, it makes no sense to interpret clauses of this kind as excluding the insurer's liability whenever there has been negligent. To put it another way, what is reasonable as between insurer and insured is not the same as what is reasonable between the insured and the third party to whom the insured becomes liable[3].

The principles laid down in *Fraser* were considered further by the Court of Appeal in *Sofi v Prudential*[4], which is of fundamental importance in the development of the modern law in this area. The claimant took out a household contents policy, which had an extension covering valuables outside the home. He went to France on holiday with his family, and he took with him a quantity of jewellery, not with the intention of wearing it while in France, but because he believed that it would be safer in his possession than left at home. On arriving at Dover he found that he had some time to wait for the ferry to France, so he parked his car and, with his family, went for a walk. The jewellery was concealed in the glove compartment of the car. On returning to the car, they found that it had been broken into and the jewellery had been stolen. The loss fell within the policy, subject to the fact that there was a reasonable care clause in the following terms:

> '**2. – Prevention of Loss**
> The Insured and any person entitled to claim under this Policy must take all reasonable steps to safeguard any property insured and to avoid accidents which may lead to damage or injury. All property insured must be maintained in efficient condition and repair.'

The claimant had also taken out a travel policy with the defendants. This also contained a reasonable care clause in the following terms:

> 'Each Beneficiary shall take all reasonable steps to prevent loss, damage, injury or illness, to safeguard his property, to trace and recover property lost and to discover guilty persons.'

The question was whether the policyholder had complied with these clauses, which the Court of Appeal treated as being materially identical in their effect. The insurers argued that it was unreasonable to take the jewellery in the car and unreasonable to leave it unattended in the car, even though the car was locked and the jewellery was concealed in the glove compartment. The Court of Appeal found in favour of the policyholder. Lloyd LJ said:

> '[I]t is at once apparent that some limitation must be placed on the full width of the language of general condition 2. This follows from the fact that the condition applies to all sections of the policy; not just s 3. If the clause were to be taken as meaning that the insured must take all reasonable care of the property insured and all reasonable care to avoid accidents, then the insurers could never be liable under s 11, for liability under s 11 pre-supposes that the insured or a member of his family is legally liable to a third party. Legal liability in the great majority of cases depends on want of reasonable care. So a wide construction of general condition 2, requiring the insured to take all reasonable care, would be altogether repugnant to the cover apparently afforded by s 11 of the policy. Similarly, the insurers would escape all liability under ss 1 and 2 in the very ordinary case of damage to a house or its contents by fire (one of the insured perils) if the fire were caused by the negligence of the insured. That could not be right[5].'

The Court of Appeal sought to apply Lord Diplock's test from *Fraser v Furman*, which it treated as being a single test based on the recklessness of the policyholder. The trial judge found that the car could only have been out of sight or sound for five to seven minutes. He said that, with hindsight, the decision to leave the jewellery in the car might not have been the same, but there was not the degree of recklessness which would justify the exclusion of liability. Before the Court of Appeal it was argued for the defendants that it was reckless of the claimant not to take the jewellery with him or not to have left somebody behind in the car, having regard to the value of the jewellery. The Court of Appeal rejected that submission. If the claimant had given no thought at all to the jewellery the submission might have succeeded; or if, to take another example, the claimant had left the jewellery exposed to view. But here the claimant considered what was best to do. He and his family were not going to be absent from the car for more than half an hour at the most. In the event they were absent for much less than half an hour. They decided that in the circumstances the safest thing to do was to leave the jewellery in the locked glove compartment. That decision could not be regarded as having been taken recklessly.

1 [1967] 2 Lloyd's Rep 1.
2 At 7.
3 See also *W & J Lane v Spratt* [1970] 2 QB 480, [1969] 2 Lloyd's Rep 229, Roskill J.
4 [1993] 2 Lloyd's Rep 559.
5 At 517.

12.3 Before attempting to summarise the current state of the law in this area, it is helpful to consider four more reported cases. In *Devco Holder Ltd and Burrows & Paine Ltd v Legal & General Assurance Society Ltd*[1] the claim arose as the result of the theft of a Ferrari 400 Grand Tourer motor car. It was stolen from a car park where the driver of the car had temporarily left it unattended and unlocked, with the keys in the ignition, while he went to his office on the first floor of a building on the other side of the road opposite the station. The car was insured under a motor policy which included a reasonable care clause in the following terms:

> 'You must take all reasonable steps to protect your car against loss or damage and to maintain it in a safe and efficient condition.'

The case for the defendants was that by leaving it unlocked with the key in the ignition in a public place, the driver failed to take such reasonable steps. The trial judge found that the keys were left in the car deliberately and not inadvertently, but that it was unclear how long the car had in fact been left unattended. These findings were not challenged before the Court of Appeal, and the question was whether the claimant should be regarded as having been reckless. On behalf of the claimant it was said that it was the driver's intention to return to the car very shortly. To park a car, with keys left in it, would constitute a failure to exercise ordinary care but not recklessness. The Court of Appeal rejected this submission. The crucial point was that when the driver parked his car in the car park, he quite deliberately left the keys in the ignition. In so doing he was leaving a no doubt attractive Ferrari motor car in the public car park of a station in a country town whilst he went into his office on the first floor of a building on the other side of the road. He knew that he was taking a risk. If the keys had been left in the ignition merely by inadvertence, the legal position might well have been different.

In *Sinnott v Municipal General*[2] the policyholder was moving house and was transporting property, some of it quite valuable, by car. She left her car unattended for 30 minutes in an area known to have a high incidence of car thefts while she visited a library. The car was stolen. It was held that there was no breach of the reasonable care condition, since the goods had been locked in the boot and had not been visible to passers-by.

In *Bushell v General Accident*[3] the policyholder's car was stolen from outside his house. It was locked at the time, but the keys were in the ignition because for two years previously the policyholder had found it difficult to remove them from the ignition barrel. He had taken no steps to rectify this problem. It was held that this was a breach of the reasonable care condition.

The most recent case is *Frans Maas (UK) Ltd v Sun Alliance and London Insurance PLC*[4], which was a case of commercial insurance, with an express reasonable care clause which David Steel J found to impose duties effectively synonymous with those in *Fraser v Furman*. The policy covered goods in storage and the insured became liable to third parties (ie not customers) in respect of misdelivery of those goods and/or wrongful interference with them. The court's observations about reasonable care must be regarded as *obiter* because the primary ground of decision was that liabilities to non-customers were in any event not within the scope of the policy, but David Steel J also held that the insured had acted recklessly as to possible liabilities to customers and third parties in releasing goods without the necessary bills of lading. There were commercial reasons why this was done, but the judge took the view that this conduct was obviously inappropriate and that the insured had been well aware of the risk it was running. It is hard to see how the insured could not have appreciated the risk, given the fundamental importance attached to bills of lading in the international carriage of goods.

1 [1993] 2 Lloyd's Rep 567.
2 [1989] CLY 2051 Liverpool Cty Ct 24/2/89, Hamilton J.
3 [1992] CLY 2614 Andover Cty Ct 2/12/91, Bailey-Cox J.
4 [2004] Lloyd's Rep IR 649, David Steel J.

12.4 The principles laid down in these three cases are both difficult and contentious. On the one hand it is often said by those in the insurance industry that insurance must work on the basis that the insured takes the same care to avoid loss as would be taken if there were no insurance policy in force. On the other hand it may be said that policyholders take out insurance at least partly to relieve themselves of some of the burdens of precautions which might otherwise be necessary. It is noticeable that in all three Court of Appeal cases the policies concerned provided some protection against the risk of negligence-based liability, so that it was necessary to construe the reasonable care clause in a way which would not negate the effect of that protection. Of course, many policies do include protection of this sort, even where such protection is not the principal aspect of the cover. However, there are policies which do not include this protection, and this raises the issue of how to interpret a reasonable care clause in such a policy. On one view the absence of liability cover would negate the arguments used in these three cases, so that a higher standard of care could be expected of policyholders. It is submitted, however, that the courts would be unlikely to take this view for at least two good reasons. The first reason is that policies such as the Hearth and Home policy in *Sofi* are often designed so that policyholders can choose which sections of cover they want to buy. The result is that some policyholders subject to the reasonable care clause have liability cover, whilst others, with the same clause, have no such cover. It seems undesirable, perhaps even unworkable, to say that the clause should be interpreted differently according to which sections of the policy the policyholder has purchased. The second reason is of more general application. Now that the principles applicable to reasonable care clauses have been expounded by the Court of Appeal and developed in these three cases, it seems unlikely that that court would be sympathetic to a proposal to develop differing standards. A simple single test has much to commend it and is likely to be adopted.

The Ombudsman's approach

12.5 In examining the implications of this line of case law it is helpful to look at the approach which has been adopted by the Insurance Ombudsman has given a number of important decisions[1]. The Ombudsman first pronounced on the subject in his Annual Report for 1985, where he suggested[2] that he normally asked himself four questions:

(a) What was the value of the goods at risk?
(b) What was the reason for having them in the place from which they were stolen?
(c) What precautions were actually taken to safeguard them?
(d) Were there any alternatives open to the policyholder?

This list was referred to by Lloyd LJ in *Sofi*, though his Lordship declined either to approve or to disapprove of the list as a general guide. Since then the Ombudsman has returned to the question on a number of occasions in the IOB Bulletin. In Bulletin 7 the then Ombudsman gave a summary of his approach. A distinction has been drawn between cases of momentary forgetfulness and cases where the policyholder might be said to have been reckless in choosing to take a possibly unjustified risk. In the former event it has been held that there is no failure to take reasonable care. In the latter event it has been held necessary to enquire whether the risk was unjustified. This in turn depends upon an objective assessment of how great the risk was in the particular case, coupled with an enquiry into what alternative courses of action were reasonably available to the policyholder. The Ombudsman's approach was roundly criticised in a later issue of the IOB Bulletin[3] by a company claims manager, but has subsequently been restated[4]. The Ombudsman made the point that in fact many people simply do not consider the risk of theft, even in circumstances where, with the benefit of hindsight, the risk might be considered to be obvious.

1 Ait appears that the Insurance Ombudsman's approach has stayed broadly the same under the FSOS.
2 Paragraph 2.5.
3 IOB Bulletin 10.
4 IOB Bulletin 13.

Motor insurance

12.6 Many of the cases decided by the Ombudsman concern motor policies. A common cause of loss is theft in circumstances where the policyholder has left the keys in the car. Sometimes the keys are hidden under the seat, sometimes they are left in the ignition. Sometimes they are left in the lock. A particularly common situation occurs where the car is stolen from a petrol station, the driver having left the keys in the ignition while paying for his fuel. Examination of IOB Bulletins[1] suggests that most such cases are treated as being matters of momentary inadvertence, with the result that the claim is upheld.

The prospects of a successful claim appear to be almost as good when the policyholder has left the keys in the ignition to go shopping elsewhere. In one case a policyholder parked outside a shop from which he had arranged to collect a bulky purchase. He unlocked the boot of his car and left the keys in the lock. It was estimated that he had been in the shop for about two minutes. When he returned, the car was gone. It was held that there was no failure to take reasonable care. Although it would obviously have been possible for him to take the keys with him, the risk that the car would in these circumstances be stolen on a busy shopping street was slight enough that he should not be penalised for acting as he did. Similarly in another case the policyholder was in the habit of leaving the keys in the ignition while buying his morning paper. He had done this regularly for 15 years, and the area in question was not considered a high-crime area. It was held that he was not guilty of lack of reasonable care[2]. By contrast, in another case an insured left the keys in the car (not in the ignition) while delivering parcels to a village post office. The difference in this case was that he was aware of police warnings about thefts in the area. This claim was rejected by the Ombudsman[3]. In another case a policyholder had left the keys under the seat of the car and left the car unlocked overnight. There appeared no good reason why he had chosen to do this, and it was held that this was a failure to take reasonable care[4].

1 Particularly Nos 10 and 13.
2 IOB Bulletin 7, leading article.
3 IOB Bulletin 7, leading article.
4 Case handled by the author in 1991.

12.7 In a number of cases keys have been left in the ignition while the policy-holder left the car alone to do something else. Where the policyholder left his car in a secluded office car-park, but with the keys in the ignition because he was called away to the telephone, his claim was upheld. This may at first sight seem incompatible with *Devco Holder*, but the two cases may perhaps be reconciled on the basis that the inadvertence here was momentary rather than the deliberate taking of risk and that the reasonableness of the policyholder's actions was affected by the location. Where keys have been left in the ignition at a petrol station, claims for loss by theft have usually been rejected, though in at least one case where the car was left for only a very short time the claim was upheld[1]. By contrast, where the keys were left in the car so that a prospective purchaser could take a test drive, it was held that there had been a breach of the reasonable care clause[2].

Where property has been stolen from a car, the usual test has been whether it was sufficiently concealed from the eyes of potential thieves. Hiding it in the boot[3] or locking the car[4] appear to be sufficient precautions, but there is a conflict of case law on the effect of leaving property in the back of a hatchback. In one case this was regarded as insufficient[5], but in another[6] it was held to be sufficient. In both cases it appears that the policyholder was aware of the risk.

1 IOB Bulletin 10.22.
2 IOB Bulletin 10.24.
3 IOB Bulletin 10.1.
4 IOB Bulletin 10.2.
5 IOB Bulletin 10.9.
6 IOB Bulletin 10.10.

12.8 Partly as a result of these decisions, some insurers have taken to inserting specific exclusions for the situation where the keys have been left in the car. The effectiveness of such exclusions was upheld in *Hayward v Norwich Union Insurance Ltd*[1], where the policyholder left the key in the ignition and also left in the car a control device which was supposed to immobilise the car. A thief gained access to the car and stole it while the keys were in the ignition. The Court of Appeal held that the trial judge had been wrong to hold that the exclusion did not apply when the key was left in the ignition but the policyholder was able to observe the vehicle. These were plain English words and it was wrong to try to distort them to the benefit of the policyholder. Although the clause in question is obviously not a reasonable care clause, it is equally obvious that it is intended to replace a reasonable care clause, and it is interesting to observe the somewhat stricter construction adopted in relation to this clause as compared with the courts' rather lenient approach to reasonable care clauses.

1 [2001] EWCA Civ 243, [2001] 1 All ER Comm 545, CA.

12.9 A more surprising attempt to rely upon the reasonable care clause occurred in a case[1] where the policyholder was involved in an accident after consuming alcohol well in excess of the legal limit. The insurers argued that driving in this state was a breach of the reasonable care clause, but the Ombudsman held that this risk should have been expressly excluded, and that the reliance Upon reasonable care was inappropriate.

In all motor cases it should be noted that the reasonable care clause normally applies only to the policyholder. Thus, in a case[2] where the car was in the custody of another named driver when it was stolen, it was held that the policyholder had not breached the reasonable care clause[3].

1 IOB Bulletin 13.4.
2 Handled by the author in 1990.
3 See also the cases below on household policies.

12.10 Given the complexities and uncertainties in this area, it is perhaps not surprising to find that some insurers now expressly exclude cover if keys are left in the ignition. This is without doubt a clearer solution, though it must be noted that a clause worded in this way will have no effect where the keys are left in the lock or elsewhere in the car. There is of course very rarely any way of proving whether the keys were left in the ignition or on the seat, and it may therefore be doubted whether clauses of this kind will have much practical value. To avoid the problem it would seem necessary to exclude liability in all cases where the keys are left in or about the car.

Household policies

12.11 In one case[1] a claim was made for money stolen. It appeared that the thief was the policyholder's stepson. The insurer sought to rely Upon the reasonable care clause, on the basis that the stepson had previously stolen money from the policyholder's daughter, who had taken no action to prevent recurrence of the theft (although the report is not entirely clear on this point, it appears that the policyholder had no prior knowledge of the theft). The Ombudsman held that the daughter, who was not a party to the policy, could in any event have no obligations under it. The same result was reached in another case[2] where the alleged lack of reasonable care was by the brother of the policyholder's executor.

In another case[3] the policyholder's bag, containing his keys, was stolen. He did not have the locks of his flat changed and shortly afterwards a burglary took place. His claim for the burglary was upheld on the basis that he had been imprudent but not reckless – had he appreciated the risk he would have acted differently. It can readily be seen that this argument proves rather too much, since the same can be said in almost any case where failure to take precautions leads to loss.

1 IOB Bulletin 13.1.
2 IOB Bulletin 13.3.
3 IOB Bulletin 13.7.

Travel policies

12.12 These policies usually provide cover for loss of personal property, but this cover has usually been accompanied by a reasonable care clause. A number of common situations of loss may be identified. One is where the policyholder goes for a swim, leaving behind valuable items such as a watch, which is then stolen. More or less effort may have been made to conceal the watch. Another is where luggage is left in a car, perhaps overnight, and is stolen during that time. Insurers have tended to regard any behaviour of this kind as automatically failing to comply with a reasonable care clause, but again the Insurance Ombudsman has not been prepared to support so broad an approach. In IOB Bulletin 16 the Ombudsman suggested that the value of the property concerned must also be a relevant factor, especially where it is left unattended on a beach. There is also a tendency to ask whether the policyholder was reckless and what alternative steps could have been taken. Thus, where a holdall was stolen from the luggage rack of an unattended moped, the Insurance Ombudsman held that the policyholder must have been reckless as to the risk, which was very obvious, and had unreasonably failed to take any steps to protect against it[1].

A further development may be noted in relation to travel policies. Following *Sofi* and the cases in which the Ombudsman developed the *Sofi* principle, insurers have taken to applying to the baggage cover a clause excluding loss for any property unattended at the time of the loss. As a matter of construction of the policy, this appears to deal satisfactorily with the problem, all such losses now being excluded. However, it must be remembered that a clause of this kind might now be subject to the UTCCR 1994[2]. In addition, the Insurance Ombudsman will look at such clauses as if they were subject to UCTA 1977[3].

1 IOB Bulletin 4.15.
2 SI 1994/3159; see Chapter 16.
3 (1992) 2 Ins L & P.

Conclusion

12.13 Both the law and the Ombudsman seem to have moved in the direction of treating the issue of inadvertence as almost determinative of the question of reasonable care. Whilst the move away from strict notions of reasonable care is to be welcomed as a pragmatic attempt to balance the interests of the parties, there is no doubt that in many cases an astute policyholder can simply profess blank ignorance of the risk and thereby defeat a reasonable care clause. From this point of view it might be thought that the law had moved a little too far.

Chapter 13

The continuing duty of utmost good faith

Introduction

13.1 An important and difficult area of law which can arise during the currency of the policy concerns the continuing duties which the parties owe to each other. The pre-contractual duties of the parties are relatively well-settled[1], but until recently the law has much less clear on the question of continuing duties after the commencement of the policy. The crucial question is whether the law should recognise a continuing duty of utmost good faith over and above the obvious duty to comply with the express and implied terms of the policy. A recent House of Lords decision has significantly developed this area of the law.

In *Manifest Shipping Co Ltd v Uni-Polaris Shipping Co Ltd, The Star Sea*[2] the insured vessel under a time policy became a constructive total loss as a result of fire. A question arose whether the vessel had put to sea in an unseaworthy state with the privity of the assured[3], and it was alleged that the assured had sought to conceal expert reports on the cause of the fire which drew attention to some aspects of unseaworthiness. In dealing with these arguments the House of Lords explained the operation of the duty of utmost good faith in relation to the making of claims. The leading speech is that of Lord Hobhouse, from which the following general principles may be derived as listed below and in paragraphs 13.5 and 13.6.

(1) Utmost good faith is common to all forms of insurance, and is a bilateral duty. The first part of this proposition is uncontroversial, but the second represents the clearest general statement of the duty that there has yet been.

(2) The duty continues after the formation of the contract[4]. Although s 17 of the MIA 1906 is included in the section on pre-contractual matters, it is clear that the post-contractual duty is also derived from the principle laid down in s 17[5]. In the light of this observation it is possible to reconsider the earlier cases in this area, principally *Banque Financiere de la Cite SA v Westgate Insurance Co Ltd*[6] and *Bank of Nova Scotia v Hellenic Mutual War Risks Association (Bermuda) Ltd, The Good Luck*[7].

[1] Chapter 5.

[2] [2001] Lloyd's Rep IR 247, HL.

[3] MIA 1906, s 39(5); for this aspect of the case, see Chapter 40.
[4] See also *Fargnoli v GA Bonus plc* [1997] Re LR 374, Ct of Sess (OH).
[5] For this reason, the reasoning of Hirst J in *The Litsion Pride* [1985] 1 Lloyd's Rep 437 can no longer be treated as sound law – see per Lord Hobhouse at para 71; and see *The Captain Panagos* [1986] 2 Lloyd's Rep 470 Evans J.
[6] [1990] 2 All ER 947.
[7] [1991] 3 All ER 1, HL.

13.2 In *Banque Financiere* (above) the appellants were a bank who had advanced substantial sums of money to companies controlled by B. The loans were secured on certain gemstones and on credit insurance policies. The policies were arranged by L, a branch manager of an insurance broker, who negotiated some of the primary cover (which was in three layers) with the insurers through D, who was a senior underwriter with those insurers. The policies contained an exclusion for losses caused by fraud or attempted fraud. L was unable to place the full amount of risk, but in order to lead the appellant bank to believe that cover was in place (without which they would not have been prepared to make the loan) he persuaded D to underwrite the loan for 14 days, and issued false cover notes for the excess layers when no cover for those layers was in fact in place. D discovered L's deception in 1980, but did not inform his own employers or the brokers or the bank; instead he continued to underwrite further loans to the same companies. In due course those companies defaulted on the loans, the gemstones proved to be worth much less than the value of the loans and B absconded with the money advanced by the banks. The banks had to accept that they could not claim on the credit insurance policies in view of the very obvious fraud, but they sued the insurers contending that the insurers owed them a duty of care to disclose the existence of L's fraud once they knew of it, and that their losses stemmed from the insurers' breach of this duty. The House of Lords dismissed the bank's claim. First, there is no duty to warn the insured that the insured's own agent (here L) had committed a breach of duty towards the insured. Secondly, the loss was not caused by any omission on the part of the insurer's. There was fraud by both L and B, and either of these would have been sufficient to prevent a claim under the insurance policy, even if the insurers had made full disclosure to the bank. Lord Bridge, with whom Lord Brandon and Lord Jauncey agreed, expressly approved a passage from the judgment of Slade LJ when the case was before the Court of Appeal. The passage in question reads:

> 'In adapting the well-established principles relating to the duty of disclosure falling on the insured to the obverse case of the insurer himself, due account must be taken of the rather different reasons for which the insured and the insurer require the protection of full disclosure. In our judgment, the duty falling on the insurer must at least extend to disclosing all facts known to him which are material either to the nature of the risk sought to be covered or the recoverability of a claim under the policy which a prudent insured would take into account in deciding whether or not to place the risk for which he seeks cover with that insurer[1].'

Although Slade LJ refers to matters affecting the recoverability of a claim under the policy It should be observed that this passage relates only to the decision whether or not to place the risk with the particular insurer, and is therefore appropriate only to deal with the insurer's *pre-contractual* duty of utmost good faith. This duty is considered at length in Chapter 5, but does not fall within the scope of this Chapter. According to the view of the facts ultimately taken by the House of Lords, it was unnecessary to reach any decision on the existence of a continuing duty of utmost good faith.

1 [1990] 2 All ER 947 at 950.

13.3 In *The Good Luck* (see above) the claimants were a bank to whom a ship had been mortgaged. The defendant Protection & Indemnity club ('P & I club') were the insurers of the vessel. Notification of the mortgage had been given to the defendants, the benefit of the insurance policies had been assigned to the claimants, and the defendants had agreed to hold the insurance moneys to the order of the claimants and to inform the claimants promptly if it 'ceased to insure' the vessel. The insurer designated certain areas of the Persian Gulf as additional premium areas or prohibited areas for the ship to enter because of the Iran-Iraq war which was then taking place. The ship was struck by a missile while in one of the prohibited areas, but the owners submitted a claim on the policy under the pretence that they had given notice of the entry of the ship into an additional premium zone (as they were required to do under the policy) and that they were ignorant of the prohibited zone. At this time the bank was in the process of re-scheduling the loans it had made to the owners of the vessel; on enquiring about the casualty and the resulting claim it was told by the insurer's agent that the claim was being processed, an answer which it took to imply that there was no apparent problem with the claim, which would be paid in due course. In fact the agent knew that this claim would be rejected because of the entry into the prohibited zone. The bank went ahead and re-scheduled the loans. The insurers duly rejected the claim on the insurance policy, and the bank brought this action, alleging that it had lost the right to the insurance proceeds because of the deception by the insurer's agents. The House of Lords decided in favour of the bank on the ground that the insurer was in breach of its duty to inform the bank promptly on ceasing to insure the vessel. This in turn followed from a finding that the statements as to the areas in which the ship would be used amounted to promissory warranties under s 33 of the MIA 1906, and that the effect of the breach of such a warranty is to discharge the insurer's liability automatically, ie without the exercise of any choice on the part of the insurer, and even though the insurer is not at that time aware of the breach.

This case, too, requires careful analysis. The following points may be noted. First, the claimants were not the policyholders, although the benefit of the policy had been assigned to them. Secondly, the decision is not based upon the breach of any general duty on the part of the insurers to disclose a breach of utmost good faith, whether pre-contractual or post-contractual. Instead, it relies upon the narrow ground that the insurers had undertaken to give prompt notice of ceasing to insure the vessel, and that they were in breach of that undertaking. The breach had caused the bank's loss, since the bank had entered into the re-financing arrangement on the basis of its belief that the vessel was still insured[1].

The decision in *The Star Sea* is not incompatible with either of these decisions. What it does is develop the relevant principles from the narrow situations which arose in those cases to a principle of general application.

1 It is one of the oddities of the case that the wording of the undertaking was almost certain to lead to its being breached, since it would have been almost impossible for the insurers to know of the insured's breach of warranty promptly when it happened.

13.4 In *K/S Merc-Scandia XXXXII v Certain Lloyd's Underwriters*[1] a claim was made against the assured who held a liability policy with the defendants. An issue arose as to whether the assured had entered into a jurisdiction agreement with the claimant. Such an agreement would probably have been a breach of the liability policy. In an effort to persuade the defendants that no such agreement had been made, the assured produced a document which was later held to have been forged. Rather surprisingly, Aitkens J held that this did not amount to a breach of the continuing duty of utmost good faith. He said that this duty applies only to variations of the risk and the presentation of claims. In the present case, the deception had related only to the question of jurisdiction. It is submitted that this is a regrettably narrow view of the scope of the continuing duty of utmost good faith.

1 [2000] Lloyd's Rep IR 694, Aitkens J.

Statutory assignees

13.5 It is unclear whether the continuing duty transfers to a person who has become entitled to sue on a policy of insurance by statutory assignment, such as that effected by the TP(RAI)A 1930. The point was discussed but not decided in *Alfred MacAlpine plc v BAI (Run-Off) Ltd*[1]:

(3) There are significant differences between the pre-contractual duty and the post-contractual duty. Thus, it cannot be right to suggest that there is a continuing duty to disclose facts material to the insurer's assessment of the risk[2], and this remains so even where the policy gives the insurer a right of cancellation and the fact is one which would be material to a possible decision to cancel[3].

A further important point in this context is that post-loss avoidance of the policy is a wholly one-sided remedy, since it can never be of benefit to the insured. It is necessary to construe the post-contractual duty in such a way as to ensure that the insurer is not encouraged to act in bad faith. So far as the post-contractual situation is concerned, it is not a breach of the duty for the insured to act negligently in presenting a claim.

It should be understood that this duty would exist independently of any provision contained in the policy, though of course it could be extended or restricted by policy provisions. One matter which may be mentioned here is that policy provisions which suspend cover in the event of the policyholder doing some act, such as (in the context of life policies) leaving the country or taking up smoking, should be dealt with as a matter of express provision and not under this principle, since it is only the presence of the express provision which makes them relevant.

1 [2000] Lloyd's Rep IR 352.

2 *Cory v Patton* (1872) LR 7 QB 304; *Lishman v Northern Maritime Insurance Co* (1875) LR 10 CP 179; *Niger Co Ltd v Guardian Assurance Co Ltd* (1922) 13 Ll L Rep 75.

3 *Niger Co Ltd v Guardian Assurance Co Ltd* (1922) 13 Ll L Rep 75; *New Hampshire Insurance Co v MGN Ltd* [1997] LRLR 24; *NSW Medical Defence Union Ltd v Transport Industries Insurance Co Ltd* (1985) 4 NSWLR 107.

Duty of disclosure – bonus rates

13.6 A particular problem of recent years in this area has concerned possible changes in the terminal bonus rates on with-profits policies[1]. Insurers routinely issue to policyholders, with their annual statements, projections of terminal bonuses for policies which are due to mature shortly. It is only to be expected that policyholders will to some extent rely upon these in planning what to do with the policy proceeds. It is of course normal practice to include a disclaimer to the effect that the continuance of the rates cannot be guaranteed, and it is suggested that a change to bonus rates made after the issue of the annual statement is covered by this disclaimer. Greater difficulties have arisen where a decision to cut bonus rates has been taken before the annual statement was issued, but that statement still refers to bonuses at the old rate. This may be evidence of nothing more than administrative confusion within the insurance company, but policyholders are, not surprisingly, aggrieved by it, and there have been complaints to the Insurance Ombudsman. He has ruled that bonus projections issued with annual statements should be up-to-date, ie that they should incorporate any changes already decided upon. It is less clear, however, what consequences would follow from a breach of this principle. The policyholder is most unlikely to want to avoid the contract, unless the rates of return now expected are extremely poor, and it is clear that damages cannot be awarded at law. In any case, the policyholder will have some difficulty establishing any loss, since the actual return is what it would have been anyway, whatever the annual statement had said. The Ombudsman could award damages for maladministration or inconvenience:

(4) Fraudulent claims continue to give the insurer the right to reject all claims under the policy[2]. It is apparent that the fraudulent claim cannot succeed, but it is also important to show that the insured cannot have any incentive to make a fraudulent claim. The penalty of forfeiting all benefit under the policy achieves this objective[3].

(5) Once legal proceedings have begun between the parties, their mutual rights and duties are governed by the CPR 1998. These lay down the way in which litigation is to be conducted, as well as providing their own code of sanctions for non-compliance. The more general duty of good faith can have no application in this context[4].

[1] As is well-known, a problem of this kind eventually led to the *Equitable Life* litigation, resolved by the House of Lords in 2000 – see [2001] Lloyd's Rep IR 99 – which resulted in the collapse of that insurance company, which was held contractually bound to honour promises it had made to such policyholders, even though it was no longer financially able to do so.

[2] See further Chapter 19 on the claims process generally.

[3] See also *Goulstone v Royal Insurance Co* (1858) 1 F & F 276; *Britton v Royal Insurance Co* (1866) 4 F & F 905; *Orakpo v Barclays Insurance Services* [1995] LRLR 443.

[4] See also *Rego v Connecticut Insurance Placement Facility* 593 A2d 491 (1991) (Sup Ct of Connecticut).

Consequences of breach of the continuing duty

13.7 *The Star Sea* also provides a further reminder that the only consequence of a breach of the continuing duty of utmost good faith is that the innocent party may avoid the contract. Damages cannot be awarded. Thus, it is not open to the insurer to seek to be compensated for losses incurred in investigating and defending a claim, even where that claim is fraudulent.

Breaches by insurer

13.8 The question of the insurer's continuing duty can give rise to difficult problems when there is a breach of that duty. The usual understanding is that the consequence of such a breach is that the policy becomes voidable at the instance of the policyholder. Although this solution may work reasonably well in cases of general insurance, where the policy will normally be for a duration not exceeding one year, it may appear more problematic in life cases, where the policy may have been in existence for some considerable time. A case decided by the Insurance Ombudsman in 1991 is of some interest here. The policyholder had effected an investment policy, but some two years later his financial circumstances changed and he decided that he could no longer afford the premiums. He therefore cancelled the Direct Debit Mandate under which the premiums were being paid. The insurance company discovered this, and sent its representative to visit the policyholder to persuade him to resume the payments. The policyholder promised to consider the matter further, but the agent, on returning to his office, completed a new Direct Debit Mandate, *signed it in the name of the policyholder and submitted it to the bank*. The bank, in all innocence, paid three instalments of premiums before the policyholder drew attention to the fraud. The company accepted that these instalments must be refunded, but rejected the policyholder's claim to avoid the policy entirely. The Insurance Ombudsman upheld the policyholder's complaint and required the company to refund all premiums paid without allowing any deduction for the life cover provided. It is of course possible to view this case as an application of the Ombudsman's equitable discretion to give policyholders more than their legal entitlement, but it is submitted that it is in fact merely an application of legal principle to the facts. Many insurance companies are ready enough to rely upon technical breaches of utmost good faith by their policyholders. They should not complain when the roles are reversed. It is to be observed that they will suffer only the same fate as that which befalls an insured who commits a breach of the duty, which is to have the policy avoided against them – damages cannot be awarded[1], and in most cases the consequences of this are much less serious for them than they would be for the insured, who is deprived of the chance of recovering under the policy.

1 *Banque Financiere de la Cité SA v Westgate Insurance* [1990] 2 All ER 947, HL.

Avoidance of policy by policyholder

13.9 Where a breach of the continuing duty entitles a policyholder to avoid the policy, the question will arise, what exactly the policyholder is entitled to claim. It is submitted that the position is no different from that where the policyholder avoids for breach of the pre-contractual duty of disclosure. Thus, the policyholder is entitled to the return of his premiums, plus interest, and the company is not entitled to make any deduction for the life cover provided. This last point has proved particularly controversial within the insurance industry, and many companies adopt the practice of making a deduction for the life cover already provided. Although there is apparently no modern authority directly on the point in an insurance context, it is submitted that the correct answer may be deduced from an application of ordinary legal principles. What is happening is the rescission of the contract, and it is well settled that rescission of a contract requires *restitutio in integrun* ie the parties must be restored to their original positions. Thus, any property transferred under the contract must be returned. Once the contract is rescinded it is treated as void *ab initio*; thus it is deemed never to have existed. If it never existed, then it must follow that no life cover was ever provided, and if no life cover was ever provided there can be no possible justification for attempting to make a charge for it. Support for this general principle of contract law may be found in the case of *Rowland v Divall*[1], where the purchaser of a car was able to rescind the contract of sale on the ground of a defect in the formation of the contract. Although he had used the car for some time, thereby deriving a benefit, and although the value of the car had diminished as a result of normal wear and tear during that time, he was able to recover the purchase price in full. Although this is not an insurance case, there is no reason to think that the principles which it lays down are not applicable to insurance law.

1 [1923] 2 KB 500.

Effect of Rescission

13.10 Rescission of the contract puts an end to the continuing duty of utmost good faith, which is derived from the contract itself. Consequently, where the rescission was unjustified because of facts not known to the insurer at the time of the rescission, it cannot be a breach of continuing utmost good faith to refuse to reinstate the policy when the full facts become known[1].

1 *Drake Insurance plc v Provident Insurance plc* [2003] Lloyd's Rep IR 781, Moore-Bick J.

Conclusion

13.11 The decision in *The Star Sea* provides an authoritative answer to many of the important questions in this area, which have been debated at length at least since *The Litsion Pride*. The House of Lords has managed to strike a sensible balance between the need for continuing good faith and the need to protect the insured. However, it is to be expected that the law in this area will continue to develop.

Chapter 14

Lapse of policies

Introduction

14.1 This is a subject whose importance is largely confined to life policies, though there may also be cases in general insurance where the premium is to be paid by instalments and the payments are not made as they should be. However, these cases appear to be dealt with mostly by means of express warranties as to payment of premium[1]. Thus, the following discussion is in principle applicable to all types of insurance, but is more likely to be relevant in the context of life assurance.

1 See for example *JA Chapman & Co Ltd v Kadirga* [1998] Lloyd's Rep IR 377, CA.

Lapse, paying up and surrender

14.2 Where the assured fails to pay the premiums, whether voluntarily or involuntarily, the policy is liable to lapse. This is an application of the general common law rule that substantial failure to perform the obligations under a contract may give the other party the right to terminate that contract[1]. It is also usual for the policy to contain express provisions dealing with lapse for non-payment. The notion of substantiality in relation to failure to perform is of course one of degree. At common law it seems unlikely that failure to pay a single monthly premium instalment would give rise to a right to terminate, though failure to pay monthly instalments for a whole year presumably would do so[2].

Independently of the common law rules, however, life policies will include a clause dealing with lapse for non-payment. It is not usual to provide for the immediate lapse of the policy on the failure to pay a single premium, but a repeated failure will normally lead to lapse. In the case of life policies which qualify for Life Assurance Premium Relief ('LAPR'), the rules of the Inland Revenue require that the policy shall lapse not later than the date on which thirteen consecutive payments are due and unpaid. Non-compliance with this requirement will lead to the loss of the relief, though this point is of course of declining importance in view of the non-availability of the relief on policies taken out after 18 March 1984.

Problems in this area are not limited to policies which qualify for LAPR. Even where the policy is ineligible for LAPR it will normally be a 'qualifying policy'[3], which means that any gain accruing at maturity will be tax-free. However, this status is lost where the policy lapses and is subsequently reinstated[4].

[1] Thus the non-payment may be accepted by the insurer notifying the insured that the policy is at an end. In the absence of a policy provision it appears that such notice is required.
[2] The leading cases are *Boone v Eyre* (1779) 1 Hy Bl 273n, 2 Wm Bl 1312; and *Duke of St Albans v Shore* (1789) 1 Hy Bl 270.
[3] ICTA 1988, s 656.
[4] As to reinstatement see below.

Payment by standing order

14.3 In many cases premium payments are made through the policyholder's bank by means of a standing order. If one or more such payments are not made, the question may arise, who bears the responsibility for this failure. The general rule in relation to standing order payments[1] is that the bank makes these payments as agent for its own customer. Consequently, any failure on the part of the bank is the responsibility of the principal, ie the policyholder, and it is not open to the policyholder to lay the blame at the door of the insurance company. He may of course have a remedy against his own bank if the non-payment causes him loss. Sometimes the failure to pay will result from a lack of funds in the account, and in this event the policyholder clearly has only himself to blame, and will have no remedy against anyone.

[1] For direct debit payments see below. The different consequences of standing orders and direct debits are well analysed in FOS 38, and the case studies given there also illustrate the potential liabilities of banks for administering the system incorrectly, though none of them directly deals with an insurance policy.

Company's failure to collect premiums

14.4 Difficult problems arise where the lapse (or apparent lapse) of the policy arises from the company's failure to collect the premiums. This situation most commonly occurs where the premiums are being paid by direct debit, though it may also be relevant in the relatively few remaining cases of industrial assurance business where the premiums are collected at the policyholder's home.

Direct debit payments

14.5 Where premiums for an investment policy other then an Industrial Branch policy are not collected, the usual consequence will be that the company's own computerised reminder system will be activated and will send the policyholder a request for the unpaid premiums. It is unlikely that this system will be able to detect the reason for the non-payment, since collection is usually effected by running the relevant disk through the bank's computer system. Reminders issued in these circumstances are commonly ignored by policyholders who assume (usually correctly) that they result from an error on the part of the company. In other cases they produce a justified complaint from the policyholder. In the author's experience insurance companies do not for the most part have a good record in dealing with this kind of problem. A major source of friction is the fact that in many companies the system for sending out reminders about unpaid premium is apparently separate from any system for checking that payments have been properly collected. As a result it is common to find that reminders continue to be sent (and sometimes that premiums continue not to be collected) even after the policyholder has drawn attention to the error.

Where a life policy has fallen some months into arrears through the company's failure to collect the premiums, it commonly happens that the company will require a declaration of continuing good health from the policyholder before allowing the policy to be fully reinstated. It must be stressed that the right to require such a declaration depends upon the non-payment of premiums being the fault of the policyholder. That right accordingly does not exist where the company has failed to collect the premiums. It may of course happen that the policyholder is unwilling to provide the declaration, perhaps because he does not accept that the company is entitled to demand it, or that he is unable to do so because his health has deteriorated in the intervening period. In either event it is likely that the company will eventually declare the policy to have lapsed for non-payment of the premiums. Both the Insurance Ombudsman and the PIAOB took the view that this is not a proper course, since the original fault lies with the company, and it seems likely that the FOS will adopt the same approach.

The question becomes more complicated still in those cases where the original policy qualified for LAPR, since the policy, once lapsed, cannot be reinstated with the benefit of such relief. In cases of this kind the Ombudsman has held that the company must pay a lump sum to the policyholder in compensation for the fact that the new policy is less valuable to him than the old policy. The calculation of the appropriate sum has however proved to be a matter of some difficulty. The starting point must of course be that the policyholder is entitled to be put in the same position as if the mistake had not been made. However, it is usual to apply the principle that the policyholder ought to mitigate his loss so far as reasonably practicable. Where the declaration of continuing good health could properly be made, therefore, the policyholder would be well advised to make it, since it costs him nothing to do so, and will presumably put an end to the problem. In such cases policyholders frequently become angry with the company and refuse to do anything to alleviate the situation. Understandable though this may be, it is a failure to mitigate and is therefore likely to be taken into account when assessing the compensation due if the policy subsequently lapses. Where the declaration of continuing good health is not possible, the policyholder is perhaps in a stronger position, since there is less he can do to help the company out of any difficulties which it may be facing, though it must be added that there is no justification for the response of some policyholders, who in this situation suspend payment of premiums entirely. Another argument which is tried occasionally in these cases, but which did not find favour with the PIAOB, is that this evidence of inefficiency in the company has caused the policyholder to lose confidence in the company entirely, and that he ought to be entitled to cancel the policy and recover all his premiums. Whatever the exact ambit of any continuing duty of utmost good faith[1] it seems impossible to argue that it extends to a duty of good administration. The problem of loss of LAPR has greatly diminished as the number of policies with LAPR declined. Twenty-one years after the abolition of the relief, it will only be the 25-year policies which can give rise to the problem.

[1] As to this see Chapter 13.

Standing order

14.6 The position would of course be different if the premiums were paid by standing order, since it is clear that in such cases the bank makes the payment acting as the policyholder's agent. As between policyholder and insurer the consequences of any error must therefore fall on the policyholder, whose only possible redress would be against the bank. However, the modern practice is to insist on direct debit rather than standing order, so this point is of declining importance.

Reminder notices

14.7 It is common practice for insurance companies to send reminder notices when instalments of premium are not paid. However, this is done for reasons of commercial advantage, and in the absence of a policy provision they are under no duty to do so, and the policyholder cannot rely on the lack of such notice to resist the lapsing of the policy. This rule appears to apply even where a company has sent such notices in the past but fails to do so on one occasion.

Policy provisions

14.8 It may be noted that many policies contain an express provision that the payment of the premiums is in any event the policyholder's responsibility. This clause is apparently intended to preclude the policyholder from relying on the company's failure to collect premiums by direct debit. This seems objectionable in principle where, as is usually the case, the company will only accept payment by direct debit, since it puts onto the policyholder the risk of a mistake by the company. Its legal status has not yet been tested, but it is suggested that a court could readily circumvent it if minded to do so. It would be possible to argue that the policyholder effectively makes the company his agent for the purposes of payment by authorising the use of the direct debit system. On the one hand this would mean that the policyholder must bear the consequences of any failure by the company to collect premiums; on the other hand the policyholder, as principal in this deemed agency relationship, would have a right of recourse against the company, as agent, for failure to perform the duties of the agency. Another unresolved question is what attitude the FSOS would take in cases of this kind, but it is suggested that the obvious inequity of allowing the company to rely on the clauses in these circumstances is a strong pointer to the likely outcome.

Industrial assurance cases[1]

14.9 In the case of Industrial Branch policies the most usual reason for failure of collection is that the collector has left the company and has not been replaced immediately[1]. It is then easy for policy arrears to be built up. There appear to be relatively few cases of companies attempting to treat policies as lapsed or paid up in these circumstances, and most of the problems which arise relate to policyholders complaining about non-collection of premiums or seeking to have arrears of premium written off. The policy will normally contain an express clause making payment of premiums the responsibility of the policyholder. Although it would be inequitable to treat the policy as lapsed or paid up in these cases, there is no reason to allow any write off of premium arrears; some companies are apparently willing to negotiate extended periods for the clearing of the arrears, usually without interest, and this seems an entirely equitable solution.

1 It may be noted that as long ago as 1931 the Cohen Committee recommended the enactment of a general rule that in these cases companies must make reasonable efforts to collect the premiums, but this was never done.

Days of grace

14.10 It is customary in insurance policies (both general and long-term) to allow a certain period beyond the contractual due date within which the premium may be paid. These extra days are referred to as the 'days of grace'. Where they are included in the terms of the policy, the insured is entitled to wait until the end of the days of grace before paying, and this ceases to be a matter of discretion on the part of the insurers. Where the life assured dies during the days of grace, the policy moneys are still payable, at least where the policy is expressed to continue until the end of the days of grace[1], though the unpaid premium should of course be deducted. This appears to be the usual practice at the present day.

1 *Stuart v Freeman* [1903] 1 KB 47.

Reinstatement

14.11 An area requiring careful attention is reinstatement of a policy which has already lapsed. The first point is to be clear which cases fall within this category. Where only moderate arrears of premium have been built up (usually less than three months) the policyholder is usually entitled under the terms of the policy to restore the full value of the policy by paying the arrears. This does not normally require the consent of the company, nor is it usually dependent upon the completion of a new proposal form or even in a life policy on the making of a Declaration of Continuing Good Health. Cases of this kind are not cases of reinstatement within the meaning of the present section, for the policyholder is simply correcting a minor error which has arisen, namely the arrears of premium.

Reinstatement as understood here arises only where the policy has already lapsed by reason of non-payment of premiums. The distinction between reinstatement and the creation of a new policy may be important because a claim has arisen since the lapse or because the cover is for some reason no longer available on the original terms. In the case of investment policies there is the further point that accrued investment benefits will be lost if the policy is not reinstated. General insurance policies normally have no provision for reinstatement, which is thus effectively left at the discretion of the insurer.

Life policies commonly provide for reinstatement within a certain further period on the completion of some further formality, usually a Declaration of Continuing Good Health, more rarely a Private Medical Attendant's Report or, even more rarely, the completion of a new proposal. In these cases it is important to know what is the correct legal analysis of what the parties are doing, for problems may arise where there is some irregularity in relation to the required formalities.

Reinstatement under express policy provision

14.12 Where reinstatement takes place under an express policy provision, the better view is probably that this amounts to the creation of a new contract, but that the insurer is not entitled to decline this contract, provided that the insured complies with the requirements contained in the original policy. The original policy may in effect be regarded as conferring on the policyholder an option to take out a new contract in these circumstances[1]. However, the fact that this is a new contract gives rise to certain questions. To what extent do the duties imposed on the policyholder in relation to the creation of a contract of insurance, ie the duty of disclosure, apply to the formation of this contract? The question is especially important and difficult because there will not normally be a proposal form. There may have been changes in material circumstances since the original contract was entered into. To the extent that these relate to questions of health they can be dealt with by means of the Declaration of Continuing Good Health, but if they relate to other matters this will not apply. It might be argued that the new contract brings into play all the legal rules, including the rule that the duty of disclosure is independent of the proposal form. It is submitted, however, that this is not correct. Where the original policy stipulates a procedure for reinstatement, the policyholder is entitled to the new policy so long as he complies with that procedure, and the procedure laid down by the contract is to be regarded as replacing the normal procedure for the formation of a contract of insurance. Thus, if the reinstatement procedure does not include the completion of a proposal form, it is to be assumed that questions as to health which might normally appear on such a form but which are not asked are not regarded by the insurers as relevant and failure to disclose facts relating to them cannot be a ground for avoiding the policy. This conclusion is also consistent with the Statements of Insurance Practice, which require[2] insurers to ask express questions about matters which have generally been found to be material.

Although these Statements do not have the force of law, the FSOS will continue the IOB and PIAOB practice of giving great weight to them and will not allow insurers to depart from what he regards as being the spirit of the Statements. In cases where there is no proposal form the IOB and PIAOB have been prepared to hold that insurers may not rely on any non-disclosure.

[1] Clarke *The Law of Insurance Contracts* (1999, LLP), para 11–4C; in the case of an investment policy it will be necessary to imply the further term that the accrued investment benefits of the original contract are to be preserved.
[2] Clause 1.

Reinstatement obtained by fraud

14.13 Although the above principle works well enough in the majority of cases, it may appear to produce unjust results where there is some element of fraud in the reinstatement. It would be possible to argue that the procedure for reinstatement contained in the contract excludes the very strict duty of disclosure normally imposed in relation to insurance contracts, but does not supplant the ordinary contractual rules against active misrepresentations. The point is as yet untested in any legal decision, but in a case in 1992 with facts of this kind, the Insurance Ombudsman held that the reinstated policy was vitiated by the fraud of the policyholder in relation to the reinstatement process. This was a strong case since fraud was involved, but it is suggested that any active misrepresentation would lead to the same result, provided of course that it related to a material fact and that the answer to it had caused the insurer to accept the proposal[1]. This outcome is obviously desirable, and it is thought likely that the FSO will adopt the same approach.

These problems are of course greatly reduced in those cases where a new proposal form is required. This very substantially strengthens the argument that there is a new policy, and the presence of the proposal form clearly brings the full duty of disclosure into operation.

[1] *Pan Atlantic Insurance Co Ltd v Pine Top Insurane Co Ltd* [1994] 3 All ER 581, HL.

Reinstatement as revival of original contract

14.14 An alternative analysis of reinstatement would be that it is merely a revival of the original contract. There is some support for this in the fact that the original policy terms will normally apply and in the case of an investment policy any accrued value in the policy will normally be restored. As against that it must be remembered that a lapsed policy which formerly qualified for LAPR cannot be reinstated with that relief, though that fact might plausibly be explained away as turning on a quirk of the taxation legislation. If this analysis is adopted, the question of the policyholder's duty at reinstatement becomes even more problematic. There is no obvious reason to impose any duties on the policyholder beyond those stipulated in the policy, and it might seem that this would apply even to matters of fraud. However, there is one way in which this difficulty can be circumvented, which is by reference to the concept of the continuing duty of utmost good faith[1]. If it is accepted that this duty exists, then it might be possible to apply it to this situation. The obvious difficulty is that immediately prior to the reinstatement there is apparently no policy in force, since it has lapsed. Two possible answers to this suggest themselves. The first is that the policy is merely in suspense for so long as its own provisions allow it to be reinstated in this way, though this is somewhat contrived. The second requires a more robust, but perhaps more honest approach. It is that this is a special situation in the law of insurance unlike any other, and that special rules have to be created to deal with it. Clearly the appropriate rules are that the duty of utmost good faith applies to the situation. There is no authority either for or against this approach, and a court might be reluctant to accept the creation of a completely new type of situation. Consequently, it is suggested that this situation will have to be fitted into one of the first two analyses suggested above. However, consideration of the contrivances produced by the analysis that there is no new contract points quite strongly to the advantages of holding that there is a new contract, and it is submitted that this is the better view.

[1] This is explored at length in Chapter 13.

Failure of payment under assigned policies

14.15 The assignment of a policy does not automatically transfer liability for paying the premiums to the assignee, although it is the assignee who is most likely to be prejudiced if premiums are not paid. Two situations must be distinguished. The first is where the transaction giving rise to the assignment (often a loan) is conducted on the basis that the original policyholder will continue to pay the premiums. Here the terms of the assignment should expressly require the original holder of the policy to keep up the payments. A failure to make the payments may give the lender a remedy against the borrower, but it will not give any remedy against the insurer where the policy has lapsed. This difficulty may be circumvented by making the lender and the insurer parties to a single overall agreement in which the insurer undertakes to inform the lender if the premiums fall into arrears[1]. Many insurers do as a matter of practice copy premium reminder notices to assignees of policies, but it is suggested that the practice is not sufficiently common to be regarded as a custom having the force of law. Note here that it is not sufficient to require notice once the policy has lapsed, since it is by then too late to do anything to remedy the situation. Where the insurer does not comply with this undertaking there is on the face of it a breach of contract, for which damages may be recovered. However, identifying the loss suffered by the lender is not always easy. So long as the borrower pays the instalments on the loan, there is no substantial loss, though there is the theoretical weakening of the lender's position in that it has lost the security of the life policy. If the borrower dies, the loss may be more evident, though it must of course be remembered that the borrower's estate remains liable on the loan, and that the lender's position is in the end worsened only if the estate cannot pay the loan. Many such arrangements will involve mortgages of real property, and the normal solution in such a case would be to sell the property. In these circumstances the only loss would be suffered by the policyholder's estate, which might otherwise have expected the loan to be repaid out of the policy money, so that the property would not have to be sold. Unfortunately, the insurer's undertaking will not be given to the policyholder, so the policyholder cannot sue in contract for breach of it, and the deliberate choice to give the undertaking only to the insurer is likely to lead to the conclusion that the policyholder has no action in tort either.

If the policyholder's estate is not able to pay in full, then it appears that the lender would be able to sue the insurer, but it is necessary to ask exactly what is being claimed. The answer is presumably not the policy money, since the policy has lapsed. Rather, the claim is for the loss caused to the lender by the failure to give notice of the arrears of premium. There can be loss only if the lender is able to establish that on the giving of notice, it would have been able to take some effective action to prevent the policy from lapsing. The most effective action available in such a case would be to pay the arrears of premium on behalf of the borrower.

Although it is far from clear that in such circumstances those premiums could be recovered from the borrower, the lender might well see the payment of the premiums as a sound commercial decision – in many policies the premiums for a few months will be trivial compared with the sum assured. Where this hurdle can be circumvented the loss is the difference between the amount owing and the amount which can be recovered from the policyholder's estate. An important consequence of this is that there will never be any surplus to be paid over to the policyholder's estate.

The second situation is the increasingly common one of the sale (perhaps at auction) of an endowment policy which has not yet matured. This practice does not violate the rules on insurable interest, since the policyholder need only have an interest at the time when the policy is taken out[2]. In this situation it is contemplated that the assignees will pay the future premiums, the capital sum paid for the policy representing only the market price of the accrued surrender value coupled with the potential for future growth. Thus, the original policyholder has no further liability on the policy once it is sold.

[1] This may be seen as an analogy with the marine case of *The Good Luck* [1990] 3 All ER 1, HL where the insurers undertook to inform the bank if they ceased to insure the vessel, and were held liable in damages for failure to do so.
[2] *Dalby v India and London Life Assurance* (1854) 15 CB 365; and see Chapter 4.

Lapse for non-renewal

14.16 In the context of general business it is of course possible for the policy to lapse for non-renewal[1]. However, this is in effect the expiry of the policy by effluxion of time and is therefore not a case of lapse as that term is used in the present Chapter.

[1] Renewal generally is dealt with in Chapter 7; see also *Commercial Union Assurance Co plc v Sun Alliance Insurance Group plc* [1992] 1 Lloyd's Rep 475.

Chapter 15

Assignment of policies

The concept of assignment

15.1 The possibility of assigning rights under a contract has long been recognised by English law, despite the conceptual confusion involved in treating personal obligations as though they were property. At the present day the important questions are how the assignment is to be effected and what effect the assignment has on each of the three parties concerned, assignor, assignee and obligor. Further difficulties are likely to be created where there are attempts to assign the same property more than once. The discussion of these questions in an insurance context is made more difficult by the fact that assignments may be made in equity, under the Law of Property Act 1925 ('LPA 1925'), under the Policies of Assurance Act 1867 ('PAA 1867') (life policies only) or under s 50 of the MIA 1906 (marine policies only). Assignment is principally, though not exclusively, of importance in relation to life policies, and in these cases the PAA 1867 is the method most commonly used.

Assignment at common law

15.2 The common law did not recognise assignment of choses in action, such as the rights accruing under an insurance policy, though it did accept novation. The difference between the two processes is that novation requires the agreement and participation of all three parties – former creditor, new creditor and debtor, whereas assignment does not. At the present day there are enough effective ways of assigning the benefit of a policy of insurance to make novation a matter of no practical importance.

Equitable assignment

15.3 Equity was always more flexible than the common law, and was accordingly more willing to recognise assignments of choses in action. However, equity was rightly concerned to protect the interests of all parties, and therefore insisted that an action arising from the assignment of a legal chose in action be brought at common law by the assignee using the name of the assignor. Following the fusion of law and equity this rule has been replaced by a requirement that the assignor be a party to the action, either as co-claimant or as co-defendant[1]. The practical point is that the assignor should be bound by the result of the action, and for this purpose he has to be a party to the action in some capacity. If the chose assigned is itself equitable, then the possibility of a subsequent action at law by the assignor against the obligor does not exist, with the result that there is no objection to the assignee suing in his own name, nor is it necessary that the assignor be a party to the action. Although most assignments of life policies are now made under statute, the question of equitable assignment can still arise where the formalities necessary for a valid statutory assignment have not been complied with. The difficulties resulting from successive equitable assignments of the same chose in action are considered below.

[1] *Weddell v Pearce & Major* [1988] Ch 26.

Statutory assignment

15.4 Section 136(1) of the LPA 1925[1] allows the assignment of any legal (as distinct from equitable[2]) chose in action to be effective to pass the legal right to the assignee, provided that the assignment is made in writing and that express written notice of the assignment has been given to the obligor. The assignment must be absolute (ie the assignor must not retain any interest in the property) must not be by way of charge or security and must be of the whole of the rights which the assignor previously held. Assignments of policies of assurance under these provisions may occasionally be encountered, In comparing the requirements of s 136 with those of the PAA 1867, considered below, it will be seen that the LPA 1925 does not require the assignor to have a good equitable title to the policy. The LPA 1925 is therefore likely to be used for a transfer of the legal title by persons already holding the policy on trust.

[1] This re-enacts s 25(6) of the Judicature Act 1873.
[2] *Torkington v Magee* [1902] 2 KB 427, CA.

Assignments of life policies

Modern practice

15.5 The assignment of life policies is an extremely common event. It occurs most frequently in connection with endowment mortgages. Such mortgages are required to be protected by a life policy designed to pay off the mortgage should the borrower die before the mortgage term expires, and to produce a capital sum sufficient to achieve the same result should the borrower survive to maturity, though in most versions of endowment policy the latter outcome is not guaranteed. Under the PAA 1867 it is possible to assign the benefit of a life policy to another, provided that the proper form is adopted. The assignment of the benefit of the policy does not relieve the original assured of the duty to pay the premiums.

Proof of Assignment

15.6 This is normally achieved by producing the original policy together with the original assignment(s), though it is in each case a question of fact whether sufficient evidence has been produced, and it may for example be sufficient to have notice of assignment together with evidence that the validity of the assignment has been accepted by the assignor[1].

[1] *NM Rothschild & Sons (CI) Ltd v Equitable Life Assurance Society* [2003] Lloyd's Rep IR 371, Cooke J.

The Policies of Assurance Act 1867

15.7 This Act allows for the making of a legal (as distinct from a purely equitable) assignment of a life policy. However, s 1 of the Act imposes the requirements that the assignee must have a good equitable title, that the assignment is executed in writing and that written notice thereof is given to the insurer. The second and third requirements are of course familiar from the discussion above of s 136 of the LPA 1925, but the first requirement is not found in that section.

Good equitable title

15.8 This must be understood as relating to the position in equity before the coming into force of the Judicature Acts 1873–75. The question is whether the assignee has such a title as would have allowed him to enforce the contract in a court of equity, or, in other words, is he beneficially entitled to the policy proceeds. Most of the difficult cases in this area turn on the validity or otherwise of equitable assignments. This occurs because the person claiming to be entitled may have acquired his rights under a written assignment complying with the PAA 1867, but from a person whose own title depends on the validity of an earlier equitable assignment. The cases discussed in the following paragraphs give some indication of the range of problems which have arisen here, and of the ways in which the law has dealt with them. Although not all these cases concern insurance policies, the general principles of equitable assignments appear to be the same in all cases of the assignment of choses in action.

In *Ashley v Ashley*[1] there were two successive assignments of a life policy; the first one was gratuitous, the second was for value. The question was whether the second assignee could enforce the policy. It was held that he could. Such assignments are allowed under the Judicature Acts, and there is no problem in principle about successive assignments or about gratuitous assignments. Thus, a gratuitous assignment may be one of a chain of assignments giving a good title to the ultimate holder.

In *Dearle v Hall*[2] there were successive assignments of the same interest under a trust fund. The first assignee did not give notice to the trustees. When the second assignment was proposed, the prospective assignee checked with the trustees, who said, truthfully, that they had no knowledge of any prior assignment. The second assignee gave the trustees notice of assignment. The case was a dispute between the two assignees about order of priority. It was held that the second assignee had the better claim to the fund, being a *bona fide* purchaser for value without notice of the prior interest. It is irrelevant for these purposes whether the vendor's interest is contingent, present or reversionary. This case may be contrasted with *Spencer v Clarke*[3], where the policyholder gave an equitable mortgage of a policy by depositing it with A, who did not give notice to the company. Later the policyholder persuaded B to lend money on the faith of a promise to deliver the policy document and create an effective mortgage of it. B gave notice to the company. The policyholder was never able to comply with this and died without retrieving the document from A. It was held that A's title must prevail. In the circumstances B had constructive notice that there might well be another policy and could not rely on A's failure to give notice to the company. The distinction between the two cases turns on the knowledge to be imputed to the second assignee. In the absence of other circumstances he is entitled to assume that there is no other assignment, especially if he specifically asks the trustees about this; on the other hand, the existence of suspicious circumstances, such as the unavailability of the policy document, will almost always put the second assignee on notice. It is suggested that the result in *Spencer v Clarke* would have been the same even if B had asked the company about previous assignments, for he should still have been suspicious of the absence of the policy document, and therefore could not claim to be without constructive notice of the earlier assignment.

In *William Brandt's Sons & Co v Dunlop Rubber Co Ltd*[4] sellers of goods directed the purchasers to pay the price direct to the sellers' bankers; the purchasers signed an undertaking to do so. By oversight the money was paid to the wrong bankers. It was held that there had been a valid equitable assignment of the debt for the purposes of the Judicature Act 1873[5], with the result that the assignee bank was entitled to claim the debt and the payment to the wrong party was not a valid discharge. This would have been a valid assignment before the Judicature Act, which only added new ways of making such assignments and did not take away any existing mechanism.

In *Burlinson v Hall*[6] there was an assignment of a debt on terms that the assignee should use the proceeds to discharge a debt owed to him by the assignor and should account to the assignor for the surplus. It was held that this was nevertheless an absolute assignment not purporting to be by way of charge only for the purposes of the Judicature Acts. This apparently surprising decision may be justified on the grounds that the assignee was to be entitled to claim the whole of the debt from the debtor, the assignor's claim against the debtor disappearing entirely, to be replaced by a claim against the assignee for the surplus.

In *Chapman v Chapman*[7] It was held that mere possession of title deeds, without any explanation of how they came to be held, is not sufficient to establish the existence of an equitable mortgage. Thus, it is not evidence of a valid equitable assignment.

In *Dufaur v Professional Life*[8] a life policy was to become void if the life assured should 'commit suicide' except that it would not be void against a person to whom it had been 'validly and effectually assigned'. The life killed himself while of unsound mind. It was held that 'valid and effectual assignment' included any legally valid assignment, ie any assignment which would be recognised in court, rather than one effective at law as distinct from in equity, and this covered equitable charge by mere deposit without notice to the company. The decision appears to be a sensible interpretation of the words used, though it may also be suggested that the court was reluctant to penalise an innocent assignee.

In *Howes v Prudential*[9] a man took out an own life policy and gave the policy document to his wife, on condition that she paid the premiums. She duly did so. When the man died he left his estate to the claimant (not his widow) and the question was whether this bequest included the policy. It was held that it did, since mere delivery of the policy document without more was not enough to effect an assignment of it, even if it was his intention to assign the policy by giving the document to his wife.

1 (1829) 3 Sim 149.
2 (1823) 3 Russ 1, 38 ER 475.
3 (1878) 9 Ch D 137, V-C Hall.
4 [1905] AC 454, HL.
5 The PAA 1867 was of course irrelevant because this was not a case of an insurance policy.
6 (1884) 12 QBD 347, DC.
7 (1851) 13 Beav 308, 51 ER 119.
8 (1858) 25 Beav 599, Romilly MR.
9 (1883) 48 LT 133, Lopes J.

Effect of equitable assignment

15.9 A powerful reason for using a legal assignment rather than an equitable one whenever possible is that only a legal assignment can give the assignee the right to sue on the policy using solely his own name. After an equitable assignment the action must be brought by assignor and assignee jointly. It follows that in such a case the insurer should require a joint discharge from the two parties before paying out on the policy.

The 1867 Act

15.10 These cases collectively illustrate some of the difficulties of the traditional methods of assignment – the question of giving notice to the debtor causes more problems than anything else, and successive assignments of the same interest by the same person naturally cause other difficulties. Next it is necessary to examine in detail the modes of assignment permitted under the PAA 1867.

Assignment in writing

15.11 Section 5 of the PAA 1867 Act provides that an assignment for the purposes of this Act may be made by endorsement on the policy or by a separate instrument to the same effect as that set out in the Schedule to the Act (reproduced as Appendix 1 to this work). It is clear that a valid assignment may only be made by one or other of these methods, both of which involve writing. It therefore follows that a purely oral assignment cannot be effective under the Act. It should also be noted that it is not necessary to follow exactly the form of words used in the Schedule to the Act, so long as the words used are to the same effect. For the sake of safety and certainty, however, it is obviously prudent to follow those words as closely as the circumstances of the case permit.

Written notice to insurer

15.12 Section 3 of the Act requires that a written notice of the date and purport of the assignment shall be given to the insurer. The notice is to be given at the insurer's principal place of business (or at any one of them if there be more than one). Section 4 of the Act requires the company to state on every policy the address of its principal place or places of business, at which such notices may be given, though the Act does not provide any sanction for breaches of this requirement. Until due notice is given, the assignee does not acquire the right to sue at law (though any equitable right he might have is unaffected). It follows that until such notice is given, the company may properly pay the policy proceeds to the assignor, and s 3 expressly states that any payment made bona fide before the receipt of such a notice is as valid against the assignee as if the PAA 1867 had not been passed. It is to be supposed that in such a case the assignor would hold the proceeds on trust for the assignee, but the assignee's remedy would have to lie against the assignor rather than against the obligor.

Position of assignee

15.13 The assignee is entitled to enforce the policy as against the company, provided of course that the formalities discussed above have been duly complied with. An action brought on the policy should be brought in the name of the assignee[1] Whether the assignee becomes responsible for the payment of the premiums depends on the arrangement between assignor and assignee, though such an arrangement is of course effective only between those two parties, since the burden of the contract cannot be transferred from assignor to assignee without the consent of the insurance company, a process which would require a novation.

The assignment of the policy does not affect the rule that the policy is liable to lapse if premiums are not paid. It may of course be that the premiums are no longer being paid by the person beneficially entitled to the policy, but this is not a matter with which the insurer need be concerned – any remedy of the assignee in the case of lapse for non-payment would have to lie against the assignor.

[1] PAA 1867, s 1.

Position of assignor

15.14 Under the PAA 1867 it is necessary to give notice to the insurer that the policy has been assigned. Until this is done the insurer is not bound to deal with the assignee. Where due notice has been given, the insurer should deal only with the assignee in relation to payments of claims under the policy. Until such notice is given, the insurer should normally insist on dealing with the original policyholder.

Relationship between assignor and assignee

15.15 In most cases it will be a term of the agreement (normally a mortgage) between the policyholder and the assignee that the former must continue to pay the premiums. In some cases the agreement may be that the assignee will reimburse these payments, or even that the assignee must himself be responsible for the payments. However, this is not a problem with which the insurance company needs to be concerned. This position would continue even in the case of successive assignments.

Is consideration necessary?

15.16 Some writers[1] have discussed at length the question whether consideration is necessary to support an assignment. Although the question is of some interest in relation to assignments generally, it is of little relevance in the context of insurance. First, it is clear that assignments made under statute do not have to be supported by consideration, since the relevant statutory provisions[2] list exhaustively the requirements of a valid assignment and do not mention consideration. This deals with the vast majority of assignments of life policies. As to equitable assignments it should be noted that the obligor has in any event no interest in the presence or absence of consideration, and must pay the assignee once he has notice of the assignment. The question is relevant only between assignor and assignee, and then only if the assignor is called upon to take some further step such as turning the equitable assignment into a statutory one and refuses to do so. In such a case the balance of authority[3] suggests that he will not be compelled to make good the assignment.

1 Notably Treitel in *The Law of Contract* (9th edn, Sweet and Maxwell), pp 585–592.
2 LPA 1925, s 136(1) and PAA 1867, s 1.
3 *Milroy v Lord* (1862) 4 De GF & J 264 is the leading authority.

Receipt for notice of assignment

15.17 Section 6 of the PAA 1867 requires the insurer, upon request of the person giving notice of the assignment, to issue a receipt for that notice. A receipt signed by the Manager, Secretary, Treasurer or other principal officer of the insurer is conclusive evidence against the insurer of the notice having been received by the insurer.

Assignment before notice

15.18 Section 3 of the PAA 1867 makes a payment by the insurer before receiving a proper notice of assignment valid against the assignee in the same way as if the PAA 1867 had not been passed. In such a case the assignee cannot still claim the money from the insurer, but must seek redress from the assignor.

Successive assignments

15.19 Problems may arise where the insurer receives notice of a number of assignments of the same interest. Where all assignments are of the same type (ie all statutory or all equitable) the first notice will prevail. The insurer can properly pay to the first assignee, and, it is submitted, cannot properly pay to the second assignee. Where one assignment is equitable and the other statutory, the position depends on the order in which they come. If the first assignment is statutory, evidence of a subsequent equitable assignment should not be accepted. The only proper course is to pay to the holder under the statutory assignment. Where the first assignment was equitable, the position is more difficult. Although on the face of it the statutory assignment is valid, it must be remembered that this is so only if it the assignee is a person who has a good equitable title[1], and this will depend on that person having no constructive notice of the earlier equitable assignment. The insurer is here in a difficult position, for it is not possible to know who is entitled to the money without investigating the state of mind and knowledge of the second assignee at the date of the assignment. it is suggested that this is a case for making a payment of the money into court under the Life Insurance Companies (Payments into Court) Act 1896, and leaving the two assignees to dispute title to the money between themselves.

[1] PAA 1867, s 4.

Assignment of non-life policies

15.20 The practical importance of this is relatively limited because there is less often any reason to assign a non-life policy. Transfers of insured property do not operate as automatic transfers of any insurance policy relating to that property. It is necessary to distinguish between an assignment of the policy and an assignment of an accrued claim under the policy. However, one common situation does arise in relation to ship financing, where a mortgagee bank usually takes an assignment of the owners' hull policy as collateral security[1]. However, it is important to bear in mind the rule that in cases not covered by the PAA the assignee may commence proceedings based on an equitable assignment, but may not obtain judgment until there is a legal assignment[2].

[1] It is usual for the mortgagee to also take out its own insurance policy to protect itself against the risk that the hull policy will be voidable for non-disclosure or breach of warranty by the owners.
[2] *Weddell v J.A. Pearce & Major* [1988] Ch 26, Scott J.

Assignment of the policy proceeds

15.21 This may happen either before or after the loss has occurred. Where it happens after the loss, this is a simple case of the assignment of a right of action, which is valid subject to the usual rules about such assignments[1]. Where it happens before loss, this is like the assignment of any other contractual right and should give rise to no difficulty. The policy is unaffected – the parties remain the same and their respective obligations are not altered. It follows from this that the behaviour of the policyholder after the assignment can affect the validity of the policy or the prospect of a successful claim[2]. It has even been held that the assignment is vaild notwithstanding an express prohibition on assignment[3], since the assignment does not destroy the personal character of the policy. However, this decision may be regarded as turning on its own facts and should perhaps not be accorded too much weight as a general principle at the present day.

1 See above.
2 As for example in the case of a failure to take reasonable care.
3 *Re Turcan* (1888) 40 Ch D 5, CA.

Assignment of the subject matter

15.22 This is primarily relevant in the case of tangible property (though intellectual property rights, for example, might also be capable of assignment). Where the subject matter is assigned, it is necessary to consider carefully the terms of the policy. Many policies will have an express term bringing the policy to an end in this event. This is common, for example, in motor policies, though it is usual for motor insurers to allow the substitution of a different vehicle in a motor policy, on the giving of notice and the payment of any necessary additional premium. Even where the policy does not contain a term bringing it to an end in these circumstances, questions of insurable interest and indemnity may arise. Insurable interest is relevant only in those cases to which the LAA 1774 applies[1]. Even where it is relevant, there remains the question whether the interest is required at the time of the loss or only at the time when the policy is taken out. By analogy with the MIA 1906[2] it might be thought that interest was required at the time of loss, though this cannot be regarded as definitively established. Fortunately, in virtually all these cases the application of the principle of indemnity should ensure that a sensible result is reached. An insured who by the time of loss has no further interest in the insured property is unlikely to suffer any loss, and the principle of indemnity will therefore prevent him from recovering under the policy.

However, a contract for the sale of property will not divest the policyholder of an insurable interest in the property, even though his equitable interest may have passed under the contract[3]. It also appears that in such a case the vendor will be able to recover the full value of the destroyed property[4], though presumably he would hold all or most of it on trust for the purchaser.

It may be that an unpaid vendor of personality retains an insurable interest even after the sale has been completed, based on the unpaid vendor's lien. However, this point must be regarded as doubtful in the absence of authority. If the policy is still valid, then once again the policy proceeds would have to be held on trust for the purchaser.

Some assignments happen by operation of law, as in the case of bankruptcy or death. However, in these cases the property and the policy are assigned simultaneously and to the same person. Rules as to insurable interest and as to indemnity are therefore not infringed, and, subject to any express policy term, the validity of the policy is unaffected.

[1] See Chapter 4 for a discussion of the possibility that the Act does not apply at all to indemnity policies.
[2] Section 6.
[3] *Collingridge v Royal Exchange* (1877) 3 QBD 173.
[4] See n 3 above.

Assignment of marine policies

15.23 Section 50 of the MIA 1906 provides:

> '(1) A marine policy is assignable unless it contains terms expressly prohibiting assignment. It may be assigned either before or after loss.
> (2) Where a marine policy has been assigned so as to pass the beneficial interest in such policy, the assignee of the policy is entitled to sue thereon in his own name; and the defendant is entitled to make any defence arising out of the contract which he would have been entitled to make if the action had been brought in the name of the person by or on behalf of whom the policy was effected.
> (3) A marine policy may be assigned by indorsement thereon or in other customary manner.'

This section allows a simpler method of assignment than the PAA 1867. In particular there is apparently no requirement to give notice of the assignment to the insurer, since simple indorsement is sufficient (though of course the giving of notice is likely to be a prudent step to take). Section 50(2) is a statutory mechanism by which the assignee is effectively substituted for the assignor. It offers the practical advantage that the assignor need not be a party to the action. However, the assignee, quite properly, cannot be in a better position against the insurer than was the assignor, since the insurer can rely upon any defence which would have been available against the assignor.

Assignment and the Ombudsman

15.24 The Rules of the FOS appear to have resolved problems which arose under their predecessor schemes about complaints by assignees of policies. The DISP section of the FSA Handbook contains the rules as to who is an eligible complainant, and, as with the old schemes, the starting point is that the complaint ought to be brought by someone who is or was a customer of the firm which is the subject of the complaint[1]. However, the rules also recognise the possibility of what are 'indirect complaints' and one of the bases on which such a complaint can be brought is that the complainant is a person on whom the legal right to benefit from a claim under a contract of insurance has been devolved by contract, statute or subrogation[2].

This obviously includes the case of an assignee, even an assignee for value, a category whose status was previously uncertain. The rules do not expressly say that an assignor loses the right to bring a complaint once the assignment is made, but it is suggested that the Ombudsman is unlikely to make an award in favour of a party who does not stand to suffer any loss as a result of whatever misconduct is alleged.

[1] DISP 2.4.7.
[2] DISP 2.4.12.

Assignment on trust

15.25 Where policies are written in trust for a third party, or where it is subsequently desired to create a trust of an existing policy, attention must be paid to the legal formalities.

In some cases the intention to create a trust is obvious, either because the proposal form includes a section declaring a trust or because the word trust is expressly used in a document declaring the intentions of the settlor. Unfortunately, matters are not always so well conducted, especially where the alleged creation of the trust happens after the policy has been created. The history of the law of trusts contains many cases where courts have had to consider whether a particular form of words is apt to create a trust. Ultimately, all these cases must be regarded as turning on their own individual circumstances[1], which makes it dangerous to rely too closely on the facts of any of them. A general point which may be extracted from them, however, is that courts have traditionally been reluctant to find that a trust has been created in the absence of clear words. Thus, where the policy moneys were expressed to be payable to the assured's godson[2], where the policy moneys were to be paid to the assured's son or his executors[3] and where the proposer completed the proposal form in his own name 'for my daughter'[4] it was held that there was insufficient evidence to establish the existence of a trust. On the other hand, phrases such as 'on behalf of and for the benefit of'[5] have been held to create effective trusts.

It must be remembered that under s 53 of the LPA 1925 any creation or disposition of an equitable interest is required to be in writing. Although this rule has no application to implied, constructive or resulting trusts, this will not save the creation of a trust of an insurance policy from the requirement of writing, since such trusts will always be express trusts. Another consequence is that the declaration of trust may attract stamp duty. In most cases, though, this will be of limited practical significance, since the kind of policy which is transferred into trust is usually an endowment policy, which will have very little value (if any) at the time of the transfer if the transferor follows the usual pattern of assigning the policy more or less as soon as it has come into force. Since stamp duty is charged *ad valorem* according to the value of the property transferred, a transfer of a newly executed life policy will attract only the nominal 50 pence stamp duty.

[1] *Re Webb, Barclays Bank Ltd v Webb* [1941] Ch 225, Farwell J.
[2] *Re Sinclair's Life Policy* [1938] Ch 799, Farwell J.
[3] *Re Foster, Hudson v Foster* [1938] 3 All ER 357.
[4] *Re Engelbach's Estate, Tibbetts v Englebach* [1924] 2 Ch 348.
[5] *Re Webb, Barclays Bank Ltd v Webb supra; Re Foster's Policy, Meneer v Foster* [1966] 1 WLR 222.

Trusts and insurable interest

15.26 The transfer into trust of a policy which has very recently been created may raise the question whether the original assured was ever the intended beneficiary.

This is important because of the need to name the beneficiary in the policy[1] and because of the requirement of insurable interest to create a valid life policy[2]. In practice, however, the trust device is commonly used in situations where it is obvious that the beneficiary under the trust was always the intended beneficiary and where that person clearly has no insurable interest. The most common example is where parents insure their own lives and the policy is written in trust for their children. It is common to find that the proposal form for the policy actually invites the proposers to consider writing the policy in trust. Although this practice appears to contravene totally the intention behind the LAA 1774, it is generally accepted at the present day.

[1] LAA 1774, s 2.
[2] LAA 1774, s 1.

Tax implications

15.27 The next point to be borne in mind concerns the tax implications of writing a policy in trust for someone else. The creation of such a policy will be a chargeable transfer for the purposes of inheritance tax under the Inheritance Tax Act 1984. It should be noted that a transfer into trust cannot be a Potentially Exempt Transfer under that legislation, and that it therefore attracts an immediate tax charge, though at half the rates normally applicable to chargeable transfers. In practice, though, this point is unlikely to be of great importance, since the value of most policies at the date of their creation will be very small, and it is the value of the asset transferred which determines the amount of tax paid in these cases. Indeed, the writing of a policy in trust provides an excellent example of prudent inheritance tax planning, since it involves giving away an appreciating asset.

Procedure after assignment

15.28 A trust created by the transfer of a life policy for the benefit of children of the settlor will commonly be an Accumulation and Maintenance Settlement under s 71 of the Inheritance Tax Act 1984. Where a policy has been transferred into such a trust, there are tax implications associated with the subsequent payment of premiums. If the settlor pays the premiums direct to the company, this does not involve a transfer into trust and is therefore only potentially exempt. By contrast, a payment of cash to the trustees to pay the premiums receives the more favourable tax treatment associated with this type of settlement. Such a payment will be exempt from inheritance tax.

The Married Women's Property Act 1882

15.29 This Act was passed at a time when married women did not have full contractual capacity[1]. By s 11 it allowed married women to effect policies on their own lives for their own benefit or for the benefit of their spouse and/or children. At the present day, however, the more important part of this section is that which deals with the consequences of effecting such policies. The policy does not form part of the estate of the women concerned, and is therefore not subject to her debts. The policy moneys therefore go to the intended beneficiaries even where the estate is insolvent. The only exception to this principle occurs where the policy is effected fraudulently or with the intention of defeating the creditors of the policyholder. In such a case the creditors have a claim on the policy proceeds for the premiums paid, but no more. Trustees appointed for a trust under s 11 are empowered to give a valid receipt for the policy proceeds.

[1] A status which they finally achieved with the Law Reform (Married Women and Tortfeasors) Act 1935.

Title to policy document

15.30 The ownership of the policy document should be carefully distinguished from entitlement to benefit under the policy. In *Rummens v Hare*[1] P had purported to assign a policy to D by mere delivery. After his death his widow sued for detinue of the policy document. It was held that the action must fail. Although the assignment of the policy was obviously ineffective, title to the document itself could pass by mere delivery and had done so here. Similarly, a solicitor may claim a lien (a possessory rather than a proprietary right) for unpaid costs over a policy document in his possession even though he has no claim to the proceeds of the policy.

[1] (1876) 1 Ex D 169, CA.

Other assignments

15.31 It has been assumed so far in dealing with life policies that the standard assignment operates between members of the same family and is done as a way of providing for future generations. In recent years it has become increasingly common for life policies to be sold at auction. This practice is most commonly adopted in relation to endowment policies, where the purchaser obtains the advantage of the surrender value which the vendor has been able to build up, and is able to continue payment of the premiums so as to bring the policy to maturity at the appropriate time. Once the policy has been properly assigned, it remains a policy on the life of the original life assured, but the assignee is entitled to the policy moneys if that life drops, and to the maturity value when the maturity date is reached. Although it would be possible in such a case to leave the assignor to continue to pay the premiums, this would not produce satisfactory results in most cases, since the usual reason for the sale of such policies is financial stringency, and in any case the assignor would have little interest in continuing to pay the premiums once he has ceased to be beneficially entitled to the proceeds. It is therefore usual for the purchaser to take over responsibility for payment of the premiums, the price paid for the policy being adjusted to reflect this.

Chapter 16

Construction of policies (including fairness of terms)

General principles

Common law

16.1 The construction of an insurance policy is no more than the interpretation of a contract. As such it is to be carried out in accordance with the ordinary principles of contractual interpretation in English law. The starting point is now the speech of Lord Hoffmann in *Investors Compensation Scheme Ltd v West Bromwich Building Society*[1]. This passage is of such importance that it is worth setting it out in full here:

> '(1) Interpretation is the ascertainment of the meaning which the document would convey to a reasonable person having all the background knowledge which would reasonably have been available to the parties in the situation in which they were at the time of the contract.
>
> (2) The background was famously referred to by Lord Wilberforce as the 'matrix of fact', but this phrase is, if anything, an understated description of what the background may include. Subject to the requirement that it should have been reasonably available to the parties and to the exception to be mentioned next, it includes absolutely anything which would have affected the way in which the language of the document would have been understood by a reasonable man.
>
> (3) The law excludes from the admissible background the previous negotiations of the parties and their declarations of subjective intent. They are admissible only in an action for rectification. The law makes this distinction for reasons of practical policy and, in this respect only, legal interpretation differs from the way we would interpret utterances in ordinary life. The boundaries of this exception are in some respects unclear. But this is not the occasion on which to explore them.
>
> (4) The meaning which a document (or any other utterance) would convey to a reasonable man is not the same thing as the meaning of its words. The meaning of words is a matter of dictionaries and grammars; the meaning of the document is what the parties using those words against the relevant background would reasonably have been understood to mean. The background may not merely enable the reasonable man to choose between the possible meanings of words

which are ambiguous but even (as occasionally happens in ordinary life) to conclude that the parties must, for whatever reason, have used the wrong words or syntax (see *Mannai Investment Co Ltd v Eagle Star Life Assurance Co Ltd* [1997] 3 All ER 352, [1997] 2 WLR 945).

(5) The 'rule' that words should be given their 'natural and ordinary meaning' reflects the commonsense proposition that we do not easily accept that people have made linguistic mistakes, particularly in formal documents. On the other hand, if one would nevertheless conclude from the background that something must have gone wrong with the language, the law does not require judges to attribute to the parties an intention which they plainly could not have had. Lord Diplock made this point more vigorously when he said in *Antaios Cia Naviera SA v Salen Rederierna AB, The Antaios* [1984] 3 All ER 229 at 233, [1985] AC 191 at 201: "... if detailed semantic and syntactical analysis of words in a commercial contract is going to lead to a conclusion that flouts business common sense, it must be made to yield to business common sense." '

However, the particular features of insurance policies require some amplification and modification of those principles, and these are explored in this Chapter.

[1] [1998] 1 All ER 98, HL; considered, among other places, in *GE Reinsurance Corporation v New Hampshire Insurance Co* [2004] Lloyd's Rep IR 404, CA.

16.2 It is clear that there is an element of discretion and judgment which is always involved in deciding what a contract means – the task cannot be a purely mechanical one[1].

The fact that the document is in writing involves the application of the principle that what has to be considered is the actual language used in the policy and in any documents which are contractual by virtue of being incorporated in the policy[2], this being the language which the parties themselves have chosen to express their bargain – *Forsikringsaktieselskapet Vesta v Butcher*[3]; *Hitchins (Hatfield) Ltd v Prudential Assurance Co Ltd*[4] If the words are clear, precise and unambiguous, effect must be given to them, however unreasonable the result may be – *New Hampshire Insurance Co v Strabag AG*[5] (collective insurance policy).

However, it is by no means easy to implement this principle in relation to insurance contracts, which are documents of undoubted complexity and normally in standard form.

The meaning of a word may be controlled by its context – *Youell v Bland Welch & Co Ltd*[6]; *Hitchens (Hatfield) Ltd v Prudential Assurance Co Ltd*[7].

[1] [1996] 5 Re LR 7 at 13.
[2] Relying on Lord Reid in *L Schuler AG v Wickman Machine Tool Sales Ltd* [1974] AC 235 at 251.
[3] [1989] AC 852, [1989] 1 All ER 402, HL.
[4] [1991] 2 Lloyd's Rep 580 at 586, CA, per Parker LJ.
[5] [1990] 2 Lloyd's Rep 61, CA.
[6] [1990] 2 Lloyd's Rep 423, CA.
[7] [1991] 2 Lloyd's Rep 580, CA.

Trade usage

16.3 As to the implication of a term on grounds of business efficacy or trade practice, see *Baker v Black Sea and Baltic General Insurance Co Ltd*[1]. That case must be regarded as unsatisfactory from this point of view, because much of the outcome seems to have depended upon exactly what was pleaded and what evidence was led. However, an important general point which may fairly be derived from it is that a court will require compelling evidence of a more or less universal practice within the relevant industry before being prepared to accept that a term can be implied on this basis.

1 [1998] 2 All ER 833, HL.

Alternative constructions

16.4 Where two constructions are possible, the one which tends to defeat the intention or to make it practically illusory will be rejected – *Commercial Union Assurance Co plc v Sun Alliance Group plc*[1]. Where the printed parts of a non-marine insurance policy, and usually the written parts, are produced by the insurers, it is their business to see that precision and clarity are attained and, if they fail to do so, the ambiguity will be resolved by adopting the construction favourable to the assured – *Hitchens (Hatfield) Ltd v Prudential Assurance plc*[2]. In cases of ambiguity the leaning will be in favour of the interpretation which tends to give business efficacy to the contract. Regard will also be had to the known or proved customs and usages – see *Anderson v Commercial Union Assurance Co plc*[3]. *Commercial Union Assurance Co plc v Sun Alliance Insurance Group plc*[4]. Courts are also likely to prefer an interpretation which gives continuous cover to one which creates gaps in the cover, since such gaps are in the ordinary course of things unlikely to accord with the intentions of the parties, though it cannot be said that there is a formal presumption to this effect[5]. Similarly, where there are separate layers to a policy, it will normally be assumed that the scope of the cover of the various layers, apart of course from the financial limits, is intended to be identical[6]. The argument that a particular provision is void for vagueness must be regarded as very much a last resort and one which a court will resist if at all possible[7].

1 [1992] 1 Lloyd's Rep 475.
2 [1991] 2 Lloyd's Rep 580, CA.
3 1998 SLT 826, Second Division.
4 [1992] 1 Lloyd's Rep 475.
5 *Eurodale Manufacturing Ltd v Ecclesiastical Insurance Office Plc* [2003] EWCA Civ 203, [2003] Lloyd's Rep IR 444.
6 *Friends Provident Life and Pensions Ltd v Sirius International Insurance Corpn* [2004] EWHC 1799 (Comm), [2005] Lloyd's Rep IR 135, Moore-Bick J.
7 *Charman v New Cap Reinsurance Corpn Ltd* [2004] Lloyd's Rep IR 373, CA.

Words with technical meaning

16.5 Where words are used which have some other technical legal meaning, they are to be interpreted according to that meaning, at any rate where the risk is situated in England – the principle is apparently to be applied with some flexibility in relation to risks situated abroad[1]. Some examples follow.

1 *Canelhas Comercio Importacao e Exportacao Ltd v Wooldridge* [2004] Lloyd's Rep IR 915, CA.

Riot

16.6 The word riot in a policy must be construed in accordance with the legal definition of that word, which is now contained in the Public Order Act 1986, namely 12 or more persons gathered together for an unlawful purpose[1].

[1] *London and Lancashire Fire Insurance Co v Bolands* [1924] AC 836, HL. Note that in those days the common law definition applied, and this required only three persons.

Theft

16.7 Where a policy refers to a loss by theft, the word must be interpreted in accordance with the meaning given to it in the Theft Acts 1968 and 1978[1]. Thus, an unlawful taking of a motor vehicle, contrary to s 12 of the Theft Act 1968 is not covered by such a clause, since this is not theft in the absence of an intention permanently to deprive the owner of the property[2]. For a detailed treatment of the meaning of 'theft' in insurance policies see *Dobson v General Accident Fire and Life Assurance Corpn plc*[3], where it was held that the appropriation of property by a rogue in exchange for a stolen building society cheque amounted to theft within the meaning of a household contents policy because the property did not at that moment belong to the rogue and the other elements of the statutory definition of theft were present. This seems to indicate clearly that the rule relating to technical legal meanings overrides any intentions of the parties, since the insurers almost certainly did not intend to cover this peril, and it is far from certain that any policyholder would have ever put his mind to the question.

A number of other relevant principles of construction may also be identified, though it must be said that these are no more than general principles, which may yield to other principles in appropriate cases, and which should therefore not be elevated to the status of hard and fast rules.

[1] *Grundy (Teddington) v Fulton* [1983] 1 Lloyd's Rep 16, CA.
[2] Though the resulting loss will be covered by a comprehensive policy. See also IOB 14.16, discussed below, where the technical meaning was not applied.
[3] [1989] 2 Lloyd's Rep 549, CA.

Robbery

16.8 In *Canelhas Comercio Importacao e Exportacao Ltd v Wooldridge*[1] the Court of Appeal had to construe a policy which had an exclusion for losses by 'Robbery' in relation to premises in Sao Paulo, Brazil. It appears to have common ground between the parties in this case that the term 'Robbery' was to be understood not as a technical term of English law but in the sense in which 'ordinary commercial men' would understand it. This case, and the case of *Langton*, to which it refers, seem to go against the general principle stated in this Chapter concerning the interpretation of technical words. It is interesting to note that in both cases the policyholders were foreign nationals, though it is not at all clear that this fact can be regarded as part of the *ratio* in either case.

[1] [2004] Lloyd's Rep IR 915, CA, relying on *Algemeene Bankvereeniging v Langton* [1935] 51 Lloyd's Law Reports 275, CA.

Contra proferentem

16.9 It is often said that as a general principle contractual documents should be construed *contra proferentem* ie against the interests of the party who drafted them. In the present context that will usually mean against the insurance company. This is an important principle, but it should not be taken too far, It does not mean that every document must always be construed in the way least favourable to the company. It merely allows for genuine ambiguities to be resolved in favour of the policyholder when other approaches fail. It must also be stressed that the principle is limited to *genuine* ambiguities – it is not proper to adopt a strained construction of the language in order to find an ambiguity which can then be resolved in favour of the policyholder[1]. A good example of the proper application of the principle may be found in a case decided by the Insurance Ombudsman in 1991, but which, it is submitted, would have been decided the same way by a court of law. A life policy contained an exclusion for death caused by 'alcoholism'. The policyholder went out to celebrate New Year's Eve and returned home drunk. After returning home he fell downstairs and died of the resulting injuries. The insurers sought to rely upon the exclusion, but it was held that they were liable on the policy. Although it was fairly clear that the death was caused by drunkenness, and although there was evidence that the policyholder was a heavy drinker, it was by no means clear that he could properly be called an alcoholic, far less that the alcoholism, as distinct from the one incident of drunkenness, was the cause of his death. If the insurer had wanted to exclude liability in any case where the insured was drunk at the time of death, then the policy wording should have been made much more explicit.

1 *Denby v Fuller* [1996] 5 Re LR 175, Waller J; *Eurodale Manufacturing Ltd v Ecclesiastical Insurance Office Plc* [2003] Lloyd's Rep IR 444, CA.

Written words to prevail over printed words

16.10 This principle applies in those cases where there is a standard form printed policy, which has been specifically altered to meet the needs of the particular case. The maxim is of importance in those situations where the standard form words and the specially inserted words appear to be in conflict with each other. In such cases it is obviously sensible to assume that the parties are more likely to have intended to apply the specially inserted words, though obviously even this presumption will be inapplicable if it would produce absurd results[1]. The reference to *written* words dates from the time when such alterations would normally be inserted in manuscript. Although there is no reason why this should not be done even today, it is more likely that the words will be typed, or even printed. In view of this it is suggested that the maxim might usefully be re-formulated as 'special provisions take precedence over general provisions'.

1 *Eurodale Manufacturing Ltd v Ecclesiastical Insurance Office Plc* [2003] Lloyd's Rep IR 444, CA.

Coverage and exceptions

16.11 It is initially for those claiming on the policy to prove that the insured event has happened. In the case of life polices this will normally mean only that death must be established. It is then for the insurer to establish any defence on which it wishes to rely, whether by way of public policy argument such as suicide or by way of excepted cause of death. The question of burden of proof will assume immense practical significance in those cases where the circumstances of the death are not clear, for it may be that little or nothing can be satisfactorily proved, in which case whichever party bears the relevant burden of proof will lose.

The Ombudsman's approach

16.12 The Insurance Ombudsman is not bound by strict rules of law in relation to the construction of policies. The approaches developed by Ombudsmen in the period prior to the inception of the FOS appear to have been continued by their successors.

Subjective construction

16.13 In applying the principle that the policy should give effect to the reasonable expectations of the insured it is necessary to ask what the individual policyholder understood the policy to mean. In many cases this will be of very limited value, since it is only rarely that the policyholder has seen the policy itself before the contract is entered into. In most instances the policyholder will have seen only the promotional literature and the proposal form. It may then be sought to argue that these documents should be regarded as incorporated into the policy. The proposal form will often be incorporated by express term, but the statements relied upon are more likely to be in the promotional literature, which will not normally be so incorporated. Although there have been insurance cases where these documents have been held to be incorporated[1] and such incorporation is of course possible as a matter of the general law of contract, it is submitted that this will rarely happen. The finding of a collateral contract is another possible way of dealing with this problem, but is submitted that modern courts are reluctant to resort to the device of a collateral contract. However, in those rare cases where the policyholder has seen the policy in advance or can be shown to have relied upon it in some way it may be possible to invoke this canon of construction.

[1] *Sun Life Assurance of Canada v Jervis* [1944] AC 111, HL.

Pre-contractual representations

16.14 In appropriate cases it may be possible to resolve ambiguities in the interpretation of the policy by asking what the policyholder was led to expect in the pre-contractual discussions. This is of particular importance when dealing with investment policies. It should be noted, though, that only in rare cases will the policy contain any provision as to investment return. consequently, complaints that the return has been less than was promised by the company representative in pre-contractual discussions will very rarely be supported by anything in the policy. Where the complaint is about misrepresentations as to the terms on which investment could be discontinued or the policy could be encashed, it is likely that the policy will contain express provisions, and the difficulty will be that these are inconsistent with what the policyholder claims to have been told before entering into the contract. Consequently, these cases too will involve no question of policy construction.

Hazardous activities

16.15 Although proposal forms commonly ask whether the proposed life assured engages or has any intention of engaging in hazardous activities, it is rare to find an express provision in the policy excluding liability in the event that death is caused by such an activity. Of course, death while undertaking a hazardous activity may well be evidence that a false answer was given to the relevant question on the form, so that the policy becomes voidable. It is therefore appropriate to consider what is meant by the phrase 'hazardous activity' or 'extra hazardous activity'. Unfortunately, this has not as yet been the subject of judicial interpretation. The phrase is by its nature imprecise, but it is suggested that it should be interpreted as relating primarily to leisure activities, since there will almost always be a separate question asking about the proposer's application. All activities are to some extent hazardous, and it is therefore necessary to find some sensible way of limiting the interpretation given to the phrase. The ambiguity of the phrase leads to the suggestion that it will be restrictively interpreted, but there is as yet no more definite authority on the subject.

Indisputable policies

16.16 The policy may provide that it is 'indisputable'. This is normally understood to mean only that it cannot be challenged for non-fraudulent non-disclosure. It does not prevent a challenge in the case of fraud[1]. Sometimes this will be made clear by stating that the policy is 'indisputable in the absence of fraud'. Although it might be thought that a policy which is merely described as 'indisputable' would be so under all circumstances, at least before the Insurance Ombudsman, it must be remembered that the Ombudsman acts in effect as a court of equity, and will therefore not assist a policyholder who has been guilty of fraud.

1 *Re General Provincial, ex p Daintree* (1870) 18 WR 396.

Security endorsements

16.17 The interpretation of security endorsements and inspection conditions in policies has been the subject of cases before the Insurance Ombudsman. In one such case[1] a household contents policy required all 'accessible' windows to be fitted with locks. Thieves gained access through a first-floor window via the drain and soil-pipe. The window had no lock, and the insurer therefore declined the claim. The policyholder argued that given the physical configuration of the house the window should not be regarded as having been accessible. From a legal point of view it might be thought that there was a simple answer to this contention, namely that the thieves had in fact gained access by this means, but in the event the

Insurance Ombudsman upheld the complaint on the basis that the policyholder could legitimately have believed that the window was not accessible. It was therefore not fair for the insurer to rely strictly on the wording of the endorsement. In the Ombudsman's view the insurer would have needed to bring specifically to the attention of the policyholder the need to obtain expert advice to identify all windows which could possibly be regarded as 'accessible'. The decision is very clearly an application of the fair and reasonable discretion, and it cannot be imagined that a court would come to the same conclusion.

A similar case[2] occurred in motor insurance, where a comprehensive policy was issued, subject to the proviso that cover would be third party only until the car had been inspected by the insurer's agent. The car was stolen before the inspection could take place. The Insurance Ombudsman held that the insurer must meet the claim. It appeared that the car was in fact in good condition – the policyholder was able to produce evidence to this effect – so that the inspection would have been only a formality. The premium charged had from the outset been based upon the notion that the cover was comprehensive. The result seems a sensible one, though it is again very unlikely that a court could possibly have reached it.

An IOB case on warranties occurred[3] in relation to a motor policy where the proposer was asked on the proposal form for the original policy where the car was usually left. At the time the policyholder rented a garage, so he replied that it was usually left in a locked garage. Over two years later the car was stolen, the policy having been renewed twice in the meantime. By this time the insured no longer had the use of the garage, and the car was stolen from the road outside his house. The insurer sought to rely upon a breach of policy requirements, but the Insurance Ombudsman upheld the policyholder's complaint. The policy contained no relevant condition or warranty, and the answer given on the proposal form could not be construed as amounting to a promissory warranty[4].

[1] IOB 10.19.
[2] IOB 10.20.
[3] IOB 14.7.
[4] See also *Hussain v Brown* [1996] 1 Lloyd's Rep 627.

Unattended

16.18 In *CTN Cash and Carry Ltd v General Accident Fire and Life Assurance Corpn plc*[1] the policyholders insured business premises. The policy included the following clause:

> 'It is warranted that the secure cash kiosk shall be attended and locked at all times during business hours.'

A robbery took place at a time when the kiosk had been left unattended for a short period, though it appeared likely that the robbery would have happened even if the kiosk had been attended at the material time. The judge held that the clause in question should not be regarded as being a promissory warranty, but rather a clause defining the risk[2]. As the clause was not being complied with at the time of the robbery, there could be no cover. The question of causation was of course irrelevant. It is interesting to see here a case in which a judge has refused to accept a clause as being a warranty even though it was expressly described as one. The point does not make any difference to the decision in the case itself, but it could be relevant if a robbery happened when the kiosk was attended, but there was evidence that it had on occasions been left unattended[3].

[1] [1989] 1 Lloyd's Rep 299, MacPherson J.
[2] Cf cases such as *Farr v Motor Traders Mutual* [1990] 3 KB 669, CA.
[3] It may be observed in passing that strict compliance with the wording was almost impossible in any case: if the kiosk had really been kept locked *at all times* during business hours, it would presumably have been necessary for the same person to staff it non-stop throughout the business day.

Forcible and violent entry

16.19 In *Dino Services Ltd v Prudential*[1] the policyholder was a car dealer who had insured his premises against theft, but the policy was expressed to apply only where entry to or exit from the premises was effected by 'forcible and violent means'. The policyholder's keys were abstracted from his possession, and the thieves used them to gain entry to the premises and make off with his stock of cars. His claim on the policy was rejected on the grounds that there had been no use of forcible and violent means. In analysing this phrase the Court of Appeal distinguished between that which is violent and that which is merely forcible. Forcible means are used where any element of force at all is used. Thus a person who turns a door handle in order to gain entry to a room uses forcible means, as does one who inserts the key in the lock and unlocks the door. However, neither of these methods is properly described as 'violent'; that requires some greater degree of force, usually implying that entry has been obtained in a way which is unusual and probably inappropriate in normal circumstances. A person who breaks down a door to gain entry thus uses violent means[2]. It followed that in the present case the means of access and departure had been forcible but not violent, and the policyholder's claim had to fail. The cases relied upon in reaching this decision are of some antiquity, and it was accepted by the Court of Appeal that the phrase is in modern terms an unhelpful one.

Another important aspect of the claims processing is construing the policy so as to ensure that the events which have happened do fall within the policy cover. Although the happening of death will only rarely be disputed, other problems may arise, and it is important to have some awareness of the general principles of construction.

[1] [1989] 1 All ER 422, CA.
[2] See also *Re Calf and Sun Insurance Office* [1920] 2 KB 366, CA; *Re George and Goldsmiths and General Burglary Insurance Association Ltd* [1899] 1 QB 595, CA; *Swales v Cox* [1981] QB 849.

Deliberately

16.20 An act is done 'deliberately' if it is done on purpose as opposed to accidentally. There is no requirement that it be directed at any particular person[1].

[1] *Tektrol Ltd v International Insurance Co of Hanover Ltd* [2005] 1 All ER (Comm) 132, Langley J.

Construction of policy – 'including ex-factory in PR China'

16.21 In *Wünsche Handelsgesellschaft International mbH v Tai Ping Insurance and Prudential Assurance*[1] the Court of Appeal considered the construction of an insurance policy taken out by the sellers and consigned to the Carriage Insurance and Freight ('CIF') buyer.

The cargo was transported from canning factories in inland China to a Chinese port and from there to warehouses at Hamburg. The alleged damage to the cargo occurred on the journey from the canning factories to the port. The question was whether the term in the policy providing *'including ex-factory in PR China to warehouse Hamburg'* covered the inland transport.

The court held that it did. It was held that the goods were covered from the canning plants and that there was no implied term that they were only covered while being carried in containers. It was said that one should not construe 'ex-factory PR China' as being limited to factories, much less warehouses, in the port or its immediate hinterland. The intention was said to be to insure the goods from the Chinese factories, where they were produced, to the warehouse in Hamburg.

[1] [1998] 2 Lloyd's Rep 8, CA.

Time policy – unseaworthiness warranty

16.22 In *Martin Maritime Ltd v Provident Capital Indemnity Ltd*[1] the court considered the effect of an apparently absolute warranty of seaworthiness in a time policy and also the question whether a rudder is machinery for the purposes of the Institute Machinery Damage Additional Deductible Clause.

The vessel had lost its rudder. It was common ground that this was caused as a result of negligence on the part of ship repairers at a dry docking predating the voyage. The questions were whether it was covered by the time policy and what was the correct deductible.

Dealing with each in turn:

(1) – The time policy in question included a general warranty that:

> '1. The following are warranties that must be complied with to maintain the insurance in effect. If these warranties are not complied with, the insurance will be suspended until the warranties are complied with. Any claims which occur during any period in which the insurance is suspended for failure to comply with these warranties will not be covered by this insurance.'

The specific warranties included warranty no 11 which provided:

> '11. Warranted that at the inception of this policy, the vessel named herein shall be in seaworthy condition and thereafter during the valid period of this policy, the insured

> shall exercise due diligence to keep the vessel seaworthy and in all respects fit, tight and properly manned, equipped and supplied.'

The policy in question incorporated the Institute Time Clauses Hulls 1 October 1983 which provide:

> '6.1 this insurance covers loss of or damage to the subject matter caused by …
> 6.2.2 bursting of boilers, breakage of shafts or any latent defence in the machinery or hull
> 6.2.3 negligence of master, officers, crew or pilots
> 6.2.4 negligence of repairers or charterers provided such repairers or charterers are not an assured hereunder … provided that such loss or damage has not resulted from want of due diligence by the assured, owners or managers.'

As to the question of whether warranty no 11 meant that as the vessel was unseaworthy at the time of inception of the policy there was no cover until it was rendered seaworthy, the court endeavoured to give meaning to both warranty no 11 and cl 6.2. of the Institute Time Clauses. It therefore held that warranty no 11 was worded in absolute but wholly general terms whereas cl 6 of the Institute Time Clauses dealt with certain identified perils which were specifically covered by the policy. The two were therefore interpreted to the effect that clause 6 provided, where appropriate, exceptions to the general terms in warranty no 11. This meant that the claim was covered.

(2) – The second question related to the additional machinery deductible in the policy which provided:

> 'Notwithstanding any provisions to the contrary in this insurance, a claim for loss of or damage to any machinery, shaft, electrical equipment or wiring, boiler, condenser, heating coil or associated pipework arising from any of the perils enumerated in clause 6.2.2 to 6.2.5 inclusive of the Institute Time Clauses Hulls or from fire or explosion when either has originated in the machinery space shall be subject to a deductible of …'

As to whether a rudder was 'machinery' in this clause, it was held that in the context in which the word 'machinery' appeared in the clause it was apt to refer to motors of various kinds including the motors and equipment which operate the vessel's steering gear and was not apt to refer to a vessel's rudder as such, since it should properly be regarded as a movable party of the hull rather than machinery.

[1] [1998] 2 Lloyd's Rep 652.

Aggregate extension clause

16.23 In *Yasuda Fire and Marine Insurance Company of Europe Ltd v Lloyd's Underwriting Syndicate No 229*[1] – the syndicates reinsured Yasuda by various whole account excess of loss agreements each of which contained an aggregate extension clause.

The clause provided:

'(1) As regards liability incurred by the reinsured for losses on risks covering on an aggregate basis, if required by the reinsured, this reinsurance shall protect the reinsured excess of the amounts as provided for herein in the aggregate any one such aggregate loss up to the limit of indemnity as provided for herein in all any one such aggregate loss.'

Yasuda was a participant in professional indemnity line slips arranged by JH Minet & Co Ltd. Various primary and excess policies of insurance binding upon Yasuda were issued under Minet professional indemnity ('MIPI') line slips to firms of solicitors and accountants.

The issue in the appeal from arbitration was whether for the purposes of determining the liability of the syndicates under the excess of loss agreements Yasuda was entitled to add together causally unconnected losses which it had paid under any particular MIPI policy and to present those losses to the syndicates as one loss. Yasuda would be so entitled if the underlying MIPI policy was to be regarded as a policy 'covering on an aggregate basis'.

The judge found that the risks under the MIPI policies covered on an each and every claim basis.

It was therefore held that an aggregate extension clause in a whole account excess of loss agreement, which protected the reinsured for liability incurred for 'losses on risks covering on an aggregate basis' did not cover an underlying professional indemnity policy which was expressed to cover on a per claim basis but which contained an aggregate limit or an aggregate deductible since it did not 'cover on an aggregate basis'.

1 [1998] Lloyd's Rep IR 285, CA.

Institute Frozen Meat Clauses

16.24 In *Hibernia Foods plc v McAuslin*[1] there were two slip policies by which the defendants agreed with the claimants to insure cargoes of frozen meat products declared by the claimants. The claimants' insured interest included export refunds as well as the meat itself.

The policy incorporated the Institute Frozen Meat Clauses and cl 8 provided, inter alia, that the insurance was to terminate on the expiry of 30 days in respect of frozen interests only after the final discharge of the goods from the vessel at the port of discharge.

The question arose whether this 30-day limit applied just to the meat itself or also to the loss of export refund caused by rejection of part of the cargo in Egypt and condemnation of part of the rejected cargo in Ireland.

It was held that the slip incorporated the Institute Clauses and extension clauses without distinguishing between the two interests which were being insured – the meat itself and the export refund. There was nothing in cl 8 itself which indicated that it was not applicable to both interests. It was. Both the export refund and the meat were insured by the same clause against the same risks and so the duration of the cover would be the same for both.

1 [1998] 1 Lloyd's Rep 310.

'Follow the leader' clauses

16.25 In *Roar Marine Ltd v Bimeh Iran Insurance Co*[1] the claimants sought summary judgment against the defendants as hull and machinery insurers for their proportion in respect of loss arising from an engine breakdown.

The hull and machinery insurance was spread over various co-insuring markets. Market A consisted of various Lloyd's underwriters and London companies; markets B, C, and D were elsewhere and the balance of the cover was placed with the defendants in Iran.

The terms on which markets B, C, and D and the defendants undertook to insure the vessel included a 'follow the leader' clause which stated inter alia:

> 'It is agreed with or without previous notice to follow leading British underwriters in regard to … settlements in respect of claims …'

The claimants' claim under the insurance was eventually settled by syndicate 724 on the basis that the breakdown had resulted from crew negligence. The claimants claimed against the defendants for their proportion of the loss.

The defendants denied that syndicate 724 was the leading British underwriter and/or said that by reason of the custom or practice of the London marine insurance market a follower was not obliged to pay on a claim falling outside the perils insured against irrespective of any settlements by the leading British underwriter and that they were not obliged to follow a settlement of a claim which had not been concluded in a proper business-like way.

It was held that:

- It was common ground that the leading British underwriters referred to the leading underwriters in market A. Lloyd's underwriters appeared first in the list of participants in market A and Syndicate 724 appeared first in the list of Lloyd's underwriters. The identity of the leading British underwriter was established beyond argument[2].
- For there to be any relevance in custom or practice it had to be possible to identify the custom or practice with some certainty. The matters put forward by the defendants were incapable of assisting and inadmissible. The defendants were seeking to contradict the commercial purpose of the clause – to simplify the administration and settlement of claims. The defendants had failed to show that they had any fair or reasonable probability or possibility of having a real or bona fide defence.
- There was no basis for further qualifying the follow my leader clause by providing that the settlement should be conducted in a proper and business-like way.

Accordingly, summary judgment was entered against the defendants.

[1] [1998] 1 Lloyd's Rep 423.
[2] Though there is still a minority view that 'leading underwriter' should be considered to refer to the underwriter taking the largest line, rather than to the one who appears first on the slip.

Exclusion clauses

16.26 In *Cook v Financial Insurance Co Ltd*[1] the claimant had seen his doctor for pain and breathlessness. The doctor could not diagnose the condition but referred the claimant to a cardiologist under a letter stating '... I would like to exclude angina.' The claimant entered into a contract for disability insurance on 15 October and on 16 October the cardiologist diagnosed angina.

The case turned on whether recovery under the policy was debarred by an exclusion clause dealing with a 'disability resulting from ... any sickness, disease, condition or injury for which [he] received advice, treatment or counselling from any registered medical practitioner during the 12 months preceding the commencement date [of the policy].'

The House of Lords was split 3:2. The minority were of the view that although undiagnosed at the time, the claimant had been suffering from a medical condition that was angina and in relation to which he had received advice and counselling. They could see no reason why in order to suffer a disability resulting from a condition the exact nature of that condition had to be identified.

The majority concentrated on the treatment for angina specifically and found that it was not suggested that the claimant had received counselling for angina prior to commencement of the policy. They were of the view that the claimant had not received treatment for angina nor advice for angina, but only advice in respect of symptoms that turned out to be those of angina. They held that 'condition' in the context of the clause meant a medical condition recognised as such by doctors and could not include symptoms of a generalised kind that might indicate any number of different diseases or none.

[1] [1999] Lloyd's Rep IR 1, HL.

Parties covered by insurance

16.27 In *Chrismas v Taylor Woodrow Civil Engineering Ltd and Sir Robert McAlpine Ltd*[1] the question was whether the charterers of a seabed platform who suffered loss when the platform was struck by a wave and the crane which it supported fell into the sea were owners within the insurance contract which covered persons becoming 'legally liable as owners'. It was held that the insurance contract did not apply as the provision relating to 'owner' should not necessarily be read as referring to charterer and owner. It meant that the charterer as insured was indemnified against any liabilities which the charterer might be under, against which an owner would be indemnified if sued as owner. The charterer became liable to remove the crane from the seabed as a result of the contract with the water authority and not as a result of its status as charterer.

1 [1997] 1 Lloyd's Rep 407.

The Unfair Terms in Consumer Contracts Directive[1]

16.28 This Directive required Member States to introduce into their law provisions striking down unfair terms in consumer contracts generally. English law did this originally by means of the UTCCR 1994[2], now replaced by the UTCCR 1999[3].

The following discussion must therefore be understood in the light of the fact that the regulations apply to all types of consumer contract. A consumer contract for these purposes is one between a seller or supplier and a consumer. 'Consumer' is defined[4] as a natural person who, in making the contract in question, is acting for purposes which are outside his business. In an insurance context this may be regarded as being for all practical purposes the same thing as a personal lines policy.

The scheme of the Directive is essentially[5] that terms in consumer contracts may be invalidated if, contrary to the requirement of good faith, they create a significant imbalance between the parties, to the detriment of the consumer[6]. However, terms are not subject to this test if they are 'core terms' and are expressed in plain, intelligible language[7]. It is provided that:

> '(2) In so far as it is in plain intelligible language, the assessment of fairness of a term shall not relate–
> (a) to the definition of the main subject matter of the contract, or
> (b) to the adequacy of the price of remuneration, as against the goods or services supplied in exchange[8].'

However, Recital 19 to the Directive declares that the logic of the Directive requires that in insurance contracts terms which define the risk or the insurer's liability should be covered. The existing literature in this field shows that the application of this principle is far from clear. First, it is uncertain what status the Recital has in the face of the apparently clear words of the Articles of the Directive. Secondly, it is unclear what is meant by defining the risk or the insurer's liability. There is, for example, dispute over whether warranties, especially promissory warranties, are clauses which define the risk. There is an exception in respect of any term that has been individually negotiated. A term is not individually negotiated where it is drafted in advance, and where the consumer has been unable to influence the substance of the term[9].

1 93/13/EEC. J Davey 'Unfair Terms In Consumer Insurance Contracts', paper delivered at 1997 *Insurance and the Law Conference* (Leeds University, 10 April 1997).
2 SI 1994/3159.
3 SI 1999/2083.
4 SI 1999/2083, reg 3.
5 For a fuller account see Adams and Brownsword *Key Issues in Contract Law* (1995, Butterworths), chap 8; Duffy [1993] JBL 67; Dean (1993) 56 MLR 581; Collins (1994) 14 OJLS 229; Brownsword & Howells [1995] JBL 243; and MacDonald [1994] JBL 243.
6 SI 1999/2083.

[7] SI 1999/2083, reg 6(2). Regulation 7 creates a specific obligation on the supplier to ensure that terms are in such language. However, breach of this obligation does not of itself appear to attract any penalty. Given the complexity of most insurance policies, insurers will no doubt be glad of this.
[8] SI 1999/2083, reg 6(2).
[9] SI 1999/2083, reg 5(2).

16.29 In the context of insurance policies some particular problems in interpreting the Directive may be mentioned. First, as has been pointed out in dealing with the question of burden of proof[1], it is not always easy to decide what is a matter defining the risk and what is a matter creating an exception to the definition of the risk. If the distinction drawn in relation to burden of proof is followed in relation to the fairness of terms, then the result could be the drawing of some fairly artificial lines. However, there is good reason to think that this is not a proper approach to interpretation. The Regulations implement a Directive, and it is now well-settled that so far as possible Regulations of this type are to be interpreted so as to give effect to the purposes of the Directive. It is also clear that in the context of European law substance should wherever possible prevail over form. Consequently, the result ought to be the same whichever form of drafting is used. Unfortunately, this merely throws the question back to asking whether terms of this kind should be included or excluded. It is submitted that they should be excluded from consideration. In the drafting of the Directive a policy decision was taken that terms defining the main obligations of the contract should be excluded. The reason for this decision may be thought to be that the nature and extent of these obligations is fundamentally connected with the price charged for the contract. Terms defining the risk run by the insurer fall squarely within the category of terms which are primarily determinative of the price to be charged for the contract. If this argument is accepted, it will greatly reduce those parts of the insurance contract which are subject to the UTCCR 1999. The question of warranties may still give rise to some difficulty. It was shown in Chapter 10 that warranties can be divided into warranties of fact, promissory warranties and warranties descriptive of the risk. The first category is clearly within the UTCCR 1994. These are warranties which relate to the past, but compliance with them is a pre-condition of the risk. It could happen that the proposal required the proposer to give an extensive series of warranties which went beyond what was required for the proper protection of the insurer. Such a state of affairs would seem to fall squarely within the mischief of the Regulations[2]. Warranties of the last category are equally clearly excluded from the Regulations, for the reasons already given. The difficulty is to know where to place warranties in the second category. On the one hand it might be argued that these do not define the main obligations of the contract, being instead a pre-condition of liability like those warranties in the first category. On the other hand it is in the nature of promissory warranties that they can be described as deifing the scope of the risk. A simple example will suffice. In a fire insurance policy the insured might be required to warrant that no inflammable material will be stored on the premises[3]. That is an obvious promissory warranty. Alternatively the warranty might be omitted, but the risk might be stated as being loss caused by fire not arising from inflammable material stored on the premises. The latter variant clearly makes the absence of inflammable material (or at least its lack of connection with the fire) part of the definition of the risk, so that the case falls outside the UTCCR 1999. If the former version of the drafting is held to fall within the UTCCR 1999, then form will have prevailed over substance. It is therefore submitted that promissory warranties should be held to fall outside the Regulations.

If that conclusion is ever held to be wrong, it will of course become necessary to consider how the fairness of such terms is to be evaluated. This leads into the more general question of the test of fairness. Regulation 5 of the Regulations defines an unfair term as one which is:

> '... contrary to the requirement of good faith, it causes a significant imbalance in the parties' rights and obligations arising under the contract to the detriment of the consumer.'

From the point of view of an English lawyer perhaps the first problematic aspect of this definition is the reference to the requirement of good faith. It is trite law that the English law of contract does not have a general doctrine of good faith in contracts[4], and the question therefore arises, how this requirement should be interpreted in an English law context. One extreme view would be to say that it is meaningless because of the absence of any general doctrine of good faith. This view, however, surely cannot be sustained. It is of course true that the use of a Directive rather than a Regulation as a way of introducing fairness into consumer contracts allows for the possibility that some discrepancies between national legal systems will survive even after the Directive has been fully implemented, but the notion of good faith is so integral to the Directive that it will be necessary for English courts to develop and articulate some notion of fairness, at least in relation to consumer contracts.

[1] Chapter 20.
[2] Though it may also be noted that the Statements of Insurance Practice forbid the insurer to make statements of past or present fact into warranties: see the general discussion of the Statements in Chapter 5.
[3] The example is obviously based upon *Hales v Reliance Fire* [1960] 2 Lloyd's Rep 391, Mocatta J. Although that was not a consumer contract, the point is of general application.
[4] Unlike, for example, French law, where art 1134 c civ provides that contracts must be performed in good faith.

16.30 All this must leave the question of what other terms in an insurance contract are seriously at risk of being held to infringe the 1999 Regulations. Regulation 6(1) provides that the assessment of unfairness is to be made taking into account the nature of the services in question and all circumstances, at the time when the contract was concluded, attending the conclusion of the contract and all the other terms of the contract itself and any other contract on which it is dependent. Regrettably, this form of words amounts to no more than saying that everything relevant must be considered. By itself it tells us nothing of what matters are regarded as relevant. Schedule 2 to the Regulations contains an indicative and non-exhaustive list of terms which may be regarded as unfair. The list runs to 17 items, most of which can readily be excluded from consideration here. However, it is submitted that the following items in the list are worthy of consideration in an insurance context:

> '(h) automatically extending a contract of fixed duration where the consumer does not indicate otherwise, when the deadline fixed for the consumer to express this desire is unreasonably early.'

This could be relevant if an annual policy were expressed to be subject to automatic renewal (though this is not the usual practice in personal lines policies) if the deadline for opting out of the renewal were unreasonably early. There is no obvious reason in insurance cases why there should be a long deadline at all – there is no argument for saying that insurers need adequate notice to arrange the withdrawal of cover. At most there might be some requirement of notice in motor insurance where a certificate of insurance is a statutory requirement, but even here cover notes can be provided at a few days' notice:

> '(i) irrevocably binding the consumer to terms with which he had no real opportunity of becoming acquainted before the conclusion of the contract.'

It should be acknowledged that this is an area where insurance law and practice has a major problem. It is still very uncommon for insurers to provide policy-holders with full details of the terms of the policy before the contract is entered into. Advertising literature will specify the major elements of cover (but will naturally not make much effort to draw attention to limitations and exclusions) and there may also be a summary of cover provided with the proposal form, but the policy document itself is not normally supplied until after the premium has been paid. This practice appears to be a clear contravention of paragraph (i). However, it must be remembered that Schedule 2 lists terms which *may* be regarded as unfair; merely because a term falls within the words of Schedule 2, it does not automatically follow that it *will* be regarded as unfair. In the present case it might be argued on behalf of insurers, first, that most policyholders would not read the policy even if it were provided to them in advance; secondly, that they would probably not understand it if they did read it; thirdly, that even if they read it and objected to it, the insurer would not be willing to change the term; fourthly, that none of this makes the term substantively unfair. The last point is a particularly strong one, though it is in some danger of proving too much. This paragraph appears to show once again the confusion identified earlier between the fairness of the process by which the term becomes part of the contract and the substantive fairness of the term itself as between the parties:

> '(q) excluding or hindering the consumer's right to take legal action or exercise any other legal remedy, particularly by requiring the consumer to take disputes exclusively to arbitration not covered by legal provisions, unduly restricting the evidence available to him or *imposing on him a burden of proof which, according to the applicable law, should lie with another party to the contract*.' [emphasis added]

It appears that only the italicised words in this paragraph are relevant, since there is no practice in personal lines policies of doing any of the other things mentioned. However, as is explained in the Chapter on Burden of Proof[1], policies which are drafted with exclusions sometimes seek to place the burden of proof in relation to them on the policyholder even though it properly belongs on the insurer. Such clauses would seem to be a clear contravention of paragraph (q).

It is thus apparent that relatively few of the specific items mentioned in Schedule 3 are relevant to insurance law. However, it is submitted that some other clauses found in insurance policies ought to be regarded as capable of contravening the fairness test. The major area which appears to be open for exploration is that of the claims process. Personal lines policies should not in any event have clauses requiring claims to be notified within a fixed period (since such clauses would contravene the Statements of Insurance Practice) except in relation to notification of legal proceedings against the insured, where it may be necessary for prompt notice to be given to ensure compliance with the CPR 1998, and where the Statements of Practice[2] allow an exemption to the general principle. Any clause contravening the Statements of Practice on this point would, it is submitted, also contravene the UTCCR 1999. A more difficult area concerns the other obligations of the policyholder in relation to settlements and admissions of liability. Policies frequently the forbid the policyholder to take any decision on his own initiative in this regard. These clauses are sometimes expressed as conditions precedent to recovery. Both the courts and the Ombudsman are hostile to such clauses, and do their best to interpret them merely as conditions of the policy, but in any event it is submitted that it is unfair within the UTCCR 1999 to make such clauses conditions precedent to recovery. Policyholders can easily make the mistake of saying something which can be construed as an admission of liability, especially in the immediate aftermath of an incident such as a motor accident. It is surely unfair to say that the making of such an admission disqualifies the policyholder from any recovery, especially in cases where the admission was objectively justified.

1 Chapter 19.
2 SGIP cl 2.

Consequences of unfairness

16.31 An unfair term in a consumer contract is not binding on the consumer[1], but the contract as a whole shall continue to bind the parties if it is capable of continuing in existence without the unfair term[2]. Thus, the blue pencil rule is applied and the term simply deleted. The court has no power to substitute for it a fairer alternative.

1 UTCCR 1994, reg 8(1).
2 UTCCR 1994, reg 8(2).

16.32 There is one reported case on the applicability of the UTCCR in an insurance context. In *Bankers Insurance Co Ltd v South and Gardener*[1] a travel policy had an exclusion for losses arising from the policyholder's possession or ownership of 'motorised waterborne craft'. There were also conditions requiring the notification of third party claims. As to the exclusion clause the insurers denied liability on the basis that the accident had involved a jetski. The insured sought to argue that the clause was ambiguous as to whether a jetski fell within the clause and that it was unfair to allow reliance on it. This argument inevitably failed, since the exclusion clause clearly goes to the definition of the main subject matter of the contract and therefore could not be challenged under the Regulations. So far as the claims conditions were concerned Buckley J held that these were unfair only in so far as they defeated claims where the time limits were not observed[2] regardless of the consequences of such failure. They were not unfair in so far as they allowed insurers to rely on prejudice caused to them. It was also held that the terms were in sufficiently clear language to enable insurers to rely on them. Although it is obviously dangerous to generalise too much from one case, it may be suggested that this case supports the idea that claims conditions are perhaps the clauses in an insurance contract most obviously susceptible to challenge under the UTCCR.

1 [2004] Lloyd's Rep IR 1, Buckley J.
2 The use of such time limits in relation to third party claims is expressly permitted by the SGIP.

Enforcement

16.33 The enforcement of the UTCCR 1994 in the UK is in the hands of the Director General of Fair Trading[1], who has so far taken a strongly consumerist approach to interpretation of the Regulations. In bulletins issued by the Director General[2], there are a number of statements that could be seen as supporting a wide view of this provision. In particular, it is mentioned that the use of legal terms of art is contrary to this requirement. Thus terms such as 'force majeure', and 'consequential loss' are used as examples of clauses that are not regarded as being in plain and intelligible language[3]. The Director General expressly states that contract terms must normally be 'within the understanding of ordinary consumers *without legal advice*'[4]. The view of the Director General of Fair Trading does give an indication of circumstances when enforcement will be pursued. However there are as yet no formal decisions, whether by the Office of Fair Trading ('OFT') or by the courts, to resolve any of the problems of interpretation. Now that the Regulations have been in force for some years it is becoming clear that the OFT's preferred method of enforcement is to negotiate with businesses whose terms it regards as unsatisfactory. It has been prepared on occasions to threaten proceedings for infringement of the Regulations, but has apparently not yet found it necessary to carry out such a threat. It appears that as yet no term of an insurance contract has been targeted by the OFT as an apparent breach of the Regulations.

1 Regulation 8.
2 Extensive summaries are available at http://www.open.gov.uk/oft/ofthome.htm.
3 *Unfair Contract Terms – Issue No* 2 (OFT, September 1996), p 10.
4 OFT Bulletin No 2 (n 3 above), p 10.

The Insurance Ombudsman's approach to fairness of terms

16.34 Even before the coming into force of the UTCCR 1994 the Insurance Ombudsman had begun to develop principles relevant to the notion of fairness in insurance contracts. UCTA 1977 is of course inapplicable to insurance contracts[1]. In 1992 the then Ombudsman announced that in future disputes involving questions of fairness of terms would be considered by the Ombudsman on the basis that such terms were to be required to comply with the spirit of UCTA 1977[2]. The discussion of the following cases should be understood in the light of that statement.

A policyholder claimed on a contents policy for the loss of his false teeth. He had not taken the optional accidental loss cover, so he argued that the teeth had been stolen by a pet dog, and that the loss was therefore within the theft peril. The Insurance Ombudsman held that 'theft' within the policy should be interpreted not in accordance with its technical legal meaning[3], but in the way that an ordinary person might be expected to understand it. However, even this definition required, in the Ombudsman's opinion, some element of dishonesty, which could scarcely be imputed to the dog. The claim therefore failed.

Another IOB case[4] concerned a term as to security measures in a household policy. These have been discussed elsewhere[5], but the present case is interesting because of the Ombudsman's reliance on the question of fairness. The policyholder had failed to fit a key-operated lock to a window, which was in fact used as an access by thieves. Although the requirement to fit keys is not particularly unusual, the Ombudsman took account of the fact that that it was expressed as a condition precedent to liability without a separate endorsement. A further relevant fact was that the policy was intended for shared, rented accommodation, where the policy-holder is usually not allowed to implement modifications to the property. These two points, taken together, led the Ombudsman to conclude that the term was a particularly onerous one, and that it would not be fair to allow the insurer to rely on it.

Another interesting application of the notion of fairness occurred in a household policy[6] where the policyholder claimed for the cost of repairing or replacing a faulty soil pipe. The insured peril on which she relied was loss or damage [to the buildings] by … water escaping from, or freezing of, water tanks, apparatus or pipes.

However, there was no evidence that the pipe had been damaged by freezing or escaped water (though the leak from the pipe might well cause damage to other property which would have been covered). From a strict legal point of view the position was clearly that the claim must fail. However, the policy covered an apartment in a block of flats, and the landlord had made it a condition of the lease that the tenants effect their insurance with the insurer in question. It appeared that the policyholder's neighbour had a policy issued by the same insurer, which covered accidental damage to pipes providing services to and from the home, and which therefore covered a soil pipe. On the basis that the difference in wording was probably accidental and that it would be illogical to insure adjoining properties on different terms in relation to shared facilities, the policyholder was given the benefit of the neighbour's insurance policy, and the complaint was upheld. Whilst it is easy to sympathise with the elderly policyholder in this case, the decision appears to go well beyond anything which could be regarded as a legitimate interpretation of UCTA 1977 or even of a more general notion of fairness. What would have happened, for example, if the adjoining property had been insured with a different insurer? Presumably at that point the argument would have broken down. Yet this is really a very flimsy basis for a decision which goes so far beyond the policyholder's legal rights.

The next case concerns the importance of bringing onerous terms properly to the attention of the policyholder[7]. It concerned the theft of a holdall from a car. The policyholder claimed on her contents policy, which contained an exclusion for theft from unattended vehicles unless the property in question had been 'removed from view'. The holdall was quite large, and it appeared that it might well have been visible from outside even if, as the policyholder claimed, it had been covered with a blanket. The basis of the Ombudsman's decision in favour of the complainant was that the term had not been in the original policy, and that at renewal she had been sent a renewal notice listing important changes, but not including this change. Even though the new term was included in the new policy document, the Ombudsman concluded that it had not been sufficiently brought to the attention of the policyholder. A similar result was reached in another case[8] where a contents policy included accidental damage cover, but with an exclusion for loss or damage to any items designed to be portable. The claim was for damage resulting from dropping a portable television. On the face of it the exclusion obviously applied, but the exclusion was not mentioned in the 'Application Booklet' which had been issued prior to inception. To make matters worse that booklet had expressly stated that the policy would cover televisions, without specifying that they had to be non-portable.

[1] Schedule 1 to the Act.
[2] (1992) 2 Ins Ins L & P 86.
[3] This is of course inconsistent with the approach of the courts in cases such as *Grundy (Teddington) Ltd v Fulton* [1983] 1 Lloyd's Rep 6, CA and *Dobson v General Accident* [1990] 1 QB 274, CA.
[4] IOB 14.14.
[5] Paragraph 90.15.
[6] IOB 14.15.
[7] IOB 14.16.
[8] IOB 14.18.

16.35 A more difficult case about the impact of advertising on the policyholder's expectations involved medical expenses insurance[1]. The policyholder had taken out this insurance and made five claims in the next four years. The validity of all these claims was admitted, and they were duly met, but after the last one the insurer gave 28 days' notice of cancellation of the policy, as was permitted by the policy. The policyholder, however, believed that she was entitled to lifetime cover. The promotional literature had contained the following statement:

> 'Never again face accident or illness unprepared ... Guaranteed acceptance regardless of your age, occupation or medical history. The subscriptions do not increase with age.'

The small print referred to the policy terms, but the policyholder did not have a copy of these at the time of the application. Two questions arose; first, whether cancellation was to be permitted at all; secondly, whether cancellation part-way through the policy was good insurance practice, even though it was permitted by the terms of the policy.

The first question is the more difficult of the two. On the one hand the policy was clearly expressed to be an annual policy, as is usual with policies of this type, and it would seem unreasonable to say that the insurer must maintain the cover indefinitely. On the other hand the advertisement quoted was at best severely misleading, and the insurer could not have felt too badly treated if there had been some adverse consequences. The Insurance Ombudsman held that the insurer was entitled to cancel despite the advertising. One relevant factor in this was that the policyholder had at the same time effected similar policies with other insurers, all of which were annual policies. It is perhaps surprising that the Ombudsman did not seek a compromise in the form of requiring the cover to be maintained for some longer (but finite) period. On the second point it was held that the cancellation mid-term was legitimate provided that a pro-rata refund of premium was offered. The IOB report describes this as an appropriate compromise, but in fact the decision seems unduly favourable to the insurer. The report ends by saying that insurers may be required to give effect to policyholders' legitimate expectations and that they should not normally cancel in order to avoid the effect of having made a bad bargain. Unfortunately, the decision itself does not appear to apply either of those principles properly.

[1] IOB 14.19.

'Accommodation'

16.36 The Insurance Ombudsman considered a case[1] in which a travel policy was effected to cover a trip to South Africa via Amsterdam. The policyholders were delayed in Amsterdam because one of their passports was stolen. The policy covered 'accommodation' in these circumstances, and the Insurance Ombudsman held that it was within the reasonable expectation of the insured that reasonable sustenance and the cost of luggage storage should fall within the concept of accommodation.

[1] IOB 14.20.

16.37 Another question of fairness of terms arose in a travel policy where the tour operator collapsed before the holiday started[1]. The policyholder was able to recover most of the cost of the holiday from the credit card company through which the holiday had been paid for, but he then sought a refund of premium. The insurer relied upon an exclusion for claims arising from the tour operator becoming insolvent. The Ombudsman held that this exclusion did not apply because the policyholder was not making a claim under the policy, but rather seeking a refund of premium. The Ombudsman relied further upon a statement in the 1990 Annual Report to the effect that it is unfair in travel policies to have a clause providing that the premium is never refundable. The example given in that Report[2] was that of the tour operator collapsing before travel. Consequently the insurer was required to refund the premium, less administration expenses and a deduction for the cancellation cover. It has to be said that the logic of this decision is hard to fathom. Certainly the exclusion did not apply, for the reasons given, but why was it appropriate to have any refund of premium at all? Admittedly most of the cover became irrelevant when the tour operator collapsed, but the usual principle surely is that the premium is refundable only when the policyholder has received nothing for it (ie a total failure of consideration). Here he had certainly received some cancellation cover. The logic of the decision would seem to mean that a policyholder who buys a car on a credit arrangement which makes a third party liable (as where the purchase is by credit card) can recover the insurance premium if the car is destroyed within the period covered by the third party liability. This surely cannot be right.

[1] Paragraph 2.4.
[2] IOB 14.21.

Chapter 17

Warranties and Conditions

Introduction

17.1 In insurance law, the traditional contract law distinction between warranties and conditions is reversed, ie the conditions are the less important terms of the contract, whereas the warranties are the fundamental terms. Although there is no statutory test for recognising a warranty, in the modern law the starting point is the judgment of Rix LJ in *HIH Casualty and General Insurance Ltd v New Hampshire Insurance Co*[1]:

> 'It is a question of construction, and the presence or absence of the word "warranty" or "warranted" is not conclusive. One test is whether it is a term which goes to the root of the transaction; a second, whether it is descriptive of or bears materially on the risk of loss; a third, whether damages would be an unsatisfactory or inadequate remedy. As Lord Justice Bowen said in *Barnard v Faber* [1893] 1 QB 340 at p 344: "A term as regards the risk must be a condition." Otherwise the insurer is merely left to a cross-claim in a matter which goes to the risk itself, which is unbusinesslike (ibid; see also *Ellinger & Co v Mutual Life Insurance Co of New York* [1905] 1 KB 31 at p 38). In the present case, the six film term would seem to answer all three tests. It is a fundamental term, for even if only one film were omitted, the revenues are likely to be immediately reduced. That will not matter if the revenues already exceed the sum insured, for in that case there can be no loss in any event. Where, however, the revenues fall below she sum insured, the loss of a single film may be the critical difference between a loss or no loss, and will in any event be likely to increase the loss. For the same reason the term bears materially on the risk. A cross-claim would be an unsatisfactory and inadequate remedy because it would never be possible to know how much the lost film would have contributed to revenues. The very fact that the making of the six films lies under the "INTEREST" line emphasizes the importance of the term and its direct bearing on the risk. As for the draft originating with the assured's brokers, that is nearly always the case. There is a maximum of construction which is called the contra proferentum rule; but there is no maxim to the opposite effect.'

[1] [2001] Lloyd's Rep IR 596 at para 101.

Warranties

17.2 In principle the position of insurance law on warranties is simple. Breach of warranty renders the policy voidable at the instance of the insurer, but, subject to exceptions noted below, does not automatically avoid the policy. These points were settled at a relative early stage in the development of insurance law. The two cases normally relied upon as the origin of the doctrine are *Anderson v Fitzgerald*[1] and *Duckett v Williams*[2]. In these cases there were express policy terms which provided that cover should be avoided if any statement made by the policyholder in the proposal form were 'untrue'. The direction given to the jury, later upheld on appeal, was that only the truth of the statement was in issue, it being irrelevant whether the proposer had had any sort of belief in the truth of the statement. The same sort of approach was in evidence half a century later in *Thomson v Weems*[3]. This was a life case, in which the proposal form asked whether the life assured had always been 'strictly temperate'. The answer given was 'temperate'. Two years after the issue of the policy the life assured died of liver failure, apparently caused by excessive drinking. The House of Lords again held that the warranty was one of fact rather than opinion, and that it was untrue. By modern standards the decision may seems surprising, but it must be remembered that it was made at a time when 'temperate' had a specific meaning, namely 'teetotal', with the result that the answer might reasonably be treated as a matter of fact. It might also be added that on the facts of the case the House of Lords would surely have been justified in deciding that the proposer could not possibly have had an honest belief in the truth of the statement. The basic rule as to warranties has been reaffirmed more recently in *Seavision Investment SA v Evennett and Clarkson Puckle Ltd, The Tiburon*[4] (warranted that insured vessel 'German FOM', ie flag, ownership and management). The essential characteristic of a warranty is that it is a condition which must be exactly complied with, whether it is material to the risk or not. If it is not complied with then, subject to any express provision in the policy and to the effect of waiver of the breach by the insurer, the insurer is discharged from liability as from the date of the breach of warranty but without prejudice to any liability incurred by him before that date.

However, examination of the case law shows that insurance law recognises a number of different types of warranty, and that these have different effects. This is not surprising. Given the draconian consequences of holding that a statement is a promissory warranty, it is understandable that courts have sought ways of avoiding that conclusion.

1 (1835) 4 HL Cas 484, HL.
2 (1834) 2 Cr & M 348.
3 (1884) 9 App Cas 671, HL.
4 [1990] 2 Lloyd's Rep 418, CA.

Promissory warranties

17.3 The first category of warranty to be considered is the promissory warranty. This is apparently the same as the warranty described in s 33 of the MIA 1906, though it is not clear that breach of such a warranty operates as an automatic discharge of the liability. The problem therefore is to be able to identify which warranties fall into this category. In *Hales v Reliance Fire*[1] the policyholder was a shopkeeper. When he proposed for insurance on his premises the proposal form asked whether any inflammable materials were kept on the premises. He disclosed only the existence of fuel for cigarette lighters, which was the only such material at the time of the proposal. During the currency of the policy he bought some fireworks and stored them on the premises. They caught fire, and his claim for the resulting damage was rejected on the ground that the existence of the fireworks had not been disclosed. Although the question on the proposal form was couched in the present tense, McNair J held that it must be construed as a promissory warranty, so that the insurers were entitled to succeed. The decision has been criticised, and it is certainly fair to say that the question could reasonably have been regarded as ambiguous. On the other hand it can also be said that the question really only makes sense if it is treated as referring to the future as well as to the present. The case may be thought to illustrate the difficulty of deciding in the abstract whether a particular question is to be treated as giving rise to a promissory warranty. It may usefully be contrasted with the Scottish case of *Kennedy v Smith*[2]. This was a motor insurance case, in which the policyholder had declared on the proposal form that he was a total abstainer from all forms of alcohol. During the policy he was responsible for an accident after consuming a small amount of alcohol. The Court of Session held that the statement on the proposal form was not to be regarded as promissory in nature – it referred only to the situation at the date of the proposal. It was perhaps relevant that the policy also contained a clause excluding liability if the policyholder were under the influence of alcohol at the time of the accident, which would have been unnecessary if the statement as to abstinence were promissory in nature. On balance it is probably fair to say that in almost every case a court can choose whether to categorise a warranty as promissory or not. This was implicitly recognised in *Hussain v Brown*[3], where the Court of Appeal said that in completing, signing and submitting the proposal form the proposer is providing the information upon which the insurers act in deciding whether to accept the proposal at all, and if so, at what premium. The answers given to questions in a proposal form are not necessarily to be read as an undertaking as to future conduct by the intended insured, as a continuing warranty is a draconian term.

1 [1960] 2 Lloyd's Rep 391, McNair J.
2 1976 SLT 110, Ct of Sess.
3 [1996] 1 Lloyd's Rep 627, CA.

Warranties descriptive of the risk

17.4 The second category of warranty to be considered is that which describes the risk. Such a warranty is not a promise by the assured of anything. It merely means that so long as the warranty is not complied with the risk will not attach. It should be said that strictly speaking a clause of this kind is not a warranty within the meaning of MIA 1906, s 33, though it is common practice to describe it as one. A good example of such a warranty is to be found in *Farr v Motor Traders Mutual Insurance*[1]. This was a case of the commercial insurance of a taxi business. The business had two cars, and in normal circumstances each did a single eight-hour shift per day. When the proposal form asked how long each would be used each day, the answer was given that each would be used for eight hours. The statement was, obviously, true as a general statement. However, there came a time during the currency of the policy when one of the cars was off the road for repairs, and during that time the other one was used for two eight-hour shifts each day. The proposal form contained a basis of the contract clause. Later, after usage had reverted to the normal pattern, an accident occurred. The insurers sought to deny liability on the ground of breach of warranty, but the Court of Appeal rejected this defence, saying that the warranty given was simply descriptive of the risk – so long as only one car was being used, there was no cover, but once usage reverted to the pattern described in the proposal form, cover resumed. The result is at first sight attractive, but the case gives rise to a number of difficult issues. First, it is not at all clear that the result is fair to the insurers. Most commentators on the case seem to assume that by the time of the accident the risk being run was that which the insurers had contemplated, but that is not necessarily so. The report does not make clear which of the vehicles suffered the accident, nor what the nature of the accident was. It is surely not unreasonable to suggest that the vehicle which was operated for 16 hours daily was thereby exposed to greater stresses than would otherwise have been the case, and that these could have rendered it more liable to a malfunction which might have caused an accident. Even if the accident which happened bore no relationship to this hypothesis, it remains that the risk was arguably changed by the departure from what had been stated on the proposal form. Of course there is no certainty that the insurers would have charged a different premium had this possibility been drawn to their attention, but presumably their purpose in making the statement into a warranty was to render that issue irrelevant.

The second difficulty arising from the case concerns the position while one vehicle was off the road. The Court of Appeal did not directly have to decide this point, but the logic of its reasoning is that if an accident had happened at that time, there would have been no cover. The case pre-dates the requirement of compulsory motor insurance[2], but at the present day this would appear to mean that during this time the other vehicle would have been driven without valid insurance, so that a criminal offence would have been committed. Although this would not affect the right of a third party to claim for any loss suffered[3], it could have serious consequences for the policyholder.

Finally, it may be asked whether a question such as this would be likely to be interpreted in the same way today. It is submitted that it would not. It seems fairly clear that the statement can only be regarded as a general one – much more explicit wording would be needed to make it into a promissory warranty – but it is submitted that the consequence of regarding the statement as a general one it that it would remain true as a general statement even when not being complied with. Although the Statements of Practice would not apply to this case, it being a case of commercial insurance, it seems appropriate to hold that in the absence of clear wording the cover is valid so long as the statement is an accurate statement of general practice.

More recently, the decision in Farr was applied by Morland J in *Kler Knitwear Ltd v Lombard General Insurance Co Ltd*[4], where a policy on factory premises contained a clause whereby it was 'warranted' that an inspection by a qualified engineer would be carried out within 30 days of inception, remedial work being done within 14 days thereafter. The inspection was not carried out in time, and the insurers relied upon this when rejecting a later claim for storm damage. Morland J rejected this defence, holding that the 'warranty' was merely a suspensive condition. It is not decisive that the word 'warranty' is used in the policy, since that term is used in various ways in insurance policies. Nor is it correct to say that a once and for all obligation such as this is necessarily a promissory warranty[5]. It is in all cases a matter of the construction of the policy. It must be admitted that in the present case the construction adopted produces a sensible result. The inspection had been carried out, albeit rather late, before the loss happened, and it would not have made commercial sense to allow the insurers to rely upon the technical breach of the clause. However, the case does emphasise the need for great care in interpreting clauses such as this.

In some policies a clause may be found entitling insurers to deny a claim if there is a breach of warranty as a result of which the risk of loss is increased[6]. These clauses appear to create an incoherent mix between a warranty and a condition. If the clause is truly a warranty, then it is irrelevant whether the breach increases the risk of loss, and the sanction for breach is automatic termination, not merely the right to reject the particular claim. If the clause is treated at its face value, it comes close to reducing the warranty to the status of a simple condition, though it does not quite achieve that, because the insurer can still rely on the clause if the *risk* of damage is increased, whereas in the case of a simple condition it would be necessary to show that the breach had actually *caused* the loss.

[1] [1920] 3 KB 669, CA.
[2] First introduced by the Road Traffic Act 1930.
[3] RTA 1988, s 151.
[4] [2000] Lloyd's Rep IR 47.
[5] See also *Case Existological Laboratories Ltd v Century Insurance Co of Canada* [1986] 2 Lloyd's Rep 528n; *Roberts v AngloSaxon Insurance Association Ltd* (1927) 27 Ll L Rep 313, CA.
[6] For an example see *Bennett v Axa Insurance plc* [2004] Lloyd's Rep IR 615, Tomlinson J.

Role of the Statements of Practice

17.5 In the context of personal lines policies the Statements of Insurance Practice are relevant to the question of warranties. The SGIP provides[1] that nothing in the policy shall convert statements on the proposal form as to past or present fact into a promissory warranty. Making such statements into warranties would have the effect of allowing the insurer to avoid the policy if any of the statements proved to be untrue, notwithstanding that the matter warranted was not material to the risk. The prohibition contained in the general statement is expressed to be without prejudice to the freedom of insurers to require specific warranties about matters material to the risk. At first sight the two provisions may appear to contradict each other, but it seems clear enough that the second is to be read as an exception to the first. It is not permitted to have clauses which make all the statements on the proposal form into warranties, but it is permissible to require specific warranties about individual matters, provided that these can be shown to be material to the risk.

The General Statement also limits the freedom of insurers to repudiate liability for breach of warranty. As was seen above, one of the most invidious consequences of promissory warranties is that breach of them renders the policy voidable even though the circumstances of the breach are not connected with the loss. The General Statement seeks to deal with this by providing in cl 2(b)(iii) that there shall be no repudiation for breach of warranty or condition where the circumstances of the loss are unconnected with the breach unless fraud is involved. The law is clearly that any breach of warranty allows the insurer to avoid the entire policy, and that a breach of condition may allow the repudiation of the claim. In all cases it is irrelevant whether the breach is connected with the loss. This clause varies that rule, by requiring (in the absence of fraud) a causal connection between breach and loss before the breach can be relied upon.

The corresponding provision of the SLIP[2] is worded slightly differently. Insurers agree not to rely upon breach of warranty (again in the absence of fraud) unless the circumstances of the loss are connected with the breach and unless either the warranty relates to a statement of fact concerning the life assured under a life of another policy and that statement would have constituted grounds for rejection of the claim if it had been made by the life assured under an own life policy (ie it was a fact which was material and which the proposer could reasonably have been expected to disclose) or the warranty was created in relation to specific matters material to the risk and it was drawn to the proposer's attention at or before the making of the contract.

Like all provisions of the Statements of Practice, these clauses apply only to policyholders resident in the UK and insured in their private capacity only. They have no legal force, but it is the settled practice of the FOS to insist that insurers abide by them. Where necessary this has been achieved by disregarding clauses which infringe the spirit or letter of the Statements.

1 Clause 1.
2 Clause 2(b).

When breach of warranty voids the policy

Marine insurance

17.6 Section 33 of the MIA 1906 explains the meaning and significance of warranties for the purposes of ss 34–41 of that Act. The definition is:

> 'a promissory warranty, that is to say, a warranty by which the assured undertakes that some particular thing shall or shall not be done, or that some condition shall be fulfilled, or whereby he affirms or negatives the existence of a particular state of facts.'

It is important to note that this is not accurate as a general definition of warranties in insurance law. As was shown above, these need to be more carefully subdivided according to their nature and effects.

Section 33(3) goes on to provide that a warranty in the MIA 1906 sense must be exactly complied with, whether it be material to the risk or not. Failure to comply means (subject to any express provision in the policy) that the insurer is discharged from liability from the date of the breach, though not from liability for events happening prior to that date. It has been held[1] that this discharge from liability happens immediately and automatically, even though neither party is aware that the breach of warranty has occurred. Despite this apparent automatic discharge, a breach of warranty may be waived by the insurer[2], and the effect of such waiver is apparently that the policy cover is retrospectively reinstated to the time of the breach.

Section 34 adds that non-compliance with a warranty is excused where by reason of a change of circumstances the warranty ceases to be applicable to the circumstances of the contract (though there is very little case law in which an assured has successfully used this provision) or when compliance with the warranty is rendered unlawful by any subsequent law. Where there is a breach of warranty the assured cannot rely upon the argument that the warranty has been complied with and the breach remedied before the time of loss[3]. In other words, the breach makes the policy voidable irreparably and without more.

In marine insurance there is an implied warranty that the adventure insured is a lawful one, and that so far as the assured can control the matter, the adventure is to be carried out in a lawful manner[4]. This provision has no application to non-marine insurance in respect of goods alone: *Euro-Diam Ltd v Bathurst*[5].

Other marine warranties cover seaworthiness of the ship at the commencement of a voyage policy (but not a time policy)[6], neutrality of ship or goods[7] and good safety of the ship[8].

It is thought that the MIA 1906 rules on the effect of breach of warranty are confined to the marine situation and possibly even to breaches of the particular warranties mentioned in the Act. Certainly, the normal understanding in non-marine insurance is that breach of warranty renders the policy voidable but not void.

1 *The Good Luck* [1991] 3 All ER 1, HL.
2 MIA 1906, s 34(3).
3 MIA 1906, s 34(2).
4 MIA 1906, s 41.
5 [1990] 1 QB 1, [1988] 2 All ER 23, CA.
6 MIA 1906, s 39.
7 MIA 1906, s 36.
8 MIA 1906, s 38.

Waiver of Breach

17.7 Section 34(3) of the MIA 1906 allows an insurer to waive a breach of warranty. The provision is on the face of it odd, for section 33 contemplates that discharge of liability on breach is automatic, so section 34(3) must work by a retrospective reinstatement of the cover. The requisites for such a waiver were considered in *HIH Casualty and General Insurance Ltd v AXA Corporate Solutions*[1], where it was held that waiver of breach of warranty could only be waiver by estoppel, and that this required a clear and unequivocal representation that the insurer would not stand on its right to treat the cover as having been discharged. This in turn required that the insurer must know of the facts giving rise to the breach and must understand that they amounted to breach and that it was therefore entitled to treat the cover as discharged. Only if these conditions were satisfied could there be any possibility of a suitably clear and unequivocal representation. It must then be a question of fact whether such a representation has been made. It may be added, although this point did not feature at any length in this case, that the insured would also need to establish sufficient detrimental reliance on the representation to found a waiver by estoppel.

1 [2003] Lloyd's Rep IR 1, CA.

When breach of warranty is no defence

17.8 A rare example of a case where even breach of warranty could not avoid the policy is *Kumar v AGF Insurance Ltd*[1], a professional indemnity case, where the policy provided that the insurers would not for any reason seek to avoid, rescind or repudiate the policy. On the basis of an alleged non-disclosure of a pending claim the insurers sought to refuse indemnity, pleading, among other things, breach of warranty. One argument was that repudiating liability for breach of warranty did not amount to avoidance, rescission or repudiation of the policy. Thomas J held that the clear intention of the policy was to prevent the insurers escaping liability on any ground whatsoever, so that even a breach of warranty would not provide a defence. On the facts the decision is clearly correct, but its application seems likely to be confined to the rather special situation of professional indemnity policies[2].

1 [1998] 4 All ER 788.
2 As to these see further Chapter 41.

Damages for breach of warranty

17.9 *Kumar* also confirms that where the insurers choose not to avoid the policy for breach of warranty, they can still claim damages for the breach. Usually the damages will be the amount by which the claim is increased as a result of the breach. In some cases this will be the full value of the claim, in which event the insurers will have a 100% set-off against the policyholder's claim.

Conditions

17.10 Conditions may be further divided. There are simple conditions, the breach of which merely gives rise to a right to damages. There are also conditions precedent to liability. Failure to comply with these will, as the name implies, mean that the insurer is not liable for any loss which occurred during the period of non-compliance. It will not mean, however, that the policy as a whole becomes void or voidable.

The division of conditions in this way raises the further problem of telling one type from the other. Unfortunately, there is no clear and reliable guide to how to do this. A clause which is said to be a condition precedent to liability is likely to be held to be one[1], though even this principle may have to yield in cases where such a construction would produce an absurd result. A clause which is not said to be a condition precedent to liability is unlikely to be held to be one. Moreover, where the same clause characterises some obligations as conditions precedent but is silent as to the status of others it is likely that the others will not be held to be conditions precedent[2].

1 *George Hunt Cranes Ltd v Scottish Boiler & General Insurance Co Ltd* [2002] 1 All ER 366.
2 *Friends Provident Life and Pensions Ltd v Sirius International Insurance Corpn* [2005] Lloyd's Rep IR 135, Moore-Bick J.

17.11 It appears that a claims notification and co-operation clause is not to be treated as a condition precedent to liability. In *Friends Provident Life and Pensions Ltd v Sirius International Insurance Corpn*[1] it was said that a clause of this type should be regarded as capable only of sounding in damages (ie it should be treated as a simple condition). In coming to this conclusion the Court of Appeal also cast doubt on its own earlier decision in *Alfred McAlpine plc v BAI (Run-off) Ltd*[2], where it had been suggested that such clauses could be innominate terms, so that the consequences of a breach depended on the extent of the damage suffered by the insurer as a result of the breach. Although Mance LJ[3] expressed himself as content to assume that the term was an innominate term, it seems unlikely that it could in fact be so. Indeed, it is hard to understand how innominate terms can have any place in the structure of insurance law. The *Friends Provident* decision was followed in *Ronson International Ltd v Patrick*[4] and is now to be regarded as settled law. The earlier suggestion that such a clause can be a condition precedent to liability[5] appears now to have been discarded. A notification clause should be regarded as including an implied term that notice will be given within a reasonable time[6].

1 [2005] 2 All ER (Comm) 145, CA.
2 [2000] 1 All ER (Comm) 545.
3 At para 29.
4 [2005] 2 All ER (Comm) 453, Richard Seymour J.
5 *Pilkington UK Ltd v CGU Insurance plc* [2004] Lloyd's Rep IR 891, CA.
6 *Shinedean Ltd v Alldown Demolition (London) Ltd (in liq)* [2006] 1 All ER (Comm) 224, Havery J.

17.12 In cases where the breach of a simple condition does directly cause the loss, the result will be that the insurer's damages for the breach of the condition are automatically equal to the value of any claim which the policyholder might have under the policy, so the effect will be that the breach does negate the claim. Thus the distinction between simple conditions and conditions precedent to liability is important only in those cases where a condition is breached, but the breach does not lead directly to the loss.

The tendency of insurers to draft conditions in draconian terms can produce its own difficulties. In *Kazakstan Wool Producers (Europe) Ltd v Nederlandsche Creditverzekering Maatschappij NV*[1] the insured ('KWP') took credit insurance with the defendants. The policy required KWP to submit monthly declarations of all goods despatched under sale contracts. Where appropriate a nil declaration was required. The policy provided that performance of every stipulation in the policy was a condition precedent to recovery. Any breach of the condition precedent was to give the insurer the right to terminate the policy 'and all liability under it', retaining all premiums paid. The policy was due to expire in August 1998, but KWP failed to submit a declaration for June 1998. The insurers argued that this entitled them to terminate the policy, repudiate liability for previously accrued claims and even recover back sums which they had previously paid on claims under the policy. A number of questions and issues arose. The Court of Appeal held first that the insurers could not recover back sums already paid. It is not correct to refer to such sums as 'liabilities', so there was no question of reopening matters already settled. The second question was whether the failure to submit a return for June 1998 affected claims for earlier months in respect of which there had been compliance with the policy terms. This was essentially a matter of construction, and the Court of Appeal held that the condition must be treated as applying separately to each month's claim. This is a sensible construction in the sense that the requirement to submit a return was intended to enable the insurers to monitor the position each month and see the maximum extent of their exposure. It was also pointed out that the construction favoured by the insurers would mean that no claim would have to be paid until after the expiry of the policy, since until that time there would always be the possibility that a later breach of condition precedent would entitle the insurers to repudiate the earlier claim. However, the Court of Appeal went on to hold that any breach of condition precedent would terminate all future and contingent liabilities, even if there were to be no breach of condition in relation to them. Further, the insurers would be entitled to retain the premiums in these circumstances. This outcome is obviously capable of working an injustice where the breach happens at an early stage in the policy, but the Court of Appeal was of the view that the wording was sufficiently clear to make this outcome unavoidable[2]. It is to be noted that this right to retain premiums in the event of breach of condition is in contrast to the case of avoidance of the policy, where the premiums have to be returned[3].

It is not easy to draw general conclusions from this case. The result depends to a significant extent upon the wording of the particular policy; however, it is submitted that some pointers can be identified. As usual, the court will be astute to prevent over-reliance upon technical failures to comply with policy conditions and will seek to give these conditions a commercially sensible meaning. Often, as here, the court is compelled to grapple with provisions which have been drafted with an eye to comprehensiveness rather than clarity, and in doing this the court is likely to be willing to accept interpretations which may render otiose some part of the drafting.

1 [2000] 1 All ER (Comm) 708, CA.
2 As this was a commercial policy, issues of fairness did not directly arise.
3 See Chapter 5.

Reasonableness of conditions

17.13 This is a point which will not arise outside personal lines policies, since the statutory provisions dealing with reasonableness of terms in insurance contracts[1] apply only to such policies. In *Shoshana Stern v Norwich Union Fire Insurance Society Ltd*[2] the claimant had insured a ring with the defendants for £42,849. The appellant had lent the ring to her daughter-in-law who took it to her apartment in Jerusalem and lost it on 15 May 1992. The defendants accepted this as a genuine loss but relied upon an endorsement in the insurance policy making it a condition precedent to liability that the ring and other insured items should be kept in a locked safe at all times when not being worn and kept in the personal custody of the insured at all times. The Court of Appeal upheld the decision of the trial judge to the effect that the condition had not been complied with, so that the insurers were not liable. The reasonableness of clauses of this kind has often been questioned on the basis that they are very difficult to comply with. However, it is submitted that this particular form of the clause should survive the scrutiny of both the Ombudsman and the courts by virtue of the UTCCR 1999[3]. As to the UTCCR 1999, a number of points may be made. First, it is arguable that this clause delimits the risk and should thus be regarded as a main term of the contract, in which event it would not be subject to the Regulations at all. Secondly, the clause may be regarded as a reasonable one. Given the valuable and attractive nature of jewellery, it is surely reasonable to insist on proper security precautions being taken. The position might be otherwise if the policy contained an alternative version of the clause, still sometimes encountered, which simply requires the jewellery to be kept in a locked safe at all times. Literally interpreted, this clause would prevent the jewellery from ever being worn or moved, and it is suggested that the UTCCR 1999 ought for that reason to invalidate the clause. It should be observed that the UTCCR 1999 do not allow the court to substitute a more reasonable version of the clause, which would simply be struck down in its entirety.

The position before the Ombudsman would be different in two respects. First, it is irrelevant whether the clause is regarded as a main term of the contract, since the Ombudsman can operate on the basis of UCTA 1977 principles, which do not draw this distinction. Secondly, the Ombudsman's duty to make a fair and reasonable decision[4] would allow him effectively to rewrite the clause so that there would be cover if, for example, the policyholder were mugged while wearing the jewellery, but not in the circumstances of Shoshana Stern, where there does appear to have been an undue disregard of the necessary safety precautions.

[1] See Chapter 16.
[2] 15 November 1996, CA, unreported.
[3] Which were not relevant in the present case because the policy was taken out before 1 July 1995, when the UTCCR 1994 came into force. The relevant legislation now is the UTCCR 1999.
[4] This aspect of the IOB jurisdiction is in the FOS scheme: see Chapter 21.

Part D

The insurer's liability

Chapter 18

Causation

Introduction

18.1 It is of course fundamental to insurance law that the policy covers only loss caused by an insured peril. This in turn focuses attention on the question of causation by requiring a decision to be made as to what has caused a particular loss. The question of causation generally is both philosophically and legally difficult, but there is case law which is of assistance in deciding the question in an insurance context. The principles applicable do not differ as between insurance law and other branches of the law[1].

It may be helpful to begin by expounding the relationship so far as causation is concerned between insured perils and excluded perils. A good statement of general principle is to be found in the MIA 1906, s 55, which provides:

> '(1) Subject to the provisions of this Act, and unless the policy otherwise provides, the insurer is liable for any loss proximately caused by a peril insured against, but, subject as aforesaid, he is not liable for any loss which is not proximately caused by a peril insured against.
> (2) In particular–
> (a) The insurer is not liable for any loss attributable to the wilful misconduct of the assured, but, unless the policy otherwise provides, he is liable for any loss proximately caused by a peril insured against, even though the loss would not have happened but for the negligence or misconduct of the master or crew;
> (b) Unless the policy otherwise provides, the insurer on ship or goods is not liable for any loss proximately caused by delay, although the delay be caused by a peril insured against;
> (c) Unless the policy otherwise provides, the insurer is not liable for ordinary wear and tear, ordinary leakage and breakage, inherent vice or nature of the subject-matter insured, or for any loss proximately caused by rats or vermin, or for any injury to machinery not proximately caused by maritime perils.'

In short, three possible situations arise:

(1) Loss not covered by an insured peril: the insurer is *not* liable.

(2) Loss covered by insured peril not within exclusion: the insurer *is* liable.
(3) Loss covered by insured peril but within exclusion: the insurer is *not* liable.

Some further comments on the provisions of s 55 are appropriate. First, there is the familiar difficulty that the section has formalistically no application outside marine insurance. Despite this it is submitted that the general principles it lays down are of application throughout the law of insurance (those parts of the section which by their terms are relevant only in marine insurance – essentially sub-s (2)(b) and (c) – can obviously be excluded from this). The words of s 55(1) seem to be no more than a statement of the obvious, except that the last clause may even be self-contradictory – if the policy provides that there is cover against 'a loss not proximately caused by a peril insured against' then in effect that peril has become one which *is* insured against.

Section 55(2)(a) serves as a reminder of another very important general principle, namely that insurance does not cover against losses caused by the *deliberate* wrongdoing of the insured, though losses caused by his negligence are normally insured. The former rule is obviously necessary for reasons of public policy. Without the latter rule it would be impossible to have most modern-day liability insurance policies.

[1] *Lloyd's TSB General Insurance Holdings Ltd v Lloyd's Bank Group Insurance Co Ltd* [2001] 1 All ER (Comm) 13, Moore-Bick J.

Burden of proof

18.2 The above analysis leads in turn to consideration of the burdens of proof arising in relation to insured perils and excluded perils. The general rule may be simply stated. Initially the burden is on the insured to show that the loss arose from an insured peril. Once that burden has been discharged, it is for the insurer to show that the loss arose from an excepted peril.

The crucial question in all causation problems is how to identify which events or circumstances are to be treated as being the cause of the loss against which indemnity is sought[1]. In an insurance context the matter might perhaps be expressed more exactly by saying that the question is whether the cause can be fitted within the scope of one or more of the insured perils. Sometimes it will be sufficient to know that the cause must have been one of the insured perils, without needing to specify more closely which of them applied, but in other cases a greater degree of precision will be required, perhaps because there are exclusions or limitations which are applicable to some, but not all, of the insured perils.

The next point which should to be made in any discussion of causation is that the task of assigning a *legal* cause to any event is often a somewhat artificial one. Lawyers tend to look for *the single cause* of an event, even when it is obvious that in everyday terms the event should be regarded as having more than one cause.

A further important point concerns the difficulty of distinguishing events or circumstances which cause losses from those which are merely conditions within which losses can happen. The attempt to make this distinction in a rigorously logical way has often been made, but it seems likely that the task defied pure logical analysis. The fact is that in assigning causes it is necessary to make choices which are based as much upon popular notions of common sense as upon strict logic[2]. As a very general statement it may perhaps be said that the concern of the lawyer is to know why the particular event (rather than a slightly or significantly different event) happened when it did (rather than at a slightly or significantly different time). In asking these questions it is necessary to distinguish between those circumstances which are part of the everyday course of events and thus, by implication, are likely to be found in cases where the loss in question has not happened, and those circumstances which are out of the ordinary and without which the loss in question presumably would not have happened. This may be regarded as no more than another way of expressing the distinction which lawyers have traditionally drawn between the *causa sine qua non* and the *causa causans*[3]. The former has been regarded as the background circumstance, whilst the latter has been regarded as the 'operating cause'. There are perhaps two good reasons for abandoning these older terms. The first lies in the increasing tendency to eschew the use of Latin terminology in the interests of clarity[4]. The second is that these terms may not, even in their English translation, express very accurately the rather difficult concepts which are being explored here.

The complexities of the background circumstance may be seen from the popular late 20th century notion, partly derived from Chaos Theory, that the beating of a butterfly's wings in Brazil can produce an earthquake in China. The chain of reasoning involved in drawing this conclusion is, to say the least, tortuous, but it serves to illustrate the impossibility of drawing a strict logical line. It is no doubt for this reason, albeit not fully articulated, that judges have in the past observed that the law looks only to immediate causes, not to remote causes[5].

[1] Or in the case of a contingency policy the cause of the happening of the event on which the sum assured is to be paid.

[2] An outstanding account of these issues of causation in a broader legal context maybe found in Hart and Honore, *Causation in the Law* (2nd edn, 1985, OUP).

[3] In a marine insurance context see *Greenock Steamship Co v Maritime Insurance Co* [1903] 1 KB 367, CA.

[4] This tendency now has the support of the Court of Appeal as part of the process of reforming civil justice through the CPR 1998.

[5] Lord Bacon, *Maxims of the Law*, cited in, among other places, *De Vaux v Salvador* (1836) 4 Ad & El 420.

18.3 It is to those immediate causes that we now turn. In many cases the question of causation is relatively simple, since it is soon apparent that there is only one event which can realistically be said to be the cause of the loss. Where a solicitor incurs liability to a client for giving negligent advice, it will be clear that the giving of the advice is the cause of the loss. In the client's claim against the solicitor there may of course be questions about the exact amount of the client's loss, but in the resulting claim on the solicitor's professional negligence policy, it will be clear that the amount for which he has been held liable to the client is directly caused by the negligence. Other cases may, however, be more difficult. Three particular types of case give rise to major logical difficulties in the context of causation. The first is where there appear to be two causes, neither of which is by itself sufficient to bring about the loss. The second is where there are two causes, either of which would by itself have been sufficient to cause the loss. The third is where there are two successive causes, and the question is whether the second is sufficient to break the chain of causation deriving from the first, so that the first ceases to be an operating cause.

18.4 Another important point in the area of causation is that a particular event may cause certain losses while merely drawing attention to others. An illuminating example of this in an insurance context is provided by the common case of windows and doors in household policies. A storm may result in water coming in through these, damaging carpets and furnishings. In such cases the policyholder frequently claims for the cost of replacing the window as well as for the cost of the carpets and furnishings. Although the latter claim is likely to succeed, the former will often not. The reason for this is that the storm is not the cause of the failure of the window; rather it reveals the fact that the window has failed, presumably by reason of simply wearing out. This cause of the loss is naturally not an insured peril, and the claim therefore cannot succeed.

Accidental causes

18.5 A policy may give protection specifically against 'accidental damage'. Even if the cover is not expressed in this way, it is a general principle of insurance that cover is not provided in respect of damage deliberately caused by the policy-holder or those for whom he is responsible. For these reasons it is important to understand what in an insurance context is meant by saying that something was an 'accident'.

At the simplest level this question may be answered by saying that an event is accidental if it is not caused deliberately. Thus in one IOB case[1] of building insurance the claim was for damage following the escape of water from a copper central heating pipe. Although the insurers accepted liability for the damage caused by the escape, they denied liability for the cost of tracing and repairing the leak. However, the policy provided cover against accidental damage to pipes. The Ombudsman held that the damage to this pipe was to be regarded as accidental on the basis that it had not been caused by the deliberate actions of any person.

A more dramatic example occurred in an IOB case[2] involving a PHI policy, which excluded disability 'caused or contributed to by pregnancy or childbirth'. After a difficult pregnancy, the policyholder was induced, but then an emergency caesar-ean had to be performed. Complications developed, as a result of which she suffered serious brain damage. The insurers denied liability on the basis of the exclusion, but the Ombudsman upheld the policyholder's complaint. Although the caesarean could in one sense be said to have been the cause of the brain damage, it was more appropriate to view it as no more than the background against which the wholly unexpected and radical complications developed. Insurance, like other areas of the law, looks to proximate causes, rather than to remote causes. Looking at the matter from this point of view, the only proper conclusion was that the injury was to be regarded as being an accident and thus not caught by the policy exclusion.

[1] IOB 3.15.
[2] IOB 15.1.

18.6 It is also necessary to approach realistically the identification of the cause of the loss. In *IF P&C Insurance Ltd v Silversea Cruises Ltd*[1] there was business interruption cover for the net loss causes by State Department warnings of acts of war, terrorist activities and other related events. The insured's business declined sharply following the attacks on the World Trade Center on 11 September 2001, but one of the defences put forward by the insurers was that this loss was caused not by the subsequent warnings of possible terrorist activity, but by the fact of the original attacks. The Court of Appeal rightly regarded this as unacceptably nit-picking. It was not realistically possible to distinguish the fear of further attacks generated by the original attacks from the fear of further attacks generated by the warnings of the possibility of further attacks, and this decline in business was legitimately to be regarded as resulting from the warnings and was therefore covered by the policy.

[1] [2004] Lloyd's Rep IR 217, Tomlinson J; and [2004] Lloyd's Rep IR 696, CA.

Intervening causes

18.7 In *Merchants' Marine Insurance Co v Liverpool Marine and General Insurance Co Ltd*[1] a marine policy provided cover for any damage to a ship occurring during the currency of the policy and thereafter *en route* to its final destination[2], but only for the 'immediate consequences' of any damage which happened after the expiry of the policy. The ship was damaged after the policy expired but while *en route* to its destination. Temporary repairs were made, but the ship later sank. It was held that the sinking was the 'immediate consequence' of the damage. It could not seriously be doubted that the damage caused the sinking, but the policy in this case contained a further requirement of 'immediate' consequence. This might have been interpreted in either of two ways. One view would have been that the word 'immediate' relates essentially to time, so that the lapse of time between the damage and the sinking took the loss outside the coverage of the policy. The alternative view, which appears to have prevailed here, is that 'immediate' meant only that there must be no intervening cause. The obvious objection to that interpretation is that it gives no real meaning to the word 'immediate' – it seems that the result would have been the same if that word had been omitted. Indeed, it may then be said that the result of the case would have been the same if the entire proviso about damage happening after the expiry of the policy had been omitted, since presumably the only way in which that proviso was intended to alter the position was by adding the requirement that the loss must be the 'immediate consequence' of the damage, rather than simply being caused by it[3].

In *Lloyd's TSB General Insurance Holdings Ltd v Lloyd's Bank Group Insurance Co Ltd*[4], financial adviser employed by the claimant had allegedly given negligent pensions advice. For the purposes of a clause allowing the aggregation of all claims arising from a single negligent act or omission it was necessary to decide whether the cause of the claims made against the claimant by aggrieved investors was the claimant's failure to train its staff properly, or whether each claim was to be regarded as caused by the negligent advice of the salesperson. It was held that the effective cause of the loss was the claimant's failure to train its sales force, and that the consequent failure of individual salespersons to give proper advice did not break the chain of causation. The decision is explicable on the basis that the failures in individual cases were themselves the natural consequence of the claimant's initial failure to provide proper training.

[1] (1928) 31 Ll L Rep 45, CA.
[2] This rather curious wording appears to create a strange cross between a time policy and a voyage policy. A literalist might argue that the policy did not 'expire' until the ship arrived at its final destination, so that the reference to damage happening after the expiry is meaningless, but that is clearly not what the draftsman meant.
[3] It is fair to say that the policy wording in this case was somewhat unusual.
[4] [2001] 1 All ER (Comm) 13, Moore-Bick J.

Effective causes

18.8 Some examination of the relevant case law is essential. In *Leyland Shipping Co v Norwich Union Fire Insurance Society Ltd*[1] a marine insurance policy excluded loss resulting from 'hostilities'. The ship was torpedoed and badly damaged. It reached Le Havre and a safe berth, where, apparently, it could have remained in safety in the inner harbour. However, it was later moved to the outer harbour by order of the harbour authorities, where it suffered further damage and sank. When a claim was made on the policy it became necessary to decide whether the moving to the outer harbour and the further damage then resulting constituted a *novus actus interveniens* so that the loss was not caused by hostilities. It was held that there had been no break in the chain of causation. This was still a loss from hostilities, and the policy did not provide cover. The decision seems somewhat odd, given the finding that the ship would probably not have sunk had it not been moved to the outer harbour. It is not easy to understand why Lord Finlay LC should observe[2] that the case must be decided as if the ship had never been to the inner harbour. In *Green v Elmslie*[3] a ship was insured against capture. In a storm the ship was driven onto the French coast, where it was captured. The insurers argued that this was a loss by perils of the sea and not by capture, but Lord Kenyon CJ held that it was a loss by capture. It was obviously relevant that, had the ship been driven onto the coast of any other country, it would have been in no danger.

Other marine cases have provided important illustrations of the limits of the notion of effective cause and the law's tendency to look no further than the nearest cause. In *Ionides v Universal Marine Insurance Co*[4] a ship ran aground on Cape Hatteras. The light which normally shone there had been extinguished by the Confederate forces in the American Civil War. It was held that the loss was proximately caused by the perils of the seas.

In *Hamilton, Fraser & Co v Pandorf*[5] water entered the ship and damaged cargo after rats had gnawed a hole in a pipe. It was held that the sea water was the immediate cause of the loss, rather than the rats.

These cases collectively may be taken as showing that a particular loss may have more than one effective cause. This point is illustrated by *Midland Mainline Ltd v Eagle Star Insurance Co Ltd*[6], a case arising out of the Hatfield railway accident of

October 2000. The Claimants had business interruption insurance which covered losses caused by denial of access to the railway network. Following the accident emergency speed restrictions were imposed on many parts of the network, disrupting the timetables of the Claimants. The business interruption policy also contained an exclusion for loss arising from wear and tear. When the Claimants claimed on the policy one question which arose was whether the losses brought about by the disruptions were caused by denial of access or whether they resulted from wear and tear. It was clear that the cracking of the rail which led to the accident was wear and tear. The Court of Appeal, reversing the decision of David Steel J[7], held that both the wear and tear and the denial of access were proximate causes of the loss[8].

[1] [1918] AC 350, HL.
[2] At 355.
[3] (1794) Peake 278, 170 ER 156.
[4] (1863) 32 LJCP 170.
[5] (1887) 12 App Cas 518.
[6] [2004] Lloyd's Rep IR 739.
[7] [2004] Lloyd's Rep IR 22.
[8] For the general principle that there can be more than one proximate cause see *Wayne Tank and Pump Co Ltd v Employers Liability Assurance Corporation Ltd* [1974] 1 QB 57, CA.

No cover for loss caused by avoiding action

18.9 *Becker Gray & Co v London Assurance*[1] establishes an important general point of insurance law. Cargo was laden on board a British ship bound for Germany from Malta. The insurance policy included loss arising from restraint of princes. On the outbreak of war in August 1914 the master took the view that the presence in the Mediterranean of the Goeben and the Breslau constituted a substantial risk of capture and therefore put into Messina, a neutral port, where the ship was interned. The question was whether the resulting constructive total loss was caused by restraint of princes. It was held that it was not. The loss was caused by the act of the master: this was self-restraint, not restraint of princes. No insured peril had materialised and there could be no recovery under the policy. Lord Sumner made the very important observation that a distinction must be drawn between a loss by perils insured against and a loss caused by avoiding such perils. This is a point of enormous importance, and it is obvious that it can lead to unsatisfactory results. In *Becker Gray* itself it appears that the insurers would have been liable if the master had chosen to take the risk of capture and had in fact been captured, even though the loss which happened was no greater than that which would have resulted from capture[2]. In other contexts the application of the principle means, for example, that in a household buildings policy expenditure incurred to protect a property against storm damage is not recoverable, though the loss arising from the storm damage is recoverable[3]. Obviously, a line must be drawn – if all expenditure to prevent storm damage were recoverable, the insurance policy would be turned into a maintenance contract. On the other hand *Becker Gray* illustrates the fact that there can be no recovery even when the avoiding action is taken in the fact of an immediate and credible threat of the operation of an insured peril. It may fairly be said that this is a settled and rather arbitrary rule of insurance law, rather than a strictly logical application of the ordinary principles of causation.

In *Wayne Tank and Pump v Employers' Liability Corpn*[4] the claimants were contractors engaged to build a factory. The factory burned down because the defendants had done the electrical wiring wrongly[5]. Having been held liable to their client, they sought to claim on their liability insurance. The policy contained an exception for 'damage caused by the nature or condition of any goods sold or supplied by or on behalf of the insured'. It was held that the proximate cause of the fire was the dangerously defective nature of the installation. This fell within the exception, and there was therefore no cover under the policy.

1 [1918] AC 101, HL.
2 In human terms it might well have been less, since the capture could well have involved some loss of life.
3 Provided of course that the failure to incur the expenditure cannot be regarded as amounting to a failure to take reasonable care of the property.
4 [1974] QB 57, CA, Lord Denning MR, Cairns and Roskill LJJ.
5 See *Harbutt's Plasticine Ltd v Wayne Tank and Pump Co* [1970] 1 All ER 225, CA.

Immediate causes and pre-disposing causes

18.10 In *Marcel Beller Ltd v Hayden*[1] the assured died after a road accident caused by his own drunkenness. The question was whether the death was to be regarded as 'accidental' for the purposes of a personal accident policy. It was held that it was. The law must look to the immediate cause of the death, rather than to any pre-disposing cause. Here the immediate cause was the car accident, which was clearly accidental.

Fitton v Accidental Death Insurance[2] was a personal accident case. The policy had an exception for 'hernia'. After suffering an injury the claimant underwent an operation, suffered a hernia and died of it. It was held that the death was not caused by the hernia, but by the operation. The case may perhaps be regarded as being in the same line as *Leyland*.

In one IOB case[3] the policyholder had had surgical treatment for tennis elbow before the inception of the policy. After inception she developed a post-operative wound infection. The Ombudsman held that the infection was not a natural and ordinary cause of the earlier treatment and should therefore be regarded as a new cause not caught by the exclusion. This decision seems somewhat generous from the point of view of the policyholder.

In another IOB case[4] a household policy covered accidental damage, but with an exclusion for:

> 'damage caused by … domestic animals or other household pets.'

The policyholder's adult daughter collided with a table, causing two clocks to fall from it, as she was pulled along by the policyholder's dog. The insurer sought to reject the claim on the basis of the above exclusion, but the Ombudsman held that the damage was caused by the daughter, not by the dog.

1 [1978] 3 All ER 111, Judge Edgar Fay QC.
2 (1864) 17 CBNS 122, 144 ER 50 CCP. See also Chapter 35.

[3] IOB 7.5.
[4] IOB 14.17.

Concurrent causes[1]

18.11 Here the position appears to depend upon the interaction of coverage and exclusions. If one or more of the causes is insured and none is specifically excluded, then the policy pays[2], but if any of the causes is specifically excluded, then it does not[3]. However, in such cases the IOB practice was to expect insurers to make a 'fair and reasonable' contribution, based on the extent to which the insured peril contributed to the loss[4].

In a recent IOB decision[5] there was an exclusion for depression, and it appeared that the policyholder's inability to work was caused partly by back problems and partly by depression. The Ombudsman held that the fair and reasonable outcome was that the insurers should pay 50% of the sum insured. From a strict legal point of view this case appears to depend very much upon the exact policy wording. If the policy excludes incapacity 'caused or contributed to' by depression, then it would seem that the insurer is not liable. Otherwise, it is suggested that there is liability, so long as the back problems can be considered an operating cause of the incapacity. It does not appear to be relevant that the back problems by themselves might not have been sufficient to cause the incapacity.

[1] IOB 22 leading article.
[2] *JJ Lloyd Instruments Ltd v Northern Star Insurance Co Ltd* [1987] 1 Lloyd's Rep 32, CA; *Martini Investments Ltd v McGinn* [2001] Lloyd's Rep IR 374, Timothy Walker J.
[3] See n 2 above. See also *Wayne Tank and Pump Co Ltd v Employers Liability Assurance Corpn Ltd* [1973] 2 Lloyd's Rep 237, CA.
[4] IOB 22.
[5] IOB 21.4.

When loss would have happened anyway

18.12 In *Deloitte Haskins & Sells v National Mutual Life Nominees*[1] the defendants were auditors of a public company which took unsecured deposits from the public. Under the relevant regulatory regime the company was obliged to appoint a trustee to act on behalf of the unsecured depositors. It was part of the auditors' duty to review the solvency of the company and to make reports to the trustee if they became aware of anything which was relevant to the performance of the duties of the trustee. After the company went into insolvent liquidation the trustee brought proceedings against the auditors, alleging that they had failed in their statutory duties in that they had not reported certain matters as soon as they should have done, with the result that the trustee had become liable to pay some $6.75m to the unsecured depositors. Part of the argument on behalf of the auditors (effectively the auditors' liability insurers) was that by the time the auditors became aware of the matters in issue the company was already insolvent, so that the losses would have been incurred anyway. The Court of Appeal of New Zealand[2] rejected this defence, saying that whatever the strict logic of the position, policy considerations required that the auditors should be held liable. That decision was reversed by the Privy Council. On a strict interpretation it is probably correct to say that the Privy Council's decision depends on the absence of any breach of duty rather than on the question of causation, but that court also observed that on the facts alleged it could not be said that the auditors' acts or omissions had caused the loss.

1 [1993] 2 All ER 1015, PC.
2 [1991] 3 NZBLC 102.

Remoteness of damage

18.13 In one IOB case[1] a motor policy excluded loss caused by deception[2]. It was held that this exclusion applied where the policyholder's car turned out to have been stolen, with the result that she had to return it to the true owner. The correctness of this decision appears to depend on the fact that the vendor had been prosecuted in relation to the car (presumably for receiving stolen property). If it appeared that the immediate vendor had acted innocently, then it is suggested that the deception, which must have happened at an earlier stage in the car's chain of title, would be too remote to be considered as being the cause of the loss.

1 IOB 11.27.
2 This trend is a result of the decision of the Court of Appeal in *Dobson v General Accident* [1990] 1 QB 274.

Conclusion

18.14 Questions of causation are without doubt some of the most difficult problems which arise in any area of law. It is submitted that no one has ever succeeded in explaining satisfactorily all the decisions on causation in English law. Most discussions of the subject are in the end reduced to a series of examples which seek to illustrate the typical approach of the courts, but which cannot really be said to develop any coherent principle[1]. It might justly be said that the present discussion is not exempt from this criticism. In the particular context of insurance it might also be added that the decisions discussed in this Chapter tend to support the idea that causation is an extremely flexible notion, which courts are able to use to manipulate the outcome of cases to suit their preferences. It is also certainly true that the drafting of policies in relation to issues of causation frequently leaves a good deal to be desired.

1 Without doubt the best concerted attempt at the task is Hart and Honore *Causation in the Law* (2nd edn, 1985, OUP), though even that monumental work is eventually driven to admit that logic alone will not solve all the problems in causation.

Chapter 19

The claims process and indemnity

19.1 This Chapter deals with the legal rules relevant to the process of making a claim under the policy and with issues relating to the quantum of the insurer's liability. Although the detailed procedures applicable to claims are often laid down in the policy itself, there is some case law supporting the development of general principles appropriate to all types of claim.

Making a claim

Accrual of the cause of action

19.2 No claim can be made before the date when the cause of action accrues. A number of cases have considered the problem of accrual of cause of action under indemnity contracts. The question which commonly arises is whether the claimant's cause of action accrues when he incurs the loss (which may include a liability to a third party) or only when the extent of that liability is quantified, which may be achieved by a finding of liability by a court[1].

The leading authority in this area is *Telfair Shipping Corpn v Intersea Carriers SA, The Caroline P*[2]. This was a charter-party case, in which the charter-party required the master of the vessel to sign bills of lading 'as presented.' The bills of lading which were presented imposed upon the owners obligations in respect of the cargo in excess of those provided for in the charter-party. The owners incurred liability under these obligations and sought indemnity from the charterers. The question was when the owners' right of indemnity arose.

Neill J analysed in detail the circumstances under which A, who has become liable to B, may be able to obtain redress from C. He held that these cases fell into three categories:

(a) Actions based upon breach of contract. These cases fall within the usual principles applicable to contract cases, so that time runs from the breach of contract by C.
(b) Actions based upon an express indemnity agreement. Here the date of accrual will depend upon the terms of the indemnity. If the indemnity is

expressed as being against liability then it is likely that the cause of action will accrue when the liability is incurred. In other cases, though, the cause of action will normally accrue when A's liability to B has been established and ascertained.

(c) Actions based upon an implied indemnity. It will normally be assumed that this is an indemnity against the discharge of a liability rather than against the incurring of that liability, so that the cause of action will accrue only when the liability is established and quantified. It was accepted that before the Judicature Acts 1873–75 equity might in some cases have required the defendant to set aside a fund to meet the liability in advance of its being ascertained. However, even in equity the defendant would not have been compelled to pay over this fund in advance of the establishment of the liability, and the obligation to establish the fund would not be sufficient to cause the action to accrue for limitation purposes.

The judgment in *Telfair Shipping* offers a detailed and convincing analysis of the problems of accrual of action in indemnity contracts. Nevertheless it leaves a number of potentially significant difficulties in this area unresolved. First, Neill J carefully couches his judgment in terms of general propositions, leaving open the possibility that there may be exceptions to the general principles. It is therefore necessary to consider under what circumstances these exceptions might arise. So far as express indemnity is concerned it may be suggested that only clauses which speak of indemnity against 'liability' will be construed as departing from the general rule, whilst in the case of implied indemnity it is even more unlikely that a court will be prepared to find a departure from the general principle. The second outstanding point concerns the nature of the indemnity which is implied in these cases. Neill J expressed the view that any indemnity, even if construed as an indemnity against the incurring of liability, would only cover actual, as distinct from potential liability. In other words, where only part of the liability materialises immediately, the action for the indemnity nevertheless accrues, and, if the remainder of the liability does not materialise for more than six years, the result will apparently be that it cannot be reclaimed under the indemnity.

[1] See also the discussion below on *Callaghan v Dominion Insurance* [1997] 2 Lloyd's Rep 541.
[2] [1985] 1 WLR 553.

Insurance contracts

19.3 The most common example of a contract of indemnity is of course an insurance contract. This is an example of an express indemnity, as described by Neill J in the *Telfair Shipping* case. Consequently, the date when the cause of action accrues will depend upon the terms of the contract, but the usual rule may be illustrated by reference to *Chandris v Argo Insurance Co*[1]. This was a marine insurance case which involved general average losses and particular average losses under the MIA 1906. In accordance with the usual marine insurance practice average adjusters were employed to determine the proportions in which the losses should be borne by the various cargo owners involved. Average adjustment can be a protracted process, as happened here, and the result was that the action, which was to recover sums specified in the adjusters' award, was brought more than six years after the losses happened, though fewer than six years after the making of the award. It is the practice in insurance that underwriters do not pay on a claim until the award of the average adjusters is published (since until that time the amount of the claim cannot be properly ascertained), and the claimant accordingly argued that the cause of action could not accrue until that time. Megaw J rejected this argument, holding that the cause of action accrued when the loss was incurred – the insurers' refusal to pay could not be a relevant factor in the decision. The case may be treated as showing that in insurance contracts, the right of recovery against the insurer accrues on the happening of the loss rather than at any later stage. This principle is generally sound, but Megaw J's reasoning in applying to the facts of this particular case is unconvincing. Given the custom of the market[2] that no payment is made until the award is published, it would have been better to hold that the parties have agreed that the cause of action does not accrue until that time. To adopt the classification later developed by Neill J in the *Telfair Shipping case*, this is a case of express indemnity, and the date of accrual depends on the terms of the indemnity. If one of those terms is that the indemnity is not payable until a date which will always be significantly later than the date of the loss, this must strongly suggest that it is only at the later time that the cause of action accrues. The principle was again illustrated, and this time correctly applied in *Lefevre v White*[3]. The claimant brought a personal injuries action. The defendant became bankrupt, so the claimant sought to sue the defendant's liability insurers under the TP(RAI)A 1930. The claimant argued that the cause of action against the insurers did not arise until the defendant became bankrupt, but it was held that the action against the insurers accrues at the same time as the claimant's original action against the defendant, notwithstanding that at that stage the claimant could not have sued the insurers. The present decision is to be explained on the basis that the right which is transferred to the claimant under the 1930 Act[4] is the *defendant's* right to sue his own liability insurers. Under an express contract of indemnity this of course accrues as soon as the loss occurs, notwithstanding that the quantum of loss has not at that time been established. A more unusual case about accrual is *Hardial Singh Virk v Gan Life Holdings plc*[5] Under the policy the insurer agreed to pay the claimant a 'critical illness benefit' if he suffered a stroke, provided that he survived for a period of thirty days after the stroke, failing which death benefits became payable under other provisions of the policy. On 11 August 1992 the claimant suffered a stroke. In 1993 liability was repudiated under the policy for non-disclosure. The action was commenced on 21 August 1998. The claimant contended that the 30-day survival clause was a condition precedent to liability under the policy, with the consequence that the cause of action for failure to pay under the policy did not accrue to him until after the expiry of that period, namely on 11 September 1992, such that his claim was not time-barred. The Court of Appeal held that it was open to the parties to modify or displace the general rule as to accrual by express terms, so as to create a condition precedent to the insured's right to payment. In the present case the insured event was not 'stroke' simpliciter: it was the consequent condition of 'critical illness'. The parties had expressly provided that that condition had to endure for a period of at least 30 days (so that the separate life provisions of the policy would not apply) and the right to payment in respect of that condition therefore did not arise until after the expiry of that period. Accordingly, the action was not time-barred.

[1] [1963] 2 Lloyd's Rep 65.

[2] Establishing market custom can often require extensive and expensive evidence; see *Baker v Black Sea & Baltic General Insurance Co* [1996] LRLR 353, CA, where it was suggested that this process ought to be brought under rather better control.
[3] [1990] 1 Lloyd's Rep 569, Popplewell J.
[4] For detailed treatment of this Act see Chapter 29.
[5] [2000] Lloyd's Rep IR 159, CA.

Accrual of action against broker

19.4 In *Knapp v Ecclesiastical Insurance Group plc*[1] an insurance broker had negligently advised a client to take out an insurance policy which was voidable and which the insurer avoided when the client tried to claim under it. The question to be determined by the Court of Appeal was when the cause of action against the broker arose, ie when did the claimants first suffer damage as a result of the insurance brokers alleged breach of duty – when the policy premium was paid or when the insurer avoided the policy?

The authorities considered indicated that the cause of action could accrue and the claimant had suffered damage once he had acted upon the relevant advice to his detriment and failed to get that to which he was entitled. In this case the claimants paid their renewal premiums without getting in return a binding contract of indemnity from the insurance company – the loss which they suffered was the receipt of a purported cover which was not binding, a deficiency of which they were not aware, in return for the payment of the renewal premiums. The fact that how serious the consequences of the negligence would be depended upon subsequent events and contingencies did not alter that.

Accordingly, the cause of action arose when the policy premiums were paid and not when the insurer avoided the policy.

In *Callaghan v Dominion Insurance Co Ltd*[2] the question arose as to whether the cause of action for breach of a contract of indemnity insurance arose at the date of a fire on the claimant's property in 1989 or on the avoidance of the policy in 1990, for the purposes of determining whether the claim was statute barred.

The court defined indemnity insurance as an agreement by the insurer to confer on the insured a contractual right which came into existence immediately when loss was suffered by the happening of an event insured against, to be put by the insurer into the same position in which the insured would have been had the event not occurred. Accordingly, the cause of action for breach of such an insurance contract, whether marine or property insurance, arose at the date of the loss, from the failure of the insurer to prevent the insured person from suffering loss.

[1] [1998] Lloyd's Rep IR 390, CA.
[2] [1997] 2 Lloyd's Rep 541.

Notification – time limits and need for prompt notification

19.5 The policy will normally contain a term requiring notification of claims at least within a reasonable period. In commercial policies there may be a requirement to notify within a set number of days of the claim arising. In *Cassell v Lancashire and Yorkshire Accident Co*[1] the claimant was insured against accidents. It was a condition precedent of liability that notice of any accident be given within 14 days of its occurrence. The claimant suffered an accident, but no consequences of this manifested themselves for several months, with the natural result that the claimant saw no reason to notify the insurers within the 14 days. The court upheld the insurers' repudiation of the claim on the ground that the clause was clear and unambiguous. A similar result was reached in the more modern case of *TH Adamson & Sons v Liverpool London and Globe Insurance*[2], which concerned an employees' fidelity policy. Again the losses were required to be notified within 14 days. Not surprisingly, the dishonest employee did his best to cover up the frauds, which were not discovered for some months. Lord Goddard CJ held that the clause meant what it said, with the result that very little of the total loss could be recovered. It might of course be argued in both cases (and particularly in *Adamson*) that given the nature of the risk the notification clause very substantially cut down the cover provided. However, it does not follow that the decisions were wrong. It would have been quite difficult to construe these clauses as making the 14 days run from the date of discovery without doing serious violence to the words used. Moreover, it is not obvious that such an outcome would have been fair. The premium had no doubt been calculated on the basis of the risk as described in the policy, so the policyholders had arguably got what they paid for. The application of the UTCCR 1999 to such terms is somewhat problematic[3]. However, clauses of this kind are not permitted in personal lines policies by virtue of cl 2 of the SGIP. As ever, the Insurance Ombudsman will enforce compliance with the statement by refusing to allow insurers to rely upon clauses which breach this rule. In one IOB case[4] a policyholder submitted a claim for the theft of items from property which he rented out. At the time of the theft the police had asked him not to make a claim until they had had chance to complete investigations into the letting agents. Eight months later a second theft occurred, and the policyholder notified the insurers of both claims. The insurers sought to rely upon the delay in notifying the first claim[5], but the Insurance Ombudsman held that the insurer had not been prejudiced by the failure to notify earlier[6]. In any event the SGIP[7] states that an insurer will not repudiate liability for breach of condition where the circumstances of the loss are unconnected with the breach.

[1] (1885) 1 TLR 495, DC.
[2] [1953] 2 Lloyd's Rep 355, Lord Goddard CJ.
[3] See Chapter 16.
[4] IOB 14.8.
[5] Although the report does not make this clear, the clause presumably required no more than notification within a reasonable time, since to do otherwise would breach the Statements of Practice.
[6] This must depend on the particular facts of the case: as a general point insurers have good reason to want to be notified promptly of theft claims, since they can then inspect the *locus in quo* at an early stage to satisfy themselves about the claim.
[7] Clause 2.

Notification of claim – whether there is a condition precedent to liability

19.6 In *Alfred McAlpine plc v BAI (Run-off) Ltd*[1] the insurance contract in question contained a clause providing that:

> 'In the event of any occurrence which may give rise to a claim under this policy, the insured shall as soon as possible, give notice thereof to the company in writing with full details …'

The question was whether non compliance with this provision operated as a substantive defence to the claim – ie was it a condition any breach of which would amount to a repudiatory breach or merely an innominate term, breach of which would only give rise to a right to treat the contract as terminated if the consequences were such as substantially to deprive the innocent party of the whole benefit of the contract[2]?

There was no term of general application to make the clause a condition precedent to the insurers' liability. There was also no specific express provision that this was a condition precedent, in contrast to which there was a provision that an arbitration award was to be *'a condition precedent to any right of action against the company.'* This was held to be a strong indication that the clause was not intended to be a condition precedent.

It was held that in the absence of an express or implied term to the effect that it was a condition precedent an assured who advanced a claim for an indemnity without first complying with the requirements of the clause committed a breach of the insurance contract, the remedy for which was only damages, ie there would not be a right to repudiate the policy, nor to deny the claim in its entirety[3].

In the specific context of motor insurance, insurers are entitled to rely upon the non-service of a statutory notice of intention to commence proceedings[4] even though they are in fact aware of the prospect (and actual fact) of the proceedings[5].

1 [2000] Lloyd's Rep IR 352, CA.
2 As to types of terms, see further Chapter 17.
3 See also *Friends Provident Life and Pensions Ltd v Sirius International Insurance* [2005] 2 All ER Comm 145 CA, discussed further at para 17.11, where it was suggested that as a general rule such terms should be regarded as simple conditions.
4 RTA 1988, s 152.
5 *Wake v Page* (2001) Times, 9 February, CA.

Effect of delay

19.7 In *Taylors v Builders Accident Insurance*[1] the facts were very similar to those in the *McAlpine* case. It was suggested by the court that the delay in giving notice under the policy deprived the insurers of their rights to investigate and defend their position which amounted to a breach which would enable the insurance company to repudiate notwithstanding that the condition breached was not stated to be a condition precedent. The distinction as to the remedy must rest upon the court's view that this clause was in effect a condition precedent even though the policy did not expressly say so.

1 (1997) PIQR P247.

Fraudulent claims

19.8 Policies of non-marine insurance usually contain an express condition against fraudulent claims.

Even in the absence of an express clause, there is a general duty not to make fraudulent claims. This may be viewed either as an implied term of the policy, or, perhaps better, as part of the continuing duty of utmost good faith[1]. In *Cox v Orion*[2] the claimant held motor insurance. After an accident he submitted a claim, the particulars of which were false in material respects. It was held that the insurers were entitled to repudiate liability on this ground, but it is not clear whether they were entitled to avoid the policy, as would presumably be the case if this were a breach of utmost good faith. However, the fraud must be in a matter directly related to the claim, rather than in a collateral matter[3].

An insurer who alleges fraud must prove it – *McGregor v Prudential Insurance Co Ltd*[4] where it was held that an insurer, who alleged that the insured's claim for loss by fire was fraudulent because the fire was started deliberately by the insured, had to prove the insured's responsibility and that there was no other plausible explanation for fire. This may be contrasted with the principle in *The Popi M*[5] that a claim will fail where the insured is not able to demonstrate the cause of the loss, and that the insurer does not have to establish that the cause was an excluded peril. As with any other allegation of fraud, the standard of proof is a high one[6]. The question of the effect of fraudulent claims has come before the courts on a number of occasions in recent years.

In *Manifest Shipping & Co Ltd v Uni Polaris Shipping Co Ltd (The Star Sea)*[7] it was alleged that there had been a breach of the duty of utmost good faith in failing to disclose reports of previous losses of other ships sooner and fraud in misleading the underwriters by concealing evidence. It was held that whereas it is established by the MIA 1906, s 17 that underwriters are not liable for fraudulent claims there is less agreement as to the content of the duty of utmost good faith or remedies for breach of the duty. When a claim is made the duty rests upon both assured and insurer but it is less clear whether the duty of disclosure is co-extensive with the pre-contractual duty. Such a distinction is irrelevant for s 17 as it would be inconsistent with the entitlement to avoid the contract where a party has acted innocently. No enlargement of the duty not to make fraudulent claims exists to embrace culpably made claims. There was no warrant for increasing the existing duty in the manner sought, which covered both disclosure needed for the claim and to assist the underwriters in their defence or to limit their liability. Even if the contractual duty of disclosure survives the contract itself it is then superseded by the procedures of the CPR 1998 concerning a party's disclosure obligations. In *Fargnoli v GA Bonus plc*[8] the policy provided that in the event of a fraudulent claim all benefit under the policy would be forfeited. There were two separate losses, and the insurers alleged that the second of these was caused by the wilful act of the policyholder. They sought to use this as a ground to terminate[9] the policy and to refuse to meet either claim. It was held that the fraudulent claim could operate only prospectively, voiding the claim itself and any subsequent claim, but not allowing the insurers to escape an accrued liability for a previous loss. Although this conclusion is to some extent dependent on the wording of the policy, it is suggested that a court is likely to lean to this interpretation whenever possible.

[1] *The Star Sea* [2001] Lloyd's Rep IR 247, HL; see also *Interpart Commerciao E Gestato SA v Lexington Insurance Co* [2004] Lloyd's Rep IR 690, Chambers J, where it was held that a document could be false for some purposes and not for others.
[2] [1982] RTR 1, CA.
[3] *K/S Merc-Scandia XXXXII v Certain Lloyd's Underwriters* [2000] Lloyd's Rep IR 694, Aitkens J and see Chapter 13 on the continuing duty of utmost good faith.
[4] [1998] 1 Lloyd's Rep 112 and see *Rhesa Shipping Co SA v Edmunds* [1985] 2 Lloyd's Rep 1 HL; *Waddle v Wallsand Shipping Co Ltd (The Hopestar)* [1952] 2 Lloyd's Rep 105, Devlin J.
[5] [1985] 2 All ER 712, HL.
[6] And counsel should not allege fraud unless he has before him reasonably credible material which as it stands establishes a *prima facie* case of fraud – Code of Conduct of the Bar (7th edn), para 704(c). Breach of this rule is liable to lead to a wasted costs order: *Medcalf v Mardell* [2001] OS LS Gaz R 36, CA.
[7] [1997] 1 Lloyd's Rep 360, CA. An appeal to the House of Lords was dismissed: (2001) Times, 25 January.
[8] [1997] Re LR 374 Ct of Sess (OH).
[9] The judgment speaks in terms of 'rescission', but the word is clearly not used here in its English law sense of rescission *ab initio*.

19.9 The Insurance Ombudsman has also had to pronounce on the principles applicable to dealing with fraudulent claims. Although these pronouncements do not have the force of law, it is suggested that they are worthy of consideration in relation to the duty of both sides to act in utmost good faith.

The first question concerns the attitude to be taken by insurers when dealing with possibly fraudulent claims. In one IOB case[1] the policyholder's house was burgled while he was on holiday, electrical items and jewellery being stolen. The policyholder gave a statement about this matter to the police and then claimed on his contents policy. The insurers appointed independent investigators, who took statements from the policyholder and other members of his family. As a result of the investigators' report, the insurers wrote to the policyholder, telling him that the claim was being rejected because of unspecified 'unsatisfactory matters' in connection with the claim. They refused to give more details and told him that the matter was being referred to the police. The letter was copied to his employers, a bank which had arranged the insurance for him and which was also the mortgagee of his house. The policyholder complained to the Ombudsman about the way in which the claim had been handled. The Ombudsman held that the insurers had been guilty of misadministration in a number of respects.

First, it was not good insurance practice to refuse to explain the grounds for refusing the claim. It is obviously not possible for a policyholder to respond to any of the insurer's concerns about the claim when he does not even know what those concerns are.

Secondly, there appeared to be no good reason for the insurer to decide to refer the matter to the police without at least giving the policyholder the chance to give some explanation.

Thirdly, there was no proper reason for copying the letter to the policyholder's employer. Such action would inevitably be prejudicial to the policyholder's position at the bank, especially since the letter included the statement about the matter being referred to the police[2]. It could not be good practice to send such a letter at a time when the policyholder had been given no opportunity to explain himself.

[1] IOB 8.8; for another example of insensitive case-handling see IOB 13.24.
[2] It might be thought that the innuendo behind this observation was capable of amounting to a defamatory statement.

19.10 Although this is only a single case, the points raised here may be regarded as being of general importance. It is suggested that the following principles may properly be derived from the decision:

(1) Insurers have a duty to seek explanations from the policyholder before rejecting a claim.
(2) Referring a claim to the police is to be done only in exceptional circumstances and only after allowing the possibility of an explanation.
(3) The same applies to notifying the policyholder's employers. Indeed, it may well be that an even higher standard is required here, since the police do at least have the duty to investigate alleged wrongdoing.
(4) Insurers should be slow to allege fraud in relation to the details of the claim. In this case the insurers took the view that the claim contained sufficient in the way of exaggeration to taint the whole claim. There were certainly some discrepancies in statements made at different times by different members of the policyholder's family, but the Ombudsman took the view that these could be regarded as examples of differing and sometimes confused recollection rather than as evidence of dishonesty. It was also relevant that the total claim amounted to only about 25% of the sum insured (and there was no suggestion of over-insurance or under insurance). In addition to requiring the insurers to pay the claim, the Ombudsman made one of the biggest awards for misadministration in the history of the IOB, a total of £2,000.
(5) It is necessary to remember that policyholders do not always have every detail at their fingertips, particularly when a loss, such as a burglary, has just been discovered. The IOB report observes that absence of documentary evidence of purchase or possession of goods is not, by itself, conclusive of lack of ownership. Although the report does not put matters in quite these terms, the gist of it seems to come close to saying that, once the fact of the loss is accepted, the policyholder's account of the details of what has been lost ought to be accepted in the absence of evidence to the contrary.

The second question concerns the attitude to be taken by the Insurance Ombudsman where it appears that a claim brought to the IOB is itself fraudulent. This is something which requires careful handling. In the first place the IOB has no power to summon witnesses or to require the policyholder or anyone else to give evidence. In those cases where evidence, oral or written, is obtained, there is no power to administer oaths, with the result that penalties for perjury do not apply to the making of false statements. Secondly, decisions of the IOB do not attract any privilege for the purposes of the law of defamation. It would therefore be very imprudent for the Ombudsman to issue decisions which accused a policyholder of fraud. In practice the IOB has dealt with this problem by taking advantage of the provision in the Terms of Reference under which jurisdiction may be declined if in the opinion of the Ombudsman the matter is one which is more suitable to be investigated by a court. The usual form of words has been along the lines that the factual disputes cannot properly be resolved by the informal procedure which the IOB operates, and that the policyholder is therefore left to his remedies at law.

Partially fraudulent insurance claim

19.11 In *Galloway v Guardian Royal Exchange*[1] the claimant submitted a claim under his insurance policy for loss sustained in a burglary – £16,000 and also made a false claim for an additional £2,000 in respect of a computer. The policy did not contain an express clause saying that if an insured submitted a claim that was partially fraudulent he forfeited all benefit under the policy.

The Court of Appeal held that a claim that is partly fraudulent is capable of tainting the whole of the claim so that the insured is not entitled to receive any payment provided that the fraud is material or, put another way, the claim is fraudulent to a substantial extent.

It was held on the facts that the fraudulent claim was 10% of the whole claim. That was enough to be 'substantial' so the insured was not entitled to any payment at all. Millett LJ was in favour of a harsher test by focusing solely on the fraudulent claim, not the size of the claim as a whole, to consider whether the fraudulent claim is sufficiently serious to justify characterising it as a breach of the insured's duty of good faith[2].

Although the decision is no doubt correct it may be best to treat it with some caution as the insured had also failed to disclose material facts on the insurance form (relating to obtaining property by deception) and had been convicted of attempting to obtain property by deception by making the false claim under the policy. Thus it would have been possible to reject the claim on the broader ground of pre-contractual non-disclosure. As a point of general principle it would seem that the application of the doctrine of utmost good faith to the claims process is likely to lead to the conclusion that any degree of fraud will be sufficient to taint the claim. At the same time the IOB decisions discussed above may serve as a reminder that there is a difference between making a fraudulent claim and merely making a mistake on the claim form[3]. Historically, the justification for the onerous and detailed pre-contractual duty of disclosure which is imposed upon proposers has been that proposers may be supposed to have detailed knowledge of the risk which is not available to insurers. In relation to claims it must be recognised that policyholders sometimes complete claim forms when still distressed over the circumstances of the loss and that they do not always have ready access to all the details necessary to quantify the claim exactly. These points have to be taken into account when deciding whether a claim is fraudulent or merely inaccurate.

[1] 15 October 1997, CA.

[2] See also *Orakpo v Barclays* [1995] LRLR 443, CA where the Court of Appeal held that any fraudulent claim results in the loss of all benefits under the policy. This case must be considered to be of doubtful authority in the light of the later cases cited in the text.
[3] A view supported by *Alfred McAlpine plc v BAI (Run-off) Ltd* [2000] Lloyd's Rep IR 352, CA.

Fraudulent Means

19.12 A policyholder may have a genuine claim but may put forward false evidence in order to substantiate it or in order to increase the value of the indemnity which he will receive. The consequences of such behaviour were considered in *Agapitos v Agnew*[1]. Mance LJ said firstly that a claim, which is honestly believed in when initially presented, may become fraudulent for these purposes , if the insured subsequently realizes that it is exaggerated, but continues to maintain it[2]. Moreover, a claim cannot be regarded as valid, if there is a known defence to it which the insured deliberately suppresses. To that extent, at least, fraud in relation to a defence falls within the fraudulent claim rule[3] Where there is a fraudulent claim, the law forfeits not only that which is known to be untrue, but also any genuine part of the claim. In contrast, where the use of fraudulent devices occurs, the whole claim is by definition otherwise good. At the same time it is necessary to bear in mind MIA s17 which provides that any want of utmost good faith allows the innocent party to avoid the contract, a more drastic remedy than merely forfeiting the contract prospectively. In summarising the approach to be adopted in relation to fraudulent means Mance LJ said:

> 'What then is the appropriate approach for the law to adopt in relation to the use of a fraudulent device to promote a claim, which may (or may not) prove at trial to be otherwise good, but in relation to which the insured feels it expedient to tell lies to improve his prospects of a settlement or at trial? The common law rule relating to cases of no or exaggerated loss arises from a perception of appropriate policy and jurisprudence on the part of our 19th century predecessors, which time has done nothing to alter. The proper approach to the use of fraudulent devices or means is much freer from authority. It is, as a result, our duty to form our own perception of the proper ambit or any extension of the common law rule. In the present imperfect state of the law, fettered as it is by s 17, my tentative view of an acceptable solution would be:
>
> (a) To recognize that the fraudulent claim rule applies as much to the fraudulent maintenance of an initially honest claim as to a claim which the insured knows from the outset to be exaggerated,
>
> (b) To treat the use of a fraudulent device as a sub-species of making a fraudulent claim – at least as regards forfeiture of the claim itself in relation to which the fraudulent device or means is used. (The fraudulent claim rule may have a prospective aspect in respect of future, and perhaps current, claims, but it is unnecessary to consider that aspect or its application to cases of use of fraudulent devices.)
>
> (c) To treat as relevant for this purpose any lie, directly related to the claim to which the fraudulent device relates, which is intended to improve the insured's prospects of obtaining a settlement or winning the case, and which would, if believed, tend, objectively, prior to any final determination at trial of the parties' rights, to yield a not insignificant improvement in the insured's prospects – whether they be prospects of obtaining a settlement, or a better settlement, or of winning at trial.

(d) To treat the common law rules governing the making of a fraudulent claim (including the use of fraudulent device) as falling outside the scope of s 17 (as advocated, though more generally, by Howard N. Bennett in the article to which I have already referred). On this basis no question of avoidance ab initio would arise.'

These observations must at present be regarded as authoritative on this point. It can be seen that they adopt a stern approach, under which any distinction between fraudulent claims and fraudulent means is largely elided.

1 [2002] 2 Lloyd's Rep 42, CA.
2 [2002] 2 Lloyd's Rep 42, CA at para 15; see also *Lek v Mathews* (1927) 29 Lloyd's Rep 141 HL; *Piermay Shipping Co SA v Chester (The Michael)* [1979] 2 Lloyd's Rep 1.
3 Ibid at para 18.

Proof of loss

Burden of proof

19.13 It is for the insured to prove that a loss has taken place and that this loss falls within the insuring clauses of the policy[1]. Once that has been done, it is for the insurers to establish that the loss falls within one of the exceptions[2], or that there has been a relevant breach of condition[3]. However, it appears that a clause in the policy reversing the burden of proof in relation to specified matters is effective[4]. The burden of proof is of course higher where fraud is alleged, since there is a general principle that fraud must be proved to a high standard[5].

Occasionally it may be necessary for the policyholder to begin by proving that the policy is still in force. One rather obscure area of insurance where this problem is encountered is industrial assurance business. For many years some companies sold life policies of relatively small value, the premiums for which were collected by agents of the insurer visiting the policyholders at home[6]. Some of these policies lasted for many years, and a good few of them were written well before computerisation of records existed. It is not uncommon that when the policyholder dies, the policy schedule is found among his effects, and the relatives try to claim on the policy, only to be met with the defence that the policy was surrendered many years ago. Given the fairly small value of such policies, cases of this kind inevitably end up with the Ombudsman. The IOB view was[7] that in the absence of the original policy document or a payment book showing continuing payments up until death, the likelihood was that the policy had been surrendered or had lapsed for non-payment of the premiums. It is believed that the PIA Ombudsman has taken substantially the same view, though the point does not feature in any of his Reports[8]. Similar problems have sometimes occurred at Lloyd's in relation to long-tail business such as environmental liability. In some cases the original policy documents are not readily to hand, and the original underwriters may have died.

1 MIA 1906, s 55.
2 MIA 1906, s 55.
3 *Bond Air Services Ltd v Hill* [1955] 2 All ER 476, Lord Goddard CJ.
4 *Levy v Assicurazioni Generali* (1940) 67 Lloyd's Rep 174 PC, reluctantly followed in *Grell-Taurel Ltd v Caribbean Home Insurance Co Ltd* [2002] Lloyd's Rep IR 655; for an alternative approach, not followed in *Grell-Taufel*, see *Spinney's (1948) Ltd v Royal Insurance Co* [1980] 1 Lloyd's Rep 406, Mustill J.

[5] As to the general principle see *Bater v Bater* [1951] P 35; *Hornal v Neuberger Products Ltd* [1957] 1 QB 247, CA; *Khawaja v Secretary of State for the Home Department* [1984] AC 74. In an insurance context see *Baghbadrani v Commercial Union Assurance Co plc* [2000] Lloyd's Rep IR 94; and *Strive Shipping v Hellenic Mutual War Risks Association (Bermuda) Ltd* [2002] 2 All ER (Comm) 213, Colman J.
[6] This is part of the definition of Industrial Assurance Business: see Industrial Assurance Act 1923, s 2.
[7] In the days when such things were within the IOB's remit.
[8] Fortunately the passage of time is gradually eliminating this problem, with more and more policies being within the scope of computer records.

Evidence of loss

19.14 The policyholder must take all reasonable steps to provide evidence of the loss. Often this is an express term of the policy. It does not follow that exact details of every single item of loss must be provided. In some cases, for example domestic burglary, where many items are stolen, this is an impracticable and unreasonable requirement. On the other hand the complete failure of the policyholders to substantiate any item of the alleged loss inevitably casts grave doubt on their credibility. It is a matter of degree whether reasonable steps have been taken[1]. A sworn statement by the policyholder as to the items of loss is of course evidence which the court can consider, though it cannot of itself be conclusive.

[1] IOB 11.24.

Claims Co-operation clauses

19.15 Some policies contain clauses requiring the insured to co-operate with the insurer in the handling and investigation of claims. There is some doubt about whether these are to be regarded as conditions precedent to liability or as simple conditions[1], though it is submitted that the better view is that they are simple conditions. The Court of Appeal has held that in so far as these consist of standard wording (which many of them do) their interpretation should be uniform and should not depend on which party proposes them[2].

[1] See para 17.11.
[2] *Royal and Sun Alliance Insurance PLC v Dornoch Ltd* [2004] Lloyd's Rep IR 826, Aikens J.

Claims handling by the insurer

Acknowledgment and acquiescence

19.16 Insurers will commonly acknowledge receipt of a claim, though this is not by itself intended to indicate that the claim will be paid. Unfortunately, as a result of some rather unsatisfactory judicial authority, this area of law and practice is more complicated than it needs to be. The problematic case is *Lickiss v Milestone*

Motor Policies[1]. The policyholder was a motor cyclist who was involved in an accident. In breach of the requirements of the policy he did not immediately notify the insurers of this. They found out about the accident from the police and later wrote to him asking him why he had not notified them and pointing out that this made it difficult for them to arrange his defence on any criminal charge resulting from the accident. Later they repudiated liability to indemnify him for his losses on the ground of the failure to notify. The Court of Appeal rejected this defence on two grounds. The first was that the insurers had sufficient notice of the accident, since they had heard of it from the police. This argument overlooks the fact that the relevant policy condition required the *policyholder* to notify the insurers[2]. However, it is the second ground of the decision which causes rather more problems in the present context. By a majority[3] the Court of Appeal held that the letter asking for an explanation of the failure to notify was to be construed as a waiver of the breach of condition. This appears to rest on the fact that the letter also enquired about arranging the policyholder's defence, something which would not have been an issue if the insurers were intending to repudiate liability. It is hard to avoid the feeling that this is an example of stretching the facts somewhat to give the policyholder a remedy. From the point of view of general principle the lesson of the case must be that insurers must be very careful in their claims handling, especially when dealing with policyholders who appear to have committed a breach of the policy terms such as would justify repudiation of the claim. Every case will of course depend upon its own facts, but the more recent authority of *Baghbadrani v Commercial Union*[4] suggests an approach which is somewhat more favourable to insurers. In that case the insurers had at one stage written to the policyholders saying that they did not intend to maintain their denial of liability and that loss adjusters had been instructed to negotiate a settlement. However, the continued to investigate the claim, and, following receipt of further information, they repudiated liability. Judge Gibbs held first that it is possible to have a binding partial settlement, as for example an admission of liability but not of quantum[5], but that in the present case there was nothing which amounted to a clear offer and acceptance of the alleged settlement. For a similar reason arguments based upon election, waiver and estoppel were all rejected[6], though it is suggested that any of these might be capable of succeeding on appropriate facts.

1 [1966] 2 All ER 972, CA.
2 See also *Pioneer Concrete (UK) Ltd v National Employers' Mutual* [1985] 2 All ER 395, Bingham J.
3 Lord Denning MR and Danckwerts LJ; Salmon LJ dissenting.
4 [2000] Lloyd's Rep IR 94, Judge Gibbs QC.
5 See also *The Wise* [1989] 2 Lloyd's Rep 451.
6 As they were in *Callaghan and Hedges v Thompson* [2000] Lloyd's Rep IR 125, David Steel J.

19.18 In *Cape plc v Iron Trades Employers Insurance Association Ltd*[1] insurers had continued for some years to pay a personal injury claim which they knew to be based on a type of injury which they later argued was not covered by the policy. Rix J held that the fact of continuing to pay after they knew of the basis of the claims prevented them from subsequently arguing that the policy did not extend to this type of injury.

1 [2004] Lloyd's Rep IR 75, Rix J.

Effect of denying liability

19.19 Where an insurer under a liability policy begins by denying liability, for example on the basis that the loss falls outside the policy terms, he is unlikely to be allowed at a later stage to argue that he is unreasonably prejudiced by not being allowed the chance to comment on a proposed settlement of the claim against his insured[1]. However, an insurer who pleads fraud is not thereby debarred from subsequently relying on breach of policy provisions[2].

[1] *Structural Polymer Systems Ltd v Brown* [2000] Lloyd's Rep IR 64, Moore-Bick J; see also Chapter 41.

[2] *Super Chem Products Ltd v American Life and General Insurance Co Ltd* [2004] 1 All ER (Comm) 713, PC.

Investigation

Loss adjusters

19.20 The insurers may appoint a loss adjuster to assist them in dealing with the assured's claim. As to the role of the loss adjuster see *Kitchen Design and Advice Ltd v Lea Valley Water Co*[1] where the judge set out the loss adjuster's affidavit as to his responsibilities. It is essential to remember that loss adjusters act on behalf of the insurers, to whom they owe their only duties. Although they often like to portray themselves as independent, this impression is at best misleading. They certainly do not conduct an impartial investigation, nor is it any part of their job to help the policyholder in presenting the claim. Policyholders and those advising them would do well to be aware of this, and to treat loss adjusters accordingly.

[1] [1989] 2 Lloyd's Rep 221 at 222.

Loss assessors

19.21 Loss assessors, by contrast to loss adjusters, do act for the policyholder in presenting, quantifying and defending the claim. They are remunerated either by a flat fee or by a percentage of the amounts which they succeed in recovering. Given that the majority of insurance claims are settled amicably without third party involvement, it follows that the use of loss assessors normally indicates that the claim is in some way problematic. It is important to be aware that the activity of loss assessor is not the subject of any independent regulation, nor do loss assessors have to possess any qualifications or undergo any vocational training. It is fair to say that the quality of service and standards of professional conduct found among loss assessors vary widely.

Brokers as investigators

19.22 It sometimes happens that insurers dealing with a claim will appoint the brokers who originally placed the risk with them to investigate the claim. This practice has been considered in two reported cases. In *Anglo-African Merchants Ltd v Bayley*[1] Megaw J observed, *obiter*, that this practice was plainly improper, since it involved the brokers in an irreconcilable conflict of interest between their duty to their client, the insured and their duty to the insurer. The point arose more directly in *North & South Trust Co v Berkely*[2]. The facts here were slightly different in that the brokers had attempted to distance themselves somewhat from the investigation by appointing loss adjusters on behalf of the underwriters. The point in issue in the hearing was that the insured wanted to see copies of the report prepared by the adjusters, which the insurers were not prepared to release. Donaldson J agreed with the view of Megaw J in the earlier case that the brokers had acted wrongly; he added that the practice of using the brokers to investigate claims would not be recognised by the courts as having the force of law. Despite this he went on to hold that the report itself, being a document brought into existence on behalf of the insurers in connection with contemplated litigation, was exempt from disclosure under the normal principles of the law of evidence[3]. The question which is left unanswered in this case (because it was not directly before the court) is what damages, if any, the insured could have recovered for the breach of duty by the brokers. By the application to the case of the ordinary principles of contract it can be seen that the answer must be that the insured could recover such loss as they could show had been caused to them by the breach. Unfortunately, it is hard to see how they could ever prove any loss. Even if their claim eventually failed (and it is not at all clear that it did) they would be hard-pressed to prove that it failed because of the brokers' breach of duty. It might be that the loss adjusters found something which was fatal to the claim, but if so, it is reasonable to suppose that any loss adjuster would have been likely to make the same discovery. Despite the criticisms in these two cases, the practice continues, as appears from *Callaghan and Hedges v Thompson*[4]. David Steel J said that the appointment of brokers to act on behalf of the insurer does not make them agents of the insurer, but it does amount to a breach of duty on their part. It may be doubted whether this is correct. In relation to the work which they undertake for the insurers, the brokers surely are acting as agents – were they not doing so, the conflict of interest would not arise.

[1] [1970] 1 QB 311, Megaw J.
[2] [1971] 1 All ER 980, Donaldson J.
[3] See now *Waugh v British Railways Board* [1980] AC 521, HL for the authoritative statement of the relevant principles of evidence.
[4] [2000] Lloyd's Rep IR 125, David Steel J.

Secretly obtained evidence

19.23 In *McNally v RG Manufacturing Ltd*[1] the claimant brought an action in relation to an accident at work and the alleged injury caused thereby. The defendant's liability insurers caused the claimant to be secretly videoed doing things which he alleged were made impossible by his injury. It was held that this evidence was admissible despite the secrecy. It is important to observe that the video had been made at a public place. In addition a conversation between the loss adjuster and the claimant in the claimant's house had been secretly recorded. Although this was more reprehensible, it was held that it was not of such gravity as to render the evidence inadmissible. The proper treatment of evidence in these circumstances may be derived from the overriding objective of dealing with cases justly and fairly.

In some circumstances misleading a party might be the only way of showing that he was misleading other people, even if this involved infringing his privacy. The commission of a criminal offence or a tort is not the definitive test to disqualify evidence thus obtained, although serious or grave illegality would almost always be unjustified and would lead to the exclusion of the evidence.

[1] [2001] Lloyd's Rep IR 379, Harris J.

Involving previous insurers

19.24 In *Myers v Dortex International Ltd*[1] an employer's current insurers were defending on his behalf an action brought by an employee for damages for personal injuries caused by two accidents. One of the accidents had happened while they were on risk, but the other had happened while a previous insurer was on risk. It was unclear how much each accident had contributed to the personal injuries. The previous insurers wanted to be joined as parties to the action, in order to be able to present argument on this point. The Court of Appeal upheld the trial judge's refusal of their application for joinder. It was said that such joinder was not necessary, since the trial judge could be expected to give a full and reasoned judgment, from which the two insurers would be able to work out an appropriate apportionment of liability. In addition, if joinder were allowed, the claimant might have to meet two conflicting cases on causation. It is of course accepted that joinder is a matter for the discretion of the judge, and that under RSC Order 15 it is to be allowed only where necessary in order to determine the case, but it is submitted that this decision raises some problems. First, the previous insurers would not be bound by the result of the case, since they would not be parties to it. This raises the equally disagreeable prospect of the matter having to be relitigated as against them[2]. This stems from the second problematic aspect of the decision, which is that in the absence of the previous insurers, the court is not going to hear a proper presentation of any argument for loading liability onto the current insurers. The resulting decision, whilst no doubt detailed and reasoned, will therefore have been reached without hearing the arguments of all interested parties. The difficulties for the claimant if joinder were permitted must be acknowledged, but at the same time the decision appears to cause unacceptable problems for the previous insurers.

[1] [2000] Lloyd's Rep IR 529, CA.
[2] It appears from the report that the claimant had declined to bring separate proceedings for each accident, despite that suggestion having been made to him by the previous insurers.

Late payment

19.25 Following on from *Ventouris v Mountain*, in *Sprung v Royal Insurance (UK) Ltd*[1] the insured claimed damages for losses suffered as a result of late payment of his claim. It was held by the Court of Appeal that the liability of insurers is in the nature of a payment for damages and there is no action for late payment. The insured would therefore be compensated by a payment of interest only.

In the context of personal lines insurance it is useful to note Clause 3 of the SLIP, which provides that insurers will normally pay claims within two months of being notified of them. The Insurance Ombudsman used to take the view that a failure to do this could amount to maladministration, for which an award of compensation could be made. The PIA Ombudsman took the same view, though his powers were limited to awarding a maximum of £1,500 for inconvenience. In principle it would seem appropriate that at the least an unjustified failure to meet this standard should cause the payment to carry interest from the date by which it should properly have been paid. In general insurance the Insurance Ombudsman has also said that it is proper for insurers to pay the amount of the claim, if any, which they accept as being justified, leaving the balance to be disputed. It is not proper for them to refuse to make any payment until the claim has been fully settled.

1 [1999] Lloyd's Rep IR 111.

Measure of indemnity

19.26 In marine insurance the position is regulated by the MIA 1906, ss 67 and 68:

> '**67 – Extent of liability of insurer for loss**
> (1) The sum which the assured can recover in respect of a loss on a policy by which he is insured, in the case of an unvalued policy to the full extent of the insurable value, or, in the case of a valued policy to the full extent of the value fixed by the policy, is called the measure of indemnity.
> (2) Where there is a loss recoverable under the policy, the insurer, or each insurer if there be more than one, is liable for such proportion of the measure of indemnity as the amount of his subscription bears to the value fixed by the policy in the case of a valued policy, or to the insurable value in the case of an unvalued policy.
>
> **68 – Total loss**
> Subject to the provisions of this Act and to any express provision in the policy, where there is a total loss of the subject-matter insured–
> (1) If the policy be a valued policy, the measure of indemnity is the sum fixed by the policy;
> (2) If the policy be an unvalued policy, the measure of indemnity is the insurable value of the subject-matter insured.'

Sections 67 and 68 are definitive of an insurer's liability, and an assured is not entitled to any additional special or general damages: *Ventouris v Mountain, The Italia Express (No 2)*[1]. Consequently, where there is a total loss of a vessel, the assured is not entitled to claim damages for loss of income, the increase in capital value of a replacement vessel, hardship, inconvenience and mental distress. This rule applies even where the insurers have wrongly refused to pay out on a policy.

In non-marine insurance the principle of indemnity[2] appears to produce substantially the same result, although it is not usual to see the MIA 1906 provisions cited as authority outside the marine context. The general rule is that the policyholder is entitled to be compensated for the losses which he has actually suffered, in so far as they are covered by one or more of the insuring clauses of the policy. Where property has been damaged, he is entitled to the reduction in the value of that property, but not, unless the policy states otherwise, to the cost of repairing it. Where the property is destroyed, he is entitled to the pre-loss value of the property. This is not necessarily the amount he paid for it (it might be more or less) nor is it the same as the cost of replacing it as new. It is possible, in some household policies, to obtain New for Old cover, under which the policyholder is entitled to the cost of replacing the insured items as new. It might well be argued that the policyholder's insurable interest in the property cannot really extend beyond the pre-loss value. In the case of contents policies this does not matter, because these are policies on goods, for which no insurable interest is required[3].

1 [1992] 2 Lloyd's Rep 281 at 291, Hirst J.
2 As to this see also Chapter 4.
3 LAA 1774, s 4; see Chapter 4.

Assessment of loss

19.27 In *Grimaldi Ltd v Sullivan*[1] the insurance policy provided cover against defective title (part C) and all risks cover for stock (part A). Part C provided an indemnity and the question was whether the special clause in the policy relating to the basis of valuation for the assured's own unsold stock should apply where the goods (Cartier watches) were found to be fakes. It was held by the Court of Appeal that the special clause did not apply to losses under part C. In this case the loss was what the imitation watches were worth and not what the assured had paid for them.

1 [1997] CLC 64, CA.

Rateable proportion clauses

19.28 Policies commonly contain clauses providing that where there is another policy covering the same risk, the insurer will be liable only for a rateable proportion of any loss. However, such clauses are of no effect where losses occur in different policy periods, for the risk in each policy period is a distinct risk, and the two policies do not cover the same risk[1].

1 *Phillips v Syndicate 992 Gunner* [2004] Lloyd's Rep IR 426, Eady J.

Valued Policies

19.29 These are more or less universal in marine insurance[1] but at the present day are almost unknown in other forms of insurance. An unsuccessful attempt to argue for the existence of a valued policy occurred in *Quorum A/S v Schramm*[2] where the insured item was a painting, and the clause relating to partial loss set out a formula for calculating the amount of indemnity, but then went on to add that in no case should this be more than the 'insured value of the item'. Thomas J made the obvious point that the clause was self-contradictory, but held that the most sensible way to resolve the contradiction was to treat the phrase 'insured value of the item' as meaning the sum insured. It seems clear that in general courts will be reluctant in the absence of clear wording to find a valued policy outside marine insurance. It may be added that section 3 of the Life Assurance Act (which does not apply to marine insurance[3]) would in any event create a problem in any case where the agreed value appeared to be greater than the value of the policyholder's actual interest in the property.

[1] See Chapter 40.
[2] [2002] 2 All ER (Comm) 147, Thomas J.
[3] LAA 1774, s 4.

Deductibles

19.30 Where a policy includes a deductible, also known as an 'excess' it may say that the deductible is to be applied to each 'occurrence' or each 'event'. It will then be important to know what counts as one 'event'. The classic definition was given by David Steel J, in *Midland Mainline v Commercial Union*[1]:

> 'Whether or not something which produces a plurality of loss or damage can properly be described as one occurrence therefore depends on the position and viewpoint of the observer and involves the question of degree of unity in relation to cause, locality, time, and, if initiated by human action, the circumstances and purposes of the persons responsible.'

It may be noted that an event is not the same thing as a cause. One cause may result in multiple events, or many causes may combine to produce a single event. It is also clear that the above test is not a mechanical one – it involves elements of impression and judgment based on the detailed facts of each case. However, it is unlikely that a single occurrence could happen at more than one location[2]. The result may be different where the aggregation clause applies to a series of events 'originating from a single cause' since that single cause might well produce a number of different events[3].

[1] [2004] Lloyd's Rep IR 22 at para 76.
[2] *Mann v Lexington Insurance Co* [2001] 1 All ER (Comm) 28, CA; *Scott v Copenhagen Reinsurance Co (UK) Ltd* [2003] 2 All ER (Comm) 190, CA; see also *Caudle v Sharp* [1995] LRLR 433 and *Empress Car Co (Abertillery) Ltd v National Rivers Authority* [1998] 1 All ER 481.
[3] *Countrywide Assured Group plc v Marshall* [2003] 1 All ER (Comm) 237, Morison J; see also *Axa Reinsurance (UK) plc v Field* [1996] 3 All ER 517.

Successive losses

19.31 Unless the policy otherwise provides, and subject to the provisions of the MIA 1906, the insurer is liable for successive losses, even though the total amount of those losses may exceed the sum insured. The MIA 1906, s 77(1) refers only to successive repaired losses: *Kusel v Atkin, The Catariba*[1]. In that case it was held that, applying the provisions of s 69 of the Act, where there are successive partial losses that are unrepaired at the time of termination of the policy the measure of indemnity is assessed by reference to the depreciation in value at that time. If the loss is to be assessed at the date of termination of the cover then the loss is the reduced value of the vessel, not the aggregate costs of repair. Section 69 expressly provides that the measure of indemnity might be capped by whichever is the lower of the reasonable cost of repair and the insured value of the vessel.

[1] [1997] 2 Lloyd's Rep 749.

Nature of Insured's Claim

19.32 A claim against insurers for failure to honour a valid claim is a claim for damages ie a claim for the enforcement of a secondary obligation, the primary obligation having been the obligation to pay a sum of money on the happening of the insured peril[1]. Consequently, there can be no claim in damages for the late payment of the damages[2] nor for failure to pay the damages[3]. These rules continue to apply even if the insurer's liability to pay does not arise until the happening of some event later than the insured peril[4].

[1] For the classic analysis of the distinction between the two types of obligation see *Photo Production Ltd v Securicor Transport Ltd* [1980] AC 827 at 848, Lord Diplock.
[2] *President of India v Lips Maritime Corpn* [1988] AC 395, HL.
[3] *The Italia Express (No 2)* [1992] 2 Lloyd's Rep 281, approved by the Court of Appeal in *Sprung v Royal Insurance* [1999] Lloyd's Rep IR 111.
[4] *Normhurst Ltd v Dornoch Ltd* [2005] Lloyd's Rep IR 27, Chambers J.

Settlements

19.33 It is a general principle of English law that settlements of disputes, entered into in good faith are binding on both sides. The settlement is to be regarded as a contract, and the rights arising under the contract replace any rights which the parties might previously have had against each other at law. In the great majority of cases this rule causes no difficulty, but there is a range of cases where the validity of the settlement contract may be called into question. The principles in this area are of course not limited to the law of insurance, but by coincidence most of the important cases are insurance cases.

It appears that there are essentially four grounds on which a party to a settlement contract may seek to have that contract set aside. The first two are capable of applying whether or not the terms of the contract have been executed, whereas the last two are relevant only where money has been paid under the contract. Thus the latter two exceptions can arise where an insurer seeks to recover money which it has paid in pursuance of a settled claim.

Undue influence

19.34 The leading case on this point is *Horry v Tate and Lyle*[1]. The claimant was an employee of the defendants and was injured in an accident at work. While he was recovering from his injuries, he was visited by a loss adjuster appointed by the defendants' liability insurers. In the absence of any legal advice or representation he was induced to sign a form settling his claim against his employers for £1,000. He later sought to have this agreement set aside. It was accepted at trial that the claim was worth significantly more than £1,000. Peter Pain J found that the claimant had relied upon the advice of the adjuster as to the value of the claim and that this advice had been inaccurate. He held that in the circumstances of the case the insurers were under a duty not to mislead the claimant and that they were in breach of this duty, both by misrepresenting the value of the claim and by falsely suggesting to the claimant that the form he signed was not meant as a final settlement of the claim, even though it was clearly expressed as being exactly that. Although he held that there was no inequality of bargaining power between the parties, the judge went on to hold that the misrepresentations meant that the insurers were not entitled to rely upon the signed release. It is by no means easy to interpret this decision. It is not clear to what extent it should be regarded as depending on the fact that this was a contract of insurance, for it would be perfectly possible to say that any settlement of any claim obtained by misrepresenting the nature of the document to a party who was still suffering the after effects of an injury would be voidable. Indeed, the misrepresentation as to the nature of the document might well be thought to give rise to a plea of *non est factum*. As the insurers were not in a contractual relationship with the claimant[2], it would not be appropriate to rely upon notions of utmost good faith. However, this point might be different if a policyholder were induced to settle a claim for much less than its proper value. This could even be a rare example of a case where a breach of continuing utmost good faith led to a remedy other than the avoidance of the policy.

1 [1982] 2 Lloyd's Rep 416, Peter Pain J.

2 Who was in the anomalous and uncomfortable position of a person for whose benefit the insurance was effected, but who was not himself a policyholder. At the present day it is possible that such a person might be able to enforce the policy by relying upon the Contracts (Rights of Third Parties) Act 1999.

Misrepresentation/common mistake

19.35 The classic case in this area is *Magee v Pennine Insurance*[1]. The claimant bought a car from a dealer, and a proposal form was completed with the assistance of a employee of the dealer. On the form that claimant stated that he held a full driving licence and that he would be the principal driver of the car. His son, then a minor, was named as an additional driver. In fact the purchaser had never held a driving license and it was always intended that the son would be the principal driver. Some four years later[2] an accident happened, while the son was driving. The father submitted a claim for over £600 in relation to the accident, and the insurers offered £348 in full settlement. This offer was accepted. However, before the sum was paid the insurers made further enquiries into the matter and discovered the misrepresentations which had been made to them. They thereupon repudiated both the insurance policy and the settlement contract. The policyholder sued on the settlement, and the Court of Appeal had to consider whether the agreement was valid. By a majority it was held that the agreement was not valid, and the majority reasoning was that the settlement contract was void for common mistake, the mistake in question being that the underlying contract of insurance was valid, so that the claimant was entitled to indemnity in respect of the accident. It should be mentioned that this analysis was made possible only because of a finding by the trial judge that the claimant had not acted fraudulently in presenting the proposal. It is not altogether easy to understand that finding, since it is hard to believe that the claimant did not know that he had never had a driving licence or that his son was going to be the main driver. Indeed, at first sight the case appears to be a simple example of the well-known device of a parent insuring a car for a teenage son to drive, and making false statements on the proposal form in order to secure a lower premium. However, the absence of fraud was a finding of primary fact, and any analysis of the case must respect that finding. Despite this the decision in the case causes serious difficulty, for it seems to establish too much. In any case where the policyholder's claim is for some reason invalid – even though he may not know it – the case seems to point to the invalidity of the settlement contract. Further, in any case where the claimant's claim is worth significantly less than the amount claimed, it might be said that the parties are under a common mistake as to the value of the claim, so that the settlement is not enforceable. Such a conclusion, which presumably could not be limited to the context of insurance law, would be practically unworkable, since it would threaten to undermine the whole practice of settling disputed cases at some compromise figure. In reality it must be accepted that such settlements often rest upon commercial convenience as much as on any serious attempt to value the claim. Parties, especially insurance companies, know that even the most doubtful of claims has a certain 'nuisance value', and that the time and effort which might be expended in investigating them exhaustively is not justified. Accordingly, they enter into settlements on incomplete information (rather as Pennine Insurance appear to have done in the present case). It is not generally appropriate to allow them subsequently to resile from the agreement. Fortunately the effect of this decision has been seriously undermined by a number of more recent decisions[3], in which the strictness of the decision in *Bell v Lever Bros Ltd*[4] has been reiterated, and *Magee* has been questioned to the point where it cannot really be regarded any longer as being good law. Although this turns primarily on technical points as to the scope and effect of the doctrine of common mistake in contract, it is clear that no party to an insurance contract should rely on the decision as a way of setting aside a settlement.

A more recent consideration of the enforceability of settlements came in *Fraser Shipping Ltd v Colton*[5], where a ship was insured against actual total loss only while being towed to the breakers' yard. The policy required the use of an approved tug. After the vessel was wrecked, underwriters offered to settle the claim subject to production of the policy and confirmation that the towage warranty had been complied with. Before such confirmation had been given the offer was withdrawn. Potter LJ held that the offer must be treated as conditional on complying with these terms and could therefore be withdrawn at any time before it had been validly accepted. However, it appears to have been assumed that the offer would have become a binding contract if its terms had been complied with before the withdrawal. In *Baghbadrani v Commercial Union*[6] it was said that a contract of compromise would have been voidable[7] because the insured had acted fraudulently in relation to each of the claims concerned.

1 [1969] 2 Lloyd's Rep 378, CA.

2 This must mean that the policy had been renewed several times in the interim, and the question would therefore seem to arise, what had happened at each renewal about the question of disclosure. The point is not alluded to anywhere in the judgments, which proceed entirely on the basis that the misstatements on the original proposal form were still operative. It may be observed

that judgment in this case was given *ex tempore*. In view of the complexity of the legal arguments it is hard to avoid the view that it would have been more prudent to reserve judgment.
[3] *Associated Japanese Bank (International) Ltd v Crédit du Nord SA* [1988] 3 All ER 902; *Insurance Corpn of the Channel Islands v Royal Hotel Ltd* [1998] Lloyd's Rep IR 151; *Great Peace Shipping Ltd v Tsavliris Salvage (International) Ltd, The Great Peace* [2002] Lloyd's Rep 653, CA.
[4] [1932] AC 161, HL.
[5] [1997] 1 Lloyd's Rep 586, Queen's Bench Division (Commercial Court), Potter J.
[6] [2000] Lloyd's Rep IR 94, Judge Gibbs QC.
[7] On the facts it was held that no such contract had been entered into.

Payment induced by mistake of fact

19.36 The leading old authority in this area is *Kelly v Solari*[1]. This was a life assurance case where the policy had lapsed for non-payment of premiums. The life assured died, and, for reasons which do not appear from the report[2], the insurers paid on the policy. Later, having realised their mistake, they sued for the return of the sums paid. It was held that the money would be recoverable if the insurers had never known of the lapse, but not if they had known of it but forgotten it. The case has generally been treated as authority for the proposition that money paid under a mistake of fact is recoverable. It has never been clear to what extent the mistake has to be a reasonable or excusable one. In any event the rule now appears fundamentally altered as a result of the decision in *Kleinwort Benson v Lincoln Council*, which is considered in the paragraph below.

[1] (1841) 9 M & W 54.
[2] It is reasonable to assume simple administrative error – certainly the report contains no suggestion of any fraud; had there been fraud, the position would obviously have been entirely different.

Payment induced by mistake of law

19.37 For many years the position in this situation was understood to be governed by the decision in *Bilbie v Lumley*[1]. The claimant insurer in that case had settled a claim and later brought an action to recover the money he had paid. The basis of the action was that he had not in fact been legally liable to pay and had made the payment under a misapprehension as to the law. It was held that the mistake of law was not a ground on which the money could be recovered. There matters stood for the better part of two centuries, but in late 1998 the House of Lords had the opportunity to consider the question again in *Kleinwort Benson Ltd v Lincoln City Council*[2], which is considered separately below since it impacts on the law as to mistakes of fact as well as on that as to mistakes of law.

[1] (1802) 2 East 469; followed by the Court of King's Bench in *Brisbane v Dacres* (1813) 5 Taunt 143.
[2] [1998] 4 All ER 513.

Kleinwort Benson v Lincoln Council

19.38 This was one of the many pieces of litigation arising from the ill-fated attempts by some local authorities in the 1980s to manage their finances by engaging in transactions in the commercial swaps market. After it was held that such transactions were unlawful and beyond the powers of the local authorities, the counterparties sought recovery of sums paid under the agreements. One of the defences to this claim was that the sums had been paid under a mistake of law and were therefore not recoverable. The House of Lords held that the rule in *Bilbie v Lumley* could no longer be regarded as good law. Instead, it laid down a general principle that there is a general right to recover money paid under a mistake, whether of fact or law, subject only to those defences which are available as part of the law of restitution. This in turn moves the debate on to a consideration of the nature and extent of those defences. Lord Goff, giving the leading speech in *Kleinwort Benson* says[1] that the only two properly recognised defences to such a claim are change of position and settlement of an honest claim, the latter being described by Lord Goff as 'an as yet undefined limit'.

From the point of view of an insurance lawyer it must be said that this decision causes more problems than it solves. The previous authorities may have been unsatisfactory in certain respects[2], but at least the law was reasonably clear. Now, insurance lawyers face a period of uncertainty while the parameters of the defences to recovery claims are worked out.

1 [1998] 4 All ER 513 at 530.
2 See for example the criticisms of the Law Commission in Law Com No 227 *Restitution: mistakes of law and ultra vires public authority receipts and payments*. That report recommended the abrogation by statute of the rule in *Bilbie v Lumley* (1802) 2 East 469.

Change of position

19.39 Given that the House of Lords has now chosen expressly to base the law in this area upon the notion of unjust enrichment, attention is inevitably focused on those cases where it would be inequitable to require the recipient of money paid under a mistake to repay it. The existence of the defence of change of position was recognised by the House of Lords in *Lipkin Gorman (a firm) v Carpnale Ltd*[1], but in that case the House of Lords declined to explore fully the parameters of the defence, which was said to be available where the defendant had so changed his position that it would be inequitable to require him to pay the money. However, both Lord Templeman and Lord Goff said[2] that the defence of change of position could not be established *merely* by showing that the defendant had spent the money, since it might be that the money would have been spent in any event. There is no authority on how any of this might operate in an insurance law context, but it is submitted that an appropriate approach to the problem would be as follows. First, the defence cannot possibly succeed unless the defendant is shown to have acted honestly in changing his position; thus a defendant who has paid away the money with the intention of defeating a claim for its return is not entitled to use this defence. Secondly, in the case of an indemnity policy, if it appears that the defendant has used the money to repair, reinstate or replace the damaged or destroyed property, it will usually be inequitable to require repayment of the money. However, if the money has been used for some other purpose, then it is much less likely that the defence of change of position will be established. Thirdly, in the case of a contingency policy it is much more likely that the defendant will have to repay the money, though this will not be the case where the money has been used to provide compensation against loss actually suffered, as, for example, where the proceeds of a life policy have been used to repay a mortgage.

[1] [1992] 4 All ER 512, HL.
[2] Lord Templeman at 517, Lord Goff at 524.

Settlement of an honest claim

19.40 This is likely to be of great importance in insurance law, since all claims to recovery money paid under settlements are likely to be met with this defence. The first obvious point to be made is that the claim has to have been an honest one. A consequence of this would seem to be that insurers are unlikely to seek recovery of money paid unless they have good evidence that the claim was fraudulent. Thus, the defence would apparently defeat the claim made in *Kelly v Solari*. The second point is that it is as yet uncertain whether settlement of an honest claim will always be a good defence, or whether there are further refinements to this test. Thirdly, the defence of settlement of an honest claim is not the same as the proposed defence of honest receipt, which was argued for in the Lincoln Council case, based on a suggestion by Brennan J in *David Securities Pty Ltd v Commonwealth Bank of Australia*[1]. As Lord Goff pointed out in his speech, a defence which was based solely upon the state of mind of the recipient at the time of receipt would in effect undermine the general doctrine of recoverability of money paid under mistake to a point where it would have little effect.

Until further case law emerges it is difficult to say much more about the defence of settlement of an honest claim.

[1] (1992) 175 CLR 353 at 399.

Good faith in the claims process[1]

19.41 The Insurance Ombudsman has also made certain observations on good faith in relation to settlements. IOB 9[2] deals with a case where the insurer had made a settlement offer. When that offer was refused, the insurer indicated that it was prepared to let the matter go to the IOB, but that in this event the settlement offer would be withdrawn. The Ombudsman held that this was not good insurance practice. A policyholder should not be penalised for taking his case to the Ombudsman, not least since he might well feel that he was not capable of making a proper assessment of the reasonableness or otherwise of the insurer's offer. It is therefore a firm IOB rule that offers of settlement must not be made conditional on the matter not being referred to the IOB[3].

[1] See also Chapter 13 on continuing good faith generally.
[2] Leading article.
[3] As the Ombudsman points out, the result was that the case was an expensive lesson for the insurer – it had no liability under the policy, but as a result of its behaviour it ended up paying both the offer it made to the policyholder and the IOB case fee.

Pre-emptive litigation by insurers

19.42 *New Hampshire Insurance Co v Philips Electronics Corpn North America Ltd*[1] was an example of the commencement of pre-emptive litigation by insurers. The policy in this case was an employees' fidelity policy, under which the insured had submitted claims relating to events alleged to have happened in Illinois. The policy required the insured to wait at least 90 days after submitting their proof of loss to the insurers before commencing proceedings. The insurers alleged that on the proper construction of the policies some of the alleged events did not fall within the scope of the policy. Because of the commercially sensitive nature of the alleged losses the policyholders were reluctant to begin legal proceedings, but at the end of the 90-day period the insurers began proceedings in the Commercial Court claiming declarations that the facts alleged, even if true, did not give rise to valid claims under the policies. The writ was served out of the jurisdiction, pursuant to RSC Order 11, but the policyholders sought to have the service set aside on the ground that the appropriate forum was Illinois. The Court of Appeal upheld the decision of Rix J that whilst Illinois would be the appropriate forum for resolving disputed issues of fact, England would be the appropriate forum for resolving disputed questions of law. Although a negative declaration is an unusual form of relief, which will be granted only where there are very good reasons for doing so[2], these reasons did exist in the present case because the insurers were treating these proceedings in the nature of a test case to resolve general issues about the scope of their standard-form wording for policies of this type. This effectively left them in the position of being the natural claimants. However, the court must be careful to satisfy itself that the proceedings were not merely an attempt to pre-empt litigation in another more appropriate forum. That requirement was also satisfied here; the policies were governed by English law, and the English court was an appropriate place to resolve the legal issues. It was also relevant that the answers given to the questions of law raised in these proceedings might well prove to be decisive of the whole claim, thus saving the considerable expense associated with a trial as to the disputed factual issues. It was therefore proper in the particular circumstances to proceed with the application for negative relief. The case illustrates that in relatively exceptional circumstances it may be proper for insurers to take pre-emptive action of this kind.

[1] [1999] Lloyd's Rep IR 58, CA.

[2] *Camilla Cotton Oil Co v Granadex SA and Tracomin SA* [1976] 2 Lloyd's Rep 10, HL; in the particular context of Order 11 see also *Insurance Corpn of Ireland v Strombus International Insurance Co* [1985] 2 Lloyd's Rep 138, CA.

Chapter 20

Illegality

20.1 The question of illegality in insurance contracts must be understood in the context of general principles of contractual illegality, though, as ever, there are particular insurance law connotations.

Illegality generally

20.2 The decision of Talbot J in *Geismar v Sun Alliance*[1] was for some time thought to restrict severely the cases in which a claimant could recover under an insurance policy if he had been guilty of some illegality connected with the claim. In that case the claimant tried to claim under a household policy for the loss of some goods which had been imported into the UK without payment of the appropriate duty. The claimant openly admitted that he had no intention of paying the duty if he could avoid it. Talbot J held that in these circumstances public policy barred him from claiming for the loss of the goods. The application of the general contractual doctrine of illegality in an insurance context has since been considered at greater length by the Court of Appeal in *Euro-Diam v Bathurst*[2]. This was a case of insurance on precious stones. The vendors of the diamonds were the policyholders, and they exported the stones to Germany with an invoice which understated the price of the stones by a substantial amount. It was clear that this had been done deliberately, and that the effect was to enable the recipients fraudulently to reduce or defer their tax liability on the stones in Germany. Some of the stones were subsequently stolen, but when the policyholders sought to claim for the loss they were met with a defence of illegality based on the false invoice. Having held that s 41 of the MIA 1906 was not applicable to non-marine insurance[3], the Court of Appeal went on to consider whether common law principles of illegality operated to defeat this claim. It was held that it did not, primarily because there was no connection between the illegality and the circumstances of the loss. The claimants had no need to rely upon the invoice, since they could make good their claim by showing that they had insured the diamonds, that they had an interest in them and that they had been lost in circumstances covered by the policy. Moreover the claimants had derived no tangible benefit from the illegality, which had apparently been entered into as a favour to the purchaser.

It is submitted that the decision is correct, and that it can be regarded as illustrating the application of well-known contractual principles of illegality in an insurance context. Illegality is available as a defence in three situations. The first is where the claimant founds his claim on an illegal act[4]. The second is where the grant of relief to the claimant would allow him to benefit from his own wrongful act[5] – *Geismar* can be distinguished as a case within this category. The third is where the maxim *ex turpi causa non oritur actio* applies[6]. This last category is of course very imprecisely defined, and it may be doubted whether it is likely to be of much importance in an insurance law context. In cases not falling within any of these three categories the defence of illegality is not available. It is therefore not correct to say that a claimant whose behaviour in relation to the facts of the claim has been in any way reprehensible is automatically barred from claiming on the policy[7].

[1] [1977] 3 All ER 570.

[2] [1988] 2 All ER 23, CA.

[3] See above.

[4] *St John Shipping Corpn v Joseph Rank Ltd* [1956] 3 All ER 683; *Saunders v Edwards* [1987] 2 All ER 651, CA; *Bowmakers Ltd v Barnet Instruments Ltd* [1945] KB 65; *Gascoigne v Gascoigne* [1918] 1 KB 223; *Re Emery's Investment Trusts* [1959] 1 All ER 577.

[5] See below under 'Forfeiture'.

[6] Ie the principle that no cause of action can be founded on the claimant's own wrongful act; see for example *Thackwell v Barclays Bank plc* [1986] 1 All ER 676; *Saunders v Edwards* [1987] 2 All ER 651.

[7] Though of course the claims process itself is subject to the requirements of utmost good faith, at least up to the time when proceedings are issued. Thereafter, matters are governed by the CPR 1998: *The Star Sea* [2001] Lloyd's Rep IR 247, HL.

Criminal and civil law

20.3 It is of course well known that the burdens of proof in the civil and criminal law are different. It is therefore dangerous in an insurance context to use the outcome of one set of proceedings as the basis for deciding the outcome of a different set of proceedings. In a theft claim, where the insured had been charged with attempting to obtain property by deception in conjunction with the claim, the proceedings were subsequently discontinued by the Crown Prosecution Service ('CPS'). The Insurance Ombudsman held[1] that it did not follow that the policyholder had established the validity of his claim. The dropping of the criminal proceedings showed only that the CPS believed that it would not be possible to establish the policyholder's guilt of the criminal offence beyond reasonable doubt.

[1] IOB 5.8.

Liability insurance – exemplary damages

20.4 It has been held that a policy insuring a local authority against liability to pay exemplary damages is not inherently unlawful as being contrary to public policy[1]. It is perhaps relevant to note that in that case the authority itself had not been guilty of any bad faith, its liability being only vicarious. On the other hand it is normally understood that a policy which purported to insure against the risk of liability for deliberate wrongdoing would be unlawful[2], and it may therefore be thought that in such a case a policy providing cover for exemplary damages might be found to be contrary to public policy. The question of the insurability of such awards is particularly important where US risks are being insured, since awards of exemplary damages are far more common – and often far larger – there than they are in England.

1 *Lancashire County Council v Municipal Mutual Insurance Ltd* [1997] QB 897, CA.
2 And the DTI took action some years ago to stop the practice of certain motorists organisations of offering policies under which a chauffeur was to be provided to any member who lost his licence through, *inter alia*, driving with excess alcohol levels.

Marine insurance

20.5 Section 41 of the MIA 1906 provides:

> 'There is an implied warranty that the adventure insured is a lawful one, and that, so far as the assured can control the matter, the adventure shall be carried out in a lawful manner.'

However, this provision is limited to cases of marine insurance[1], and it appears that there is no equivalent doctrine at common law, though no doubt it would be possible to draft a policy so as to incorporate such a term expressly. This is commonly done by providing that the insured must comply with all relevant rules and regulations. In the marine context it is important to observe that the Act makes this term a warranty, with the result that breach of the term automatically discharges the insurer from liability for future losses[2].

1 *Euro-Diam v Bathurst* [1988] 2 All ER 23, CA.
2 MIA 1906, s 33(3); in a non-marine context, however, attention is drawn to *Kumar v AGF Insurance* [1999] Lloyd's Rep IR 147, Thomas J, in the context of a policy drafted before the decision of the House of Lords in *The Good Luck* [1991] 2 Lloyd's Rep 191 clarified the meaning of s 33(3). It was held that a policy which excluded the right to 'avoid, repudiate or rescind' was to be construed as excluding the right to treat as discharged for breach of warranty.

Indemnity for own wrongful act

20.6 In *Haseldine v Hasken*[1] a solicitor entered into a champertous agreement. He was subsequently sued in respect of this, and the action was settled for £950. He then sought to claim on his professional indemnity policy, which covered him for 'negligence, errors and omissions'. The Court of Appeal, reversing Swift J, held that the loss which had occurred did not fall within the policy, and that, in any event, no claim could be made because the policyholder was seeking indemnity for the consequences of his own deliberate wrongdoing. In reaching this conclusion the court distinguished the decisions in *James v British General Assurance*[2] and *Tinline v White Cross Insurance Association Ltd*[3]. These were both cases where the policyholder had knocked down and killed a pedestrian and had been convicted of manslaughter[4]. In both cases the policyholder succeeded in recovering from the insurers the damages which he had had to pay in a civil action by the victim's estate. A distinction was drawn between a deliberate wrongful act and a merely negligent one. More recently this distinction has been restated in *Charlton v Fisher*[5], a motor insurance case where deliberate injury was caused away from the public road, so that there was no MIB liability. It was held that the driver's insurers were not obliged to indemnify him and were therefore not obliged to indemnify the third party who was injured. This distinction is of fundamental importance, for without it very few forms of liability insurance would be possible, since most liabilities are incurred as result of some form of negligence. The normal practice at the present day is to provide cover against the policyholder's own negligence and against the negligence or fraud of the policyholder's partners or employees. It is for this reason that a professional partnership can claim on its insurance when one of the partners commits a fraud, but a sole partner has no insurance cover in the same circumstances[6].

The question of liability for the fraud of employees continues to give trouble in modern professional indemnity policies. In *MDIS Ltd v Swinbank*[7] a policy of this type was expressed as providing cover against claims 'alleging. . .... dishonesty of employees' but with an exclusion for loss occasioned by dishonest, fraudulent, criminal or malicious acts perpetrated after the assured could reasonably have discovered or suspected the improper conduct of the employees concerned. It was held first that this clause related to the true cause of the liability, rather than to the way in which the claim was expressed, the reference to 'alleging' being insufficient to avoid this consequence. This part of the decision appears to have been based on the sensible view that the outcome of the policyholder's claim should not depend upon the way in which a third party chose to frame its claim against the policyholder. Secondly, it was held that the effect of the clause referred to above was primarily to provide cover against claims based upon dishonesty. This cover was expressly limited where the dishonesty occurred after the policyholder had reasonable cause to suspect it. In such a case (of which this was one) it would be necessary for the policyholder to show that the claim was really based upon negligence rather than dishonesty. In the present case that was not possible, so the claim must fail. The effect of the clause is thus to put an onus on the policyholder to take action to control dishonesty once it is suspected.

The case is also important for its consideration of the application of clauses of this kind to cases where the third party's claim against the policyholder is settled out of court. This situation gives rise to particular difficulties because the settlement, even if recorded in writing, is not likely to state clearly the form of liability on which it is based. Indeed, it may well be made expressly on the basis of there being no admission of liability. The Court of Appeal held that in this event it is nevertheless necessary to decide on what basis the settlement has really been reached. It is submitted that this threatens to be a somewhat problematic task, for the reasons already given. Indeed, an astute policyholder might well wish to influence what was written in the settlement agreement with an eye to protecting his insurance cover. This, if done in bad faith, would no doubt by itself be a ground for refusing indemnity, and where the insurer is involved in negotiating the settlement it may be more difficult to do.

1 [1933] 1 KB 822, CA.
2 [1927] 2 KB 311, Roche J.
3 [1921] 3 KB 327, Bailhache J.
4 This predates the introduction of the specific offence of causing death by dangerous driving.

[5] [2001] 1 All ER (Comm) 769 CA; see also *Hardy v MIB* [1964] 2 All ER 742; and *Gardner v Moore* [1984] 1 All ER 1100, CA. For the MIB generally, see Chapter 28.
[6] This in turn leads to the use of devices such as the Law Society's Compensation Fund, which exists to provide cover for third parties who suffer loss in such cases.
[7] [1999] Lloyd's Rep IR 516, CA.

Forfeiture

20.7 In life policies the issue of forfeiture may arise where the assured has by some unlawful means caused or contributed to the death of the life assured. At common law the position was governed by the forfeiture rule, but the law has now been modified by the provisions of the Forfeiture Act 1982 ('FoA 1982').

The common law rule was stated by Geoffrey Lane LJ in *Gray v Barr*[1]:

> 'The logical test ... is whether the person seeking the indemnity was guilty of deliberate, intentional and unlawful violence of threats of violence.'

Although this passage contains a reference to the seeking of an indemnity, there is no reason to doubt that it applies equally to claims under a contingency policy.

Where the claimant has murdered the life assured, the common law rule clearly applies[2], since Geoffrey Lane LJ's test will inevitably be satisfied, and the murderer will be unable to take any benefit from the deceased's estate (whether in the form of insurance moneys or otherwise). Equally, a claim under a life of another policy will be barred.

Where it is held that the claimant is guilty only of manslaughter, the position is less clear, for manslaughter is an offence which may be committed in a variety of different states of mind, ranging from that just short of having the necessary intention for murder to that which consists merely of culpable negligence[3]. However, at common law it seems that the forfeiture rule will normally apply, since there will have to be unlawful violence, which will often be deliberate and intentional, though there may be cases of complete accident which fall outside the rule although the circumstances are sufficient to amount to manslaughter[4]. The sole exception to this appears to be *Re H (decd)*[5], where there was a conviction for manslaughter based upon diminished responsibility, and it was held that on the facts the act of killing could not be considered to have been deliberate or intentional. The rule does apply to cases of suicide pacts[6]. In cases where the common law rule does apply, the FoA 1982 is likely to be of relevant. This Act gives the court discretion to relieve a person from the consequences of the common law prohibition on profiting from one's own wrong in cases where it appears just to do so.

The clearest evidence for the application of the forfeiture rule will naturally be that the person seeking to recover on the policy has been convicted of murder or manslaughter. However, this is not the only acceptable evidence. If the claimant has never been tried in connection with the death, then it is open to the insurers to defend the claim on the basis that the claimant is culpably responsible for the death. They will then bear the burden of proving this fact, but in a civil trial they will only need to establish it on the balance of probabilities, rather than being subject to the criminal standard of proof beyond reasonable doubt.

Even where the claimant has been tried in connection with the death of the life assured and has been acquitted, that is not conclusive evidence for the purposes of the civil law that he is not responsible. The insurers can still allege that he was responsible, and again will only bear the civil burden of proof, for the acquittal means only that the jury did not regard the case as proved beyond reasonable doubt. On the other hand it is suggested that both a court and the Ombudsman would be naturally reluctant to find the claimant responsible for the death after an acquittal, and that it might be prudent to accept the acquittal as decisive of the matter, at least in the absence of some new evidence.

1 [1970] 2 All ER 702 at 710.
2 Celebrated early cases include *Re Crippen (decd)* [1911] P 108; and *Cleaver v Mutual Reserve Fund Life Association* [1892] 1 QB 147, CA. See also *Beresford v Royal Insurance* [1938] AC 586, CA.
3 *R v Chief National Insurance Comr, ex p Connor* [1981] QB 758, DC.
4 *Re Hall's Estate, Hall v Knight* [1914] P 1, CA; *Gray v Barr* [1971] 2 QB 554, CA; *Re Giles (decd)* [1972] Ch 544, Pennycuick V-C.
5 [1991] 1 FLR 441, Peter Gibson J.
6 *Dunbar v Plant* [1997] 4 All ER 289, CA.

The Forfeiture Act 1982

20.8 This Act was passed in an attempt to modify the unfairnesses which were perceived to result from the common law forfeiture rule. Section 1 of the Act defines the 'forfeiture rule' for the purposes of the Act as:

> 'the rule of public policy which in certain circumstances precludes a person who has unlawfully killed another from acquiring a benefit in consequence of the killing.'

Section 1(2) glosses this by adding:

> 'References in this Act to a person who has unlawfully killed another include a reference to a person who has unlawfully aided, abetted, counselled or procured the death of that other and references in this Act to unlawful killing shall be interpreted accordingly.'

Thus, for these purposes unlawful killing includes the offence of assisting in the suicide of another, contrary to the Suicide Act 1961, as well as aiding and abetting the killing of a non-consenting third party.

Under s 2 of the Act where a court determines that the forfeiture rule has precluded a person who has unlawfully killed another from acquiring any interest in property, the court may make an order modifying the effect of the forfeiture rule. However, such an order is to be made only if the court is satisfied that having regard to the conduct of the offender and of the deceased and to such other circumstances as appear to the court to be material, the justice of the case requires the rule to be so modified.

In *Re Royse (deceased)*[1] the claimant had been convicted of the manslaughter of her husband and had been sent to a mental hospital. She was the sole beneficiary of his will and the only person entitled on his intestacy. She applied under the Inheritance (Provision for Family and Dependants) Act 1975 for provision out of her husband's estate, but it was held that her action was time-barred and would in any event have fallen foul of the common law forfeiture rule. The FoA 1982 came into force after the commenced proceedings, but it was held that this Act did not have retrospective effect. A similar point subsequently arose in *Re S (Deceased)*[2]. H and W married in 1985 and had a son in 1988. In 1991 they took out a joint life endowment, payable on first death. In 1993, H killed W. He was convicted of manslaughter and detained in a mental hospital. H was clearly prevented from taking any benefit under the policy, but on his behalf an order was successfully sought, varying the forfeiture rule so that the proceeds could be paid for the benefit of the son. This appears a clear enough case of modifying the forfeiture rule, since H did not seek to take any benefit from the policy proceeds, the offence was manslaughter not murder and there was apparently no one else interested in the policy. It may perhaps be contrasted with *Davitt v Titcumb*[3], though in the latter case no application for relief from forfeiture was or could have been made. The defendant bought a house with his then partner. The property was held on an equitable tenancy in common, and the purchase was financed primarily by an endowment mortgage (though the purchasers also provided some funds of their own), the life policy being assigned to the mortgagee as usual. The defendant then murdered his co-tenant, for which offence he was sentenced to life imprisonment. The mortgagee claimed under the life policy, and the insurers duly paid the sum assured, thus discharging the mortgage. The mortgagee was clearly entitled to claim as assignee, and it could not have been suggested that there was any public policy objection to this claim. The house was sold for a sum greater than that which the purchasers had paid for it, and the question arose as to entitlement to that part of the net proceeds which represented the defendant's share of the equity. The claimants in the action were the personal representatives of the defendant's late partner, who argued that the defendant could not be allowed to receive this money, since that would infringe the rule against forfeiture. The obvious difficulty with this argument is that the defendant was not claiming the insurance proceeds – such a claim would on the authorities have been doomed. Instead, he was claiming to exercise his proprietary rights in the house (or in the net proceeds of sale). These rights had of course existed prior to his murdering his partner and were not affected by the murder. Scott J held that the forfeiture rule applied to this case on the ground that the fund which the defendant was claiming would not have come into existence but for his wrongful act. Once it was decided that the forfeiture rule was in principle applicable, there was no prospect of a successful application to have the rule varied. The decision is evidently an extension of the doctrine as it has been traditionally understood, but it would clearly have been unacceptable for the defendant to receive any part of the money.

1 [1984] 3 All ER 339, CA.
2 [1996] 1 WLR 235, Rattee J.
3 [1989] 3 All ER 417, Scott J.

20.9 More problematic is the second part of this decision, in which Scott J held that the share of the fund which would otherwise have gone to the defendant belonged to the claimants as executors of the deceased tenant in common. It is to be noted that both the Crown and the insurers expressly disclaimed any interest in the fund, and from that point of view there was obvious pressure on the judge to hold that the money should go to the claimants. Although Scott J declares in his judgment that this conclusion is also in strict accordance with the law, it may be doubted whether this is correct. Although it is true that the deceased and the defendant between them held the equity of redemption in the property, they did not hold it as beneficial joint tenants (in which case the defendant's share would presumably pass to the claimant by an extension of the doctrine of survivorship), but as beneficial tenants in common. In these circumstances it is not obvious why the loss of the defendant's entitlement to a share of the fund automatically passes that entitlement to the deceased. It is submitted that the mortgagee would have had a good claim to retain the balance of the money on the simple ground that there was no one with a better claim to it. However, it cannot be doubted that the solution reached by Scott J accords with many peoples' notions of justice in such a case. In *Re K (deceased)*[1] the facts were similar in that a woman had been convicted of the manslaughter of her husband following many years of violent and abusive behaviour on his part. She was a major beneficiary under his will, though not the sole beneficiary. The Court of Appeal held that there was jurisdiction to relieve the widow from the effect of the forfeiture rule, and that in the circumstances the fair solution would be to allow the provisions of the will to take effect unaltered. There is no rule that on an application under the FoA 1982 the court is restricted to awarding the applicant what she would have received in an application under the Inheritance (Provision for Family and Dependants) Act 1975.

In *Dunbar v Plant*[2] the Court of Appeal, having held that the common law rule applies to suicide pacts, had to consider the possibility of granting relief in such a case. In so doing it commented on general issues as to the exercise of the discretion. First, it is not correct to treat the matter as being simply a dispute between the immediate parties. Rather, it is necessary to have regard to all the consequences of any order which is proposed. The starting point is to ask whether the beneficiary's conduct was so culpable as to justify the application of the forfeiture rule at all. In the case of a suicide pact the usual answer will be that it is not[3], though this of course cannot be a universal rule. Beyond that the discretion is at large for the judge.

More recently *Dalton v Latham*[4] provided what is apparently the first recorded example of a refusal of relief. The applicant had been convicted of the manslaughter (on the ground of diminished responsibility) of an elderly man, with whom he had at one time had a sexual relationship, and whose house he had shared at the time of the victim's death. Patten J rejected the argument that in cases of manslaughter there should be relief more or less automatically. On the facts, which included some evidence of abusive behaviour by the applicant towards the victim, he held that the applicant could not discharge the burden of showing that fairness required the modification of the forfeiture rule.

[1] [1985] 2 All ER 833, CA.
[2] [1997] 4 All ER 289, CA.
[3] That answer was applied in *Dunbar v Plant*, full relief against forfeiture being given.
[4] [2003] EWHC 796 (Ch), Patten J.

Limitation period

20.10 Where a person stands convicted of an offence of which unlawful killing is an element, the court shall not make an order modifying the effect of the forfeiture rule in that case unless proceedings for this purpose are brought before the expiry of the period of three months beginning with his conviction[1]. This rule applies only where a person has been convicted. The forfeiture rule itself may apply even in the absence of a conviction, and where the person concerned has not been convicted, there is no limitation period applicable to the bringing of the action. Some uncertainty surrounds the position where the offender has been convicted but that conviction is subsequently quashed after the expiry of the three month limitation period. The principles underlying the Act would suggest that the possibility of making an application for relief from the forfeiture rule should in such a case be revived by the quashing of the conviction, and it is submitted that this is the correct answer, notwithstanding that there is apparently no other case in English law where an action can be revived after the limitation period has expired.

[1] FoA 1982, s 3.

Chapter 21

Arbitration and alternative dispute resolution

21.1 For the purpose of insurance practice it is necessary to divide this topic into two distinct areas. The first concerns commercial *disputes*, whereas the second concerns disputes arising under personal lines policies.

Commercial policies – arbitration

21.2 It is common, though by no means universal, for commercial insurance policies to provide for arbitration in respect of disputes arising under them. The principal Act is now the Arbitration Act 1996 ('AA 1996')[1]. No more than a brief account of that Act will be given here, since in the present context it is the specific issue of arbitration in insurance which is of interest.

[1] Which repealed the Arbitration Acts 1975 and 1979, and Pt I of the Arbitration Act 1950, which was previously the principal statute.

Major features of the Arbitration Acts

21.3 The AA 1996 is founded on the principles that the object of arbitration is to obtain the fair resolution of disputes by an impartial tribunal without unnecessary delay or expense and that the parties should be free to agree how their disputes are resolved, subject only to such safeguards as are necessary in the public interest[1]. To these ends the Act lays down schemes for the appointment (and, where necessary, removal) of arbitrators, for the conduct of the arbitration and for the making and enforcing of arbitration awards.

[1] AA 1996, s 1.

Application of the Arbitration Acts to insurance cases

21.4 A number of important cases have considered the operation of arbitration provisions in an insurance context. By coincidence the very first case in which the enforceability of arbitration provisions was accepted – *Scott v Avery*[1] – was itself an insurance case. There it was held that it was legitimate to have a contractual provision requiring the parties first to submit their dispute to arbitration, so long as that was only a precursor to going to court. In other words it was not acceptable to seek to oust the jurisdiction of the court entirely by providing that arbitration was to the exclusion of court proceedings.

Later cases have continued the development of the relationship between arbitration proceedings and conventional judicial proceedings. In *Smith v Pearl Assurance*[2] the claimant was injured in a road accident through the negligence of a third party. He obtained judgment, but the third party was insolvent, so he sought to sue the insurers under the TP(RAI)A 1930[3]. The insurers relied on an arbitration clause in the insurance contract. The claimant sought to have the arbitration clause set aside on the ground that he could not afford to go to arbitration (legal aid not being available for this purpose). The Court of Appeal held that the claimant's impecuniosity was not a reason for overriding the contractual term. This strict approach was somewhat refined in *Fakes v Taylor Woodrow*[4]. the claimant was a plumber, employed on a sub-contract basis by the defendants. They did not pay him for his work, and he became insolvent after being sued by his creditors. He obtained legal aid to sue the defendants. The sub-contract contained an arbitration clause, which the defendants sought to invoke. The Court of Appeal[5] declined to apply the principle laid down in *Smith v Pearl Assurance*, on the ground that the claimant had been able to raise a triable issue that his insolvency was due to the very breach of duty for which he was suing. However, in *Goodman v Winchester and Alton Rly plc*[6] this test was further qualified when the Court of Appeal said that the poverty of the claimant could be taken into account but was not decisive. Rather, the task of the court was to balance properly the interests of the parties. On the facts of the case the court took the view that the absence of legal aid would not seriously prejudice the claimant, since the matters in dispute were within his own knowledge, and there was no reason why he could not handle the case for himself.

It is to be observed that all these cases involve claimants who were consumers or small businessmen. In the context of commercial insurance, arbitration clauses are very commonly encountered, and it seems most unlikely that a party to such a policy would seek to escape the operation of the arbitration clause.

Section 6 of the AA 1996 provides:

> 'a document containing an arbitration clause constitutes an arbitration agreement if the reference is such as to make that clause part of the agreement.'

In *Trygg Hansa Insurance v Equitas*[7] the court considered the effect of this section on the incorporation of arbitration clauses into reinsurance contracts. There were arbitration clauses in the underlying insurance policies which the reinsurers argued were incorporated in the reinsurance policy by the provision 'to follow the same terms exclusions conditions … as the policy of the primary insurers.'

It was held that s 6 allowed the court to consider the previous authorities on the incorporation of arbitration clauses. The court concluded that there were no special circumstances which indicated an intention to incorporate the arbitration provisions of the direct policies in the reinsurance. The general rule of construction is that generally expressed words of incorporation have the effect of incorporating only terms relating to the subject matter of the contract unless circumstances prevailing when the contract was made show that it was the parties' intention to adopt an ancillary term.

Where there is a contract between the parties which incorporates an arbitration clause, the AA 1996, s 9 would effectively require the court to grant a stay. Section 9(4) reads:

> '(4) on an application under this section the court shall grant a stay unless satisfied that the arbitration agreement is null and void, inoperative, or incapable of being performed.'

Thus the exceptions to the grant of a stay are very limited, and in all other cases a stay must be granted, provided of course that the agreement does in fact cover the events which have happened[8].

1 (1856) 5 HL Cas 811.
2 [1939] 1 All ER 95, CA.
3 Which allows (subject to important qualifications) an action to be brought directly against the liability insurers of an insured defendant: see Chapter 29.
4 [1973] 1 All ER 670, CA.
5 Megaw LJ dissenting.
6 [1984] 3 All ER 594, CA.
7 [1998] 2 Lloyd's Rep 439.
8 For a rare example of a refusal to grant a stay, see *T&N Ltd v Royal & Sun Alliance plc* [2004] Lloyd's Rep IR 102, Lloyd J.

Personal lines policies – Ombudsman schemes

21.5 Ombudsman schemes have been in use in the insurance sector since 1981, when the IOB was created. In 1994 the establishment of the Personal Investment Authority led to the creation of the PIAOB, and the two schemes have operated side-by-side since that date.

This area has undergone substantial change in recent years, and the new arrangements provided by way of the Financial Services Ombudsman have now had several years in which to establish a distinctive approach, though it remains the case that they build in recognisable ways on their predecessors, notably the old Insurance Ombudsman Bureau.

The Financial Services Ombudsman

21.6 The FSO was created by the FSMA 2000, as part of the radical restructuring, for the third time in 15 years[1], of the system of financial services regulation in the UK. From an insurance point of view it is important to understand that the current scheme combines the functions formerly held by the Insurance Ombudsman and the PIAO.

Section 225(1) of the FSMA 2000 creates:

'a scheme under which certain disputes may be resolved quickly and with minimum formality by an independent person.'

Schedule 17 to the Act makes the FSA the 'scheme operator' with the power to make detailed rules for the operation of the scheme, which include the creation of a Board to manage the scheme and ensure the independence of the Ombudsman. An Annual Report must also be produced.

The scheme is divided between the compulsory jurisdiction and the voluntary jurisdiction. All member firms of the FSA are subject to the compulsory jurisdiction, but a firm may choose whether it will participate in the voluntary jurisdiction. The FSA, as scheme operator, is required to make rules specifying which activities fall within the compulsory jurisdiction, but may only specify activities which are or could be regulated under s 20 of the Act[2]. The rules may include provision for persons other than individuals to be eligible; but may not provide for authorised persons to be eligible except in specified circumstances or in relation to complaints of a specified kind[3]. The voluntary jurisdiction is available where the member firm was participating in that scheme at the time of the act or omission in question and has not withdrawn from it at the time of the complaint[4]. Again, the only activities which may be covered are those falling within s 20. The overall effect of this is that the FSOS is empowered to set up two classes of regulated activity. All member firms of the FSA will be subject to the FSOS jurisdiction in relation to the first class, but the firms will have the choice of whether or not to be subject to that jurisdiction in relation to the second class.

Section 228 of the Act then deals with the determination of complaints falling within the compulsory jurisdiction. Such complaints are is to be determined by reference to what is, in the opinion of the ombudsman, fair and reasonable in all the circumstances of the case[5]. This is a provision of crucial importance. The IOB and Office of the Banking Ombudsman ('OBO') have always had a clause to this effect in their terms of reference, but the PIAOB did not. It is submitted that an essential part of the purpose of Ombudsman schemes in the private sector is that they should be able to mitigate the deficiencies of the law from the point of view of private investors. In order to do this it is necessary to give the Ombudsman power to make a fair and reasonable decision even when this involves departing from the strict letter of the law.

1 The first was in the FSA 1986, whilst the second occurred in 1994 with the merger of LAUTRO and Financial Intermediaries Managers Brokers Regulatory Association into the PIA.
2 This includes the selling of all types of insurance and the management of the resulting policies.
3 Section 226(7).
4 Section 227.
5 Section 228(2).

21.7 When the ombudsman has determined a complaint he must give a written statement of his determination to the respondent and to the complainant. The statement must give the ombudsman's reasons for his determination, be signed by him and require the complainant to notify him in writing, before a date specified in the statement, whether he accepts or rejects the determination. To a large extent this provision merely embodies in statute the existing practices of the major Ombudsman schemes. One element which may give rise to some problem is the requirement that every decision be signed by the Ombudsman personally. Given the number of complaints received by all the major schemes, it has long been the practice to delegate the initial investigations to case officers, who also write letters to complainants setting out their views of the case. It would be quite impracticable to depart from this by requiring every letter to a complainant to be signed by the Ombudsman. These letters are normally referred to an an 'Initial view', leaving the complainant free to present further arguments, which can then be submitted to the Ombudsman for a final decision, though in practice initial view letters which are unfavourable to the complainant are expressed in terms making clear the case officer's view that the complaint would be rejected by the Ombudsman if referred to him[1].

If the complainant notifies the Ombudsman that he accepts the determination, it is binding on the respondent and the complainant and final[2]. If, by the specified date, the complainant has not notified the ombudsman of his acceptance or rejection of the determination he is to be treated as having rejected it[3]. Although the statute does not say so in as many words, the effect of this is presumably that the decision is not binding on either side. Thus, the complainant will not be entitled to any redress awarded to him by the decision. The Ombudsman must in any event notify the respondent of the outcome[4].

1 Section 228(5).
2 The FSO claims that 90% of its complaints are resolved by the case officers without needing to go before an Ombudsman.
3 Section 228(6).
4 Section 228(7).

21.8 Section 229 of the FSMA 2000 deals with awards made under the compulsory jurisdiction.

If a complaint which has been dealt with under the scheme is determined in favour of the complainant, the determination may include an award against the respondent of such amount as the Ombudsman considers fair compensation for loss or damage suffered by the complainant ('a money award'); A money award may compensate for any loss or damage of a kind in respect of which a court would have power to award damages if it were deciding an action for breach of contract or of a kind specified in the scheme rules. The FSA may specify the maximum amount which may be regarded as fair compensation for a particular kind of loss or damage specified in this way. It is likely that the only additional loss which will be specified is inconvenience. Under the old PIAOB scheme this could be compensated up to a maximum of £1,500, though in practice the awards were usually much more modest. For loss which is legally recoverable the scheme rules will set a monetary limit (probably £100,000 initially, since that was the limit operated by the predecessor schemes). A money award may not exceed the monetary limit, but the Ombudsman may, if he considers that fair compensation requires payment of a larger amount, recommend that the respondent pay the complainant the balance. A money award may provide for the amount payable under the award to bear interest at a rate and as from a date specified in the award and is enforceable by the complainant. These provisions again mirror those of the IOB and PIAOB.

Alternatively, a determination in favour of the complainant may include a direction that the respondent take such steps in relation to the complainant as the Ombudsman considers just and appropriate (whether or not a court could order those steps to be taken). Compliance with such a direction is enforceable by an injunction, though only the complainant may bring proceedings for such an injunction.

Section 230 of the FSMA 2000 deals with the question of costs. The scheme operator may by rules ('costs rules') provide for an ombudsman to have power, on determining a complaint, to award costs in accordance with the provisions of the rules. Costs rules may not provide for the making of an award against the complainant in respect of the respondent's costs, but they may provide for the making of an award against the complainant in favour of the scheme operator, for the purpose of providing a contribution to resources deployed in dealing with the complaint, if in the opinion of the Ombudsman the complainant's conduct was improper or unreasonable or the complainant was responsible for an unreasonable delay. This aspect of the rules represents a major departure from previous practice. Until now it has been treated as axiomatic that Ombudsman schemes in the financial services sector cannot possibly make costs orders against complainants. The new scheme offers a limited departure from that principle, though in factno use has been made of this new power.

Sections 231 and 232 of the FSMA 2000 give the Ombudsman extensive powers to require any party (not just a member firm or a complainant) to produce relevant, non-privileged information for the purposes of dealing properly with a complaint. Section 232 provides that a person who without reasonable excuse fails to produce relevant information in his possession is guilty of contempt of court.

21.9 The new scheme is funded by means of a levy on the industry in accordance with rules set by the FSA[1]. In recent years the levy has been refined to help smaller members, especially small brokers who have come within the scheme for the first time as as result of the implementation in January 2005 of the new regulatory scheme provided by the FSMA 2000[2]. The effect now is to provide a lower fee for each firm's first few complaints in eachyear, thereby rewarding those who have fewer complaints.

The new scheme brings together no fewer than eight previously existing Ombudsman schemes. These are the IOB, the OBO, the Building Societies Ombudsman, the PIAOB, the Financial Services Authority Independent Adjudicator, the Securities and Futures Authority and the Personal Insurance Arbitration Service.

1 Section 234.
2 For a fuller account of this scheme, see Chapter 6.

Outstanding questions

21.10 The new scheme may be regarded as being in some ways a hybrid of the various schemes which have been merged into it.The scheme is headed by the Chief Ombudsman, a post held in the first instance by Walter Merricks, formerly the Insurance Ombudsman. At the level below the Chief Ombudsman are a number of 'principal ombudsmen' a title which seems to be used to cover people with senior managerial responsibilty but who do not actually decide cases. Below them what might be called the sectoral Ombudsman, (the 2000 Act refers to the 'panel of Ombudsmen', though this phrase perhaps fails to convey the fact that there is to be subject specialisation, closely based on the pre-Act Ombudsman schemes). These posts largely mirror the roles formerly held by the Ombudsmen within the original schemes which make up the new FSOS. Among the Ombudsmen are five who are said to have lead responsibility for respectively mortgage endowments, general insurance banking & credit, pensions & securities and general investment1,and who may be regarded as roughly the equivalent of the former sectoral ombudsmen. The scheme rules provide a hybrid between the former PIAOB rules and the former IOB rules. Membership of the scheme is compulsory for members of the FSA. Decisions are made on a fair and reasonable basis, rather than in strict accordance with the law, and are binding on both sides (this was a rule which applied neither in the PIAOB nor in the IOB) up to a maximum of £100,000.

Perhaps the most important departure from the rules of the former schemes is to be found in the provisions relating to oral hearings of disputes. The tradition of FSOSs in the UK has from the earliest days[1] been that oral hearings are to be regarded as very much the exception, most cases being decided purely on the papers. This tradition has now had to be abandoned as a result of the coming into force of the Human Rights Act 1998, which implements into English law the European Convention on Human Rights. Article 6 of the Convention confers on individuals a right to have their cases decided by means of a hearing. Somewhat reluctantly the FSA has had to accept that the determination of complaints to the FSO'S is caught by Article 6, given that decisions are to be binding on both sides. Consequently, the rules of the scheme, rather like the CPR 1998, have had to be structured around the idea of a hearing, even though it is clear to all parties that by no means all cases will in fact end in a hearing.

1 Taken from the FSO website www.financial-ombudsman.org.uk as at November 2005.
2 Ie the creation of the IOB in 1981.

21.11 it is easy to recognise that the current scheme builds on the success of its predecessors. These have been undeniable successes in the sense that during their existence they have attracted increasing amounts of public awareness and steadily increasing levels of complaint. It is of course impossible to tell whether this reflects increasing dissatisfaction, or increasing willingness to complain or increasing public confidence that the system can provide some avenue of redress.

There is no doubt that the current scheme is highly organised and regulated, and that a good deal of effort has been put into ensuring the quality and consistency of decision-making. Moreover, the principles upon which Ombudsman schemes should operate have been extensively developed and refined in the quarter of a century since the IOB first came into existence. This consistency has perhaps been achieved at the expense of some of the creativity which characterised earlier periods of the IOB, especially when Julian Farrand was Insurance Ombudsman, but the greater certainty is something to be welcomed. On the other hand it may be doubted whether the current scheme does a great deal to improve, as distinct from merely maintain, standards of fairness and customer service in the industry.

Part E

Settlement

Chapter 22

Subrogation and other consequences of settlement

The principle

22.1 Subrogation may be expressed as being the doctrine that a person who undertakes a contractual obligation to another to provide indemnity against loss[1] is entitled to stand in the shoes of that other in relation to that other's rights to receive or claim any money which would go to diminish the loss.

[1] Thus the doctrine is not limited to policies of insurance, though of course insurance is the context in which the doctrine most commonly arises. *Morris v Ford Motor Co Ltd* [1973] 2 All ER 1084, CA is perhaps the best-known example of a disoute about subrogation in the context of an indemnity contract which was not a policy of insurance.

History

22.2 The doctrine has a lengthy history. In *Randal v Cockran*[1] Lord Hardwicke LC referred to the insurers as having the 'plainest equity' to enforce subrogation rights[2], whilst later in the same century the Court of Kings Bench, in two seminal cases, accepted the principle of subrogation. The cases were *Mason v Sainsbury*[3] and *Clark v Inhabitants of Blything*[4]. In both cases the insureds had suffered losses as a result of civil disorder. They had claimed on their insurance policies, and the insurers had paid. They then sought to sue their local authorities[5], who were statutorily liable for the damage[6]. The authorities resisted the action on the basis that the claimants had already been indemnified by their insurers, but in both cases it was held that this was no defence. However, in both cases it was also assumed (the point not being directly before the court) that the insurers would then be able to recover from their policyholders the sums which they recovered from the local authority.

The circumstances in which the doctrine of subrogation applies were considered by the Court of Appeal in *Colonia Versicherung AG v Amoco Oil Co*[7]. The debate in this case centred on the principle, laid down as long ago as 1882 in *Burnand v Rodocanachi*[8], that the insured is required to account to the insurer for sums received in diminution of his loss, but not for sums which are properly regarded as gifts. In that case the insured effected with underwriters valued policies of insurance[9] (including war risks) on a cargo, which was afterwards destroyed by the *Alabama*, a Confederate cruiser, and the underwriters paid to the insured as on an actual total loss the valued amounts, which were less than the real value. After the end of the Civil War, the US, out of a compensation fund created after the loss and distributed under an Act of Congress passed subsequently to the loss, paid the insured the difference between their real total loss and the sum received from the underwriters. The House of Lords held that the underwriters were not entitled to recover the compensation from the insured. The facts of the *Colonia* case were that ICI were purchasers of oil from Amoco (through a chain of intermediate buyers). ICI was also an assignee of a policy of insurance taken out by one of the intermediate buyers covering the oil against contamination. On delivery the oil was found to be contaminated, and it was subsequently established that this resulted from the fault of Amoco. ICI's claim against Amoco was settled on terms which included an assignment to Amoco of ICI's rights under the insurance policy. Amoco then sought to claim on the policy, either as assignees of ICI or as a co-assured of ICI. The obvious difficulties with this attempt were that Amoco had caused the contamination, and if ICI had first claimed on the policy, then the insurers would have expected to exercise subrogation rights against Amoco. In order to avoid this consequence, Amoco needed to argue that the payment it had made to ICI was not intended to diminish the insured loss, but was intended to benefit ICI to the exclusion of the insurers. Both at first instance and in the Court of Appeal this argument failed. It is a matter of construction whether in any given case the payment is intended solely to benefit the insured to the exclusion of the insurer. In practice, however, it will be very rare for a payment made by a wrongdoer to his victim and calculated in some way by reference to the loss caused by the wrongdoing, to be considered as something other than a compensation payment such as must be taken into account as between insured and insurer. *Burnand v Rodoconachi* remains the only case where a payment has been held to have this characteristic, and it is noticeable that in that case the US Government was clearly under no legal liability to pay the money, which could only really be described as amounting to an *ex gratia* payment.

[1] (1748) 1 Ves Sen 98, 27 ER 916. See also *Yates v Whyte* (1838) 4 Bing NC 272.

[2] It may be noted that this was actually a claim to recover from the insured compensation subsequently obtained from a third party. The Court of Equity dealt with the matter by holding that this compensation was held *on trust* for the insurer. This approach to analysing the first limb of subrogation does not appear to have been followed in later cases – it would in any event not have been available to a common law court.

[3] (1782) 3 Doug KB 61.

[4] (1823) 2 B & C 254.

[5] Or the equivalent at that time, the term local authority not being then in common usage.

[6] Riot Act 1714.

[7] [1997] Lloyd's Rep IR 261, CA.

[8] (1882) 7 App Cas 333, HL.

[9] As is the usual practice in marine insurance: see Chapter 40.

Extent

Applicable to all indemnity policies

22.3 The doctrine of subrogation is applicable in any case where a party has been obliged under contract to indemnify another party. Although insurance contracts are by far the most important example of such contracts, they are not the only one[1].

[1] See eg *Morris v Ford Motor Co* [1973] 2 All ER 1084, CA.

Not applicable to contingency policies

22.4 On the other hand, the doctrine has no application to contingency policies, even where these are policies of insurance. Thus, insurers who have paid on a life or personal accident policy cannot claim to be subrogated to the rights of the insured against any wrongdoer.

Two limbs

22.5 It can be seen from these cases that here are essentially two limbs to the doctrine of subrogation. The first is the rule that the insurer may recover from the insured any sum which the insured recovers from a third party in diminution of his insured loss. The second is the rule that the insurer may require the insured to lend his name to an action against a third party from whom he has the opportunity to recover such sums. The first limb deals with the case where the insured has already recovered from the third party, whilst the second deals with the case where the insured has not already recovered and might be reluctant to do so, given that he has already been compensated by the insurer. Each of the limbs requires some further examination and elucidation.

Insurer may recover from the insured

22.6 The insurer is entitled to recover from the insured any payment which the insured has received which goes to diminish his loss, but is not entitled to any payment which is not paid in respect of legal liability for the loss.

Amount of recovery

22.7 In *Yorkshire Insurance Co Ltd v Nisbet*[1] the defendants insured a ship for £72,000. It was wrecked in a collision, and the insurers paid for a total loss. The accident was caused by a ship of the Canadian Navy, and the Canadian Government subsequently paid compensation in Canadian dollars. Because of changes in the rate of exchange, by the time of the payment the money was worth £127,000. The insured were willing to hand over £72,000, but the insurers sought to claim all the £127,000. Diplock J held that the insurers' claim failed. The purpose of the doctrine of subrogation is to ensure that insurers can recoup themselves up to the amount which they have paid out, but no more.

In *England v Guardian Insurance Ltd*[2] the relationship between subrogation claims and the rights of the Legal Aid Board were considered. The claimants brought an action against their buildings insurers in relation to damage suffered to their property. At the same time they sued those allegedly responsible for the damage. The claim against the insurers was settled by the acceptance of a payment into court of £102,000. Then judgment was given against one of the alleged wrongdoers (W) for £126,000. Of that amount, £102,000 was covered by a payment into court by W, though the court ordered that £40,000 be set aside to cover the costs of another alleged wrongdoer (G), who had been exonerated. The insurers sought a declaration that, subject to the £40,000 payable to G, they were entitled to exercise rights of subrogation by means of a lien over the sums paid into court by W. The insured argued that no lien could arise, partly because of the prior statutory charge in favour of the Legal Aid Board and partly because they were entitled to deduct from any recoupment by the insurers certain irrecoverable costs which they had incurred in their unsuccessful efforts to obtain judgment against G and others. It was held that subrogation does operate by means of imposing a lien on money payable to the insured in diminution of the insured loss. This included the fund of £62,000 (£102,000 – G's £40,000). The insurers' lien took priority over the Legal Aid Board's statutory charge because the money could not be said to have been 'recovered' by the insured until that lien had been discharged. At the same time the lien was a matter of equity, and it was open to the court to decide how much of the money should be subject to the lien. In making this decision, the court should allow the deduction by the insured of legal costs reasonably incurred in attempts to recoup the loss from elsewhere, even if those attempts had been unsuccessful, provided that the court was satisfied that in the circumstances it would be inequitable to allow the insurer to benefit from the sums received without giving credit for the expenses incurred in securing those sums.

1 [1962] 2 QB 330, Diplock J.
2 [1999] 2 All ER (Comm) 481, Judge Thornton QC as High Court Judge.

22.8 The damages recoverable in a subrogation action are not limited to the amount paid by the insurers under the policy. The insurers may keep what is recovered in the action up to the amount so paid; any excess belongs to the assured, unless the policy modifies the rights of the parties or the assured has assigned his rights to the insurers – *Lonrho Exports Ltd v Export Credits Guarantee Department*[1] (sums received by the Crown, its in sovereign capacity, under international agreement, absolute property of state; assured had no proprietary or other interest in any such sums until payments made to it by the Crown, as a matter of bounty; no interest recoverable).

1 [1996] 4 All ER 673.

Insurer may require the insured to lend his name to an action

22.9 The first point to be made in relation to this limb is that any action brought to recover against a third party must be brought in the name of the insured[1]. Subrogation is not the same thing as assignment[2]. It is for this reason that the law is prepared to require the insured to lend his name to the action[3]. It follows that the only rights which can be exercised are those of the insured, and that the third party may take advantage of any defence which may be available to him. In practice it is now usual to find policy provisions which entitle the insurer to take over the conduct of any action already begun by the insured in respect of the loss, as well as entitling the insurer to commence proceedings in the name of the insured.

[1] This statement refers to the position in English law. It should not automatically be assumed that the position is the same in other jurisdictions.
[2] Though it is of course possible for the insured to assign his rights to the insurer, in which case the insured effectively drops out of the picture: *King v Victoria Insurance Co Ltd* [1896] AC 250.
[3] *Wilson v Raffalovich* (1881) 7 QBD 553, CA. If the insured will not co-operate in this arrangement, then since the Judicature Act 1873 the practice has been to join the insured as co-defendant. This practice survives the introduction of the CPR 1998, which do not cover the point.

Legal or equitable rights?

22.10 An important and difficult case in the context of subrogation is *Morris v Ford Motor Co*[1]. Although it is not an insurance case, the decision has considerable implications for the operation of the doctrine of subrogation in an insurance context. The defendants engaged the third party, a firm of cleaners, to clean their factory. The third party agreed to indemnify the defendants against all losses arising from the cleaning, even if caused by the defendant's negligence. The claimant was an employee of the third party and was injured by the negligence of the fourth party, the defendant's employee. The claimant sued the defendant on the basis of vicarious liability and won. The defendant brought in the third party, relying on the indemnity clause and again won. The defendant would have had a *Lister v Romford Ice*[2] action against the fourth party, and the third party, having admitted liability to the defendant, sought to be subrogated to the defendant's rights against the fourth party. Neither the defendant nor its insurers would ever have contemplated exercising those rights. Hollings J held in favour of the third party, acting through the defendant as nominal claimant. The fourth party appealed. There was no doubt that indemnity had been given, but the Court of Appeal by a majority held that subrogation was not to be permitted. The judgments of the Court of Appeal raise and discuss questions as to the origins and basis of the doctrine of subrogation. Lord Denning MR said that the doctrine is equitable in origin[3]. It therefore followed that the exercise of subrogation rights lay in the discretion of the court, rather than being a matter of right. On the rather special facts of the case Lord Denning held that it would not be equitable to allow the exercise of subrogation rights. Whilst the conclusion reached is likely to strike most lawyers as a desirable one, it is submitted that the reasoning employed is not as fully developed as it might be. Lord Denning does not distinguish in his judgment between the two limbs of subrogation, which is unfortunate, because an examination of the history of subrogation appears to support the conclusion that the two limbs have different origins. The first limb has its origins in the two decisions of the Court of Kings Bench mentioned above[4], and it is indisputable that the Court of Kings Bench was a common law court. It is scarcely surprising that a remedy which operated against the defendant's property rather than his person should have been available in the common law courts.

The origins of the second limb of the doctrine are more obscure. *Randal v Cockran*[5] is sometimes suggested as the earliest case showing this limb, but the report of the case is so short and unsatisfactory that it should not really be relied upon as authority for anything. Some assistance towards the correct classification of this limb may perhaps be obtained by considering the nature of the remedy involved. It is a remedy which operates upon the person of the defendant rather than upon his property, since it requires him to do something. Thus it is by its nature likely to have been a remedy granted by the courts of equity rather than by the courts of common law. It is of course this limb which Lord Denning was considering in *Morris*, and it therefore seems likely that he was right to assume that the case before him was governed by equitable considerations. However, it should not be assumed that the same is true of the first limb of the doctrine.

Before leaving this case it is also appropriate to consider the rather different approach taken by the other two members of the Court of Appeal. Both Stamp LJ and James LJ took the view that subrogation is more properly to be treated as an aspect of the contract of insurance, ie that subrogation rights are a matter of implied terms of the contract. However, they then differ in their approach to the interpretation of the relevant implied terms. James LJ holds that it is an implied term of any contract of indemnity that subrogation rights will exist, but that it is open to the parties to agree to exclude this term if they so choose. In the present case there was clearly no express exclusion of subrogation rights – the contract was silent on the question of subrogation – but James LJ was prepared to hold that the rights should be held to have been excluded by implied term. It will be apparent that this analysis is extremely contrived and artificial – to find one term implied in fact excluding another implied by law might reasonably be regarded as a fairly extreme case of judicial ingenuity. If the implied term approach is to be adopted at all, then it is submitted that the reasoning of Stamp LJ is to be preferred. He held that subrogation is a matter of implied term, but then observed that in the circumstances there was nothing to suggest the exclusion of that term by any wish of the parties. This appears to accord with reality in the sense that it is very unlikely that the parties ever turned their minds to the issue at all in the contractual negotiations. It is unfortunate that this analysis should lead to a conclusion which is likely to be regarded as unacceptable.

In the light of these three judgments it is submitted that the technical exercise of extracting a *ratio decidendi* from the case is probably impossible and almost certainly pointless. What can be said is that Lord Denning's equity-based approach seems to produce the best outcomes in this case and in any others which might be like it. It is desirable that this approach should be followed and likely that it will be.

1 [1973] 2 All ER 1084, CA.
2 [1957] AC 555.
3 Stamp LJ in his dissenting judgment points out that this point was not argued by the parties.
4 *Mason v Sainsbury* (1782) 3 Doug KB 61 and *Clark v Inhabitants of Blything* (1823) 2 B & C 254.
5 (1748) 1 Ves Sen 98, 27 ER 916.

22.11 Questions about the fairness of the exercise of subrogation rights were also considered in *Woolwich Building Society v Brown*[1], which concerned mortgage indemnity guarantee ('MIGs') policies. These policies are effected by mortgage lenders to protect against the risk of default by borrowers. The premium is charged to the borrower, but the policy is in the sole name of the lender. In the present case the insurers settled a claim on the policy, then sought to exercise subrogation rights against the borrower. On behalf of the borrower it was argued that subrogation ought not to be available, either because the borrower was a person for whose benefit the policy was effected or because, by analogy with *Morris v Ford Motor Co* it would be unfair to allow the exercise of subrogation rights. Both arguments were rejected. As to the first, it was clear that the borrower was not a party to the policy, which gave no indication that it was intended to enure for the borrower's benefit. As to the second the judge said:

> 'the case may recognise the possibility of excluding by implication in the indemnity contract itself a right of subrogation in certain circumstances ... It may even be some support for asserting that equity will in certain circumstances not assist by compelling a party to use its name for the benefit of another so as to enforce a subrogated claim. But, if the common law were to imply such an exclusion, it would only do so in extreme cases, since the natural implication in the case of an indemnity is for there to be a right of subrogation. If equity were to refuse a right of subrogation, that would only be in circumstances where it would not be just and equitable that someone should be compelled to lend their name to sue.
>
> There is simply no basis for implying into the insurance contract an exclusion of the right of subrogation; indeed to do so would be contrary to its express terms ... What is more, I do not see that if the insurers have to pay because the defendant borrower has failed or refuses to pay, that it is unjust or inequitable that the insurers should be entitled to pursue their rights of subrogation if they have them'.

It is submitted that the decision is to be regretted. The essence of MIG policies is that the borrower pays the premium and might reasonably suppose that he has insured himself against the risk of subsequent default, whereas this case in effect decides that the borrower pays to insure the lender against that risk. It is surely unrealistic to say that the borrower should not be allowed to gain protection from the risk of his own default – all forms of liability insurance effectively provide such protection. The arguments would of course be quite different if mortgage lenders were in the habit of paying for such policies out of their own pockets.

1 [1996] CLC 625, Waller J.

Requirement of indemnity

22.12 Subrogation rights arise only where the insurer has indemnified the insured to the full extent required under the policy. In *Page v Scottish Insurance Corpn*[1] the limits of this principle were tested by a curious combination of facts. The claimant was the driver of a car damaged in an accident (but was not the insured). The insurers chose to entrust the task of repairing the damage to the claimant, who was an expert in this field. They then declined to pay the claimant for the repairs, alleging that the accident was his fault. When he sued for the cost, they counter-claimed for the same sum on the basis of exercising subrogation rights in the name of their insured. The Court of Appeal held that their subrogation rights had not arisen because they had not actually indemnified their insured. The unsatisfactory nature of the decision is readily apparent. The consequences must be that the insurers have to pay the claimant the cost of the repairs (acting in the name of their insured). They can thereupon say that they have indemnified their insured, so that their subrogation rights arise, and they become entitled to recover those costs from the person responsible for the accident, namely the original claimant. Thus, the money simply goes round in a circle.

In *Brown and Brown v Albany Construction*[2] the insured's house suffered heave damage. The insurers indemnified their insured by buying the house at the full market value prior to the damage. They then sold it on at a much lower price, no doubt reflecting the damage which had happened. The insurers then sought to exercise rights of subrogation against the engineer who had designed the foundations. Their claim would have had to be limited to their net loss, but the engineer sought to argue that the sum paid was to be regarded as being paid under the contract of sale rather than as being an indemnity, and that the doctrine of subrogation was limited to cases where the insurer paid the actual sum due under the policy. These rather formalistic arguments were rightly rejected in the Court of Appeal, where it was pointed out that the insurers would not have paid the sum they did unless they had been legally liable to indemnify their insured. The only realistic view of the purchase of the house was that it was the chosen way of effecting an indemnity. The insured had received the full value of their house only because of this behaviour on the part of the insurers, and there was no reason why the engineer should benefit from that.

1 (1929) 98 LJKB 308, CA.
2 [1996] CLY 3554, CA.

Insurers' duties

22.13 It is common practice for insurers in these circumstances to seek in the claim to recover any uninsured loss (eg the policy excess) on behalf of the insured. However, there is apparently no authority on the nature of the insurer's duties when exercising subrogation rights. The point is of practical importance because of the rule that only one action may be brought on any given cause of action. An insurer who brings an action in the name of the insured but chooses not to seek the recovery of all the insured's losses will prejudice the insured's position in the sense that the insured will not thereafter be able to bring a separate action to recover the remaining losses. It would thus seem reasonable to suggest that an insurer should owe at least some duty to the insured in these circumstances, just as the insured owes a duty not to prejudice the insurer's position by settling or waiving the claim against the third party without the insurer's consent. It is therefore somewhat surprising to find that there is apparently no authority dealing with the point. It is submitted that an insurer does have a duty to the insured to act reasonably in exercising subrogation rights. Although this cannot be construed as a blanket obligation always to seek recovery of all uninsured losses, it will in many cases impose a duty to do so. Failure to comply with the duty should be regarded as a breach of an implied term of the policy (but not as a breach of the continuing duty of utmost good faith) and the damages awarded for it should be equal to the loss thereby caused to the insured. In a clear case this will be the difference between the amount actually recovered and the amount which would have been recovered if the uninsured losses had been included in the claim. The position is more difficult where the recoverability of these losses is uncertain. In such cases there may have to be some apportionment of the losses.

Waiver of subrogation rights

22.14 In *The Surf City*[1] the insurers claimed to exercise subrogation rights in the name of CIF buyers of a lost cargo, who had obtained open cover for the cargo. The policy[2] provided that there was to be no subrogation against a cargo being carried by an affiliated or subsidiary company of the policyholder, the obvious intention being to prevent the subsidiary from being obliged to reimburse sums which had been paid to the parent under an insurance claim. It was held that no subrogation rights could exist here, since they had effectively been waived by the policy, which protected ships owned by subsidiaries or affiliates of the insured, as the ship in this case was.

1 [1995] 2 Lloyd's Rep 242.
2 Bulk Oil Clauses 1962, cl 6.

Co-assurance and subrogation

22.15 In *The Yasin*[1] D were carriers of goods to P. The contract required D to insure the goods, which they duly did. Ship and cargo became a total loss, and the insurers paid P as owners of the goods. Then they sought to bring a subrogated action against D on the basis that the ship had been unseaworthy at the start of the voyage. D argued, inter alia, that D and P were co-assured, and it is a fundamental rule of insurance that insurers cannot exercise a right of subrogation in the name of one co-assured against another, and that it was an implied term of the contract of insurance that no subrogation rights would exist in this case.

Both arguments were rejected. As to the first, there is no such rule, though principles of circuitry of action might defeat many actions of this type: see *Samuel v Dumas*[2]. As to the second, there was no ground for implying such a term here. The case, being entirely commercial, is distinguishable from *Morris v Ford Motor Co*. The same result would be reached if the test were Lord Denning's equitable test from that case. Some doubt was cast on this decision in *Petrofina (UK) Ltd v Magnaload Ltd*[3]. The claimants were main contractors in the building of an oil refinery. They insured the property, the insured being defined in the policy as the contractors and all sub-contractors. The works were damaged by the negligence of a sub-contractor. The insurers settled the claim and then sought to exercise subrogation rights against the sub-contractor. Lloyd J held that no subrogation rights could exist, since the sub-contractors were to be regarded as one of the insured, as stated in the policy, and it must follow that the insurers could not seek compensation from the insured for the very loss which was insured. Lloyd J expressed some doubt as to whether he had been right in *The Yasin* to allow subrogation rights to be exercised against a co-assured. It is submitted, however, that both decisions are correct on their facts. Whether subrogation rights can be exercised against a co-assured depends on substance, not on the formal point that the defendant is a co-assured. The question is whether the defendant is substantively one of the insured, as in *Petrofina* or merely on the policy as a matter of form, having insured for others without himself having any real interest in the goods, as in *The Yasin*. The analysis also deals satisfactorily with *Mark Rowlands Ltd v Berni Inns Ltd*[4]. In that case there was a sub-lease of part of a building in which it was provided that the tenants were to pay insurance and rent and the landlords were to insure the whole. Policy moneys were to be applied to reinstating fire damage, and in this event the tenant was to be released from repairing obligations. The whole building was destroyed in a fire caused by the tenant's negligence. The insurers paid, but then sought subrogation against the tenant. It was held that subrogation rights were not available because the insurance enured for the tenant's benefit, although the tenant was not expressly made a party to the contract.

It is of course a question of construction in each case whether the policy is intended to turn a sub-contractor or other third party into a co-assured – *Stone Vickers Ltd v Appledore Ferguson*[5], where the Court of Appeal held that a nominated sub-contractors was not entitled to the protection of a policy. Also in *BP Exploration Operating Co Ltd v Kvaerner Oilfield Products Ltd*[6] the question of whether the defendant was to be treated as a co-assured on the claimant's policy was resolved by reference to the commercial agreement between claimant and defendant which provided the background for the policy, rather than simply by reference to the policy itself. It was further held in *National Oilwell (UK) Ltd v Davy Offshore*[7] that it is possible for insurers to become bound to a co-assured on terms which differ from those on which it is bound to the principal assured.

In *Caledonia North Sea Ltd v London Bridge Engineering Co*[8] similar questions again arose. The case arose out of the Piper Alpha disaster in 1987. The operators of the platform sued various of the sub-contractors under indemnity clauses contained in the sub-contracts. The actions were in fact brought on behalf of the operator's insurers, who were seeking to exercise rights of subrogation. One argument raised on behalf of the sub-contractors was that they, being liable under the indemnity clauses, were to be considered as being co-obligors with the insurers, so that subrogation rights could not arise against them. This argument was rejected by the Court of Session. There is no general principle that obligations under an indemnity clause in a contract are to be put on a par with obligations under an express contract of insurance. Here the sub-contractors were not co-obligors.

More recently these questions have been considered by the Court of Appeal in *Co-Operative Retail Services Ltd v Taylor Young Partnership Ltd*[9] In that case it was emphasised that the crucial question is what the contract of insurance provides. If an insurer has provided a full indemnity to one co-assured, it will usually have fully discharged its liability under the policy so that a second co-assured cannot expect the losses to be paid a second time. The use in *The Yasin*[10] of reference to circuity of action as a reason why such claims cannot succeed was disapproved as being unhelpful.

1 [1979] 2 Lloyd's Rep 45, Lloyd J.
2 (1924) 18 Lloyd's Rep 211.
3 [1984] QB 127, Lloyd J.
4 [1985] 3 All ER 473, CA.
5 [1992] 2 Lloyd's Rep 578, CA, Anthony Colman QC.
6 [2004] 2 All ER (Comm) 266, Colman J.
7 [1993] 2 Lloyd's Rep 582, Colman J.
8 [2000] Lloyd's Rep IR 249, Ct Sess.
9 [2001] Lloyd's Rep IR 122, CA.
10 [1979] 2 Lloyd's Rep 45, Lloyd J.

Reinstatement and subrogation

22.16 In *Darrell v Tibbits*[1] the landlord of premises had insured them against fire. They burned down, and the tenant, in accordance with a clause in the lease, re-instated. The insurers had indemnified the landlord, but sought to reclaim the insurance money. The Court of Appeal held that the claim must succeed. It is notable that the landlord never received any payment in cash from the tenant, and both Cotton and Thesiger LJJ accepted that the juridical basis of the insurer's claim is by no means obvious. Nevertheless, the decision appears still to be good law.

1 (1880) 5 QBD 560, CA.

Subrogation and contribution

22.17 Where the policyholder has been fully indemnified by one insurer, he has no further right of action against another insurer who has covered the same risk. It follows that the first insurer cannot exercise subrogation rights against the second insurer[1]. Any claim between the insurers must be founded on the doctrine of contribution[2].

1 *Bovis Construction Ltd v Commercial Union Assurance Co plc* [2001] Lloyd's Rep IR 321, Steel J.
2 For contribution generally, see Chapter 24.

Order of application of payments

22.18 In *Napier v Kershaw*[1] the House of Lords had to consider a complex issue about the exercise of subrogation rights in relation to the settlement of some of the claims arising out of the problems suffered by Lloyd's in the 1980s. The essential facts were that the claimants were Lloyd's Names who obtained a sum of £116m in settlement of an action against their managing agents. They held stop-loss policies which covered one layer of their losses, and they had received payments under these policies. The £116m had been paid to the claimant's solicitors, and the stop-loss insurers claimed an equitable proprietary right in the fund on the basis of subrogation. It was held that there was a proprietary interest in the fund; as the fund was held in a separate account, this was effectively enforceable, and there would be an order restraining payment of the fund to the claimants without providing for the repayment of money due under the principle of subrogation. The claimants were their own insurers for sums below and above the insured layer. The correct order of payment of the sums received in the settlement was top-down, ie first to sums above the insured layer, then to the insured layer, then to sums below the insured layer. In the instant case the effect of this was to deprive the stop-loss insurers of most of the benefit of the settlement, but that outcome depends on the fact that most of the Names had substantial losses over and above the insured layer. The position would clearly be different if all or nearly all of the loss were covered by the sum recovered.

Some care is, however, needed in the application of this principle to the much more commonplace case of motor accidents where there may be uninsured losses such as the costs of hiring a replacement car. It does not follow that any recovery made by the insurers must be applied first in covering these uninsured losses. The reason for this is that the insurers' action will not include a claim for these uninsured losses. Thus the correct order of application is to set the money first against the insured losses and only then to apply any surplus to the policy excess.

The insured must account to the insurers for the money received from the third parties to the extent of the amount which they have paid him – *Lord Napier and Ettrick v Hunter*[2] (stop-loss insurance). The case is also authority for the proposition that the damages recovered by the insured from a wrongdoer are subject to an equitable proprietary lien or charge in favour of the insurers.

1 [1993] 1 All ER 385, HL.
2 [1993] AC 713, [1993] 1 All ER 385, HL.

Settlements

22.19 Because insurers bring subrogated claims in the name if the insured, it follows that the conclusion of such an action will normally bring to an end the rights of the insured. In *Kitchen Design and Advice Ltd v Lee Valley Water Co*[1] the claimants were insured under a policy which provided cover against both loss of or damage to property and loss of profits due to business interruptions. The policy allowed the insurers to undertake in the name of, and on behalf of, the Insured the absolute conduct, control and settlement of any proceedings, and at any time to take proceedings at its own expense and for its own benefit, but in the name of the insured, to recover compensation or secure indemnity from the third party in respect of anything covered by this policy. A water main burst causing damage to the claimants' stock, fixtures and fittings The claimants claimed under their insurance policy in respect of physical damage to their property. That claim was settled for some £18,000. The defendants, as the statutory water undertakers were the owners of the burst water main. They settled the claim against their insured for £15,000, and the claimant's insurers signed a form of discharge expressed to relate to all claims arising out of the burst water main. Later the claimants advanced for the first time to their insurers a claim for loss of profits in consequence of business interruption. This was settled for some £17,000, and the insurers sought to recover this amount from the defendants. The defendants contended that their liability had been discharged under the terms of the form of discharge. Phillips J held that the natural meaning and effect of the form of discharge was that the defendants were to be discharged of all liability in respect of claims by the claimants to which their insurers were or might become subrogated; the risk of further claims was one of the very matters against which the discharge was intended to protect the defendants and their underwriters and there was no doctrine of mistake that the claimants could invoke which avoided the effect of the form of discharge. Moreover, the claimants' policy expressly entitled their insurers to undertake in the name of the claimants the conduct, control and settlement of any proceedings and to recover compensation or secure indemnity from a third party in respect of anything covered by this policy; it was implicit in the clause not merely that the insurers had authority to settle a claim once proceedings had been commenced but they had authority to settle that claim if an offer of settlement was made prior to and without the requirement for issue of the writ; thus the insurers had authority on behalf of the claimants to compromise the claim advanced in the action. This was a single claim for physical damage and resultant consequential loss so far as the defendants were concerned; both heads of damage to settle both elements of the claim; the form of discharge did provide a defence to the claim and it was signed with the authority of the claimants.

In *Buckland v Palmer*[2] the claimant brought an action against the defendant for his uninsured losses after a motor accident. The defendant paid the sum into court, and the claimant accepted it, with the result that the action was stayed. It then appeared that the defendant was uninsured, so the claimant's insurers started a second action against him. This was struck out as an abuse of process in view of the existence of the first action, but the Court of Appeal suggested that the problem might be dealt with by applying to have the stay on the first action lifted. In *Hayler v Chapman*[3] the sequence of events was somewhat different. The claimant's car collided with the defendant's car. The claimant's insurers paid the claimant the write-off value of the car, and then sought to recover their outlay from the defendant's insurers by way of subrogation. The claimant, without informing his insurers, sought to recover his uninsured loss from the defendant's insurers and subsequently succeeded in obtaining judgment, which the insurers satisfied. The subsequent subrogated claim for the value of the car was resisted on the ground that the claimant's rights were exhausted by the judgment. The claimant's insurers applied to have the claimant's judgment set aside so that these proceedings could be amended to include the claimant's claim as well as the uninsured loss. The Court of Appeal held that before a court took the unusual step of setting aside a judgment given after a contested hearing there would have to be evidence as to the conduct of the parties showing that it was unjust and inequitable for the judgment to stand and thereby bar any additional claim. Such evidence was entirely lacking here – there was nothing to suggest that the defendant's insurers had acted so as to deliberately exploit the misunderstanding between the claimant and his insurers. The difference between the two cases lies in the fact that in *Buckland* the action had not proceeded to judgment.

1 [1989] 2 Lloyd's Rep 221, Philips J.
2 [1984] 3 All ER 554, CA.
3 [1989] 1 Lloyd's Rep 490, CA.

Insured's duties

22.20 It is clear from the cases discussed above that it is possible for an insured to prejudice the insurer's chances of recovering sums it has paid out under the policy. This may happen in a number of ways. The insured may bring a claim for only part of the loss, as happened in the cases discussed above. Or the action may be brought for the whole loss but pursued in such a way that some or all the loss is not recovered. Alternatively the claim may be settled out of court for less than the full loss, or the insured may in the conduct of the action do other things prejudicial to the insurer, such as making damaging admissions. Since the insurer can have better rights than does the insured, any of these things will be prejudicial. It is therefore a general principle of insurance law that the insured should not act to the prejudice of the insurer's subrogation rights without the insurer's consent. To do so is a breach of the insurance contract, but at common law does not automatically entitle the insurer to reject the claim – it is a matter of fact in each case what loss has been caused to the insurer by the breach. Clearly there will be cases where the insured's actions in fact cause no loss because the case was unwinnable anyway. In other cases it may be that some recovery was possible and that the insured's actions have prejudiced that to some extent. In that event the insurer is entitled to retain or recoup, as the case may be, the loss caused by the insured's breach.

In order to deal with the problems arising from the common law position it is common for insurers to insert into policies express clauses forbidding the insured to deal with the claim without reference to the insurers and giving the insurers the right to take over the conduct of any proceedings arising out of insured events. Compliance with such clauses is often stated to be a condition precedent to the insurer's liability under the policy. In personal lines policies the Insurance Ombudsman has tended to refuse to give effect to the condition precedent element of such clauses, reducing the insurers to their rights at common law. In commercial policies there appears no reason why full effect should not be given to these clauses, though the courts would no doubt require clear wording before concluding that compliance is a condition precedent to recovery.

Other consequences of settlement

Salvage

22.21 Once the insurer has paid for a total loss of insured property, including a constructive total loss, anything that remains of the property belongs to the insurer, who is entitled to take it and dispose of it as he sees fit[1], keeping the proceeds for himself. The doctrine also applies where insurers pay for a total loss by theft and the property is later recovered[2], though in such cases insurers under personal lines policies commonly sell the recovered property back to the policyholder for a nominal sum.

It is uncertain how, if at all, salvage applies where the insurer has paid only for part of the loss as a result of the operation of average.

1 MIA 1906, s 79, but considered to apply equally to non-marine insurance.
2 IOB 5.3.

Termination of the policy

22.22 Where the whole of the insured property has been destroyed or has become a constructive total loss, and the insurers have paid on that basis, the contract of insurance is at an end. This is because the contract has been fully performed – the insurers have discharged the whole of their obligations under that contract. It follows that the insured is not entitled to claim that the policy continues to apply to replacement property which he has bought, nor is there any entitlement to a refund of premium. The most likely example of the application of this rule is in motor insurance where the policyholder's car is destroyed.

The position is of course different where not all the insured property is destroyed. Thus, in a household contents policy a theft claim will not bring about the termination of the policy unless the policy itself expressly so provides.

Chapter 23

Reinstatement

23.1 In the present context reinstatement means the restoration of damaged or destroyed property to its pre-loss condition[1]. In practice it is an issue which arises mainly in the case of real property, though it is not unknown to find policies on personal property, especially household contents, which also allow for this possibility. There is no statutory definition of the concept of 'reinstatement', and, as appears below, this lacuna can in some cases give rise to practical difficulties.

The law relating to reinstatement must be considered both under statute and under the terms of the policy.

[1] The phrase is also sometimes used to refer to the revival of a policy by paying a premium to reinstate capital which has been depleted by the payment of a loss.

Statutory provisions

23.2 The major statutory provision in this area is the Fires Prevention (Metropolis) Act 1774, s 83. This section provides:

> '... that it shall and may be lawful to and for respective governors or directors of the several insurance offices for insuring houses or other buildings against loss by fire, and they are hereby authorised and required, upon the request of any person or persons interested or intitled unto any house or houses or other buildings which may hereafter be burnt down, demolished or damaged by fire, or upon any grounds of suspicion that the owner or owners, occupier or occupiers, or other person or persons who shall have insured such house or houses or other buildings have been guilty of fraud or of wilfully setting their house or houses or other buildings on fire, to cause the insurance money to be laid out and expended as far as the same will go, towards, rebuilding, reinstating or repairing such house or houses or other buildings so burnt down, demolished or damaged by fire, unless the party or parties claiming the insurance money shall within sixty days after his, her or their claim is adjusted, give a sufficient security to the governors or directors of the insurance office where such house or houses or other buildings are insured, that the said insurance money shall be laid out or expended as aforesaid, or unless the said insurance money shall be in that time settled and disposed of to and amongst all the contending parties, to the satisfaction and approbation of such governors or directors of such insurance office respectively.'

The original intention of the statute was to take away an insured's incentive to destroy his own property by providing that where such behaviour was suspected the insurers would be entitled to reinstate rather than to pay over the pre-loss value of the property. However, the importance of the statute at the present day may be regarded as being limited for a number of reasons. The first is that the wording of the statute is far from satisfactory. It is, for example, by no means easy to work out from the section the exact circumstances under which it applies. The section also appears to contradict itself as to the effect on the insurer. It begins by declaring that reinstatement is 'lawful', which implies that insurers have a choice, but goes on to say that insurers are 'authorised and required' to reinstate in the specified circumstances. Eighteenth century statutes are often somewhat obscure in their wording, and it is dangerous to be too dogmatic in drawing conclusions, but it is suggested that the proper resolution of this point must be that reinstatement is compulsory if the conditions of the section are met. Declaring that reinstatement is lawful is not inconsistent with making it mandatory, whereas the contrary conclusion leaves at least part of the section with no meaning at all. Nevertheless, the already prolix and convoluted drafting is not at all helped by the addition of this ambiguity.

A pragmatic answer to these points would be that they are of little practical importance at the present day because of the practice of including express reinstatement clauses in policies where it is appropriate to do so. Certainly, modern authority on the section is very scarce, which is perhaps an indication that it is not regarded as being practically important or difficult. Given the very robust attitude which the courts have begun to take towards the interpretation of some poorly-drafted statutes of this vintage[1], it is impossible to discount the idea that a modern court might decide that the section should be effectively emasculated. On the other hand, it cannot be denied that the wording of the section allows of an argument that its application is in certain circumstances mandatory, and it is therefore necessary to give some account of it.

[1] Notably the LAA 1774, as to which see Chapter 4.

23.3 The section is expressed to apply to some parts of the City of London only, though it has previously been held, in flagrant disregard of this, that it applies throughout England and Wales[1]. This oddity immediately suggests a way in which a modern court might restrict the operation of the section – it could simply revert to a strict interpretation of the geographical extent of the section. The section is expressed to cover only buildings, not fixtures and fittings.

The case law upon the section indicates that the section does not give the insured any right to insist upon reinstatement[2]. At first sight this may seem odd, since the assured is clearly a person interested and apparently entitled to the insurance money. However, the provision would make little sense if it applied to the assured. In the first place, it is always open to the assured to spend the insurance money on reinstatement if he so chooses, so there is no need to deal with this by statute. Secondly, it must be remembered that the section is intended as a discouragement to wilful burning of buildings by assureds. Such conduct is usually motivated by a desire to obtain the cash rather than by an interest in reinstatement. The provision that others can insist on reinstatement is intended to offer a way in which the fraudulent aims of the assured can be circumvented.

However, this point leads inevitably to the question of who can exercise the rights conferred by the section. There are of course various categories of person who may be in some way interested in a building without being the assured under a policy insuring that building. These would include tenants[3] (though possibly not mere licensees) and mortgagees[4]. The category might also be extended to those with contingent interests, such as remaindermen. An equitable interest, such as that of the purchaser of a building, might also suffice. The right of an interested third party to require reinstatement is apparently not limited to cases where there is suspicion that the building has been burned down deliberately. On the other hand, where there is such suspicion, the insurers are apparently entitled to insist on reinstatement even though there is no request to that effect from an interested third party.

1 *Re Barker, ex p Gorely* (1864) 4 De GJ & SM 477.
2 *Reynolds amd Anderson Phoenix Assurance Co* [1978] 2 Lloyd's Rep 440.
3 *Vernon v Smith* (1821) 5 B & Ald 1.
4 *Sinnott v Bowden* [1912] 2 Ch 414.

23.4 The reference in the section to the application of the insurance money would seem to have the effect that interested third parties have no relevant rights unless and until a valid claim is made on the policy, since until that point there will be no insurance money to apply. The logic of this would be that the operation of the section could be frustrated if the assured did not make a claim. Two points may be made about this. The first is that such a conclusion is not wholly illogical – the purpose of the section was not to protect the interests of the third parties, but to use the third parties as a way of discouraging arson. An assured who fires his own building but then does not make a policy claim is at least prevented from profiting from his own wrong. The second point raises a more serious objection to this view. In the case where there is suspicion of fraud or arson the obvious course for the insurers is to refuse to pay on the policy at all, rather than to insist on reinstatement. On the other hand it must be acknowledged that in practice insurers who have some suspicion of arson but who do not consider that they have sufficient grounds to reject the claim entirely may seek to compromise by insisting on reinstatement. It would therefore seem that there is at least some room for the view that a third party could require the insurers to reinstate even in the absence of a valid claim by the insured. Such a conclusion would have the desirable effect of giving greater protection to interested third parties. It might be said that the doctrine of privity of contract provides an insurmountable obstacle to this view, but the argument would have to be that the statute effectively provides an express exemption from the operation of that doctrine. If the independent right of third parties to insist on reinstatement is to be recognised, it will presumably also have to be accepted that the insurer can, as against the third party, take advantage of any defence which would have been available as against the assured (including fraud and arson).

23.5 It must be noted that the section does not require the insurer to restore the property to its pre-loss condition. It provides that the insurance money is to be applied in reinstatement as far as it will go. Where the sum insured is inadequate for reinstatement, the effect will be that the insured gets less than he had before. The section is silent on the issue of how the insurer should cope with that situation. If full reinstatement is not possible, what principles can be used to decide what should be built in place of the destroyed building? The question is of some practical significance, for the insured may reasonably say that having half of the building restored (or all the building half-restored) is of no use to him. It is no doubt open to him to make proposals to the insurers about what form the reinstatement should take and even to offer to supplement the restoration costs out of his own pocket, but it is not at all clear that he can insist on having any of his suggestions taken up.

In *Beaumont v Humberts*[1] it was held that a valuer's reinstatement value, which was based upon reconstruction in the same style and general shape, but redesigned in parts according to modern practice, was not negligent although it did not provide for an exact or nearly exact copy of the original house. This is not a decision on the application of the LAA 1774 and must therefore be treated with caution in the present context. However, it may perhaps be regarded as a relatively modern recognition of the need for some flexibility in interpreting the notion of reinstatement.

The section provides that the insurer's obligation to reinstate is excluded if the policyholder gives adequate security for the application of the insurance money in reinstatement or if the distribution of the money is within 60 days after the adjustment of the claim paid out among the various interested parties in a way which is acceptable to all of them. The section does not define what security is to be regarded as adequate. In the first instance this is presumably a matter for the insurers to decide, though it may be that a court would be prepared to set aside a wholly unreasonable decision on this matter. The alternative possibility of general agreement about the distribution of the money is one which scarcely needed to be stated in the statute, since in this event it would seem unthinkable that any attempt should be made to insist on reinstatement.

[1] [1990] 2 EGLR 166, CA.

Reinstatement under contract

23.6 It is usual in modern practice for reinstatement to be at the option of the insurers rather than the insured. There will of course be many cases where reinstatement is a good deal more expensive than merely paying the pre-loss value of the property. For this reason it is usual in buildings insurance, especially policies effected in conjunction with a mortgage, to insist that the property be insured for its estimated rebuilding cost. Of course there is no guarantee that this estimate will prove accurate should it ever have to be tested.

Relationship between reinstatement and subrogation

23.7 In *Darrell v Tibbits*[1] the landlord of premises had insured them against fire. They burned down, and the tenant, in accordance with a clause in the lease, re-instated. The insurers had indemnified the landlord, but sought to reclaim the insurance money. The Court of Appeal held that the claim must succeed, even though the landlord never received any payment in cash from the tenant[2].

[1] (1880) 5 QBD 560, CA.

[2] See also Chapter 22.

Chapter 24

Double insurance, contribution, over-insurance

24.1 This chapter deals with a number of related but distinct topics. Reference should also be made to Chapter 25, dealing with under-insurance.

Double insurance and contribution

24.2 Double insurance occurs where the same risk is separately insured by two or more insurers. It is customary to limit use of the term 'double insurance' to those cases where it is the same interest which is insured more than once against the same risk. A number of different situations may arise. The insured may have recovered the whole of his loss from one of the insurers. In this case the insurer who has paid may seek contribution from the other insurer(s) on risk. This aspect of the matter is dealt with below, under contribution. Alternatively, the insurer who is sued for the loss may seek to rely upon the existence of other policies as a basis for restricting or excluding his liability.

The MIA 1906, s 32 lays down some principles for resolving cases of double insurance, which appear to be of general application:

> '(1) Where two or more policies are effected by or on behalf of the assured on the same adventure and interest or any part thereof, and the sums insured exceed the indemnity allowed by this Act, the assured is said to be over-insured by double insurance.
>
> (2) Where the assured is over-insured by double insurance:
>
> (a) The assured, unless the policy otherwise provides, may claim payment from the insurers in such order as he may think fit, provided that he is not entitled to receive any sum in excess of the indemnity allowed by this Act[1];'

In relation to non-marine insurance this must be read as a reference to recovering more than a full indemnity, which would obviously infringe the principle of indemnity.

> '(b) Where the policy under which the insured claims is a valued policy, the assured must give credit as against the valuation, for any sum received by him under any other policy without regard to the actual value of the subject-matter insured;'

Valued policies are in practice found only in marine and aviation insurance, so this provision may be ignored in other contexts.

> '(c) Where the policy under which the assured claims is an unvalued policy he must give credit, as against the full insurable value, for any sum received by him under any other policy;'

The effect of this appears to be that where the assured has already recovered part of his loss under one policy, the total which he can recover in a subsequent action on another policy covering the same risk is reduced by the amount already recovered.

> '(d) Where the assured receives any sum in excess of the indemnity allowed by this Act, he is deemed to hold such sum in trust for the insurers, according to their right of contribution among themselves.'

The reference to contribution emphasises the close link between double insurance and contribution.

1 In a marine context s 16 of the Act explains the insurable value in unvalued policies, whilst s 27 deals with valued policies.

Contribution

24.3 This may be divided into two major questions. First, when does the right of contribution exist? Secondly, in cases where the right exists, how is the proportion of contribution to be decided?

When the right exists

24.4 The first point which requires to be clearly understood is that contribution can apply only where both policies do in fact insure the same risk. Where two policies relate to different policy periods they do not cover the same risk for this purpose[1]. In *North British and Mercantile Insurance Co v London, Liverpool and Globe Insurance Co*[2] wharfingers had effected fire insurance on property of which they were bailees. This policy contained a rateable contribution clause. Some grain belonging to a client was destroyed while in their possession. The client had also insured this grain against fire, under a policy with a similar rateable contribution clause. The wharfingers recovered indemnity from their own insurers, and this action was brought to determine the rights of the insurers *inter se*. It was held that the rateable contribution clauses did not apply, for the two policies were covering different interests – one related to the wharfingers' interest as bailees, whilst the other related to the owners' rights. The correct analysis of the position was that the wharfingers were liable to the owners as bailees, but could recover from their own insurers, who were not then entitled to claim contribution from the owners' insurers. In *Zurich Insurance Co v Shield*[3] the claimant was injured in a road accident caused by the negligence of a person acting in the course of his employment. He sued both the driver and the employer; it was held that the employer was entitled to indemnity from the employee[4]. The employer's motor insurer satisfied the judgment, then sought contribution from the employer's liability insurer. The Irish Supreme Court considered the *North British* case and held that there was no double insurance because the motor policy covered the vicarious liability of the employer for an employee's breach of duty to the general public, whereas the employer's liability policy covered liability to the employee[5]. However, it is not essential that the two policies shall be co-extensive so long as they in fact cover the risk which has materialised[6].

In *Gale v Motor Union Insurance Co*[7] G drove L's car. G's motor insurance covered this, as did L's. There was an accident falling within the compulsory risks. Both policies had a rateable contribution clause. The question was as to the proper rates of contribution. It was held, without apparent ratiocination, that each insurer should pay 50%.

In *Legal and General Assurance Society Ltd v Drake Insurance*[8] the claimant insurers insured A under a motor policy. During the currency of the policy he knocked down a pedestrian. Proceedings were commenced and the claim was settled. Meanwhile P had discovered that A was also insured by defendant insurers, and they claimed 50% contribution. Both policies had rateable proportion clauses. D would have had a good defence against A, who had failed to give them prompt notice of the claim against him, but P argued that contribution was based upon equity, not on transfer of policyholder's contractual rights. It was held, first, that the right to contribution was equitable, not contractual, and, secondly, that the presence of a rateable proportion clause excluded the right of contribution in cases where the insurer made a voluntary payment in excess of the rateable proportion. The payment here was a voluntary payment for these purposes, even though the third party could enforce a judgment against P without regard to the rateable proportion clause (RTA 1988, s 149) since the insurer could recover the excess against its own insured[9]. However, the relevance of that point was doubted in the most recent case on the subject, *Drake Insurance plc v Provident Insurance plc*[10]. In that case the Court of Appeal focused on the question whether the payment was voluntary as against the co-insurer, so as to remove the equity for the prima facie right to contribution. The point was relevant in that case because it was at least arguable that Drake was a volunteer as against the policyholder, because of s 151 of the Road Traffic Act 1988. However, an insurer who made a payment when his co-insurer has repudiated liability may still be a volunteer.

Eagle Star Insurance Co Ltd v Provincial Insurance[11] was a motor insurance case from the Bahamas. P was injured through the negligent driving of D, who was driving a car lent to him by a car repairer. P obtained judgment against D and, when that was not satisfied, sued both D's insurers and the repairer's insurers. D's insurers had cancelled the policy before the accident, but were still statutorily liable because they had not obtained the surrender of the policy documents. The repairer's insurers could have avoided liability to D because he had not given them the necessary notice of the claim, but this did not protect them against liability to P. The question was as to the proportions in which the liability was to be shared. It was held that where both insurers are under a purely statutory liability to a third party for the same loss, the extent of their respective liabilities is to be determined by reference to their liabilities under the contracts of insurance. Here, both insurers would have been able to repudiate the contractual liability (albeit for different reasons) so both insurers had the same contractual liability (ie nil) and it followed that the statutory liability was to be shared equally.

[1] *Phillips v Syndicate* 992 Gunner [2004] Lloyd's Rep IR 426, Eady J.

[2] (1877) 5 Ch D 569, Jessel MR and CA.
[3] [1988] IR 174.
[4] Presumably on the principles of *Lister v Romford Ice and Cold Storage Ltd* [1957] AC 555.
[5] See also *Godin v London Assurance* (1758) 1 Burr 489.
[6] *Bovis Construction Ltd v Commercial Union Assurance Co plc* [2001] Lloyd's Rep IR 321, Steel J.
[7] [1928] 1 KB 359, Roche J.
[8] [1992] 1 All ER 283, CA.
[9] See also *Bovis Construction Ltd v Commercial Union Assurance Co plc* [2001] Lloyd's Rep IR 321, Steel J for a case where a voluntary payment was irrecoverable and see *Weddell v Road Transport and General Insurance Co Ltd* [1932] 2 KB 563, Rowlett J.
[10] [2004] Lloyd's Rep IR 277, CA.
[11] [1993] 3 All ER 1, PC.

24.5 Each policy must be in force at the time of the loss. There is no contribution if one of the policies has already become void or the risk under it has not yet attached; the insurer from whom contribution is claimed can repudiate liability under his policy on the ground that the assured has broken a condition – *Eagle Star Insurance Co Ltd v Provincial Insurance plc*[1]. Cf *Legal and General Assurance Society Ltd v Drake Insurance Co Ltd*[2].

Where the insured has already been fully indemnified by one insurer, he cannot make a further claim on another policy. Consequently it is not possible for the insurer who has indemnified him to exercise any right of subrogation against the other insurer, since in subrogation the insurer merely exercises the rights of the insured[3].

[1] [1994] 1 AC 130, [1993] 3 All ER 1, PC.
[2] [1992] QB 887, [1992] 1 All ER 283, CA.
[3] *Bovis Construction Ltd v Commercial Union Assurance Co plc* [2001] Lloyd's Rep IR 321, Steel J. For subrogation generally, see Chapter 22.

Where there are exclusion clauses

24.6 One or both of the policies may contain a clause excluding liability if the loss is covered by any other policy. Where at least one of the policies does not have such a clause, no difficulty arises from this – the policy with such an exclusion clause is not on risk, the loss being borne by the policy which has no such clause. Where both policies have such clauses, the law has to avoid the absurd conclusion that no policy is on risk. English law has solved this dilemma by deciding that in such cases the exclusion clauses are to be ignored and all policies are on risk[1].

[1] See *Weddell v Road Transport and General Insurance Co Ltd* [1932] 2 KB 563; *Structural Polymer v Brown* [2000] Lloyd's Rep IR 64, Moore-Bick J.

Determining the proportions

24.7 The point is to some extent dealt with in the MIA 1906, s 80(1) which provides that each insurer shall be liable 'in proportion to the amount for which he is liable under the contract'. It is unclear to what extent this applies outside marine insurance. The leading case on the proportion of contribution in English law is *Commercial Union Assurance Co Ltd v Hayden*[1]. The policyholder had taken out liability insurance covering the same risk with both parties. The claimant's policy gave cover up to £100,000, whereas the defendant's policy gave cover only up to £10,000. A loss of about £4,000 occurred. The claimant paid on the policy, then sought contribution of 50%, and the question was whether this was the correct proportion. The defendant argued that the proper approach was to look at the maximum amount for which each insurer could have been liable and divide the losses in proportion to that figure. On this basis the defendant's liability would have been only 1/11 of the loss (10000/1000+100000). The Court of Appeal rejected this method of calculation, holding that the proper answer is the so-called 'independent liability' approach. Under this approach the court asks how much each insurer would be liable for in the absence of the other policy. The ratio between these amounts then determines the ratio in which the insurers are liable for the loss which has occurred. In the present case the loss was below the lower of the two policy limits, with the result that each insurer would have been independently liable for the full amount of the loss. Consequently, the appropriate contribution was 50%. Clearly, if the loss had been over £10,000, the independent liability approach would have begun to shift the balance of ultimate liability towards the claimant. It may be observed that the choice between the maximum liability approach and the independent liability approach reveals the ambiguity inherent in s 80 of the MIA 1906[2], which does not specify how to calculate the amount for which the insurer is liable.

[1] [1977] QB 804, CA.
[2] See per Cairns LJ in the *Hayden* case.

24.8 A further unresolved question is whether the rules on this point are the same for all forms of insurance. In *Commercial Union v Hayden* Cairns and Stephenson LJJ both questioned this point, observing that in the particular case of liability insurance premiums are not strictly proportionate to the limit insured – in that case the premium of the £100,000 policy was only 120% of the premium on the £10,000 policy. However, there is apparently no authority for saying that any branch of insurance does in fact operate the maximum liability approach. It may also be observed that the maximum liability approach is logically impossible in those areas, such as motor insurance, where cover is statutorily required to be for an unlimited amount. It is suggested that the most likely result of all this is that the independent liability approach will be adopted in all areas.

24.9 A situation which has given rise to much debate is that where neither policy contains any clause dealing with contribution, but one or both policies cover a wider range of property than that which is lost. Ivamy, for example[1], believed that it was necessary to distinguish so-called 'concurrent' and 'non-concurrent' policies, and that the latter gave rise to the greatest difficulties. It is submitted that this makes the problem appear more difficult than it really is, and that the matter can be resolved by reference to first principles. In the case presently being considered, any one of the policies involved would, independently of the others, have to bear at least some of the loss. It is therefore possible to apply the independent liability approach this case and obtain a result with is clear and simple to calculate. The objection to this is said to be that it treats both policies as if they were identical and ignores the fact that they are not limited to the same subject-matter and may differ widely in their scope and character[2]. It is submitted that this objection misses the point. *Ex hypothesi* all policies do cover the loss which has happened – beyond that their differences of scope and cover are irrelevant. It would in any event be quite impossible to devise any principle which would adequately account for all the possible differences between policies; the law would be forced to resort to giving judges a general discretion as to the proportions of contribution, but there is no apparent basis on which such a discretion could be exercised. Moreover, it is commercially undesirable that the matter should need judicial intervention: insurers need to be able to calculate accurately for themselves the basis on which contribution is to be paid.

[1] Ivamy *General Principles of Insurance Law* (6th edn, 1993, Butterworths).
[2] See n 1 above.

Exclusion of contribution

24.10 Section 32 of the MIA 1906 is expressed to be subject to any provision of the policy, and it sometimes happens that policies seek to exclude the possibility of contribution. A number of different situations need to be distinguished:

(1) Some, but not all, relevant policies exclude contribution. This is usually done by providing that the policy shall not be on risk if the loss is covered by any other policy. So long as there is at least one policy covering the loss which does not have such a clause, these clauses appear to be fully effective, and the whole of the loss can be cast on the policy which lacks such a clause.
(2) All relevant policies have clauses providing that the policy shall not be on risk if the loss is covered by any other policy. This situation threatens to create an unbreakable circle in which none of the policies is on risk. The law solves this problem by providing that all are on risk as if none had a contribution clause.
(3) Some, but not all, of the policies have clauses excluding or limiting liability if the risk is 'more particularly' (or some similar phrase) covered by another policy[1]. The standard wording defines more particular insurance as referring to the case where the specific policy insures only the property which is lost, and it is to be noted that this greatly restricts the scope of such clauses. Where the clause applies, the wording goes on to provide that cover is restricted to the case where the specific policy does not cover the full loss. Thus, in effect the wider policy is postponed to the specific policy. The result is that there is not in effect any double insurance, since the insurance on the property concerned is arranged in layers which do not overlap.

[1] This clause has sometimes been referred to as the 'second average clause', but this term appears misleading, since the clause does not really deal with issues of average.

Enforcement of contribution

24.11 It is settled law that insurers seeking contribution do so on the basis of an equitable right which they have against other insurers[1], rather than by exercising a right vested in the insured. The point is of some practical importance. It means that a claim for contribution should be brought in the insurer's own name. It also means that the insurer's right to contribution is not liable to be prejudiced by any action or inaction on the part of the insured.

[1] *Legal and General Assurance Society Ltd v Drake Insurance Co Ltd* [1992] 1 All ER 283, CA.

Over-insurance

24.12 Over-insurance arises where the insured value is greater than the value of the property insured. It often occurs in cases of double insurance, though it can occur without any element of double insurance.

The existence of over-insurance in any given case may give rise to the suspicion that the insured has acted fraudulently. It is not unknown for insureds to insure property for more than it is worth in the hope of making a profit from its subsequent destruction. The mere fact of effecting a policy on this basis probably does not amount to a criminal offence (insufficient steps having been taken to amount to an attempt to obtain property by deception). The more interesting question for present purposes is whether it has any effect on the policy. In the case of an unvalued policy the principle of indemnity would in any event restrict the insured to recovering his actual loss. This argument would not apply in the case of a valued policy. The question therefore is whether the overinsurance can by itself vitiate the policy entirely. The point was considered in the context of a marine policy in *Glafki Shipping Co SA v Pinios Shipping Co (The Maira (No 2))*[1], where Hobhouse J said that the vitiation of the policy could only be on the basis that the contract was one of gaming or wagering and accordingly void under s 4(2) of the MIA 1906[2]. In a non-marine context s 18 of the Gaming Act 1845 could produce the same result. Neither of those sections gives any definition of gaming or wagering, and it is presumably a question of fact in each case to decide whether the policy is of this type. Despite Hobhouse J's disapproval of earlier authorities focusing on the intention to make a profit out of the policy, it is hard to avoid the view that this will be at least strong *prima facie* evidence that the policy is by way of gaming or wagering. Clearly the point is only of real importance in valued policies.

[1] [1984] 1 Lloyd's Rep 660.
[2] Disapproving *Herring v Janson* (1895) 1 Com Cas 177, where it was suggested that the test was whether the sum insured was so excessive as to show that the insured must have intended to make a profit. That case of course pre-dated the MIA 1906, though the Marine Insurance Act 1745 was in more or less identical terms as to this point.

Over-insurance and valued policies

24.13 In *Elcock v Thomson*[1] premises had been insured under a valued policy. The value was some £196,000 but the insurers were not to be liable for more than £186,000. The premises were damaged, but not destroyed in a fire. It then became apparent that the claimant had bought the premises for £40,000, and that they were about to be compulsorily purchased for £50,000, this sum not being materially affected by the fire damage. The case concerned the proper basis of indemnity. The claimants argued for one of:

(a) 186/196 x the difference between the agreed value and the real value after the fire;

(b) the proportion of percentage depreciation in real value due to the fire, as applied to the agreed value;
(c) a proportion of the cost of reinstatement.

The defendants argued for either:

(a) the actual depreciation in real value caused by the fire; or
(b) such percentage of the agreed value as the cost of reinstatement bore to the cost of erecting a new building.

Understandably the insurers were anxious to downplay as far as possible the significance of the agreed value in view of the enormous disparity between the agreed value and the actual value. However, Morris J held that the agreed value could not simply be ignored.

> 'When parties have agreed upon a valuation, then, in the absence of fraud or of circumstances invalidating their agreement, they have made an arrangement by which for better or worse they are bound[2].'

These observations follow closely the provisions of s 27 of the MIA 1906; though this was of course not a case of marine insurance, it appears that the same principles are generally applicable. On this basis it was held that claimant's option (b) was the correct measure of indemnity. Where there is a valid agreed value, the starting point for measuring indemnity must be that immediately before the loss the property was worth that amount. If the property has been reduced in value by x %, then for the purposes of the policy, the loss is x % of the agreed value. In the present case the outcome of applying this rule may appear unacceptable, but it is submitted that this results from the enormous over-insurance which had happened here. However, it is not proper to deal with this point by finding some other basis of indemnity. Either the valuation is valid, in which case the outcome must be that specified here, or it is not, in which case the whole policy may well be voidable for want of good faith. The point is illustrated by *O'Connell v Pearl*[3], where a horse was insured for £200,000, but was found to be worth no more than £20,000. It was held that the over-valuation was so large that the policyholder must have known of it. However, the logic of this conclusion does not appear to have been followed through with full rigour, for the policy also insured the foal which the horse was carrying. The insured value of the foal was £60,000, and it was held that this claim should succeed, the valuation not being excessive. The difficulty is that, if the valuation of the dam was fraudulent, it would appear that the whole policy should have been voidable.

1 (1949) 82 Ll L Rep 892, Morris J.
2 At 899–900.
3 [1995] 2 Lloyd's Rep 479.

24.14 Where the over-insurance is deliberate, this gives rise to a potential moral hazard, since the policyholder has an obvious incentive to bring about a loss. Despite this, it is not uncommon, at least in marine and aviation insurance, to find valuations which are obviously excessive. One reason why insurers may be prepared to collude in these, at least with insureds whom they regard as trustworthy, is that the premium is to some extent based on the valuation, so a larger valuation produces a larger premium.

Chapter 25

Under-insurance

25.1 Under-insurance is the situation which arises where property is insured for less than its full value (the converse situation of over-insurance is examined in Chapter 24). Two separate but related issues are considered in this Chapter:

(a) the amount of indemnity payable in an under-insurance situation;
(b) avoidance for misrepresentation/non-disclosure of the true value of the property.

The doctrine of average

25.2 This may be summarised as being the principle that where property is insured for less than its true value and an insured loss occurs, the insurer is liable only for the proportion of the loss which the sum insured bears to the true value of the property. Many insurers appear to regard the principle as more or less self-evident, but it is submitted that it is no such thing[1]. There are logically two ways of dealing with the situation where the insured value is less than the real value. The doctrine of average is one, but the other is simply to say that the policy covers all loss up to the insured value but not beyond. The two solutions obviously produce different results, but there is no inherent reason why one is superior to the other. Moreover, it is submitted that the average policyholder, if he were ever to put his mind to the question, would be more likely to assume that the second solution was the correct one. Whilst policyholder expectation is of course not by itself conclusive of the law, it is submitted that in a case of this kind where either solution is equally logical, it ought to be allowed to have some weight.

[1] See, for example, *Carreras v Cunard Steamship Co* [1918] 1 KB 118, where Bailhache J held that the presence of an average clause in a fire policy was so much a part of normal practice as to be taken for granted.

25.3 In the context of marine insurance the principle of average is recognised in s 67(2) of the MIA 1906:

> 'Where there is a loss recoverable under the policy, the insurer, or each insurer if there be more than one, is liable for such proportion of the measure of indemnity as the

> amount of his subscription bears to the value fixed by the policy in the case of a valued policy, or to the insurable value in the case of an unvalued policy.'

This provision deals both with aspects of double insurance[1] and with the consequences of under-insurance in a single policy. However, it is not certain that s 67 does not apply outside marine insurance; and there is no clear doctrine of average in non-marine policies. It should be added that some commentators assume that s 81 of the MIA 1906 adds statutory force to the doctrine of average. That section provides:

> 'Where the assured is insured for an amount less than the insurable value or in the case of a valued policy[2] for an amount less than the policy valuation, he is deemed to be his own insurer in respect of the uninsured balance.'

It should scarcely need to be stated that this provision says nothing about whether the division of responsibility between assured and insurer is to be made on a proportionate basis or on a first loss basis. If anything, the latter interpretation seems more plausible. Of course it must be admitted that s 67(2) does effectively apply average to marine policies, though even this can be excluded by express agreement.

Despite the difficulties here alluded to, it is clear that both the courts and the Insurance Ombudsman[3] do accept that the doctrine of average is an appropriate one to apply, at least where it is clearly set out in the policy.

[1] See Chapter 24. Double insurance occurs where the same risk is separately insured by two or more insurers. It is customary to limit use of the term 'double insurance' to those cases where it is the same interest which is insured more than once against the same risk.

[2] Valued policies are more or less universal in marine insurance, but are very rarely encountered elsewhere.

[3] See for example IOB 14.24, 14.26 and 14.27.

Proposer's duties

25.4 Many policies, especially household contents policies, now expressly state that the sum insured must be adequate to meet the replacement cost of the items. Quite apart from the difficulties of principle identified in the previous paragraph, it may also be observed that it is not always easy for the policyholder to make an accurate estimate of the replacement cost of all items covered by such a policy. Where the estimate given, on which the sum insured (and the premium) is calculated proves to be significantly inaccurate, insurers may seek to avoid the policy for non-disclosure. A case of this kind was *Economides v Commercial Union*[1], one of the very few personal lines cases to come before the courts since the creation of the IOB in 1981. The value of the contents was found to be of the order of £40,000, whereas the sum insured was only £16,000. The Court of Appeal held that the statement of value made by the policyholder on the proposal form was not a warranty as to value. Rather, it was a statement of his belief, within s 20(5) of the MIA 1906 and was therefore true if honestly made, notwithstanding that the valuation might be inaccurate. Obviously, the more inaccurate a valuation, the more the suspicion might arise that it was not honestly made, but an honest inaccurate valuation does not amount to a non-disclosure or a misrepresentation.

Thus the policy must be considered to be valid, though the Court of Appeal did not have to consider the question of how the loss would be adjusted in the light of the obvious under-insurance.

The principle laid down in *Economides* must apply all the more strongly in cases where there is no proposal form and the policyholder is not clearly asked about the replacement cost. In one IOB case[2] insurance was taken out over the telephone and it appeared that the policyholder had merely been asked for what sum he wanted to insure the contents, which is not at all the same question as asking what is the replacement value. Although the sum he gave was much less than the replacement cost, it was held that the insurer could not avoid the policy.

1 [1997] 3 All ER 636, CA.
2 IOB 17.8.

Under-insurance of valuables

25.5 A further refinement of the under-insurance question arises where the policy has a separate limit for items of particular value, sometimes called high-value or high-risk items. In principle under-insurance has to be calculated separately in respect of items falling within whatever definition the policy gives for this clause. Thus, there may be cases where the total sum insured is not an underestimate but the high-risks valuation is. This may occur especially where the policy automatically applies a limit to high-risk items as a proportion of the total sum insured. This practice is in some ways unsatisfactory, since it may lead the policyholder to have to insure for more than the total value of the contents in order to obtain full cover for the high-risk items. An important question in such cases is whether the nature and extent of the high-risks provision has been adequately brought to the policyholder's attention[1].

1 IOB 14.25.

Inconsistent remedies

25.6 Problems are caused by the practice of some insurers in describing the consequences of under-insurance. The following IOB case provides a good illustration[1]. In a household contents policy claim it was found that the sum insured for valuables was substantially less than the replacement value claimed by the policyholder for replacing jewellery which had been lost. The policy prospectus contained a statement that '[the sum insured] must be sufficient to meet the full cost of replacing all your contents' though without specifying what would happen if the sum were inadequate. The policy document stated that the insurer would have the option to make a deduction for wear and tear and betterment or to pay for the reduction in value resulting from the loss or damage if 'the total replacement value exceeds the sum insured'.

The insurer sought to avoid the policy entirely on the basis that there had been non-disclosure of some of the valuable items and that no cover would have been granted if the full facts had been disclosed. Even if this was true, the difficulty was that the policy document appeared to provide a different remedy from avoidance. The Insurance Ombudsman held that only this remedy was to be available to the insurer. From a strict legal point of view the case is not without difficulty. Although the IOB report asserts that avoidance would not have been legally possible, it is not clear that this is so. The policyholder had clearly committed non-disclosure on the proposal form, and it appeared that this non-disclosure had induced the insurer to enter into the policy. It would be perfectly possible to construe the words on the policy document as applying only to the case where the sum insured was adequate at the inception but not at the time of the claim (perhaps because more items had been acquired in the interval). On the other hand the insurer's failure to specify in the proposal form any consequence resulting from under-insurance does not make it any easier to hold that avoidance should be available. A final point in relation to this case is that the Ombudsman apparently accepted that the non-disclosure of the items of jewellery was on the facts to be accepted as entirely innocent.

It is submitted that as a matter of strict law this policy should have been voidable for non-disclosure, since the requirements of the *Pan Atlantic* test are met and there is nothing in the proposal form to waive the full duty of disclosure. At the same time it is a case where the strict application of the law appears to produce a harsh outcome, and the Ombudsman was therefore correct, in the context of his terms of reference, in the conclusion to which he came.

[1] IOB 5.4.

Wear and tear clauses

25.7 In two cases the Ombudsman has had to consider the effect of wear and tear clauses ie clauses which provide that in the event of under-insurance the insurer may make a deduction for wear and tear. A clause of this kind does not import into the policy the doctrine of average. Rather, the effect is that the insurer is only required to pay the second-hand replacement value of goods rather than the cost of replacing them new[1]. The effect of this will naturally differ according to the nature of the items in question. Thus, for example, valuable coins are unlikely to suffer much, if anything, in the form of wear and tear[2].

[1] IOB 11.22.
[2] IOB 15.18.

Abandonment and salvage

25.8 It is not clear from the authorities whether the doctrine of salvage[1] applies in the case of an insured who, by reason of the operation of average, has received only a partial indemnity. One solution is to say that insured and insurer hold as equitable tenants in common in proportion to their respective interests.

[1] See Chapter 22.

Subrogation

25.9 Equally it is not clear whether subrogation rights[1] are available to an insurer who by reason of the operation of average has paid only for part of a loss. It is submitted that as a matter of principle they should be available once the insurer has done all that he is obliged to do under the policy. It is instructive to consider the example of the insurer who, in the case of a total loss, has paid up to the limit of his liability on the policy. It surely cannot be suggested that such an insurer is prohibited from exercising subrogation rights merely because there has been under-insurance. Yet once this proposition is accepted, it is very hard to see why it does not also apply to an insurer who has settled his share of a partial loss. Obviously the insurer cannot be allowed to make a profit out of exercising those rights, so, as is usual in cases of subrogation, if he recovers from the wrongdoer more than he has paid to the insured, the excess must be paid over to the insured. A more difficult situation might arise if the right against the wrongdoer is founded on tort and the insurer recovers only a portion of the loss because of a finding of contributory negligence. Here it is suggested, admittedly without authority, that the insurer is entitled to keep the amount recovered up to the amount he has paid out.

[1] See Chapter 22.

Chapter 26

Costs

Introduction

26.1 The general principle of costs is that they follow the event, ie that the losing party must pay the winning party's costs[1]. The operation of this is clear enough when the defendant is an insurance company, but some difficulties have been found to arise when the nominal defendant is a policyholder who has liability insurance. In such cases the policy will normally give the insurance company the right to take over the conduct of the defence, though the policyholder will remain the nominal defendant. If the claimant is ultimately successful, a question of costs may arise. The costs of the action may be provided for in the policy, but this will normally be subject to the policy limit. In these circumstances successful claimants have resorted to the use of s 51 of the SCA 1981, which allows costs orders to be made against non-parties to the action in specified circumstances. The principles generally applicable to s 51 applications have been worked out in a series of cases involving applications against legal practitioners[2]. In brief, they are that applications are appropriate only in straightforward cases, where the procedure can be conducted in hours rather than days; the application should normally be made to the trial judge; elaborate pleadings should be avoided; discovery and interrogatories are inappropriate; the ordinary rules of evidence will normally apply and there will be no cross-examination on affidavits or, as is more usual at the present day, witness statements.

There are a number of recent decisions of the Court of Appeal which consider the question whether the insurer of the unsuccessful party in litigation who finances that party's conduct of the litigation may be ordered by the court to pay the successful party's costs of that litigation. These cases are considered below, but this discussion must be understood subject to the caveat that this is an emerging area of the law and one where the House of Lords has not yet had the opportunity to lay down a definitive set of principles.

1 CPR 1998, 44.2(a), though 44.2(b) adds that the court may make a different order. There is a gradually emerging body of case law and practice on the circumstances when split costs orders will be made. It appears that the general rule is still quite strongly enforced, and it is clear that trial judges have a very wide discretion as to costs which is extremely difficult to challenge on appeal.
2 See *Ridehalgh v Horsfield* [1994] Ch 205, CA.

The authorities

26.2 In *TGA Chapman Ltd v Christopher*[1] the Court of Appeal considered s 51 of the SCA 1981 and, in particular, the liability of an insurer of a negligent defendant to pay the claimant's costs of the action.

The Court of Appeal held that as the insurance company in this case, who were named as second defendants in the action, had decided to defend the claimants' action and the claimants had succeeded in their action, the insurance company was liable to pay the claimants' costs in addition to making payment to the defendant up to the limit of the insurance policy.

It was held that the judges, in exercising their discretion under s 51 of the SCA 1981 to award the costs of an action against the losing defendants' insurers should consider whether:

(1) the insurers determined that the claim would be fought;
(2) the insurers funded the defence of the claim;
(3) the insurers had the conduct of the litigation;
(4) the insurers fought the claim exclusively to defend their own interests;
(5) the defence failed in its entirety.

In *Murphy v Young*[2] it was held that costs would be appropriately awarded against a non-party under the SCA 1981, s 51 in exceptional circumstances, for example: where there had been wanton meddling; where there was funding by a trade union with an interest in supporting the claim and with responsibility for whether and how the litigation was to be pursued and where an insurer provided unlimited cover against liability. Legal expenses insurance policies, where the insurer's liability was limited, were in the public interest and a decision to award non-party costs would depend upon the facts of the case. Funding of litigation alone, for example by a disinterested relative out of natural affection would not make a s 51 order appropriate. In this case the insurer had funded the litigation under a commercial agreement but had neither initiated it nor controlled its course and it would be unreasonable to make a s 51 order.

This decision may helpfully be contrasted with that in *Tharros Shipping Co Ltd v Bias Shipping Ltd*[3], heard at the same time and by the same Court of Appeal. In that case a P & I club had originally agreed to support its members defence of a claim, but had withdrawn the support shortly before trial on the basis of advice as to the likely outcome. The insured abandoned its defence fairly early in the trial and judgment was given against it. When it was unable to satisfy either the judgment or the order for costs, the claimant sought to make the club liable for the costs. This attempt failed, the Court of Appeal holding that there is no general principle that insurers are liable if the defence fails and that, on the facts, the club had acted properly both in granting cover originally and in withdrawing it shortly before trial.

The case of *Gloucestershire Health Authority v MA Torpy and Partners*[4] may also provide some comfort for liability insurers. Judge Bowsher QC held that professional negligence insurers were not liable for costs in excess of the limit on the policy of insurance. It appears that the reason for the departure from the ruling of the Court of Appeal in *Chapman v Christopher* was the extent to which it could be said that the insurers were conducting the appeal solely for their own account. It appears that if the insured has an interest in the proceedings, even if he is not active in them, this will enable the insurers to rely on the limit in the policy[5]. This will surely be the normal case, and it is to be noted that since this early flurry of attempts to impose greater costs liability on insurers, this area of law seems to have gone quiet.

In *Bristol and West plc v Bhadresa*[6], the SIF had initially supported the defence of a claim, but had withdrawn cover shortly before trial on concluding that the defendants had been dishonest. The claimants sought a s 51 order against the SIF. Lightman J held that there was jurisdiction to make such an order, but declined to make one on the facts because the SIF had done no more than investigate the claim thoroughly before withdrawing cover. The judge alluded to the very serious consequences for a practising solicitor if the SIF seeks to settle a claim against him or withdraws cover, said that it would be contrary to the public interest if the SIF were put under pressure to make decisions of this kind hastily[7].

1 [1998] Lloyd's Rep IR 1.
2 [1997] 1 WLR 1591, CA.
3 [1997] 1 Lloyd's Rep 246, CA.
4 [1999] Lloyd's Rep IR 203.
5 See also *Cormack v Washbourne* [2000] 15 LS Gaz R 39, CA where an application for a costs order in excess of the policy limit was rejected.
6 [1999] Lloyd's Rep IR 138, Lightman J.
7 Although the Law Society has now changed the basis of its professional indemnity cover and the SIF is now in run-off, it is inevitable that cases involving the SIF will continue to come before the courts for some years.

26.3 It is important to note that in the *Torpy* case the defendant was not impecunious, and that he had always wanted the claim to be defended robustly. Also, the policy included what is known as a QC clause by which the insurers agree to pay claims which may arise under the insurance without requiring the insured to dispute any claim unless a Queen's Counsel advises that the claim could be contested with a reasonable prospect of success by the insured and the insured consents to such claim being contested, but such consent is not to be unreasonably withheld. At no time did the defendants ask the insurers to pay the claim in full or ask for the opinion of a QC to be taken[1].

It was said that in any case where the insurance involved is professional indemnity there is a question of professional reputation to consider with the result that it is unlikely that it will be possible to say in that the defence is conducted solely for the insurers' benefit.

Most importantly, the judge in the *Torpy* case said:

> 'I ask myself what is the exceptional feature of this case which should cause me to exercise my discretion in favour of making the order sought. I have to say that I do not see any exceptional feature. It could be strongly argued that whenever an insurer supports a defendant, the insurer should pay the claimant's costs if the defendant loses and the defendant cannot pay the costs, but that is not the law ... What has happened is not unusual ...'

Accordingly the case of *Chapman v Christopher* should be treated as applying only in limited circumstances where there is something over and above the usual situation of an insurer supporting its insured in the defence of a claim against it.

1 As to QC clauses generally, see Chapter 41.

26.4 In *Citibank NA v Excess Insurance Co Ltd*[1] the defendants were the insurers of a company (Lebihan) which was found to be liable for a fire' due to negligence on its part. Two other companies were also found liable to a lesser extent. A number of issues arose:

(1) Was the policy inclusive or exclusive of defence costs? It was held that the policy was exclusive of defence costs. This was a matter of construction and turned on the meaning of the word 'payable' in the context of costs where the insured company only paid the VAT on the costs and not the whole amount, which was payable by the insurers.

(2) What was the policy limit? The policy provided that the limit of £2m applied to '*any one claim or series of claims arising out of any one original cause.*' The question therefore turned on whether there was one claim or two', ie £2m or £4m. It was held that the original cause was only relevant if there was a series of claims and that if there was one claim then it did not matter how many causes there were of the claim because the limit attached to that one claim' this meant that the limit was £2m.

(3) As regards the liability of the insurers for costs over and above the limit of the policy, the court obviously referred to the *Chapman v Christopher* decision in which the five criteria referred to above at paragraph 26.3 were set down as being those which would justify a costs order being made. The judge said that in all such cases two of these criteria will be present, namely (2) and (5) which means that in each case it is necessary to consider (1), (3) and (4).

The judge then proceeded to look at each of these in turn on the facts of the particular case:

(i) the insurers determined that the claim would be fought – It was found on the facts that the primary decision to defend the claim made in 1994 was that of the insurers' they had assumed the defence and settlement of the claim under the policy. Although the insured would have wanted the claim to be defended to protect its interest that was not an overwhelming factor for if the case could have been settled for less than the policy limit then it was irrelevant what view the insured had as the insurer would have been entitled to insist on settlement. The judge therefore concluded that at least until judgment had been given against the insured it did have an interest in the claim being defended.

(ii) the insurers had the conduct of the litigation – Here, the judge drew a distinction between (a) the obtaining of information for the purposes of the defence and (b) the giving and receiving of advice and the taking of decisions as to whether to defend the case through to trial or to attempt to settle the litigation. It was held that it is (b) which determines who is controlling and directing the litigation. In this case it was found to be the insurers. Before the judgment on liability the judge was satisfied that the insurers had the control and direction of the litigation and, certainly after the trial on liability when two settlement offers were made without consulting the insured it was clear that the litigation was being entirely conducted, directed and controlled by them.

(iii) the insurers fought the claim exclusively to defend their own interests – It was found that until the judgment on liability, the protection of the insured's reputation, although not the dominant reason for the defence of the claim, nonetheless played some material part in the motivation for defending. After the determination of the issue on liability that cannot have been any motivation for defending the claim and the judge found that at that stage the defence was conducted exclusively in the interest of the insurers and motivated entirely by their own interests. It should be noted that the insurers' solicitor never considered that the policy limit might be exceeded.

The judge therefore held that he should exercise his discretion under s 51 of the SCA 1981 to hold the insurers liable for the costs of defending the claim over and above the limit of the policy but only from the time after the judgment on liability was given. This was because until the judgment on liability he did not believe that the decision to defend the case was taken solely by the insurers or that the case was defended solely for the benefit of the insurers:

(4) It is worth noting that the court also considered whether the delay in the bringing of the s 51 application was fatal. In this case, the s 51 application was made about 12 months after it was appreciated that the insured could not pay the costs and about 16 months after the conclusion of the trial. Although generally such applications should be made immediately after the trial, it was held that as the delay had caused no prejudice to the insurer it should not debar the application.

(5) Finally, the s 51 application was only made by the claimants after a s 51 application had been made by the two other defendants who would be liable for the insured's proportion of the claimants' costs if they were not paid by the insured or its insurers. The judge held that if the claimants had not made an application it would have been right to make an order in favour of the co-defendants under s 51 as they would ultimately be the parties that would have had to suffer the loss as a result of the third party's conduct' ie the insurers' in pursuing the defence.

The judge recommended that in such cases where solicitors are appointed by insurers to defend a claim where the indemnity is limited, consideration should be given to spelling out clearly the terms of the solicitors' retainer and recording contemporaneously the involvement of the insurer and the insured in the decision making process.

As the insured's ability to pay may not always be relevant, insurers may be encouraged to use QC clauses which tend to make it more difficult to show that the insurer had the conduct and control of the action.

1 [1999] Lloyd's Rep IR 122, Thomas J.

Other costs issues

Indemnity costs awarded – disgraceful conduct of insurers

26.5 In *Wailes v Stapleton Construction and Commercial Services Ltd (Unum Ltd, Second Defendant)*[1] the insurers were criticised for their behaviour during the litigation' it was said that they had acted in a way which could be described as disgraceful or deserving of moral condemnation. The litigation had proceeded on a misconceived basis with a view to creating sufficient prejudice at trial to avoid a valid claim. Indemnity costs were therefore awarded in favour of the claimant. The principle of this case is applicable to all forms of insurance, but will be relevant only in wholly exceptional cases[2]. In any event it may be observed that an award of indemnity costs rather than costs on the standard basis is of little practical significance. The relevant rule is CPR 44.4(2):

> '(2) Where the amount of costs is to be assessed on the standard basis, the court will–
> (a) only allow costs which are proportionate to the matters in issue; and
> (b) resolve any doubt which it may have as to whether costs were reasonably incurred or reasonable and proportionate in amount in favour of the paying party.
>
> (Factors which the court may take into account are set out in rule 44.5.)
>
> (3) Where the amount of costs is to be assessed on the indemnity basis, the court will resolve any doubt which it may have as to whether costs were reasonably incurred or were reasonable in amount in favour of the receiving party.'

In other words the difference between the standard basis and the indemnity basis is only a reversal of the presumption as to the reasonableness of particular items of cost in cases of doubt.

[1] [1997] 2 Lloyd's Rep 112.

[2] It appears that awards of this kind are rather more common in the US, where at least some states allow a jury to award damages for bad faith by the insurers in defending a claim. The point is of some practical importance, since the London insurance market insures many US risks.

Settlements as to costs

26.6 Where a claims settlement includes a provision for payment of the insured's costs, the court may be asked to consider whether those costs are reasonable and whether taxation of them should be ordered. In *Barclays plc v Villers*[1] Langley J held that the court had discretion to order taxation in favour of the insurer, even though the legal services were provided to the insured rather than to the insurer. In deciding whether to order such taxation it is necessary to take into account the fact that the settlement (which expressly provided a mechanism for settling the costs) was intended to achieve finality. On the facts, Langley J declined to order taxation.

[1] [2001] Lloyd's Rep IR 162.

Company reimbursement policy

26.7 In *New Zealand Forest Products Ltd v New Zealand Insurance Co Ltd*[1] the question was whether a policy which covered amounts which a director was 'legally obligated to pay on account of any claim … made against him.' covered amounts paid in relation to settling litigation affecting another person who was also a defendant to the same action. It was held that any expense which was reasonably related to the director's defence was covered' ie in this case an expense relating to another defendant's defence whose costs did not fall within the scope of the policy was covered.

[1] [1997] 1 WLR 1237, PC.

Conclusion

26.8 It is only in very recent years that the question of the insurer's liability for costs has come to be considered judicially. This may perhaps be explained by the increasing tendency of liability insurers to take an aggressive view of the business of defending claims.

The general issue is now to receive authoritative consideration from the House of Lords, and it is necessary to await their decision before drawing firm conclusions. However, it seems clear that s 51 of the SCA 1981 will be available in at least some circumstances, notably where it appears that the insurers have defended the action for their own benefit rather than for the benefit of the insured. It is inevitably going to be a matter for the discretion of the trial judge whether such a test is satisfied in any given case.

Part F

Protection of third parties

Chapter 27

The Financial Services Compensation Scheme

27.1 The FSCS has replaced the Policyholders Protection Acts 1975–1997 as the source of financial protection for policyholders in the event that their insurer becomes insolvent. The PPA have accordingly been repealed[1].

[1] FSMA 2000 (Consequential Amendments and Repeals) Order 2001, SI 2001/3649, reg 3.

27.2 Part XV of FSMA 2000 contains the statutory authority for the FSCS, and the detailed rules of the Scheme are then contained in the Comp section of the FSA Handbook. There is also a Memorandum of Understanding[1] between the FSA and the FSCS which sets out their mutual understanding as to how their activities interrelate. The FSCS applies across all activities regulated under FSMA 2000, but the account in this Chapter focuses principally on its application to insurance.

[1] Available at http://www.fsa.gov.uk/pubs/mou/fsafscs.pdf.

Legislative Framework

27.3 Under s 212 of the FSMA the FSA must establish a body corporate ('the scheme manager') to exercise the functions conferred on the scheme manager and must take such steps as are necessary to ensure that the scheme manager is, at all times, capable of exercising those functions.

27.4 Under s 213 the FSA must by rules establish a scheme for compensating persons in cases where relevant persons are unable, or are likely to be unable, to satisfy claims against them. This scheme is the Financial Services Compensation Scheme The compensation scheme must, in particular, provide for the scheme manager to assess and pay compensation, in accordance with the scheme, to claimants in respect of claims made in connection with regulated activities carried on (whether or not with permission) by relevant persons; and to have power to impose levies on authorised persons, or any class of authorised person, for the purpose of meeting its expenses (including in particular expenses incurred, or expected to be incurred, in paying compensation, borrowing or insuring risks).

27.5 Section 216 is of particular relevance to insurance because it provides that the compensation scheme may include provision requiring the scheme manager to make arrangements for securing continuity of insurance for policyholders, or policyholders of a specified class, of relevant long-term insurers ie those who have permission to effect or carry out contracts of long-term insurance and are unable, or likely to be unable, to satisfy claims made against them.

27.6 Section 217 further allows the compensation scheme to include provision for the scheme manager to have power to take measures for safeguarding policyholders, or policyholders of a specified class, of relevant insurers ie those who have permission to effect or carry out contracts of insurance and are in financial difficulties.

27.7 The detailed rules of the FSCS are set out in the COMP section of the FSA Handbook, and are summarised here.

27.8 The FSCS must administer the compensation scheme in accordance with the rules in the COMP section and any other rules prescribed by law to ensure that the compensation scheme is administered in a manner that is procedurally fair and in accordance with the European Convention on Human Rights[1]. These requirements are not further developed in the Handbook, but it is easy to see that openness and ensuring that all parties have a right to be properly heard before any decision is reached must be central to this requirement.

[1] Comp 2.2.1.

27.9 The FSCS may pay compensation to eligible claimants or secure continuity of insurance for eligible claimants when a relevant person is unable or likely to be unable to meet claims against it and may make levies on participant firms to enable it to pay compensation, secure continuity of insurance, or meet the costs of discharging its statutory functions. It may also agree to pay the reasonable costs of an eligible claimant bringing or continuing insolvency proceedings against a relevant person (whether those proceedings began before or after a determination of default), if the FSCS is satisfied that those proceedings would help it to discharge its functions under the requirements of this sourcebook.

[1] Comp 2.2.2.
[2] Comp 2.2.4.

The qualifying conditions for paying compensation

27.10 The FSCS may pay compensation to an eligible claimant where the regulated person is in default and in the case of a claim under a protected contract of insurance it is not reasonably practicable or appropriate to make, or continue to make, arrangements to secure continuity of insurance[2] or it would not be appropriate to take, or continue to take, measures under COMP 3.3.3 R to safeguard policyholders of an insurance undertaking in financial difficulties. The FSCS may also require an applicant to assigned the whole or any part of his rights against the relevant person or against any third party to the FSCS, on such terms as the FSCS thinks fit.

[1] Comp 3.2.1.
[2] Under Comp 3.3.1.

27.11 The FSCS may pay compensation to a person who makes a claim on behalf of another person if the FSCS is satisfied that the person on whose behalf the claim is made:

(1) is or would have been an eligible claimant; and
(2) would have been paid compensation by the FSCS had he been able to make the claim himself, or to pursue his application for compensation further[1].

This covers situation such as the following:

(1) when personal representatives make a claim on behalf of the deceased;
(2) when trustees make a claim on behalf of beneficiaries;
(3) when the donee of an enduring power of attorney makes a claim on behalf of the donor of the power;
(4) when the Master of the Court of Protection makes a claim on behalf of a person incapable by reason of mental disorder of managing and administering his property and affairs;
(5) when an eligible claimant makes a claim for compensation but dies before his claim is determined[2].

[1] Comp 3.2.2.
[2] Comp 3.2.3.

27.12 The FSCS may also pay compensation to a firm, who makes a claim in connection with protected non-investment insurance mediation on behalf of its customers, if the FSCS is satisfied that:

(1) each customer has borne a shortfall in client money held by the firm caused by a secondary pooling event arising out of the failure of a broker or settlement agent which is a relevant person in default;
(2) the customers in respect of which compensation is to be paid satisfy the conditions set out in COMP 3.2.2 R (1)[1];
(3) the customers do not have a claim against the relevant person directly, nor a claim against the firm, in respect of the same loss;
(4) the customers would have been paid compensation by FSCS if the customers had a claim for their share of the shortfall, and if the firm were the relevant person; and
(5) the firm has agreed, on such terms as the FSCS thinks fit, to pay, or credit the accounts of, without deduction, each relevant customer in (1), that part of the compensation equal to the customer's financial loss[2].

It is to be noted that compensation under this provision will in the end be paid to the firm's customers, and the payment to the firm is merely a mechanism by which the payment can in the end be transferred to those customers.

[1] See para 27.11 above.
[2] Comp 3.2.4.

Securing continuity of long term insurance cover[1]

27.13 The FSCS must make arrangements to secure continuity of insurance for an eligible claimant under a protected contract of insurance which is a long term insurance contract with a relevant person, if:

(1) the relevant person is the subject of any of the proceedings listed in COMP 6.3.3 R(1)–(5) 2;
(2) it is reasonably practicable to do so;
(3) the cost of doing so would, in the opinion of the FSCS at the time it proposes to make the arrangements, be likely to be no more than the cost of paying compensation under COMP 3.2; and
(4) where the relevant person is a member, the FSCS is satisfied that the amounts which the Society is able to provide from the Central Fund are or are likely to be insufficient to ensure that claims against the member under a protected contract of insurance will be met to the level of protection which would otherwise be available under this sourcebook.

27.14 In order to secure continuity of insurance under COMP 3.3.1 R the FSCS may take such measures as it considers appropriate to:

(1) secure or facilitate the transfer of the business of the relevant person in default which consists of carrying out long-term insurance contracts or any part of that business, to another firm; and
(2) secure the issue of policies by another firm to eligible claimants in substitution for their existing policies.

[1] Comp 3.3.1.

27.15 The FSCS's duty to pay compensation in respect of a long term insurance contract is limited to ensuring that the claimant will receive at least 90% of any benefit under his contract of insurance, subject to and in accordance with terms corresponding (so far as it appears to the FSCS to be reasonable in the circumstances) to those which have applied under the contract of insurance[1]. If the FSCS secures less than 100% of any benefit of a claimant under a contract, then FSCS must ensure that any future premiums that the claimant is committed to paying under the contract will be reduced by an equivalent amount[2].

[1] Comp 3.3.2A.
[2] Comp 3.3.2B.

27.16 In any period when the FSCS is seeking to secure continuity of insurance, it must secure that 90% of any benefit under a long term insurance contract which:

(a) falls due, or would have fallen due, to be paid to any eligible claimant; or
(b) had already fallen due to be paid to any eligible claimant before the beginning of that period and has not yet been paid;

is paid to the eligible claimant in question as soon as reasonably practicable after the time when the benefit in question fell due, or would have fallen due, under contract.

Any such payment is made subject to and in accordance with any other terms which apply or would have applied under the contract, but is not subject to the FSCS deciding that the cost of the making the payment would be likely to be no more than the cost of paying compensation under COMP 3.2.

[1] Comp 3.3.2.

27.17 Unless the FSCS has decided to treat the liability of the relevant person under the contract as reduced or (as the case may be) disregarded under COMP

12.4.14 R, it must not treat as a reason for failing to secure, or for delaying the securing of, payments under COMP 3.3.2C R at the level prescribed in that rule the fact that:

(1) it considers that any benefit referred to in COMP 3.3.2C R is or may be excessive in any respect; or
(2) it has referred the contract in question to an independent actuary under COMP 12.4.13 R; or
(3) it considers that it may at some later date decide to treat the liability of the relevant person under a contract as reduced or disregarded under COMP 12.4.14 R;

save where the FSCS decides to exclude certain benefits to the extent that they arise out of the exercise of any option under the policy and for this purpose the option includes, but is not restricted to, a right to surrender the policy.

[1] Comp 3.3.

Insurance undertakings in financial difficulties[1]

27.18 The FSCS may take such measures as it considers appropriate for the purpose of safeguarding the rights of eligible claimants under protected contracts of insurance which are:

(a) general insurance contracts with a relevant person which is an insurance undertaking in financial difficulties; or
(b) long-term insurance contracts with a relevant person which is an insurance undertaking in financial difficulties but in respect of which the FSCS is not securing continuity of insurance within COMP 3.3.1 R;

if at the time it proposes to take the measures, it considers that the cost of doing so is likely to be no more than the cost of paying compensation under COMP 3.2.

Such measures may be taken on such terms (including terms reducing or deferring payment of any liabilities or benefits provided under any protected contract of insurance) as the FSCS considers appropriate.

[1] Comp 3.3.4.

27.19 The measures referred to in the previous paragraph include measures to:

(1) secure or facilitate the transfer of the insurance business of the relevant person, or any part of the business, to another firm;
(2) give assistance to the relevant person to enable it to continue to effect contracts of insurance or carry out contracts of insurance; and
(3) secure the issue of policies by another firm to eligible claimants in substitution for their existing policies.

27.20 If it thinks appropriate, the FSA may in relation to any insurance undertaking which is in financial difficulties[1]:

(1) give the FSCS assistance in determining what measures under COMP 3.3.3 R are practicable or desirable;
(2) impose constraints on the measures which may be taken by the FSCS under COMP 3.3.3 R;
(3) require the FSCS to provide it with information about any measures which it is proposing to take under COMP 3.3.3 R[2].

[1] A relevant person who is an insurance undertaking is in financial difficulties if: (1) a liquidator, administrator, provisional liquidator, administrative receiver or interim manager is appointed to the relevant person, or a receiver is appointed by the court to manage the relevant person's affairs; or (2) there is a finding by a court of competent jurisdiction that the relevant person is unable to pay its debts; or (3) a resolution is passed for winding up of the relevant person, unless a declaration of solvency has been made in accordance with section 89 of the Insolvency Act 1986; or (4) the FSA determines that the relevant person who is an insurance undertaking is likely to be unable to satisfy protected claims against it; or (5) approval is given to any company voluntary arrangement made by the relevant person; or (6) the relevant person makes a composition or arrangement with any one or more of its creditors providing for the reduction of, or deferral of payment of, the liabilities or benefits provided for under any of the relevant person's policies; or (7) the relevant person is dissolved or struck off from the Register of Companies; or (8) a receiver is appointed over particular property of the relevant person; or (9) any of (1) to (8) or anything equivalent occurs in respect of the relevant person in a jurisdiction outside England and Wales; or (10) in the case of an insurance undertaking which is a member, the FSCS is satisfied that any of sub-paragraphs (1) to (9) apply to the member, and the amounts which the Society is able to provide from the Central Fund are or are likely to be insufficient to ensure that claims against the member under a protected contract of insurance will be met to the level or protection which would otherwise be available under this sourcebook. COMP 3.3.6.
[2] COMP 3.3.4A.

Eligibility[1]

27.21 An eligible claimant is any person who at any material time is not excluded by virtue of the following table[2], subject to the exceptions in COMP 4.2.3 which are listed below that table.

COMP 4.2.2: Persons not eligible to claim unless COMP 4.3 applies

(this version of the table has been edited to take out those categories which are of no relevance in an insurance context)

(1) Firms (other than a sole trader firm, a credit union, a trustee of a stakeholder pension scheme (which is not an occupational pension scheme) or a small business whose claim arises out of a regulated activity for which they do not have a permission).

(4) Pension and retirement funds, and anyone who is a trustee of such a fund. However, this exclusion does not apply to:

(a) a trustee of a personal pension scheme or a stakeholder pension scheme (which is not an occupational pension scheme); or

(b) a trustee of a small self-administered scheme or an occupational pension scheme of an employer which is not a large company, large partnership or large mutual association.

(12) Persons who, in the opinion of the FSCS, are responsible for, or have contributed to, the relevant person's default.

(13) Large companies or large mutual associations.

(14) Large partnerships.

(15) Persons whose claim arises from transactions in connection with which they have been convicted of an offence of money laundering.

(16) Persons whose claim arises under the Third Parties (Rights against Insurers) Act 1930.

(17) Where the claim is in relation to a protected contract of insurance or protected non-investment insurance mediation, body corporate, partnerships, mutual associations and unincorporated associations which are not small businesses.

[1] Comp 4.2.1.
[2] Comp 4.2.2.

27.21A A person who is a small business is an eligible claimant in respect of a relevant general insurance contract entered into before commencement only if the person is a partnership[1].

[1] Comp 4.2.3.

Long term insurance as an exception

27.22 A person other than one which comes within any of categories (7)–(12) and (15) of COMP 4.2.2R is eligible to claim compensation in respect of a long term insurance contract[1]:

(1) A person falling within categories (1)–(4) of COMP 4.2.2 R is eligible to claim compensation in respect of a relevant general insurance contract if, at the date the contract commenced he was a small business.
(2) Where the contract has been renewed, the last renewal date shall be taken as the commencement date[2].

A 'partnership which falls' within category 14, or category 17, or both[1] of COMP 4.2.2R is eligible to claim compensation in respect of a relevant general insurance contract entered into before commencement[3].

A person who comes within category (16) of COMP 4.2.2R (a 'category 16 person') is eligible to claim compensation if:

(1) the person insured would have been an eligible claimant at the time that his rights against the insurer were transferred to and vested in the category 16 person; or
(2) the liability of the person insured in respect of the category 16 person was a liability under a contract of employer's liability insurance which would have been a liability subject to compulsory insurance had the contract been entered into after 1 January 1972 or (for contracts in Northern Ireland) 29 December 1975; or
(3) the extent of the liability of the person insured in respect of the category 16 person had been agreed in writing by the insurer, or determined by a court or arbitrator, before the date on which the insurer is determined to be in default[4].

A person who comes within COMP 4.2.2R is eligible to claim compensation in respect of a liability subject to compulsory insurance if the claim is:

(1) a claim under a protected contract of insurance; or
(2) a claim in connection with protected non-investment insurance mediation[5].

[1] COMP 4.3.2.
[2] COMP 4.3.3.
[3] COMP 4.3.4.
[4] COMP 4.3.5.
[5] COMP 4.3.6.

Protected contracts of insurance

27.23 A protected contract of insurance is:

(1) (if issued after commencement) a contract of insurance within COMP 5.4.2 R (Contracts of insurance issued after commencement);
(2) (if issued before commencement) a contract of insurance within COMP 5.4.5 R (Contracts of insurance issued before commencement)[1].

[1] COMP 5.4.1.

Contracts of insurance issued after commencement[1]

27.24 A contract of insurance issued after commencement which:

(1) relates to a protected risk or commitment as described in COMP 5.4.3 R, ie:
  (a) in the case of a contract of insurance falling within COMP 5.4.2 R(2)(a), it is situated in an EEA State, the Channel Islands or the Isle of Man;
  (b) in the case of a contract of insurance falling within COMP 5.4.2 R(2)(b), it is situated in the United Kingdom;
  (c) in the case of a contract of insurance falling within COMP 5.4.2 R(2)(c), it is situated in the United Kingdom, the Channel Islands or the Isle of Man.
(2) is issued by the relevant person through an establishment in;
  (a) the United Kingdom; or
  (b) another EEA State; or
  (c) the Channel Islands or the Isle of Man;
(3) is a long-term insurance contract or a relevant general insurance contract;
(4) is not a reinsurance contract; and
(5) if it is a contract of insurance entered into by a member, was entered into on or after 1 January 2004 is a protected contract of insurance.

[1] COMP 5.4.2.

Contracts not evidenced by a policy

27.25 If it appears to the FSCS that a person is insured under a contract with an insurance undertaking which is not evidenced by a policy, and it is satisfied that if a policy evidencing the contract had been issued, the person in question would have had a protected contract of insurance, the FSCS must treat the contract as a protected contract of insurance[1].

[1] COMP 5.4.6.

Liabilities giving rise to claims under a protected contract of insurance

27.26 The FSCS must treat liabilities of an insurance undertaking which is in default, in respect of the following items, as giving rise to claims under a protected contract of insurance[1]:

(1) (if the contract is not a reinsurance contract and has not commenced) premiums paid to the insurance undertaking; or
(2) proceeds of a long-term insurance contract that is not a reinsurance contract and that has matured or been surrendered which have not yet been passed to the claimant; or
(3) the unexpired portion of any premium in relation to relevant general insurance contracts which are not reinsurance contracts; or
(4) claims by persons entitled to the benefit of a judgment under s 151 of the Road Traffic Act 1988 or Article 98 of the Road Traffic (Northern Ireland) Order 1981.

[1] COMP 5.4.7.

Who is a relevant person?

27.27 A relevant person is a person who was, at the time the act or omission giving rise to the claim against it took place:

(1) a participant firm; or
(2) an appointed representative of a participant firm[1].

[1] COMP 6.2.1.

When is a relevant person in default?

27.28 A relevant person is in default if: (the FSCS has determined it to be in default under COMP 6.3.2 R, COMP 6.3.3 R, COMP 6.3.4 R or COMP 6.3.5 R; or a judicial authority has made a ruling that had the effect of suspending the ability of eligible claimants to bring claims against the participant firm, if that is earlier than the FSCS's determination of default[1]. The FSCS (or, where COMP 6.3.1 R(2)(a) applies, the FSA) may determine a relevant person to be in default when it is, in the opinion of the FSCS or the FSA:

(1) unable to satisfy protected claims against it; or
(2) likely to be unable to satisfy protected claims against it[2].

[1] COMP 6.3.1.
[2] COMP 6.3.227.29.

27.29 Subject to COMP 6.3.6 R the FSCS may determine a relevant person to be in default if it is satisfied that a protected claim exists (other than an ICD claim or DGD claim), and the relevant person is the subject of one or more of the following proceedings in the United Kingdom (or of equivalent or similar proceedings in another jurisdiction):

(1) the passing of a resolution for a creditors' voluntary winding up;
(2) a determination by the relevant person's Home State regulator that the relevant person appears unable to meet claims against it and has no early prospect of being able to do so;
(3) the appointment of a liquidator or administrator, or provisional liquidator or interim manager;
(4) the making of an order by a court of competent jurisdiction for the winding up of a company, the dissolution of a partnership, the administration of a company or partnership, or the bankruptcy of an individual;
(5) the approval of a company voluntary arrangement, a partnership voluntary arrangement, or of an individual voluntary arrangement[1].

[1] COMP 6.3.3.

27.30 For claims arising in connection with protected investment business or protected non-investment insurance mediation, the FSCS has the additional power to determine that a relevant person is in default if it is satisfied that a protected claim exists, and[1]:

(1) the FSCS is satisfied that the relevant person cannot be contacted at its last place of business and that reasonable steps have been taken to establish a forwarding or current address, but without success; and
(2) there appears to the FSCS to be no evidence that the relevant person will be able to meet claims made against it.

[1] COMP 6.3.4.

Assignment of Rights under COMP 7

27.31 The FSCS may make any payment of compensation to a claimant in respect of a protected claim conditional on the claimant assigning the whole or any part of his rights against the relevant person, or against any third party, or both, to the FSCS on such terms as the FSCS thinks fit[1]. If a claimant assigns the whole or any part of his rights against any person to the FSCS as a condition of payment, the effect of this is that any sum payable in relation to the rights so assigned will be payable to the FSCS and not the claimant[2]. If the FSCS takes assignment of rights from the claimant under COMP 7.2.1 R, it must pursue all and only such recoveries as it considers are likely to be both reasonably possible and cost effective to pursue. If the FSCS makes recoveries through rights assigned under COMP 7.2.1 R, it may deduct from any recoveries paid over to the claimant under COMP 7.2.4 R part or all of its reasonable costs of recovery (if any)[3].

[1] COMP 7.2.1.
[2] COMP 7.2.2.
[3] COMP 7.2.3.

27.32 Unless compensation was paid under COMP 9.2.3R, if a claimant agrees to assign his rights to the FSCS and the FSCS subsequently makes recoveries through those rights, those recoveries must be paid to the claimant: to the extent that the amount recovered exceeds the amount of compensation (excluding interest paid under COMP 11.2.7R) received by the claimant in relation to the protected claim; or in circumstances where the amount recovered does not exceed the amount of compensation paid, to the extent that a failure to pay any sums recovered to the claimant would leave a claimant who had promptly accepted an offer of compensation at a disadvantage relative to a claimant who had delayed accepting an offer of compensation[1].

[1] COMP 7.2.4.

Rejection of application for compensation

27.33 If an application for compensation contains any material inaccuracy or omission, the FSCS may reject the application unless this is considered by the FSCS to be wholly unintentional[1], but a rejection under COMP 8.2.1 R does not mean that the claimant cannot receive compensation. A rejected application may be resubmitted, with the appropriate amendments[2]. Rejection under the provision is in any event purely discretionary where the error is not wholly unintentional. The rule appears to mean that a wholly unintentional error cannot lead to rejection, though it does not explain what the FSCS should then do. Presumably the proper course would be to allow the applicant the opportunity to amend the error and then to proceed to consider the application as amended.

[1] COMP 8.2.1.
[2] COMP 8.2.2.

27.34 The FSCS must reject an application for compensation if:

(1) the FSCS considers that a civil claim in respect of the liability would have been defeated by a defence of limitation at the earlier of:
   (a) the date on which the relevant person is determined to be in default; and
   (b) the date on which the claimant first indicates in writing that he may have a claim against the relevant person;

except that for claims made in connection with protected investment business or protected non-investment insurance mediation, the FSCS may disregard a defence of limitation where the FSCS considers that it would be reasonable to do so[1], or:

(2) the liability of the relevant person to the claimant has been extinguished by the operation of law, unless COMP 8.2.5 R applies[2].

An application rejected under COMP 8.2.3 R may be resubmitted if COMP 8.2.5 R applies[3].

[1] COMP 8.2.4.
[2] COMP 8.2.3. COMP 8.2.5 provides For claims made in connection with protected investment business or protected non-investment insurance mediation, if a relevant person, incorporated as a company, has been dissolved with the result that its liability to the claimant has been extinguished by operation of law, the FSCS must treat the claim, for the purposes of paying compensation, as if the relevant person had not been dissolved.
[3] COMP 8.2.2.

Withdrawal of offer of compensation

27.35 The following rules are found in COMP 8.3.1–5.

The FSCS may withdraw any offer of compensation made to a claimant if the offer is not accepted or if it is not disputed within 90 days of the date on which the offer is made.

Where the amount of compensation offered is disputed, the FSCS may withdraw the offer but must consider exercising its powers to make a reduced or interim payment under COMP 11.2.4 R or COMP 11.2.5 R before doing so.

The FSCS may repeat any offer withdrawn under COMP 8.3.1 R or COMP 8.3.2 R.

The FSCS must withdraw any offer of compensation if it appears to the FSCS that no such offer should have been made.

The FSCS must seek to recover any compensation paid to a claimant if it appears to the FSCS that no such payment should have been made, unless the FSCS believes on reasonable grounds that it would be unreasonable to do so, or that the costs of doing so would exceed any amount that could be recovered.

When must compensation be paid?

27.36 The FSCS must pay a claim as soon as reasonably possible after it is satisfied that the conditions of eligibility have been met and it has calculated the amount of compensation due to the claimant; and in any event within three months of that date, unless the FSA has granted the FSCS an extension, in which case payment must be made no later than six months from that date. However, the FSCS may postpone paying compensation if:

(1) in the case of a claim against a relevant person who is an appointed representative, the FSCS considers that the claimant should make and pursue an application for compensation against the appointed representative's relevant principal; or
(2) in the case of a claim relating to protected investment business which is not an ICD claim or a claim relating to protected mortgage business, the FSCS

considers that the claimant should first exhaust his rights against the relevant person or any third party, or make and pursue an application for compensation to any other person; or[1]

(3) in the case of a claim relating to a protected contracts of insurance, the FSCS considers that the liability to which the claim relates or any part of the liability is covered by another contract of insurance with a solvent insurance undertaking, or where it appears that a person, other than the liquidator, may make payments or take such action to secure the continuity of cover as the FSCS would undertake; or

(4) the claim is one which falls within COMP 12.4.5 R or COMP 12.4.7 R and it is not practicable for payment to be made within the usual time limits laid out in COMP 9.2.1 R[2]; or

(5) the claimant has been charged with an offence arising out of or in relation to money laundering, and those proceedings have not yet been concluded; or

(6) the claim relates solely to a bonus provided for under a protected contract of insurance the value of which the FSCS considers to be of such uncertainty that immediate payment of compensation in respect of that bonus would not be prudent and a court has yet to attribute a value to such bonus.

1 COMP 9.2.1.
2 COMP 9.2.2.

Limits on compensation payable

27.37 COMP 10.2 sets out the limits on compensation payable. The limits apply to the aggregate amount of claims in respect of each category of protected claim that an eligible claimant has against the relevant person. The limits so far as they relate to insurance contracts are as follows:

Type of claim	Level of cover	Maximum payment
Protected contract of insurance when the contract is a relevant general insurance contract	(1) Where the claim is in respect of a liability subject to compulsory insurance: 100% of claim.	Unlimited
	(2) Where the claim arises under the Third Party (Rights against Insurers) Act 1930, is in respect of a liability within COMP 5.4.5R(1)(b), and is in connection with an Article 9 default: 90% of the claim.	Unlimited
	(3) In all other cases: 100% × first £2,000 90% of remainder of the claim.	Unlimited
Protected contract of insurance when the contract is a long-term insurance contract	100% × first £2,000 At least 90% of the remaining value of the policy as determined in accordance with COMP12.	Unlimited

Protected non-investment insurance mediation	(1) where the claim is in respect of a liability subject to compulsory insurance: 100% of claim.	Unlimited[2]

[1] COMP 10.2.2.

27.38 Claims against more than one member in respect of a single protected contract of insurance to be treated as a single claim In applying the financial limits in COMP 10.2, and in calculating the amount of a claim in respect of a protected contract of insurance arising from the default of one or more members, a policyholder is to be treated as having a single claim for the aggregate of all such amounts as may be payable on the claim in respect of the protected contract of insurance.

[1] COMP 10.2.8.

Reduced or interim payments

27.39 If the FSCS is satisfied that in principle compensation is payable in connection with any protected claim, but considers that immediate payment in full would not be prudent because of uncertainty as to the amount of the claimant's overall net claim, it may decide to pay an appropriate lesser sum in final settlement, or to make payment on account. Similarly, the FSCS may also decide to make a payment on account or to pay a lesser sum in final settlement if the claimant has any reasonable prospect for recovery in respect of the claim from any third party or by applying for compensation to any other person.

[1] COMP 11.2.4.
[2] COMP 11.2.5.

Paying interest on compensation

27.40 The FSCS may pay interest on the compensation sum in such circumstances as it considers appropriate[1].

[1] Comp 11.2.5.

Quantification

27.40 The following is a summary of the effect of Rule 12.2.

The amount of compensation payable to the claimant in respect of any type of protected claim is the amount of his overall net claim against the relevant person at the quantification date. However, this is subject to the other provisions of COMP, in particular those rules that set limits on the amount of compensation payable for various types of protected claim. The limits are set out in COMP 10.

A claimant's overall net claim is the sum of the protected claims of the same category that he has against a relevant person in default, less the amount of any liability which the relevant person may set off against any of those claims.

In calculating the claimant's overall net claim, the FSCS may rely, to the extent that it is relevant, on any determination by:

(1) a court of competent jurisdiction;
(2) a trustee in bankruptcy;
(3) a liquidator;
(4) any other recognised insolvency practitioner;

and on the certification of any net sum due which is made in default proceedings of any exchange or clearing house.

In calculating the claimant's overall net claim, the FSCS must take into account any payments to the claimant (including amounts recovered by the FSCS on behalf of the claimant) made by the relevant person or the FSCS or any other person, if that payment is connected with the relevant person's liability to the claimant.

The FSCS must calculate the amount of compensation due to the claimant as soon as reasonably possible after it is satisfied that the conditions in COMP 3.2.1 R have been met.

In calculating the claimant's overall net claim the FSCS must take into account the amounts paid by, or expected to be paid by, the Society from the Central Fund to meet a member's liabilities under the contract which gives rise to the claim.

Quantification date

27.41 For a claim under a protected contract of insurance that is a long-term insurance contract, the FSCS must determine as the quantification date a specific date by reference to which the liability of the relevant person to the eligible claimant is to be determined[1]. For a claim under a protected contract of insurance that is a relevant general insurance contract, the FSCS must determine as the quantification date a specific date by reference to which the liability of the relevant person to the eligible claimant is to be determined[2]. For a claim in respect of the unexpired premiums under a protected contract of insurance that is a relevant general insurance contract (see COMP 5.4.7 R (3)), the quantification date, being the date by which the liability of the relevant person to the eligible claimant is to be determined, is the date the policy was terminated or cancelled[3]. For a claim made in connection with protected non-investment insurance mediation, the FSCS must determine a specific date as the quantification date, and this date may be either on, before or after the date of determination of default[4].

[1] COMP 12.3.2.
[2] COMP 12.3.3.
[3] COMP 12.3.4.
[4] COMP 12.3.8.

The compensation calculation

27.42 COMP 12.4 contains the following rules as to the calculation of compensation.

If the claimant has a DGD claim against an incoming EEA firm which is a credit institution, the FSCS must take account of the liability of the Home State deposit-guarantee scheme in calculating the compensation payable by the FSCS. The FSCS must pay a sum equal to 100% of any liability of a relevant person who is an insurance undertaking in respect of a liability subject to compulsory insurance to the claimant as soon as reasonably practicable after it has determined the relevant person to be in default. The FSCS must calculate the liability of a relevant person to the claimant under a relevant general insurance contract in accordance with the terms of the contract, and (subject to any limits in COMP 10.2.3R) pay that amount to the claimant. Unless the FSCS is making arrangements to secure continuity of insurance cover under COMP 3.3.1R to COMP 3.3.2ER, the FSCS must calculate the liability of a relevant person to the claimant under a long-term insurance contract in accordance with the terms of the contract as valued in a liquidation of the relevant person, or (in the absence of such relevant terms) in accordance with such reasonable valuation techniques as the FSCS considers appropriate:

(1) Unless the FSCS is seeking to secure continuity of cover for a relevant person under COMP 3.3.1 R to COMP 3.3.2E R, it must:
   (a) pay compensation in accordance with COMP 12.4.11 R for any benefit provided for under a protected long-term insurance contract which has fallen due or would have fallen due under the contract to be paid to any eligible claimant and has not already been paid; and
   (b) do as soon as reasonably practicable after the time when the benefit in question fell due or would have fallen due under the contract (but subject to and in accordance with any other terms which apply or would have applied under the contract).
(2) If the FSCS decides to treat the liability of the relevant person under the contract as reduced or (as the case may be) disregarded under COMP 12.4.14 R then, for the purposes of (1), the value of benefits falling due after the date of that decision must be treated as reduced or disregarded to that extent.
(3) Unless it has decided to treat the liability of the relevant person under the contract as reduced or disregarded under COMP 12.4.14 R the FSCS must not treat as a reason for failing to pay, or for delaying the payment of compensation in accordance with (1), the fact that:
   (a) it considers that any benefit referred to in (1) is or may be excessive in any respect; or
   (b) it has referred the contract in question to an independent actuary under COMP 12.4.13 R; or
   (c) it considers that it may at some later date decide to treat the liability of the relevant person under a contract as reduced or (as the case may be) disregarded under COMP 12.4.14 R;

save where the FSCS decides to exclude certain benefits to the extent that they arise out of the exercise of any option under the policy (for this purpose option includes, but is not restricted to, a right to surrender the policy).

The FSCS must not treat any bonus provided for under a long-term insurance contract as part of the claimant's claim except to the extent that:

(1) a value has been attributed to it by a court in accordance with the Insurers (Winding Up) Rules 2001 or any equivalent rules or legislative provision in force from time to time; or
(2) the FSCS considers that a court would be likely to attribute a value to the bonus if it were to apply the method set out in those rules.

If the FSCS is:

(a) seeking to secure continuity of cover under COMP 3.3.1 R to COMP 3.3.2E R or to calculate the liability owed to an eligible claimant under COMP 12.4.11 R; and
(b) considers that the benefits provided for under a protected long-term insurance contract are or may be excessive in any respect,

it must refer the contract to an actuary who is independent of the eligible claimant and of the relevant person.

In this rule and in COMP 12.4.14 R, a benefit is only 'excessive' if, at the time when the relevant person decided to confer or to offer to confer that benefit, no reasonable and prudent insurer in the position of the relevant person would have so decided given the premiums payable and other contractual terms.

If the FSCS is satisfied, following the actuary's written recommendation, that any of the benefits provided for under the contract are or may be excessive, it may treat the liability of the relevant person under the contract as reduced or (as the case may be) disregarded for the purpose of any payment made after the date of that decision.

The FSCS may rely on the value attributed to the contract by the actuary when calculating the compensation payable to the claimant, or when securing continuity of cover.

Protected non-investment insurance mediation

27.43 This is subject to the special restriction that the FSCS may pay compensation for any claim made in connection with protected non-investment insurance mediation only to the extent that the FSCS considers that the payment of compensation is essential in order to provide the claimant with fair compensation[1]. It is by no means obvious to what extent this will really restrict the FSCS, since in any event it would not normally expect to pay more than was necessary to secure fair compensation.

[1] COMP 12.4.20.

Reduction of compensation

27.44 The FSCS may decide to reduce the compensation that would otherwise be payable for a claim made in connection with protected non-investment insurance mediation if it is satisfied that there is evidence of contributory negligence by the claimant; or payment of the full amount would provide a greater benefit than the claimant might reasonably have expected or than the benefit available on similar contracts with other relevant persons and it would be inequitable for FSCS not to take account of these matters[1]. Again this seems to leave FSCS with a very broad discretion. Certainly there is no general rule that contributory negligence leads to a reduction in compensation. The rule is worded in a negative way – there is a reduction only if it inequitable not to make one.

[1] COMP 12.4.21.

Quantification: trustees, personal representatives, agents, and joint claims

Trustees

27.45 COMP 12.6 has special provisions covering the quantification of claims by trustees, personal representatives, agents, and joint claims. If a claimant's claim includes a claim as trustee, the FSCS must treat him in respect of that claim as if his claim as trustee were a claim of a different person. If a claimant has a claim as a bare trustee or nominee company[1] for one or more beneficiaries, the FSCS must treat the beneficiary or beneficiaries as having the claim, and not the claimant[2].

[1] COMP 12.6.1.
[2] COMP 12.6.2.

Group Claims

27.46 If any group of persons has a claim as trustees, the FSCS must treat them as a single and continuing person distinct from the persons who may from time to time be the trustees[1]. Where the same person has a claim as trustee for different trusts, COMP applies as if the claims relating to each of these trusts were claims of different persons[2]. Where the claimant is a trustee, and some of the beneficiaries of the trust are persons who would not be eligible claimants if they had a claim themselves, the FSCS must adjust the amount of the overall net claim to eliminate the part of the claim which, in the FSCS's view, is a claim for those beneficiaries[3].

[1] COMP 12.6.3.
[2] COMP 12.6.4.
[3] COMP 12.6.5.

Quantum

27.47 Where compensation is paid to a trustee the FSCS must try to ensure that it is for the benefit of beneficiaries who would be eligible claimants if they had a claim themselves; and does not exceed the amount of the loss suffered by those beneficiaries[1].

[1] COMP 12.6.6.

Personal representative

27.48 Where a person numbers among his claims a claim as the personal representative of another, the FSCS must treat him in respect of that claim as if he were standing in the shoes of that other person[1].

1 COMP 12.6.8.

Chapter 28

The Motor Insurers' Bureau

Introduction

28.1 The Motor Insurers' Bureau ('MIB') exists to provide indemnity for those who suffer in Great Britain[1] loss of a kind which is required to be covered by a policy of motor insurance under the RTA 1988[2], but where no such policy is in fact in force at the time of the loss. This may happen because it is not possible to locate the driver responsible, or because that driver has no insurance[3].

1 Not the UK – the Agreements do not apply to Northern Ireland.
2 For the scope of the compulsory insurance requirement, see Chapter 37.
3 Much useful information is available on the MIB website: www.mib.org.uk

The status of the Motor Insurers' Bureau

28.2 The arrangements under which the MIB operates are a remarkable example of the English gift for pragmatism. The two Agreements discussed in this Chapter are made between the Secretary of State for Transport and the MIB, which is a company registered in England. The MIB is owned and controlled by the motor insurers of the UK collectively. A theoretical consequence of this is that no one who suffers injury, loss or damage in a road accident should be able to enforce the Agreements, to which they will of course not be party. Thus, it would appear to be a matter of discretion for the MIB whether to pay any given claim. The pragmatic response of the courts to this situation has been to ignore the absence of privity of contract and allow such claimants to enforce the terms of the Agreements. The MIB has of course never attempted to take the privity point: indeed, to do so would entirely defeat the purpose of the scheme[1]. This position will apparently not be affected by the Contracts (Rights of Third Parties) Act 1999 ('C(RTP)A 1999'), since that Act cannot apply to agreements made before it came into force[2].

1 And would presumably lead very rapidly to the putting of the scheme on a statutory footing. For a discussion of the courts' attitude see *Albert v Motor Insurers' Bureau* [1972] AC 301.
2 Section 10.

The Agreements

28.3 There are two Agreements, one relating to uninsured drivers, the other to untraced drivers[1]. Both Agreements have undergone revisions, with the result that different provisions may apply according to the date of the accident. At present this point is significant only in relation to the Uninsured Drivers Agreement, which was revised in 1999, the new version applying to accidents after 30 September 1999.

1 Both Agreements are reproduced in Appendix 3.

Meaning of 'road'

28.4 Because the requirement for insurance applies only to the driving of a vehicle on a road, there is substantial case law on what amounts to a 'road' for these purposes. In *McGurk & Dale v Coster*[1] the second claimant was driving the first claimant's car on Southport beach when a motor car driven by X collided with it. Judgment was obtained against X and was not satisfied. However, the MIB refused to satisfy the judgment on the basis that the part of the beach in question was not a road. This defence was upheld. Although a substantial part of the public had access to that part of the beach, there was no definable way between two points. The part of the beach in question was used as a car park, but no parking spaces were marked on the sand and on one side the area was bounded only by the sea (with the result that its limits would change with the tides). It was irrelevant that the area in question was not covered with tarmac, or whether a parking fee was charged or whether the area was formally dedicated to the public.

In *Cutter v Eagle Star Insurance Co Ltd*[3] the court had to decide whether an injury sustained in a multi storey car park was sustained on a 'road' within the definition in the act. It was held that the question was whether there was a roadway in the car park and it was found that there was.

In *Clarke v Kato*[4] it was held that a route from a car park to a parade of shops which was used on a regular basis solely by pedestrians constituted a road – all that was needed was that such a route was definable.

1 [1995] CLY 2912, Bernstein J.
2 [1997] 1 WLR 1082.
3 [1997] 1 WLR 208.

The Uninsured Drivers Agreement

28.5 This section deals firstly with the current version of the Agreement, which applies to accidents on or after 1 October 1999. This is followed by a brief summary of the rules applying to accidents happening before that date.

MIB's obligation to satisfy compensation claims

28.6 Subject to the exceptions described below, if a claimant has obtained against any person in a Court in Great Britain a judgment which is an unsatisfied judgment, then the MIB will pay the relevant sum to, or to the satisfaction of, the claimant or will cause the same to be so paid. This applies whether or not the person liable to satisfy the judgment is in fact covered by a contract of insurance and whatever may be the cause of his failure to satisfy the judgment.

Exceptions

28.7 The basic obligation does not apply in the case of an application made in respect of a claim of any of the following descriptions (and, where part only of a claim satisfies such a description, the basic obligation does not apply to that part):

'(1)

(a) a claim arising out of a relevant liability incurred by the user of a vehicle owned by or in the possession of the Crown, unless:
 (i) responsibility for the existence of a contract of insurance under Part VI of the RTA 1988 in relation to that vehicle had been undertaken by some other person (whether or not the person liable was in fact covered by a contract of insurance), or
 (ii) the relevant liability was in fact covered by a contract of insurance;

(b) a claim arising out of the use of a vehicle which is not required to be covered by a contract ofinsurance by virtue of s 144 of the RTA 1988, unless the use is in fact covered by such a contract;

(c) a claim by, or for the benefit of, a person ('the beneficiary') other than the person suffering death, injury or other damage which is made either:
 (i) in respect of a cause of action or a judgment which has been assigned to the beneficiary, or
 (ii) pursuant to a right of subrogation or contractual or other right belonging to the beneficiary;

(d) a claim in respect of damage to a motor vehicle or losses arising therefrom where, at the time when the damage to it was sustained:
 (i) there was not in force in relation to the use of that vehicle such a contract of insurance as is required by Part VI of the RTA 1988, and
 (ii) the claimant either knew or ought to have known that that was the case;

(e) a claim which is made in respect of a liability incurred by the owner or registered keeper or a person using the vehicle in which the claimant was being carried, by a claimant who, at the time of the use giving rise to the relevant liability was voluntarily allowing himself to be carried in the vehicle and, either before the commencement of his journey in the vehicle or after such commencement if he could reasonably be expected to have alighted from it, knew or ought to have known[1] that:
 (i) the vehicle had been stolen or unlawfully taken,
 (ii) the vehicle was being used without there being in force in relation to its use such a contract of insurance as would comply with Part VI of the RTA 1988,
 (iii) the vehicle was being used in the course or furtherance of a crime, or
 (iv) the vehicle was being used as a means of escape from, or avoidance of, lawful apprehension.'

[1] A person does not 'know' of these matters within the meaning of the Agreement merely ecause he is negligent or even reckless as to the possibility: *White v White* [2001] UKHL 9, [2001] 2 All ER 43, HL.

28.8 The burden of proving that the claimant knew or ought to have known of any matter set out in paragraph (1)(e) is on the MIB but, in the absence of evidence to the contrary, the MIB proves the claimant's knowledge by showing any of the following things:

(a) that the claimant was the owner or registered keeper of the vehicle or had caused or permitted its use;
(b) that the claimant knew the vehicle was being used by a person who was below the minimum age at which he could be granted a licence authorising the driving of a vehicle of that class;
(c) that the claimant knew that the person driving the vehicle was disqualified for holding or obtaining a driving licence;
(d) that the claimant knew that the user of the vehicle was neither its owner nor registered keeper nor an employee of the owner or registered keeper nor the owner or registered keeper of any other vehicle.

Knowledge which the claimant has or ought to have for the purposes of paragraph (1)(e) includes knowledge of matters which he could reasonably be expected to have been aware of had he not been under the self-induced influence of drink or drugs.

For the purposes of Clause 1:

(a) a vehicle which has been unlawfully removed from the possession of the Crown shall be taken to continue in that possession whilst it is kept so removed;
(b) references to a person being carried in a vehicle include references to his being carried upon, entering, getting on to and alighting from the vehicle; and
(c) 'owner', in relation to a vehicle which is the subject of a hiring agreement or a hire-purchase agreement, means the person in possession of the vehicle under that agreement.

Applying to the MIB

28.9 The MIB shall incur no liability under its obligation unless an application is made to the person and in such form and with such information as the MIB may reasonably require.

The MIB shall incur no liability under its obligation unless proper notice of the bringing of the relevant proceedings has been given by the claimant not later than 14 days after the commencement of those proceedings:

'(1)
(a) in the case of proceedings in respect of a relevant liability which is covered by a contract of insurance with an insurer whose identity can be ascertained, to that insurer;
(b) in any other case, to the MIB (the "proper person").
(2) in this clause "proper notice" means, except in so far as any part of such information or any copy document or other thing has already been supplied:
(a) notice in writing that proceedings have been commenced by Claim Form, Writ, or other means,

(b) a copy of the sealed Claim Form, Writ or other official document providing evidence of the commencement of the proceedings and, in Scotland, a statement of the means of service,

(c) a copy or details of any insurance policy providing benefits in the case of the death, bodily injury or damage to property to which the proceedings relate where the claimant is the insured party and the benefits are available to him,

(d) copies of all correspondence in the possession of the claimant or (as the case may be) his Solicitor or agent to or from the defendant or the defender or (as the case may be) his Solicitor, insurers or agent which is relevant to:

  (i) the death, bodily injury or damage for which the defendant or defender is alleged to be responsible, or

  (ii) any contract of insurance which covers, or which may or has been alleged to cover, liability for such death, injury or damage the benefit of which is, or is claimed to be, available to defendant or defender,

(e) subject to paragraph (3), a copy of the Particulars of Claim whether or not indorsed on the Claim Form, Writ or other originating process, and whether or not served (in England and Wales) on any defendant or (in Scotland) on any defender, and

(f) a copy of all other documents which are required under the appropriate rules of procedure to be served on a defendant or defender with the Claim Form, Writ or other originating process or with the Particulars of Claim,

(g) such other information about the relevant proceedings as the MIB may reasonably specify.

(3) If, in the case of proceedings commenced in England or Wales, the Particulars of Claim (including any document required to be served therewith) has not yet been served with the Claim Form or other originating process paragraph (2)(e) shall be sufficiently complied with if a copy thereof is served on the MIB not later than seven days after it is served on the defendant.'

Notice of service of proceedings

28.10 Where the relevant proceedings are commenced in England or Wales the MIB shall incur no liability under its obligation unless the claimant has, not later than the appropriate date, given notice in writing to the proper person of the date of service of the Claim Form or other originating process in the relevant proceedings. 'The appropriate date' means the day falling:

'(a) seven days after the date when the claimant receives notification from the Court that service of the Claim Form or other originating process has occurred, the date when the claimant receives notification from the defendant that service of the Claim Form or other originating process has occurred, or the date of personal service, or

(b) 14 days after the date when service is deemed to have occurred in accordance with the CPR 1998, whichever of those days occurs first.'

Further information

28.11 The MIB shall incur no liability under MIB's obligation unless the claimant has, not later than seven days after the occurrence of any of the following events, namely:

(a) the filing of a defence in the relevant proceedings,

(b) any amendment to the Particulars of Claim or any amendment of or addition to any schedule or other document required to be served therewith, and
(c) either:
 (i) the setting down of the case for trial, or
 (ii) where the court gives notice to the claimant of the trial date, the date when that notice is received,

given notice in writing of the date of that event to the proper person and has, in the case of the filing of a defence or an amendment of the Particulars of Claim or any amendment of or addition to any schedule or other document required to be served therewith, supplied a copy thereof to that person.

The MIB shall incur no liability under its obligation unless the claimant furnishes to the proper within a reasonable time after being required to do so such further information and documents in support of his claim as the MIB may reasonably require.

Notice of intention to apply for judgment

28.12 The MIB shall incur no liability under its obligation unless the claimant has, after commencement of the relevant proceedings and not less than 35 days before the appropriate date, given notice in writing to the proper person of his intention to apply for or to sign judgment in the relevant proceedings. In this clause, 'the appropriate date' means the date when the application for judgment is made or, as the case may be, the signing of judgment occurs.

Section 154 of the Road Traffic Act 1988

28.13 The MIB shall incur no liability under its obligation unless the claimant has as soon as reasonably practicable demanded the information and, where appropriate, the particulars specified in s 154(1) of the RTA 1988, and if the person of whom the demand is made fails to comply with the provisions of that subsection made a formal complaint to a police officer in respect of such failure, and used all reasonable endeavours to obtain the name and address of the registered keeper of the vehicle or, if so required by the MIB, has authorised the MIB to take such steps on his behalf.

Prosecution of proceedings

28.14 The MIB shall incur no liability under its obligation unless the claimant has, if so required by the MIB and having been granted a full indemnity by the MIB as to costs, taken all reasonable steps to obtain judgment against every person who may be liable (including any person who may be vicariously liable) in respect of the injury or death or damage to property, or if the claimant, upon being requested to do so by the MIB, refuses to consent to the MIB being joined as a party to the relevant proceedings.

Assignment of judgment and undertakings

28.15 The MIB shall incur no liability under its obligation unless the claimant has assigned to the MIB or its nominee the unsatisfied judgment, whether or not that judgment includes an amount in respect of a liability other than a relevant liability, and any order for costs made in the relevant proceedings, and undertaken to repay to the MIB any sum paid to him by the MIB in discharge of its obligation if the judgment is subsequently set aside either as a whole or in respect of the part of the relevant liability to which that sum relates or by any other person by way of compensation or benefit for the death, bodily injury or other damage to which the relevant proceedings relate.

Compensation for damage to property

28.16 Where a claim under this Agreement includes a claim in respect of damage to property, the MIB's obligation in respect of that part of the relevant sum which is awarded for such damage and any losses arising therefrom (referred to in this clause as 'the property damage compensation') is limited as follows.

Where the property damage compensation does not exceed the specified excess, the MIB shall incur no liability.

Where the property damage compensation in respect of any one accident exceeds the specified excess but does not exceed £250,000, the MIB shall incur liability only in respect of the property damage compensation less the specified excess.

Where the property damage compensation in respect of any one accident exceeds £250,000, the MIB shall incur liability only in respect of the sum of £250,000 less the specified excess.

Compensation received from other sources

28.17 Where a claimant has received compensation from the PPB under the PPA 1975, or an insurer under an insurance agreement or arrangement, or any other source, in respect of the death, bodily injury or other damage to which the relevant proceedings relate and such compensation has not been taken into account in the calculation of the relevant sum, the MIB may deduct from the relevant sum, in addition to any sum deductible under cl 16, an amount equal to that compensation.

Recoveries

28.18 Nothing in the Agreement prevents an insurer from providing by conditions in a contract of insurance that all sums paid by the insurer or by the MIB by virtue of the Principal Agreement or this Agreement in or towards the discharge of the liability of the insured shall be recoverable by them or by the MIB from the insured or from any other person.

Apportionment of damages, etc

28.19 Where an unsatisfied judgment which includes an amount in respect of a liability other than a relevant liability has been assigned to the MIB or its nominee, the MIB shall apportion any sum it receives in satisfaction or partial satisfaction of the judgment according to the proportion which the damages awarded in respect of the relevant liability bear to the damages awarded in respect of the other liability, and account to the claimant in respect of the moneys received properly apportionable to the other liability.

Where the sum received includes an amount in respect of interest or an amount awarded under an order for costs, the interest or the amount received in pursuance of the order shall be dealt with in the manner provided in the previous paragraph.

The 1988 Agreement

28.20 This provides that if judgment in respect of any relevant liability is obtained against any person or persons in any court in Great Britain, whether or not the person is covered by a contract of insurance and any such judgment is not satisfied in full within seven days from the date on which the person in whose favour the judgment was given became entitled to enforce it, the MIB becomes liable. The MIB will then pay or satisfy, or cause to be paid or satisfied, to or to the satisfaction of the person in whose favour the judgment was given any sum payable or remaining payable in respect of the liability, including sums awarded for interest and any taxed costs or costs awarded by the court without taxation (or such proportion as is attributable to the liability). This applies whatever may be the cause of the judgment debtor's failure to satisfy the judgment. An interim payment order is a judgment for the purposes of the agreement: *Sharp v Pereria*[1].

The doctrine of direct effect is inapplicable to enforce an EU Council Directive against the MIB: *Mighell v Reading; Evans v Motor Insurers' Bureau; White v White*[2].

The conditions precedent to the Bureau's acceptance of liability under this agreement are: notice in writing of the bringing of the proceedings must be given within seven days after the commencement of the proceedings. Proceedings commence from the issue of the summons for service, and there is no implied term that the date of commencement is to be postponed until the claimant knows of the issue by receipt of the summons from the court: *Silverton v Goodall*[3] The notice must be accompanied by a copy of the writ, summons or other document initiating the proceedings: ibid cl 5(1)(a). See *Cambridge v Motor Insurers' Bureau*[4] (supply of notice of issue of a default summons, rather than a copy of an officially stamped summons, held to be sufficient evidence of the instigation of proceedings).

1 [1998] 4 All ER 145, CA.
2 [1999] Lloyd's Rep IR 30, CA.
3 [1997] PIQR P451, CA.
4 [1998] RTR 365, CA.

28.21 Clause 6 of the Agreement specifies a number of cases where the MIB's liability is expressly excluded. The most important of these is that the MIB is under no liability where at the time of the use which gave rise to the liability the person suffering death or bodily injury or damage to property was allowing himself to be carried in or on the vehicle and, either before the commencement of his journey in it or after such commencement if he could reasonably be expected to have alighted from it, he knew or ought to have known that it had been stolen or unlawfully taken, or knew or ought to have known that it was being used without there being in force in relation to its use a contract of insurance: cl 6(1)(e). The consent to be carried is judged at the start of the journey and not at the time of the accident – an applicant cannot avoid this clause by saying that he initially gave consent to be carried, but withdrew it before the time of the accident[1]. This exception applies only where the judgment in respect of which the claim against the MIB is being made was obtained in respect of a relevant liability incurred by the owner or a person using the vehicle in which the person who suffered death or bodily injury or sustained damage to property was being carried: cl 6(2). References to a person being carried in a vehicle for the purpose of this exception include references to his being carried in or upon or getting on to or alighting from the vehicle: cl 6(3)(b). 'Owner', in relation to a vehicle which is the subject of a hiring agreement or a hire-purchase agreement, means the person in possession of the vehicle under that agreement: cl 6(3)(c). The words 'being a person using the vehicle' in the 1972 Agreement, cl 6(1)(c) refer to control and management or a joint venture[2], but also include situations in which a person allows himself to be carried in the vehicle in pursuance of a joint venture as in *Stinton v Motor Insurers' Bureau*[3], where the claimant allowed himself to be carried in the car driven by his drunken brother who was, as he knew, uninsured. A similar conclusion was reached in *O'Mahoney v Joliffe*[4], where the parties were a courting couple who went on a motorbike ride. On the other side of the line was *Hatton v Hall*[5], another case of a motor-bike ride, but where the Court of Appeal considered that there was insufficient evidence that the claimant was a controlling influence in the use of the vehicle so as to be a user. This exception is inserted on public policy grounds, and may be regarded as mirroring the position where such a person tries to bring an action against the driver of the car. These cases, although recent, are of no relevance under the new Agreement, because the MIB no longer needs to establish that the claimant was a user of the vehicle – it is now sufficient to show that the claimant was aware that the driver was uninsured.

1 *Pickett v Motor Insurer's Bureau* [2004] Lloyd's Rep IR 513, CA.
2 By analogy with the definition in the RTA 1988, s 143: see *Hatton v Hall* [1999] Lloyd's Rep IR 313, CA.
3 (1994) 159 JP 656, [1999] Lloyd's Rep IR 305, CA.
4 [1999] Lloyd's Rep IR 321, CA.
5 [1999] Lloyd;s Rep IR 313, CA.

Limit of liability

28.22 The MIB's liability under this Agreement is limited to £250,000 in respect of property damage, though it is unlimited in relation to personal injuries. This figure corresponds to the minimum legally permitted level of cover for property damage in a policy complying with the requirements of the RTA 1988.

In *Limbrick v French and Farley*[1] the claimant was insured with the second defendant, under which the claimant and her mother were the only insured drivers.

The claimant allowed the first defendant to drive her in her own car. The first defendant crashed the car, injuring the claimant. It then transpired that the first defendant had been uninsured. The MIB nominated the second defendant to deal with the claim. On behalf of the second defendant it was argued that the insurance of a policyholder was not a 'relevant liability' for the purposes of MIB liability[2]. The insurer also claimed that it would be able to rely on the terms of its policy with the claimant to recover an indemnity from her as soon as it had to pay out under its liability under the RTA or the 1988 MIB Agreement[3]. Thus, the money paid to the claimant would have been immediately recoverable from her, and her claim would have failed on the basis of circuitry of action. These arguments were rejected. The insurance of a policyholder is a relevant liability[4]. Moreover, the contract of insurance between the claimant and the insurer was irrelevant, because that referred only to cases where the insurer discharged a liability under that contract. In the present case the insurer would be discharging the MIB's liability as its nominee.

[1] [1993] PIQR P121, Simon Brown J.
[2] Although this case arose under the Road Traffic Act 1972 and Agreement, the position appears to be the same at the present day.
[3] Clause 4 of the Uninsured Drivers Agreement expressly preserves the right of insurers to insert such clauses in their policies.
[4] And the headnote in *Cooper v Motor Insurers' Bureau* [1985] QB 575, CA is wrong to the extent that it suggests otherwise.

Victims of untraced drivers – Untraced Drivers Agreement of 1996

28.23 This is the second of the MIB Agreements. It is intended to ensure that compensation is provided in those cases where the person responsible for the accident cannot be traced. Where the agreement applies, the bureau must award the applicant a payment of an amount assessed in the same manner as a court would assess the damages which the applicant would have been entitled to recover from the untraced person in respect of that death or injury if proceedings to enforce a claim for damages were successfully brought by the applicant against the untraced person. The amount to be paid by the MIB is to be calculated by reference to an assessment of damages and not to the other elements that a court would have to consider, such as interest: *Evans v Motor Insurers' Bureau*[1]. The agreement expressly excludes from cover[2] the situation where the death or injury was caused by the use of the vehicle by the untraced person as a weapon, that is to say in a deliberate attempt to run down the person injured or killed. Clause 2 of the Agreement also excludes liability to a person who at the time of the accident is allowing himself to be carried in a vehicle and he knows or had reason to believe that it has been unlawfully taken without the consent of the owner (unless he discovered that only after the start of the journey and it would have been unreasonable to expect him to get out of the vehicle – as perhaps where it is being driven at high speed).

[1] [1997] 3 CMLR 1218 (affirmed on other grounds: (1998) Times, 12 October, CA).
[2] Clause 1(e).

28.24 Clause 3 of the Agreement provides that a person making a valid application under the Agreement is to receive such sum as a court would have awarded him in an action against the untraced driver, less any amount which he has in fact received in respect of earnings from his employer during the period for which any loss of earnings claim is made.

28.25 Clause 5 of the Agreement applies where damage or injury falling within the compulsory risks is caused partly by an untraced person and partly by a person who can be traced and held responsible (whether personally or vicariously). This situation gives rise to a special difficulty because the liability for the loss is borne only partly by a person whose liabilities the MIB is required to discharge. The complicated provisions of cl 5 show how the MIB's liability is calculated in such a case. First, where judgment has been obtained against one or more identified persons responsible[1] for the loss, but that judgment remains wholly unsatisfied three months after its date, the MIB's contribution is equal to what the Agreement defines as the untraced person's contribution to a full award[2]. A full award is the amount which would have been awarded to the claimant if the untraced persons had been wholly responsible for the accident. The untraced person's contribution to that award is the amount which the untraced person would have been held liable to contribute in judicial proceedings to recover damages if proceedings had been brought by the applicant against the untraced person and all other persons partly responsible for the accident. The effect of this provision must be carefully noted. It does not allow the applicant to recover the same amount as he would have recovered simply by suing the untraced person (assuming that that person could be traced) for an action against one of the tortfeasors will enable to claimant to recover all his recoverable losses, the defendant tortfeasor being left to recover an appropriate proportion of that loss from the other tortfeasors. Here the MIB assumes liability only for the net proportion for which the untraced driver might have been expected to be held liable.

Secondly, where judgment is obtained, but at the expiry of three months from the date of judgment, and has been satisfied in part but not in whole, the amount for which the MIB is liable is the untraced person's contribution to a full award or, if less, the unsatisfied part of the judgment. The effect of this is that the MIB accepts that payments made in satisfaction of the judgment by other responsible parties are in the first instance to be set against the liabilities of those persons rather than against the liabilities of the MIB.

[1] Including cases of vicarious responsibility.
[2] Clause 5(6).

28.26 Clause 6 of the Agreement deals with conditions precedent to the MIB's liability under the Agreement. The applicant must give the MIB all reasonable assistance in the carrying out of its investigations under the Agreement. This extends to providing written statements and, if so required, attending oral interviews. The applicant must also, if the MIB so requires, take all reasonable steps to obtain judgment against any other person specified by the MIB in respect of their liability for the losses incurred. In this event, the MIB must indemnify the applicant against any costs reasonably[1] incurred by him in the proceedings, unless the proceedings materially contribute to establishing that the untraced person was not in fact responsible for the losses. The MIB may require the applicant to assign to it any judgment which the applicant has obtained against third parties in respect of the losses, but this must be on terms that the MIB will in due course be accountable to the applicant for any sums recovered in excess of the applicant's liability to the MIB in respect of the accident.

Where the MIB give the applicant notice that his claim is to be rejected, cl 11 of the Agreement gives him a right of appeal to an arbitrator[2] on the ground that, as the case may be, the MIB was wrong to reject the case as falling outside the terms of the Agreement, or was wrong to refuse to make an award, or has awarded him an amount less than the proper amount, or was wrong to refuse to make an award of costs in his favour. The applicant must give notice of appeal to the MIB within six weeks of receiving the decision against which he wishes to appeal. The notice of appeal must be accompanied by an undertaking to accept the decision of the arbitrator. The appeal is decided on the documents provided by the MIB, being the papers relevant to the making of the original decision, and no further evidence is permitted. The arbitrator may reverse the MIB's decision to reject the case after preliminary investigation, in which event the matter is referred to the MIB for substantive investigation. Alternatively he may reverse a decision that no award should be made or may vary the amount of the award. The normal principle is that each side must bear its own costs, though the arbitrator has power to make an award of costs against the appellant if he considers that there was no proper ground for bringing the appeal.

[1] A dispute as to the reasonableness of any costs incurred may be referred to the Secretary of State.
[2] The arbitrator must be a QC appointed from a panel approved by the Lord Chancellor (for cases in England and Wales) or the Lord Advocate (for cases in Scotland): cl 18.

EU Law

28.27 In *Evans v Secretary of State for the Environment, Transport and the Regions*[1] the ECJ considered questions relating to the conformity of the MIB scheme with the provisions of Article 1(4) of the Second Motor Insurance Directive[2], which requires the creation of a body having functions similar to those of the MIB[3]. The ECJ held that Article 1(4) requires Member States to have in place rules under which the MIB or its national equivalent pays interest on awards, but that Article 1(4) does not require costs to be awarded to applicants except to the extent necessary to safeguard the rights of victims. It is for national courts to consider whether existing costs rules provide the necessary protection.

[1] [2004] Lloyd's Rep IR 391; the questions were referred by the High Court in the case of *Evans v Secretary of State for the Environment, Transport and the Regions*, and the High Court's eventual decision was upheld by the Court of Appeal: see [2002] Lloyd's Rep IR 1.
[2] Directive 84/5/EEC.
[3] Although the MIB pre-dates this Directive, it is nevertheless the means by which the UK discharges its obligations under the Directive.

28.28 The effect of this decision is that interest will in future have to be awarded, though it is, according to the ECJ, for national authorities to lay down rules as to the period and basis of calculation of the interest. It appears that the existing costs rules are to be regarded as adequate.

Relationship with the Criminal Injuries Compensation Scheme

28.29 In *R v Criminal Injuries Compensation Board (Respondent), ex p Wayne Joseph Marsden*[1] it was held that compensation under the Criminal Injuries Compensation Scheme is not available where the injury was not caused intentionally. The point is of some small relevance in the context of the MIB, because it shows that in cases of negligent but unintentional injury the MIB cannot escape liability by arguing that the applicant should apply to the Criminal Injuries Compensation Board ('CICB') instead. By contrast, the Untraced Drivers Agreement expressly excludes the case of deliberately caused injury, presumably because that is a case where the applicant should go to the CICB.

1 [2000] RTR 21, CA.

Civil liability for permitting uninsured use

28.30 A person who permits another to use a vehicle without insurance is liable in damages to a person injured through the negligent driving of that vehicle, because the RTA 1988, s 143 gives rise to an action for breach of statutory duty. Such a right of action was originally recognised in *Monk v Warbeys*[1], in relation to the slightly different wording under the RTA 1930, s 35. In *Norman v Aziz*[2] it was held that this rule survived the change of wording under the RTA 1988 and was not affected by the EC Directive[3] requiring Member States to provide effective forms of compensation for the victims of uninsured drivers.

1 [1935] 1 KB 75.
2 [2000] Lloyd's Rep IR 395, CA, Judge Kershaw QC.
3 84/5/EC.

Criminal Injuries Compensation Board

28.31 Where injuries are deliberately caused in the course of committing a criminal offence, the injured person may also have recourse to the CICB, though the details of this scheme lie outside the scope of the present work.

Conclusion

28.32 The MIB Agreements provide an important additional element in the protection of road users and pedestrians. So long as some people drive irresponsibly and without the protection of insurance, this scheme or some variant of it will remain necessary. In any event the existence of such a scheme is now required under the First Generation of Insurance Directives.

Chapter 29

The Third Parties (Rights Against Insurers) Act 1930

Introduction

29.1 The purpose of the TP(RAI)A 1930 is to allow proceedings to be taken directly against a liability insurer where the insured person has become insolvent or has otherwise entered into a composition with creditors. The intention is that the person to whom the liability is incurred should be able to circumvent the normal statutory order of payment of debts. In practice the interpretation given to the Act by the courts has severely undermined the value of the statute.

When the Act applies

29.2 The Act applies where under any contract of insurance a person is insured against liabilities to third parties which he may incur, and one of the following events occurs:

(a) he becomes bankrupt or makes a composition or arrangement with his creditors; or

(b) in the case of the insured being a company, in the event of:
   (i) a winding-up order or an administration order being made;
   (ii) a resolution for a voluntary winding-up being passed, with respect to the company;
   (iii) of a receiver or manager of the company's business or undertaking being duly appointed;
   (iv) of possession being taken, by or on behalf of the holders of any debentures secured by a floating charge, of any property comprised in or subject to the charge; or
   (v) of a voluntary arrangement proposed for the purposes of Part I of the Insolvency Act 1986 ('IA 1986') being approved under that Part.

It is important to observe that the Act is not limited to cases where the company goes into liquidation. The list above includes the standard forms of corporate rescue procedure – Administration Order and Company Voluntary Arrangement – as well as the appointment of a receiver. None of these necessarily implies the end of the company's existence, but any of them will still have the effect of bringing the TP(RAI)A 1930 into operation. Moreover, in *Centre Reinsurance International Co v Curzon Insurance Ltd*[1] it was held that section 1(3) applies also to other events (i.e. events not falling within the statutory defintion) which are said by the policy to lead to an alteration of the rights of the parties so long as they are sufficiently closely connected with the happening of one or more of the statutory events. It is a matter of fact and degree in each case whether there is a sufficiently close connection.

[1] [2004] Lloyd's Rep IR 622, Blackburne J.

29.3 The Act does apply to contractual liabilities as well as to tortious liabilities. This was established by the decision of the Court of Appeal in *Re OT Computers (In Administration)*[1]. Moreover the court suggested, *obiter*, that the Act applies also to liabilities voluntarily incurred[2].

[1] [2004] Lloyd's Rep IR 669, following In *Re Compania Merabello San Nicholas SA* [1973] Ch 75; *Cox v Bankside Members Agency Ltd* [1995] 2 Lloyd's Rep 437; and *Centre Reinsurance International Co v Curzon Insurance Ltd* [2004] Lloyd's Rep IR 622, and overruling *Nigel Upchurch Associates v The Aldridge Estates Investment Co Ltd.*
[2] Doubting the decision in *Tarbuck v Avon Insurance plc* [2002] QB 571.

What the Act does

29.4 In those cases where the Act applies, if, either before or after the happening of the event which triggers the application of the Act, any insured liability is incurred by the insured, his rights against the insurer under the contract in respect of the liability are transferred to and vest in the third party to whom the liability was so incurred.

This is the crucial provision of the Act, and it is one which has given rise to substantial difficult case law.

The rights transferred to the third party under the TP(RAI)A 1930 are the rights of the assured against the insurers under the contract of insurance in respect of the liability in question; rights which are not referable to that liability are not transferred. Thus in *Firma C-Trade SA v Newcastle Protection and Indemnity Association)*[1] (often referred to as *The Fanti* or *The Padre Island*) the assured, because of failure to comply with a prior payment condition, had no rights against the insurers. It was held that there could be no rights capable of transfer to the third party. This decision of the House of Lords settled a long-standing controversy in this area over the effect of so-called 'pay and be paid' clauses, which are commonly used by P & I clubs. The effect of this is that in many cases those insured under arrangements containing such terms will never be able to recover on the policy because their own lack of funds will prevent them from paying the claim in the first instance.

In *Pioneer Concrete (UK) v National Employers' Mutual*[2] the claimants had a claim against a third party, the defendants being the third party's insurers. The third party went into liquidation without notifying the insurers of the claim (although they had given notice of the accident which led to the claim). The claimants sought to sue under the TP(RAI)A 1930, but it was held that the defendants could have pleaded the failure to give notice of the claim if their insured had sued them. It followed that the same defence was available against the claimants. This case emphasises the point that what is transferred to the third party is the rights which the insured had against the insurers, subject to whatever defences and limitations applied to those rights.

[1] [1990] 2 All ER 705, [1990] 2 Lloyd's Rep 191, HL.
[2] [1985] 2 All ER 395, Bingham J.

29.5 The phrase 'his rights against the insurer under the contract in respect of the liability' in s 1(1) was considered by Blackburne J in *Centre Reinsurance International Co v Curzon Insurance Ltd*[1], where the clause which gave rise to the difficulty was a clause which purported to transfer claims handling rights from the insured to the insurers. The question was whether this was 'in respect of the liability'. It is obviously not a clause which affects the existence or amount of the liability, though it does provide a mechanism for determining those matters. Further, the rights conferred by the clause would not be transferred to the third party by virtue of s 1(1). Blackburne J held that the rights under the claims handling clause were not caught by s 1(3), apparently because the transfer did not materially affect the third party's enjoyment of his rights against the insurers. However, he commented that there may be rights which are not transferred under s 1(1), whose alteration on the happening of one of the statutory events does materially prejudice the third party. He suggested that the alteration of such rights would be caught by s 1(3), given that that provision is intended to protect the third party against the effect of avoidance provisions which attempt to undermine or devalue the statutory transfer of rights under s 1(1)[2]. It will presumably be a question of fact in each case to determine whether a particular clause is sufficiently important to the rights of a third party to be caught by s 1(3).

[1] [2004] Lloyd's Rep IR 622.
[2] See also *The Allobrogia* [1979] 1 Lloyd's Rep 190 at 198 per Slade J and the observations of Bingham LJ in the Court of Appeal's decision in *The Fanti* [1989] 1 Lloyd's Rep 239 at 248.

Discretionary payments

29.6 In *The Vainqueur José*[1] the rules of the P & I club allowed the committee, at its discretion, to make an *ex gratia* payment in respect of forwarding expenses. Mocatta J held that the third party claimant could have no right to any such payment, since the insured had had none. Whilst it is obviously correct to say that the insured had no vested right to such a payment, it would have been possible to argue that there was at least an implied term that the committee would give fair consideration to any request for such a payment, and that the benefit of this term could have been passed on to the third party.

[1] *CVG Siderurgicia del Orinoco SA v London SS Owners' Mutual Insurance Association Ltd, The Vainqueur José* [1979] 1 Lloyd's Rep 557, Mocatta J.

The anti-avoidance provision

29.7 Section 1(3) of the TP(RAI)A 1930 purports to prohibit contracting out of the Act. It provides that anything in any contract of insurance which purports, whether directly or indirectly, to avoid the contract or to alter the rights of the parties thereunder upon the happening to the insured of any of the events which trigger the operation of the Act, is of no effect. The effect of this provision was considered in the *Firma C-Trade* case[1], where it was argued that the standard pay and be paid clause used by P & I clubs violated this rule because it had the effect that the third party could never become entitled to payment. The reasoning behind this argument was as follows. The Act says that the insured's rights against the insurer are transferred to the third party. The right of the insured under the policy is to obtain payment of the claim from the insurer upon paying the claim to the person entitled. But that person is the third party, and if the third party succeeds to the insured's rights, then it appears that the third party will have to pay itself in order to trigger payment of the claim. Since this is obviously impossible, there would seem to be two possible outcomes. The first is that it becomes impossible to invoke the Act in these circumstances, whilst the second is that the law should decline to insist on compliance with an impossible condition and should instead say that the claim is payable immediately. The latter appears to achieve the purposes of the TP(RAI)A 1930, whereas the former appears to frustrate them. Unfortunately, in *Firma C-Trade*[2] the House of Lords held that the former construction was the correct one. The basis of the decision was, first, that until the member paid the claim it had only a contingent right against the club and, secondly, that s 1(3) had no application because the clause did not effect any change in the legal rights of the parties on the happening of any of the specified events. Whilst the second of these arguments appears sound, the first does not. Section 1(3) does not say that the third party can never be in a better position that the insured. It merely says that the rights of the insured are transferred to the third party. The correct approach is to recognise that transfer and then see what follows. In the case of pay and be paid clauses, what should follow is that the third party acquires the insured's contingent right against the insurer, but performance of the contingency is no longer required because it is impossible. Thus, the third party would acquire the right to claim against the insurer. The Court of Appeal[3] had felt able to come to just this conclusion. The decision of the House of Lords is greatly to be regretted[4], but it clearly represents the law now and for the foreseeable future.

[1] [1991] 2 AC 1, HL. Lord Goff described the question in the case as 'one which has troubled maritime lawyers ... ever since the enactment of the [1930 Act]'.
[2] [1991] 2 AC 1, HL.
[3] [1989] 1 Lloyd's Rep 239, CA.
[4] Indeed it is easy to agree with Stuart-Smith LJ's observation in the Court of Appeal that the conclusion eventually reached by the House of Lords drives a coach and horses through the scheme of the Act. It is also interesting to note the decision of the Court of Appeal in *Charter Reinsurance Co Ltd v Fagan* [1996] Lloyd's Rep IR 7, where, on slightly different wording, a different result was reached.

Need to establish liability

29.8 In *Post Office v Norwich Union*[1] a contractor damaged a cable belonging to the Post Office. Proceedings were brought, but the contractor denied negligence.

Before the matter could be settled or come to trial the contractor went into liquidation. The Post Office sued the contractor's liability insurers, but it was held that the TP(RAI)A 1930 could not be relied upon. The contractors could not at the date of liquidation have brought an action against their own insurers, since their liability had not been established. Under the TP(RAI)A 1930 the third party could not have any greater rights than the insured had had. In *Bradley v Eagle Star Insurance Co Ltd*[2] the claimant was an ex-employee of the defendants. She brought an action in 1984 against the defendant's former liability insurers in respect of industrial injury allegedly suffered between 1933 and 1970 while she was working for the defendants, who were dissolved in 1976. The House of Lords held that she could not rely upon the TP(RAI)A 1930 because the defendants' liability to her had never been established. However, it is clear that the insured's inchoate right against the insurer is transferred to the third party. Consequently, if liability is established subsequent to the statutory transfer of rights, the third party will be able to sue the insurer[3].

1 [1967] 1 All ER 577.
2 [1989] 1 All ER 961, HL.
3 *Centre Reinsurance International Co v Curzon Insurance Ltd* [2004] Lloyd's Rep IR 622, Blackburne J.

Unequal liabilities

29.9 Where s 1(1) takes effect, the insurer is under the same liability to the third party as he would have been under to the insured, but if the liability of the insurer to the insured exceeds the liability of the insured to the third party, nothing in the Act affects the rights of the insured against the insurer in respect of the excess. Conversely, if the liability of the insurer to the insured is less than the liability of the insured to the third party, nothing in the Act affects the rights of the third party against the insured in respect of the balance.

Obstructing settlements

29.10 In *Normid Housing Association Ltd v Ralphs & Mansell*[1] the claimant brought an action for damages for alleged professional negligence. The defendants' insurers offered to settle the defendants' claim for £250.000. However, the sum claimed against the defendants was £5.7m. The claimants were concerned that acceptance of this offer would prejudice their position under the TP(RAI)A 1930 if, as appeared likely, the defendants went into liquidation. They therefore sought an injunction to restrain the defendants from accepting this offer. The Court of Appeal held that the action was misconceived. The claimants were evidently not party to the contract of insurance; the only way in which they could acquire any rights under it was by the operation of the TP(RAI)A 1930, but this could not happen until one of the specified events occurred.

A similar point arose in *Jackson v Greenfield*[2] where a professional firm had sued one of its clients for unpaid fees and the client counterclaimed for negligence. The firm's professional indemnity insurers subsequently repudiated cover for the claim, because they alleged that the firm knew of the potential counterclaim but did not notify them of it, and the firm ceased to trade. Two of the partners in the firm entered into individual voluntary arrangements ('IVAs') with their creditors.

The insurers sought to settle the claim with the firm and a settlement was proposed. Somehow, and it is not clear how, the client with the counterclaim heard about the proposed settlement and sought an injunction preventing the firm entering into such an agreement with its insurers.

The supervisor of the IVA's decided that the best course was for her to make an application to the court for directions as to the steps she could take regarding settlement with the firms' indemnity insurers.

The question was whether the TP(RAI)A 1930 gave the client any third party rights against the insurers of the firm which was subject to insolvency proceedings. It was held that it did not. The effect of s 1(1) of the TP(RAI)A 1930 was that no rights of the insolvent former partners in the firm against their professional indemnity insurers transferred to, or vested in, the client until such time as it had been ascertained and determined that there was a liability of the partnership to the client.

In this case the rights of the insolvent partners against their indemnity insurers were assets in the IVA's and so the supervisor of the IVA's was entitled to compromise a claim on the indemnity policy.

1 [1989] 1 Lloyd's Rep 265, CA.
2 [1998] BPIR 699.

29.11 A further important point about the interaction of the TP(RAI)A 1930 and IVA was considered in *Sea Voyager Maritime Inc v Bielecki*[1]. This case concerned an IVA entered into by a solicitor. A former client wished to bring a professional negligence action against the solicitor (who denied negligence), but claimed that it was unable to do so because of the IVA. It was therefore unable to establish the solicitor's legal liability to it and unable to take advantage of the operation of the TP(RAI)A 1930. It therefore sought to challenge the IVA under the IA 1986, s 262, which allows a creditor to apply to court on the ground that it is unfairly prejudiced by the IVA. It was held that the company did count as a creditor for these purposes, having had a value put on its claim by the chairman on the meeting which approved the IVA[2]. Moreover, it was unable to pursue its claim against the solicitor because of the IVA, and this did have the effect of precluding the operation of the TP(RAI)A 1930. On the question whether this amounted to unfair prejudice it was said that there could be unfair prejudice even where the terms of the IVA treated all creditors identically. This is because there might be situations where fairness required that some creditors be given preferential treatment. In the present case the effect of the IVA was to prejudice the company's interests.

However, the most interesting aspect of this case is the conclusion which followed from this. It might have been expected that the IVA would have been set aside on the basis of the unfair prejudice. In fact both parties were of the view that this consequence should be avoided if at all possible. Had the IVA been set aside it seems likely that the next step would have been a petition for the bankruptcy of the solicitor, which he would have been quite unable to resist. Given that the question of his liability to the company was still in dispute, this would not at all have suited the company's interests, since the chance to take advantage of the TP(RAI)A 1930 would then have been lost for ever. What the company presumably wanted was some arrangement by which it could have pursued its claim against him while keeping the IVA alive. Unfortunately it is not easy to see how this could have been achieved, and the report of the case gives no indication as to what order was eventually made. The case provides another illustration of the practical difficulties caused by the rule in *Post Office v Norwich Union*[3] that the TP(RAI)A 1930 is not available if liability has not been established when the triggering event under s 1 of the Act occurs.

1 [1999] Lloyd's Rep IR 356, Richard McCombe QC.
2 In accordance with Insolvency Rule 5.17.
3 [1967] 2 QB 363, CA.

Professional indemnity insurance – fraud and non-disclosure under policy

29.12 In *Arab Bank plc v John D Wood (Commercial) Ltd*[1], Arab Bank plc and BBL obtained judgments against John D Wood Commercial Ltd ('JDW') for negligent valuations carried out by its managing director.

JDW went into liquidation and the banks sought to enforce the judgments directly against JDW's insurers, Zurich, under the TP(RAI)A 1930.

The court was asked to consider preliminary issues on whether the assumed fraudulent conduct or knowledge of the two directors – alleged fraud in the making of the valuations and non-disclosure in the policy of the fraudulent valuations which it was known might give rise to a claim – was to be attributed to JDW so entitling Zurich to refuse cover and/or to avoid the policy. Issues of construction, as well as non-disclosure, misrepresentation and breach of warranty arose.

The policy in question provided an indemnity against civil liability subject to the proviso that the definition of the term 'insured' shall 'NOT be construed to mean that the Company shall indemnify any person knowingly committing, making or condoning any dishonest, fraudulent or malicious act or omission.' It was a composite policy so there were several insureds with separate interests. There was also an innocent non-disclosure clause and one entitling Zurich to forfeit the policy for fraudulent claims on the policy.

The judge held that as it was a composite policy the director and the company were separately insured for their own separate interests. He held that the policy would respond, in the case of the dishonesty of any of the insureds, in favour of another insured who was not complicit in that dishonesty.

The judge emphasised that the rules of attribution (it was submitted by Zurich that the dishonest acts and knowledge of the director should be attributed to JDW because the managing director was its alter ego or directing mind and will – although this was not one of the agreed facts) vary depending on the context. In this case the ordinary rules of vicarious liability and agency by which a company may be made liable for the dishonesty of an employee would not fit and any rule of attribution applicable had to be consistent with the policy's clear guidance that it was intended to provide cover to other innocent insureds even in circumstances where a director of the primary insured had been dishonest.

It was held that where the parties are insured separately under the definitions in the policy each separate person is a separate insured and in the absence of an assumed fact to the effect that the managing director was the alter ego or directing mind and will of the company, the rules of attribution did not apply.

It was therefore held that the innocent insureds of which the company JDW was one were insured for the dishonest acts of two of its directors and that Zurich had no right to avoid the policy for their fraudulent non-disclosure.

It is worth noting that the warranty in this policy was that the statements made in the proposal 'are to the best of my/our knowledge true and complete' and that it was held that the decision would have been different if the warranty had been absolute as to the truth of the statements as in those circumstances the ignorance of the company would have been no defence.

[1] [2000] Lloyd's Rep IR 471, CA.

Time for claiming

29.13 In *Lefevre v White*[1] it was held that the third party must claim within the limitation period[2]; the third party's rights against the insurers are to be regarded as founded on contract, since the third party is merely the statutory assignee of the insured party's rights. This is so even where the third party's original claim against the insured was based upon some other ground, such as personal injuries. It will still be the case that the insured's rights against the insurer are contractual rights – what the insured claims against the insurer in such a case is not damages for personal injuries but damages for breach of contract in not paying the original claim[3].

[1] [1990] 1 Lloyd's Rep 569, Popplewell J.
[2] The general question of when time starts to run under a contract of insurance is discussed at length in Chapter 19; see also *Callaghan v Dominion Insurance* [1997] 2 Lloyd's Rep 541.
[3] Cf *Ackbar v Green* [1975] QB 582, Croom-Johnson J.

Provision of Information

29.14 Section 2 of the 1930 Act provides for third parties to request information concerning the insurance policies held by parties against whom they have a claim. Once one of the statutory insolvency events has occurred it is the duty of the insured to give at the request of the third party such information as may reasonably be required by him for the purpose of ascertaining whether any rights have been transferred to and vested in him by the Act[1]. If the information given in pursuance of subsection (1) discloses reasonable ground for supposing that there have or may have been transferred to him under this Act rights against any particular insurer, that insurer shall be subject to the same duty to give information as is imposed on the insured[2]. The duty to give information arises once there is a claim against the insured. It is not limited to cases where liability has already been established[3].

[1] Section 2(1).
[2] Section 2(2).
[3] *Re OT Computers (In Administration)* [2004] Lloyd's Rep IR 669, CA, overruling *Woolwich Building Society v Taylor* [1995] 1 BCLC 132.

Part G

European aspects

Chapter 30

European aspects: the Treaty Provisions

The four freedoms

30.1 The EU is built on the foundation of the so-called 'four freedoms', the right of free movement of goods, persons, capital and services. The Treaty of Rome, in its original form, contained very broad provisions recognising these freedoms, though it is fair to say that in the years between 1957 and 1985 the full extent of the freedoms conferred by the Treaty were not always recognised. The free movement of goods was the area in which most progress was made through the jurisprudence of the European Courts of Justice ('ECJ'), perhaps because this is the area where the principles are easiest to state and where the Treaty contained provisions which were obviously capable of direct application. Although some progress was made in relation to the other freedoms, it was only in 1985 with the development of the Commission's program for completing the Internal Market that real impetus was given to this process. Much of the Single Market Program may legitimately be seen as the full working out of the implications of the four freedoms within the EU. In this sense it may be said that the 1992 Program did no more than make explicit what had always been implicit within the original Treaty. The Treaty on European Union ('TEU'[1]), despite its immense political importance, does not make major changes in relation to the Four Freedoms.

1 Commonly known as the Treaty of Maastricht, and in force from 1 November 1993. The Treaty of Amsterdam (in force 1 May 1999) made a number of further amendments as well as consolidating and renumbering the Articles of the Treaty. The Treaty of Nice (in force 1 February 2003) makes no amendments relevant to the provision of services and is therefore not considered further here.

Free movement of services

30.2 Insurance is a service, and the provision of services within the EU is dealt with by Articles 43–55[1] of the TEU. The major provisions of these Articles are examined below, but it will immediately be clear that they do not by themselves provide an adequate framework for the regulation of insurance services.

However, the complexities of achieving free movement across all service sectors prevented the framers of the TEU from conferring a simple across-the-board right to freedom in this area. Instead the TEU sets out general principles, the detailed application of which is then left to further Directives and Regulations. The TEU provisions are considered in this Chapter, whilst the detailed provisions of the Directives and Regulations will be considered in Chapter 31.

This section of the TEU may be subdivided into those Articles dealing with freedom to provide services and those Articles dealing with the right of establishment.

[1] All Article references are to the numbers applying *after* the renumbering exercise.

Freedom to provide services

30.3 Articles 52–58 deal with the right of establishment. Articles 52–54 confer the relevant rights, whilst Articles 55–58 deal with restrictions on those rights and other related matters. The basic provision is Article 52, which provides:

> 'Within the framework of the provisions set out below, restrictions on the freedom of establishment of nationals of a Member State in the territory of another Member State shall be abolished by progressive stages in the course of the transitional period. Such progressive abolition shall also apply to restrictions on the setting up of agencies, branches or subsidiaries by nationals of any Member State established in the territory of any Member State.
> Freedom of establishment shall include the right to take up and pursue activities as self-employed persons and to set up and manage undertakings, in particular companies and firms within the meaning of the second paragraph of Article 58, under the conditions laid down for its own nationals by the law of the country where such establishment is effected, subject to the provisions of the Chapter relating to capital.'

It is important to note that the TEU gives no further guidance on what is meant by the term 'establishment'. This is a point of some significance, for the rules on establishment are different from those on freedom to provide services, discussed later, and the drawing of the line between the two categories is thus important. It will also be seen later that the ECJ has chosen to draw that line in a way which expands the category of establishment at the expense of the category of freedom to provide services.

30.4 Article 54 requires the Council, on a proposal from the Commission, to draw up a general plan for implementing the objectives of Article 52. Thereafter, the Council is to proceed towards the overall objective by means of Directives.

Article 54(3) gives further guidance on the principles to be adopted by the Council and Commission in carrying out these tasks. Some of these principles are relevant to the insurance sector. Principle (b) requires Council and Commission to ensure close co-operation between the competent authorities at national level in order to ascertain the particular situation within the Community of the activities concerned. This is inevitably important in any sector where there is already a substantial level of regulation at national level, which needs to be respected and harmonised in developing the Internal Market. Principle (c) calls for the abolition of those administrative practices and procedures the maintenance of which would form an obstacle to freedom of establishment. Again, this is relevant in areas which have established regulatory regimes, since it is quite likely that practices and procedures developed over the years will be found, on careful examination, to include aspects which are unnecessarily restrictive. (Principles (d) and (e) are not relevant in the present context). Principle (f) calls for the progressive abolition of restrictions on freedom of establishment in all branches of activity; this is to extend to the conditions for setting up agencies, branches and subsidiaries in other Member States and to the rules relating to the entry of personnel belonging to the main establishment into managerial or supervisory posts in such agencies, branches or subsidiaries. The importance of the first part of this principle scarcely calls for comment, but it is also worth noting the second part of the principle. In a business such as insurance which relies heavily on the expertise of employees and in particular on their familiarity with the complex technical details of the product being sold, an enterprise which is unable to choose which personnel it will assign to branches and agencies outside its own home territory will thereby be placed at a significant competitive disadvantage. Finally, principle (g) calls for co-ordination to the necessary extent of the safeguards which, for the protection of members or others are required of companies or firms with a view to making such safeguards equivalent throughout the Community. Insurance, like other financial services, is an area where various safeguards are universally accepted as being necessary, and this principle is therefore of obvious importance in the insurance sector.

The very broad nature of the freedoms described in Articles 52–54 must be emphasised. The clear aim is to create an Internal Market without national boundaries, though at the same time these provisions, especially Article 44, recognise the considerable practical difficulties arising from this ambitious plan.

30.5 Article 45 makes a very important exception to the Article 42 principles by declaring them inapplicable, so far as any Member State is concerned, to activities which in that State, are connected, even occasionally, with the exercise of official authority. However, this exception appears to have no relevance to the insurance sector, which in all Member States is apparently carried on entirely as a private sector activity. Even if a Member State were to operate an insurance company as a nationalised enterprise, it is not clear that this would amount to the 'exercise of official authority', a phrase which is not further defined in the TEU.

The same Article also authorises the Council, acting by qualified majority on a proposal from the Commission, to rule that Articles 43–48 shall not apply to specified activities[1].

[1] This does not appear to have been done in any case. Certainly it is clear that the provisions do apply in the insurance sector.

30.6 Article 46 allows a derogation from the general Article 43 principle in the case of national rules which provide for special treatment for foreign nationals on grounds of public policy, public security or public health. It seems unlikely that this article will be of major importance in the insurance sector. Although there will no doubt be specific cases where it is appropriate to object to the involvement of individuals in the conduct of an insurance business (a possibility expressly dealt with in the Third Directives[1]) insurance is not a sector where blanket rules against foreign nationals could ever be justified.

[1] Article 32.3 in both the life and non-life Directives.

30.7 Article 47 deals with the question of mutual recognition of diplomas, certificates and other evidence of formal qualifications[1]. This is a potentially important area in the present context because in relation to some activities the laws of at least some Member States require evidence of proficiency before allowing individuals to undertake the activity in that Member State. It is necessary to ensure that qualifications obtained in one Member State are recognised in other Member States, since it could otherwise become effectively impossible for individuals to move freely between Member States to carry on the activity. Mutual recognition must of course take account of the need to ensure that all Member States set adequate and roughly comparable standards for particular qualifications. Within this constraint Article 57(1) calls on the Council to issue Directives for mutual recognition. The harmonisation of laws in this area is to be achieved using the co-decision procedure under Article 189b of the TEU[2].

Article 47(2) extends the idea of mutual recognition to domestic legal requirements governing the taking-up and pursuit of activities of self-employed persons. The co-decision procedure is to be used where the proposed legislation does not involve amendments to existing domestic law, but where such amendment is required, the Council must decide unanimously.

The question of mutual recognition does not appear to be of general practical importance for those directly employed by insurance companies, since such people are not generally subject to qualification requirements. The position may, however, be different in relation to insurance intermediaries, who may be subject to registration requirements[3] or even to authorisation requirements[4].

1 For a general account of this subject see H Schneider *Anerkennung von Diplomen* (1995, Blackstone).
2 Article 47.
3 Eg the IBRA 1977.
4 Eg the FSMA 2000.

30.8 Article 48 equates the position of companies and firms (ie those constituted under civil and commercial law other than those which are not profit-seeking) with the position of natural persons by providing that companies and firms formed in accordance with the law of a Member State and having their registered office, central administration or principal place of business in a Member State are to be treated in the same way as nationals of a Member State. In the case of insurance the right of establishment and the right to provide services will in practice always be vested in companies rather than in individuals or unincorporated firms, since the First Directives contain provisions[1] requiring insurance undertakings to adopt the form of a limited company.

The simplest form of the exercise of the freedom to provide services occurs where an insurance undertaking operates within a State other than its home state without having any branch or permanent establishment in that State. On the one hand it might be said that this form of activity is of less concern to the authorities of the host State than is the case of establishment of a permanent presence. On the other hand it must be admitted that some serious issues can arise. First, there is the question of which regulatory system is to apply to this activity – should it be a matter of host country control or of home country control. Whichever answer is chosen it is easy to see that the answer needs to be clear and to be consistently applied. Secondly, the occasional nature of the activity may give rise to as many problems as it solves, for the host country may not be very willing to deploy its full regulatory apparatus to deal with occasional provision of services, yet may equally not be happy to have insurers engaging in such occasional provision without being subject to the same rules as those with permanent establishments. The problem is exacerbated when it is remembered that operation in a Member State on a services basis does not by any means have to be an occasional activity – the only requirement in order to fall within this definition is that there is no permanent establishment within the Member State concerned. Thus, an insurer could in theory set up an office in an adjoining Member State, from where mail and telephone sales campaigns could be conducted into the Member State without ever creating a permanent establishment in that State and thus without ever falling within the right of establishment rules. This example immediately brings into question the soundness of making any absolute distinction between the services basis and the establishment basis, for it becomes clear that the damage which can be done to consumers by an incompetent and/or dishonest insurer does not principally depend on whether or not the insurer is established in the Member State where the services are provided.

[1] Article 8, as amended, in both the life and non-life Directives.

Right of establishment

30.9 Articles 49–55 deal with the provision of services without establishment. The basic provision is Article 49, which provides:

> 'Within the framework of the provisions set out below, restrictions on freedom to provide services within the Community shall be progressively abolished during the transitional period in respect of nationals of Member States who are established in a State of the Community other than that of the person for whom the services are intended.
> The Council may, acting by a qualified majority on a proposal from the Commission, extend the provisions of this Chapter to nationals of a third country who provide services and who are established within the Community.'

Services are defined by Article 50 as extending to any services normally provided in exchange for remuneration (it is unclear whether 'normally' refers to the character of the services or the practice of the person providing them, though it is suggested that the former interpretation is more in keeping with the objectives of Articles 59–66). Article 60 goes on to create a further right, which is of considerable importance in the context of the insurance industry. This allows a person providing a service temporarily to pursue his activity in the State where the service is provided, under the same conditions as are imposed by that State on its own nationals. In effect, this provision allows an insurance salesperson, for example, to provide investment advice and even to sell a policy in another country to a policyholder resident there, even though the sales person is not ordinarily authorised to carry on business in that other Member State. This right was not available to those who were in fact established in the territory of the Member State concerned, since such people were expected to rely upon the right of establishment in so far as it applied to them. Before the enactment of the Third Generation of Directives, considered in detail in the next Chapter, this was a freedom of some importance, since it could allow insurers to circumvent host country controls on the conduct of insurance business, at least on an occasional basis.

30.10 Article 51, paragraph 2 adds an important further provision of special relevance in the present context, by providing that the liberalisation of banking and insurance services connected with movements of capital is to be effected in step with the progressive liberalisation of movement of capital, which is dealt with in Articles 56–60.

30.11 Article 52 is the equivalent of Article 44 in the previous Chapter of the TEU, laying down similar principles to underpin a programme of measures aimed at achieving full freedom to provide services.

30.12 Article 53 is a declaration of general intent in which the Member States affirm their willingness to extend liberalisation of services beyond the scope laid down in Article 52 if the general economic situation and the situation of the particular sector permit. The Commission is to make recommendations to Member States to this end. The Article is expressed in such vague terms that it cannot possibly give rise to any specific enforceable obligations.

30.13 Article 54 requires Member States to apply any surviving restrictions on freedom to provide services without distinction on grounds of nationality, whilst Article 66 makes the provisions of Articles 45–48 applicable also to the right of establishment.

The question of the right of establishment gives rise to issues somewhat different from those presented by the simple freedom to provide services. A permanent establishment of an insurance undertaking in a State other than its home State more naturally falls to be regulated by the host State than does a mere branch or agency or the provision of services on an occasional basis by a travelling representative, though, as was shown in the previous paragraph, this is a distinction which should not be insisted upon too strictly. In any event, the full programme for completing the Internal Market in insurance has distinguished between freedom to provide services and right of establishment, dealing with the former in the Second Directives and the latter in the Third Directives. The Third Directives have adopted the principle of home country regulation rather than that of host country regulation, though some small residual powers are reserved to the host State. In practical terms it might be thought that the effective implementation of the right of establishment renders the freedom to provide services a question of largely academic importance. In fact, the Second Directive provisions remain largely in force, though it is true that the Commission is now considering whether to move towards a system in which both freedom to provide services and right of establishment are treated in more or less the same way.

Free movement of insurance services

30.14 It can readily be seen that the provisions of Articles 43–55 provide only the most basic framework for the creation of freedom to provide services, much of the detail being left to be filled in by means of Directives applicable to particular sectors of the economy. In considering these TEU provisions and the ways in which the Commission and the Council have discharged their duties under Articles 44 and 52, it is necessary to understand the difficulties which affect attempts to secure the free provision of services across national boundaries but within the EU.

30.15 First, services raise different issues from goods. In the case of goods there will be a physical object moving across a national boundary, but in the case of services this will most often not be so. In the specific case of insurance the only physical cross-border movement is likely to involve proposal forms and/or policy documents (and in some cases even this may not happen). Since these are likely to be transmitted by post, or even in some cases by fax, there is no practical way in which their passage across borders can be prevented or even monitored. Thus, to put the matter in terms of the types of barrier to the exercise of the four freedoms which have commonly been identified, there is no physical barrier to the cross-border provision of insurance services. Secondly, there may well be technical barriers, since the existence in all Member States of a system for regulating the freedom to carry on insurance business means that individual insurers may be unable to comply with technical requirements imposed by the authorities of a particular Member State. Alternatively, individual insurance products may be found not to comply with such technical requirements. The harmonisation of such technical requirements in order to reduce or eliminate this type of barrier has necessarily formed a major part of the process of developing the Single Market in insurance.

30.16 The third commonly recognised type of barrier, namely fiscal barriers, may also be relevant to services generally, since the provision of services may be subject to different tax regimes in different member states. In the particular case of insurance further complexities arise because of the possibility of differential tax treatments for the policy document itself, for the premiums and for sums paid by the insurer in settlement of claims or on the maturity of an endowment policy. The recitals to both the Second and the Third Generations of Directives recognise the existence of taxation differences as a possible distorting factor in the creation of the Internal Market, though there has as yet been no progress on the harmonisation of tax treatment. In practice it appears that differential tax treatment for the proceeds of investment policies has proved to be the major source of difficulty. Most systems recognise the need to avoid the double taxation of such proceeds which would arise if they were subject to tax as capital gains in the hands of the insurer and then subject to a second tax charge, either as income or as capital gains, in the hands of the policyholder. The logical solution to this problem is to exempt either the insurer or the policyholder from the tax charge, but logic alone cannot determine which should be exempt. It is perhaps not surprising that different legal systems have made different choices about this question. A policyholder living in a State which taxes the proceeds in the hands of the policyholder and who takes out a policy in a State which taxes the insurer instead, faces a double charge, whereas it appears that a policyholder who lives in a state which taxes the insurer and who takes out a policy in a country which taxes the policyholder, may escape liability entirely[1]. The resulting distortion of the market through capricious competitive advantages and disadvantages is obvious and clearly incompatible with the Single Market concept.

1 Wills (1992) 2 Ins L & P 45.

30.17 The fourth type of barrier, that represented by differences in legal systems, may also be relevant to any service, since the provision of a service will normally involve the existence of a contract, oral or written, and the private international law question of the law applicable to the contract is therefore likely to arise. The problem is particularly acute in the case of insurance because of the extreme importance and complexity of the policy document. Prospective policyholders may find that their willingness to enter into contractual arrangements with particular insurers is affected by their lack of familiarity with another legal system. Similarly, given the considerable level of regulation which exists in relation to the process of selling and marketing policies, individual insurers may find that detailed differences between the systems of different Member States impede their activities by making it difficult if not impossible to have a single set of marketing literature which simultaneously meets the requirements of all the relevant authorities[1]. There has been no progress in attempts to harmonise the various national laws on insurance contracts, the 1979 Draft Directive[2] on that subject not having been taken up. The nearest approach to any attempt to deal with choice of law questions is found in the Second Directive provisions on determining the applicable law of an insurance contract; these do at least try to give policyholders some protection by making the law of the policyholder's habitual residence the applicable law in most cases.

[1] In the UK such requirements are generally found in the FSMA 2000, replacing the earlier scheme of the FSA 1986.
[2] The Draft Directive on Insurance Contract Law (OJ C190/2 28.7.79).

Case law

30.18 The most authoritative consideration of the practical application of these provisions in an insurance context came in *EC Commission v Germany*[1], which concerned rules of German law purporting to limit the freedom of foreign insurers to sell insurance in Germany without having a permanent establishment there. A number of important points about the application of Articles 49 and 50 of the TEU emerged from that case.

[1] Case 205/84 [1986] ECR 3775, ECJ.

30.19 First, a permanent presence in another Member State is in principle covered by the rules on right of establishment, rather than by those on freedom to provide services. This is so even where the presence does not take the form of a branch but consists merely of an office managed by the enterprise's own staff or by a person who is independent but is authorised to act on a permanent basis for the enterprise (ie what English law would describe as an 'agent'). The line between cases subject to the rules on freedom to provide services and cases subject to the rules on right of establishment is a fine one, and this case emphasises how easy it is to fall on the establishment side of that line. The distinction is important because of the differences between the two sets of rules alluded to above. An enterprise which maintains an establishment (as here defined) in another Member State cannot in respect of that establishment take advantage of the rules relating to freedom to provide services.

30.20 Secondly, a Member State is entitled to restrict the freedom to provide services under Article 49 in the case of an enterprise abroad whose activity is entirely or mainly directed towards its territory and which is thereby intending to evade the rules of conduct which would be applicable to it if it were established in the target State. This exemption is sufficient to deal with the possible problem of enterprises which establish themselves just across the border from the target State and then concentrate their activities on that State. To this extent it can provide some measure of protection against a possible 'Race to the Bottom', but it is to be observed that it does not protect against an enterprise which establishes itself in the Member State which is perceived to have the laxest regulatory regime in the EU and then proceeds to sell insurance to a wide range of other Member States. In such a case, no one Member State can claim that the enterprise's activities are directed 'entirely or mainly' towards its territory.

30.21 Thirdly, Articles 49 and 50 became directly applicable at the end of the transitional period (1969 in the case of the original six Member States) and this direct applicability did not depend on the harmonisation or co-ordination of the laws of the Member States. These Articles require the removal not only of all discrimination against a provider of services on the ground of his nationality, but all the removal of all restrictions on his freedom to provide services imposed by reason of the fact that he is established in a Member State other than that in which the service is to be provided. In particular, Article 50(3) aims to allow a service provider to offer that service in another Member State without suffering from discrimination in favour of nationals of that State. However, it does not automatically follow that all national legislation applicable to local nationals and the permanent activities of locally established enterprises may be applied to the temporary activities of enterprises which are established in another Member State. As an example of the difficulties in this area it is possible to contrast rules as to solvency margins on the one hand with rules as to technical reserves and conditions of insurance on the other. The First Directives contain enough rules on solvency to apply to the supply of services as well as to purely domestic provision of insurance. Consequently the authorities of the target state must accept as sufficient evidence of solvency a certificate of solvency issued by the authorities of the Member State of main establishment. The same does not apply to rules on technical reserves and conditions of insurance, with the result that the target state is justified in imposing its own rules in these areas, provided that those rules do not exceed what is necessary in order to ensure the protection of policyholders and insured persons. The observations on this point are of course now obsolete in view of the Third Directive provisions on home country authorisation.

30.22 Fourthly, national law requiring an insurer established in another Member State to have a permanent establishment within the jurisdiction and to obtain a fresh authorisation from the local authorities before he may provide insurance services amounts to a restriction on the freedom to provide services, and is incompatible with Articles 49 and 50 of the TEU unless there are imperative reasons relating to the public interest, and that public interest is not adequately protected by the rules of the state of establishment and the same result cannot be achieved by less restrictive means. These observations by the ECJ are of importance in the context of the discussion of the expression 'the general good', which appears in the Third Directives. It is thought that the general good is the same thing here as the 'public interest'[1], and the formulation of the public interest exception offered here by the ECJ is notably restrictive, taking into account the role of the

State of establishment as well as the doctrine of proportionality. At the same time the ECJ goes on to acknowledge that in the case of insurance services there are imperative reasons relating to the public interest which *may* justify restrictions on the freedom to provide services.

[1] The original French expression is 'intérêt général', for which 'general good' is at best an approximate translation.

30.23 Fifthly, a system of prior authorisation for the right to provide insurance services, although an obvious restriction on the freedom to provide services, is compatible with Articles 49 and 50, provided that authorisation is granted in accordance with criteria laid down by law and which are no more than is necessary for the protection of policyholders and insured persons. Moreover, restrictions imposed on insurers operating under the freedom to provide services may not duplicate equivalent statutory conditions which have already been satisfied in the State of main establishment. By contrast, if there is a requirement that an enterprise must be established in a State in order to provide services in that State, the result is a complete negation of freedom to provide services and is therefore calculated to deprive Article 49 of all effectiveness. A requirement of this kind cannot therefore be accepted unless it is shown to be indispensable for attaining the objectives pursued. There is in fact no objective justification for such a requirement, since any legitimate objective in relation to the supervision of insurance business and the protection of policyholders and insured persons can be achieved by means of lesser restrictions.

30.24 This case was decided before the enactment of the Second and Third Generations of Insurance Directives, and perhaps its most striking feature is the broad view which it takes of the rights and freedoms conferred by Articles 49 and 50. Although, as has already been pointed out, these Articles are couched in general terms and appear to provide little more than a framework to be completed by means of Directives, the ECJ was prepared to hold that the Articles became directly applicable on the expiry of the transitional period and were therefore capable of giving rise to rights and duties. It will be seen in the next Chapter that subsequent generations of Directives have developed the position in relation to freedom to provide services and right of establishment. The form which these Directives have taken may well be seen as having been influenced to a significant degree by the decision in this case and in particular by the views of the ECJ about the very limited nature of the restrictions on freedom to provide services which can be justified under the TEU.

Chapter 31

European aspects: the First Directives

31.1 The previous Chapter showed the ways in which the TEU provisions provide an essential framework for the development of the free provision of services but cannot by their nature deal adequately with the many different situations which arise in different service sectors. The detailed working out of principles for individual sectors has therefore been left to be carried out by means of Directives applicable to these sectors.

Regulation

31.2 In the case of the insurance sector there have been three generations of Directives in the area of regulation, each generation containing two Directives, one dealing with life assurance, the other with non-life assurance. In each generation of Directives the same matters are covered by both Directives, the same principles being applied to their resolution so far as possible, allowing only for changes made necessary by the different characters of life and non-life business. The three generations of Directives are considered in detail below and in the following Chapters. The present Chapter deals only with the First Generation Directives. Although as a matter of general EU law, Directives are not directly effective in English law, all the First Generation Directives have now been implemented into English law, and the present position can accurately be derived from a consideration of the implementing legislation.

Insurance contract law

31.3 In addition to these three generations of Directives dealing with the regulation of the insurance market, there have also been some Directives dealing with the harmonisation of certain matters of insurance contract law. However, as a general point it is fair to say that harmonisation of insurance contract law has made relatively little progress. At June 2005 the only proposed legislation in the area of insurance was a 5th Motor Insurance Directive.

First Generation

31.4 The First Generation of Directives[1] necessarily started from a very low base in terms of regulatory standards and common provisions, since prior to these Directives each Member State had simply adopted whatever solutions it thought fit to whatever problems it had identified in relation to the regulation of insurance business. The following discussion refers primarily to the First Non-life Assurance Directive, though differences between the Non-life and Life Directives are noted where appropriate. The Life Directive covers[2] life assurance, annuities, personal injury policies when offered by life assurance companies and PHI (the last-named apparently existing only in Ireland and the UK). No undertaking may be authorised under both the First Life Directive and the First Non-life Directive[3], except that undertakings already authorised for classes of business falling under both Directives at the time of the notification of the Directive are allowed to continue in that way provided that the life and non-life sides of the business are separately managed, subject to the power of the authorities of the home state of such an undertaking at any time to require it within a specified time to cease to carry on both life and non-life business within the same undertaking[4]. The apparent prohibition on the creation of new businesses carrying on both types of insurance is much less significant in practice than may at first appear, since it is possible to circumvent it by creating a holding company with two subsidiaries, one of which carries on life business, while the other carries on non-life business. This arrangement contravenes neither the letter nor the spirit of Article 13 of the First Non-life Directive, the purpose of which is to ensure that the management and funds of the life business are not mixed with the management and funds of the non-life business. The device of allocating the two sides of the business to separate companies achieves that objective.

1 Directive 73/239, as amended by Directive 84/641 and Directive 90/618/EEC (non-life); Directive 79/267/EEC (life).
2 First Life Directive, Art 1.
3 First Life Directive, Art 13.
4 First Life Directive, Art 13.6.

31.5 All references are to the current text of the Directives, which have in a number of cases been modified by the later generations of Directives. In particular, the First Generation Directives were extensively modified by the Third Generation Directives. The concerns of the Commission at the time of the First Generation Directives may be gleaned from examining the Recitals to the First Generation Directives. The more important points emerging from these Recitals include: the need to eliminate divergences between national supervisory legislation, including in particular the need to make the provision of insurance services subject to a requirement of prior authorisation and the need to co-ordinate the provisions relating to the financial guarantees required of insurance undertakings, and in that connection the need to adopt a satisfactory system of classes of insurance. Two especially important matters are mentioned towards the end of the Recitals. These are the need to provide that the rules on the taking-up or pursuit of direct insurance apply equally to all undertakings entering the market, wherever their headquarters are situated and the need to include transitional provisions for the benefit of small and medium-sized undertakings so as to allow them time to adjust to the new requirements.

31.6 Articles 6 and 7 of the Directive then impose the requirement of authorisation and define the classes into which insurance is divided for the purposes of authorisation. Articles 8–12 detail the administrative requirements for obtaining authorisation. The important aspects of these are that the business must take one of the approved forms (essentially a limited liability company)[1], must seek authorisation for one or more specified classes of insurance[2], must submit to the regulatory authorities a scheme of operations[3] covering the nature of the risks to be covered, the guiding principles as to reinsurance, the items constituting the minimum guarantee fund, estimates of the costs of setting up the administrative services and the organisation for securing business. In relation to the first three years of the business the scheme must also show estimates of management expenses other than installation costs, estimates of premiums and claims, a forecast balance sheet and estimates of the financial resources intended to cover underwriting liabilities and the solvency margin. These provisions are intended to ensure that insurance undertakings setting up business make full disclosure of their intentions to the regulatory authorities and that they begin with a sound financial base and business plan.

1 Article 8.
2 Article 7.2.
3 Article 9.

31.7 Articles 13–20 of the Directive then deal with the conditions for exercise of business. The conditions stated in these Articles are entirely concerned with financial supervision and accounting questions. They say nothing about questions relating to the ethical conduct of business[1], nor do they deal with ensuring that the business is managed by fit and proper persons[2]. In their current form these provisions make all supervisory matters with which they deal the responsibility of the insurer's home State, in accordance with the general principle of home country control. Article 13.2 provides that the concept of 'financial supervision' includes verification of the insurer's state of solvency, establishment of technical provisions and of the assets covering them. Article 13.3 provides that the regulatory authorities in each Member State must require insurers to have sound administrative and accounting procedures and adequate control mechanisms. Article 15 requires the imposition of rules to ensure that insurers have adequate technical provisions, which are in turn covered by matching assets. Under Article 20 the consequence of failure to comply with the technical provisions rules imposed under Article 15 is that the authorities of the insurer's home State may prohibit the free disposal of its assets, after communicating its intention to do so to the regulatory authorities of the States in which the risks are situated.

1 The Directives do not at any point require Member States to adopt conduct of business rules, though many Member States in fact do so.
2 Article 37 of the First Non-life directive makes limited reference to existing national rules of this kind, but does not insist that Member States should introduce such rules. In the UK the relevant provisions are in the ICA 1982, ss 60–64.

31.8 Article 16 deals with solvency margins. Member States must require insurers whom they authorise to establish adequate solvency margins. The term 'solvency margin' is defined in Article 16.1 as being the assets of the business free of any foreseeable liabilities less any intangible items. The remainder of Article 16.1 lists in detail the matters to be included in the calculation of the solvency margin. Article 16.2 explains in detail how the solvency margin is then calculated, offering two alternative bases, the premium basis and the claims basis. As the names indicate the former places more emphasis on the net levels of premium received in the last year, whereas the latter emphasises the amounts paid out by way of claims. Article 16.3 sets out the calculations to be performed to determine the current solvency margin and imposes a minimum acceptable result. Article 20.2 deals with the situation which arises if the calculation in Article 16.3 produces a result less than the minimum acceptable. In such cases the Member State must require that the insurer submits for its approval a plan for the restoration of a sound financial situation. If the authorities of the home state thinks that the financial situation of the insurer will deteriorate further, it may also restrict of prohibit the free disposal of the undertaking's assets. The measures taken must be notified to the authorities of other Member States in which the undertaking carries on business. These authorities shall, if so requested by the authorities of the home State, take the same measures in respect of assets within their jurisdiction.

31.9 Article 17 then relates the guarantee fund to the solvency margin. The guarantee fund is one third of the total solvency margin, subject to specified minimum amounts for particular types of business. If the solvency margin falls below the amount of the guarantee fund (which would indicate a very serious financial situation for the insurer concerned) Article 20.3 requires the authorities of the insurer's home State to insist that the insurer submits a short-term finance scheme for approval. This requirement can be seen as part of a system of graded responses to financial difficulty experienced by insurers. An inadequate solvency margin calls for a plan to restore financial stability, but a solvency margin below the level of the guarantee fund calls for a more urgent and short-term response because it represents a greater degree of financial difficulty. The right to prevent free disposal of the insurer's assets is available in this case as it is in the less serious case where the solvency margin falls below acceptable levels.

31.10 Article 19 deals with accounts. Member States are required to compel insurers whom they regulate to produce annual accounts covering all types of operation and dealing with its financial situation and solvency. Member States are required to give their supervisory authorities the powers and means necessary for effective supervision of insurers within their territory. Article 19.3 goes on to list a number of specific powers which these authorities must have. These are: the power to make detailed enquiries about the insurer's situation and the whole of its business by gathering information or requiring the submission of documents concerning insurance business; carrying out on-the-spot investigations at an insurer's premises; the power to take any measures with regard to the undertaking which are appropriate and necessary to ensure that the activities of the undertaking conform with the laws of the Member State and in particular with the scheme of operations (submitted under Article 8) in so far as it remains mandatory and to prevent or remove any irregularities prejudicial to policyholders; the power to ensure that measures required by the supervisory authorities are carried out, if need be by enforcement, where appropriate, through judicial channels. In addition Member States may (but need not) make provision for the supervisory authorities to obtain information regarding contracts which are held by intermediaries.

31.11 Article 22 lists the circumstances in which an authorisation to conduct business given to an insurer by the authorities of its home State may be withdrawn. These are: where the insurer does not make use of the authorisation within 12 months of its being granted or ceases to carry on business under the authorisation for more than six months (unless the law of the Member State provides for automatic lapse in such cases); where the insurer no longer fulfils the conditions for the granting of authorisation; where the insurer has been unable within the time allowed to correct a deficient solvency margin (or solvency margin below the level of the guarantee fund) in accordance within Article 20; where the insurer fails seriously in its obligations under the regulations to which it is subject. There is no further definition of the very imprecise concept of 'serious failure', the interpretation of which is therefore left to the authorities of individual Member States. It is to be observed that these are all cases which give the home State authorities a discretion to withdraw the authority. In none of these cases is the withdrawal compulsory. If the power to withdraw authorisation is exercised, the authorities of the home State must notify the authorities of the other Member States, who must take appropriate measures to prevent the insurer concerned from commencing operations in their territory under either the right of establishment or the freedom to provide services. The authorities of the home State shall take all measures necessary to safeguard the interests of policyholders and in particular are required to restrict the free disposal of the insurer's assets. Insurers are given some protection against arbitrary or unjustified use of the power to withdraw authority by Article 22.2, which requires the authorities exercising the power to give the insurer precise reasons for the withdrawal. Most developed legal systems than have some system equivalent to the English law concept of judicial review which would allow insurers aggrieved by the decision to challenge it before a court. It is to be noted that the First Life Directive contains a specific provision[1] requiring Member States to allow an application to the court in the case of a refusal of authorisation.

[1] Article 12.

31.12 Articles 23–29 contain provisions dealing with agencies or branches established within the Community and belonging to undertakings whose head offices are outside the Community. Special rules are needed for such cases because the basic system of home country regulation is clearly inapplicable where the home state is not a Member State. Article 23.1 lays down the basic principle that the setting up of a branch or agency by such an insurer must always be subject to official authorisation. Article 23.2 lists the conditions which must be satisfied before the authorities of a Member State are at liberty to grant the necessary authorisation. These are that the insurers must be entitled to carry on insurance business under the law of its home State, must establish an agency or branch in a Member State, must undertake to establishment at the place of management of the agency or branch accounts specific to the business which it undertakes there, must designate an authorised agent to be approved by the authorities of the Member State where the agency or branch is established, must possess in that Member State assets of at least half the amount required for the guarantee fund under Article 17, must deposit one quarter of that amount as security, must submit a scheme of operations in accordance with Articles 11.1 and 11.2 in the same way as an insurer with its head office in a Member State, and must undertake to maintain a solvency margin which must be of the same percentage as is required for any insurer under Article 16, though the assets and liabilities taken into account in calculating the solvency margin of the branch are only those relating to the business of the branch or agency concerned.

31.13 Articles 24 and 25 impose requirements of technical provisions and solvency margins similar to those applying under Articles 16 and 17, but with the additional requirement that the assets and liabilities concerned must be situated in the Member State. Article 26 goes on to create a derogation from the general principles of financial supervision for undertakings with its head office outside the Community but which have established branches or agencies in more than one Member State. Such undertakings may apply to have its Community branches and agencies effectively treated as a unit, so that the solvency margin is calculated by references to all the branches and agencies combined instead of being calculated separately for each, the deposit of funds required under Article 23 is lodged in only one Member State instead of being required separately in each Member State where the undertaking has a presence and the assets representing the guarantee fund may be localised in any one of the Member States where the undertaking carries on business instead of being required separately in each such Member State. The application for the benefit of these privileges (which can only be granted jointly) must be made to the authorities of all Member States where the undertaking carries on business. One Member State must be named in the application as being responsible in the future for the overall supervision of the undertaking within the Community, ie taking on the role of *de facto* home State for the undertaking. The privileges may be granted only if the authorities of all Member States concerned agree, and must be withdrawn if a request to this effect is made at any time by the authorities of any Member State in which the undertaking carries on business.

31.14 Article 27 applies the provisions of Articles 19 (accounts) and 20 (failure to comply with requirements as to technical provisions, solvency margin or guarantee fund) to undertakings authorised under Article 23.

31.15 Article 29A makes special provision for subsidiaries of parent undertakings governed by the laws of a third country and for acquisitions of holdings by such parent undertakings. The competent authorities in Member States are required to inform the Insurance Committee of the Commission of any authorisation granted to a direct or indirect subsidiary, one or more of whose parent undertakings are governed by the laws of a third country and whenever such a parent undertaking acquires a holding in a Community insurance undertaking which would turn the latter into its subsidiary. These requirements are in addition to all the pre-conditions for authorisation already mentioned.

31.16 Article 29B deals with problems which can arise in the mirror-image situation of that above, ie where Community insurance undertakings seek to establish themselves in third countries. Member States are required to report to the Commission any difficulties encountered by their insurance undertakings in establishing themselves or carrying on their activities in a third country. The Commission is required to present to the Council at six-monthly intervals a report summarising the experiences of the various Member States in this regard. If the Commission concludes that a third country is not granting Community insurance undertakings effective market access comparable with that granted by the Community to insurance undertakings from that third country, the Commission may submit to the Council proposals for the appropriate mandate to open negotiations with a view to redressing the situation. If the Commission concludes that Community insurance undertakings already established in a third country are not receiving national treatment offering the same competitive opportunities as are available to domestic insurance undertakings in that third country, the Commission may initiate negotiations with a view to remedying the situation. The differences between the two situations should be observed. When it is a question of obtaining authorisation, the only permissible response is to open negotiations to remedy the situation, and this requires the consent of the Council. When it is a question of discriminatory treatment against insurers already established in third countries, there is an alternative response of immediate retaliation, and this may be instigated by the Commission without reference to the Council. In such cases the Commission may also decide that the authorities of the Member States must limit or suspend their decisions regarding authorisation of direct or indirect subsidiaries of third country insurers and regarding the acquisition by such insurers of holdings in insurance undertakings with head offices in the Community. When taken on the initiative of the Commission these measures against third countries may not last for more than three months, though within that time the Council may decide to continue them.

If the Commission considers that either of the above situations has arisen it may require Member States to notify it of any request for the authorisation of a direct or indirect subsidiary of a parent company governed by the laws of a third country and of any plans for such a company to become a parent company of a Community insurance undertaking.

31.17 Articles 30–32 contain transitional provisions on the coming into force of the Directive. Article 30 requires Member States to allow undertakings already established in their territories at the coming into force of the Directive a period of five years to comply with the requirements of Articles 16 (solvency margin) and 17 (guarantee fund). This period may be extended by a further two years in the case of the solvency margin for an undertaking which submits to the authorities a plan showing what steps it will take to bring its solvency margin up to the requisite standard within the additional two-year period.

31.18 Articles 33–37 are the Final Provisions of the Directive. Article 33 calls on the Commission and the authorities of the Member States to collaborate closely for the purpose of facilitating the supervision of direct insurance within the Community and of examining any difficulties which may arise in the application of the Directive. Article 34 requires the Commission to submit to the Council, within six years from the date of notification of the Directive, a report[1] on the effects of the financial requirements imposed by this Directive on the situation of the insurance markets in the Member States. The time limits imposed by Article 35 for the implementation of the Directive have now expired, and implementation has been completed in all Member States.

1 No such report has ever appeared in the Official Journal.

31.19 The First Generation Directives must be seen in context. They had to start from a more or less blank sheet; before they were enacted there was no harmonisation of even the most basic matters in the regulation of insurance. They therefore have very limited aims, and must be considered in the context of the 1970s, when the term 'Internal Market' was not in general use, and when it was clearly premature to think in terms of creating a genuine Single Passport System. On this basis it is readily understandable that they should follow the approach of other Directives of the time[1] by aiming for no more than the attainment of certain minimum standards by a process of harmonisation. In attempting this it was obviously desirable to deal with what were perceived as the most important and pressing aspects of the regulatory system. Thus, they deal with the process of authorisation, and in particular they co-ordinate the rules relating to financial stability. It was inevitable that authorisation should be the starting point, since everything else within the regulatory structure naturally follows from the basic authorisation process. In is also understandable, though perhaps not inevitable, that financial stability should feature high on the list of priorities. Such stability is one of the major objectives of any system of financial services regulation, and failure to address this point would have exposed the First Directive regime to serious criticism in the event of failure of major insurers. At the same time it is clear that the First Directives cannot be regarded as being aimed at creating the Internal Market, since they do not attempt to deal with issues about the cross-border provision of services or the right of establishment. Despite their limited aims they represent the essential first step in applying the principles of Articles 43–55 to the insurance sector. They provide the foundation on which subsequent generations of Directives have been able to build.

[1] The company law Directives provide a good example. Eg First Company Law Directive: 68/151 [1968] OJ 41; and Second Company Law Directive 77/91 [1977] OJ L26/1.

Chapter 32

European aspects: the Second Directives – choice of Law[1]

32.1 The Second Generation of Directives[2] dealt with a number of matters relating to the provision of services on a cross-border basis but not to the right of establishment. The two Directives are a further step in the creation of the Single Market in insurance, and their general approach was to facilitate what is sometimes called 'passive' provision of cross-border services, ie the situation where a proposer in one country approach an insurer in another country with a view to obtaining cover. The facilitation of 'active' provision of cross-border services, ie where the initial approach comes from the insurer was left to the Third Generation Directives[3]. This account is based upon the Non-life Directive, but relevant differences in the Life Directive are noted.

1 For more general choice of law and conflict of laws issues, see Chapter 51.
2 Directive 88/357, as amended by Directive 90/618/EEC (non-life); Directive 90/619/EEC (life).
3 As to which see Chapter 33.

Second Generation

32.2 First, it is helpful to draw attention to a few of the statements made in the Recitals to the Non-life Directive, which give some indication of the thinking behind the substantive provisions and of the context in which the Non-life Directive was prepared.

One significant Recital is that which declares the desirability of separating the treatment of the right of establishment from the right of free provision of services. It is of course true that the TEU provisions[1] make this distinction, but the Recital gives no reasoned argument to show why in this particular context it is appropriate to treat them differently. The Commission has continued to struggle with the practical difficulties caused by this distinction, as is perhaps not surprising, bearing in mind that the Recital makes no attempt to explain why the two things have to be treated differently. A later Recital refers to difficulties caused by differences in the tax regimes applicable to insurance contracts in different Member States, some imposing no charge on policies but most imposing some form of indirect taxation. The Recital refers to the obvious danger that these differences may lead to distortion in the pattern of competition within the Member States and suggests that the adoption of the system of taxation prevailing in the Member State where the risk is situated is best adapted to remedying this problem pending any future harmonisation of tax regimes.

1 Articles 43–49.

Situation of the risk

32.3 The early Articles of the Non-life Directive provide definitions of a number of very important concepts for the development of the Internal Market in insurance. Article 2 defines the 'Member State where the risk is situated', an expression used later in the Non-life Directive in determining questions about the proper law of the policy. The definition distinguishes between different types of policy and is worth detailed attention. The general rule is that the risk is considered to be situated in the Member State where the policyholder has his habitual residence, or, if the policyholder is a legal person, where his establishment to which the policy relates is situated. The effect of this rule will normally be to ensure that the policy is subject to the system of law with which the policyholder is likely to be most familiar. However, the exceptions to this general principle are also important. In the case of a buildings policy or a combined buildings and contents policy the risk is situated in the country where the property is situated. This reflects the general rule of private international law that in cases of immovable property the proper law is normally the *lex situs*, but it also has the effect that in these cases the applicable law may not be the law with which the policyholder is most familiar.

Motor insurance Directive 73/239/EC (non-life); Directive 79/267/EC (life)

32.4 Where the insurance relates to any type of vehicle, the risk is situated in the Member State where the vehicle is registered. This creates the possibility that the risk could be situated in different Member States for two or more vehicles insured under the same policy but registered in different Member States.

In the case of travel or holiday risks where the policy lasts for four months or less the risk is situated in the country where the policy was taken out, even if, as will commonly be the case, the holiday is to be taken in another country.

These provisions have to be understood in conjunction with Article 7 of the Non-life Directive, which lays down the principles for determining the law applicable to contracts of insurance. The simplest case occurs where the policyholder has his habitual residence[1] in the State where the risk is situated. In this case the law of that Member State is presumed to be the applicable law. However, the parties may choose to apply the law of another Member State where the law of the State in which the risk is situated allows them to do so. In the typical case, certainly in most cases where the policyholder is an individual, the choice of another system of law is unlikely to be appropriate. However, English law does generally recognise the freedom of contracting parties to choose which law shall apply to their contract, and it would be possible for an insurer established in another country to produce a policy document which contained an express choice of law clause nominating the law of the insurer's home State. Obviously, the choice of an alternative applicable law requires the consent of both parties, but the application form for the policy will normally be drafted (by the insurer) as a request for insurance on the insurer's standard terms. This situation is to some extent dealt with by paragraph (g) of Article 7.1, which states that an express choice of law shall not override mandatory rules of Member States forbidding the choice of another legal system when all the other elements of the contract point to a connection with only one Member State. However, English law has no such rule, the relevant rule of English law being only that the express choice of law must be made *bona fide*[2].

[1] Throughout the following discussion the term 'habitual residence', which is strictly applicable only to individuals, is used to refer also to the central administration of a legal person.
[2] *Vita Food Products Inc v Unus Shipping Co* [1939] AC 277, PC.

32.5 Where the policyholder's habitual residence is not in the State where the risk is situated, the parties may choose to apply either the law of the policyholder's habitual residence or the law of the State where the risk is situated. This paragraph of the Article does not say what will happen if the policy makes no express choice as between these options. In terms of the general principles of private international law, which are declared by Article 7.3 to be applicable in the absence of any express provision in the Non-life Directive, the answer ought to be that the applicable law is that of the country with which the contract has its *closest connection*. This principle is introduced into the Non-life Directive by paragraph (h) of Article 7.1. However, this leaves open the question, with which country is the contract considered to have its closest connection. So far as English private international law is concerned, the place where the contract is entered into is commonly taken as a significant consideration in answering this question[1]. Similarly an express choice of jurisdiction will often be regarded as pointing towards an implied choice of law, even though jurisdiction and choice of law are logically distinct[2]. Unfortunately, the application of these tests to cases involving insurance policies may prove somewhat problematic. In the common case where the contract is entered into after the policyholder has submitted an application and proposal form, English law at least is far from clear on the question of when and where the contract comes into existence. What is clear is that the proposal form is at most an offer of a contract (since the insurer is still at liberty to decline the proposal) so the submission of the proposal form does not by itself create a contract. The acceptance of the offer must then come from the insurer, and it is only on the happening of this acceptance and its communication to the proposer that there can be a contract. However, the decision to accept the proposal will normally be made in the insurer's office. These need not give rise to problems where the insurer's office is in the same State as that where the policyholder has his habitual residence, but it will surely be relatively uncommon for a policyholder and an insurer in the same State to be insuring a risk situated in another State, given the definition of the situation of the risk explained above. Much more commonly the parties will be in different States and the risk will be situated in one of those States. Given that the acceptance is made in the insurer's office, it seems that many contracts in this category will be made in the insurer's State rather than in the policyholder's State; thus, in the absence of an express choice of law, the applicable law is again likely to be the insurer's law. This tendency is reinforced by the fact that any express choice of law clause is much more likely to nominate the insurer's law than the policyholder's law. In some legal systems it might be possible to circumvent this result by arguing that the acceptance does not take effect until received, so that it takes place in the policyholder's State. English law is of course unable to adopt this convenient solution because of its rule that an acceptance made by post takes effect when posted[3]. So far as arbitration is concerned, there may or may not be an arbitration clause. Paragraph (h) tries to resolve some of these difficulties by providing that the contract is rebuttably presumed to be most closely connected with the Member State in which the risk is situated. Unfortunately, paragraph (h) gives no indication of what evidence will be sufficient to rebut that presumption. In English law the general rule about presumptions is that they apply only so long as there is no evidence at all; once there is evidence, the presumption disappears and the matter must be decided according to the evidence.

In the end it appears that these provisions of the Non-life Directive add little to the general private international law rule that the court must decide what is the proper law of the contract, either by applying some (often fairly notional) idea of the intentions of the parties or by deciding what would be the fairest solution.

1 *R v International Trustee for the Protection of Bondholders AG* [1937] AC 500.
2 *Vita Food Products Inc v Unus Shipping Co* [1939] AC 277, PC.
3 *Adams v Lindsell* (1818) 1 B & Ald 681.

Business insureds

32.6 Paragraph (c) of Article 7.1 extends the freedom given in the previous paragraph. It applies where the policyholder pursues a commercial or industrial activity or a liberal profession and where the contract covers two or more risks relating to those activities and situated in different Member States. In this situation the parties may choose the law of any of the Member States where an insured risk is situated or the law of the Member State where the policyholder has his habitual residence. Paragraph (h), discussed above, is again applicable in cases where the policy contains no express choice of law clause.

Both these paragraphs also raise the question of the validity of express choice of law clauses which purport to choose a legal system other than those which they authorise. Paragraph (d) of Article 7.1 attempts to deal with this situation by providing that where the Member States referred to in those paragraphs grant greater freedom of choice of applicable law, the parties may take advantage of that freedom. Unfortunately, this is another paragraph which raises as many questions as it answers. By definition this question arises only where there is more than one Member State whose law could conceivably apply to the situation. If the laws of all the Member States concerned allow the parties greater freedom of choice, then it is clear that paragraph (d) applies, but what is the situation if the laws of only some of the Member States concerned allow this freedom? The reference to the laws 'of *the* Member States' seems to imply that all relevant Member States must permit this freedom if it is to be available to the parties. It is submitted, however, that this is not the correct interpretation. It is sufficient if the law of any of the Member States referred to in the two paragraphs permits a wider choice of law, for in that event the parties can then effectively choose the law of that Member State and then take advantage of the freedom which it grants. It is submitted that this interpretation is the most appropriate one to give effect to the apparently liberal intentions of this part of Article 7, even though it may at first sight appear to run contrary to the English law principle that the doctrine of *renvoi* does not apply in contractual cases[1]. In fact this is not an attempt to apply *renvoi*, since that doctrine refers to the mandatory reference from one legal system to another in cases where private international law initially assigns the case to one legal system rather than to the case where the parties expressly and freely choose a particular legal system to govern their legal relations.

Paragraph (h) also contains an important exception applicable where one severable part of a contract has a close connection with a Member State other than that applicable to the rest of the contract. In such a case that severable part may by way of exception be governed by the law of the State with which it has the closest connection. It is suggested, however, that there will be very few cases falling into his category, given the two requirements which must be fulfilled part of the contract must be severable, a relatively rare phenomenon in itself, and that part must have its closest connection with a Member State other than the one with which the rest of the contract is most closely connected.

1 *Re United Railways of the Havana and Regla Warehouses Ltd* [1960] Ch 52.

32.7 Paragraph (i) then deals with the problems arising in states which are made up of a number of territorial units each having its own rules for contractual obligations. These rules are of course of relevance in the context of the UK, where Scotland does have its own law of contract. For the purposes of Article 7 each territorial unit within a Member State is considered a separate country for the purposes of identifying the applicable law. This simply means that, for example, a contract made in Scotland between a Scots policyholder and a Scots insurer will be subject to Scots law, it being impossible in this context to speak of the law of the UK. However, paragraph (i) also provides that the provisions of Article 7 do not apply to resolving conflicts between different territorial units of the same Member State unless that Member State chooses to make them applicable.

Article 7.2 reinforces the general rule that Member States may override the general principles of Article 7.1 by providing that in certain situations (determined by the law of the Member State) the application of the *lex fori* is mandatory, whatever law would otherwise have been applicable to the contract. Rules of this kind are normally imposed on grounds of public policy, and it is to be noted that they have nothing to do with any choice of law on the part of the parties to the contract.

The overall effect of Article 7 is thus to provide something of a gloss on the traditional choice of law rules applied in private international law. To the extent that the Non-life Directive rules differ from the ordinary English law rules, it was therefore necessary to have implementing legislation to bring English law into line with the Non-life Directive. This was achieved through the Contracts (Applicable Law) Act 1990 ('C(AL)A 1990'), which is discussed in Chapter 51.

Large risks

32.8 Article 5 of the Non-life Directive deals with the concept of 'large risks'. The definition of this concept is important because, as appears below, policyholders seeking cover for large risks are generally treated as being in less need of protection than those seeking cover for mass risks and the rules regarding the free provision of services to them are therefore more lax.

There are three groups of large risks which the Non-life Directive identifies, and in all three cases a vital consideration is the *class* of risk, using the classifications adopted for the purposes of the Annex to the first Directive. In the case of the second and third categories of large risk there are also other criteria.

The first group of large risks are those falling under classes 4 (damage to or loss of railway rolling stock), 5 (damage to or loss of aircraft), 6 (damage to or loss of river and canal vessels, lake and sea vessels, 7 (all damage to or loss of goods in transit or baggage, irrespective of the form of transport), 11 (all liability arising out of the use of aircraft, including carrier's liability) and 12 (all liability arising out of the use of ships, vessels or boats on the seas, lakes, rivers or canals, including carrier's liability) of point A in the Annex. These risks are large risks without reference to the characteristics of the policyholder.

The second group of large risks are those falling under classes 14 (insolvency, general, export credit, instalment credit, mortgages, agricultural credit) and 15 (direct and indirect suretyship) of point A of the Annex. However, these are large risks only where the policyholder is engaged professionally in an industrial or commercial activity or in one of the liberal professions and the risks relate to such activity.

The third group of large risks are those falling under points 8 (damage to or loss of property through fire and natural forces), 9 (damage to or loss of property due to hail or frost and any event such as theft, other than those falling under point 8), 13 (all liability claims under than those falling under points 10, 11 and 12) and 16 (miscellaneous financial loss) of point A of the Annex. These risks are large risks only where the policyholder meets at least two of the following three criteria[1]:

(1) balance sheet total 6.2m ECU;
(2) net turnover 12.8m ECU;
(3) average number of employees during the financial year 250.

These definitions of large risk are relevant to the question of choice of law, since Article 7.1(f) provides that in the case of large risks the parties to the contract are free to choose any law as the applicable law, though it is to be assumed that, as in other cases under Article 7, an express choice can be overriddden on grounds of public policy or because the law of the Member State requires the adoption of the *lex fori*.

The definition of large risk is relevant also to the freedom to provide services, though the provisions on this subject contained in the Second Directive have now been repealed and replaced by provisions in the Third Directive.

[1] The criteria in this form apply from 1 January 1993; prior to that date the figures were approximately twice their present level.

32.9 Article 8 of the Non-life Directive deals with contracts for compulsory insurance, ie those cases, such as motor insurance, where the law of a Member State forbids the carrying on of any activity without an appropriate insurance policy. The Article allows the offering and conclusion of compulsory contracts in accordance with the First and Second Directives. A problem which may arise is that the law of the Member State imposing the obligation and the law of the Member State where the risk is situated may conflict as to the requirements of an appropriate compulsory policy. In this event Article 8.3 makes the former law prevail. In order to make Article 8 practically workable, Article 8.5 requires each Member State to inform the Commission of the risks against which insurance is compulsory under its legislation, stating the specific legal provision relating to that insurance and the particulars which must be given in the certificate which an insurer must issue to an insured person where that State requires proof that the obligation to take out insurance has been complied with. A Member State may require that those particulars include a declaration by the insurer to the effect that the contract complies with the specific provisions relating to that insurance. Where a certificate is issued which conforms with these requirements, a Member State must accept it as proof that the insurance obligation has been fulfilled.

When Member States have notified the Commission in the above terms, the Commission must publish the particulars supplied in the Official Journal.

32.10 Article 12 of the Non-life Directive applies where an undertaking, through an establishment situated in a Member State covers a risk situated in another Member State. The latter State shall be the State of provision of services.

32.11 Under Article 14 of the Non-life Directive an undertaking which intends to carry on business for the first time in one or more Member States under the freedom to provide services must first inform the authorities of its home Member State, indicating the nature of the risks it proposes to cover. This requirement, inserted into the Second Directive by the Third Directive, accords with the general principle of home State regulation. Article 16 goes on to stipulate how the home State authorities must respond to such a notification. The essence of Article 16 is that it provides for co-operation between the home State authorities and those of the other Member States where the insurer proposes to carry on business. Within one month of receiving a notification under Article 14 the authorities of the home State must inform the authorities of each Member State where the undertaking proposes to carry on business of the notification, providing a certificate that the undertaking has the necessary solvency margin, calculated in accordance with the provisions of the first Directive, discussed above, and stating the classes of risks which the undertaking has been authorised to cover and the nature of the risks which the undertaking proposes to cover in the Member State where it wishes to provide services. The same notification must be given to the undertaking concerned, which may start to provide the services as from the date of that notification. Article 16.2 gives the authorities of the home state a residual right to refuse to provide this notification, thereby preventing the undertaking from starting to provide the services, but this refusal is subject to a right of appeal to the courts of the home State.

The same procedure of notification to the authorities of the home state followed by communication to the authorities of the other Member States concerned is also required if there is any change in the information provided under Article 14, ie the nature of the risks to be covered[1].

[1] Article 17.

32.12 Article 12A of the Non-life Directive makes special provision for insurers offering motor insurance under the free provision of services. The particular difficulty which arises in this context is that every Member State is required[1] to operate a national bureau and guarantee funds along the lines of the UK's MIB, designed to ensure that there is compensation for the victims of road accidents caused by the negligence of a driver, even where that driver has failed to comply with the requirement to have an insurance policy in force. In each country this scheme is funded by a levy on all the motor insurers in that country. Clearly, it would not be acceptable for an insurer to provide motor insurance in a Member State on the basis of free provision of services without bearing an appropriate share of the costs of the levy for that State. Article 12A therefore compels the Member State of provision of services to require all insurers providing motor insurance in its territory, whether established there or not, to become members of the bureau and guarantee funds and to contribute to the funding of the scheme. The undertaking is required to ensure that persons claiming in respect of risks in the State of provision of services are not in a worse position as a result of the fact that they have insured with an insurer who is not established in that State. For this purpose the Member State where the services are provided shall require the undertaking to appoint a resident representative to collect all information relating to claims and where necessary to represent the undertaking in the courts or before the authorities of the Member State where the services are provided in dealing with claims and with questions about the existence and validity of motor vehicle liability policies. On the other hand the contribution required to the guarantee fund must be calculated on the same basis for non-established insurers as for established insurers. Article 26 of the Non-life Directive deals with co-insurance, and should be understood in the context of Directive 78/473/EC, under which a doubt had arisen as to the need for authorisation of the leading insurer and the co-insurer(s) in the state where the insurance is to be provided. Article 26 resolves these doubts by providing that the lead insurer must either be regulated in the State where the risk is situated or must comply with the provisions discussed above as to the exercise of the right to provide services; by contrast, the co-insurer(s) need not meet either of these requirements.

1 Article 12A.2.

32.13 Articles 28–35 of the Non-life Directive are the Final Provisions. Article 28 mirrors the First Directive in calling on the Member states and the Commission to collaborate closely for the purpose of facilitating the supervision of direct insurance within the Community. It also requires Member States to inform the Commission of any major difficulties to which the application of the Non-life Directive gives rise. A particular concern to which Article 28 alludes is the risk that a Member state will suffer an abnormal transfer of insurance business to the detriment of undertakings established in its territory and to the advantage of branches and agencies located just beyond its borders. This situation is perhaps hard to imagine in the case of the UK, given its geographical position, but it could happen to other states more centrally located. If it did occur, it might be seen as evidence that the Member State suffering this transfer was perceived as having higher regulatory standards than its neighbours, so that insurers found it to their advantage to sell insurance in that territory without being fully subject to the regulatory standards normally applied there. A simple way to achieve this would be to operate from a branch or agency just outside that territory.

Article 28 also authorises the Commission to submit to the Council appropriate proposals for dealing with any problems which might arise. As yet it has not been necessary for the Commission to make use of these powers, though the current review of the Internal Market in insurance, resulting from the Green Book of May 1996, may lead to legislative proposals.

Article 29 requires the Commission to forward to the Council regular reports on the development of the market in insurance transacted under the freedom to provide services.

Conclusion

32.14 In summary it can be seen that the Second Directives represent an important stage in the development of the Internal Market in insurance. Although they do not by themselves create a complete Internal Market, since they do not allow an automatic right of establishment in other Member States for insurers authorised in one Member State, they do for the first time expressly open up the possibility that an insurer established and authorised in one Member state may by virtue of that authorisation be able to provide insurance services in another Member State.

The Second Generation Directives are perhaps more difficult to evaluate than are their predecessors. These two Directives must clearly be set in the context of the 1992 Single Market Programme, of which they form part, both temporally and in intention. At the same time they are no more than an interim measure on the path to the Single Market, and the question must be asked, why take these measures at this time? The answer clearly lies in a conscious decision to prioritise the develop of the freedom to provide services ahead of the right of establishment. This decision can be justified, not on the basis that freedom to provide services is more important than the right of establishment – it clearly is not – but on the pragmatic grounds that the legal issues to which it gives rise are simpler than those relating to the right of establishment. In particular, freedom to provide services can be achieved without imposing major additional duties on regulatory authorities, whereas realising the Single Passport System creates a need for considerable additional bureaucracy. Indeed, it is one of the most noticeable features of the Second Generation Directives that they require little or nothing of the national regulatory authorities. From one point of view this might even be said to be a weakness of these Directives. They create various freedoms for insurers and policyholders, but do not address important questions about how the national regulatory authorities are to ensure that these freedoms are not abused. It appears to be assumed that home State regulation will operate, since there is no provision for insurers wishing to avail themselves of the freedom to provide services to notify the authorities of the host State of what they are doing. This is a logical arrangement, since it is inherent in the freedom to provide services that the service is provided from the home State (otherwise there would be an attempted exercise of the right of establishment) but the obvious danger is that policyholders in the State where the services are received will think that they are dealing under the regulatory arrangements obtaining in their home State and that the rules relating to the marketing and selling of the policy are those of the receiving State. It is not at all clear that this is the case, since these rules are not part of the proper law of the contract, not being terms of the contract. It might well be thought that the Second Generation Directives are the least satisfactory of the three generations of Directives, principally because of their failure to integrate properly the regulatory and contractual issues. At the same time it might also be surmised that the Commission saw these Directives as no more than an interim measure on the way to the creation of the full Single Passport System. Such a view, while understandable, would also be unfortunate, for it appears likely that freedom to provide services will continue to be an important aspect of the insurance market even after the introduction of the Single Passport System. Provision of insurance on a services basis is always likely to be easier and cheaper than the creation of a permanent establishment, and the recent growth in the market for provision of insurance services by telephone only serves to emphasise this point. Once it becomes culturally acceptable to buy insurance by telephone (a process already well advanced in the UK) the arguments in favour of creating a permanent establishment in a foreign country are significantly weakened. These issues are explored more fully in the next Chapter, where the history of the Third Directives is charted.

Chapter 33

European aspects: the Single Passport System of the Third Directives

Third Generation

33.1 The Third Generation of Directives[1] was designed to complete the Single Passport System, and the changes to which it led represented the most important development of the System of insurance regulation in the EU since regulatory systems became commonplace in the nineteenth century. The Third Generation put in place the system of home country regulation, combining this System with a right of residual control for the authorities of host States.

The Third Life Directive[2] operates according to broadly similar principles, but it is necessary to draw attention to some important differences between the Life Directive and the Non-life Directive. Turning first to the Recitals to this Directive, it can be seen that in the interval between the enactment of the Second Non-life Directive and the enactment of this Directive, the Commission's understanding of some of the issues relating to the Internal Market generally had developed. This is reflected in particular in the reference to the extent to which account needs to be taken of the differing levels of development of different economies within the EU and thus of the efforts which some Member States need to make in order to bring their economies into line with the general EU standard.

In the substantive provisions of the Directives, four major points of difference may be noted between the Life Directive and the Non-life Directive. These concern the notion of the Member State of commitment, the choice of law, rights of cancellation and the differing levels of protection afforded to different policyholders.

[1] Directive 92/49/EC (non-life); Directive 92/96/EC (life).
[2] Directive 90/619/EC.

33.2 The Member State of the commitment is the term used in place of the expression 'Member State where the risk is situated' in the Non-life Directive. It is defined by Article 2 of the Non-life Directive as meaning the Member State where the policyholder has his habitual residence[1]. Article 4 then goes on to deal with choice of law questions. The presumption is always that the applicable law of a life policy is the law of the Member State of the commitment. However, where the law of that State allows, the parties may choose another law. By Article 4.2 where the policyholder is a natural person and has his habitual residence in a Member State other than that of which he is a national, the parties may choose the law of the State of which he is a national. This rule appears to be unnecessary, since the general rule that the parties may choose the law which they prefer surely includes the possibility of making this choice. In any event, Article 4.4 makes clear that the general freedom to choose is subject to rules requiring the mandatory application of the *lex fori*.

[1] In the consideration of this Directive, as in that of the non-life Directive, 'habitual residence' includes the place of establishment of a legal person.

33.3 Article 15 of the Life Directive deals with rights of cancellation. There is of course no corresponding provision in the Non-life Directive, since it is not customary to allow rights of cancellation in non-life policies. Article 15 requires Member States to include in their law a provision giving policyholders a period of between 14 and 30 days in which to cancel a policy, the time to run from the date on which the policyholder is informed that the policy has been concluded. Where the policyholder gives notice of cancellation, this must have the effect of releasing him from any future obligation arising under the contract. It is important to note that the Directive says nothing about releasing the policyholder from past obligations or from the effect of transactions already executed. This is of great importance in dealing with investment policies, especially single-premium investment policies, where it is still possible for a policyholder to be exposed to the risk of a fall in the value of the fund between the execution of the policy and the exercise of the right of cancellation. These questions, as well as everything else relating to the conditions of cancellation are expressly left to be determined by the law of the Member State of the commitment. The only permissible derogations from the general rules about the right of cancellation arise in relation to policies of a duration not exceeding six months and cases where because of the status of the policyholder or the circumstances in which the contract is concluded, the policyholder does not need this special protection. The cases in this latter category are not further explained in the Life Directive, and the interpretation of the provision is therefore left to the Member States, subject to the right of the Commission to bring Article 226 proceedings alleging a failure to implement the Life Directive correctly.

Implementation

33.4 The First and Second Generation Directives were implemented some years ago throughout the Member States. The implementation date for the Third Generation of Directives was 1 July 1994, and this deadline was met by the majority of Member States. All Members States have now complied.

The Third Generation of Directives are intended to realise the vital final stage in the process of creating the Single Market. They make rational (perhaps inevitable) decisions about the regulatory structure to be adopted. What they of course cannot do is to create the necessary market culture to make the Single Market a reality.

A proper evaluation of the approach adopted to date requires the development of some criteria by which existing legislation can be judged. At the simplest level it is possible to enquire how far the legislation goes in creating a Single Market in insurance. From this point of view it would inevitably be judged that the project is more or less complete on the regulatory side (though questions remain about the regulation of marketing and selling practices, which are not as yet harmonised) though not on the contract law side. It is submitted, however, that such an approach is simplistic. The question is not simply whether *a* Single Market has been completed, but whether the best achievable Single Market has been created. The question is deliberately formulated in this limited way because it is clear that the ideal Single Market has not been and will not be created. Such a Market would involve identity of laws throughout the Member States, coupled with a single regulatory authority. For reasons discussed in this Chapter, this is not likely to happen at any time in the foreseeable future.

It can be seen that the Directives enacted and implemented to date have largely completed the process of establishing the regulatory framework for the Internal Market in insurance, though this has been achieved at the cost of treating insurance as an area separate from other types of financial service.

33.5 The implementation in the UK of the Third Life Assurance Directive and the Third Non-life Assurance Directive by the Third Directives Regulations 1994 has finally completed the process of liberalising the insurance market within the EU so as to allow the selling of policies throughout the EU by insurers with an authorisation anywhere in the EU. This Chapter provides an overview of the regulatory requirements affecting insurers who wish to sell policies outside their home State, and may therefore be of interest both to UK insurers seeking to expand their markets and to non-UK insurers seeking to sell within the UK.

The basic principle underlying the Third Directives is that authorisation in any Member State of the EU entitles an insurer to do business through out the EU. However, the doing of business needs to be further sub-divided according to the manner in which the business is conducted. The Directives distinguish between the setting up of a permanent establishment in the country concerned (the Establishment Basis of operations) on the one hand and, on the other hand, the use of agents to sell in that country without a permanent establishment and the selling of policies into that country without any presence (ie telephone or direct mail selling), the latter being known as the Services Basis of operation. It is convenient here to summarise the effects of each of the three Life Assurance Directives so as to give a proper indication of the current position.

Establishment basis

33.6 As already indicated establishment includes setting up an agency or a branch in a foreign country. The Second Directive makes it clear that establishment is also to embrace setting up any office staffed solely by persons directly employed by the company and using tied agents based in the foreign country (Article 3). The First Directive makes establishment subject to authorisation by the foreign country in question (Article 6). In order to obtain this authorisation, a number of steps (laid down by Article 10) have to be taken. The company has to submit to the relevant authorities of the foreign country its memorandum and articles of association together with a list of its directors and managers. It also has to provide a certificate from the competent authorities in the country where its head office is (in the UK this means the DTI); this must state:

(a) the types of activity the company is authorised to undertake and actually undertakes; and
(b) that it has the requisite assets.

In addition, the company must present a scheme of operations, giving a long list of items of information prescribed by Article 11 and detailing, *inter alia*, the company's financial status and past performance and the financial arrangements and prospects for the agency, branch etc being established. Finally, the company must name a general representative in the foreign country, having full powers to bind the company and to represent it before administrative and judicial authorities.

Before making a decision, the foreign authorities will consult the authorities in the country where the company has its head office. The foreign authorities should make their decision within six months; if they do not, the application will be deemed refused. Reasons must be given for refusal, and refusal can be challenged in the courts of the country concerned. The foreign country may insist on its approval being sought for the terms of policies, premium scales and other documents (Article 10(3)).

Services basis

33.7 As indicated earlier, the cross-frontier provision of services covers both situations where the company has only a temporary presence in the foreign country and situations where it has no presence there at all. Under the first head would come visits made by an employee or tied agent from this country; the second head includes introductions made by independent agents based in the foreign country, direct contact made by agents in this country with prospective clients abroad (eg by letter or telephone) and direct contact made by prospective clients abroad with agents here (eg in response to advertising material).

Where authorisation is required, but the company has not obtained it, activity by agents will cause major problems. For example, an agent in the south of England may cross the Channel to sell policies; or an agent, while on holiday abroad, may take the opportunity to generate business. In such a situation, this activity will generally give rise to criminal liability, both on the part of the agent and, possibly, on the part of the company, and may render policies unenforceable. The precise implications will depend on the law of the country in question; but it is clear that there are distinct problems here. It is recommended, therefore, that agents' contracts should expressly restrict their activities, unless otherwise authorised, to the UK. This still leaves it open for an insurer to apply for authorisations and then allow agents to go to the relevant countries, and equally allows an insurer to permit agents to go to countries where authorisation is not required. The important point, however, is that an insurer should control the overseas activity of its agents, so as to minimise the risks. Nevertheless, it should be borne in mind that the risks cannot be entirely eliminated: even prohibited activities may attract criminal liability for the company and may taint its policies with illegality, depending on the legal rules of the foreign country involved.

The post-Directive law: unauthorised activity

33.8 Even after the implementation of the Directives insurers do not have unfettered access to European markets: other EU countries remain free to insist on authorisations being obtained. Insurers therefore remain in the position of having to choose whether or not to obtain authorisations. To the extent that they choose not to do so, the problems of unauthorised activity discussed above continue to arise, and the recommendation made above remains highly relevant. In fact, the problems have become more acute: previously, where authorisation was not required, the company's agents could act freely; but the Directives insist that, before any activity can take place, the company must have to submit certain documents to the authorities of the other country. Moreover, under the Directives irregular activity in the foreign country may have repercussions here: the DTI[1] is obliged to take action against the company to prevent any repetition.

Insurers should also be aware that the Directives may entail restrictions on policies negotiated and concluded in this country, and which therefore may appear to have no EU dimension. The Directives regard the insurance service as being provided in the country where the policyholder habitually resides, not where the contract is formed (Article 2(e)). It follows that if a Frenchman visiting England takes out a policy through an agent there, this constitutes the provision of services in France. The consequences of this are: the contract is presumed to be governed by French law, the terms of the policy and the premiums are subject to the restrictions of French law and the policy is subject to French indirect taxation (if any). In addition, an offence may have been committed under French law. These consequences will apply equally if the policyholder is an Englishman who has taken up temporary residence in France. Agents' contracts should therefore forbid them to accept proposal forms from persons who appear to be resident outside the UK without referring the matter to Head Office. Although this may at first sight appear to be a discriminatory rule, it is not unlawful. The discrimination is only indirect, since the criterion is residence rather than nationality. It is therefore lawful if objectively justified, and the justification is found in the regulatory regime which prohibits the transacting of such business.

[1] A term which appears likely to remain appropriate, despite a short-lived attempt to substitute a different name in the wake of the 2005 General Election.

The post-Directive law: authorised activity

33.9 If an insurer does decide to obtain authorisation to provide services in another EU country, the conditions that have to satisfied are laid down by the Second Directive. This also deals with a number of consequential issues: the regulatory regime governing an insurer's activities abroad; the law applicable to policies; and the tax treatment of policies. In relation to authorisations and to all the consequential issues other than tax treatment, a distinction is drawn according to whether the initiative comes from the client or the company: if it comes from the client the company's activities are subject to less stringent controls. The client is deemed to have taken the initiative either if the initial contact between the company and him is made by the client or if the contract is made in this country and there was no prior contact between client and company in the country where the client habitually resides. The company's activities here are limited to publishing notices indicating its address and the types of cover it is authorised to provide.

Conditions to be satisfied

33.10 A company cannot provide services abroad unless it already authorised to provide them in its own country (Article 10(4)). The intention to provide services to other countries must be notified to the competent authorities in the country where the company has its head office (in the UK this means the DTI), and the company must indicate which countries will be involved and the nature of the cover to be provided (Article 11). If the business in question is to be conducted from a branch or office or by a tied agent in a country other than the one where the head office is, the authorities of that country must also be notified.

A foreign country which the company is targeting is allowed to insist that official authorisation be obtained from it (Article 12). This may involve providing certain certificates: one from the authorities of the country where the company's head office is, confirming that it has the requisite assets; and one from the authorities of the country from which the services will be provided, stating that the company is authorised to provide them and that the authorities have no objection to the company's acting across frontiers. In addition, as a condition of obtaining authorisation, the foreign country may insist on being given (if it wishes, in its own language) details of the intended operations, including particulars of the terms of the company's policies, its premium rates and the forms and other documents it intends using. The relevant authorities of the foreign country have six months to make a decision; if no decision is made within that time, the application is deemed refused. The reasons for refusal must be given, and the company will be able to challenge the refusal in court.

Where, however, the company intends solely to allow clients in foreign countries to take the initiative, the process is much simpler. The company will have to provide the two certificates mentioned above, and in addition it will have to indicate the nature of the cover to be provided. As soon as this is done, the company will be able to start providing the services in question: the foreign country has no say in the matter.

The regulatory regime

33.11 The Second Directive itself provides that, before any policy is concluded, the client must be told in which country the head office, agency or branch with which the contract is to be made is established (Article 22). This information must be on all documents issued to the policyholder. Moreover, policy documents must give the address of establishment with which the contract is made and also (if different) of the company's head office. This will become a practical problem if an insurer sets up operations in another country which are co-ordinated through a head office in that country.

In addition, the foreign country to which the company provides services may impose restrictions with a view to protecting policyholders (Article 19). These may deal with such matters as the terms of policies, premium scales and the nature of forms and other documents used. However, such restrictions are only allowed in so far as the rules in the country from which the services are provided are 'insufficient to achieve the necessary level of protection'; equally, the restrictions themselves must not go beyond what is necessary. No restrictions can be imposed where the client takes the initiative; however, the client does have the protection of a 30-day cancellation period (Article 15).

A foreign country can punish irregularities committed within its territory. It can also report failure to comply with its legal provisions to the authorities of the country from which the services are being provided and, if different, those of the country where the company has its head office. These authorities are obliged to act; but if their action proves inadequate, the foreign country can take appropriate action, including preventing the company from providing cover in its territory.

Applicable law[1]

33.12 Normally, the law applicable to policies will be the law of the country where the policyholder habitually resides (Article 4(1)). Thus, subject to what follows, English law will not apply to policies covering the life of someone living in France even if the contract is made in this country. However, the Directives allow the parties to select a different law, provided that this is permissible under the law of the country where the policyholder habitually resides. Thus, the effectiveness of including a clause in a policy applying English law to it cannot be guaranteed.

In general, the nationality of the policyholder is irrelevant: it is simply a question of where he resides. Thus, French law *prima facie* applies to a policy entered into by an Englishman living in France. However, where the initiative for the policy comes from the client and he does not reside in the country of which he is a national, the policy may provide that the applicable law shall be that of the country of which he has nationality. Nevertheless, this flexibility does not apply if the policyholder is not a national of an EU country. In this case residence is the only possible criterion.

[1] It is to be noted that the Rome Convention on Choice of Law does not apply to contracts of insurance.

The Third Life Directive

33.13 This Directive contains few provisions directly relating to the marketing of policies, being more concerned with the general question of authorisation to carry on business within a particular country. It seeks to erode the distinction between the services basis and the establishment basis by providing that authority to carry on business in any Member State is sufficient authorisation to carry on business in *all* Member States, subject only to the possibility that Member States may restrict this freedom in the interests of the 'general good'. The scope of this exception is far from clear.

Selling and marketing regulations

33.14 Some care is needed when considering the consequences of the Third Directive for marketing practices. The so-called 'Single Passport System' relates to the freedom to carry on business, and ensures that improper behaviour by an insurer or its agents will be dealt with by the authorities of its home State rather than by those of any host State where the impropriety has taken place. However, when determining whether laws have been broken, the relevant laws are those of the host State, not those of the home state. In other words, insurers doing business in other Member States need to be familiar with the regulations governing the marketing and selling of policies in those countries. As these regulations have not yet been harmonised, it cannot safely be assumed that they all follow the UK model, nor that they are all the same. Indeed, few follow the UK model of insisting on strict polarisation and there are many differences of detail between Member States.

Recognition in the UK of EU and EFTA companies[1]

EU companies carrying on business in the UK

33.15 References in this section to the provision of insurance in the UK are references to the covering (otherwise than by way of reinsurance) of a risk or commitment situated in the UK through an establishment in another Member State[2].

An EU company may not carry on direct insurance business through a branch in the UK unless it is authorised in accordance with Article 6 of the First Long-term Insurance Directive to carry on insurance business of that class or part of a class; and the supervisory authority in the company's home State has sent to the Secretary of State a notice which contains the requisite details; and a certificate given in respect of the company by the supervisory authority in its home State which attests that the company has the minimum margin of solvency calculated in accordance with Articles 18, 19 and 20 of the First Long-term Insurance Directive; and indicates the classes of business which the company is authorised to carry on in accordance with Article 6 of the First Long-term Insurance Directive and either the Secretary of State has informed that authority of the conditions which, in the interest of the general good, must be complied with by the company in carrying on insurance business through the branch; or) the period of two months beginning with the day on which the Secretary of State received the notice and certificate has elapsed.

An EU company may not change the requisite details of a branch which has been established by it in the UK; and through which it carries on direct insurance business, unless the company has given a notice to the Secretary of State, and to the supervisory authority in its home State, stating the details of the proposed change not less than one month before the change is to take place and the Secretary of State has received from that authority a notice stating that it has approved the proposed change; and either the Secretary of State has informed that authority of any consequential changes in the conditions which, in the interest of the general good, must be complied with by the company in carrying on insurance business through the branch; or the period of two months beginning with the day on which the company gave the Secretary of State the notice above has elapsed.

If the change is occasioned by circumstances beyond the company's control, the requirements of this paragraph are that the company shall as soon as practicable (whether before or after the change) give a notice to the Secretary of State, and to the supervisory authority in its home State, stating the details of the change.

[1] These rules were added by SI 1994/1696, reg 45(2), Sch 6.
[2] However, an EU or EFTA company shall not be regarded for this section or the next section of the Act as carrying on insurance business in the UK by reason only of the fact that it provides insurance in the UK.

Requisite details

33.16 The requisite details are the name of the company; the address of the branch in the UK and confirmation that it is an address for service on the company's authorised agent; the name of the company's authorised agent; a scheme of operations prepared in accordance with such requirements as may be imposed by the supervisory authority in its home State.

Requirements for providing insurance

33.17 An EU company shall not provide insurance of a class or part of a class in the UK unless the company is authorised in accordance with Article 6 of the First Long-term Insurance Directive to carry on insurance business of that class or part of a class and either the supervisory authority in the company's home State has sent to the Secretary of State a notice containing the requisite details and a certificate which attests that the company has the minimum margin of solvency calculated in accordance with Articles 18, 19 and 20 of the First Long-term Insurance Directive; and indicates the classes of business which the company is authorised to carry on in accordance with Article 6 of the First Long-term Insurance Directive. The company must also have been notified by that authority that it has sent such a notice to the Secretary of State or the insurance is provided by the company participating in a Community co-insurance operation otherwise than as the leading insurer.

An EU company shall not change the requisite details relating to the provision of insurance in the UK unless the company has given a notice to the supervisory authority in its home State stating the details of the proposed change; and that authority has passed to the Secretary of State the information contained in that notice. In the case of a change occasioned by circumstances beyond the company's control, the requirements of this paragraph are that the company shall, as soon as is practicable, give a notice to the supervisory authority in its home State stating the details of the change.

Requisite details

33.18 The requisite details for the purposes of the two preceding paragraphs are the name and address of the company, and the nature of the risks or commitments which the company proposes to cover in the UK.

Powers of intervention

33.19 Where it appears to the Secretary of State that an EU company has failed to comply with any provision of law applicable to its insurance activities in the UK, he may require it to take such steps as he may specify to comply with the provision. If the company fails to comply with such a requirement above, the Secretary of State shall notify the supervisory authority in the home State. If the company still persists in contravening the provision in question, the Secretary of State may, after informing the supervisory authority of the home State, direct the company to cease to carry on insurance business or provide insurance, or to cease to carry on insurance business or provide insurance of any specified description, in the UK. Such a direction under this paragraph does not prevent the company from effecting a contract of insurance in pursuance of a term of a subsisting contract of insurance.

Power to withdraw recognition

33.20 Where an EU company is carrying on insurance business or providing insurance in the UK; and the Secretary of State is notified by the supervisory authority in the home State that the company's authorisation has been withdrawn, or has lapsed, in accordance with Article 26 of the First Long-term Insurance Directive. the Secretary of State may direct the company to cease to carry on insurance business or provide insurance, or to cease to carry on insurance business or provide insurance of a specified description, in the UK through all, or any specified, establishments. Such a direction does not prevent the company from effecting or carrying out a contract of insurance in pursuance of a term of a subsisting contract of insurance.

EFTA companies providing insurance in the UK

33.21 References in this section to the provision of insurance in the UK are references to the covering (otherwise than by way of reinsurance) of a risk or commitment situated in the UK through an establishment in another EEA State.

An EFTA company which intends to provide insurance in the UK shall send to the Secretary of State a certificate, issued by the supervisory authority in the EFTA State in which the company's head office is situated, which attests that the company possesses for its activities as a whole the minimum solvency margin calculated in accordance with the relevant provisions; and that the company's authorisation in accordance with Article 7(1) of the First Long-term Insurance Directive[1] and enables the company to operate outside the EEA State in which the establishment through which the insurance will be provided is situated ('the EEA State of establishment'); a certificate, issued by the supervisory authority in the EEA State of establishment, which indicates the classes of insurance business which the company has been authorised to undertake through that establishment and states that the authority does not object to the company providing insurance in the UK; and confirms that all the commitments which the company intends to cover fall within the classes of insurance business which the company has been authorised to undertake through that establishment; and a statement by the company of the nature of the risks or commitments which it proposes to cover in the UK.

Where an EFTA company wishes to provide insurance in the UK in respect of risks or commitments other than those mentioned in the statement given in accordance with the previous paragraph it shall give written notice to the Secretary of State amending that statement; and it shall not provide insurance in the UK in respect of such risks or commitments before the date certified as that on which written notice of the amendment was received by the Secretary of State. Any insurance which is provided by the company participating in a Community co-insurance operation otherwise than as the leading insurer shall be disregarded for the purposes of this paragraph.

1 79/267/EEC.

Powers of intervention

33.22 Where it appears to the Secretary of State that an EFTA company providing insurance in the UK has failed to comply with any provision of the ICA 1982 he may require it to take such steps as he may specify to comply with that provision. If the company fails to comply with such a requirement the Secretary of State shall notify the supervisory authority in the EEA State in which the establishment through which the insurance is provided is situated. If the company still persists in contravening a provision which has been the subject of such a requirement, the Secretary of State may, after informing that supervisory authority, direct the company to cease to provide insurance, or insurance of any specified description, in the UK. Such a direction under this paragraph does not prevent the company from effecting a contract of insurance in pursuance of a term of a subsisting contract of insurance.

Power to require information

33.23 The Secretary of State may, for the purpose of facilitating the exercise by him of his regulatory functions in relation to EFTA insurers require an EFTA company providing insurance in the UK to furnish him, at specified times or intervals with information about such matters as he may specify being, if he so requires, information verified in a specified manner.

Withdrawal of authorisation

33.24 Where an EFTA company is providing insurance in the UK and the Secretary of State is notified by the supervisory authority in the EEA State in which the establishment through which the insurance is provided, or the company's head office, is situated that the authorisation of the company has been withdrawn in accordance with Article 26 of the First Long-term Insurance Directive, he may direct the company to cease to provide insurance, or insurance of any specified description, in the UK through all, or any specified, establishments. Such a direction under this paragraph does not prevent the company from effecting a contract of insurance in pursuance of a term of a subsisting contract of insurance.

EFTA companies providing insurance through establishments in the UK

33.25 References in this section to the provision of insurance through an establishment in the UK are references to the covering (otherwise than by way of reinsurance) of a risk or commitment situated in another EEA State through an establishment in the UK.

Where an EFTA company intends to provide insurance through an establishment in the UK, it shall before doing so notify the Secretary of State of its intention. The notification shall indicate the EEA State in which the insurance is to be provided, and the nature of the risks or commitments which the company proposes to cover. Where the company intends to provide insurance in more than one EEA State, the information specified above may be contained in a single notification but must be set out separately in relation to each such State. Any insurance which is provided by the company participating in a Community co-insurance operation otherwise than as the leading insurer shall be disregarded for the purposes of this paragraph.

Issue of certificates by the Secretary of State

33.26 An EFTA company which intends to provide insurance through an establishment in the UK may apply to the Secretary of State for a certificate indicating the classes of insurance which the company is authorised to carry on in the UK, and stating that the Secretary of State does not object to the company providing the insurance, and the Secretary of State may issue such a certificate if he sees fit.

Offences

33.27 An EU company commits an offence if it carries on insurance business in the UK without the necessary authorisation or if it changes the requisite details of a branch established by it in the UK without following the procedures described above or if it provides insurance in the UK from a branch elsewhere without the necessary authorisation or if it changes the requisite details relating to the provision of insurance in the UK without following the prescribed procedures.

An EFTA company commits an offence if it provides insurance in the UK without having the necessary authorisation.

UK insurers carrying on business etc in other Member States[1]

Requirements for carrying on direct insurance business

33.28 A UK insurer shall not carry on direct insurance business of a class or part of a class through a branch in a Member State other than the UK unless the insurer is authorised under ss 3 or 4 of this Act to carry on insurance business of that class or part of a class or is a member of Lloyd's, and the insurer has given to the Secretary of State a notice containing the requisite EU details and, in the case of a company, the requisite UK details; and the Secretary of State has given to the supervisory authority of the Member State in which the branch is to be established ('the Member State of the branch') a notice which contains the requisite EU details; and a certificate which attests that the insurer has the minimum margin of solvency calculated in accordance with Articles 18, 19 and 20 of the First Long-term Insurance Directive, and indicates the classes of insurance business which the insurer is authorised to carry on in the UK. It is also necessary that either that authority has informed the Secretary of State of the conditions which, in the interest of the general good, must be complied with by the insurer in carrying on insurance business through the branch; or the period of two months beginning with the day on which the Secretary of State gave that authority the certificate mentioned in paragraph (b) above has elapsed.

[1] These rules were added by SI 1994/1696, reg 46(2), Sch 7.

33.29 The Secretary of State shall, within the period of three months beginning with the date on which the insurer's notice was received, give the notice and certificate referred to above; or refuse to give either or both of those documents. He shall, within the same period , notify the insurer that he has given the notice and certificate referred to above, stating the date on which he did so; or that he has refused to give either or both of those documents, stating the reasons for the refusal. In the case of a UK company, the Secretary of State shall not refuse to give the notice referred to above unless, having regard to the business to be carried on through the branch, it appears to him that the criteria of sound and prudent management would not or might not continue to be fulfilled in respect of the company.

33.30 A UK insurer shall not change the requisite EU details of a branch which has been established by it in a Member State other than the UK ('the Member State of the branch') and through which it carries on direct insurance business unless the insurer has given a notice to the Secretary of State, and to the supervisory authority in the Member State of the branch, stating the details of the proposed change not less than one month before the change is to take place and the Secretary of State has sent to that authority a notice informing it of the proposed change and either that authority has informed the insurer of any consequential changes in the conditions which, in the interest of the general good, must be complied with by the insurer in carrying on insurance business through the branch or the period of two months beginning with the day on which the insurer gave that authority the notice of the proposed change has elapsed. In the case of a change occasioned by circumstances beyond the insurer's control, the requirements of this paragraph are that the insurer shall as soon as practicable (whether before or after the change) give a notice to the Secretary of State, and to the supervisory authority in the Member State of the branch, stating the details of the change.

33.31 The Secretary of State shall, as soon as is practicable after receiving a notice of a proposed change either give the necessary notice to the authority in the Member State of the branch or refuse to give such notice. He must then notify the insurer that he has given the notice stating the date on which he did so or that he refused to give the notice, stating the reasons for that refusal. In the case of a UK company, the Secretary of State shall not refuse to give the notice unless, having regard to the proposed change, it appears to him that the criteria of sound and prudent management would not or might not continue to be fulfilled in respect of the company.

A UK company shall not change the requisite UK details of a branch which has been established by it in a Member State other than the UK; and through which it carries on direct insurance business, unless the company has given a notice to the Secretary of State stating the details of the proposed change at least one month before the change is effected, though in the case of a change occasioned by circumstances beyond the company's control, it is sufficient that the company shall as soon as is practicable (whether before or after the change) give a notice to the Secretary of State stating the details of the change.

33.32 The requisite EU details for the purposes of paragraphs 9.43–9.45 above in the case of a life assurance company are the Member State in which the branch is to be or has been established ('the Member State of the branch'), the address of the branch and confirmation that it is an address for service on the insurer's authorised agent, the name of the insurer's authorised agent and, in the case of a member of Lloyd's, confirmation that the authorised agent has power to accept service of proceedings on behalf of Lloyd's, the classes or parts of classes of business to be carried on, and nature of the risks or commitments to be covered, in the Member State of the branch. Details of the structural organisation of the branch, estimates of the costs of installing administrative services and the organisation for securing business in the Member State of the branch and the resources available to cover those costs; for each of the first three financial years following the establishment of the branch estimates of the insurer's margin of solvency and the margin of solvency required, and a statement showing how both have been calculated, estimates relating to expenses of management (other than costs of installation), and in particular those relating to current general expenses and commissions, estimates relating to premiums or contributions (both gross and net of all reinsurance ceded) and to claims (after all reinsurance recoveries); and estimates relating to the financial resources intended to cover underwriting liabilities.

33.33 The requisite UK details are the names of the company's managers and main agents in the Member State of the branch, particulars of any association which exists or is proposed to exist between the directors and the controllers of the company; and any person who will act as an insurance broker, agent, loss adjuster or reinsurer for the company in the Member State of the branch, the names of the principal reinsurers of business to be carried on in the Member State of the branch, the sources of business in the Member State of the branch (for example, insurance brokers, agents, own employees or direct selling) with the approximate percentage expected from each of those sources, copies or drafts of any separate reinsurance treaties covering business to be written in the Member State of the branch, any standard agreements which the company will enter into with brokers or agents in the Member State of the branch, any agreements which the company will enter into with persons (other than employees of the company) who will manage the business to be carried on in the Member State of the branch. It is also necessary to supply details of the technical bases which the actuary appointed in accordance with s 19 above proposes to use for each class of business to be carried on in the Member State of the branch, including the bases needed for calculating premium rates and mathematical reserves, a statement by the actuary so appointed as to whether he considers that the premium rates which will be used in the Member State of the branch are suitable, the technical bases used to calculate the statements and estimates referred to above.

Requirements for providing insurance

33.34 A UK insurer shall not provide insurance of any class or part of a class in a Member State other than the UK unless the insurer is authorised under ss 3 or 4 of the ICA 1982 to carry on insurance of that class or part of a class or is a member of Lloyd's and either the insurer has given to the Secretary of State a notice containing the requisite details; and the Secretary of State has given to the supervisory authority in the Member State in which the insurance is to be provided a notice which contains the requisite details; and a certificate which attests that the insurer has the minimum margin of solvency calculated in accordance with Articles 18, 19 and 20 of the First Long-term Insurance Directive; and indicates the classes of insurance business which the insurer is authorised to carry on in the UK, or the insurance is provided by the insurer participating in a Community co-insurance operation otherwise than as the leading insurer. Where the insurer intends to provide insurance in more than one Member State, the requisite details may be contained in a single notification but must be set out separately in relation to each Member State.

The Secretary of State shall, within the period of one month beginning with the date on which the insurer's notice was received give the notice and certificate referred to above to the supervisory authority in the Member State in which the insurer intends to provide insurance or refuse to give either or both of those documents. He shall also within the same period notify the insurer that he has given the notice and certificate to the supervisory authority in the Member State in which the insurer intends to provide insurance, stating the date on which he did so or that he has refused to give either or both those documents, stating the reasons for the refusal. In the case of a UK company, the Secretary of State shall not refuse to give the notice unless, having regard to the insurance to be provided in the Member State, it appears to him that the criteria of sound and prudent management would not or might not continue to be fulfilled in respect of the company.

A UK insurer shall not change the requisite details of the provision of insurance in a Member State other than the UK unless the insurer has given a notice to the Secretary of State stating the details of the proposed change and that the Secretary of State has sent to the supervisory authority in the Member State in which the insurance is provided a notice informing it of the proposed change, though in the case of a change occasioned by circumstances beyond the insurer's control, the requirements of this paragraph are that the insurer shall as soon as practicable give a notice to the Secretary of State stating the details of the change.

The Secretary of State shall, as soon as is practicable notify the insurer that he has given the necessary notice stating the date on which he did so or, if he exercises his discretion to refuse to give such a notice, that he has done so, stating the reasons for the refusal. In the case of a UK company, the Secretary of State shall not refuse to give the notice referred to in sub-paragraph (4)(a) above unless, having regard to the proposed change, it appears to him that the criteria of sound and prudent management would not or might not continue to be fulfilled in respect of the company.

Requisite details

33.35 The requisite details are the Member State in which the insurance is to be provided and the nature of the risks or commitments which the insurer proposes to cover in that State.

Requirement to notify cessation of insurance business etc

33.36 A UK insurer which has ceased to carry on direct insurance business through a branch in a Member State other than the UK or to provide insurance in such a Member State shall as soon as is practicable notify the Secretary of State in writing that it has done so. Any insurance which is provided by the insurer participating in a Community co-insurance operation otherwise than as the leading insurer shall be disregarded for these purposes.

UK insurers providing insurance in EFTA States

33.37 Where a UK insurer intends to provide insurance in an EFTA State, it shall before doing so notify the Secretary of State in writing of its intention. The notification shall indicate the EFTA State in which the insurance is to be provided, the EEA State in which is situated the establishment through which the insurance will be provided ('the EEA State of establishment'), and the nature of the risks or commitments which the insurer proposes to cover. Where the insurer intends to provide insurance in more than one EFTA State, the information specified above may be contained in a single notification but must be set out separately in relation to each such State.

Where a UK insurer has duly notified the Secretary of State of its intention to provide insurance in an EFTA State where administrative authorisation is required for the provision of insurance, then, if the original notification related only to risks or commitments in respect of which such authorisation is required, or only to risks or commitments in respect of which such authorisation is not required and the insurer subsequently intends to extend its activities to risks falling within the other category, it shall before doing so comply with the above rules as if it were starting to provide insurance in that country for the first time. Any insurance which is provided by the insurer participating in a Community co-insurance operation otherwise than as the leading insurer shall be disregarded for the purposes of this paragraph.

Issue of certificates by the Secretary of State

33.38 A UK insurer which intends to provide insurance in an EFTA State may apply to the Secretary of State for a certificate attesting that the insurer possesses for its activities as a whole the minimum solvency margin calculated in accordance with the relevant provisions, indicating the classes of business which the insurer is authorised to carry on in the UK, stating that the Secretary of State does not object to the insurer providing the insurance; and in the case of a company, attesting that the company's authorisation to carry on business in the UK, issued in accordance with Article 7(1) of the First Life Assurance Directive, enables the company to carry on business outside the EEA State of establishment.

If it appears to the Secretary of State that a certificate applied for ought to be issued, he shall issue the certificate accordingly. If the Secretary of State refuses to issue a certificate, he shall inform the company in writing of his decision and of the reasons for it.

Recognition in other EEA States of UK insurers

33.39 Where a UK insurer intends to provide insurance in the UK through a branch in another EEA State, it must first notify the Secretary of State in writing of its intention. The notification must indicate the EEA State in which is situated the branch through which the company intends to provide insurance in the UK; and the nature of the risks or commitments which the insurer proposes to cover in the UK. Where the EEA State in which is situated the branch through which the company intends to provide insurance in the UK is an EFTA State, the notification shall be accompanied by a certificate, issued by the supervisory authority in that State, which- indicates the classes of insurance business which the company has been authorised to undertake through that branch and states that the authority does not object to the company providing insurance in the UK; and confirms that all the commitments which the company intends to cover fall within the classes of insurance business which the company has been authorised to undertake through that branch. The insurer shall notify the Secretary of State in writing if it changes either of the details notified to the Secretary of State or if it ceases to provide insurance in the UK. Any insurance which is provided by the insurer participating in a Community co-insurance operation otherwise than as the leading insurer shall be disregarded for these purposes.

Offences

33.40 A UK insurer commits an offence if it carries on insurance business in a Member State other than the UK without the necessary permissions as described in the previous paragraph or if it changes the requisite EU details or, as the case may be, the requisite UK details of a branch established by it in such a Member State without following the procedure set out in the previous paragraph or if it provides insurance in such a Member State without the necessary authorisations or if it changes the requisite details relating to the provision of insurance in such a Member State without following the prescribed procedures.

Definitions

33.41 In this Chapter references to the provision of insurance in a Member State other than the UK are references to the covering (otherwise than by way of reinsurance) of a risk or commitment situated in that Member State through an establishment in another Member State. References to the provision of insurance in an EFTA State are references to the covering (otherwise than by way of reinsurance) of a risk or commitment situated in that EFTA State through an establishment in another EEA State. References to the provision of insurance in the UK are references to the covering (otherwise than by way of reinsurance) of a risk or commitment situated in the UK through an establishment in another Member State or through an establishment in an EFTA State.

Law applicable to certain contracts of insurance (s 94A of the ICA 1982)[1]

33.42 In relation to long-term business, the law applicable to the contract is the law of the Member State of the commitment. However, where the law of that Member State so allows, the parties may choose the law of another country. Where the policyholder is an individual and has his habitual residence in a Member State other than that of which he is a national, the parties may choose the law of the Member State of which he is a national.

[1] See Chapter 51 for more detailed consideration of general conflict of laws issues in insurance.

Mandatory rules

33.43 None of the above restricts the application of the rules of a part of the UK in a situation where they are mandatory, irrespective of the law otherwise applicable to the contract.

Supplementary provisions

33.44 Where a Member State includes several territorial units, each of which has its own rules of law concerning contractual obligations, each unit shall be considered as a country for the purposes of identifying the applicable law. This applies also to conflicts between the laws of the different parts of the UK. Subject to the foregoing, a court in a part of the UK shall act in accordance with the provisions of the C(AL)A 1990. In particular, reference shall be made to those provisions to ascertain what freedom of choice the parties have under the law of a part of the UK.

Conclusion

33.45 The Single Passport System has now been in place for several years. It can be seen that it has worked well in the sense that it has offered insurers the opportunity to operate relatively freely throughout the EU. On the other hand, at least in the UK, it has not led to a major influx of foreign insurers (the position is perhaps different in mainland Europe). This can be explained partly by the very competitive nature of the UK insurance market and partly by problems of cultural and legal difference, which are by their nature not susceptible to being addressed by legislation. The Commission has also recognised that it may in due course be necessary to pass further Directives in order to develop this area of the Internal Market further.

Part H

Particular types of policy

Chapter 34

Life assurance

34.1 Life assurance is one of the major traditional types of insurance cover. It differs from most other types of cover in a number of important respects. The subject is well served by some specialist texts[1], but the most important aspects of it will be dealt with here.

[1] Houseman and Davies *Law of Life Assurance* (2001, Butterworths); McGee *The Law and Practice of Life Assurance Contracts* (2nd edn, 2005, Cavendish).

Types of life policy

34.2 The basic distinction in this area is between *term assurance* and *endowment assurance*.

Term assurance is the simplest form of life policy. It covers only the risk that the life assured will die during the term of the policy. It has no investment element, so that there is no maturity sum – indeed the very concept of maturity is irrelevant in a term policy.

Endowment assurance is a form of assurance which is both insurance and investment. In addition to providing cover against the risk of death during the term it also provides a lump sum of money payable when the policy matures. Although modern financial services practice recognised various different forms of endowment, all share this basic common feature.

What is a life policy?

34.3 The question of what is a life policy, indeed what is a contract of insurance at all, has been extensively considered in *Fuji Finance Inc v Aetna Assurance*[1], which is discussed in Chapter 1. For the most part it may safely be said that definitional questions give rise to few, if any, problems. The crucial feature of a life policy is that the insured event is the death of the life assured (who need not be the policyholder). In this sense it may be distinguished from a personal accident policy[2], which pays out not only on death but also on personal accident not causing death. The modern practice of at least some life assurers is to pay the sum assured if the life assured is diagnosed as being critically ill (the definition of this is usually that the prognosis is less than six months to live). This variant does not appear to prevent the policy from being a life policy for the purposes of regulatory classification.

1 [1997] Ch 173, CA.
2 Dealt with in Chapter 35.

Mis-selling of investment policies

34.4 Given that many life policies are in fact sold as investment vehicles, it is inevitable that many issues of mis-selling arise. The basic problem may be said to arise from the fact that there are inherent problems in mixing insurance with savings. Historically, there were some advantages in saving by means of an insurance policy in the form of favourable tax treatment of premiums[1] and/or maturity proceeds. These have gradually been eroded over the years, but the insurance industry continues to sell life policies as savings vehicles. Problems resulting from this are of two major types. The first arises where the policyholder discovers that the investment performance is less than he had expected, whilst the second arises where the policyholder is unable to continue paying the premiums and then discovers the severe effect which this is likely to have on his investment return.

1 Although LAPR was prospectively abolished by the Finance Act 1984, there are still a few policies in force which benefit from it.

Nomination of beneficiary

34.5 In *Gold v Hill; Hill v Gold*[1] the deceased whose life was assured had nominated a Mr Gold as the beneficiary under his life assurance policy. At a dinner shortly before his death the deceased informed Mr Gold that he had been nominated under the policy and asked that he should look after his common law wife and children if anything happened to him.

It was held that the nomination of a beneficiary under a life insurance policy when the insured did not intend that nominee to take in a personal capacity, but had asked him to apply any funds arising under the policy to look after the insured's family, was analogous to a secret trust. However, the requirements of s 53(1)(c) of the LPA 1925 (which provides that '*a disposition of an equitable interest … subsisting at the time of the disposition, must be in writing …*') did not need to be complied with because the nomination did not operate as a disposition of an equitable interest. The trust did not crystallise until the sum became payable upon death and until then there was no subsisting equitable interest capable of being disposed of within the meaning of s 53 of the LPA 1925.

Where the person paying premiums in an endowment policy is not the intended beneficiary of the policy, the Insurance Ombudsman had held[2] that the person paying the premiums has no power to require the insurer to delay paying the policy proceeds to the beneficiary. This is clearly legally correct.

[1] [1999] 1 FLR 54.
[2] IOB 3.14.

Death as stipulated contingency

34.6 Under a policy of life insurance in the strict sense the event which gives the right to payment is death during the currency of the policy. Generally the cause of the death is immaterial. All cases of death, whether due to natural or accidental causes, fall within the policy; even death caused by the wilful act of a third party is covered as was held in *Cleaver v Mutual Reserve Fund Life Association*[1] Although the fact that the assured was killed by a third party does not affect the liability of the insurers to pay the policy money, it may affect the title to the policy money since it is contrary to public policy that a man not mentally disordered who has killed another should be allowed to benefit from his crime. The 'forfeiture rule' has been mitigated in certain circumstances, eg where the killing constitutes manslaughter, by the Forfeiture Act 1982[2]. The forfeiture rule applies to aiding and abetting suicide, but the interests of justice may require that relief against forfeiture be granted: *Dunbar (administrator of Dunbar (deceased)) v Plant*[3]. In that case the deceased and his partner had entered into a suicide pact, but the partner survived the attempt at suicide. The deceased's executors sought to exclude the partner from any benefit under the deceased's estate, but the court held that in the circumstances of the case it was just that she should be able to recover on a life assurance policy made for her benefit.

[1] [1892] 1 QB 147, CA.
[2] The Act, considered in more detail in Chapter 20, allows the court a discretion to dispense a party from the operation of the forfeiture rule.
[3] [1997] 4 All ER 289, CA.

Maturity of policy

34.7 When an endowment policy matures, the policyholder or other nominated beneficiary can claim the maturity sum, which may be a fixed amount or, more commonly at the present day, may depend on the performance of funds invested during the lifetime of the policy.

Position of third party

34.8 The nomination of a beneficiary under a life assurance policy where it is the duty of the nominee to apply the funds for the benefit of a third party upon the death of the policy holder operates in the same manner as a secret trust: *Gold v Hill*[1].

[1] [1999] 1 BCLC 192.

Meaning of 'long term business' in the Insurance Companies Act 1982[1]

34.9 In *Re Friends Provident Linked Life Assurance Ltd*[2] it was held by a court in the Chancery Division that the reference to 'long term business' in para 1(1) of Sch 2C to the ICA 1982 applies equally to reinsurance business as it does to insurance business where all or part of the risk undertaken by an insurer under a contract which constitutes 'long term business' is laid off under the reinsurance contract. An arrangement which is in reality a surrender or cancellation of an insurance policy should not, however, be treated as if it were a transfer of business.

1 ICA 1982, Sch 2C, para 1(1).
2 [1999] 1 BCLC 192.

Maturity

34.10 Maturity can occur in endowment and whole of life policies and in a slightly different form in pension policies. In the case of endowment policies maturity occurs when the designated term of the endowment policy has expired, the life assured not having died in the meantime. If the life dies before this date, the matter should be dealt with under the heading of 'Claims' (Chapter 19). The same point arises in the case of pension policies, but it must be borne in mind that the usual arrangement in relation to money purchase pension schemes is that the policyholder is allowed to convert the fund into a pension at any time after the age of 50. Although the policy is likely to mention a planned retirement age, this is merely the age used as the basis for the projections of investment return on encashment. It will have been chosen by the policyholder and will no doubt represent his best estimate of likely retiring age, but it does not bind either party to the contract, and the policyholder is in effect free to determine the maturity date.

Proof of age

34.11 The age of the life assured is always a material fact, since it influences the level of premium charged for a particular level of cover. It is not always the practice to require the age to be proved by production of a Birth Certificate or other suitable evidence before the policy is issued. In these cases the policy should state that age is not admitted, and the company should reserve, by means of an express policy term, the right to insist on such proof before making any payment under the policy. If it subsequently appears that the age has been mis-stated, the insurer has two options. One is to avoid the policy entirely on the ground of mis-statement of a material fact. Prior to the decision of the House of Lords in *Pan Atlantic Insurance Co Ltd v Pine Top Insurance Co Ltd*[1] it would have been possible to argue that this was a legitimate application of the rules on non-disclosure, though it would almost certainly not have found favour with the Insurance Ombudsman, unless it could be shown that proper disclosure would have caused the risk to be declined completely. This will rarely be the case. After the decision in *Pan Atlantic* it appears that avoidance is not available unless the risk would have been declined or the premium altered. Consequently, it will no doubt continue to be usual to adopt the second option, which is to recalculate the sum due on maturity on the basis of the premiums actually paid, but taking into account the actual age of the life. Where the age has been understated (as is much more common than overstatement) this will produce a reduction in the maturity sum, and this reduction serves to ensure that the insurer is not prejudiced by the mis-statement. In the rare case where the age has been overstated, it is suggested that there is no onus on the company to adjust the maturity value upwards. In such cases it appears that the proposer will not have been guilty of non-disclosure, since this is an overstatement of the risk, which, on the basis of *Carter v Boehm*[2], does not give rise to a right to avoid.

[1] [1994] 3 All ER 581, HL.
[2] (1766) 3 Burr 1905.

Title to proceeds

34.12 It is obviously important to ensure that the policy proceeds are paid to the right person, since a payment to the wrong person will not discharge the insurer's liability and will leave it exposed to an action for payment from the person truly entitled. In the case of a matured endowment there should be little difficulty, since the policyholder will still be alive, but more care is needed when the payment is made because of the death of the life assured[1].

[1] For the complexities which may arise in the law of tracing when premiums are paid with money misappropriated from an innocent third party, see *Foskett v McKeown* [2000] Lloyd's Rep IR 627, HL.

Life of another policies

34.13 Where the policy is written on the life of another it is of course essential to ensure that the proceeds are paid to the assured, not to the life assured.

Policies in trust

34.14 If the policy is written in trust, the maturity value should be paid to the trustees, whose receipt acts as a good discharge to the company. It is then for the trustees to apply this money in accordance with the terms of the trust, and the fate of the money after it is paid to the insurance company is not a matter with which the company need concern itself. The proceeds should not be paid to anyone claiming or appearing to be a beneficiary, since the beneficiaries do not have legal title to the proceeds and it is not possible for the company to be sure that any one or more beneficiaries has an unencumbered right to the proceeds without making exhaustive investigations as to the history of the trust.

Assigned and mortgaged policies

34.15 In the same way the proceeds of policies which have been assigned or mortgaged must be paid to the person beneficially entitled. It is likely that an assignor or mortgagor to whom the proceeds are wrongly paid will hold them on trust for the rightful owner, but the company should not rely on this, since the rightful owner may still choose to sue the company, which will have no defence, and may be forced to do so if the assignor or mortgagor has disposed of the proceeds or has disappeared.

Misapplication of maturity proceeds

34.16 In theory this should never happen, provided that the principles set out above are correctly applied. In practice, however, there are always a number of ways in which things can go wrong. Although these ways generally do no more than illustrate some important general rules of law, it may be useful to discuss them at this point.

Payment of cheques

34.17 The rules relating to the payment and collection of cheques are well-established, but there is sometimes confusion about their operation. The changes introduced in this area by the Cheques Act 1992 also need to be noted.

The basic rules are contained in the Bills of Exchange Act 1882, as amended by the Cheques Acts 1957 and 1992. It is necessary to distinguish between the *paying* bank and the *collecting* bank. The paying bank is the bank on whom the cheque is drawn, ie the bank with which the drawer of the cheque has an account. The collecting bank is the bank into which the cheque is paid by the payee. Sometimes the same bank will act in both capacities, but this does not affect the operation of the general principle.

It is a more or less invariable practice at the present day for cheques to be crossed. Under the Bills of Exchange Act 1882 a cheque may be crossed generally or specially. A cheque crossed generally may be collected by any bank, but a specially crossed cheque may only be collected by the bank to which it is crossed. In practice specially crossed cheques are rarely if ever found at the present day. In the simple case where the cheque is paid to a bank by the original payee and is properly collected by that bank from the drawer's bank, no difficulty should arise. The situation which is in practice most likely to give rise to problems is that which occurs where the cheque has been (or apparently been) indorsed by the payee in favour of a third party.

'Indorsement' literally means no more than writing on the back of the cheque. Where it is desired to indorse a cheque the usual practice is to write on the back of it an instruction to pay the cheque to some third party, and to sign it. It goes without saying that a valid indorsement can only be made by the person for the time being entitled to the cheque or his agent. There is, however, the obvious risk of fraudulently forged indorsement.

Where a crossed cheque is properly indorsed and is paid without negligence on the part of the paying bank the effect of s 80 of the Bills of Exchange Act 1882 is that the paying bank is put in the same position as if the cheque had come into the hands of the true owner thereof. In other words, the bank is entitled to accept the indorsement and pay the indorsee, and, provided that there has been no negligence on the part of the bank, the original payee will have no action against them. Where the cheque has come into the hands of the indorsee, the same protection is afforded to the drawer of the cheque (which in the cases presently under consideration will be the insurer). It is to be noted that the protection of the drawer applies only where the cheque has actually come into the hands of the payee. It does not apply where a third party has fraudulently secured payment of an indorsed cheque, even though the paying bank would normally be protected in such a case. These principles must now be read subject to the amendments made by the Cheques Act 1992, discussed below.

The position of the collecting bank is dealt with by s 4 of the Cheques Act 1957. This provides that a bank which is acting in good faith and without negligence collects a cheque does not incur liability merely because the cheque is improperly indorsed. It is of course clear that the person to whom the money is wrongly paid will normally be liable to repay it, but the practical difficulty in the great majority of cases is that the wrongful payment involves a fraud on the part of the person presenting the cheque, and that person will have absconded and/or spent the money by the time the fraud comes to light.

Payment to wrong person

34.18 Administrative error may occasionally lead to a cheque being issued in favour of the wrong person. The consequences of this will almost inevitably fall on the company, since there is a strict obligation to pay the person properly entitled, which cannot be discharged by paying anyone else without the consent of the person entitled. This rule also applies where an application for the maturity proceeds is submitted under a forged signature purportedly of the person entitled. Since a forged document is a nullity[1] it follows that the company cannot rely upon having paid the proceeds in response to it. There is of course a right of recourse against the fraudster to whom the money has been paid. It is also likely that the company will have a right to recover money wrongly paid to a third party as a result of simple mistake, since in cases of this kind the mistake will usually be one of fact[2] rather than one of law[3], though it is no longer a complete bar to recovery that the mistake is one of law.

1 *Ruben v Great Fingall Consolidated* [1906] AC 439.

2 *Kelly v Solari* (1841) 9 M & W 54.

3 *Kleinwort Benson v Lincoln CC* [1999] 2 AC 349, HL, overruling *Bilbie v Lumley* (1802) 2 East 469.

Maturity cheque misappropriated by intermediary

34.19 Where a maturity cheque is entrusted to an intermediary for transmission to the policyholder it is not unknown for the cheque to be misappropriated. In this very difficult situation the first question to be asked is as to the character of the intermediary. where the intermediary is a company representative, the position is quite clear. The company has not discharged its obligation to pay the proceeds to the policyholder, who is entitled to demand them afresh. The company is left with a right of action against the intermediary, though in many cases this will no doubt be useless, since the intermediary will have vanished or will be insolvent.

Where the intermediary is an independent financial adviser, the position is less clear. In principle such a person is agent for the policyholder rather than for the company, and payment to him is payment to the policyholder, provided that he has actual or apparent authority to receive maturity cheques. This is of course a question of fact in each case. If he has no such authority, then this is to be treated as a case of mistaken payment to a third party. If, for any reason, he can be treated as the agent of the insurer for these purposes, there is no payment to anyone until the intermediary deals with the cheque.

Maturity cheque misappropriated by stranger

34.20 Here there is little doubt that the company is liable to pay the maturity sum to the policyholder, provided of course that the misappropriation happens before the cheque reaches the policyholder. The only possible exception arises where the misappropriation occurs through some negligence on the part of the policyholder. A possible situation of this kind would be where the policyholder has given the insurer the wrong address to send the cheque to.

It is assumed in the foregoing paragraphs that the maturity cheque has been made payable to the policyholder rather than to the intermediary. If the cheque is payable to the intermediary, then the latter can only misappropriate the proceeds, not the cheque itself. It is thought that no insurance company would be likely to make a maturity cheque payable to one of its own agents, so the only serious possibility here is that the cheque has been made payable to an independent intermediary. Here it seems that the payment must be made to the intermediary as agent of the policyholder. Consequently, assuming that the intermediary has apparent authority for this purpose, the loss will be borne by the policyholder. However, the practice of making cheques payable to the intermediary is so obviously dangerous that it may be doubted whether a company is justified, in the absence of specific authority, in assuming that the intermediary is authorised to receive payment in this way.

Precautions to be taken

34.21 Given the obvious risks inherent in the dispatch of maturity cheques, it is appropriate to draw attention to certain security precautions which may be found worthwhile. First, maturity cheques should always be sent by post *directly* to the policyholder. They should never be entrusted to representatives. As an additional precaution the cheques should be made payable to the policyholder (never to an intermediary for reasons discussed in the previous paragraph), and should be marked 'Not Transferable' and 'a/c payee only'. Cheques for this purpose should not include the words 'or order' after the payee's name. Note that it is not sufficient to mark the cheque 'Not negotiable', since this does not prevent an endorsement. The position in this respect was altered somewhat by the Cheques Act 1992, which provides that a cheque marked 'Not Negotiable' shall not be a negotiable instrument, and shall therefore not be capable of being transferred. Unfortunately, this provision appears to fall some way short of providing full protection in these cases. It does not prevent such a cheque being made into a cheque payable to cash by the addition of the words 'Pay Cash' across the crossing (a change which could readily be made by a rogue) nor does it prevent the transferability of cheques not so marked.

The bank's position

34.22 Where the proceeds have been paid to the wrong person, the insurer is likely to want to know whether it has any remedy against the bank or banks involved in the collection and payment of the cheque. The position in such a case depends largely upon the provisions of the Cheques Acts 1957 and 1992 and the terms on which the insurers bank provides it with banking services.

It is again necessary to distinguish between the *paying* bank and the *collecting* bank. The collecting bank will rarely have any liability, since the duty which it owes to the insurance company is no more than an ordinary common law duty of care. Unless there are circumstances which ought to put the bank on notice that the payment is likely to be improper, it does not seem that this duty will be breached. The position of the paying bank is more difficult. This will be the insurer's bank, and will therefore be in a contractual relationship with the insurer. The result is therefore likely to depend on the terms of that contract; in general it may be supposed that those terms are likely to exclude liability in the absence of negligence.

Choices available at maturity

Continuation options

34.23 Some policies provide that on maturity the policyholder has the option to leave the proceeds invested with the company, either as part of a new policy or on the same terms as the original policy. This may be an attractive option to a policyholder who has no immediate need of the money and who wishes to give it the opportunity to grow further. At least two problems arise here. The first is that the policyholder will normally need to notify the insurer of his wish to exercise this option before the maturity date, since the insurer is otherwise obliged to pay the maturity value not later than the maturity date. The second problem arises where for some reason the policyholder does not give notice in time. Both insurer and policyholder may be prepared to allow the reinvestment of the money after the maturity date, but there are tax implications to this. Where the original policy was a qualifying policy this status will be lost unless the reinvestment takes place not later than 21 days after the maturity date. Because this is an Inland Revenue rule, it is not open to the parties to dispense with it. Disputes may therefore arise where the company has failed to notify the policyholder of the impending maturity and to ask him whether he wants to exercise the continuation option. The general principle is that there is no duty on the company to do this, though it is accepted as being good insurance practice to do so. It appears unfortunately to be the practice of some companies to ask policyholders about reinvestment options after the policy has matured rather than before and close enough to the 21-day deadline to make tax-efficient reinvestment impossible. The Insurance Ombudsman has taken the view that this practice is improper and has required companies engaging in it to put policyholders in the same position as if they had had proper notice of the continuation option.

Bonuses

34.24 In a with-profits policy a significant part of the total return will be made up of reversionary bonuses and terminal bonuses. The former are normally declared annually, and cannot be taken away once declared (it is in this respect that a with-profits policy differs from a pure unit-linked policy). The latter are determined only at the maturity date, and their level will depend on the recent performance of the underlying fund. In practice the terminal bonus often represents a major part of the maturity sum, and questions relating to it have naturally arisen.

Bonuses not guaranteed

34.25 It is integral to the notion of terminal bonuses that their level cannot be guaranteed in advance. Many companies issue projections of maturity values based upon the assumption that terminal bonus rates will not change. This is an understandable practice, but also a dangerous one, for policyholders tend to rely upon these projections and are disappointed when they are not met. The point is of course especially important in an era when bonus rates have tended to drop because of poor economic conditions – few policyholders complain when the maturity sum is greater then they expect. The projections may be issued in response to a specific request from the policyholder or may be contained in annual statements issued as a matter of routine. In either case it is important to ensure that the projection is accompanied by a suitable disclaimer referring to the uncertainty of the continuation of bonus rates and the risk that the projected value will not be achieved.

Where the company is aware that the projection will almost certainly not be achieved – as where the policy is very close to maturity and a decision has already been taken to cut bonus rates – the Insurance Ombudsman ruled in 1993 that the projection should be accompanied by a suitable statement to this effect. Although there is no reported case on the matter, it is submitted that this is merely an application of the continuing duty of utmost good faith. However, this does not altogether resolve the difficulty. It may be that there has not yet been any formal decision to cut rates, but that the likelihood of such a cut is in the mind of senior executives of the company. In such a case it is suggested that it is impossible to draft any satisfactory statement to policyholders, for no information can be given as to the extent of any cut; indeed it cannot even be confirmed that there will be a cut. The only workable rule in such a case appears to be that no statement need be made until a formal decision has been taken. The statement does of course require very careful wording, for it is easy to confuse policyholders by sending them simultaneously two apparently contradictory projections, both of which may ultimately prove to be inaccurate. In more recent times insurance companies have adopted the practice of reducing the annual bonuses declared on policies with the intention of leaving themselves as much flexibility as possible in dealing with the terminal bonus.

It may be added that events over the past few years, in particular the collapse of Equitable Life after it was held liable to honour promises it had made to its with-profits policyholders[1], have cast grave doubt on the survival of with-profits policies at all in the coming years. It seems highly likely that far fewer such policies will be begun in future, though of course there will for many years be a residue of such policies, so that it will still be necessary to be familiar with the issues to which they give rise.

1 *Equitable Life Assurance Society v Hyman* [2002] 1 AC 408, HL.

Surrender

34.26 Where the policyholder wishes to surrender the policy before the maturity date various problems may arise. These are considered in the following paragraphs.

Calculating surrender value

34.27 In a unit-linked policy the surrender value is normally calculated by ascertaining the value of the units allocated to the policy at the surrender date. As this value is subject to market fluctuations it cannot be guaranteed in advance. This can be a source of difficulty when policyholders ask for the surrender value before submitting a surrender request and are dismayed to discover that the value has fallen by the date of surrender. This risk is inherent in the contract, but any quotation of surrender value given by the company should be expressly stated to be valid only for the day on which it is given.

Joint policies

34.28 Where a policy is in joint names (a joint endowment to support a mortgage is the most common example) it is necessary to have the consent of both policyholders for a surrender request. This may cause difficulties where only one party wants to surrender, but it must be understood that the company cannot properly accept a surrender request from only one of the policyholders. A purported surrender in response to such a request would leave the company obliged to reinstate the policy at the request of the other policyholder or, if this were impossible, to put the other policyholder in as good a position as if the policy had not been surrendered. The calculation of what this principle would require in any given case may cause some difficulty. This is particularly difficult where one of the joint policyholders induces the insurer to pay him/her the whole policy proceeds, perhaps by misrepresenting that the other policyholder consents to this. The non-consenting policyholder appears to have an unanswerable claim to have the policy reinstated at the insurer's expense, leaving the insurer to pursue its remedies against the policyholder who induced the surrender. If a cash payment is to be made, then one half of the surrender value at the date of surrender would seem to be a reasonable starting point, but this will not in fact represent full compensation, since the system of front-loading commission charges means that the policyholder could not immediately use it to recreate a valid policy with the same surrender value. An additional sum would have to be added to cover this.

A different issue about joint policies arose in *Murphy v Murphy*[1], where husband and wife took out a pure term assurance on a first life basis. Later they divorced, but payments on the policy were maintained. When the ex-husband died it became necessary to decide for the purposes of the Inheritance (Provision for Family and Dependants) Act 1975 whether his estate was entitled to half the policy proceeds. The Court of Appeal held that he was not because the purpose of the policy was pure protection, ie there was no investment element and the logical conclusion was that husband and wife were to be severally entitled to the policy proceeds, rather than jointly entitled.

1 [2003] EWCA Civ 1862, [2004] Lloyd's Rep IR 744, CA.

Delays in implementing surrender request

34.29 If a surrender request is not promptly implemented the policyholder may suffer loss in either of two ways. First, in a unit-linked policy the value of the units may decline between the date when the surrender should have happened and the date when it in fact happens. Secondly, the policyholder may have been planning to use the surrender proceeds to finance some other transaction, which may be made more expensive or even impossible by the delay. In the first case the position seems clear enough. The policy will normally lay down the rules applying in relation to surrender – it is common to provide that the surrender will be calculated at the values prevailing on the day after a properly completed surrender request is received by the company. Here the company is obliged to provide a surrender value calculated on that basis. If through administrative error the relevant units are not sold at the correct time, that loss falls on the company and not on the policyholder. If the policy says nothing about the date of surrender, it is suggested that a court would imply a requirement to effect the surrender reasonably promptly, but it is by no means clear that this would always mean the next day after the surrender request was received. So long as there was not undue delay, the policyholder would probably have to accept whatever unit value prevailed on the day of surrender. In the second case considered above the policyholder's position appears to depend on the ordinary rules of remoteness of damage in contract, according to which damages for breach of contract are recoverable only to the extent that the defendant could see the resulting loss as likely to result from the breach in question[1]. Although the exact level of probability required is a matter of some doubt and dispute it is suggested that in the great majority of cases the company is not required to assume that the policyholder has any other transaction depending on the receipt of the surrender value. The only exception to this would appear to be the case where the policyholder specifically informs the company that the money is required by a given date.

1 *Hadley v Baxendale* (1854) 9 Exch 341; *The Heron II* [1969] 1 AC 350; *H Parsons (Livestock) Ltd v Uttley Ingham* [1978] QB 791.

Mortgages of life policies

34.30 Mortgages may be of importance in two related but distinct situations when dealing with life policies. The more common situation is that of a mortgage of land secured by an endowment mortgage. The less common situation is where the policy itself is mortgaged to secure a loan not associated with land.

Mortgages of land

34.31 It may be helpful to begin with a brief account of the nature of mortgages of land. A mortgage is an interest in land created in order to provide security for a loan. The owner of the land becomes the mortgagor and the lender becomes the mortgagee. A mortgage does not normally[1] involve the transfer of the legal ownership of the property to the mortgagee, who obtains only a limited interest. An important consequence of this is that the mortgagor retains the right to deal with the land. The mortgage is capable of being transferred with the land, and will be so transferred unless it is discharged by the vendor. It is for this reason that a purchaser will normally insist that the vendor must discharge the mortgage out of the proceeds of sale.

The terms of a mortgage will normally state the date on which it is to be redeemed, and this date is often a relatively short time after the date of creation. In practice it is of course contemplated that most mortgages of land will last for many years, and the parties do not really intend that the mortgage shall be redeemed on the stated date. This curious fiction has its origins in the land law of an earlier generation. What is important to understand at the present day is that the mortgagor retains the right to redeem the mortgage even after the legal date for redemption has passed. This right is known as the equity of redemption, and may be exercised at any time before the lender has foreclosed on the loan.

The equity of redemption is a fundamental right of the borrower, which cannot be taken away by any provision in the mortgage[2].

It is usual for the mortgagee to require the documents of title to the property to be deposited with him. The practical reason for this is that it is not normally possible to sell or mortgage the land without these documents, and a mortgagee who has possession of them is therefore in a position to prevent the mortgagor from dealing with the land without his consent[3].

A mortgage will always be granted at a rate of interest, which will be payable at intervals. In a repayment mortgage the capital sum will also be repaid over the mortgage term. If the mortgagor defaults in making payments on the due date it may become possible for the mortgagee to foreclose on the mortgage. Foreclosure involves the mortgagee taking possession of the land and selling it in order to discharge the sums outstanding on the mortgage. After these sums have been discharged any remaining proceeds of sale belong to the mortgagor. Where the mortgaged property is over a dwelling house, the mortgagee may not take possession of the property without a court order[4].

[1] Although it is possible to create a mortgage in this way, this is never done in the modern practice in relation to land.

[2] *Toomes v Conset* (1745) 3 Atk 261; *Samuel v Jarrah Timber* [1904] AC 323.
[3] Though it should be noted that it is possible to grant a lease without these documents, since a lessee has no right to see the lessor's documents of title: LPA 1925, s 44.
[4] AJA 1970, s 35.

The borrower's position

34.32 This section deals with the position of a borrower under an endowment mortgage backed by a policy of life assurance. The mortgage must be assigned to the lender, a practice permitted by the PAA 1867. For the rules relating to assignment of policies see Chapter 15. The borrower is nevertheless obliged to continue to pay the premiums on the policy in order to protect the lender's position. If the borrower is able to repay the mortgage before the policy matures, he is entitled to maintain the policy if he continues to pay the premiums. He may also be entitled to insist that the policy be re-assigned to him by the lender, if the mortgage terms so provide. Even if he is not entitled to insist on re-assignment, the mortgagee would of course have to hold the policy proceeds on trust for the mortgagor, since there would no longer be any mortgage left to discharge out of those proceeds.

If the borrower defaults in paying the premiums, there is an obvious risk that the policy may lapse or may become paid up. This will amount to a breach by the borrower of the terms of the mortgage, and may well render him liable to the direct enforcement by the borrower of the original security. The benefit, such as it is, of the policy, will remain with the lender, who will be entitled to claim any surrender or paid-up value to be used in discharge of the borrower's liability.

Where a dispute arises between borrower and insurer as to the terms of the insurance policy, the position of the borrower is somewhat unclear. He no longer has the beneficial interest in the policy, and it may therefore be that he is not entitled to bring an action in respect of the dispute. It is necessary to examine those provisions of the Judicature Acts which deal with the consequences of assignment.

The position with regard to a complaint to the FSO is also uncertain. The Ombudsman's Terms of Reference preclude a complaint by a third party who has acquired the interest in the policy for value, and the mortgagee is obviously in that position. Although the point does not appear to have arisen as yet in any case before the Ombudsman, it is generally thought that no company would wish to take this point, though it appears that the Ombudsman would have to honour any such refusal to accept the jurisdiction. Of course the point could fairly readily be circumvented if the original policyholder were prepared to participate in the complaint. In some cases of course the borrower will have no real incentive to give this agreement, because he does not stand to gain anything from the resolution of the dispute. However, it is necessary for these purposes to distinguish between cases where the real complaint is by the borrower and cases where the real complaint is by the lender. In the former event, it appears that the borrower may complain to the Ombudsman, notwithstanding that he has assigned the policy. Presumably he will have some pecuniary interest in the matter, since he would otherwise be unlikely to bother complaining, and it would be possible to argue that he retains some interest in the policy since he has the expectation that it will be re-assigned to him if he repays the mortgage and that he will on maturity receive any excess of the policy value over the amount needed to repay the mortgage. The Ombudsman apparently has jurisdiction, and it is unlikely that he would decline to help the policyholder merely on the technical ground of the assignment. If the policyholder no longer had any real interest in the dispute, then it is suggested that the Ombudsman may well decline to intervene, although the matter would technically be within his powers.

The lender's position

Death or default

34.33 On the death of the borrower before the expiry of the mortgage term the policy moneys will become payable. As the policy will have been assigned to the lender, it is the lender who is entitled to receive those moneys, which will be applied to the reduction of the mortgage debt.

Discharge of mortgage

34.34 It may happen that the mortgagor is able to discharge an endowment mortgage before the intended maturity date if he acquires the necessary money from some other source. Although the mortgage and the policy are linked in the sense that one was taken out to secure the other, it does not follow that the policy automatically comes to an end on the discharge of the mortgage. The policy is, despite its purpose, merely a life policy, and the assured is entitled to keep it on foot by paying the premiums, and will then be entitled to the sum due at maturity in the usual way. The point which should, however, be noted, is that on the discharge of the mortgage the borrower is entitled to have the policy re-assigned to him by the lender, since the lender's charge over the property no longer exists, and there is no longer any need for the policy to secure that charge.

Position at maturity

34.35 Where the policy has been assigned to support a mortgage, some at least of the policy proceeds will normally be required in order to discharge the mortgage. However, the mortgagee is naturally entitled only to sufficient money to discharge the mortgage, and any surplus belongs to the policyholder. The company should therefore take care to pay to the mortgagee only the amount outstanding on the mortgage.

Forfeiture[1]

34.36 In exceptional cases the common law doctrine of forfeiture may need to be considered in relation to a life policy which is supporting a mortgage. The most vivid example is provided by the case of *Davitt v Titcumb*[2]. A man and a woman who were cohabitees, bought a house as tenants in common in unequal shares. The purchase was funded largely by means of an endowment mortgage. Then the man murdered the woman, and was in due course sentenced to life imprisonment. The policy was written on a first life basis, so that the policy moneys became payable on the woman's death. Although there were obvious objections to allowing the man to benefit from his own wrongful act, a refusal to pay the policy moneys would have been prejudicial to the estate of the deceased woman, since her estate remained liable for the payment of the mortgage. The insurers accordingly paid the policy proceeds to the estate of the deceased woman. The proceeds were insufficient to discharge the mortgage, but when the house was subsequently sold a question arose as to entitlement to the net proceeds of sale. It was ultimately held that these should go in their entirety to the estate of the deceased woman, notwithstanding that she and the man had held the house as tenants in common rather than as joint tenants. From an insurance point of view the interest of the case lies less in the ultimate destination of the proceeds of sale, since the insurers had no control over these, than in the treatment of the policy proceeds. In the event the insurers paid these to the estate without a court order. It seems clear that they were right to do so, following two decisions arising out of celebrated murder cases in the late nineteenth and early twentieth centuries. in *Re Crippen's Estate (decd)*[3] Evans P said:

> 'It is clear that the law is that no person can obtain, or enforce, any rights resulting to him from his own crime; neither can his representative, claiming under him, obtain or enforce any such rights.'

However, in *Cleaver v Mutual Reserve Fund Life Assurance*[4], which arose out of the case of James and Florence Maybrick, the Court of Appeal held that the proceeds of a Married Women's Property Act policy on the life of the deceased could be paid to the deceased's executors, notwithstanding that the terms of the trust required those proceeds to be held on trust for his wife, who had murdered him. The undesirable consequence of the wife benefiting from the murder was avoided by holding that the proceeds were to be held for the beneficiaries of the estate other than the wife. In the present case the matter is slightly different because the parties were not married to each other, and the policy was not a Married Women's Property Act policy. In fact, this serves to simplify the position, since the man was not entitled to any of the deceased woman's property on an intestacy, even if he had no responsibility for her death.

1 For a fuller account of this topic, see Chapter 20.
2 [1989] 3 All ER 417, Scott J.
3 [1911] P 108, Evans P.
4 [1892] 1 QB 147, CA.

Mortgages of the policy

34.37 Where the policy is not taken out in connection with a mortgage of land, it may be used as a security for some other loan (including but not limited to a loan secured on a mortgage). Indeed, some insurance companies are willing to lend money on the security of a policy effected with themselves. The amount of the loan which may be obtained will naturally depend on the surrender value of the policy at the time of the loan, and will usually be only a proportion of that value.

A mortgage of a life policy is significantly different from a mortgage of land, for the policy is personal property, whereas the land is real property. For this reason it is usual for a mortgage of a policy to take the form of a conveyance of the ownership of the policy to the mortgagee, together with a proviso that the mortgagee's ownership shall cease when the loan secured on the policy is redeemed.

Surrender of policy documents

34.38 It does not appear to be the usual practice to require the policyholder to deposit the policy documents with the mortgagee of the policy. This opens the possibility of successive mortgages of the same policy. This practice is not necessarily objectionable – the surrender value may have been greater than the original loan, and may have increased since the original loan was taken out – but it does create problems in relation to the priority as between successive mortgagees. This point will become relevant where it becomes necessary to foreclose on one or more of the loans, and it then becomes apparent that the policy is not sufficient security for all the loans which have been made on it, and that the policyholder does not have sufficient other resources to discharge the outstanding debts. If the first mortgagee has protected himself by requiring the deposit of title deeds, then this will effectively protect him, for no subsequent mortgagee can claim to be unaware of the existence of the prior mortgage[1]. In all other cases it is necessary to identify the date of creation of each of the mortgages and the date on which notice of them was given to the prior mortgagees, since a mortgage not protected by deposit of the title deeds will be a purely equitable mortgage, and whether a second or subsequent mortgagee takes free of prior encumbrances will depend upon whether he can claim to be a *bona fide* purchaser for value without notice (actual or constructive) of those prior encumbrances. Since constructive knowledge will extend to any information which would have been obtained by the making of reasonable enquiries (whether these were in fact made or not) the subsequent mortgagee is unlikely to succeed unless he can show that he asked the policyholder about the existence of prior mortgages and was told that there were none. If his ignorance results from a failure to enquire, he will take subject to the earlier mortgage(s).

[1] *Dearle v Hall* (1823) 3 Russ 1, 38 ER 475; *Spencer v Clarke* (1878) 9 Ch D 137, V-C Hall.

Position of insurance company

34.39 If the policy matures or is the subject of a claim while subject to a mortgage of this type, the company should pay the policy proceeds to the holder of the first mortgage of which it has notice. The question of any surplus will not arise as between the company and any other party, since the policy is mortgaged as a whole rather than in part. If the policy proceeds are more than sufficient to discharge the debt, the mortgagee will hold the proceeds for the benefit of the mortgagor, to whom he will be obliged to account, but the company need not concern itself with this process.

Charges

34.40 Charges should be distinguished from mortgages. In a charge no proprietary interest in the property is transferred, but the property is charged with the performance of another obligation (usually a debt). This means that if the obligation is not performed, the chargee may take and sell the charged property as a means of recouping his debt, accounting to the chargor for any remaining surplus. As the chargee is not as such entitled to possession of the charged property, a court order for the sale of the property will be required.

Other remedies of the chargee, such as the appointment of a receiver, are of little relevance to life policies.

In a few cases it may be important to know whether a security interest created over a life policy is a mortgage or a charge. This will most commonly occur where the borrower commits some default, for the remedies available differ as between the two types of security. In the context of life policies[1] the principal distinction is that a mortgagee may sell the charged property without applying to the court, whereas a chargee may not.

Although a mortgagee is entitled to possession of the mortgaged property, whereas a chargee has no right to possession of the charged property, it is not safe to attempt to distinguish the two types of security interest according to whether possession has been taken, for, as mentioned above mortgagees of life policies do not normally take possession of them, particularly where the mortgagee is the insurance company itself.

In the end, the distinction rests on the intention of the parties, though this will have to be judged by the external evidence of what they did at the time the security interest was created[2]. In case of doubt the only safe course for the holder of the security is to apply to court for an order for sale, but this may be slow and prohibitively expensive. Ideally, the loan documentation should make clear the nature of the agreement; if this is not done, it may be necessary to seek some solution other than sale of the policy even in the case of default on the mortgage.

[1] For a fuller account of the differences see Bridge *Personal Property Law* (1993, Blackstone).
[2] Bridge (n 1 above) mentions various cases on the distinction, but these are all cases involving land and appear to turn very much on their own facts.

Mis-selling of whole of life policies and long-term savings policies

34.41 The mis-selling of life assurance is a major problem within the financial services industry. Some of the issues in this regard were explored in Chapter 6 Intermediaries. This section deals with one specific problem, namely the sale of long-term savings policies, including whole of life policies.

It is commonplace for company representatives to sell life assurance policies essentially as savings vehicles. It can be argued very strongly that this fundamentally confuses the nature of insurance as a means of protection and the nature of savings and investment, but the practice continues unabated. However, the sale of such products raises serious difficulties in relation to the requirement that only suitable products should be sold. Two broad questions may be identified. The first is, when is an insurance policy a suitable savings vehicle? The second is what steps should be taken to provide adequate recompense when a mis-sale is found to have occurred?

The complexities of the first question are perhaps best explained by a consideration of some of the essential elements of long-term insurance policies. Such contracts obviously provide life cover, though at a cost. The standard charging structure means that these contracts yield their best benefits only if they are allowed to continue for some considerable time. On the other side of the case it may be said that over the medium to long term investment contracts based on equities have always outperformed those which are purely savings vehicles. It follows that these contracts are suitable for those people who can meet certain requirements at the point of sale. These may be expressed as follows:

(1) A genuine need for life assurance. In the absence of this need some other investment contract, such as a regular investment in a unit trust or investment trust, may be suitable.
(2) A reasonable expectation of being able to continue the payments regularly throughout the projected period of the policy. Without this it may be more appropriate to have an equity-based investment which can accept one-off payments at irregular intervals.
(3) A reasonable expectation that there will be no need to take money out of the policy before the maturity date[1]. Without this, it is more appropriate to have other types of equity-based investment or even a simple savings account.
(4) A willingness to accept that the value of the investment is liable to fluctuate. Without this, a simple savings account is the appropriate product.

The difficulty is that these requirements, taken cumulatively, eliminate from consideration a very large number of people. They appear to eliminate all those who have no dependents, since they have no apparent need for life assurance. They appear to eliminate all those who cannot be sure of remaining in gainful employment or otherwise having sources of income for the full duration of the policy. This would include virtually all women of child-bearing age who have not yet completed their families. In an era when guaranteed employment is scarcely to be found, it might be thought that many men were eliminated for the same reason. The proportion of people eliminated under this criterion naturally varies with the length of the policy. Criterion 3 eliminates those for whom the purpose of saving is to put aside money against some unforeseen need. In other words the funds for these policies need to come from disposable income. Criterion 4 further eliminates those who are risk-averse.

It would be absurd to suppose that in practice long-term insurance policies are sold only to those who fully meet all four of the above criteria. Policies of ten years and upwards are routinely sold to groups other than those for whom they are suitable.

[1] Though some policies do allow a limited amount of borrowing against the accrued value of the policy.

Compensation and redress

34.42 Where a mis-sale of this kind is found to have occurred, the proper approach to redress is, as always, to put the investor back to the position as it would have been in the absence of the mis-sale. This will usually involve setting aside the policy and ordering a return of premiums paid, with interest. At the same time the investor will of course lose any accrued benefit in the investment fund built up from the premiums. In returning the premiums no deduction should be made for life cover, since the setting aside of the policy operates *ab initio*, and the life cover must therefore be treated as never having existed.

Selling a whole of life policy as something else

34.43 One further particular problem to which attention should be drawn is that of the mis-selling of whole of life policies by leading investors to believe that they are in fact ten-year savings plans. PIAOB has commented on these mis-sales on a number of occasions[1]. The mis-sale appears often to take the form of the representative telling the investor that the policy can be cashed in tax-free after ten years. The statement is literally true, but is misleading in two important respects. First, the tax benefits are really only of value to higher-rate taxpayers, since standard rate taxpayers would have no tax liability in any event. Secondly, and much more seriously, it is not true to say that by the end of ten years the policy will necessarily have absorbed all the very considerable upfront charges, so that the investor gets a proper return on the investment. Of course the statement made by the representative does not specifically say otherwise, but it is designed to concentrate the mind of the investor on the idea that this is really a ten-year policy. It might be asked why a representative would engage in misleading statements of this kind. The answer is that a whole of life policy attracts a higher level of commission than does a ten-year policy. A good example of a mis-sale may be found at PIAOB 98–99, paragraph 15.5. The complainant was a 19-year-old receptionist, single with no dependants. Her main need was for a savings plan, but she was sold a whole of life policy with an initial sum assured of over £12,000. There was no possible justification for this sale, which was set aside, premiums being returned, plus interest and an additional payment of £100 for distress and inconvenience. In that case there was no reason to sell a life policy at all, but the position is more complicated where a life policy is in principle suitable, but the length of the policy sold is excessive. As a matter of law it would appear that in such a case the only available remedy is still the return of premiums with interest. In practice, however, the Ombudsman has been inclined to approach the problem somewhat differently. It can be argued that the fairest solution is to re-write the policy, so that it retrospectively becomes a policy for the proper length in the circumstances. This involves a reduction in the charges levied on the plan and a recalculation of the number of units credited to the policy. The PIA Ombudsman routinely required companies to do this in appropriate cases, and, given that FOS, unlike PIAOB, has a fair and reasonable clause in its terms of reference, it seems reasonable to assume that the practice will continue under FOS.

[1] PIAOB 95–96, 96–97, 98–99.

Chapter 35

Personal accident policies

Introduction

35.1 Personal accident policies are first-party contingency policies which pay specified amounts on the happening of particular accidents. It is usual to determine the amount payable by reference to the nature of the injury suffered by the policyholder. These policies are not liability policies, and one important consequence of this is that the amounts recoverable for particular injuries do not need to have any relationship with the amounts which might be recovered for those injuries in legal proceedings.

It must be acknowledged at the outset that there is a problem with the marketing of personal accident policies, which is the direct cause of many of the difficulties in this area. These policies are often presented to policyholders as offering extensive cover at a relatively low premium. The truth is that the low premium is achieved only by including quite significant restrictions and exceptions of the cover. Difficulties inevitably arise at claims stage when policyholders realise for the first time that the cover is not what they had been led to believe.

Policy coverage

Meaning of 'accident'[1]

35.2 This is a question which is a good deal more difficult than might at first appear. It is suggested that the difficulty comes largely from the fact that the notion of an accident may be regarded as having two principal characteristics. The first is that the event was unexpected and the second is that it is unintended. In both cases the matter should be looked at from the point of view of the person suffering the accident. Thus, it has been observed[2] that it would be a misuse of language to say that Charles I died after meeting with an accident, though his death was from his point of view unplanned and undesired. Equally, a person who suffered injury as the result of a practical joke or even as the result of a deliberate attack might well regard himself as having suffered an accident, though in either case it might equally be said that the consequences were neither unexpected nor unintended from the point of view of the other parties.

[1] This may be contrasted with the term 'occurrence', which is considered in Chapter 41 and with 'loss' and 'damage' which are considered in Chapters 38 and 39.
[2] Atiyah *Accidents, Compensation and the Law* (1999, Butterworths).

35.3 The classic judicial statement on this subject is found in *Sinclair v Maritime Passengers' Assurance Co*[1].

It is difficult to define the term accident as used in a policy of this nature so as to draw with perfect accuracy a boundary line between injury or death from accident and injury or death from natural causes, such as shall be of universal application. At the same time we may safely assume that, in the term 'accident' as so used, some violence, casualty or *vis major* is necessarily involved. We cannot think disease produced by the action of a known cause can be considered as accidental.

This passage emphasises the sudden, external and normally violent nature of an 'accident', and in so doing contrasts injury or, more particularly, death caused by accident from that resulting from natural causes[2]. The distinction is fundamental, for a personal accident policy is not the same thing as a life policy. The latter would normally cover death from natural causes, but the former would not.

In *Hamlyn v Crown Accident Insurance Co Ltd*[3] the policyholder bent down to pick up a marble and in so doing injured his knee. It was held that the injury was accidental. Although the policyholder had obviously intended to bend down, he did not intend or expect to injure his knee in doing so. The Insurance Ombudsman took a similar approach in a case[4] where the policyholder fell forward while working in a physical occupation and slipped a disc. The insurers sought to argue that the accident was not fortuitous, since it happened in the course of the policyholder's normal work activity. Not surprisingly, this line of argument was rejected, and the injury was held to be accidental. However, the IOB report of the decision contains the suggestion that the result might be different if the injury could be said to be of a kind which was 'routine, regular and everyday'. Presumably the explanation for this is that such an injury could not readily be classed as unexpected. This point may be illustrated by another IOB case[5], where the policyholder strained his back while playing baseball – he swung at the ball, but missed and strained his back in the process. It was held that the circumstances of the injury were to be regarded as a normal and commonplace part of playing baseball; thus they could not be considered to be unexpected, and the injury was not caused by an accident.

A case often quoted in the UK is the American decision in *Preferred Insurance Co v Clark*[6], where it was said that death during a common operation such as an appendectomy would not be considered accidental. However, the Insurance Ombudsman has held that contracting a rare disease during an operation might well nowadays be regarded as an accident within the meaning of a personal accident policy[7], though it might be different if the problem were something relatively common such as a septic infection. A similar view was taken in the New Zealand case of *Groves v AMP Fire and General Insurance Co*[8] where the policyholder died after having an adverse reaction to an anaesthetic. The chances of death from this cause were estimated on the medical evidence to be 1 in 125,000 operations. The insurers argued that the death was not accidental because the administration of the anaesthetic was deliberate, but Jeffries J held that this was not the critical test. An accident is something which is 'unforeseen unexpected, extraordinary, an unlooked for mishap', and what happened in this case fell within those words.

In one IOB case[9] it appeared that the policyholder had died from auto-erotic asphyxiation. As he had held a personal accident policy, the question was whether the death resulted from 'accidental bodily injury …' This was a case which might be regarded as at the borderlines of what can properly be called an accident, since it is generally accepted that part of the attraction of this practice is the element of danger which it involves. The inquest verdict was accidental death, but that should not be regarded as conclusive, since this verdict is chosen from among a relatively limited range of available verdicts. Despite this it was concluded that the death should be regarded as an accident, since there was no evidence that the deceased had tried or intended to kill himself. Insurers who wish to exclude liability in cases of this kind need to insert at least an exclusion for wilful exposure to risk, though in the light of *Morley* it may be questioned whether that would be sufficient.

In *Connelly v New Hampshire Insurance Co*[10] it was held that PTSD amounted to accidental bodily injury for the purposes of a personal accident policy, since it is a specifically defined condition, whose effects can be regarded as giving rise to bodily injury.

1 (1861) 3 E & E 478 per Cockburn CJ; see also *Lawrence v Accidental Insurance* (1881) 7 QBD 216; *Re Etherington and Lancashire and Yorkshire Accident Insurance Co* [1909] 1 KB 591, CA; *Theobald v Railway Passengers Insurance Co* (1854) 10 Ex 45.
2 As in *Sinclair* (1861) 3 E & E 478, above, where death caused by sunstroke was held not to be accidental.
3 [1893] 1 QB 750.
4 IOB 4.1.
5 IOB 4.2.
6 [1944] 144 F 2d 165.
7 IOB 4; leading article.
8 [1990] 1 NZLR 122, Jeffries J.
9 IOB 8.13.
10 [1997] 6 Re LR 367 Ct Sess (OH).

35.4 Injury or death caused by lightning, sunstroke or earthquake has been held not to be accidental in *De Souza v Home and Overseas Insurance Ltd*[1], where it was considered that the term 'accidental bodily injury' had to be construed together with 'outward violent and visible means' with the result that a death from heat-stroke was not covered and the insurers avoided liability. Here it was said that an accident is something which is fortuitous and unexpected, rather than simply the result of a natural cause[2].

These cases, taken together, illustrate the difficulties in this area. Indeed, it is far from clear that *De Souza* can properly be reconciled with *Groves*. On one view each is simply an application of the general principle to the particular facts, but on another view they represent fundamentally different approaches to the notion of an accident. It is perhaps best to reconcile these difficulties by reference to the fact that in *De Souza* the policy referred to 'outward violent and visible means' a phrase which was not in evidence in the other cases. The Insurance Ombudsman has of course the option of disregarding both decisions in order to make a fair and reasonable decision.

1 [1995] LRLR 453, CA.
2 See also *Sinclair v Maritime Passengers Assurance Co* (1861) 3 E & E 478.

35.5 The test of what is unexpected is whether the ordinary reasonable man would not have expected the occurrence, it being irrelevant that a person with expert knowledge, for example of medicine, would have regarded it as inevitable – *Dhak v Insurance Company of North America (UK) Ltd*[1] (death direct consequence of deceased drinking to excess; she had to be taken to have foreseen what might happen in such an event).

1 [1996] 2 All ER 609, CA.

Periodical payments during disablement

35.6 The injury, in addition to causing pain and suffering, may disable the assured from attending to his affairs and thus cause him pecuniary loss. This loss is in the nature of a consequential loss; the injury is not its proximate, but only its remote cause, and unless the policy so provides the assured cannot claim compensation in respect of it. For meaning of 'permanent total disablement from attending to any occupation' see *Sargent v GRE (UK) Ltd*[1] In that case the policy in question had been taken out when the assured was in the army. It was held that the relevant clause in the policy was unclear and a broader approach to its construction was needed. The phrase 'alternative occupation' was not caught by the expression 'any occupation' which was to be limited in its context to any relevant occupation. As the assured was no longer in the army he was therefore entitled to payment as he was permanently disabled from carrying on his occupation and it was irrelevant to inquire whether he was also disabled from attending to an alternative occupation. It must be said that this decision is somewhat problematic. There is an obvious distinction between being unable to attend to a 'relevant occupation' and being unable to attend to any occupation. The latter form of words provides much more restricted cover, and it seem sensible to assume that insurers are aware of the difference between the two forms of wording and will set premiums accordingly. It may be added that the number of people unable to follow any occupation as a result of accident is perhaps less than it once would have been in view of the greater number of technology-oriented jobs which can be done by those with physical disabilities. The value of policies which provide only the narrower form of cover is thus further reduced.

1 [2000] Lloyd's Rep IR 77, CA.

'Wilful exposure to needless peril'

35.7 In a case where injury caused by 'wilful exposure to needless peril' was excluded from cover, it was not enough to show an intentional act which caused the peril; rather there had to be a conscious act of volition (including recklessness) directed to the running of the risk – *Morley and Morley v United Friendly Insurance plc*[1] where the assured jumped onto the bumper of car which was then driven by his fiancée, who inadvertently accelerated instead of stopping. It was held that although the peril was clearly unnecessary, the assured's act was a 'momentary act of stupidity', but that that did not amount to wilful exposure to the peril. The case may be regarded as a development from the much older case of *Sangster's Trustees v General Accident*[2], where the Court of Session held that there was no wilful exposure to risk by a policyholder who went bathing alone in a loch on a cold evening.

Although it is not usual in personal accident policies to express the policyholder's obligations in terms of taking reasonable care to avoid accident, it is obvious that clauses excluding cover in the case of wilful or needless exposure to peril are an attempt to achieve a similar objective. The fairly generous interpretation given to wilful exposure clauses may perhaps best be understood in the light of the modern case law[3] on reasonable care clauses, where it has become clear that only a relatively low standard of care is required of the policyholder. In *Connelly v New Hampshire Insurance Co*[4] the claimant was a fireman who had suffered post traumatic stress disorder ('PTSD') after attending at a fire. One of the grounds of defence to his claim was that his injury was not 'accidental' because he had knowingly and voluntarily attended at the fire. This defence failed on the ground that PTSD was not a normal and foreseeable consequence of his service as a fireman.

In *Fitton v Accidental Death Insurance*[5] the policy had an exception for 'hernia'. After suffering an injury the claimant underwent an operation, suffered a hernia and died of it. It was held that this was not within the exception, which was restricted to hernia arising independently of any accident covered by the insured perils clause. In effect it appears that this is a decision on causation, the court taking the view that the true cause of death is not the hernia but the operation or perhaps even the accident.

1 [1993] 1 Lloyd's Rep 490, CA.
2 (1896) 24 R 56, Ct Sess.
3 Notably *Sofi v Prudential Assurance* [1993] 2 Lloyd's Rep 559, CA; and see Chapter 12 for detailed discussion of reasonable care clauses.
4 [1997] 6 Re LR 367, Ct Sess (OH).
5 (1864) 17 CBNS 122, 144 ER 50 CCP.

Permanent and total disablement

35.8 Where a personal accident policy provides for the payment of a sum if the policyholder is permanently and totally disabled from engaging in any kind of profession or occupation, it is not necessary to show that the policyholder is bed-bound and unable to carry out any function without assistance[1]. It is sufficient that his mobility and other functions are limited to the point where no gainful occupation can realistically be expected. In *Johnson v IGI Insurance Co Ltd*[2] the policy required only that the policyholder be disabled from following a 'similar gainful occupation' to the one which he had been pursuing at the time of the policy. It was held that in order to be 'similar' an alternative occupation must be as capable of generating a living wage as the policyholder's original occupation. Thus, a policyholder who was now limited to less gainful employment was disabled within the meaning of this clause[3]. On the other hand, in *McGeown v Direct Travel*

Insurance[4] the policy provided cover where the accident resulted in a permanent disability which 'prevents you from doing all your usual activities'. It was held that this applied only where the injury was so serious that the policyholder could do none of her usual activities; it was not sufficient that she was unable to do all her usual activities but could still so some of them. Although the wording is to some extent ambiguous, the Court of Appeal commented that it needed to be understood in the context of an all-or-nothing clause which provided for a substantial lump sum payment if its conditions were met.

1 IOB 3.6.
2 [1997] 6 Re LR 283, CA.
3 Although this was a PHI case, the principle appears to be of general application.
4 [2004] Lloyd's Rep IR 599, CA.

Disablement and retirement

35.9 Personal accident policies commonly refer in their disablement provisions to disablement from following the policyholder's usual occupation. Where the policyholder is already retired at the time of the accident, the insurer's may seek to argue that he has no usual occupation, so that no benefit is due. This argument was rejected by the Insurance Ombudsman[1] in a case where the policyholder had taken early retirement. The Ombudsman held that the term 'usual occupation' must be taken to mean the policyholder's most recent occupation. The position would clearly be different if the policy referred to disablement from following the policyholder's 'actual occupation'. What is less clear is whether the result should be the same if the policyholder has already reached normal retiring age. In the IOB case mentioned the policyholder was able to show that he had had offers of re-employment, which he had declined on medical grounds. It is submitted that this form of wording should still be held to provide cover in the case of a policyholder who has reached normal retirement age. Although it might be thought that there is no loss in such a case, that is not the point – the policy is a contingency policy, not an indemnity policy. If insurers want to exclude or restrict this benefit in the case of those over a certain age, they should do so by means of an express clause.

1 IOB 9.19.

Alternative employment

35.10 In considering whether the policyholder is totally disabled from any occupation, it is necessary to take account of the particular characteristics of the policyholder. This is a sensible and necessary rule, for anyone who is not totally immobilised and helpless is likely to be physically capable of following some kind of occupation. However, it would be unrealistic to suggest that a policyholder who has spent a lifetime engaged in manual labour should be expected, relatively late in life, to take up clerical work after suffering an accident which disables him from manual labour. The Insurance Ombudsman has upheld this pragmatic construction of total disability[1], and it is submitted that the same result would be reached at law.

1 See, for example, IOB 15.11.

Partial disablement

35.11 Most personal accident policies provide cover only if the disablement is permanent and total. There is generally no provision for lesser disablement. In one IOB case[1] a policyholder suffered an accidental shoulder injury which left her with pain in the shoulder and partial loss of power, sensation and grip in her hand. She gave up work as a result, though the medical evidence suggested that this was probably not a medical necessity. At the suggestion of the IOB the insurers agreed to pay 50% of the benefit due for the loss of use of a hand[2]. This appears to be a case where the Ombudsman's approach is significantly more generous than that likely to be adopted by the courts. Indeed, the Ombudsman's approach is open to quite serious criticism. Premiums on personal accident policies are relatively low, precisely because cover is restricted to cases of *total* loss of use, and it seems an unnecessary piece of policy re-writing to require proportionate payments in cases of this kind.

[1] IOB 11.29.
[2] This was greater than the sum due for loss of a shoulder.

Transport-related clauses

35.12 Personal accident policies sometimes have specific clauses dealing with accidents suffered in, on or around various forms of transport[1]. Two IOB cases illustrate some of the problems which can arise[2]. In the first[3] the policy provided cover if an accident occurred:

> 'whilst travelling in or getting on or off any public or hired transport conveyance'.

The policyholder got out of a hired car and went to remove a jacket from the boot. While doing so, she was hit by another vehicle and suffered injuries. It was held that the policy did not apply because she had already got out of the car. In the second case[4] the policy, misleadingly described as a 'Road & Travel Plan' provided cover in the event of an accident:

> 'while ... as a fare paying passenger boarding, travelling in or alighting from any bus, train, taxi, ship, ferryboat or hovercraft'.

The policyholder got off a train, tripped over an uneven paving stone, fell and suffered injury. At first sight the case appears identical to the previous one, but the Ombudsman was able to draw a distinction on the basis that the policyholder had not completed her journey, but was in fact changing from one train to another. It was therefore held that she was not to be regarded as having 'alighted' within the meaning of the policy. Although this is an attempt at bringing the events within the policy wording, it is submitted that the case can only properly be regarded as an example of the Ombudsman making a decision which he regards as fair and reasonable. In both cases the policy wording is fairly clearly designed to restrict cover to accidents suffered in the process of entering or leaving the vehicle (but not at any stage in between), and as a matter of law the only proper conclusion is that there is no cover in either case.

[1] See also *Theobald v Railway Passengers Assurance Co* (1854) 10 Exch 45, where the policyholder was injured falling from a train. The defendants in that case were apparently set up precisely to provide protection against the risks of travelling by the new-fangled invention of the railways.

[2] A more dramatic illustration can be found in the celebrated film *Double Indemnity*, where a clause providing for double benefit if the insured died by falling from a train led to an ingenious murder plot.
[3] IOB 11.30.
[4] IOB 8.14.

Burden of proof

35.13 As in all insurance policies, the policyholder bears the burden of showing that the injury was caused by an insured peril, namely an accident. This can give rise to practical difficulties where the injury does not immediately follow on from the alleged cause and where there is a difference of medical opinion about the cause of the injury. In a court of law this is of course merely a fairly routine problem of the law of evidence, and the claim is either established on the balance of probabilities or it is not. The Insurance Ombudsman, by contrast, has sometimes been prepared[1] to require insurers to pay part of the relevant benefit in cases where the evidence is ambiguous.

[1] See, for example, IOB 13.25.

Policyholder's wrongful acts

35.14 The general prohibition against making a claim for injuries which are the consequences of one's own wrongful acts applies to personal accident cases. Thus, where the policyholder became involved in a fracas and was subsequently convicted of assault occasioning actual bodily harm, the Insurance Ombudsman rejected his attempt to claim on his personal accident policy for his injuries[1].

[1] IOB 13.26.

Suicide

35.15 Where personal accident policies cover accidental death, it is common to find an exclusion couched in terms such as 'suicide, or attempted suicide or intentional self-injury'. A number of cases arising out of such exclusions have come before the Insurance Ombudsman. Two in particular are worthy of mention[1]. In the first the policyholder jumped from a bridge into the path of a lorry. There was some suggestion that he thought he was being followed and had tried to escape. The Death Certificate gave 'multiple injuries and acute paranoia' as the cause of death, but the inquest returned a verdict of accidental death. The insurer nevertheless sought to rely upon the exclusion, arguing that the deceased's actions showed a clear intention to die. The Ombudsman held that the insurer had not discharged the burden of proving that this had been the intention. There was evidence to suggest that the policyholder had been in a disturbed state of mind, and the evidence was equally consistent with the conclusion that he had not been capable of forming the necessary intention[2] to do himself harm. In the second case the policyholder threw herself from the third floor of a multi-storey car park. On the face of it this might be thought to provide clear evidence of an intention to do herself harm, but there was compelling medical evidence that the policyholder was in a state of psychotic delusion where she believed that she could not be killed by anything except decapitation. Thus it was plausible to suppose that she had acted in this way in order to prove that it would not kill her, rather than in order to kill herself. Therefore the exclusion did not apply.

The two cases illustrate an essential point in this area, namely that these exclusion clauses apply to those who *intentionally* bring about their own harm, but not to those people who are so ill that they are incapable of understanding the nature and quality of their own actions[3] or of forming the necessary intention[4].

[1] Both are to be found at para 7.15 of the Annual Report for 1993.
[2] This view about the lack of intention may also be regarded as rebutting the suggestion that the necessary element of fortuity was lacking.
[3] Historically this test applied at common law, where it was only *sane* suicide that was a crime. It was no doubt for this reason that so many coroners' juries returned verdicts of 'suicide while of unsound mind'. This usually preserved the claim to the insurance money, as well as allowing burial in consecrated ground.
[4] See also Chapter 34 Life Assurance on the relevance of suicide.

'Sole and independent cause'

35.16 Another way in which the cover provided by personal accident policies is commonly restricted is by requiring that the accident be the 'sole and independent' cause of the injury. In practice this is a significant restriction, since there are many accidents which cause injuries, whose effect is made greater when combined with some other cause[1]. When this restriction is combined with the common requirement of permanent and total disablement, it can be seen that its effect is to exclude many cases. Not surprisingly, this issue has come before the Insurance Ombudsman at various times. The IOB's approach[2] has been to say that where the accident is a significant contributing cause of the disability, it is fair and reasonable for the insurers to make a proportionate settlement of the claim. However, the proportion to be paid is often quite small. In two of the cases mentioned here the awards were for 10% and 8% respectively of the sum assured. This is clearly an approach based upon the fair and reasonable jurisdiction rather than on the strict application of the law, under which the complaint would be bound to fail in total.

[1] See also Chapter 18 for a discussion of the general principles applicable in cases of dual cause.
[2] See, for example, IOB 13.31, 13.32 and 15.10.

Chapter 36

Permanent health insurance and critical illness cover

Introduction

36.1 Policies within this Chapter are of two kinds. PHI policies protect against the risk of loss of income arising from illness (they do not provide cover for the costs of medical treatment – for medical expenses policies see Chapter 43). They are therefore indemnity policies. Critical illness cover is a form of contingency policy which pays out on the policyholder being diagnosed as suffering from one or more of the particular diseases covered by the policy. Both are long-term business within the categorisation of the ICA 1982. So long as premiums are paid, the insurer is not entitled to cancel the cover by reason of a deterioration in the health of the insured. However, where policies lapse by reason of non-payment of premiums it is usual and permissible to require a declaration of continuing good health in the same way as is normally done in relation to life policies.

PHI and critical illness cover are areas where, in the nature of things, most of the policies are personal lines policies[1], with the result that there is relatively little judicial authority, but the Ombudsman has had to consider issues in this area in a number of cases, the more important of which are discussed in this Chapter.

[1] Ie the policyholder does not act in the course of any business of his.

Policy coverage

Eligibility

36.2 Perhaps the first major problem of PHI policies concerns the question of eligibility for the policy. Most PHI policies severely limit cover for any condition for which the policyholder has received treatment within one or two years preceding the inception of the policy, as well as excluding entirely cover for any condition which exists at the date of inception. Although these clauses do not make it logically impossible for a person to have cover, the presence of a serious medical condition may make a PHI policy inappropriate. The Insurance Ombudsman has on occasion taken this view where, for example[1] a policyholder had for many years suffered from ankylosing spondylitis, but not in another case where the policyholder had had long-term depression since 1979 but had nevertheless been able to continue working until 1996, the policy having been issued in 1993.

It is possible for a condition to 'exist' even though it has not been diagnosed. This is obviously problematic for proposers, who are at risk of being caught by the exclusion for pre-existing conditions. For this reason the ABI has issued a Statement of Practice for Health-Related Insurances, which distinguishes three different situations with regard to pre-existing conditions and the proposer's knowledge of them. The first situation is where the proposer has consulted his doctor and a diagnosis has been received. The proposer's knowledge is thus limited to the diagnosis, and he is entitled to assume that the diagnosis is correct. The second situation is where the proposer has consulted for certain symptons, but no diagnosis has been made. This is more difficult than the first situation, for the proposer cannot make assumptions about the nature of the condition. It is then a question of fact what previous condition existed. The third situation concerns asymptomatic conditions, where the proposer will not normally have any reason to be aware of the condition, and where a pre-existing condition exclusion will not normally apply. The overall effect of the Statement of Practice is to move emphasis away from what condition existed and in the direction of the state of the proposer's knowledge.

The leading judicial authority in this area is *Cook v Financial Insurance Co*[2], which is considered in Chapter 43 in the context of payment protection policies.

[1] The examples in this paragraph are taken from the introduction to IOB 15.
[2] [1999] Lloyd's Rep IR 1, HL.

Causation

36.3 In one IOB case[1] the policy excluded disability 'caused or contributed to by pregnancy or childbirth'. After a difficult pregnancy, the policyholder was induced, but then an emergency caesarean had to be performed. Complications developed, as a result of which she suffered serious brain damage. The insurers denied liability on the basis of the exclusion, but the Ombudsman upheld the policyholder's complaint. Although the caesarean could in one sense be said to have been the cause of the brain damage, it was more appropriate to view it as no more than the background against which the wholly unexpected and radical complications developed[2].

[1] IOB 15.1.
[2] For the causation aspects of this case, see Chapter 18.

Critical illness

36.4 The proposal form in a critical illness policy normally requires detailed disclosure of medical history. The Insurance Ombudsman has held[1] that the need for such disclosure is so obvious that there can be no justification for failing to disclose it, even if the insurer's agent suggests that the disclosure is not necessary. It is open to argument whether the policyholder would have a remedy against the insurer's agent personally for a misrepresentation of this kind[2].

[1] IOB 8.2.
[2] Clearly there would be a remedy against a broker who made such a suggestion.

Permanent health insurance

36.5 In *Napier v Unum Ltd (formerly Nel Permanent Health Insurance Ltd)*[1] the insured had left his employment with the company through which the policy was effected. The scheme provided that in that case he would be provided with an individual policy. A dispute arose over whether the insured was covered and what the burden of proof was. It was held that there had been no suggestion that the medical reports provided by the insured were not satisfactory to constitute proof. Rather the insurers contended that they had evidence which pointed to the contrary conclusion. It was not suggested that in this the insurers were acting in bad faith. The 'proof satisfactory' requirement was simply a vouching provision requiring 'production of the insured's entitlement to benefit.' The issue was therefore whether the insured had been unable to work as a result of sickness in the period covered by the claim and on the facts that was found to be so. The insurers had also sought to recover overpaid benefit but it was held that they could not do so because they could not prove that such payments were made as a result of a mistake.

[1] [1996] 2 Lloyd's Rep 550.

Private health insurance

36.6 In *Johnson v IGI Insurance Co Ltd*[1] the insured was a taxi driver. He was offered medical insurance when purchasing a taxi on hire purchase and the question arose whether it covered him in a situation where he could no longer drive a taxi because of a bad back or whether he could arguably carry on a 'similar gainful occupation'. It was held that the term 'similar gainful occupation' meant an occupation which could generate a living wage which was what the insurance policy was supposed to cover. The question of whether the insured could have operated a taxi service and rented out his taxis to other drivers had not been raised at the court below and so the judge was entitled to find on the evidence that the insured's disability prevented him from performing the work for which he was qualified. As there had been no questions on the hire purchase application form about health the judge had been right to find that the insurer had not satisfied him that there had been non disclosure of material facts. The case is interesting for the implicit assumption that material facts should have been the subject of questions on the proposal form. Although as a general proposition this is not the law, it is suggested that the judge was justified in focusing on the curious fact of a medical insurance policy without questions as to health. The only conclusion which can really be drawn in such a case is that the insurers are proposing to resort to the common, but undesirable, practice of doing their underwriting at the claims stage.

It cannot then be legitimate for them to claim the extra protection of the doctrine of utmost good faith by relying upon the policyholder's failure to disclose information which was never asked for.

1 [1997] 6 Re LR 283, CA.

Permanent and total disablement

36.7 PHI policies commonly require the policyholder to be permanently and totally disabled in order to qualify to receive benefits. Sometimes the disablement must be from following any occupation at all, in which event the cover is very restricted. At the other extreme the disablement may only be from following the policyholder's usual occupation. An intermediate position is taken by policies which require disablement from following an occupation to which the policyholder is suited by reason of training, experience, qualifications etc. This form of words can have unfortunate effects for a policyholder who is possessed of a good range of skills. In an IOB case[1] with wording of this kind the policyholder was a police officer who suffered knee ligament damage. Although he had retired from the police force on medical grounds, the Ombudsman held that the range of skills he had acquired as a police officer left him with a reasonable prospect of finding alternative work, so that he did not meet the policy conditions.

PHI cases were subsequently transferred to the PIAOB[2], and the Ombudsman has occasionally reported on such cases. In one[3] the complainant was a dentist who had a PHI policy expressed to apply if he became incapable of following his own occupation. He developed a phobia of dentistry and, on medical advice, took early retirement. He therefore received a substantial NHS pension. The insurer objected to paying on the PHI policy on two grounds. The first was that it did not consider the phobia to be a recognised medical condition. The second was that the NHS pension plus the PHI policy would leave the complainant with as much income as he had had when working, with the result that he would have no incentive to return to work. As to the first point, the complainant had had two independent psychiatric assessments, which confirmed that the phobia was genuine. It should be fairly obvious that a dentist with a phobia of dentistry cannot practise his profession, with the result that the complainant met the definition of disability in the policy. As to the second point it is only necessary to observe that the policy contained no condition limiting the total amount which the complainant could receive, either by reference to his previous earnings or otherwise. If the insurer had wanted to insert such a condition, or had wanted to require policyholders to take steps to rehabilitate themselves, it could have done so expressly[4]. The FOS has subsequently taken the view that clauses requiring the policyholder to be unable to perform 'any occupation' should be regarded as referring to 'any relevant occupation', ie an occupation to which the policyholder is suited by reason of education, training, experience, social standing etc[5] This obviously involves detailed analysis of the facts of each case, but it does show that the FOS may take a more lenient view than do the courts.

An unusual case in this area is *Howells v IGI Insurance Co Ltd*[6] where the policyholder was a professional footballer, and the definition of 'total disablement' precluded him from playing more than 12 'games' within a specified period. The Court of Appeal rejected his contention that this referred only to first-team games, holding that any competitive professional game would be sufficient, including reserve team games. Given that the policy did not define the word 'game' the Court of Appeal's approach appears correct. As is usual in such policies, the cover was intended to be restricted to serious injury effectively precluding the policyholder from playing professionally at all, and there was no reason to restrict it in the way contended for.

On the other hand in *Walton v Airtours plc*[7] the Court of Appeal focused on the phrase 'follow any occupation', which is commonly found in policies requiring that the policyholder be 'unable to follow any occupation'. In that case it appeared that the policyholder might have been able to start working in some occupation, but would have been unable to continue in it without a degree of structured support. On that basis the Court held that he was not able to 'follow any occupation', the notion of following an occupation being different from that of starting an occupation. This appears a very sensible decision, since it cannot be fair to expect a policyholder to begin a job which can last for only a very short time.

1 IOB 11.14. The case actually concerned a payment protection policy, but the issues appear to be the same in relation to PHI policies.
2 They now go to the FOS.
3 PIAOB 97–98, para 12.13.
4 Though it is not at all easy to see what steps this particular policyholder could have taken.
5 FOS 40, leading article.
6 [2003] EWCA Civ 03, [2003] Lloyd's Rep IR 803, CA.
7 [2002] EWCA Civ 1659, [2004] Lloyd's Rep IR 69, CA.

Subjective or Objective Test?

36.8 In *Haghiran v Allied Dunbar Insurance*[1] it appeared that the policyholder genuinely believed himself to be incapable of carrying on any occupation, but the insurer declined liability on the basis that this belief was unfounded. The question was whether the subjective belief was enough or whether the test was an objective one. The Court of Appeal held that, although psychological factors can affect the severity of an illness, there must come a point where an individual's belief about his state of health was so far away from the objective evidence as to be simply incorrect. Ultimately it is a question of objective fact whether a policyholder is capable of working. The same principle must apply to any other form of words which requires an evaluation of capacity or health.

1 [2001] 1 All ER (Comm) 97, CA.

Survival clauses

36.9 In *Hardial Singh Virk v Gan Life Holdings plc*[1] a PHI policy agreed to pay the claimant a 'critical illness benefit' if he suffered a stroke, provided that he survived for a period of 30 days after the stroke, failing which death benefits became payable under other provisions of the policy. It was held that the insured event was not 'stroke' simpliciter: it was the consequent condition of 'critical illness'. The parties had expressly provided that that condition had to endure for a period of at least 30 days (so that the separate life provisions of the policy would not apply) and the right to payment in respect of that condition therefore did not arise until after the expiry of that period.

1 [2000] Lloyd's Rep IR 159, CA, Eady J.

Nature of illness covered

36.10 *Satish Khanna v Prosperity Life Assurance Ltd*[1] was a claim for declaratory relief against four defendant insurance companies. the claimant contended that owing to his ill health he was variously entitled to a waiver of premiums or to the payment of regular sums of money under the terms of insurance products that he had bought. These products ranged between flexible mortgage plans, personal pension plans and PHI polices. Each claim depended on the claimant being able to demonstrate that he was permanently prevented through sickness from carrying on his practice as a doctor, and in some cases from carrying on alternative employment. The central issue was therefore to what extent this was true: liability rather than quantum was in dispute. The claimant was 52 years old and had retired from general medical practice. He had qualified as a doctor in July 1969 and eventually decided to retire in December 1994 with the support of medical advice. The claimant was described in evidence as a competent and dedicated sole general practitioner from 1989 to 1993. In his final year of practice however, matters deteriorated and two doctors advised that he should retire, making their diagnosis on the basis of the claimant's own account that he was suffering from obstructive sleep apnoea ('OSA'). The General Medical Council ('GMC') accepted the claimant's application for exemption from subscriptions on health grounds and prevented the claimant from returning to practice unless he satisfied the GMC that he was once again fit. The defendant insurance companies however became suspicious as to the genuineness of the claimant's contention that he retired for medical reasons when it emerged that he had spoken to the two doctors about his condition at a time when he was under extreme financial pressures: the bank was about to withhold further funding thus leaving him unable to practice. The defendants contended that the claimant did not actually qualify as having OSA or alternatively, if he does, that the steps taken by the claimant to assist his condition should have rendered him capable of doing a day's work. Two objective medical experts gave conflicting reports as to the nature of the claimant's condition and whether he was in fact suffering from OSA. Eady J said that he test was whether the claimant could show, on the balance of probabilities, that he had been truly prevented from working, at the material times, by a medical condition to which it had been shown that OSA had made at least a material contribution. Medical understanding of OSA was imperfect. Research evidence was also ambivalent and the disorder had only recently been recognised. As such it was understandable that the expert evidence was divided. The defendants had been unable to challenge the claimant's evidence that he genuinely felt that his faculties had deteriorated to the extent that he was no longer safe with patients. There was evidence that he was struggling in late 1994 and that even after his financial troubles were at their highest the claimant was still hoping to get work as a police surgeon. The evidence was therefore that the claimant did have genuine problems, probably a mixture of physical illness and stress, from about November 1994. No one had seriously suggested that the claimant was fit to return to work as a doctor. There was a difference between full-time and part-time work but if the claimant was a risk to patients it did not matter: any kind of risk was unacceptable. If the claimant was not suffering to a material degree from OSA then that would have meant that two doctors had been treating him for nearly five years for a condition he did not have. OSA had not been dreamed up to fit the wording of the claimant's insurance policies. It had made a material contribution to his inability to function as a General Practitioner. There was therefore judgment and declaration for the claimant with quantum to be assessed.

[1] 18 December 2000, unreported, CA.

Cumulative conditions

36.11 This problem arises where the policyholder suffers from a number of conditions, none of which individually would be sufficient to warrant a claim on the policy, but which cumulatively may do so. The problem is made more complex if some of the conditions are covered by the policy whilst others are excluded. In an IOB case[1] the policyholder was a personnel director of a large company, but took early retirement after suffering illness. He claimed on his PHI policy, alleging that he was suffering from five different conditions. The insurers took the view that the physical conditions were adequately controlled by medication, and that any inability of the policyholder to work was caused by anxiety, which was an excluded condition. The Ombudsman held that it was not reasonable to expect a person to continue working when suffering from five different conditions, even if none of these was by itself sufficient to cause incapacity. Although the brief IOB report does not make the matter clear, it must of course be the case that that conditions taken cumulatively have to be enough to prevent the policyholder from working. It must also be the case that any of those conditions which falls within an excluded cause has to be disregarded in making the assessment of inability to work. In a more recent IOB decision[2] there was an exclusion for depression, and it appeared that the policyholder's inability to work was caused partly by back problems and partly by depression. The Ombudsman held that the fair and reasonable outcome was that the insurers should pay 50% of the sum insured[3].

[1] IOB 8.18.
[2] IOB 21.4.
[3] This case is also considered, from a causation point of view, in Chapter 18.

Rehabilitation in PHI policies

36.12 Where a PHI claim is accepted, the policy will normally provide that entitlement to benefit lasts only as long as the illness or incapacity. The insurers naturally have a vested interest in seeing that the policyholder does not remain incapacitated for longer than necessary and does not continue to claim benefit once the incapacity has ceased. For this reason insurers will want to continue to monitor the condition of anyone claiming benefit. In an IOB case on this point[1] the policy defined incapacity by reference to inability to follow the particular occupation mentioned in the policy, which was that of insurance broker, though at the time when he suffered a heart attack he was working in a different occupation. He was given early retirement from that job, but the insurers objected to paying on the PHI policy because they were not satisfied that he was incapable of working as an insurance broker. The nub of the dispute was that the policyholder's main reason for not being able to return to work was his fear that he would be at risk of further heart attacks, notwithstanding that in purely physical terms he appeared to be capable of working. Both his doctor and a rehabilitation consultant concluded that it would not be in his best interests to return to work. On the basis of this evidence the Ombudsman held that the insurer was not justified in rejecting the claim; it was necessary to consider the policyholder's medical condition as a whole, not just his cardiac condition. However, the Ombudsman added that the insurer was entitled to have the policyholder reassessed periodically to see whether he had become fit to work again, since it was possible that his psychological condition might improve. These assessments could, where appropriate, include assessment by a psychiatrist.

[1] IOB 3.7.

Chapter 37

Motor policies

Introduction

37.1 The importance of motor policies is beyond dispute. The RTA 1988 makes it a criminal offence to drive a motor vehicle on a public road without holding an appropriate insurance policy. Given the financial liabilities which can result from motor accidents, such insurance is essential in any developed society.

When insurance is compulsory

37.2 The requirements of insurance are contained in Part VI of the RTA 1988.

It is forbidden to use a motor vehicle on a road unless there is in force in relation to the use of the vehicle by that person a policy of insurance or a security in respect of third party risks which complies with the requirements of Part VI[1]. Further, a person must not cause or permit any other person to use a motor vehicle[2] on a road unless appropriate insurance or security is in place[3]. Contravention of these prohibitions is a criminal offence[4].

Subject to certain qualifications, it is unlawful for any person to *use*, or to *cause or permit* any other person to use, a motor vehicle on a road unless there is in force in relation to the use of the vehicle by that person or that other person, as the case may be, such a policy of insurance, or such a security, in respect of third party risks as complies with the statutory requirements: *Jones v DPP*[5].

[1] Section 143(1)(a).
[2] Not including an invalid carriage: s 143(4).
[3] Section 143(1)(b).
[4] Section 143(2).
[5] [1999] RTR 1, DC.

The statutory requirements

37.3 In order to comply with the statutory requirements, a policy must provide insurance cover in respect of any liability which may be incurred by such persons or classes of persons as are specified in the policy in respect of the death of, or bodily injury to, any person, or damage to property caused by, or arising out of, the use of the vehicle on a road in Great Britain. An accident is considered to arise out of the use of a person's car if the person is injured when crossing the road to get petrol when the car breaks down: *Dunthorne v Bentley*[1].

The requirement of third-party insurance does not apply to a vehicle owned by a person who has deposited and keeps deposited with the Accountant General of the Supreme Court the sum of £500,000, at a time when the vehicle is being driven under the owner's control[2]. Section 144(2) provides further exceptions for vehicles owned by county councils, police authorities, NHS Trusts and others.

The policy must be issued by an authorised insurer[3], ie a company authorised under the IFSMA 2000 to offer motor insurance and which is a member of the MIB[4].

It must insure such person, persons or classes of persons as may be specified in the policy in respect of any liability which may be incurred by him or them in respect of the death of or bodily injury to any person or damage to property caused by, or arising out of, the use of the vehicle on a road in Great Britain. In the case of a vehicle normally based in the territory of another member State, insure him or them in respect of any civil liability which may be incurred by him or them as a result of an event related to the use of the vehicle in Great Britain if according to the law of that territory, he or they would be required to be insured in respect of a civil liability which would arise under that law as a result of that event if the place where the vehicle was used when the event occurred were in that territory, and the cover required by that law would be higher than that required in Great Britain.

1 [1996] PIQR P323, CA.
2 Section 144(1). The sum required may be varied by statutory instrument.
3 Section 145(2).
4 For the MIB generally, see Chapter 28.

37.4 In the case of a vehicle normally based in Great Britain it must insure him or them in respect of any liability which may be incurred by him or them in respect of the use of the vehicle and of any trailer, whether or not coupled, in the territory other than Great Britain and Gibraltar of each of the Member States of the Communities according to the law on compulsory insurance against civil liability in respect of the use of vehicles of the State in whose territory the event giving rise to the liability occurred, or, if it would give higher cover, the law which would be applicable if the place where the vehicle was used when that event occurred was in Great Britain. It must also insure him or them in respect of any liability which may be incurred by him or them under the provisions of this Part of this Act relating to payment for emergency treatment[1].

However, the policy need not cover liability in respect of the death, arising out of and in the course of his employment, of a person in the employment of a person insured by the policy or in respect of bodily injury sustained by such a person arising out of and in the course of his employment, provided that cover in respect of the liability is in fact provided pursuant to a requirement of the EL(CI)A 1969[2]. This provision seeks to mark the dividing line between coverage under the RTA 1988 and coverage under the EL(CI)A 1969. The idea is to ensure that the liabilities here specified will always be covered, but that they do not need to be covered twice over.

The policy need not provide insurance of more than £250,000 in respect of all such liabilities as may be insured in respect of damage to property caused by, or arising out of, any one accident involving the vehicle, or cover liability in respect of damage to the vehicle, or cover liability in respect of damage to goods carried for hire or reward in or on the vehicle or in or on any trailer (whether or not coupled) drawn by the vehicle, or cover any liability of a person in respect of damage to property in his custody or under his control, or cover any contractual liability[3].

1 Section 144(3).
2 Section 144(4)(a).
3 Section 144(4).

37.5 Where a security is used rather than a policy of insurance, s 146 imposes the following conditions.

The security must be given either by an authorised insurer or by some body of persons which carries on in the UK the business of giving securities of a like kind and has deposited and keeps deposited with the Accountant General of the Supreme Court the sum of £15,000 in respect of that business.

The security must consist of an undertaking by the giver of the security to make good, subject to any conditions specified in it, any failure by the owner of the vehicle or such other persons or classes of persons as may be specified in the security duly to discharge any liability which may be incurred by him or them, being a liability required under s 145 to be covered by a policy of insurance.

However, in the case of liabilities arising out of the use of a motor vehicle on a road in Great Britain the amount secured need not exceed £25,000 in the case of an undertaking relating to the use of public service vehicles within the meaning of the Public Passenger Vehicles Act 1981 or £5,000 in any other case.

37.6 Section 147 deals with the issue and surrender of certificates of insurance and of security. A policy of insurance is ineffective for the purposes of this Part of this Act unless and until the insurer delivers to the person by whom the policy is effected a certificate in the prescribed form and containing such particulars of any conditions subject to which the policy is issued and of any other matters as may be prescribed[1]. The same rule applies in relation to a security[2].

Where a certificate has been delivered under this section and the policy or security to which it relates is cancelled by mutual consent or by virtue of any provision in the policy or security, the person to whom the certificate was delivered must, within seven days from the taking effect of the cancellation surrender the certificate to the person by whom the policy was issued or the security was given, or if the certificate has been lost or destroyed, make a statutory declaration to that effect[3].

1 Section 147(1).
2 Section 147(2).
3 Section 147(4). Non-compliance is an offence: s 147(5).

37.7 Section 148 restricts the freedom of insurers to insert terms into policies which restrict the cover afforded. Anything in the policy which purports to restrict the insurance of the persons insured by the policy, or the operation of the security by reference to any of the following matters is void as regards the liabilities required to be insured under s 145. The matters are:

(a) the age or physical or mental condition of persons driving the vehicle;
(b) the condition of the vehicle;
(c) the number of persons that the vehicle carries;
(d) the weight or physical characteristics of the goods that the vehicle carries;
(e) the time at which or the areas within which the vehicle is used;
(f) the horsepower or cylinder capacity or value of the vehicle;
(g) the carrying on the vehicle of any particular apparatus; or
(h) the carrying on the vehicle of any particular means of identification other than any means of identification required to be carried by or under the Vehicle Excise and Registration Act 1994.

37.8 The effect of this list of prohibitions is that none of these matters can be used by the insurer to resist paying a claim made by a third party in respect of risks required to be insured. Section 148(4) goes on to say that any sum paid by an insurer or the giver of a security in or towards the discharge of any liability of any person which is covered by the policy or security by virtue only of this list of prohibitions is recoverable by the insurer or giver of the security from that person. Thus the insurer must compensate the third party, but then has a right of recovery from the policyholder. In practice the right of recovery appears to be seldom used, perhaps because the sums involved are either too small to justify the effort involved or so large that there is no real prospect that the individual policyholder will be able to pay them.

A condition in a policy or security issued or given for the purposes of Part VI of the RTA 1988 providing that no liability shall arise under the policy or security, or that any liability so arising shall cease in the event of some specified thing being done or omitted to be done after the happening of the event giving rise to a claim under the policy or security, shall be of no effect in connection with such liabilities as are required to be covered by a policy under s 145 of the Act[1]. However, this does not render void any provision in a policy or security requiring the person insured or secured to pay to the insurer or the giver of the security any sums which the latter may have become liable to pay under the policy or security and which have been applied to the satisfaction of the claims of third parties[2].

[1] Section 148(5).
[2] Section 148(6).

37.9 Section 149 renders void in cases where anyone other than the user of the vehicle is carried in or upon the vehicle any agreement or understanding between them made at or before the time when the liability arises (whether intended to be legally binding or not) which purports to negative or restrict any such liability of the user in respect of persons carried in or upon the vehicle as is required by s 145 of the Act to be covered by a policy of insurance, or to impose any conditions with respect to the enforcement of any such liability of the user. This prohibition is absolute and without exception.

37.10 Section 150 deals with insurance or security in respect of private use of the vehicle to cover use under car-sharing arrangements. Where a group of people agree to travel together in a car and to share the costs, the fact that 'fares' are being paid by some of them will not prevent the use of the car from being considered as being of a non-commercial character for the purposes of insurance cover, provided that the following conditions are met:

(a) the vehicle is not adapted to carry more than eight passengers and is not a motor cycle;
(b) the fare or aggregate of the fares paid in respect of the journey does not exceed the amount of the running costs of the vehicle for the journey (which for the purposes of this paragraph shall be taken to include an appropriate amount in respect of depreciation and general wear);
(c) the arrangements for the payment of fares by the passenger or passengers carried at separate fares were made before the journey began.

It may be observed that paragraph (b) of these conditions in practice allows considerable scope in the amounts charged, since the calculation of rates of depreciation per mile is far from being an exact science.

Insurers' duty to satisfy judgments

37.11 Section 151 sets out the duty of insurers or persons giving security to satisfy judgment against persons insured or secured against third-party risks. The section applies to judgments relating to a liability with respect to any matter where liability with respect to that matter is required to be covered by a policy of insurance under s 145 of the RTA 1988, where either it is a liability covered by the terms of the policy or security to which the certificate relates, and the judgment is obtained against any person who is insured by the policy or whose liability is covered by the security, as the case may be, or it is a liability, other than an excluded liability, which would be so covered if the policy insured all persons or, as the case may be, the security covered the liability of all persons, and the judgment is obtained against any person other than one who is insured by the policy or, as the case may be, whose liability is covered by the security.

In deciding for these purposes whether a liability is or would be covered by the terms of a policy or security, so much of the policy or security as purports to restrict, as the case may be, the insurance of the persons insured by the policy or the operation of the security by reference to the holding by the driver of the vehicle of a licence authorising him to drive it shall be treated as of no effect[1].

An 'excluded liability' means a liability in respect of the death of, or bodily injury to, or damage to the property of any person who, at the time of the use which gave rise to the liability, was allowing himself to be carried in or upon the vehicle and knew or had reason to believe that the vehicle had been stolen or unlawfully taken, not being a person who did not know and had no reason to believe that the vehicle had been stolen or unlawfully taken until after the commencement of his journey, and who could not reasonably have been expected to have alighted from the vehicle[2].

Notwithstanding that the insurer may be entitled to avoid or cancel, or may have voided or cancelled, the policy or security, he must pay to the persons entitled to the benefit of the judgment the following amounts:

(a) as regards liability in respect of death or bodily injury, any sum payable under the judgment in respect of the liability, together with any sum which, by virtue of any enactment relating to interest on judgments, is payable in respect of interest on that sum;

(b) as regards liability in respect of damage to property, where the total of any amount paid, payable or likely to be payable under the policy or security in respect of damage to property caused by, or arising out of, the accident in question does not exceed £250,000, the payment of any sum payable under the judgment in respect of the liability, together with any sum which, by virtue of any enactment relating to interest on judgments, is payable in respect of interest on that sum. If that total exceeds £250,000, the required sum is either such proportion of any sum payable under the judgment in respect of the liability as £250,000 bears to that total, together with the same proportion of any sum which, by virtue of any enactment relating to interest on judgments, is payable in respect of interest on that sum, or the difference between the total of any amounts already paid under the policy or security in respect of such damage and £250,000, together with such proportion of any sum which, by virtue of any enactment relating to interest on judgments, is payable in respect of interest on any sum payable under the judgment in respect of the liability as the difference bears to that sum, whichever is the less, unless not less than £250,000 has already been paid under the policy or security in respect of such damage (in which case nothing is payable)[3]. In addition the insurer must pay any amount payable in respect of costs.

The remaining provisions of s 151 enable an insurer who has made a payment only because of the provisions of s 151 to recover that payment (or the part of it which he would not have had to make but for s 151) from the person whose liability he is discharging.

1 Section 151(3).
2 Section 151(4).
3 Section 151(6).

37.12 Section 152 lists certain exceptions to s 151. The most important of these are as follows. No sum is payable by an insurer under s 151:

(a) in respect of any judgment unless, before or within seven days after the commencement of the proceedings in which the judgment was given, the insurer had notice of the bringing of the proceedings, or

(b) in respect of any judgment so long as execution on the judgment is stayed pending an appeal.

In *Desouza v Waterlow*[1] it was held that a notice under s 152(1)(a) of the RTA 1988 need only evince an intention to bring such proceedings against a motor insurer. The notice does not have to be in writing or take a specific form.

However, in *Wake v Page*[2] it was held that failure to give a notice at all is fatal to the s 152 claim. It is irrelevant that the insurer is in fact unaware of the proceedings. What constitutes sufficient notice is a question of fact and degree[3]. In *Nawaz and Hussain v Crowe Insurance Group*[4] notice was given orally to a secretary in the firm of solicitors acting for the insurers. On the facts it was held that this notice was sufficient.

No sum is payable by an insurer under this section if, in an action commenced before, or within three months after, the commencement of the proceedings in which the judgment was given, he has obtained a declaration that, apart from any provision contained in the policy or security, he is entitled to avoid it on the ground that it was obtained by the non-disclosure of a material fact, or by a representation of fact which was false in some material particular, or if he has avoided the policy or security on that ground, that he was entitled so to do apart from any provision contained in it. An insurer who delays seeking such a declaration, and at the same time leads the insured to believe that he will not do so (as for example by contriving to deal with the claim) may find that he is held to have waived his right to a declaration[5]. However, obtaining such a declaration does not benefit the insurer as respects any judgment obtained in proceedings commenced before the commencement of that action unless before, or within seven days after, the commencement of that action he has given notice of it to the person who is the claimant in those proceedings specifying the non-disclosure or false representation on which he proposes to rely.

[1] [1999] RTR 71, CA.
[2] (2001) Times, 9 February, CA.
[3] *McBlain v Dolan Churchill Insurance Co Ltd* [2001] Lloyd's Rep IR 309, OH. See also *Ceylon Motor Insurance Association Ltd v Thambugala* [1953] AC 584, PC; *Harrington v Link Motor Policies at Lloyd's* [1989] 2 Lloyd's Rep 310, CA.
[4] [2003] EWCA Civ 316, [2003] Lloyd's Rep IR 471.
[5] *McBlain v Dolan*, above.

37.13 An insurer who has indemnified a third party under section 151 is entitled to recoup from the negligent driver any sum which he would not have had to pay but for the effect of section 151. Thus, there is a right of recoupment in any case where the insurer would have had a defence to a claim by the negligent driver (based on the non-existence, non-applicability or voidability of a policy) but is nevertheless required to indemnify the third party[1]. Section 151(8) further provides that where an insurer becomes liable to provide indemnity in respect of a liability of a person who is not insured by a policy, he is entitled to recover that amount from that person or from any person who is insured by the policy by the terms of which the liability would be covered if the policy insured all persons or from anyone who caused or permitted the use of the vehicle which gave rise to the liability in question. In *Lloyd-Wolper v Moore*[2] it was held that permission for these purposes is not vitiated when it is given on the basis of a mistake as to whether the person to whom it was given would be covered by the policy (in that case the person concerned was not covered because he was under age and because the policy purported to cover him only for driving vehicles up to 1600cc, whereas the vehicle in question was 1760cc)[3].

[1] RTA 1988, s 151.
[2] [2004] EWCA Civ 766, [2004] Lloyd's Rep IR 730.
[3] Applying *Monk v Warbey* [1935] 1 KB 75; *Lyons v May* [1948] 2 All ER 1062; *Baugh v Crago* [1975] RTR 453; *Ferrymasters Ltd v Adams* [1980] RTR 139; *DPP v Fisher* [1992] RTR 93.

37.14 Section 153 deals with the effect of an insured person becoming bankrupt. The basic principle is that where a policyholder becomes bankrupt, this should not affect his liability for a compulsory risk. Section 153 applies where the insured person becomes bankrupt or makes a composition or arrangement with his creditors or his estate is sequestrated or he grants a trust deed for his creditors, or where he dies and:

(i) his estate falls to be administered in accordance with an order under s 421 of the IA 1986, an award of sequestration of his estate is made, or
(ii) the insured person is a company, a winding-up order or an administration order is made with respect to the company, a resolution for a voluntary winding-up is passed with respect to the company,

a receiver or manager of the company's business or undertaking is duly appointed, or possession is taken, by or on behalf of the holders of any debentures secured by a floating charge, of any property comprised in or subject to the charge. However, the person to whom liability is incurred is protected by TP(RAI)A 1930 in these circumstances[1].

[1] Section 153(3). For the TP(RAI)A 1930, see Chapter 29.

Coverage of other cars

37.15 Motor insurance certificates are commonly expressed to cover any car owned by the policyholder. However, it is generally understood that they cover only one car at a time. Thus, in one IOB case[1] the policyholder insured one car, but she and her partner then acquired an additional car. It was held that the certificate did not cover this. In part this appears to be an application of general principle, but in part it depends on the fact that the policy schedule made clear that only one car was covered. However, it is usual for policy schedules to include this information, so the decision appears to be of general application.

In *Dodson v Peter H Dodson Insurance Services*[2] the insured held a policy in respect of a named car, which had the usual extension for driving other cars not owned by him. He sold the named vehicle and, in the interval before acquiring a replacement, drove his mother's car (with her permission). He was involved in an accident, and the Court of Appeal held that he was still covered by his own policy. The decision came as something of a surprise to much of the insurance industry because it had long been assumed that cover either lapsed or was suspended in such circumstances[3]. It should be noted that the decision turns to a large extent on the particular wording of the policy. It should not be assumed that the same result will e reached in al! motor policies.

[1] IOB 11.26.
[2] [2001] Lloyd's Rep IR 278, CA.
[3] The principal cases were *Rogerson v Scottish Automobile and General Insurance Co Ltd* (1931) 48 TLR 17, HL; *Tattersall v Drysdale* [1935] 2 KB 174; *Boss v Kingston* [1962] 2 Lloyd's Rep 431; *Wilkinson v General Accident Fire and Life Assurance Corpn Ltd* [1967] 2 Lloyd's Rep 182.

Social domestic and pleasure use

37.16 Motor policies commonly restrict usage to 'social domestic and pleasure'. The intention is to exclude business use, but travel to and from the policyholder's place of employment is conventionally covered by this phrase, thus leading to the gibe that insurers think that going to work is a pleasure (since it is neither social nor domestic). In a case[1] where the policy had this limitation and the policyholder had, in breach of the policy terms, been using the car as a minicab an accident occurred after he had dropped the last passengers of the night and was returning home. The Court of Appeal held that this fell within the policy, notwithstanding the earlier improper use and notwithstanding that the 'accident' consisted of the policyholder deliberately driving the car at his former passengers and injuring one of them[2]. Brooke LJ observed that the statutory scheme of road traffic insurance is intended to protect innocent third parties and that it is consequently necessary to adopt a benevolent interpretation of policy wordings in order to achieve that effect.

1 *Keeley v Pashen* [2004] EWCA Civ 149, [2005] Lloyd's Rep IR 289.
2 The claim against the insurers was brought under s 151 of the RTA 1988.

Offences in conjunction with compulsory insurance

Driving whilst uninsured

37.17 In *Adams v Dunne*[1] the defendant was disqualified for holding a driving licence. He obtained an insurance cover-note by telling the insurers that he was not disqualified. The question was whether he was guilty of driving while uninsured at a time when the insurers had not discovered the fraud and had therefore not cancelled the cover-note. It was held that he was not; the policy was of course voidable, but until it was avoided it remained effective[2].

1 [1978] RTR 281, DC.
2 Relying upon *Durrant v Maclaren* [1956] 2 Lloyd's Rep 70, DC.

The MIB

37.18 A person who suffers loss in circumstances where a motor policy is required to be in force may find that no such policy in fact existed. This may occur because the driver had no insurance, or because the policy did not cover the events which happened, or because the driver cannot be traced. In these circumstances a claim may be made against the MIB. The rules relating to such claims are examined in detail in Chapter 28.

Contractual issues

37.19 In addition to questions about compulsory insurance, motor insurance gives rise to some difficult issues about the contract of insurance itself.

Non-disclosure of convictions

37.20 As a general proposition criminal convictions of the proposer are regarded as going to moral hazard and therefore require to be disclosed. In personal lines policies, where the SGIP requires material facts to be the subject of specific questions[1], failure to draft the question properly can be a trap for unwary insurers. In one IOB case[2] the question about convictions made no mention of fixed-penalty notices (ie speeding offences), although the insurer's underwriting guide indicated that these were not acceptable. The Ombudsman took the view that a proposer might reasonably regard fixed penalties as being different from convictions, since, although they involved a licence endorsement, there was no court proceeding and the penalty was not fixed by a judge. The logic of this is that insurers need to take care to ask specifically about such matters if they want to be able to rely upon them.

[1] Clause 1(f).
[2] IOB 7.4.

Meaning of 'disability or prohibition' under the Rehabilitation of Offenders Act 1974[1], s 5

37.21 Section 5(8) of this Act provides:

> '(8) Where in respect of a conviction an order was made imposing on the person convicted any disqualification, disability, prohibition or other penalty, the rehabilitation period applicable to the sentence shall be a period beginning with the date of conviction and ending on the date on which the disqualification, disability, prohibition or penalty (as the case may be) ceases or ceased to have effect'.

In *Power v Provincial Insurance plc*[2] it was held that an endorsement of a license following a conviction of drink driving was not a disability or prohibition under s 5(8) of the Act as the expression meant an order restricting the subject from undertaking certain activities for a limited period and did not contemplate the activity of applying for a new driving licence. By contrast it seems that an order disqualifying a person from driving clearly does fall within this provision.

[1] For the ROA 1974 generally, see Chapter 5; the statute causes some criminal convictions to be 'spent' after a certain period, with the result that they do not need to be disclosed, even if they would otherwise be material.
[2] [1998] RTR 60, CA.

No claims discounts[1]

37.22 In one IOB case[2] the policyholder had obtained insurance by misrepresenting that he was entitled to three years' no claims discount ('NDC'). This inaccuracy only came to light when a claim was made. The insurer sought to avoid the policy, saying that it would not have given cover at all if it had known the true situation. The Insurance Ombudsman upheld the policyholder's complaint, taking the view that the proper course in such circumstances was a proportionate settlement, based on the fact that most insurers would have charged an increased premium for the policyholder's circumstances, but would not have refused cover. An oddity of this case is that the insurer concerned had a policy of not giving cover at all to anyone with less than three years' NCD. The decision clearly goes far beyond the policyholder's legal rights, since there had been a blatant misrepresentation when the policy was taken out[3].

A common cause of complaint by policyholders is that their NCD is reduced when they make a claim, even though the accident is not their fault. However, the policy wording is normally clear, and, as is often pointed out in such cases, the discount is a No *Claim* Discount, not a No *Blame* Discount.

1 Also commonly – though inaccurately – referred to as 'No Claims Bonus'.
2 IOB 10.28.
3 Although the IOB report is not clear on the point, it must be assumed that the Ombudsman found the misrepresentation to be innocent, since the normal policy has been not to give any relief in respect of deliberate or negligent misrepresentations.

Theft and TWOCing

37.23 Many motor policies provide cover for loss by theft. It is a basic rule of insurance law that technical words in a policy receive their technical legal meaning[1], and the definition of theft[2] requires an intention to permanently to deprive the owner of the property. Consequently, there is no theft when the vehicle is taken by joyriders, and the theft clause does not provide cover if those joyriders then destroy or damage the vehicle (the joyriders commit the separate offence of Taking Without Owner's Consent – 'TWOCing' – contrary to s 12 of the Theft Act 1968). In the absence of clear evidence to the contrary the taking of a car for no other purpose than joyriding, especially if done by a member of the policyholder's family, is very likely to be treated as TWOCing rather than as theft[3].

The position is of course different if the policy provides comprehensive cover, since there is then no need for the policyholder to show that the vehicle has been stolen, merely that it has been damaged by an external cause. In recent years it has been known for insurers to restrict their exposure to this particular risk by excluding cover where the car has been taken or driven by a person not permitted to drive who was a member of the policyholder's family. Such a clause is intended to deal with the case where the joyrider is a child (usually, but not necessarily, under-age) of the policyholder. Although such clauses are of course capable of being effective, the Insurance Ombudsman has held[4] that they are sufficiently unusual to need to be brought specifically to the attention of the policyholder when the policy is taken out.

1 See further Chapter 16.
2 Theft Act 1968, s 1.
3 See IOB 15.20, where an argument to the contrary was rightly rejected.
4 IOB 8.10.

Loss by deception

37.24 Motor policies, like household policies, now sometimes exclude loss caused by deception[1]. In one IOB case[2] it was held that this exclusion applied where the policyholder's car turned out to have been stolen, with the result that she had to return it to the true owner. The correctness of this decision appears to depend upon the fact that the vendor had been prosecuted in relation to the car (presumably for receiving stolen property). If it appeared that the immediate vendor had acted innocently, then it is suggested that the deception, which must have happened at an earlier stage in the car's chain of title, would be too remote to be considered as being the cause of the loss.

[1] This trend is a result of the decision of the Court of Appeal in *Dobson v General Accident Fire and Life Assurance Corpn plc* [1989] 3 All ER 927, CA.
[2] IOB 11.27.

Selling and buying cars

37.25 A policyholder who sells his car and buys another during the term of the policy must take care to avoid being uninsured. Policies are commonly restricted to the car declared by the policyholder at inception, though insurers will normally arrange a transfer of the cover to a new car on the basis of an appropriate adjustment of premium and a small administration fee. However, it must be remembered that this should be arranged *before* the change of vehicles takes place. In one IOB case[1] the Insurance Ombudsman appears to have taken a somewhat generous view of this requirement. The policyholder sold his car of Friday and bought another on Sunday. He intended to notify the insurer of the change on Monday, but before he could do so the car was involved in an accident. The Ombudsman, being satisfied that the failure to notify was an 'oversight', held that the insurer should indemnify the policyholder as if notice had been given (it was accepted that cover would have been provided if notice had been given). The company also provided evidence to the police that there was insurance cover in place at the time of the accident. It is submitted that this decision, whilst understandable, goes some way beyond the strict legal rights of the policyholder.

[1] IOB 10.25.

Recovery of stolen vehicle – agents of necessity

37.26 In *Egertons v KGM Motor Policies at Lloyd's*[1] the claimant sought to recover storage and recovery charges as a result of recovery of an abandoned and partly burnt out vehicle. It was held that there was no contract between the claimant, the insurers or the owner and that the claimant was not acting as an agent of necessity in recovering the vehicle.

[1] [1997] CLY 3168, county court.

Measurement of loss

37.27 Quantum of loss is a difficult issue in motor insurance cases[1], especially where the vehicle is entirely written off. A common problem is that the policyholder finds that the sum offered by the insurance company is not enough to replace the car he previously had. Another aspect of the same problem arises where the car is written off very soon after the policyholder has bought it, yet the insurers offer a sum much less than he paid for it. The explanation of both situations is the same. The policyholder is entitled to receive what the car was worth *to him* immediately before the accident, which is the sum for which he could have sold it on the open market. That is not the same as the sum which he would have had to pay to buy an identical car from a dealer. The inevitable consequence of this is that even under an indemnity policy the policyholder loses out in that he has to fund the dealer's profit out of his own pocket. Unfortunately, the problem is aggravated by the tendency of insurers to take as the basis for their valuation of the car the amount which a dealer would have paid for it. This is of course somewhat less than the policyholder could have expected to obtain by selling the car on the open market. It may be added that in many cases the figure quoted in the standard guides for trade-in[2] are somewhat on the conservative side, and an astute owner can often get a rather higher figure. Thus, although insurers are right in the basis of their valuation, the way in which they apply that basis is sometimes not fair to policyholders, who might do well to be prepared to challenge it.

Quantum of compensation causes many problems in motor insurance cases, and one of the reasons for this is the practice of insurers who ask the policyholder to declare the value of the vehicle on the proposal form. In the first place it may be said that the valuation of a motor vehicle is not an exact science, so that it is simply not possible to give a precise answer to the question. In the second place it is necessary to remember that motor policies are not valued policies – the universal practice is that indemnity is based upon the pre-accident value of the vehicle[3] (which might be different from the value stated on the proposal form, even if that value could be taken for practical purposes as being accurate at the time when stated). Unfortunately, many policyholders appear, perhaps understandably, to be under the impression that the value stated on the proposal form states the basis of indemnity in the case of a total loss. Indeed, as the Insurance Ombudsman has pointed out[4], the asking of the question is itself problematic if the value is not conclusive. In fact, insurers do have good reason for asking this question, not least because the existence of a high value may lead them to restrict the scope of cover in various ways.

[1] Unlike marine insurance, motor insurance does not in practice use agreed values.
[2] Parker's and Glass's.
[3] See also IOB 9.15.
[4] IOB 7.

Post-accident residual depreciation

37.28 This is a phenomenon which arises only where a car has been repaired after an accident. It is based upon the argument that a car which has been involved in an accident is, *for that reason alone,* worth less than an otherwise identical car which has not suffered an accident. This is said to arise from the fact that purchasers are wary of such cars, believing that the consequences of the accident may have weakened the vehicle in some way. The logic of this theory is that the value of a car is reduced post-accident, even though the physical damage caused by the accident has been repaired. It is therefore said that insurers ought properly in such cases to add a sum over and above the cost of repairs in order to indemnify the policyholder for the post-accident residual depreciation. The Insurance Ombudsman has been prepared to recognise the existence of post-accident residual depreciation and to award appropriate (though generally fairly small) sums to cover it.

Previously written-off cars

37.29 In one IOB case[1] the policyholder's car was written off, and the insurers made an offer of settlement, which the policyholder rejected. Then the insurers discovered that the car had previously been written off. They therefore reduced the offer to reflect the previous writing-off. The Ombudsman upheld the policyholder's complaint. He had bought the car in good faith (having no access to the register which would have told him of the car's history) and the Ombudsman considered that an insurer wishing to make a deduction in these circumstances should tell the policyholder of this specifically and should check the Motor Insurers Anti Fraud and Theft Register before entering into the policy. In another IOB case[2] the insurer offered less than the guide price for a written-off car on the basis that it had suffered previous damage, with the result that its pre-accident value was less than the guide price. The Ombudsman agreed that the previous damage had to be taken into account, but the appropriate reduction was not the cost of repairing that damage. Rather it was the amount by which the damage reduced the value of the car.

[1] IOB 10.30.
[2] IOB 10.32.

The recovery of stolen vehicles

37.30 *Service Motor Policies at Lloyds v City Recovery Ltd*[1] resolved an important practical question about the right to reclaim stolen vehicles which are later recovered. The case concerns the provisions of the Road Traffic Regulation Act 1984 ('RTRA 1984'), where there is conflict between the interests of innocent victims of car theft or, perhaps more importantly, their insurers and those whose services are used to remove abandoned cars from places in which they have been dumped.

In the two test cases here considered, stolen cars were recovered by the defendants at the request of the police. The insurers had settled theft claims in respect of these cars, and were thus in accordance with normal principles the owners of the cars[2].

The defendants' position was that neither vehicle would be returned until the claimants or their agents paid for the appropriate recovery charges and storage fees. The defendants claimed a lien on each car and a right to possession until such payment.

The current legislation stems from the Refuse Disposal (Amenity) Act 1978 and is now set out in the RTRA 1984. Section 99 of the RTRA 1984 provides for circumstances in which abandoned or broken down vehicles may be removed from the position in which they have been found.

[1] [1997] CLY 3167, CA.
[2] See Chapter 22.

37.31 By contrast with s 100, which provides for the interim disposal of such vehicles and arrangements for their safe custody, s 101 of the RTRA 1984 provides for their 'ultimate' disposal.

The relevant part of s 101(1) provides:

> 'a competent authority may, in such manner as they think fit, dispose of a vehicle which appears to them to be abandoned …'

The local police fall within the definition of 'competent authority', and when the defendants acted as they did in relation to each vehicle their actions were authorised in accordance with an agreement between them and the police which was known as the Garage Call Out Scheme. Assuming that the time for disposal in accordance with s 101(3) had arrived, the powers granted under s101(1) are wide enough to enable the competent authority to override the wishes of the true owner over abandoned vehicles which have been removed in accordance with the provisions of the Act. Nevertheless they remain subject to the limitation imposed by s 101(4). This provides:

> 'If, before a vehicle (found outside Greater London) is disposed of by an authority … the vehicle is claimed by a person who satisfies the authority that he is its owner and pays such sums in respect of its removal and storage as may be prescribed to the authority entitled to those sums, the authority shall permit him to remove the vehicle from their custody within such period as may be prescribed.'

37.32 Section 101(5) provides:

> 'If, before the end of the period of one year beginning with the date on which a vehicle (found outside Greater London) is sold by an authority in pursuance of this section, any person satisfies that authority that at the time of the sale he was the owner of the vehicle, that authority shall pay him any sum by which the proceeds of sale exceed the aggregate of such sums in respect of the removal, storage and disposal of the vehicle as may be prescribed.'

This subsection underlines the statutory entitlement to prescribed sums for storage and removal; the original owner of the vehicle does not recover the proceeds of sale in their entirety but simply the balance left after deduction of the prescribed sums.

37.33 Section 102 is directly concerned with the charges which may be made by an authority exercising the statutory duties under the legislation which are recoverable from the person 'responsible' for them whether he applies for the return of the vehicle or not. He is defined for the purposes of s 102 alone as:

> '(a) the owner of the vehicle at the time when it was put in the place from which it was removed … unless he shows that he was not concerned, and did not know of its being put there
> (b) any person by whom the vehicle was put in that place
> (c) any person convicted of an offence under s 2(1) of the Refuse Disposal (Amenity) Act 1978 in consequence of the putting of the vehicle in that place.'

Neither of the owners of the stolen cars nor their insurers was concerned with or knew of the dealings of the thieves with their respective vehicles and none of them fell within this definition. Accordingly they were exempt from charges made under s 102.

It was argued that as the defendants could not establish their entitlement to make charges against the owners of the vehicles under s 102 they lacked any justification for their refusal to restore the vehicles to their owners unconditionally. The defendants suggested that their justification was provided by s 101(4) and that they were not required to return the vehicles to their owners until the prescribed sums for removal and storage had been paid. The question was whether s 101 is subject to s 102 or whether it stood alone. The Court of Appeal held that it stood alone. Unless ss 101 and 102 were concerned with different situations it would not have been necessary to enact them both nor to provide a separate regulation making power in each of them. The provision exempting innocent vehicle owners from charges is confined to s 102 itself. No similar saving provision appears or is applied to s 101 and if it had been intended that the exemption in s 102 should extend to the circumstances covered by s 101 the section would have been drafted accordingly. Section 101 focuses on prescribed 'sums' whereas s 102 focuses on prescribed 'charges', a distinction highlighted by the regulations made under both sections which throughout maintain the distinction between prescribed sums and prescribed charges, a distinction highlighted by the reference in the title to prescribed charges and sums.

37.34 The difference between the two sections is identified in the heading to s 101 which is concerned with the ultimate disposal of abandoned vehicles after the appropriate time and circumstances for disposal have arisen. In such cases the owner is not precluded from seeking the return of his vehicle. If he does so then the prescribed sums for removal and storage must be paid. If he does not, the vehicle is disposed of, and if that happens he must give credit for the removal and storage sums before he can recover the balance of the proceeds of sale. In other words, although not strictly speaking a lien, before a vehicle to which s 101 applies must be returned to its owner there is a price to be paid for its recovery and storage, but once it has been paid or a genuine offer to pay has been made) the garage cannot then continue to retain the vehicle.

By contrast liability to pay charges under s 102 arises against those responsible for dumping a vehicle or parking or leaving it in an inappropriate place. It is unnecessary for the purposes of this judgment to recite all the situations in which s 102 will arise. But the charge under s 102 arises whether or not a claim is made for the return of the vehicle and this no doubt explains why it was felt appropriate to provide a measure of protection from such liabilities for the innocent owner.

The defendants were therefore not required to surrender up possession of either vehicle until the prescribed sums for removal and storage had been paid.

Credit hire agreements

37.35 Where the policyholder's car is rendered unusable as a result of an accident it is common practice for motor insurers to offer arrangements (known as 'credit hire agreements') under which a replacement car can be provided while the policyholder's car is repaired. If the accident is the fault of someone other than the policyholder, the insurer will seek to recover the cost of the hire from the party responsible for the accident. A refinement on this simple scheme is that the policyholder is not required to pay the hire costs until the conclusion of the litigation, the expectation being that they will be recovered from the negligent defendant. However, such agreements routinely provide that the policyholder remains liable for the costs in the event that they cannot be recovered from the defendant. The legality of such schemes has been challenged on the ground that they are champertous. The arguments in relation to this point were exhaustively analysed by the House of Lords in *Giles v Thompson*[1].

The defendants argued that the agreements contained an element of champerty, and that the claimants had suffered no relevant loss since they had been provided with the car hire free of charge. The House of Lords held that the agreements were not champertous. The hire companies had no proprietary right in sums recovered from the defendants, they made their money from the hiring, not from the litigation, the claimant remained personally liable for the hire charges and the solicitors acting for the claimants, even if nominated by the hire companies, would have had to act in the interests of the claimants rather than in the interests of the hire company: consequently, the claimants remained in control of the litigation and there was no risk to the proper administration of justice. Moreover, the car hire had not been provided free of charge; although payment had been deferred, it was an essential element of the agreement that the claimants remained liable if the costs were not recovered from the defendant. A question which does not appear to have been considered in *Giles v Thompson* is whether credit hire agreements are caught by the Consumer Credit Act 1974 ('CCA 1974'). This point was raised in *Dimond v Lovell*[2]. The claimant's car was damaged in an accident with a car driven by the defendant. While the claimant's car was being repaired, she hired a vehicle under a credit hire agreement The defendant's insurers resisted the claim for the hire charges on the ground that the agreement was a consumer credit agreement within the meaning of s 8(2) of the CCA 1974, that it had not been properly executed in accordance with the statutory requirements and that accordingly it was unenforceable against the claimant. It therefore followed that the claimant was not obliged to pay the hire charges, and thus she could not claim them as damages. The claimant contended, inter alia, that, even if the agreement was a consumer credit agreement, it was enforceable since it was possible for the prescribed requirements to be varied or waived by an application under s 60(3) of the Act. Alternatively, she contended that the unenforceability of the agreement did not prevent her from recovering the hire charges as damages.

The House of Lords held that for the purposes of the CCA 1974, debt was deferred, and credit extended, whenever a contract entitled the debtor to pay later than the time when payment would otherwise have been earned under that contract. Thus the credit was the difference between the contractual date of payment and the date when payment would have been required but for that stipulation. Furthermore, an agreement for the hire of an article involved the acquisition of a service, and accordingly the deferment of an obligation to pay hire charges constituted the provision of credit. Thus the agreement allowed the claimant credit and was, inter alia, a personal credit agreement and a consumer credit agreement within the meaning of s 8 of the Act. That agreement was not enforceable against the claimant since it did not contain all the terms prescribed by the CCA 1974. Section 127(3) prevents the court from making an order correcting defects of this kind. Accordingly, the claimant was under no legal liability to pay the hire charges. Where a claimant receives, at no cost to himself, a benefit from a third party which offsets loss caused by the defendant's negligence, the claimant cannot recover damages to recompense that third party unless a trust can be imposed on those damages for the latter's benefit. Such a trust would not be imposed to remedy a situation where the third party's failure to comply with statutory requirements had rendered unenforceable an agreement between it and the claimant. Nor could arguments relating to unjust enrichment be used, because it was clear that Parliament had intended the formal requirements of the CCA 1974 to be mandatory. The only proper way to achieve this result was to hold that an improperly executed agreement could not be enforced by any means at all. It followed that in the instant case the claimant could not recover the hire charges as damages[3]. The consequence appears to be that a whole generation of credit hire agreements is effectively wiped out, with claimants being required to meet the costs of hiring replacement cars. However, the decision does not lead to the conclusion that credit hire agreements can never be effective. Presumably care will be taken to ensure that the next generation of such agreements complies properly with the requirements of the CCA 1974.

[1] [1993] 3 All ER 321.
[2] [1999] 3 All ER 1, [2000] 1 QB 216, [1999] RTR 297, CA, upheld by the House of Lords in a judgment as yet unreported. See also *Stares v Deradour* (24 May 1999, unreported); *Perehenic v Deboa Structuring* [1998] CLY 1467; *Bucknall v Jepson* [1998] CLY 1456; *Spence v United Taxis* [1998] CLY 1465; *Giles v Thompson* [1993] 3 All ER 321; *McAll v Brooks* [1984] RTR 99, CA.
[3] See also *Hunt v Severs* [1994] 2 All ER 385.

Approved repairers

37.36 It is an increasingly common practice for motor insurers to include in policies arrangements whereby an approved repairer is nominated to deal with the repair of accident damage. These schemes often include provision for a courtesy car, with free collection and return of the damaged vehicle, guaranteed repairs and automatic acceptance of the approved repairer's estimate. Such schemes have the potential to be very useful, but they can also go badly wrong when it is alleged that the standard of service offered by the approved repairer is less than ideal[1]. The general principle to be applied in resolving cases of this kind must be that the approved repairer acts as the insurer's agent, with the result that the insurer is liable for failings in the standard of workmanship or service provided. Complaints about such matters have frequently come before the Insurance Ombudsman, where the difficult issues appear to have been evidential questions about the quality of the work and questions about the appropriate level of compensation in cases where failings have been discovered.

As to the evidential questions, it must be for the policyholder to substantiate his case, as always, though the Ombudsman is prepared to bear in mind the difficulties of obtaining clear proof, even in a justified case[2]. On the question of compensation, it is necessary to distinguish the provable costs of correcting defective repairs from the more nebulous claims for inconvenience and consequential expense resulting from poor workmanship and/or delays in returning the car. There is no reason why the former should not be recoverable in full, subject to the necessary evidence. So far as the latter are concerned, the Ombudsman's approach, in line with the treatment of claims of the same kind in other contexts, has been to award only relatively modest sums for inconvenience[3].

[1] A good account of the various difficulties may be found in IOB 22.

[2] IOB 22.
[3] For examples, see IOB 22.15–22.18.

Chapter 38

Household contents policies

Introduction

38.1 Household contents policies protect against the risk of loss or damage to the contents of the house. They should be contrasted with household buildings policies (Chapter 39), which deal with the fabric of the house[1]. By their nature these are personal lines policies, which means that this is an area in which the Insurance Ombudsman is the principal arbiter. The Chapter therefore concentrates largely on IOB decisions, though there are also a few decisions of the courts. Some contents policies also have extensions for public liability. These clauses are considered in Chapter 50.

[1] In practice, buildings and contents policies are often combined, and either or both may also be combined with public liability insurance.

Coverage

What are 'contents'?

38.2 There is no general legal definition of household contents, the matter being left to individual policies. Problems of two kinds may be identified. The first is where something is within the house which is not of a kind normally expected to be found within a dwelling place. In the absence of an express policy term it is submitted that anything which is within the boundaries of the house is for the time being 'contents', though issues of non-disclosure could arise if at inception[1] there were something on the premises which was wholly outside the range of what might normally be found within a house. Of course, if it does not belong to the policy-holder (or a member of his family) the principle of indemnity is likely to restrict severely the amount which can be recovered in respect of it. The policy may also define how far the boundaries of the home extend – do they include domestic outbuildings, or garages, for example? And what about furniture in the garden? Where these limits are broadly drawn, apparently odd results may arise. In one IOB case[2] four car wheels were stolen from the parking area of the block of flats in which the policyholder lived. Although such a loss would not normally be covered, this policy defined contents as 'household goods or other articles in the house or its domestic outbuildings or garages'. Car wheels might not normally be thought of as contents, but in the absence of an exclusion for motor vehicle accessories, they fell within the scope of this policy.

[1] The question of whether it was a 'normal' household item might also arise in relation to something bought during the policy.
[2] IOB 5.6.

What are 'personal possessions'?

38.3 Some contents policies offer extended cover to personal possessions when these are outside the home, the term 'personal possessions' usually being defined by reference to clothing, valuables, sports equipment and other items which are worn or normally carried. In one IOB case[1] it was held that an electric guitar could fall within this definition.

[1] IOB 17.5.

When loss happens

38.4 Contents policies often contain exclusions for theft of property from unattended road vehicles. In a case[1] where the policyholder's car was stolen, complete with contents, the Insurance Ombudsman held that the theft had not been *from* the car, so that the exclusion did not apply. In another case[2] belongings were mislaid. The policyholders replaced them, but they were later recovered. The Ombudsman held that there had nevertheless been a loss, since the policy did not restrict cover to permanent loss. The insurers were of course in theory entitled to take possession of the recovered items as salvage.

[1] IOB 6.1.
[2] IOB 13.13.

Meaning of 'jewellery'

38.5 In *Whitby, Re, Public Trustee v Whitby*[1] Lord Greene MR said:

> '... the word jewellery would cover jewels collectively and would cover gems sold by jewellers, just as it covers the case of jewels made up into an article of adornment such as a brooch or anything of that kind[2].'

[1] [1994] Ch 210, [1944] 1 All ER 299.
[2] See also IOB 7.3, where the Ombudsman followed this approach.

'Recording, audio and video equipment'

38.6 Video tapes, CDs and video games do not fall within this definition, since they are not equipment for the purpose of recording[1].

[1] IOB 8.3.

Windows

38.7 Where a policy provides that all opening or accessible windows must be fitted with specified security precautions, questions arise as to which windows are 'opening' and which are 'accessible'. A window which is clamped and padlocked shut is not an opening window[1]. Accessibility is more difficult. From one point of view it might be thought that any window through which an intruder enters is by definition accessible, since someone has managed to gain access to it[2]. However, the Insurance Ombudsman has held[3] that this is too broad an interpretation, and that accessible must mean *reasonably* accessible. It may be doubted whether this is legally correct. Equally doubtful from a strict legal point of view is another IOB decision[4], where reliance was placed upon the fact that the policyholder might well not have appreciated that a particular window was accessible.

1 IOB 9.6.
2 IOB 10.19, where this was argued.
3 IOB 9.6.
4 IOB 10.19.

Family members

38.8 Where a proposal form asked about the criminal convictions of 'any member of your family or any other person living with you' this did not extend to family members not living with the proposers[1]. To hold otherwise would bring into the equation distant relatives who could not possibly be thought material to the granting of insurance.

1 IOB 11.23.

Theft

38.9 *Dobson v General Accident Fire & Life Assurance Corpn*[1] required the Court of Appeal to consider an important general point about the meaning of 'theft' in a household contents policy. The policyholder owned some jewellery which he advertised for sale in a local newspaper. A prospective purchaser rang up to discuss the items, then came round to the policyholder's house. A price was agreed, and the purchaser later returned with a building society cheque for the agreed amount. The policyholder allowed him to take the items away. The cheque proved to have been stolen, and was therefore worthless. The policyholder claimed on the policy on the basis that the jewellery had been stolen. It is of course normally understood that technical words in an insurance policy must be given their technical legal meaning[2], so the question was whether the requirements of s 1 of the Theft Act 1968[3] were satisfied. Given that the purchaser was obviously dishonest, this resolved itself into an issue of whether property in the goods had passed to the purchaser before the appropriation. The starting point is ss 17 and 18 of the Sale of Goods Act 1979, which provide that property passes when the parties intend it to pass[4], but in the absence of any contrary indication it is assumed that in a contract for the sale of specific goods property is intended to pass at the time when the contract is made[5]. The application of this presumption would have led to the conclusion that property had passed before the goods were handed over. The Court of Appeal was able to avoid this outcome by holding that the intention of the seller was that property should pass only in exchange for a *valid* form of payment. As no such payment had been received, it followed that property had not been passed, the purchaser had appropriated property belonging to another, and there had been a loss by theft. The decision has been much criticised, not least on the ground that it conflates the offence of theft with that of obtaining property by deception contrary to s 15 of the Theft Act 1968. The question of whether the offence of theft is committed in such cases has also been considered in a criminal context in *R v Gomez*[6], where it was held that the offence of theft could be (and on facts materially similar to those of *Dobson* had been) committed even though the circumstances might also fall within s 15. It is to be noted that since this case some insurers have adopted the practice of adding to the theft section of household contents policies an exclusion for loss caused by deception. This would appear to be effective to exclude cover in cases such as *Dobson*.

[1] [1990] 1 QB 274, CA.
[2] See for example cases such as *Dobson v General Accident*, where the court spent much time on an analysis of whether the events which had happened amounted to theft.
[3] Anyone who dishonestly appropriates property belonging to another with the intention of permanently depriving that other of it shall be guilty of theft.
[4] Section 17.
[5] Section 18, r 1.
[6] [1993] 1 All ER 1.

Flood

38.10 In *Young v Sun Alliance*[1] the Court of Appeal offered a definition of flood in an insurance context as:

> 'Something large, sudden and temporary, not naturally there, such as a river overflowing its banks'.

On that basis it was held that there was no flood where seepage of water caused an accumulation of a few inches depth. In *Computer & Systems Engineering plc v John Leliot (Ilford) Ltd*[2], a case concerning the escape of water from a sprinkler system, but in the context of the standard Joint Contracts Tribunal ('JCT') contract, Beldam LJ added:

> 'Flood, in my view, imports the invasion of the property … by a large volume of water from an external source, usually but not necessarily confined to the result of a natural phenomenon such as a storm, tempest or downpour'.

In *Rohan Investments Ltd v Cunningham and Members of Syndicate 877 at Lloyds (t/a Criterion Insurance Services)*[3] the Court of Appeal considered both these definitions. The evidence showed that the accumulation of water had happened over a period of about nine days, during which there had been severe weather conditions. It was held that the latter case did not prescribe rigid criteria for determining whether there had been a flood. The Court considered that the important issues were whether: (1) the accumulation had been sufficiently rapid to be abnormal; (2) a sufficient amount of water had found its way into the house to cause damage to the contents; and (3) any condition or warranty in the policy could be invoked. It held that unless the terms of the insurance policy restricted the definition of the word 'flood' it should be given its normal and ordinary meaning and that the size and nature of the property and the circumstances which may give rise to flooding and consequent damage should also be taken into account – it is all a matter of degree.

[1] [1976] 3 All ER 561, CA.
[2] (1990) 54 BLR 1, CA.
[3] [1999] Lloyd's Rep IR 190, CA.

Entry by forcible and violent means

38.11 This phrase, which has been in use for over a hundred years, is often found in household policies as a means of restricting cover for loss by theft. Its meaning was authoritatively reconsidered by the Court of Appeal in *Dino Services Ltd v Prudential Assurance Co Ltd*[1], where the policyholder's business premises had been burgled by thieves who had obtained the keys. It was held that there is forcible entry where even minimal force is used. Thus, an entry obtained by turning the handle of an outside door or by using a skeleton key is made by forcible means. However, violent entry requires a much greater degree of force, such as breaking down a door or smashing a window. Thus, turning the handle or using the skeleton key, though sufficient to constitute a criminal offence, is not within the policy since the element of violence is absent[2].

In an IOB case[3] there was an exclusion of this type. The policyholder's property was in storage and there was evidence of forcible and violent entry to that part of the building where his property was stored, but no evidence of such entry to the building itself. It was held that it would not be fair and reasonable for the insurer to decline cover on these facts. The decision clearly does not represent the law.

[1] [1989] 1 All ER 422, [1989] 1 Lloyd's Rep 379, CA.
[2] See also *Re Calf and the Sun Alliance Insurance Office* [1920] 2 KB 366; and see IOB 5.2 for a case where the Ombudsman followed the *Dino* approach.
[3] IOB 8.4.

Works of art

38.12 Where household policies cover damage to works of art, the question may arise whether a particular item of property meets this definition. There appears to be no decision of the courts on the point, but the matter has been considered by the Insurance Ombudsman. In his 1986 Annual Report he stated that the three questions to be asked were:

(a) Has the object any use other than decoration or communication of ideas?
(b) If so, which is the prime function, the use or the decoration/communication?
(c) If the decoration/communication is the sole or prime function, is it the artist's original?

A later Ombudsman[1] glossed that by adding that the time for deciding whether something is a work of art is the time when the policy is taken out, not the time when the item is made. Something originally intended to be functional could by the passage of time become a work of art, though no firm rule could be laid down about the circumstances in which or the time at which this would happen. Thus a nineteenth century French rosewood clock was held to be a work of art within the meaning of the policy.

[1] IOB 6.5.

Repairs – role of insurer

38.13 As a general rule the insurer is not to be held responsible for the standard of workmanship and service provided by those repairing damage covered by a claim. However, the position is likely to be different where the insurer has chosen to repair the property and has engaged the contractor[1].

[1] IOB 13.10.

Matching items

38.14 A common provision in contents policies restricts the insurer's liability for costs of replacing matching items. This is designed to apply especially where for example one item in a three-piece suite is damaged and the material cannot be matched with the original. Policyholders will then naturally wish to have all the items recovered, including those which are not damaged. In the early days of the IOB it was held that in the absence of an express policy provision insurers ought to pay half the cost of recovering the undamaged items. As a result of this it became common for insurers to insert express clauses disclaiming any liability in such circumstances. An unusual application of a clause of this kind arose in one IOB case[1], where the damage was water damage to carpets and the carpets in a number of different rooms matched. As the damaged pieces could not be matched, the policyholder wanted to re-carpet all the matching areas. The insurer argued that each room, being separated from the other rooms by a door, was to be regarded as a clearly identifiable area, so that there was no liability to pay. The Ombudsman took the view that a single area for these purposes included all the rooms which could not be visually isolated from each other. As some of the doors between the rooms were glazed, this meant that a number of rooms had to be considered a single area for these purposes, and the insurer was obliged to pay for the re-carpeting of them.

[1] IOB 13.12, which also appears at IOB 18.12.

Property left unattended

38.15 It has become common for contents policies to contain an exclusion for property outside the home if it is left unattended. The term 'unattended' is not normally defined in policies, but the Ombudsman has held[1] that as a general rule property is unattended if it is out of sight of the person who has charge of it, with the result that that person is not able to look after it or prevent any attempt to interfere with it. By similar reasoning a policyholder had his complaint upheld[2] when his mobile phone was stolen, apparently from beside him, while he was in a public house. Although, obviously, he had not been able to prevent the theft, it did not follow that the phone had been unattended at the relevant time.

[1] IOB 13.16.
[2] IOB 21.21.

Responsible person

38.16 'Left unattended' clauses sometimes have a qualification that the property will remain covered if left in a room occupied by a responsible person. The Ombudsman has held that this means a person who has expressly or implicitly accepted responsibility for the property[1]. It is not sufficient that the person concerned is generally of an honest and trustworthy disposition. In *Shoshana Stern v Norwich Union Fire Insurance Society Ltd*[2] the appellant had lent a ring to her daughter-in-law who took it to her apartment in Jerusalem and lost it on 15 May 1992. The defendants accepted this as a genuine loss but relied upon an endorsement in the insurance policy making it a condition precedent to liability that the ring and other insured items should be kept in a locked safe at all times when not being worn and kept in the personal custody of the insured at all times. The Court of Appeal adopted a literal approach to the interpretation of the condition precedent and upheld the insurers' refusal to pay. This may perhaps be thought justified on the basis that the insurers had agreed to trust the policyholder to look after the item when it was out of the safe, but had not agreed to extend this trust to anyone else.

[1] IOB 15.16.
[2] 15 November 1996, unreported, CA.

Glass and furniture

38.17 In an IOB case[1] the policy covered escape of water from any 'fixed domestic water installation'[2]. It was held that a fish tank was not a fixed installation for these purposes. However, the policy also covered accidental damage to 'fixed glass in furniture'. The insurers argued that this clause did not apply because the fish tank was made almost entirely of glass, whereas the clause was intended to refer only to cases where the glass was a relatively small part of the furniture. This argument was rejected. The tank was made of glass panels fixed into place.

[1] IOB 23.10.
[2] See Chapter 39 for a case on the same phrase in relation to a buildings policy (IOB 23.8).

Valuation

38.18 Difficult questions of valuation and under-insurance can arise in household contents policies. Where the policy is written on the standard basis of settlement, the policyholder is entitled only to the marker value of the item immediately before the loss. Since the item would by definition have had to be sold as second-hand, that value will be much less than the cost of repairing it as new. Indeed, the second-hand value may in many cases be no more than nominal. For this reason many household policies are written on a new-for-old basis, where the policyholder receives the cost of replacing the item as new. Although this appears to breach the indemnity principle, it must be remembered that this principle is no more than a presumption and can be displaced by agreement.

38.19 Under-insurance causes problems in household policies because, especially where the policy is new-for-old because many policyholders underestimate the cost of replacing all their possessions as new. From the point of view of non-disclosure *Economides v Commercial Union Assurance Co plc*[1] establishes that in a household policy the only duty is to give an honest valuation, but under-insurance may still affect the amount recovered, at least where the policy has an average clause (since it appears that in the absence of express provision the doctrine of average does not apply to such policies).

[1] [1998] QB 587, CA.

Chapter 39

Household buildings policies

Introduction

39.1 Household buildings policies protect against the risk of damage to the fabric of the building. They should be contrasted with household contents policies (Chapter 38) which protect against damage to the contents. The dividing line between the two classes of policy can sometimes give rise to difficulty. This is of course an area concerned exclusively with personal lines policies, so the Chapter concentrates largely on decisions of the Insurance Ombudsman, though there are of course some important pre-1981 cases which establish important points of principle.

The National House Builders' Council ('NHBC') Agreement

39.2 In addition to any buildings policy which they may have effected, the purchasers of new homes will also normally have the benefit of the warranty offered by the NHBC. This warranty is available on all new properties built by builders who are members of the NHBC. In effect, the purchaser pays for the warranty, which is included in the price of the house. The builder purchases a bond, under which the NHBC provides the cover, and this is then transferred to the purchaser. It provides cover during the first two years from the first purchase of the building in respect of most defects which may appear during that time. For the following eight years it provides cover only against the risk of major structural defects. The warranty applies to the house rather than to the purchaser, so its validity is unaffected by sales of the house during that period. The householder is expected in the first instance to call on the builder to rectify any defects which fall within the scope of the cover. Only if the builder does not rectify them can the householder invoke the benefit of the NHBC cover by calling on the NHBC to cause the remedial work to be done. The NHBC will then look to the builder to make good the cost of the work, though in practice, the NHBC is very commonly called upon to do the work because the builder is insolvent. Disputes over the application of the NHBC scheme to any given case are within the jurisdiction of the Insurance Ombudsman.

Coverage

Central heating

39.3 Damage arising from central heating systems has been considered by the Insurance Ombudsman in a number of cases. In one case[1] there had been an escape of water from a copper central heating pipe in the floor of a flat. The pipe had a six-inch split which was consistent with frost damage. The insured claimed for the cost of tracing and repairing the leak and for internal redecoration. The insurers accepted the claim for redecoration, but declined the claim for tracing and repairing the leak. The policy provided cover against damage caused by the escape of water, but the damage to the pipe was obviously not caused by an escape of water. However, the policy also provided cover for accidental damage to service pipes for which the insured was responsible. It was held that the pipe was a service pipe, since these did not have to be external to the property, and the central heating was obviously a service.

In another case[2] the claim was for damage to the insured's property caused by fumes[3] from the central heating boiler passing up an unlined flue and causing staining and damage to the decoration of adjoining rooms. The policy provided cover against damage arising from water escaping from fixed water or heating installations. It was held that the damage was covered, since what went up the flue was largely made up of water, some of which escape through the unlined walls of the flue and caused the damage. The central heating system was indisputably a fixed heating installation.

[1] IOB 3.15.
[2] IOB 3.16.
[3] This is the word used in the IOB Bulletin, but it appears that is may be misleading in so far as it implies that these were *gas* fumes. The report makes sense only on the assumption that what escaped was primarily *steam*.

Proof of theft

39.4 The Insurance Ombudsman has held that where there is an allegation of theft in a claim on a household policy, the allegation need only be proved to the civil standard, ie on the balance of probabilities, rather than to the criminal standard, ie beyond reasonable doubt. Thus, where workmen who had not been paid for installation work entered the premises and removed some of the items which they had installed it was held that this was sufficient evidence of theft within the meaning of the policy, notwithstanding that they arguably intended to return them once they had been paid. It is submitted that the decision is correct on the point of law, but that its application to the facts is very questionable.

Subsidence

39.5 Subsidence is understood to relate to the collapse (total or partial) of property as well as to its settlement[1]. The latter point rests on a pre-war case, and it may well be that at that time the difference between the two was not so well understood as it now is. However, the point seems to be too well-settled to allow of any challenge at the present day. It may be said that subsidence occurs where the property moves, but not where the problem is caused by a bulging of the soil, which is more properly called heave. The modern tendency to include heave as a specific risk largely removes any significance this point might have had.

[1] *David Allen & Sons Billposting Ltd v Drysdale* [1939] 4 All ER 113.

Subsidence and non-disclosure

39.6 Claims for subsidence give rise to many difficulties. One concerns the possibility that the risk of subsidence has not been properly disclosed to the insurer at the outset. In some cases the survey report obtained by purchasers of a house mentions evidence of cracking, though it may not explicitly put this down to subsidence. As a general rule items of this kind require to be disclosed to insurers. Even where there is no evidence of damage to the insured property itself, it not infrequently happens that the property is in an area known to suffer badly from subsidence[1]. This is why proposal forms often ask whether other houses in the locality have suffered from subsidence. In the case of a personal lines policy the proposer is of course only required to answer this question to the best of his knowledge, information and belief, but an answer which does not comply with this standard will still be a material non-disclosure[2]. A point which does not appear to have been taken in any reported case, either before the courts or before the Insurance Ombudsman, is that insurers must have available to them information about areas which have particularly bad subsidence records. It might therefore be argued in at least some cases that this information does not require to be disclosed by the policyholder.

[1] Some areas are particularly at risk because of the character of the local soil; London Clay, for example, is notoriously prone to drying out and causing subsidence.
[2] IOB 4.7.

Accrual of cause of action for subsidence

39.7 It is in the nature of subsidence that it may go undetected for some time. In this event it may be difficult to decide which policy was current when the damage happened and thus difficult to decide which insurer should bear the risk. Of course the point is important only if insurers have changed during the relevant period. This happens especially often where ownership of a dwelling has changed and subsidence damage is discovered shortly thereafter. In order to deal with this problem some major insurance companies have adopted the practice of sharing liability between themselves, though as a general rule the policyholder should start by claiming against the insurer whose policy is current when the damage is discovered.

Subsidence repairs and betterment

39.8 In one case[1] the insurers agreed to pay for repairing damage caused by subsidence. In the course of the work it became apparent that two walls which were being repaired had additional, previously undiscovered defects. The insurer offered a 60% contribution to the cost of remedying these defects, on the basis that the defects were not caused by an insured peril and that there was an element of betterment in this repair. The Ombudsman decided that the insurer should meet the cost in full, apparently on the basis that the additional work was a necessary part of repairing the subsidence damage, that the repairs would not be visible once completed and that there was unlikely to be any significant increase in the value of the house resulting from the work. A similar result was reached in another case[2] where storm force winds caused cracking in a wall. It was accepted that hairline cracks had been present before the storm, but it was not possible to repair the storm damage without repairing the hairline cracks. The Ombudsman rejected the insurer's attempt to deduct the cost of repairing the hairline cracks. It is submitted that these decisions can only be regarded as an example of the Ombudsman's power to make a decision which he regards as fair and reasonable in all the circumstances. The legal position must surely be that the additional work was not covered on the simple ground that there was no evidence that it resulted from an insured peril[3].

[1] IOB 6.8.
[2] IOB 17.3.
[3] Though it might be argued that this is simply an example of inevitable betterment, so that the decision is right in law.

Subsidence and underpinning

39.9 A subsidence claim should not lead to payment for underpinning unless it can be shown that this is necessary in order to repair the damage. If it is purely a preventative measure to avoid future damage, then, in accordance with normal insurance principles, it is not in respect of loss caused by an insured peril and is therefore not recoverable[1].

[1] IOB 17.4.

Flood

39.10 The leading authority on what constitutes a 'flood' for the purposes of a household buildings policy is *Young v Sun Alliance*[1] where it was said that a flood must involve a large volume of water as well as some element of violence and suddenness. Thus, water seeping into a basement from failed basement tanking could not amount to a flood[2].

[1] [1977] 1 WLR 104, CA.
[2] IOB 4.8; see also *Rohan Investments Ltd v Cunningham* [1999] Lloyd's Rep IR 190, CA, which emphasised that the extent and speed of the inundation are matters of degree. See also Chapter 38.

Storm

39.11 The generally accepted definition of 'storm' for insurance purposes is that it consists of high winds accompanied by rain. Insurers adopt a rule of thumb that the wind must be of a speed of at least 35mph. The availability in many parts of the country of detailed weather records can allow insurers to determine with a high degree of accuracy whether there has been a storm in a given place at a given time. However, the Insurance Ombudsman has held that there can be cases where very heavy rainfall can by itself amount to a storm[1] even without the presence of high winds. It is submitted that this decision is not legally correct and must be regarded as being made under the fair and reasonable jurisdiction.

[1] IOB 17.2.

Storm as part cause of loss

39.12 A storm can lead to loss in the sense that it can identify damage which is not previously recognised as having occurred. A simple example would be where in a storm rain enters through a window of the policyholder's home and causes damage to carpets. This damage is clearly covered, but the policyholder may also seek to claim for the cost of replacing the window, alleging that it has been damaged beyond repair by the storm. The insurer's answer is likely to be that the damage to the window was not caused by the storm. Rather, the window is worn out, ie the problem is one of wear and tear and the storm has merely brought this to the policyholder's attention. Most buildings policies contain an exclusion along the lines of 'wear and tear or any other gradually operating cause'. It may be clear on the facts that the problem really is just wear and tear, but a more difficult case is that where the evidence suggests that the storm may have been the final straw which brings about the loss. Here the storm is a contributory factor in the loss, but is by no means the only cause. In a case of this kind[1] the Insurance Ombudsman held that the insurer should make a contribution to the cost of repair, that contribution apparently being assessed according to the role of the storm in causing the damage. It is not at all clear whether this conclusion accords with general insurance law. If the storm is an operating cause of the loss, especially if it is the last operating cause, then it would appear that the insurer ought to be liable to meet the claim in full.

[1] IOB 5, leading article.

Tempest

39.13 It is commonly supposed[1] that for insurance purposes a tempest is no more than a severe storm, although the point does not appear to have been authoritatively considered.

[1] *Young v Sun Alliance* [1976] 2 Lloyd's Rep 189, Shaw LJ.

Collision

39.14 One of the more unusual cases considered by the Insurance Ombudsman[1] occurred where the lining of the policyholder's swimming pool was damaged when one of his goats fell into it. He attempted to claim on the basis that this was damage caused by collision, but the Ombudsman rejected the claim, saying that it would be a misuse of language to describe what had happened here as a collision. The decision is clearly right as a matter of law.

[1] IOB 6.9.

Occupation of premises

39.15 Household buildings policies commonly contain exclusions which apply if the premises are 'vacant' or 'unoccupied' at the time of loss. Sometimes the proposal form also has questions about the occupation of the premises. The notion of 'occupation' is not defined and gives rise to difficulties when the policyholder is absent for a period of time. The Insurance Ombudsman has taken the view[1] that occupation should usually be understood as meaning occupation as a residence without any requirement of actual attendance. Thus the premises are still occupied during the day even though every member of the family is out at work or school. On the other hand when the family goes and lives somewhere else for six months, the premises are no longer occupied.

Where the proposal form has a question as to whether the premises will be unoccupied for more than a certain number[2] of days continuously, this is likely to be taken as meaning that shorter periods of unoccupancy do not need to be disclosed and have no effect on the cover[3]. The Ombudsman has held that a property is occupied for the purposes of a clause of this type even when the occupants are squatters[4].

An insurer seeking to rely upon an unoccupancy clause bears the burden of establishing that the loss occurred at a time when the clause was in force, ie after the premises had been unoccupied for the requisite time[5].

Some policies make the test not whether the premises are occupied, but whether they are furnished. In one IOB case[6] the policy further defined 'unfurnished' as 'insufficiently furnished for normal living purposes'. The Ombudsman held that premises were unfurnished when, despite containing a bed, cooker, fridge and fitted wardrobes, they had neither a table nor a chair[7].

[1] IOB 8, leading article.
[2] Commonly 30, but 45 is also sometimes found.
[3] IOB 9.4.
[4] IOB 20.14; though it may be observed that the presence of squatters is surely something which would need to be disclosed at renewal.
[5] IOB 10.14. This also seems to accord with the general law on burden of proof, as to which see Chapter 20.
[6] IOB 9.3.
[7] See also *Hair v Prudential Assurance* [1983] 2 Lloyd's Rep 667.

Impact damage

39.16 Where a buildings policy provides cover for impact damage the Ombudsman has taken a broad view of what amounts to impact. In one somewhat unusual case[1] one of the complainant's ponies escaped from its paddock and fell through the solar cover of the swimming pool. The pony also damaged the lining of the pool in its attempts to climb out. The Ombudsman held that this was impact damage because it could be said to be caused by the impact of the pony's hooves on the lining.

1 IOB 20.7.

Trees and shrubs

39.17 Buildings policies often exclude cover for damage to trees, but not hedges. In one case[1] the Insurance Ombudsman held that a row of leylandii, 2.5 metres high, planted to mark the boundary of the policyholder's property, were a hedge rather than trees.

1 IOB 10.18.

Time of damage and time of loss

39.18 In *Kelly v Norwich Union*[1] the claimant had a household buildings policy with the defendants. The policy was expressed to provide insurance against 'events occurring during the period of insurance'. Before the policy came into force a water pipe burst, causing an extensive discharge of water. The water caused damage to the house during the currency of the policy. It was held that the insurers were not on risk because the policy covered only loss from perils which materialised during the policy. It did not cover the situation where the peril occurred before the policy but damage was first suffered during the period of the policy. It may be that this decision can be explained on the basis that the policy referred to 'events' rather then 'losses' so that the vital date was when the water pipe burst. If the policy had been expressed – as many such policies are – to cover 'losses happening during the period of insurance' then it may well be that the loss would have been covered.

1 [1989] 2 All ER 888, CA.

Accidental damage

39.19 The Insurance Ombudsman has held[1] that damage to a floor and the ceiling below it caused by moving furniture across the room is accidental damage within the meaning of a household buildings policy. The insurer's defence that this was a normal household process and not an accident was rejected. It is submitted that the decision is correct in law. The moving of furniture may well be a normal household process, but the damage which resulted from it was clearly accidental.

1 IOB 17.1.

Quantum

39.20 It is usual for household buildings policies to leave the insurer with the option to repair, replace or pay the diminution in value resulting from the loss. In the ordinary case most insurers are willing to allow the policyholder to choose which of these options will apply, though they are not strictly obliged to do so. An unusual dispute over the measure of loss occurred in an IOB case[1] where an oil spillage had resulted in damage including contamination of the land. The insurer offered a sum based upon diminution in value, but the policyholder, who alleged delay in the handling of the claim, wanted compensation based upon the loss of his opportunity to sell the house for a larger sum. The Ombudsman held that this claim was far too speculative to succeed. It was not possible to be certain that the house could in fact have been sold for that or any price. Accordingly, the insurer had acted reasonably in dealing with the matter on the basis of diminution in value. It seems that the result would be the same at law. The policyholder might have been able to establish breach of contract by the insurer in not dealing with the claim promptly, but his only effective remedy would have been to claim damages for the loss resulting from this breach, whereupon he would again have been confronted with the problem of proving and quantifying that loss.

1 IOB 20.10.

'Defective design'

39.21 Buildings polices frequently have an exclusion for loss resulting from defective design, though that term is not usually defined. In one IOB case the damage resulted from the fact that the foundations of the extension to the policyholder's house had not been designed properly to suit the underlying subsoil conditions. The insurers relied upon the defective design exclusion, but the Ombudsman rejected this defence, observing that the design had obtained Building Regulations approval at the time. The decision may perhaps be regarded as somewhat generous to the insured, since the events which had happened surely established beyond doubt that the design was in fact defective. The remedy, if any, lay against the builder[1]. It is also interesting to observe that the policy had a separate exclusion in respect of 'inadequate foundations which do not meet Building Regulations at the time of construction'. This exclusion was clearly inapplicable.

1 And the insurer would no doubt have been subrogated to the policyholder's rights in this regard.

Damage by external means

39.22 In one IOB case[1] the policy covered damage to pipes by external means, but without any exclusion for wear and tear, gradually operating cause or defective design. The drains were made of pitch fibre, a notoriously poor quality material, which is prone to deterioration. The pipes became blocked. The Ombudsman held that the insurers were liable. The damage to the pipes had been caused by the ingress of ground water into the material of the pipe. Moreover, the blockage itself could be regarded as 'damage' to the pipes.

1 IOB 23.4.

Damage over a period of time

39.23 Another issue arising in the case discussed in the previous paragraph was that the deterioration of the pipes had happened over a period of time, and the insurer had not been on risk for all of that time. As to this point the Ombudsman observed that the blockage had occurred while the insurer was on risk, with the result that the insurer must meet the full cost. A similar result was reached in a case[1] where the drains needed to be re-lined because there were a number of misplaced joints. The insurers argued that they had been on risk for only one year, but that the damage must have occurred over a much longer period. The Ombudsman considered that the insurer was unable to establish clearly which damage was recent and which was older, with the result that the claim had to be met in full.

1 IOB 23.5.

Fixed domestic water installation

39.24 The Ombudsman has held[1] that a watergate on the roof of a house is not a 'fixed domestic water installation'[2].

1 IOB 23.8.
2 See also Chapter 38 for the same phrase in the context of contents policies.

Chapter 40

Marine insurance

Introduction

40.1 Marine insurance is governed by the MIA 1906[1], and is thus unique in being the only area of insurance contract law which is the subject of comprehensive codification. The MIA 1906 was always intended as a codification of the common law, and, as has been shown at various points throughout the present work, many of the most important provisions of the MIA 1906 are commonly treated as being applicable also in non-marine insurance[2]. The present Chapter concentrates mainly on those parts of the MIA 1906 which are primarily of importance in a marine context. Thus, for example, questions of non-disclosure and utmost good faith are not considered here. These do not appear to give rise to any issues which are specific to marine insurance. Accordingly they are examined only in Chapter 5.

1 The full text of the MIA 1906 is reproduced in Appendix 1.

2 Perhaps the most conspicuous modern example is to be found in *Pan Atlantic Insurance Co Ltd v Pine Top Insurance Co Ltd* [1995] 1 AC 501, HL, the leading case on non-disclosure. This was a case of long-tail environmental liability insurance, in which the extensive analysis by the House of Lords of the issues relating to the law of non-disclosure was conducted almost entirely by reference to ss 18 and 20 of the MIA 1906.

Marine insurance defined

40.2 Section 1 of the MIA 1906 defines a contract of marine insurance as:

> 'a contract whereby the insurer undertakes to indemnify[1] the assured[2], in manner and to the extent thereby agreed, against marine losses, that is to say, the losses incident to marine adventure.'

This is a somewhat self-referential definition, but it serves effectively to delineate the scope of the Act. The apparent limitations of the section are to some extent alleviated by s 2, which provides for the extension of a contract of marine insurance so as to protect the assured against losses on inland waters or on any land risk which may be incidental to any sea voyage[3]. Similarly, where a ship in course of building, or the launch of a ship, or any adventure analogous to a marine adventure, is covered by a policy in the form of a marine policy, the Act applies.

[1] Thus marine insurance is essentially indemnity insurance: *Kent v Bird* (1777) 2 Cowp 583 per Lord Mansfield, but the indemnity is by no means a perfect one, the most obvious exception being the universal practice of issuing valued policies, under which the indemnity may be exceeded.
[2] A peculiarity of the Act is that it invariably refers to the *insurer* but to the *assured.*
[3] Section 2(1).

Insurable interest[1]

40.3 The rules on insurable interest in a marine policy differ from those applicable to non-marine policies. Section 4 of the MIA 1906 declares void *ab initio* contracts of marine insurance 'by way of gaming or wagering'. A contract of marine insurance is deemed to be a gaming or wagering contract where the assured has no insurable interest, and the contract is entered into with no expectation of acquiring such an interest[2]. The assured must be interested in the subject matter insured at the time of the loss though he need not be interested when the insurance is effected[3]. Where the assured has no interest at the time of the loss, he cannot acquire interest by any act or election after he is aware of the loss[4]. Thus, it is not possible to circumvent the rule requiring interest at the time of loss by any act done after the assured is aware of the loss.

The rule requiring interest at the time of the loss differs from that applicable in life assurance, where interest is required at the time of the contract but not at the date of death[5]. The policy is also deemed to be by way of gaming or wagering if it is expressed to be made 'interest or no interest,' or 'without further proof of interest than the policy itself,' or 'without benefit of salvage to the insurer,' or subject to any other similar term, though, where there is no possibility of salvage, a policy may be effected without benefit of salvage to the insurer[6]. This latter provision also has no equivalent in non-marine insurance, where the use of such phrases might well give rise to a suspicion of lack of interest, but would not automatically void the policy. These or similar phrases void the policy even where the policyholder in fact has an insurable interest[7].

Where the subject matter is insured 'lost or not lost,' another practice which appears to be confined to marine insurance, the assured may recover even if he did not acquire his interest until after the loss. However, this rule does not apply if at the time of effecting the contract of insurance the assured was aware of the loss, and the insurer was not[8]. This is probably an unnecessary provision, since a failure on the part of the assured to disclose such knowledge would surely amount to a non-disclosure such as would allow the insurer to avoid the policy anyway.

In addition the Act specifically recognises the insurable interest of a certain other group: the master or any member of the crew of a ship has an insurable interest in respect of his wages[9]. This rule may be regarded as being derived from the common law rule that 'freight is the mother of wages' which meant that the master and crew did not get paid until the freight had been earned. Thus it is appropriate for them to be allowed to insure against the risk that loss of or damage to the ship might prevent the freight from being earned.

In the case of advance freight, the person advancing the freight has an insurable interest, in so far as such freight is not repayable in case of loss[10].

Where the subject matter insured is mortgaged, the mortgagor has an insurable interest in the full value of it, and the mortgagee has an insurable interest in respect of any sum due or to become due under the mortgage[11]. Thus a mortgagee, consignee, or other person having an interest in the subject matter insured may insure on behalf and for the benefit of other persons interested as well as for his own benefit[12], and the owner of insurable property has an insurable interest in respect of the full value of it, notwithstanding that some third person may have agreed, or be liable, to indemnify him in case of loss[13]. However, s 14(2) does not confer a statutory authority to insure. It is a question of fact whether the person purporting to insure on behalf of another has authority to do so, or, if not, whether there has been rstification[14]. The last part of this rule is similar to the non-marine principle established in *Hepburn v Tomlinson*[15].

1 On insurable interest generally, see Chapter 4.
2 See *Anderson v Morice* (1876) 1 App Cas 713, HL.
3 Section 6(1).
4 Section 6(2).
5 *Dalby v India and London Life* (1854) 15 CB 365. See Chapter 34.
6 Section 4(2).
7 *Thomas Cheshire & Co v Vaughan Bros* (1919) 25 Com Cas 51; affd [1920] 3 KB 240, CA.
8 Section 6(1).
9 Section 11.
10 Section 12.
11 Section 14(1).
12 Section 14(2).
13 Section 14(3).
14 *O'Kane v Jones* [2005] Lloyd's Rep IR 174, Richard Siberry QC.
15 [1966] AC 451.

Meaning of Insurable Interest

40.4 Section 5(2) contains a partial definition of insurable interest[1] However, this is only a partial definition, and in *O'Kane v Jones*[2] it was said that there are normally three characteristics which must be present in order to create insurable interest in a marine policy. First, that the assured may benefit by the safety or due arrival of insurable property or be prejudiced by its loss, damage or detention or in respect of which he may incur legal liability. Second, that the assured stood in a legal or equitable relation to the adventure or to any insurable property at risk in such adventure. Third, that the benefit, prejudice or incurring of legal liability must arise as a result of the said legal or equitable relation[3]. The definition can be seen to draw to some extent on that propounded in *Lucena v Craufurd*[4]. It is to be noted that neither proprietary nor possessory title to any property is made essential here, and it may be suggested that this offers a good starting point for a definition to be used in non-marine insurance as well. The judge went on to draw further conclusions about when insurable interest could exist in marine insurance as follows:

'(1) Ownership or possession (or the right to possession) of the property insured is not a necessary requirement of an insurable interest therein;

(2) Commercial convenience can be a relevant factor in determining the existence of an insurable interest;

(3) A person exposed to liability in respect of the custody or care of property may, as an alternative to taking out liability insurance to protect his exposure, insure the property itself, and in the event of loss or damage thereto by a peril insured against may recover in respect thereof up to the full sum insured, even if that exceeds the amount for which he is liable and even if the loss or damage has occurred without any actionable fault on his part. If and to the extent that he has suffered no personal loss he will be liable to account to the owner of the goods who has suffered the loss;

(4) A legal right to the use of goods, the benefit of which would be lost by their damage or destruction, may be sufficient to constitute an insurable interest therein;

(5) A person may also have an insurable interest in property if loss of or damage to that property would deprive him of the opportunity of carrying out work in relation to that property and being remunerated for such work – see also *Thames & Mersey Marine Insurance Co Ltd v Gunford Ship Co Ltd*, [1911] AC 529, where at page 549 Lord Robson referred to the practice of over-valuing a vessel under a H&M policy, relying among other things "on the interest that the managing owners or the managers have in preserving the ship as a source of business profit to themselves"[5].'

[1] See Appendix 1.
[2] [2005] Lloyd's Rep IR 174, Richard Siberry QC.
[3] See n 2 above at para 145.
[4] (1806) 2 Bos & PNR 269; see also *The Moonacre* [1992] 2 Lloyd's Rep 501.
[5] At para 154; see also *Hepburn v Tomlinson* [1966] AC 451 HL; *Petrofina v Magnaload* [1984] 1 QB 127; *National Oilwell (UK) Ltd v Davy Offshore Ltd* [1993] 2 Lloyd's Rep 582, Coleman J; *Deepak Fertilisers and Petrochemicals Corpn v ICI Chemicals and Polymers Ltd* [1999] 1 Lloyd's Rep 387, CA.

Measure of insurable value

40.5 The MIA 1906 also contains provisions aimed at assessing the value of the insurable interest. Subject to anything to the contrary in the policy, the following rules apply[1]:

(1) Where a ship is insured, the insurable value is the value, at the commencement of the risk, of the ship, including her outfit, provisions and stores for the officers and crew, money advanced for seamen's wages, and other disbursements (if any) incurred to make the ship fit for the voyage or adventure contemplated by the policy, plus the charges of insurance upon the whole.
In the case of a steamship it is necessary to add to this the machinery, boilers, and coals and engine stores if owned by the assured, and, in the case of a ship engaged in a special trade, the ordinary fittings requisite for that trade: The fact that steamships are dealt with separately and as an additional item reflects the fact that the statute is a century old and that even in 1906 it consolidated some fairly old case law.

(2) Where the subject matter of the insurance is freight, whether paid in advance or otherwise, the insurable value is the gross amount of the freight[2] at the risk of the assured, plus the charges of insurance.

(3) Where goods are insured, the insurable value is the prime cost of the property insured, plus the expenses of and incidental to shipping and the charges of insurance upon the whole[3].

(4) In insurance on any other subject matter, the insurable value is the amount at the risk of the assured when the policy attaches, plus the charges of insurance.

These specific rules, when analysed, do little more than show that what is insurable is that which the assured is at risk of losing in the event of a calamity.

The wording of s 16 reflects a fundamental uncertainty at the heart of the law of marine insurance. Given that marine insurance is supposed to be a contract of indemnity, it is necessary to decide what is the measure of the indemnity at which it aims. Does it seek to restore the assured to the position in which he was before the adventure was undertaken (which may be taken to be roughly a tort-based measure) or does it aim to put him in the position in which he would have been if the adventure had been successful (which may be taken to be roughly a contract-based measure)? The MIA 1906 vacillates between the two measures without ever coming to a clear decision on the point of principle[4]. Moreover, s 16 is of very limited importance in practice because of the universal adoption of valued policies, as permitted by s 27 of the MIA 1906. That section provides that a policy may be either valued or unvalued. An unvalued policy is a policy which leaves the insurable value to be subsequently ascertained in accordance with s 16. This may be seen as being comparable with the normal non-marine practice. A valued policy is a policy which specifies the agreed value of the subject matter insured. Subject to the provisions of the MIA 1906 and in the absence of fraud[5], the value fixed by the policy is binding as between the insurer and assured for the purpose of determining the insurable value of the insured property. This applies in the case of both total and partial loss. However the value fixed by the policy is not conclusive for the purpose of determining whether there has been a constructive total loss, unless the policy expressly says that it is conclusive for these purposes. In practice all marine policies are valued policies, but valued policies are very rarely encountered outside marine insurance[6].

1 Section 16.
2 As defined in s 90: 'freight includes the profit derivable by a shipowner from the employment of his ship to carry his own goods or moveables, as well as freight payable by a third party, but does not include passage money'. The definition is obviously not intended to be exhaustive.
3 See *Usher v Noble* (1810) 12 East 639.
4 See also the commentary on s 16 in Chalmers *Marine Insurance Act 1906* (9th edn, 1983, Butterworths), ed Hardy Ivamy.
5 For a case in which the conclusiveness of the valuation was undermined by fraud see *Eagle Star Insurance Co v Games Video Co* [2004] EWHC 15 (Comm), [2004] Lloyd's Rep IR 867, Simon J.
6 Aviation insurance is one of the other areas where they may also be encountered.

Apportionment of valuation

40.6 Where different species of property are insured under a single valuation, the valuation must be apportioned over the different species in proportion to their respective insurable values, as in the case of an unvalued policy. The insured value of any part of a species is such proportion of the total insured value of the same as the insurable value of the part bears to the insurable value of the whole[1]. Where a valuation has to be apportioned, and particulars of the prime cost of each separate species, quality, or description of goods cannot be ascertained, the division of the valuation may be made over the net sound values at arrival of destination of the different species, qualities, or descriptions of goods[2].

[1] Section 73(1).
[2] Section 73(2).

Cover

Floating policy by ship or ships or cargo

40.7 A floating policy is a policy which describes the insurance in general terms, and leaves the name of the ship or ships and other particulars to be defined by subsequent declaration[1]. Policies of this kind are useful where the insured wants to be able to change cargoes and/or ships at short notice. The subsequent declaration or declarations may be made by indorsement on the policy, or in any other customary manner. Unless the policy otherwise provides, the declarations must be made in the order of dispatch or shipment. They must, in the case of goods, comprise all consignments within the terms of the policy, and the value of the goods or other property must be honestly stated, but an omission or erroneous declaration may be rectified even after loss or arrival, provided the omission or declaration was made in good faith[2]. Unless the policy otherwise provides, where a declaration of value is not made until after notice of loss or arrival, the policy must be treated as an unvalued policy as regards the subject matter of that declaration. Floating policies are obviously commercially convenient, but the law is quite strict about insisting on prompt and accurate declarations. The requirement to include all relevant goods appears to prevent the former practice of choosing which of one or more floating policies should provide the cover for a particular consignment.

[1] Section 29(1); such policies are also referred to as 'open covers'.
[2] The requirement of good faith is an essential qualification, since open covers by their nature offer the assured ample opportunity for abuse by declaring only those consignments on which losses occur.

Formalities

Requirements of form

40.8 A contract of marine insurance is inadmissible in evidence unless it is embodied in a marine policy in accordance with the MIA 1906. The policy may be executed and issued either at the time when the contract is concluded, or afterwards[1]. It may be noted that this is a departure from the rule at common law, where there is apparently no requirement for a written policy at all.

A marine policy must specify the name of the assured, or of some person who effects the insurance on his behalf[2]. The subject matter insured must be designated in a marine policy with reasonable certainty[3], but the nature and extent of the interest of the assured in the subject matter insured need not be specified in the policy[4]. Where the policy designates the subject matter insured in general terms, it is construed to apply to the interest intended by the assured to be covered[5]. All these rules may fairly be regarded as no more than obvious applications of the common law principle that a contract is invalid unless its terms are spelt out with sufficient certainty to enable the court to give effect to it. However, section 26(3) has been regarded as a difficult section because it is not clear what the word 'interest' in that section means. In *Allison v Bristol Marine Insurance Co*[6] the House of Lords took the advice of the judges on this question, and Brett J's answer has often been relied upon[7]. Brett J said:

> 'Wherever the subject-matter is described in general terms, it is to be taken to cover the interest which is within its terms, which the assured has at risk, unless the contrary appears to have been the intention of the assured from other parts of the policy or other proof.'

The MIA 1906 contains no other rules as to what the policy must contain, though s 30 provides that a marine policy *may* be in the form appearing in Schedule 1 to the Act. In practice there are numerous standard forms for different marine polices, notably the Institute Clauses.

1 Section 22.
2 Section 23.
3 Section 26(1).
4 Section 26(2).
5 Section 26(3).
6 (1875) 1 App Cas 209, HL.
7 Most recently by Richard Siberry QC in *O'Kane v Jones* [2005] Lloyd's Rep IR 174 at para 140.

Signature of insurer

40.9 A marine policy must be signed by or on behalf of the insurer. In the case of a corporation the corporate seal may be sufficient, but is not necessary. Where a policy is subscribed by or on behalf of two or more insurers, each subscription, unless the contrary is expressed, constitutes a distinct contract with the assured[1]. It appears that at common law there is no requirement for the policy to be signed by or on behalf of the insurer. Many non-marine policies are not so signed, though of course they will carry on their face evidence of the identity of the insurer[2].

1 Section 24.
2 See also Chapter 7.

Types of policy

Voyage and time policies

40.10 Marine policies are either voyage policies or time policies. Where the contract is to insure the subject matter 'at and from', or from one place to another or others, the policy is called a 'voyage policy', and where the contract is to insure the subject matter for a definite period of time the policy is called a 'time policy'. A contract for both voyage and time may be included in the same policy[1]. Clearly, the two types of policy delimit the temporal scope of the risk in different ways. Each has its advantages and disadvantages. The vital point in any given case is to be clear which type of policy has been issued.

[1] Section 25; see *Gambles v Ocean Insurance Co* (1876) 1 Ex D 141, CA.

Premium

Premium – general rule

40.11 The MIA 1906 has rules on payment of the premium which are not replicated in non-marine insurance. These rules apply only to contracts whose proper law is English law1. Moreover, as will appear, these rules are in practice to a large extent superseded. First, the presumption is that the duty of the assured or his agent to pay the premium, and the duty of the insurer to issue the policy to the assured or his agent, are concurrent conditions, and the insurer is not bound to issue the policy until payment or tender of the premium[2]. There is a further presumption that where a marine policy is effected on behalf of the assured by a broker, the broker is directly responsible to the insurer for the premium, and the insurer is directly responsible to the assured for the amount which may be payable in respect of losses, or in respect of returnable premium[3]. This rule makes it necessary to give the broker some protection in his dealings with the assured, and this is achieved by the further rule that the broker is presumed to have, as against the assured, a lien upon the policy for the amount of the premium and his charges in respect of effecting the policy; and, where he has dealt with the person who employs him as a principal, he has also a lien on the policy in respect of any balance on any insurance account which may be due to him from such person, unless when the debt was incurred he had reason to believe that such person was only an agent[4].

Where a marine policy effected on behalf of the assured by a broker acknowledges the receipt of the premium (which in practice it always does), such acknowledgment is, in the absence of fraud, conclusive as between the insurer and the assured[5], but not as between the insurer and broker[6].

In practice marine insurance is conducted by means of electronic account debits and credits between insurer and broker. When the system works properly this should produce the result that the premium is always properly paid, so that the assured is protected as against the insurer, and the only effective issue is the broker's right of recoupment against the assured. Although the system generally works well, cases of broker's insolvency may give rise to difficulties if premium has been paid by the assured to the broker but has not been fully paid over to the insurer.

Accrual and Section 53 MIA – In *Heath Lambert Ltd v Sociedad de Corretaje de Seguros*[7] the Court of Appeal considered the question of when the broker's claim against the insured for reimbursement of premium accrued. It was held that the starting point is that the premium becomes due from broker to insurer when the contract is made (which may be before the risk attaches) and at that point the broker's claim against the insured also accrues. However, the position will be different where the terms of the policy provide for cash payment by a later date, thereby departing form the normal accounting method. In those circumstances the effect of section 53 is that the fiction of payment by the broker is displaced, and the claim against the assured arises when the premium is paid.

[1] *Heath Lambert v Sociedad de Corretaje* [2004] EWCA Civ 792, [2004] Lloyd's Rep IR 905.
[2] Section 52.
[3] Section 53(1); however, it is not the modern practice to rely on this rule.
[4] Section 53(2); See also Chapter 3 for the relevance of this in the context of the formation of the policy.
[5] And possibly an assignee for value without notice: *Roberts v Security Co Ltd* [1897] 1 QB 111. Although that case is not about a marine policy, the point appears to be of general application.
[6] Section 54.
[7] [2004] Lloyd's Rep IR 905, CA.

Premium to be arranged

40.12 The practice of stipulating for a premium (or additional premium) to be arranged appears to be confined to marine insurance. It may be used where there is urgency about the effecting of the insurance or where insufficient information is available at the time to allow the underwriter to set the premium accurately. This sometimes happens where a policy provides the possibility of extending cover, perhaps to another geographical area at a premium to be agreed[1]. Where an insurance is effected at a premium to be arranged, and no arrangement is made, a reasonable[2] premium is payable. Where an insurance is effected on the terms that an additional premium is to be arranged in a given event, and that event happens but no arrangement is made, then a reasonable additional premium is payable[3]. In default of agreement it will be for a court to decide what additional premium is reasonable.

[1] This is often expressed on the slip by saying that the additional premium is 'TBA L/U', ie to be agreed by the leading underwriter.
[2] What is reasonable in any given case is a question of fact: s 88.
[3] Section 31.

Return of premium

40.13 Sections 82–84 of the MIA 1906 deal with the return of premium. Section 83 deals with return by agreement. Where the policy provides for the return of the premium, or a proportionate part of it, on the happening of a certain event, and that event happens, the premium (or the proportionate part of it) is thereupon returnable to the assured. This section is no more than declaratory of an obvious principle.

Section 84 deals with the more difficult topic of return of premium for failure of consideration. First, where the consideration for the payment of the premium totally fails, and there has been no fraud or illegality on the part of the assured or his agents, the premium is returnable to the assured[1]. This accords with general principles of contract law. Secondly, where the consideration for the payment of the premium is apportionable and there is a total failure of any apportionable part of the consideration, a proportionate part of the premium is, subject to the same conditions, returnable to the assured[2]. Section 84(3) gives particular examples, as shown below:

(1) Where the policy is void, or is avoided by the insurer as from the commencement of the risk, the premium is returnable, provided that there has been no fraud or illegality on the part of the assured; but if the risk is not apportionable, and has once attached, the premium is not returnable. This again is an application of the general law of contract.

(2) Where the subject matter insured, or part thereof, has never been imperilled, the premium, or a proportionate part of it is returnable. This rule can be justified as being an example of total failure of consideration. It is essential to remember that the doctrine of total failure is strict – once there has been even a very small element of consideration, it can no longer be invoked.
However, where the subject matter has been insured 'lost or not lost' and has arrived in safety at the time when the contract is concluded, the premium is not returnable unless the insurer knew at that time of the safe arrival. This is because there has been part performance once the insurer genuinely assumes, even for a very short time, the risk that the subject matter has not arrived or will not arrive. The exception made here is limited to the case where the insurer knows that the risk is non-existent because the subject matter has arrived safely.

(3) Where the assured has no insurable interest throughout the currency of the risk, the premium is returnable (except in the case of a policy effected by way of gaming or wagering). This appears to be an exception to the general common law rule[3], which is that a policy made without the necessary insurable interest is void and illegal, so that the premium is not recoverable, unless the insurer was also aware of the lack of interest, so as to render the parties equally guilty. Marine policies made without interest are of course not subject to the LAA 1774, since s 4 of that Act declares it inapplicable to marine policies.

(4) Where the assured has a defeasible interest which is terminated during the currency of the risk, the premium is not returnable. This is because there has been partial performance during the period when the assured had an interest.

(5) Where the assured has over-insured under an unvalued policy, a proportionate part of the premium is returnable. This rule appears to be confined to marine insurance. In other areas of insurance it is certainly not the practice to recognise a right to partial return of premium on the ground of over-insurance.

Subject to the foregoing provisions, where the assured has over-insured by double insurance, a proportionate part of each of the several premiums is returnable.

However, if the policies are effected at different times, and any earlier policy has at any time borne the entire risk, or if a claim has been paid on the policy in respect of the full sum insured thereby, no premium is returnable in respect of that policy, and when the double insurance is effected knowingly by the assured no premium is returnable.

Section 82 amplifies ss 83 and 84 by providing that where the premium or a proportionate part of it is returnable, then if already paid, it may be recovered by the assured from the insurer and if unpaid, it may be retained by the assured or his agent. In practice, where there are commonly ongoing relations between broker and insurer, any sums due will no doubt simply be added to the account between the parties.

1 Section 84(1).
2 Section 84(2).
3 See eg *Harse v Pearl Life Assurance Co* [1904] 1 KB 558, CA.

Warranties

40.14 Sections 33–41 of the MIA 1906 deal with the subject of warranties in marine insurance. Section 33(1) defines a warranty as:

> 'a promissory warranty, that is to say, a warranty by which the assured undertakes that some particular thing shall or shall not be done, or that some condition shall be fulfilled, or whereby he affirms or negatives the existence of a particular state of facts.'

This may be regarded as no different from the non-marine position. However, s 33(3) adds that:

> 'A warranty, as above defined, is a condition which must be exactly complied with, whether it be material to the risk or not. If it be not so complied with, then, subject to any express provision in the policy, the insurer is discharged from liability as from the date of the breach of warranty, but without prejudice to any liability incurred by him before that date.'

The House of Lords has held[1] that in marine insurance this provision means that discharge is immediate and automatic without any need for action on the part of the insurer. Indeed, the discharge happens even if the insurer is not immediately aware of the breach. It follows that in marine insurance where a warranty is broken, the assured cannot avail himself of the defence that the breach has been remedied, and the warranty complied with, before loss[2].

Although this rule may appear to open up an undesirable clash between marine and non-marine insurance, examination of the warranties implied by the MIA 1906 shows that they are so specific to marine insurance, that the point is not a significant one. The warranties are as follows:

(1) Where insurable property, whether ship or goods, is expressly warranted neutral, there is an implied condition that the property shall have a neutral character at the commencement of the risk, and that, so far as the assured can control the matter, its neutral character shall be preserved during the risk[3]. Where a ship is expressly warranted 'neutral'[4] there is also an implied condition that, so far as the assured can control the matter, she shall be properly documented, that is to say, that she shall carry the necessary papers to establish her neutrality, and that she shall not falsify or suppress her papers, or use simulated papers. If any loss occurs through breach of this condition, the insurer may avoid the contract[5]. In many parts of the world this warranty is less important than it once would have been, though the continuing risk of warfare in some areas means that it is not wholly obsolete.

There is no implied warranty as to the nationality of a ship, or that her nationality shall not be changed during the risk[6]. An insurer which regards the nationality of the ship as material should therefore require an express warranty on the point.

(2) Where the subject matter insured is warranted 'well' or 'in good safety' on a particular day, it is sufficient if it be safe at any time during that day[7]. This rule is of course in addition to and not in substitution for the general duty of disclosure.

In a voyage policy there is an implied warranty that at the commencement of the voyage the ship shall be seaworthy for the purpose of the particular adventure insured[8].

(3) Where the policy attaches while the ship is in port, there is also an implied warranty that she shall, at the commencement of the risk, be reasonably fit to encounter the ordinary perils of the port[9].

(4) Where the policy relates to a voyage which is performed in different stages, during which the ship requires different kinds of or further preparation or equipment, there is an implied warranty that at the commencement of each stage the ship is seaworthy in respect of such preparation or equipment for the purposes of that stage[10].

In a time policy there is no implied warranty that the ship shall be seaworthy at any stage of the adventure, but where, with the privity[11] of the assured, the ship is sent to sea in an unseaworthy state, the insurer is not liable for any loss attributable to unseaworthiness[12]. It should be noted that this focuses attention on the question of causation – it is not like a warranty, where the effect of breach would be the automatic discharge of the policy.

In a policy on goods or other moveables there is no implied warranty that the goods or moveables are seaworthy[13].

In a voyage policy on goods or other moveables there is an implied warranty that at the commencement of the voyage the ship is not only seaworthy as a ship, but also that she is reasonably fit to carry the goods or other moveables to the destination contemplated by the policy[14].

There is an implied warranty that the adventure insured is a lawful one, and that, so far as the assured can control the matter, the adventure shall be carried out in a lawful manner[15]. This provision has no direct equivalent in non-marine insurance, though of course questions of illegality may still arise[16].

1 *The Good Luck* [1991] 3 All ER 1, HL.
2 Section 34(2).
3 Section 36(1).
4 Ie not belonging to any country engaged in hostilities.
5 Section 36(2).
6 Section 37.
7 Section 38.
8 Section 39(1).
9 Section 39(2).
10 Section 39(3).
11 Ie the knowledge and consent: *Compania Maritima San Basilia SA v Oceanus Mutual Underwriting Association* [1976] 2 Lloyd's Rep 171, CA.
12 Section 39(5); for a recent case where this subsection was vital, see *The Star Sea* [2001] Lloyd's Rep IR 247, HL.

13 Section 40(1).
14 Section 40(2).
15 Section 41.
16 On illegality generally, see Chapter 20.

The voyage

40.15 Sections 42–49 contain provisions dealing with the insured voyage.

Where the subject matter is insured by a voyage policy 'at and from' or 'from' a particular place, it is not necessary that the ship should be at that place when the contract is concluded. However, there is an implied condition (but not warranty) that the adventure will be commenced within a reasonable time. Failure to comply with this condition allows the insurer to avoid the contract[1]. This implied condition does not apply if the delay was caused by circumstances known to the insurer before the contract was concluded. Alternatively it may be waived by the insurer[2].

Where the place of departure is specified by the policy, and the ship instead of sailing from that place sails from any other place, the risk does not attach[3]. The same rule applies where the destination is specified in the policy, and the ship sails for any other destination, the risk does not attach[4]. In either case the risk undertaken is simply not the risk insured[5]. It is a question of fact what is the intended destination of the ship – the answer does not depend simply on what is shown in the documents[6].

Where, after the commencement of the risk, the destination of the ship is voluntarily changed from the destination contemplated by the policy, there is said to be a change of voyage[7]. The presumption (subject to contrary provision in the policy) is that the insurer is then discharged from liability as from the time of change, that is to say, as from the time when the determination to change it is manifested; and it does not matter that the ship may not in fact have left the course of voyage contemplated by the policy when the loss occurs[8]. A loss occurring before the change of voyage will still be covered in a case such as this.

Where a ship, without lawful excuse, deviates from the voyage contemplated by the policy (ie changes *route* as distinct from changing *destination*), the insurer is discharged from liability as from the time of deviation, and it does not matter that the ship may have regained her route before any loss occurs[9]. Again, a loss occurring before the deviation will still be covered.

Where several ports of discharge are specified by the policy, the ship may proceed to all or any of them, but the presumption is that she must proceed to them, or such of them as she goes to, in the order designated by the policy. If she does not there is a deviation[10], unless it can be shown that there is a usage or other sufficient reason to justify the order chosen. In the case of deviation, as distinct from change of voyage, it is irrelevant that the intention has been formed and manifested – only an actual deviation will allow the insurer to escape liability[11]. The same rule applies where the policy is to 'ports of discharge', within a given area, which are not named[12].

In the case of a voyage policy, the adventure insured must be prosecuted throughout its course with reasonable[13] dispatch. Otherwise the insurer is discharged from liability as from the time when the delay became unreasonable[14].

Deviation or delay in prosecuting the voyage contemplated by the policy is excused where authorised by any special term in the policy or where caused by circumstances beyond the control of the master and his employer or where reasonably necessary in order to comply with an express or implied warranty or where reasonably necessary for the safety of the ship or subject matter insured or for the purpose of saving human life, or aiding a ship in distress where human life may be in danger or where reasonably necessary for the purpose of obtaining medical or surgical aid for any person on board the ship; or where caused by the barratrous conduct of the master or crew, if barratry is one of the perils insured against[15].

1 Section 42(1).
2 Section 42(2).
3 Section 43.
4 Section 44.
5 *Sellar v M'Vicar* (1804) 1 Bos & PNR 23.
6 *Nina v Deves Insurance* [2002] Lloyd's Rep IR 752, CA.
7 Section 45(1).
8 Section 45(2).
9 Section 46(1); *Phyn v Royal Exchange Assurance Co* (1798) 7 Term Rep 505.
10 Section 47(1).
11 Section 46(3).
12 *Marsden v Reid* (1803) 3 East 572; and see s 47(2).
13 A question of fact – s 88; *Niger Co Ltd v Guardian Assurance Co* (1922) 13 Ll L Rep 75, HL.
14 Section 48.
15 Section 49(1).

Assignment of policy

40.16 A marine policy is assignable unless it contains terms expressly prohibiting assignment. It may be assigned either before or after loss[1]. This rule is identical to the rule at common law.

Where a marine policy has been assigned so as to pass the beneficial interest in such policy, the assignee of the policy is entitled to sue on it in his own name[2]; and the defendant is entitled to rely upon any defence arising out of the contract which would have been available to him if the action had been brought in the name of the person by or on behalf of whom the policy was effected[3].

The position is more complex where the assured has parted with or lost his interest in the subject matter insured. He may not subsequently enter into an agreement to assign the policy, but a subsequent assignment will remain effective if no later than the time when his interest in the subject matter ceased, he expressly or impliedly agreed to assign the policy[4]. This provision apparently exists to reduce the risk of gaming. Once the assured has lost his interest, he would not be allowed to recover on the policy himself, since in marine insurance it is the time of loss which is vital for determining insurable interest. It is clearly not desirable to allow him to assign he policy as a separate matter from any assignment of the subject matter.

[1] Section 50.
[2] This provision resolves any question which might otherwise have arisen about the procedure to be followed in relation to assigned marine policies under the Judicature Act 1873. For assignment generally, see Chapter 15.
[3] Section 50(2); but not a set-off arising against the assignor under a different policy: *Baker v Adam* (1910) 15 Com Cas 227.
[4] Section 51.

Losses

Included and excluded losses

40.17 Unless the policy otherwise provides, the insurer is liable for any loss proximately caused by a peril insured against, but, subject to the aforesaid, he is not liable for any loss which is not proximately caused by a peril insured against[1]. Where there is more than one proximate cause, it is sufficient that one of them is caused by a peril insured against, so long as the other is not specifically excluded[2]. This may legitimately be regarded as a statement of the obvious, and the rule is necessarily the same in all forms of insurance.

The insurer is not liable for any loss attributable to the wilful misconduct of the assured, but, unless the policy otherwise provides, he is liable for any loss proximately caused by a peril insured against, even though the loss would not have happened but for the misconduct or negligence of the master or crew. Again, this is a formulation of a general insurance law principle, namely that wilful wrongdoing will invalidate the cover, but mere negligence will not normally do so.

Unless the policy otherwise provides, the insurer on ship or goods is not liable for any loss proximately caused by delay, even where the delay is caused by a peril insured against; unless the policy otherwise provides, the insurer is not liable for ordinary wear and tear, ordinary leakage and breakage, inherent vice or nature of the subject matter insured, or for any loss proximately caused by rats or vermin, or for any injury to machinery not proximately caused by maritime perils[3]. This is another reiteration of general principle. Indeed, it is fair to say that section 55 appears to add nothing to the ordinary principles of causation as applied in English law.

[1] Section 55(1); See further Chapter 18 for a general discussion of causation issues.
[2] *Seashore Marine SA v The Phoenix Assurance plc* [2002] 1 All ER (Comm) 152, Aikens J.
[3] Section 55(2); in practice the scope of the insurer's liability is significantly widened by the use of the so-called 'Inchmaree Clause' which reads: 'This insurance also specially to cover (subject to the free of average warranty) loss of or damage to hull or machinery through the negligence of master, mariners, engineers, or pilots, or through explosions, bursting of boilers, breakage of shafts, or through any latent defect in the machinery or hull, provided such loss or damage has not resulted from want of due diligence by the owners of the ship, or any of them, or by the manager.

Partial and total loss

40.18 A loss may be either total or partial. A total loss may be either an actual total loss, or a constructive total loss. The presumption is that an insurance against total loss includes a constructive, as well as an actual, total loss[1]. Where goods reach their destination in specie, but by reason of obliteration of marks, or otherwise, they are incapable of identification, the loss, if any, is partial, and not total[2].

1 Section 56; *Adams v Mackenzie* (1863) 13 CBNS 442.
2 Section 56(5).

Actual total loss

40.19 Where the subject matter insured is destroyed, or so damaged as to cease to be a thing of the kind insured, or where the assured is irretrievably deprived thereof, there is an actual total loss[1]. In the case of an actual total loss no notice of abandonment need be given[2]. Where the ship concerned in the adventure is missing, and after the lapse of a reasonable time no news of her has been received, an actual total loss may be presumed[3]. An insurer who pays for a loss in these circumstances if of course entitled to the ship as salvage should she later reappear[4].

1 *Fleming v Smith* (1848) 1 HL Cas 513, HL; *Francis v Boulton* (1895) 65 LJQB 153.
2 Section 57.
3 Section 58.
4 *Houstman v Thornton* (1816) Holt NP 242.

Effect of transhipment

40.20 Where, by a peril insured against, the voyage is interrupted at an intermediate port or place, under such circumstances as, apart from any special stipulation in the contract of affreightment, to justify the master in landing and re-shipping the goods or other moveables, or in transhipping them, and sending them on to their destination, the liability of the insurer continues, notwithstanding the landing or transhipment[1].

1 Section 59.

Constructive total loss

40.21 Subject to any express provision in the policy, there is a constructive total loss where the subject matter insured is reasonably abandoned because its actual total loss appears to be unavoidable, or because it could not be preserved from actual total loss without an expenditure which would exceed its value when the expenditure had been incurred. In particular, the following situations are treated as a constructive total loss:

(i) where the assured is deprived of the possession of his ship or goods by a peril insured against, and (*a*) it is unlikely that he can recover the ship or goods, as the case may be, or (*b*) the cost of recovering the ship or goods, as the case may be, would exceed their value when recovered;
(ii) in the case of damage to a ship, where she is so damaged by a peril insured against that the cost of repairing the damage would exceed the value of the ship when repaired. An important question in this area is whether the value to

be taken is the agreed value or the actual value. As a general rule the agreed value in a marine policy is conclusive[1], but in practice the agreed value is more than the actual value, which gives rise to the temptation for the assured to argue that a slightly damaged vessel can be a constructive total loss (based on actual value) so that the agreed value can be claimed and the assured can make a profit. To some extent this problem is a logically inevitable consequence of the use of valued policies, but it is submitted that the answer ought to be that the calculation of constructive total loss ought to be based upon the agreed value rather than on the actual value.

In estimating the cost of repairs, no deduction is made in respect of general average contributions to those repairs payable by other interests, but account is taken of the expense of future salvage operations and of any future general average contributions to which the ship would be liable if repaired;

(iii) in the case of damage to goods, where the cost of repairing the damage and forwarding the goods to their destination would exceed their value on arrival[2].

[1] Section 27.
[2] Section 60.

Effect of constructive total loss

40.22 Where there is a constructive total loss the assured may either treat the loss as a partial loss, or abandon the subject matter insured to the insurer and treat the loss as if it were an actual total loss[1]. There may be a claim for constructive total loss by an insured peril even where that is very shortly followed by an actual total loss which cannot be shown to have been caused by an insured peril[2]. It is of course a question of fact whether and when the vessel became a constructive total loss before the time of the actual total loss. No notice of abandonment is needed in the case of a constructive total loss which the assured is content to treat as a total loss[3].

[1] Section 61; subject to the possibility of a clause in the policy which removes the assured's right to abandon.
[2] *Kastor Navigation v AGF MAT* [2004] EWCA Civ 277, [2004] Lloyd's Rep IR 481; and see *Bank of America National Trust and Savings Association v Chrismas: The Kyriaki* [1993] 1 Lloyd's Rep 137.
[3] See n 2 above.

Particular average loss

40.23 A particular average loss is a partial loss of the subject matter insured, caused by a peril insured against, and which is not a general average loss. Particular average loss is therefore to be regarded as the default category for partial losses[1]. Expenses incurred by or on behalf of the assured for the safety or preservation of the subject matter insured, other than general average and salvage charges, are called particular charges. Particular charges are not included in particular average[2].

[1] For general average losses, see s 66 below.
[2] Section 64.

General average loss

40.24 A general average loss is a loss caused by or directly consequential on a general average act. It includes a general average expenditure as well as a general average sacrifice. There is a general average act where any extraordinary sacrifice or expenditure is voluntarily and reasonably made or incurred in time of peril for the purpose of preserving the property imperilled in the common adventure[1]. Where there is a general average loss, the party on whom it falls is entitled to a rateable contribution from the other parties interested. This contribution is called a general average contribution. Subject to any express provision in the policy, where the assured has incurred a general average expenditure, he may recover from the insurer in respect of the proportion of the loss which falls upon him; and, in the case of a general average sacrifice, he may recover from the insurer in respect of the whole loss without having enforced his right of contribution from the other parties liable to contribute (though the insurer would then be subrogated to that right of contribution). Where the assured has paid, or is liable to pay, a general average contribution in respect of the subject insured, he may (unless the policy says otherwise) recover this from the insurer. The insurer is not normally liable for any general average loss or contribution where the loss was not incurred for the purpose of avoiding, or in connection with the avoidance of, a peril insured against. Where ship, freight, and cargo, or any two of those interests, are owned by the same assured, the liability of the insurer in respect of general average losses or contributions is to be determined as if those subjects were owned by different persons[2].

[1] A simple example would be where containers on deck are jettisoned during a storm in order to make the vessel lighter and more stable.
[2] Section 66.

Quantum

40.25 Where there is a loss recoverable under the policy, the insurer, or each insurer if there is more than one, is liable for such proportion of the measure of indemnity[1] as the amount of his subscription bears to the value fixed by the policy in the case of a valued policy, or to the insurable value in the case of an unvalued policy[2]. This rule does not prejudice the right of the insured to recover from whichever insurer he chooses; it merely fixes the operation of the doctrine of contribution among the various insurers.

[1] Ie the total recoverable – the agreed value in a valued policy, otherwise the insurable value.
[2] Section 67.

Total loss

40.26 Subject to the provisions of the Act and to any express provision in the policy, where there is a total loss of the subject matter insured, if the policy be an unvalued policy, the measure of indemnity is the insurable value of the subject matter insured[1].

[1] Section 68.

Partial loss of ship

40.27 Where a ship is damaged, but is not totally lost, the measure of indemnity, subject to any express provision in the policy, is as follows: Where the ship has been repaired, the assured is entitled to the reasonable cost of the repairs, less the customary deductions, but not exceeding the sum insured in respect of any one casualty.

Partial loss of freight

40.28 Subject to any express provision in the policy, where there is a partial loss of freight, the measure of indemnity is such proportion of the sum fixed by the policy in the case of a valued policy, or of the insurable value in the case of an unvalued policy, as the proportion of freight lost by the assured bears to the whole freight at the risk of the assured under the policy[1].

[1] Section 70.

Partial loss of goods, merchandise, etc

40.29 Where there is a partial loss of goods, merchandise, or other moveables, the measure of indemnity, subject to any express provision in the policy, is as follows:

> 'Where part of the goods, merchandise or other moveables insured by a valued policy is totally lost, the measure of indemnity is such proportion of the sum fixed by the policy as the insurable value of the part lost bears to the insurable value of the whole, ascertained as in the case of an unvalued policy: where part of the goods, merchandise, or other moveables insured by an unvalued policy is totally lost, the measure of indemnity is the insurable value of the part lost, ascertained as in case of total loss: where the whole or any part of the goods or merchandise insured has been delivered damaged at its destination, the measure of indemnity is such proportion of the sum fixed by the policy in the case of a valued policy, or of the insurable value in the case of an unvalued policy, as the difference between the gross sound and damaged values at the place of arrival bears to the gross sound value: 'gross value' means the wholesale price or, if there be no such price, the estimated value, with, in either case, freight, landing charges, and duty paid beforehand; provided that, in the case of goods or merchandise customarily sold in bond, the bonded price is deemed to be the gross value. "Gross proceeds" means the actual price obtained at a sale where all charges on sale are paid by the sellers[1].'

[1] Section 71.

Particular average warranties

40.30 Where the subject matter insured is warranted free from particular average, the assured cannot recover for a loss of part, other than a loss incurred by a general average sacrifice unless the contract contained in the policy be apportionable; but, if the contract be apportionable, the assured may recover for a total loss of any apportionable part[1]. Where the subject matter insured is warranted free from particular average, either wholly or under a certain percentage, the insurer is nevertheless liable for salvage charges, and for particular charges and other expenses properly incurred pursuant to the provisions of the suing and labouring clause in order to avert a loss insured against[2]. Unless the policy otherwise provides, where the subject matter insured is warranted free from particular average under a specified percentage, a general average loss cannot be added to a particular average loss to make up the specified percentage[3]. For the purpose of ascertaining whether the specified percentage has been reached, regard shall be had only to the actual loss suffered by the subject matter insured. Particular charges and the expenses of and incidental to ascertaining and proving the loss must be excluded[4].

[1] Section 76(1).
[2] Section 76(2).
[3] Section 76(3).
[4] Section 76(4).

Successive losses

40.31 These are dealt with by s 77 of the MIA 1906. Unless the policy otherwise provides, and subject to the provisions of this Act, the insurer is liable for successive losses, even though the total amount of such losses may exceed the sum insured[1]. It is not at all clear whether this rule applies outside marine insurance. It is presumably a question of construction of the policy whether the sum insured is a total limit or a limit for each claim. Where, under the same policy, a partial loss, which has not been repaired or otherwise made good, is followed by a total loss, the assured can only recover in respect of the total loss[2]. This represents a codification of the general principle that an assured under an indemnity policy should not recover more than his actual loss. This rule does not apply where a constructive total loss is followed by an actual total loss within the policy period[3].

Moreover, s 77 does not affect the liability of the insurer under the suing and labouring clause, which is considered next.

[1] Section 77(1).
[2] Section 77(2).
[3] *Kastor Navigation v AGF MAT* [2004] EWCA Civ 277, [2004] Lloyd's Rep IR 481.

Suing and labouring clause

40.32 Section 78 of the MIA 1906 deals with the suing and labouring clause which is commonly encountered in marine and aviation policies, but which appears to be much less common in other types of insurance. The form of the clause as contained in Schedule 1 to the MIA 1906 appears at Appendix 1.

Where the policy contains a standard form suing and labouring clause, the engagement thereby entered into is deemed to be supplementary to the contract of insurance, and the assured may recover from the insurer any expenses properly incurred pursuant to the clause, notwithstanding that the insurer may have paid for a total loss, or that the subject matter may have been warranted free from particular average, either wholly or under a certain percentage[1].

General average losses and contributions and salvage charges, as defined by this Act[2], are not recoverable under the suing and labouring clause[3].

Expenses incurred for the purpose of averting or diminishing any loss not covered by the policy are not recoverable under the suing and labouring clause[4].

It is the duty of the assured and his agents, in all cases, to take such measures as may be reasonable for the purpose of averting or minimising a loss[5]. The difficult question of the duty to take reasonable care in non-marine insurance is discussed extensively in Chapter 12.

In *State of the Netherlands (Represented by the Ministry of Defence) v Youell*[6] the Dutch Royal Navy insured under marine policies issued by the defendants against builders' risks in relation to two submarines which were being built for them by a Dutch shipyard ('RDM'). The navy became aware that the paint on the submarines was debonding and they found that this was attributable to RDM's application of excessive primer.

The navy claimed under their policies in respect of the debonding and cracking of the paintwork applied by RDM to the submarines.

The issue for decision was whether RDM were the navy's agents for the purposes of s 78(4) of the MIA 1906 which provides:

> 'It is the duty of the assured and his agents, in all cases, to take such measures as may be reasonable for the purpose of averting or minimising a loss.'

There is House of Lords' authority – *British and Foreign Marine Insurance Co v Gaunt*[7] – to the effect that s 78(4) only relates to suing and labouring clauses. It therefore comes as no surprise that the judge held that s 78 was directed to the effect of a suing and labouring clause and s 78(4) had to be read in that context. It was held that s 78(4) could have no application to the activities of RDM that formed the subject of the action and that the duty of agents to sue and labour referred to in s 78(4) was a duty that arose in relation to a maritime adventure by reason of the delegation to a master, crew and other agents of the conduct of that adventure and that there was no scope for the application of such a duty in relation to an assured who insured as purchaser of a ship under a building contract.

A charge in money's worth or a loss which is not quantifiable on a quantum meruit basis may be recoverable under a suing and labouring clause: *Royal Boskalis Westminster NV v Mountain*[8].

The provision in the original suing and labouring clause was of a permissive character, but it is and has long been the duty of the assured and his agents, in all cases, to take such measures as may be reasonable for the purpose of averting or minimising a loss – see *State of the Netherlands (Represented by the Minister of Defence) v Youell and Hayward*[9]. However, it is a question of fact what steps are reasonable, and the court will not require steps to be taken where the assured reasonably judges that they would be fruitless[10].

The claim under a suing and labouring clause is a separate head of claim and is not merely ancilliary to other claims, as may be seen from the fact that such a claim can arise even if the absence of any other claim. Consequently, it must be properly pleaded as a separate claim[11].

[1] Section 78(1).
[2] Sections 65 and 66.
[3] Section 78(2).
[4] Section 78(3).
[5] Section 78(4).
[6] [1997] 2 Lloyd's Rep 440, CA.
[7] [1921] All ER Rep 447, HL.
[8] [1999] QB 674, [1997] 2 All ER 929, CA.
[9] [1997] 2 Lloyd's Rep 440, CA.
[10] *Mitsui Marine & Fire Insurance Co v Bayview Motors Ltd* [2003] Lloyd's Rep IR 117, David Steel J and CA.
[11] *North Star Shipping Ltd v Sphere Drake Insurance plc* [2005] 1 All ER (Comm) 112, Colman J.

Seizure

40.33 Goods may be warranted free of seizure and capture. Misappropriation by those already in possession of a cargo does not amount to seizure[1]. Seizure does not have to be lawful, but is more likely to be established when it is lawful and done by an organ of the state. Seizure is thus not the same thing as theft[2].

[1] *Mitsui Marine & Fire Insurance Co v Bayview Motors Ltd* [2003] Lloyd's Rep IR 117, David Steel J and CA.
[2] See n 2 above.

Abandonment, salvage, subrogation and consequences of settlement

Notice of abandonment

40.34 Where the assured elects to abandon the subject matter insured to the insurer, he must give notice of abandonment. If he fails to do so the loss can only be treated as a partial loss. Notice of abandonment may be given in writing, or by word of mouth, or partly in writing and partly by word of mouth, and may be given in terms which indicate the intention of the assured to abandon his insured interest in the subject matter insured unconditionally to the insurer. Notice of abandonment must be given with reasonable diligence after the receipt of reliable information of the loss, but where the information is of a doubtful character the assured is entitled to a reasonable time to make inquiry. Where notice of abandonment is properly given, the rights of the assured are not prejudiced by the fact that the insurer refuses to accept the abandonment. The acceptance of an abandonment may be either express or implied from the conduct of the insurer. The mere silence of the insurer after notice is not an acceptance. Where a notice of abandonment is accepted the abandonment is irrevocable. The acceptance of the notice conclusively admits liability for the loss and the sufficiency of the notice. Notice of abandonment is unnecessary where, at the time when the assured receives information of the loss, there would be no possibility of benefit to the insurer if notice were given to him. Notice of abandonment may be waived by the insurer. Where an insurer has reinsured his risk, no notice of abandonment need be given by him[1]. The cause of action arises on the date of the casualty and not on the date of the giving of the notice of abandonment – *Bank of America National Trust and Savings Association v Chrismas, The Kyriaki*[2].

1 Section 62.
2 [1993] 1 Lloyd's Rep 137, CA.

Effect of abandonment

40.35 Where there is a valid abandonment the insurer is entitled to take over the interest of the assured in whatever may remain of the subject matter insured, and all proprietary rights incidental thereto. Upon the abandonment of a ship, the insurer thereof is entitled to any freight in course of being earned, and which is earned by her subsequent to the casualty causing the loss, less the expenses of earning it incurred after the casualty; and, where the ship is carrying the owner's goods, the insurer is entitled to a reasonable remuneration for the carriage of them subsequent to the casualty causing the loss[1].

1 Section 63.

Salvage charges

40.36 Subject to any express provision in the policy, salvage charges incurred in preventing a loss by perils insured against may be recovered as a loss by those perils. 'Salvage charges' means the charges recoverable under maritime law by a salvor independently of contract (though in practice most salvage is carried out under contract, usually the Lloyd's Open Form). They do not include the expenses of services in the nature of salvage rendered by the assured or his agents, or any person employed for hire by them, for the purpose of averting a peril insured against. Such expenses, where properly incurred, may be recovered as particular charges or as a general average loss, according to the circumstances under which they were incurred[1].

Where the ship has been only partially repaired, the assured is entitled to the reasonable cost of such repairs, computed as above, and also to be indemnified for the reasonable depreciation, if any, arising from the unrepaired damage, provided that the aggregate amount shall not exceed the cost of repairing the whole damage, computed as above: Where the ship has not been repaired, and has not been sold in her damaged state during the currency of the policy, the assured is entitled to be indemnified for the reasonable depreciation arising from the unrepaired damage, but not exceeding the reasonable cost of repairing such damage, computed as above[2].

1 Section 65.
2 Section 69.

General average contributions and salvage charges

40.37 Subject to any express provision in the policy, where the assured has paid, or is liable for, any general average contribution, the measure of indemnity is the full amount of such contribution, if the subject matter liable to contribution is insured for its full contributory value; but, if such subject matter be not insured for its full contributory value, or if only part of it be insured, the indemnity payable by the insurer must be reduced in proportion to the under-insurance, and where there has been a particular average loss which constitutes a deduction from the contributory value, and for which the insurer is liable, that amount must be deducted from the insured value in order to ascertain what the insurer is liable to contribute. Where the insurer is liable for salvage charges the extent of his liability must be determined on the like principle[1].

[1] Section 73.

Right of subrogation[1]

40.38 Where the insurer pays for a total loss, either of the whole, or in the case of goods of any apportionable part, of the subject matter insured, he thereupon becomes entitled to take over the interest of the assured in whatever may remain of the subject matter so paid for, and he is thereby subrogated to all the rights and remedies of the assured in and in respect of that subject matter as from the time of the casualty causing the loss. However, subject to this where the insurer pays for a partial loss, he acquires no title to the subject matter insured, or such part of it as may remain, but he is thereupon subrogated to all rights and remedies of the assured in and in respect of the subject matter insured as from the time of the casualty causing the loss, in so far as the assured has been indemnified, according to this Act, by such payment for the loss[2]. In *Colonia Versicherung AG v Amoco Oil Co*[3] the question was whether the supplier of a cargo of contaminated cargo was disentitled to claim under the insurance policy as assignees of the buyers and as to whether the supplier was a co-insured under the contract of insurance by virtue of holding the bearer certificates. The suppliers had settled the buyers' claim for losses on taking an assignment of the buyers' rights under an insurance contract.

On the facts it was held that a narrow interpretation of the doctrine of subrogation should be rejected. Whether or not the supplier had any direct liability to the buyer, the deed of assignment had settled any possible claim and had expressly allowed the insurers' subrogation rights in full. On a true construction of the deed the clear intention was not to exclude the insurer from the benefit of the payment to the buyer. It was also held that the benefit of a floating policy could not be extended to a party who, though a bearer of a certificate, had not been in the contemplation of those making the contract.

[1] On subrogation generally, see Chapter 22.
[2] Section 79.
[3] [1997] 1 Lloyd's Rep 261.

Right of contribution[1]

40.39 Where the assured is over-insured by double insurance, each insurer is bound, as between himself and the other insurers, to contribute rateably to the loss in proportion to the amount for which he is liable under his contract. If any insurer pays more than his proportion of the loss, he is entitled to maintain an action for contribution against the other insurers, and is entitled to the like remedies as a surety who has paid more than his proportion of the debt[2]. It is to be assumed that the right of contribution under this section is not affected by the passing of the Civil Liability (Contribution) Act 1978[3] This section takes effect at the time of the loss, so the existence and extent of any over-insurance must be judged as at that date alone[4].

1 On contribution generally, see Chapter 24.
2 Section 80.
3 *O'Kane v Jones* [2005] Lloyd's Rep IR 174, Richard Sibbery QC at para 189.
4 See n 3 above.

Double insurance

40.40 Where two or more policies are effected by or on behalf of the assured on the same adventure and interest or any part of it, and the sums insured exceed the indemnity allowed by this Act, the assured is over-insured by double insurance[1]. In this event the assured, unless the policy otherwise provides, may claim payment from the insurers in such order as he may think fit, but is not entitled to receive any sum in excess of the indemnity allowed by the Act. To this point the MIA 1906 rule merely states the common law principle that the assured cannot recover more than an indemnity[2]. Matters become more difficult where there is more than one policy and at least one of them is a valued policy[3]. Where the policy under which the assured claims is a valued policy, the assured must give credit as against the valuation for any sum received by him under any other policy without regard to the actual value of the subject matter insured, ie the full amount received is deducted from the agreed value. Where the policy under which the assured claims is an unvalued policy he must give credit, as against the full insurable value, for any sum received by him under any other policy. Where the assured receives any sum in excess of the indemnity allowed by this Act, he is deemed to hold such sum in trust for the insurers, according to their right of contribution among themselves[4].

1 Section 32(1); for over-insurance generally, see Chapter 24.
2 With the result that the first insurer, having paid, cannot be subrogated to the assured's rights against the second insurer, though he may be able to exercise rights of contribution.
3 As will normally happen, given the prevalence of valued policies in marine insurance.
4 Section 32(2).

Effect of under-insurance[1]

40.41 Where the assured is insured for an amount less than the insurable value or, in the case of a valued policy, for an amount less than the policy valuation, he is deemed to be his own insurer in respect of the uninsured balance. This mirrors the rule in non-marine insurance, and it appears – though this by no means follows necessarily from the words used – that the rule of under-insurance is applied also to a partial loss.

1 On under-insurance generally, see Chapter 25.

Chapter 41

Professional indemnity policies

Introduction

41.1 Professional indemnity policies (also known as 'Errors and Omissions' or 'E & O' policies) are an area of central importance in most professional life at the present day. They provide cover against the risk of the insured incurring liability for negligence or other breach of duty arising in the conduct of the profession. Many professions[1] require their members to have insurance as a condition of practice, whilst in many other professions the holding of such insurance is more or less universal.

[1] Including barristers, solicitors and accountants.

Coverage

41.2 In order to succeed in a claim on a professional indemnity policy the insured must show that it is under a legal liability to one or more of those claiming against it and that the loss in question is covered by the policy[1]. The simplest proof of this will be that the insured has been held so liable in legal proceedings[2]. It also follows that, in the absence of special wording, there is no cover where the insured is not held liable[3]. It is for this reason that PI policies normally deal separately with indemnity for costs incurred in defending a claim. Where the case is settled out of court, the position is a little more complex. In most cases the insurers will of course be involved in the handling and defending of the claim. However, if the insured settles the claim independently of the insurer, then he also needs to be able to prove that the settlement reached was reasonable in the sense that the amount which he claims from the insurer is no greater than the amount which he could have expected to pay had the matter gone to court[4].

[1] *Rigby v Sun Alliance* [1980] 1 Lloyd's Rep 359; *Peninsular & Oriental Steam Navigation Co v Youell* [1997] 2 Lloyd's Rep 136, CA.
[2] *Skandia International Insurance Corpn v NRG Victory Reinsurance Ltd* [1998] Lloyd's Rep IR 439, CA.

[3] *Thornton Springer v NEM Insurance Co Ltd* [2000] 1 All ER (Comm) 486, Colman J.
[4] *Structural Polymer v Brown* [2000] Lloyd's Rep IR 64, Moore-Bick J.

Claims basis v occurrence basis

41.3 A fundamental distinction in professional indemnity policies is that between the occurrence basis and the claims-made basis. Under the occurrence basis the risk attaches to the policy year in which the event or occurrence giving rise to the liability arises, even if the liability does not become apparent until much later. Under the claims-made basis the risk attaches to the policy year in which the claim is made against the insured. The choice between the two has obvious implications for premium levels, for the application of policy limits and excess levels and for the rules on disclosure; a policy written on a claims made basis will have more stringent requirements as to disclosure, since the insurer is exposed to claims of which the insured has prior knowledge, but which have not yet materialised.

Discovery extension cover

41.4 Where policies are written on a claims-made basis, discovery extension cover is sometimes included in respect of claims reported within a certain period after the policy ends. The operation of such clauses can be especially significant where the insured changes insurers. In *Touche Ross & Co v Colin Baker*[1] the policies provided that in the event of the underwriters refusing to renew there was to be discovery extension cover for 'Incurred But Not Reported' claims reported within a certain period after the end of the policies. When the policies were terminated by the Lloyd's underwriters, most underwriters were prepared to negotiate alternative terms, but the defendant was the representative underwriter of those who refused to do so. The question was whether the insured could choose to apply the discovery extension cover only against those who were not agreeing new terms, or whether it had to be exercised against all underwriters or none. The House of Lords held that there were in fact many separate contracts, since Lloyd's underwriters contract 'each for himself not one for another'. There was thus no reason to hold that the position had to be the same as against all underwriters, and discovery extension cover could be claimed against those who refused to renew.

[1] [1992] 2 Lloyd's Rep 207, HL.

Confidentiality and 'QC' clauses

41.5 Many policyholders under professional indemnity policies will want to be able to settle claims without going to court even where the validity of the claim is uncertain. Even the issue of proceedings for professional negligence puts the matter to some extent in the public domain, and many professionals are naturally anxious to avoid this if at all possible. Insurers, by contrast, are naturally anxious to avoid incurring liability under the policy where this is reasonably possible, and thus have a vested interest in defending doubtful claims. In professional indemnity policies it is usual to deal with this problem by means of a clause commonly known as a 'QC' clause. This provides that the insurer will meet any claim which the insured reasonably objects to defending unless the insurer can obtain leading counsel's opinion to the effect that the claim can be successfully defended. For the most part clauses of this kind work well, but some difficulties may arise where there is dispute over whether the claim which has been made falls within the policy anyway. This is not strictly a matter within the QC clause, and it may therefore be necessary to litigate it is as a preliminary question, notwithstanding that this will destroy the very confidentiality which the clause seeks to achieve[1]. Of course this problem may be (and often is) circumvented by providing for arbitration rather than litigation.

In *Kumar v AGF Insurance Ltd*[2] it was held by the Commercial Court that contracts have to be interpreted against their background which in this case was the SIF Rules, particularly rr 29 and 30 and the fact that the scheme of the insurance was meant to provide an indemnity to clients in circumstances where they had been caused loss by a solicitor which was exemplified by para 5 of the policy. It was clear that the intention of the parties was to prevent insurers escaping from liability under the policy and it was held that the alleged breach of warranty did not have the effect of providing the defendants with a defence to the claimant's claim. This is a case of some general importance in the context of professional indemnity policies. The policy was not an SIF policy; rather, it was a top-up policy to cover the risk of liability for sums exceeding £1m. The policy contained a clause providing that the insurers would not on any ground seek to avoid, repudiate or rescind the policy. The insurers alleged (and for the purposes of this action it had to be assumed) that there had been a basic non-disclosure in that a possible claim had not been disclosed. It was for that claim that the indemnity was subsequently sought. The insurers put their case on the alternative grounds of implied term, breach of warranty and misrepresentation. On the face of it the non-disclosure would seem to give the insurers a strong case, but Thomas J held that the clause outlined above prevented them from seeking to rely in any way upon the non-disclosure. Although this might at first sight seem extraordinary, it is in fact entirely explicable and sensible. The purpose of the policy was to ensure that clients were protected against the financial consequences of negligence. It was for this reason that the policy also gave the insurers a right of reimbursement against a principal under the policy who prior to inception committed a fraudulent non-disclosure or misrepresentation of circumstances which might give rise to a claim. The effect of the non-disclosure was thus that the insurers were still obliged to pay out on the policy, but would have a right of reimbursement if they could show that the non-disclosure was fraudulent. On slightly different wording it was held in *Toomey v Eagle Star Insurance Co Ltd (No 2)*[3] that the policy excluded the right to rescind for purely innocent non-disclosure or misrepresentation, but did not affect the right to rescind for negligent non-disclosure or misrepresentation.

1 *West Wake Price & Co v Ching* [1957] 1 WLR 45, Devlin J.
2 [1998] 4 All ER 788.
3 [1995] 2 Lloyd's Rep 88, Colman J.

'Claims-made' professional indemnity policy

41.6 In *Robert Irving & Burns v Stone*[1] the defendants were the insurers of the claimants under a policy of professional indemnity insurance covering liabilities incurred in the course of the claimants' business. It was a claims-made policy. The significance of this was that the policy expired between the issue and service of the writ and the question to be determined by the Court of Appeal was whether the claim was made when the writ was issued or only when it was served.

The Court of Appeal held that for the purposes of a claims-made policy of professional indemnity insurance, a claim was not made until it was communicated to the insurer. This did not occur until the writ was served and that was therefore the date on which the claim was made. In the circumstances of the case that meant that the insurers were not liable under the policy because it had expired before the claim was made.

The case is of most significance to those dealing with disputes relating to professional negligence and third party liability, where policies of insurance are often written on a claims-made basis.

The case highlights the importance in claims-made policies of notifying the insurer of any claims brought against the policyholder or, indeed, any complaint which may give rise to a claim.

In *J Rothschild Assurance plc v Collyear*[2] a life assurance company sought to be indemnified by its professional indemnity insurance underwriters for the losses it had sustained or might yet sustain by reason of the need to compensate investors for the mis-selling of pensions. One of the main issues was whether the claims made clause, which referred to 'any claim or claims ... made against them ... in respect of any civil liability' had been satisfied.

The defendants main defence was that, with rare exceptions, no claims had ever been asserted against the claimants as the pensions industry had itself gone out to uncover non-compliance and to volunteer recompense, rather than the more normal situation where an assured awaited claims to which he was then forced to respond, a situation to which, on the underwriters' case, such 'claims made' policies were simply not designed to respond.

His Lordship accepted that the words 'claim ... made' require not only the assertion of a claim, of some remedy as due, but also the bringing of that assertion to the notice of the assured. In this case the investors concerned had answered questionnaires sent to them as part of the LAUTRO review and/or by agreeing to the offers of redress in the terms in which such offers were made and accepted. When the investors accepted the 'full and final settlements' they did so on terms that 'Completing this letter and returning it prevents you from making any further claim against [the claimants] in respect of this matter.'

It was held that the court had to take an overall view of the review process. In the context of the regulatory regime of the pensions industry it was held that if claiming was easy it was because of the policy of the Act, the complexities of the subject matter and the sake of the good name of the industry. Further, the defendants were familiar with the regulatory regime and could not complain that they were being asked to underwrite risks of a different nature from those they entered upon. The claimants were therefore able to recover under the terms of the policy.

Although the case is limited to the pensions industry, in a world of increased self regulation and 'best practice' it could have wider implications in the future.

1 [1998] Lloyd's Rep IR 258, CA.
2 [1999] Lloyd's Rep IR 6, Rix J.

How many claims/occurrences?

41.7 In a claims made policy it is often necessary to decide how many 'claims' within the meaning of the policy have been made. This is because there may be a deductible for each claim and/or a limit of cover for 'any one claim'. The leading English authority is *Lloyds TSB General Insurance Holdings Ltd v Lloyds Bank Group Insurance Co Ltd*[1] where there was a deductible of £1 million per claim, but the policy also provided:

> 'If a series of third party claims shall result from any single act or omission (or a related series of acts or omissions) then irrespective of the total number of claims all such third party claims shall be considered to be a single third party claim for the purposes of the application of the Deductible.'

A large number of claims for pensions mis-selling arose and were within the policy. The question was whether these were individually subject to the Deductible or whether the terms set out above applied so that they were to be regarded as a single claim. At first instance Moore-Bick J accepted the argument that all the claims resulted from the failure of the insured to give proper training to its staff. This he characterised as a single act or omission, so that the clause applied. The Court of Appeal took the view that the clause required an analysis of the true cause of the losses, and that the true cause was in each case an individual failure to give Best Advice under the LAUTRO Rules then in force. Although this was not a single act or omission, the Court of Appeal took the view that it was a related series of acts or omissions, so that the parenthetical part of the clause applied. The House of Lords approached the matter very differently. Although they agreed that this was not a single act or omission, they did not accept that it was a related series of acts or omissions. The crucial point was that the failure to give proper training to staff, whilst undeniably a breach of regulatory obligation, was neither a necessary nor a sufficient cause of the claims, with the result that it could not be a unifying factor for the purposes of a related series of acts or omissions. To hold otherwise would be to allow the policyholders to use the parenthetical part of the clause as a way of standing the clause on its head. The substantial level of the Deductible was evidence that the parties had intended that the policy would cover only very substantial individual claims.

1 [2003] UKHL 48, [2003] Lloyd's Rep IR 623; for earlier authorities see *Australia and New Zealand Bank Ltd v Colonial and Eagle Wharves Ltd* [1960] 2 Lloyd's Rep 241, McNair J.; *Pennsylvania Co v Mumford* [1920] 2 KB 537; *Equitable Trust Co of New York v Whittakers* (1923) 17 Ll L Rep 153; *Philadelphia National Bank v Price* (1937) 58 Ll L Rep 238. *Mann v Lexington Insurance Co* [2001] Lloyd's Rep IR 179, CA.

41.8 Although the decision on the particular facts of the case may be regarded as sensible, it cannot be denied that the words in parentheses do on the face of it appear to undermine the narrow ambit of the principal part of the clause. It is also dangerous to draw over general conclusions from the decision, since it is clear that each case must depend on the exact wording of the clause. One point which can perhaps fairly be made is that in clauses of this kind it is essential to focus on the question of the causes of the various losses. It must also follow that the decision of Morrison J in *Countrywide Assured Group plc v Marshall*[1], which holds, albeit in the context of aggregates rather than deductibles that on similar facts there was a common cause, namely the failure to give proper training, can no longer be considered good law.

[1] [2002] EWHC 2082 (Comm), [2003] Lloyd's Rep IR 195; these issues, especially in relation to aggregates, are not confined to professional indemnity policies. For more general consideration of the problem see Chapter 19.

41.9 It appears that in professional indemnity policies which have a limit of cover applied to each claim it is not usual to imply into the policy a provision restricting cover in respect of errors or omissions which cause more than one event of loss[1]. In subsequent litigation arising out of the same facts[2] it was held that where design faults were found in a number of bridges designed by the insured, each bridge gave rise to a potential separate claim, so that the limit of indemnity for each claim was to be applied separately. As ever, this decision is heavily dependent on the detailed facts of the case, but it is important to note that the task for the court is to analyse the underlying reality of the case other than merely looking at the way it is expressed on behalf of the third party making the claim. Here there were separate contracts for each bridge, and the design work was somewhat different in each case, although there were certain common elements.

[1] *Mabey and Johnson Ltd v Ecclesiastical Insurance Office plc* [2001] Lloyd's Rep IR 369, Morrison J.
[2] *Mabey and Johnson Ltd v Ecclesiastical Insurance Office plc* [2004] Lloyd's Rep IR 10, Morrison J.

Payment on basis of settlement

41.10 In *Structural Polymer Systems Ltd v Brown (Lloyd's Syndicate 702)*[1], the claimant's claim under the insurance policy arose out of a liability arising in a claim against it in New Zealand, which had been settled after mediation. The claimant insured therefore requested summary judgment against the defendant professional indemnity insurers for the sums agreed in settlement in New Zealand plus the costs of the New Zealand proceedings. The insurer wanted to argue its case at a full trial. The terms of the policy were that the insurer would indemnify the insured against sums they were 'legally liable to pay'. In *Skandia v NRG* it was held that in such cases (ie where the liability arises under a settlement rather than a judgment) it is necessary for the insured to show he was in fact liable 'on a correct view of the law' – which in this case would mean that the claimant was liable under its contract 'in an amount not less than that paid under the settlement agreement.' The judge was satisfied that the claim against the insurers did not represent more than the insured's liability, when the settlement agreement payment was compared with the size of the total claim and having regard to the apparent strength of the claim.

Of relevance was the fact that the insurer had only just become involved in the action at the time of the settlement in New Zealand. During the mediation the insurer had believed the claim was outside the policy but the judge said it must have realised the insured was likely to claim under the policy and that the question of its liability under the contracts would arise. The insured's documents had been available for inspection for a considerable period of time and the insurer had chosen not to inspect the material. That was not grounds for giving leave to defend so it might now do so.

Accordingly the insured was entitled to judgment in the amount paid under the settlement agreements and the relevant part of the costs of defending the New Zealand proceedings.

In *MDIS Ltd (Formerly McDonnell Information Systems Ltd) v Swinbank*[2] the claimant, a computer company, compromised a claim by one of its clients ('S') before discovery. The claim was for, inter alia, misrepresentation but S did not allege fraud. In this action the claimant sought an indemnity in respect of that liability from its professional indemnity insurers. Its claim was under one of four perils in the operative clause, cl 2. Clause 2(a) stated that the assured was indemnified, inter alia, 'against any claim for which the assured may become legally liable ... arising out of the professional conduct of the assured's business ... alleging: (a) any neglect or omission including breach of contract occasioned by the same'. It was common ground that under cl 2(b), where the assured was indemnified if the claim alleged dishonesty by an employee, there was an exception to the effect that, whatever the nature of the claimant's allegation, the underwriters were not liable if they could prove that the proximate cause of the loss was dishonesty perpetrated after the insured could reasonably have discovered or suspected improper conduct. The defendant underwriters' case was that in order to succeed under cl 2(a) of the policy the claimant had to show that it was legally liable to S in respect of 'neglect, error or omission including breach of contract occasioned by the same'. The loss had to be proximately caused by a peril insured against, namely neglect. If, as the defendant alleged, the loss was caused by the dishonesty of the claimant's employees then there was no claim. The claimant argued that so to hold was to disregard or to give insufficient weight to the word 'alleging' in cl 2. It argued that it was not necessary for the insured to prove that the proximate cause of the loss as so established was the neglect itself. It was sufficient if the liability was for or in respect of a claim alleging such neglect.

The Court of Appeal held that:

(1) The effect of the claimant's submissions was that where the claim which was settled was advanced by the claimant only as a claim for neglect, the underwriters were liable even if they could prove that the proximate cause of the liability was the dishonest or fraudulent act of an employee of the assured, perpetrated after the assured could reasonably have discovered or suspected improper conduct. A consideration of cl 2 as a whole led to the conclusion that the parties did not intend such a result.
(2) The judge was correct in his conclusion both that cl 2 could not be read entirely literally and that it was concerned to impose liability where the proximate cause of the liability to the claimant was one of the insured perils in one of its sub-clauses.

(3) When cl 2(a) was read in the context of cl 2 as a whole and when it was borne in mind that this was an indemnity policy, the correct construction was as follows: underwriters were not liable, not only if the proximate cause of the loss was the dishonesty of the assured itself, but also if the proximate cause of the loss was not neglect but dishonesty of an employee perpetrated after the assured could reasonably have discovered or suspected the improper conduct of the employee concerned.

(4) Underwriters' liability depended upon the true facts and not simply the way in which the claimant chose to put its case.

(5) This approach was consistent with the approach in *West Wake Price & Co v Ching*[3].

(6) While, by reason of the compromise, the claimant had proved a loss, it had to be established that the loss was proximately caused by neglect. It was open to the underwriters to assert that the loss resulted from the dishonest acts of the assured's employees, perpetrated after the claimant could reasonably have discovered or suspected the improper conduct of such employees. In that event, the loss would not have been caused by neglect and the claimant would not be able to recover under the policy.

The importance of the case lies in the reaffirmation of a general principle that in liability policies the decision whether the claim falls within the class of claim covered depends upon the true characterisation of the claim rather than on the label which a third party claimant may choose to give to it.

1 [2000] Lloyd's Rep IR 64, Moore-Bick J.
2 [1999] Lloyd's Rep IR 516, CA.
3 [1957] 1 WLR 45.

Effect of non-disclosure by one partner

41.11 In *Burgess Wreford & Unsworth (A Firm) v Aegon Insurance Co (UK) Ltd*[1], which was a claim for damages against professional indemnity insurers, it was held that a non-disclosure by one of the partners of the claimant firm amounted to a breach of warranty in the proposal forms, thus depriving the claimant of the whole of their right to an indemnity.

The claimant firm ('BWU'), former independent mortgage financial consultants, sought damages against their former professional indemnity insurers ('Aegon') for the latter's refusal to provide an indemnity, in respect of a claim made against BWU by a building society in relation to a commercial property transaction. In its defence, Aegon argued breach of warranty. The underlying factual allegation was one of fraud on the part of BWU by one of its partners ('W'), which led to the building society's claim. The following issues arose:

(i) whether there was a failure to disclose, in the policy renewal proposal form or its amendment, any circumstances which were likely to give rise to a loss, or a claim against BWU;

(ii) precisely what W knew at the time these proposal forms were completed;

(iii) whether the building society claim arose by reason of any dishonest or fraudulent act or omission by W.

Clause 4 of the policy excluded the person guilty of dishonesty or fraud from obtaining an indemnity, but not his innocent partners. If an indemnity was sought by BWU in respect of a liability arising out of W's fraud, W himself would be debarred from an indemnity under cl 4 but the other partners would be entitled to an indemnity under cl 1, though W would be liable to reimburse Aegon in respect of the indemnity afforded to his fellow partners. This follows the normal practice in relation to insurance of a partnership. However, if there was a breach of warranty as a result of the proposal form (which contained a basis of the contract clause) none of the partners would be entitled to an indemnity. There was nothing in the wording of Aegon's right of reimbursement which depended upon the way in which the claim was formulated by the building society (ie in negligence and not in deceit) rather than the effective cause of the loss resulting from the claim. The allegation of fraud against W was material both to Aegon's claim that non-disclosure and breach of warranty occurred, and to its assertion that W, rather than being entitled to an indemnity, was liable to reimburse it. On the facts W had been fraudulent and must have known by the time that he filled in the proposal form that circumstances had arisen which might give rise to a claim. There was thus non-disclosure amounting to breach of warranty in the proposal forms filled out by W. This, in turn, deprived BWU as a whole of their right to an indemnity, and their claim failed. In any event W himself would not be entitled to succeed in the action and Aegon would be entitled to succeed on their counterclaim against him in respect of the claim by his fellow partners, which Aegon would then have to meet.

The emphasis here placed on the proposal form is of some importance in considering the effect of fraud. It may justly be said that any professional who commits fraud will be aware that he is doing so and thus aware of the possibility of a claim. A failure to disclose this at renewal will always be a non-disclosure of a material fact. Subject to the question of actual inducement[2], it appears that the effect will always be to render voidable any professional indemnity policy written on a claims-made basis. Even if the policy is on an occurrence basis, underwriters may well be able to show that they would have made a different decision had they been aware of the fraud.

[1] (12 May 1999, unreported), Judge Hegarty QC.

[2] *Pan Atlantic Insurance Co Ltd v Pine Top Insurance Co Ltd* [1994] 3 All ER 581, HL. See generally Chapter 5.

41.12 Where the policy has a condition forfeiting cover if the insured is guilty of fraud, this will not prevent non-guilty co-insureds from recovering on the policy, as where one partner in a firm involves the firm in liability through his fraud[1].

[1] *Arab Bank plc v Zurich Insurance Co* [1999] 1 Lloyd's Rep 262, Rix J.

The conduct of the defence

41.12A In a professional indemnity policy[1] it is usual to find a term empowering the insurers to take over and conduct the defence of any claim against the insured which may lead to a claim on the policy. In practice this will mean that the insurers instruct lawyers to deal with the claim. A significant grey area is the role and duty of those lawyers. To what extent do they act for the insurer and to what extent do they act for the insured?

In *Brown v Guardian Royal Exchange*[2] Mr Brown was a sole practitioner solicitor, insured under the Master Policy Scheme. A claim arose against him, and he duly notified his insurers, who instructed solicitors. As a result of a conference with counsel, at which Mr Brown apparently made certain admissions, insurers repudiated liability, and the solicitors decided that they could no longer act for him because of a conflict of interests. The question before the Court of Appeal concerned privilege in relation to documents prepared by Mr Brown and other parties for the purposes of advising him in the period before the solicitors withdrew. The Court of Appeal held that the matter was resolved by the wording of the policy, which specifically gave the insurers the right to receive reports prepared by the solicitors. These reports, said the Court of Appeal, could properly contain anything which the solicitors had learned about the claim (including any view which they had formed about the possibility that the insured had been fraudulent). Even where the retainer was terminated by the solicitors, insurers were still entitled to know of anything which had happened during the currency of the retainer. This decision must of course be taken to depend upon the particular wording of the policy. Some of the more general issues in this area were canvassed in *TSB Bank plc v Robert Irving and Burns*[3]. The defendants were a firm of valuers who had carried out a valuation for the claimants of a property which was proposed to be used as the security for a commercial loan. The allegation against the defendants was that the valuation had been performed negligently. The defendants' liability insurers instructed solicitors to conduct the defence of the claim, and a meeting took place between the solicitors and a representative of the defendants, at which the representative was questioned about the details of what had happened. Although the insurers were unconvinced that they were liable for the loss which had happened (because of doubts about the sequence of events) they received counsel's advice that they had no ground to deny liability, and their subsequent behaviour left the defendants with the impression that liability had been accepted, though they never expressly confirmed this. At a further conference with counsel the defendants' representative was again questioned about the sequence of events, which was crucial to the issue of the insurers' liability, but no indication was ever given that the purpose of the questioning was to look for grounds on which liability might be repudiated. Following the conference the insurers did repudiate liability. The defendants began third party proceedings against their insurers, claiming that there was liability under the policy, alternatively that as a result of their conduct the insurers were estopped from denying liability. By their defence the insurers indicated that they intended to rely upon answers given by the defendants' representative in the course of the cross-examination. The defendants applied to strike out this part of the defence; they also sought an order restraining the insurers from relying upon those answers.

1 As in most forms of liability policy.
2 [1994] 2 Lloyd's Rep 325, CA.
3 [1999] Lloyd's Rep IR 528, CA.

41.13 The case clearly raises some of the general issues mentioned above about the role of lawyers instructed by the insurers. In this case the lawyers appear to have regarded themselves as acting for the insurers and not for the defendants. At first instance it was held, first, that the proper analysis of the position was that the lawyers had been retained by the defendants and their insurers jointly, though this was not to be construed as meaning that under no circumstances could the insurers repudiate liability if the evidence appeared to establish that they were otherwise entitled to do so. Secondly, it was said that as a general rule where solicitors are instructed by two parties with a common interest, neither can maintain a claim for privilege against the other in respect of matters within the common retainer. However, a distinction must be drawn between those matters which are within the common retainer and those which are not. Thus, in the present case the insurers could claim privilege in relation to communications to the solicitors about the scope of the policy cover. Similarly, the communications made by the defendants to the solicitors about the circumstances of the valuation were privileged against the insurers. An appeal to the Court of Appeal against this ruling failed, though that court went some way towards clarifying the ambiguities present in the first instance decision. The Court of Appeal said that the retainer of the solicitors was clearly a joint one, and it did not matter whether there might also have been two separate retainers. This is to be welcomed, since the idea of three simultaneous retainers, one joint and two separate, seems more than a little contrived. However, this approach focuses attention on the question of what happens in a joint retainer such as this where the parties fall out with each other or where it otherwise becomes apparent that there is an actual conflict of interest between them. On this point the Court of Appeal said that as a general rule neither party can maintain privilege against the other in relation to documents which have come into existence earlier in the litigation[1]. However, the terms of the implied waiver of privilege as between the parties at the outset of the litigation are such that the waiver does not extend to communications made to the solicitors after an actual conflict of interest has arisen. In the present case it was clear by the time of the conference with counsel that there was an actual conflict of interest, since the possibility of repudiating liability was being actively considered. Thus the things said at that conference were privileged as against the insurers.

[1] *CIA Barca de Panama SA v George Wimpey & Co Ltd* [1980] 1 Lloyd's Rep 598; *Brown v Guardian Royal Exchange Assurance plc* [1994] 2 Lloyd's Rep 325, CA.

41.14 The decision is greatly to be welcomed, but some further points may usefully be made. First, it seems obvious enough in retrospect that the solicitors were not as astute as they might have been in considering whether they found themselves in a position of conflict of interest. In effect the crucial conference was allowed to proceed on the basis of what amounted to a cross-examination of the defendants' representative on behalf of the insurers. From this point of view the case highlights the need for solicitors and counsel in such cases to think carefully about possible conflict. Secondly, this need for reflection goes beyond the question of the admissibility of evidence. Once it becomes apparent that there is a significant likelihood that the insurers will want to repudiate liability, it must follow that a conflict of interest has arisen, and the solicitors will need to take action to draw this to the attention of both parties. For reasons of professional conduct they may also need to stop acting for either party.

Indemnity insurance and the pensions review

41.15 The review of the selling of personal pensions between 1988 and 1992 ordered by the SIB and later continued by the FSA has given rise to litigation between the providers of such pensions and their indemnity insurers. The points raised are in some instances of an importance which goes beyond the scope of pensions mis-selling. In *J Rothschild Assurance plc v John Robert Collyear*[1] the claimants' insurance policy required them to give notice of circumstances which 'may give rise to a claim'. When renewing the policy in January 1994 the claimants drew the attention of their insurers to some 2,500 policies which they had sold, but which they had not yet had time to review in detailed as required by the SIB. They notified the insurers that any or all of these policies might possibly be found in due course to be non-compliant and thus to give rise to a claim. However, the claimants were not at that time in a position to say with certainty how many of these policies would give rise to claims. By the middle of 1998 they had identified 400 priority cases as being non-compliant sales, and had made offers of redress. The policy contained an exclusion in a form common to such policies, under which there was no cover for claims arising from circumstances or occurrences known to the insured prior to the inception of the policy, where the non-disclosure was fraudulent, and the underwriters sought to rely upon this provision as excluding their liability for the 400 priority cases, and, by necessary implication, for any further claims which might arise from the review of the 2,500 cases identified by the insured. Rix J held that this defence must fail. The primary reason for this decision was that the insured were not considered to have had the necessary prior knowledge of the claims. In reaching this conclusion Rix J had to consider the interaction of the requirement to notify any event which might give rise to a claim with the exclusion of matters where there was prior knowledge. He held that notification is proper in relation to any event which *may* give rise to a claim, ie it is not necessary to be certain that there will in fact be a claim. He rejected the allegation that the notification of the 2,500 claims was merely speculative. As later events showed, a significant proportion of these did give rise to claims, a fact which appeared to vindicate the decision of the insured to notify them. At the same time the fact that the claims were uncertain meant that they were not matters of which the insured had knowledge prior to the inception of the policy.

[1] [1999] Lloyd's Rep IR 6, Rix J; and see above for other aspects of this case.

41.16 The importance of this case is likely to be considerable. The probable costs of the pensions review have been discussed elsewhere in this work[1], and it is obvious that the present case is a test case selected to allow judicial determination of some important questions about where the insurance risk for the review is going to fall. The policies in question were all written on a claims made basis, and it is of course usual in such policies to exclude claims which were or should have been notified under any previous policy, as well as any other matters outstanding, of which the insured is or should be aware. The purpose of this is to secure a clear allocation of risk between different policies; naturally, the underwriters for each year seek so far as possible to refer the risk back to earlier policies. Consequently, the real issue in this case is not whether there is going to be cover, but which policy year is to bear the risk. In effect Rix J has held that the risk attaches to the year in which the claim moves from being a mere possibility to being established as giving rise to a definite liability, but that the possibility of claims should properly be notified as soon as it is recognised.

[1] Chapter 44.

Chapter 42

Mechanical breakdown and extended warranty insurance

Introduction

42.1 This Chapter deals with two important types of modern insurance. The first is mechanical breakdown, a type of policy normally encountered in connection with privately owned motor cars[1], which aims to provide cover against the risk of breakdown, a risk which is not covered by standard motor insurance policies. The second is extended warranty insurance, commonly sold in conjunction with household electrical goods and intended to extended the warranty period beyond the standard 12 months normally provided by the manufacturer.

[1] Also sometimes in aviation and shipping, where it may be linked to loss-of-use insurance.

Mechanical breakdown

42.2 Mechanical breakdown cover suffers from one major problem, which is arguably close to being insuperable. By its nature this type of cover resembles a maintenance arrangement – in effect the insurer promises (or *appears* to promise) that if something goes wrong with the car, the insurer will meet the cost of repair. Such an arrangement may legitimately be regarded as contravening a basic principle of insurance, which is that it is intended to cover the exceptional and unexpected event, rather than to meet the cost of routine maintenance. Certainly, a contract which really gave the kind of extended cover just described would be prohibitively expensive – a policyholder would be better off simply paying for the maintenance as the cost arose. It is therefore not surprising to find that in practice mechanical breakdown policies provide a somewhat more restricted cover. Of course this simply gives rise to another common problem of insurance practice, namely the gap between policyholders' expectations and the actual scope of the cover.

42.3 The restrictions on cover provided by mechanical breakdown policies usually take one of three forms. First, there are restrictions on the parts of the car which are covered, either by having a list of exclusions, or by having a list of those parts which are covered, all others being by implication excluded. Secondly, there are restrictions on the causes of damage which will give rise to a claim on the policy. It is common to exclude loss arising from normal wear and tear. This may be regarded as no more than an expression of the fundamental insurance principle identified earlier – certainly it mirrors clauses commonly found in, for example, household policies – but it does focus attention on the cause of any given loss. In practice many losses will be caused by wear and tear. The difficulties are illustrated by an IOB case[1], where the policyholder claimed for the cost of renewal of the clutch fork, the clutch centre plate and the clutch pressure plate, which the repairer recommended should be replaced at the same time. The policy had exclusions for 'components that are replaced at the time of repair which have not actually failed' and 'repairs or replacements due to wear, tear, deterioration and corrosion'.

The clutch fork was not one of the insured items at all, and the engineer's report showed that the other items had not failed, but had merely deteriorated due to wear and tear.

The Ombudsman upheld the insurer's view that it was not obliged to pay any part of the claim. In the absence of evidence of mis-selling (of which there was none) it is hard to see how the decision could have been different, but the case shows the limited nature of the cover provided. As the IOB report of the case observes, there was no cover because no sudden mechanical failure had occurred. It is generally only failures meeting that description which will be covered under a mechanical breakdown policy. At the same time questions of causation are always important. In one IOB case[2] the policyholder's car broke down after engine coolant leaked into the head gasket over a period of time. There was a policy exclusion for 'mechancial or electrical failure resulting from lack of coolant'.

[1] IOB 19.4.
[2] IOB 18.13.

42.4 On the facts the Ombudsman was able to hold that the engine failure was not caused by lack of coolant, even though it was obvious that the leaking of coolant into the head gasket reduced the level of coolant in the engine. Another IOB case concerning wear and tear[1] occurred where a policyholder bought a second-hand car from a garage, and, five months later, it was confirmed that there were problems with the gearbox, carburettor and exhaust. The insurer relied upon the wear and tear exclusion, but it appeared that the dealer who originally sold the car had agreed to waive about half the costs of repair. On this basis the Ombudsman took the view that the problem was likely to have existed prior to the sale[2].

[1] IOB 17.12.
[2] An odd feature of this case is that pre-existing faults were apparently also excluded. The Ombudsman is reported as taking the view that these were the responsibility of the dealer and that the insurer should seek recovery from the dealer. Although the report does not say so in as many words, it appears that the Ombudsman refused to let the insurer rely upon the pre-existing fault, presumably on the basis that it was unreasonable for him to do so.

42.5 Thirdly, there are requirements that the insured comply with specified servicing standards (usually those recommended by the manufacturer). This compliance is usually required to be proved by proper servicing records. It may happen that a claim occurs under the policy, which would be admissible but for this non-compliance. The policy will usually be drafted to make compliance a condition precedent to any recovery, even in the absence of any causal link between the non-compliance and the loss. The Insurance Ombudsman has held[1] that it is not good insurance practice to rely upon a breach of this requirement where the breach does not appear to be causally connected to the failure. Where the obligation is expressed in terms of taking reasonable care to safeguard the vehicle against loss or damage, the usual *Sofi*[2] test of recklessness will be applied in determining whether there has been a failure to take reasonable care[3].

1 IOB 19.3.
2 [1993] 2 Lloyd's Rep 559, CA; and see Chapter 12 on the duty to take reasonable care.
3 IOB 18.13.

Point of sale issues

42.6 Mechanical breakdown policies are normally sold as add-ons to the sale of a car. Thus, the sale is effected through an intermediary who is not a registered insurance broker. The problems of this system, discussed below in relation to extended warranties, would therefore seem to be fully applicable to this situation. However, in practice, cases arising in this area do not appear to centre on point of sale issues.

Conclusion

42.7 Mechanical breakdown policies for the most part offer poor value to policyholders. The problems discussed in this part of this Chapter are an inevitable consequence of the conflict between the nature of the policies and the fundamental characteristics of insurance.

Extended warranty

42.8 These policies usually provide an extra two or four years' cover. However, the scope of cover varies widely[1]. Some policies cover loss of or damage to the item, as well as breakdown cover[2]. Some policies will also provide cover for food spoiled if the freezer fails.

Valuation of a claim is another matter which varies widely between policies. Given that the appliances insured will be more than a year old when any claim arises[3], it is inevitable that their market value will have depreciated significantly. If the appliance proves to be a constructive total loss, some polices provide a new for old replacement, whereas other provide no more than market value, based either upon an actual assessment of that value or on depreciation at a fixed rate from the original purchase price.

In practice, however, the major difficulties have centred less on the scope of the cover provided than on what the policyholder can expect if a claim arises. In such circumstances a policyholder is naturally anxious to obtain the services of a competent engineer as soon as possible. Extended warranty policies normally require the policyholder to use the services of an authorised engineer[4], but they never give any guarantees about how quickly service will be available. A further unresolved question is how many times must the policyholder allow the insurers to attempt to repair an item before concluding that it is beyond repair, so that he can invoke a policy clause entitling him to a replacement. The question obviously does not admit of a single correct answer, and it is fair to say that insurers are likely to be more willing to try to repair than to replace.

[1] IOB 19, leading article.
[2] Thus giving rise to double insurance for the policyholder who already has contents insurance.
[3] Since the policy cover will not take effect until the manufacturer's guarantee expires.
[4] This link with the manufacturer or vendor of the goods provides one of the ways in which insurers are able to make these policies profitable.

Point of sale issues

42.9 Extended warranties are another example of a type of insurance policy commonly sold through intermediaries who are not registered insurance brokers[1]. The ABI Code of Practice for such sales is therefore relevant. It assumes that in such sales the intermediary (who will commonly be a dealer in motor cars or other electrical goods) acts as agent of the proposer rather than as agent of the insurer (since otherwise the insurer would clearly be liable for all that the agent did and there would be no need for a separate Code. The Code requires that the insurers concerned take all reasonable steps to ensure that the intermediaries explain the nature of the cover, particularly any exclusions and unusual or onerous conditions. In one IOB case[2] the policyholder claimed for the write-off of a microwave oven, whose paint had peeled and rusted, allegedly as a result of the policyholder's failure to keep it properly cleaned and maintained. The insurer sought to rely upon an exclusion for damaged caused by 'other objects or substances'. The Ombudsman held that the inclusion of such a clause imposed an unduly onerous limitation on the normal scope of cover. Accordingly the insurer was required to meet the claim.

[1] For other examples see travel insurance (Chapter 46) and payment protection insurance (Chapter 43).
[2] IOB 19.1.

42.10 It is perhaps not surprising to find that in many disputes about this class of insurance the policyholder alleges that little or no explanation was given – certainly it is rare for the details of the cover to be explored in any depth. The provisions of the ABI Code are of course not enforceable by policyholders, but the Insurance Ombudsman does take them into account when deciding cases. The IOB's position[1] is that in cases of apparent misunderstanding the onus is on the insurer to prove that it has taken the required steps to comply with the Code. It is submitted that in practice this requirement will very rarely be met, with the result that many complaints of this type will in principle be successful[2]. However, in one IOB case[3] the policyholder bought a camcorder, and the associated insurance cover was described as 'Theft and Frozen Food Insurance'. The camcorder was stolen, but the insurers relied on a clause excluding theft cover unless the theft was effected by forcible and violent means, of which there was here no evidence. The claim was rejected by the Ombudsman, as it appeared that the policy had been properly explained at the point of sale, and the policyholder had in any event had a 14-day cooling-off period in which to read the policy again and change his mind if he wished.

Where such complaints do succeed, the question of the remedy will also arise. As with many cases of mis-sale, the policyholder is likely to want what he thought he was getting, but it by no means follows that this will be the proper remedy. If the essence of the policyholder's argument is that he would not have bought the policy had it been properly explained to him, then the appropriate remedy is to set aside the sale and order the return of the premiums, with interest. The alternative situation is that the policyholder can demonstrate that if he has been aware of the situation he could have obtained elsewhere an alternative policy which would have covered the events which happened. This is perhaps not very likely in relation to extended warranties, since these are generally made available only at the point of sale and only by the vendor of the goods, but where it does arise, the result is likely to be that the Ombudsman will require the insurer to meet the claim.

[1] IOB 19, leading article.

[2] It is interesting to note that IOB 23 has three extended warranty cases, taken from different types of business; in all of them the complaint succeeded essentially because the policyholder had not been given proper information at the point of sale.

[3] IOB 19.2.

Conclusion

42.11 Extended warranty policies continue to present many problems. Although they are insurance policies, they are not drafted as such, and those involved in selling them are frequently unaware of their complexities.

Chapter 43

Mortgage and credit protection

Introduction

43.1 The growth in home ownership and in consumer credit has in turn promoted a growth in the market for policies protecting borrowers against the risk of being unable to maintain repayments under their loan agreements. Such policies are commonly referred to as payment protection insurance ('PPI'). In practice PPI policies have been found to give rise to a number of difficulties. As a result of these difficulties the ABI has issued a Code of Practice[1] (now governed by the GISC Codes) dealing with the sale of such policies. There is apparently only one court case in which PPI policies have been considered[2]. This no doubt reflects the fact that the popularity of such policies dates from a time after the creation of the IOB, so that any issue arising under such a policy is likely to go to the IOB rather than to court. As the rest of this Chapter reveals, the Ombudsman has had many occasions to consider PPI policies.

[1] 27 September 1995.
[2] *Cook v Financial Insurance Co Ltd* [1999] Lloyd's Rep IR 1, HL; considered below.

PPI policies

43.2 From the point of view of borrowers the risk which needs to be covered by PPI policies is that the borrower will be unable to work and thus unable to earn the money to meet the loan repayments. Such inability may occur either through ill-health or because the borrower loses his job because of redundancy or dismissal.

Annual policies

43.3 Although PPI policies are commonly effected in conjunction with a mortgage, which is by its nature a long-term commitment, the policies themselves are annual policies. As the Insurance Ombudsman has observed[1], the point is of considerable importance because it means that the premium and the scope of cover can be reviewed annually, and a policyholder may find that after some years of the mortgage the cover which he has is significantly different from that which he originally took out[2].

[1] IOB 3, leading article.
[2] IOB 3.3.

No proposal form

43.4 Another notable feature of PPI policies is that there is frequently no proposal form. They are sold as add-ons to what the purchaser regards as the main contract, namely the loan agreement[1]. As a result no effective underwriting is done at this time, so the policies are written with significant exclusions and limitations. The underwriting is done at claims stage, with predictable consequences for all concerned. It is also relevant to observe that the market is not generally a free one. A borrower who wants loan protection usually has to take the policy offered by the lender, who therefore has little incentive to improve the terms of the policy or to trim the considerable profit margins to which PPI policies give rise. Moreover, such selling of PPI policies as goes on is commonly done by employees of the lender who are not expert in the selling of insurance[2].

[1] It has been observed that from this point of view they bear some similarities to travel insurance: IOB 11: Deputy Ombudsman's Casebook; and see Chapter 46 for the similar problems which arise in travel insurance.
[2] See n 1 above.

Exclusion of pre-existing circumstances

43.5 It is usual for PPI policies to exclude cover for pre-existing conditions. In relation to medical conditions a common exclusion is for any condition for which the policyholder has received advice or treatment within a given period (often 12 months) preceding the inception of the policy. This exclusion applies only where the condition for which treatment is subsequently required is one which existed previously. Consequently it may be necessary to examine carefully what condition is being treated and what condition had previously existed[1].

In applying this exception, it is necessary also to have regard to causation. In one IOB case[2] the policyholder had had surgical treatment for tennis elbow before the inception of the policy. After inception she developed a post-operative wound infection. The Ombudsman held that the infection was not a natural and ordinary cause of the earlier treatment and should therefore be regarded as a new cause not caught by the exclusion. A more difficult case about pre-existing conditions occurred in a case[3] where the policyholder was disabled as a result of a heart attack. The insurer sought to reject the claim because the policyholder had been treated for hypertension for many years before the policy began, and at the same time had been a smoker with a raised cholesterol level. It was argued that these things, *taken together*, amounted to a pre-existing condition, which had led to the disability (it was accepted that the medical evidence could not support a contention that the hypertension alone was the cause of the heart attack, though it had no doubt increased the risk). The Ombudsman held that the smoking was not a 'condition' within the meaning of the policy, and that the raised cholesterol level was, on the evidence, not severe enough to be considered a 'condition'. The case is interesting because it emphasises the need to analyse with great care the policyholder's physical condition at inception in order to see whether he is caught by the standard exclusions. No doubt the insurers, had they known at proposal stage what they discovered at claims stage, would have restricted the cover or even refused the risk entirely. This is one of those rare cases where the failure to do proper underwriting at the outset worked in the policyholder's favour.

[1] See IOB 23.30 for a case where the distinction proved vital. Cf IOB 23.31, which fell on the other side of this admittedly fine line.
[2] IOB 7.5.
[3] IOB 11.7.

43.6 The only known judicial decision in this area concerns pre-existing conditions. In *Cook v Financial Insurance Co Ltd*[1] the claimant was a self-employed businessman who took out a PPI policy in connection with a business loan. The following day he was diagnosed as suffering from angina, and two months later he had to give up work. The exclusion for pre-existing conditions was in the following terms:

> 'Exclusions: No benefit will be payable for disability resulting from:
> (a) Any sickness, disease, condition or injury for which an insured person received advice, treatment or counselling from any registered medical practitioner during the 12 months preceding the commencement date'.

Although the angina was not diagnosed until just after the inception of the policy, the claimant had been taken ill a few months before, but his GP initially thought that this was no more than a fainting fit, then suspected a viral infection, for which an antibiotic was prescribed. Later she prescribed a Ventolin inhaler (which is used for asthmatics). It was only when she asked for a second opinion that angina was diagnosed. The questions to be decided therefore were:

(1) Did the claimant receive advice, treatment or counselling for angina prior to the inception of the policy?
(2) If not, is it enough to bring the case within the exclusion that he received advice, treatment or counselling for symptoms which later turned out to be those of angina?

As to the first question it could not be suggested that he received counselling for angina. Nor, in the view of the majority of the House of Lords, did he receive treatment for angina, since neither Ventolin nor a mild antibiotic could possibly be regarded as a treatment for angina. Equally, he did not receive advice for angina. He received advice in respect of symptoms which turned out to be those of angina, but he did not receive advice for angina.

As to the second question, the majority held that it was not enough that the claimant received advice for symptoms which turned out to be those of angina. Lord Lloyd of Berwick, giving the only substantial speech on behalf of the majority, said that to hold otherwise would be to read the word 'condition' as including symptoms of a generalised kind which might indicate any number of different diseases, or none. He saw no justification for so reading the word, especially in the context of 'sickness, disease ... or injury'. 'Condition' in this context means a medical condition recognised as such by doctors.

Lord Lloyd went on to explore some of the difficulties inherent in this approach:

> 'Take a man who complains to his doctor that he is suffering from headaches. The doctor can find nothing wrong, and recommends a strong painkiller. Eventually it transpires that the man has a brain tumour. Can it really be said that he received advice for his brain tumour when he first went to see his doctor? Clearly not. Nor, I think, can it be said that he received advice for his condition.
>
> At the other end of the scale one might take the case of a man with a very high temperature who is taken to an isolation hospital suffering from Cape Congo Fever or some other rare disease. Obviously he is receiving treatment within the meaning of the exclusion clause from the moment of his arrival in hospital, even though the disease cannot at first be diagnosed. Where the present case fits on the scale was a question of fact for the judge.
>
> It is said that the purpose of the exclusion clause is to exclude liability for disability which may eventuate, not for disability which must eventuate. But if this were the purpose, then it would be easy enough to exclude liability for any disability resulting from sickness, disease or injury from which the insured was in fact suffering before the commencement of the policy. But the insurers did not mean to go that far. Hence the qualification introduced by the words "for which". If there were any doubt as to the meaning of the exclusion clause, which I do not think there is, then on well known principles of construction I would not hesitate to construe it against the defendants, all the more so because of the terms of the undertaking in the application form.'

Both the majority and the minority in this case were at pains to say that the case raised no point of general importance in insurance law. It is submitted, however, that this is not so. Lord Lloyd's distinction between suffering from a condition and receiving treatment etc for it is an important one. The contention on behalf of the insurers that the exclusion was *intended* to catch cases of the present kind is almost certainly true, though of course that is of no avail if the clause has been defectively drafted. It may be supposed that the case will lead to revisions of this policy wording.

1 [1999] Lloyd's Rep IR 1, HL.

43.7 A clearer case on a related point is an IOB decision[1] where in the course of a routine medical consultation a doctor had noticed signs of a particular condition and had commented on them in the medical notes but had not said anything to the patient. It was held that the patient could not be said to have 'consulted' the doctor about this condition. It is interesting to contrast an IOB case[2], in which exactly the same point appears to arise. In that case the Ombudsman took the view which subsequently appealed to the minority in *Cook v Financial Insurance*.

In another case[3] the policy excluded: 'Disability resulting from any pre-existing condition or circumstances of which you were aware …'

When the policyholder was signed off work with depression the insurers discovered that 16 months before the inception date the policyholder had been off work for six weeks suffering from depression. The insurers argued that the policyholder was vulnerable to depression and had been aware of this when he took out the policy. However, the proposal form had asked: 'Do you suffer from any medical conditions of a persistent or recurring nature …?'

The Ombudsman held that being vulnerable to a condition is not the same as suffering from it. On the evidence the two episodes of depression were not connected. There was thus no pre-existing condition and no proper ground for rejecting the claim.

[1] IOB 11.11.
[2] IOB 15.3.
[3] IOB 11.15.

43.8 The Insurance Ombudsman has subsequently published general advice on the treatment of pre-existing conditions and the application of the *Cook* case[1]. He points out that these clauses usually have two limbs, the first relating to conditions of which the policyholder is aware or which exist at inception, the second for conditions for which the policyholder has received advice, treatment or counselling within a specified period before inception (it is one of the oddities of the *Cook* case that the policy there had only the second type of clause). Clauses of the first type are effectively subject to the Statement of Practice on Health-Related Insurance, discussed in Chapter 36. Clauses of the second type focus exclusively on the moment of inception and look at what conditions had been recognised at the time and treated at the time. 'Condition' means a recognised medical condition. It does not include symptoms of a general kind, which might indicate any number of different diseases or none. The Ombudsman offers a non-exhaustive list of factors which may be relevant in determining whether a condition is caught by a clause of this type:

(1) the previous medical history of the policyholder;
(2) the intensity of the symptoms;
(3) the seriousness with which the symptoms have been regarded;
(4) whether any alternative diagnosis has been made;
(5) whether there is a significant difference in kind between the symptoms and the condition which is finally diagnosed;
(6) what the policyholder has been told.

It should be added that where there has been a wrong diagnosis prior to inception, the policyholder cannot be considered to have received advice, treatment or counselling for the condition which is eventually identified[2].

[1] IOB 23.
[2] IOB 23.34.

Declaration of good health

43.9 In addition to or instead of the exclusion for pre-existing conditions, the proposal form may require the policyholder to sign a declaration of good health. This is an example of an attempt at proper underwriting at the proposal stage. However, the normal principles relating to disclosure apply to this situation. Thus, a fact disclosed to the lender, who usually acts as the insurer's agent[1], may be considered to have been sufficiently disclosed. The Insurance Ombudsman had to consider[2] a case where the policyholder had attended at the lender's office on crutches. He held that this was a sufficient disclosure of the policyholder's condition.

[1] It is important to bear in mind that the lender is authorised by the insurer to sell policies in conjunction with the loan transaction. Usually the lender will be associated with only one insurer, for whom it clearly acts as agent. Thus, disclosure to the lender is normally disclosure to the insurer, and representations made by the lender to the borrower/policyholder are likely to bind the insurer.
[2] IOB 15, leading article.

Permanent and total disablement

43.10 Some PPI policies provide cover only if the policyholder suffers a permanent and total disablement. For the issues arising in relation to such wording, see Chapter 36.

Mental health and redundancy

43.11 It is increasingly common for policies to exclude cover where illness is caused (or exacerbated) by mental or nervous conditions. This is a significant limitation of cover and the sale is unlikely to comply with the GISC Code if the limitation is not brought to the insureds attention at the point of sale[1].

A further difficulty arises where an insured is made redundant and then suffers depression. A disability claim may fail because of the mental illness, whilst an unemployment claim normally requires proof that the insured is actually seeking work, but a sick claimant will not be able to sign on. In one IOB case, it was held that in such circumstances the fair and reasonable solution was for the insurer to pay 50% of the clause[2].

1 *Ombudsmans News* (April 2001).
2 *Ombudsmans News* (April 2001).

Notice of loss of job

43.12 In relation to unemployment it is usual to exclude any loss of employment of which the policyholder has notice at the inception of the policy. In one IOB case[1] the exclusion provided that no claim was to be payable if the unemployment 'occurs or becomes expected within 90 days after the date of the certificate [of insurance]'.

The policyholder was a company director, whose company went into receivership just over four months after the date of the certificate. He argued that he had not expected to lose his job until the very last minute; indeed, he had been optimistic about the company's prospects of survival. The Ombudsman held that in order to rely upon the exclusion the insurer would have to show that the loss of employment was probable, rather than merely possible. There is an obvious problem about the wording of the exclusion, in that it does not say by whom the loss of employment must be expected. It would not be surprising to find that an objective observer would have concluded rather earlier that the company's survival prospects were poor, but to rely on that would be to import an objective test of expectation. In the absence of clear policy wording, the Ombudsman was correct to apply the test more favourable to the policyholder. In another IOB case[2] the policyholder was required to declare on the proposal form that he did not know of any 'impending unemployment'. He worked in the defence industry on secondment in West Germany. Such work is normally on the basis of being employed on individual projects, and, before the date of the proposal form, he had received a letter from his employer telling him that his employment could not be guaranteed beyond a certain date. After inception he received another letter saying that he would be made redundant unless a suitable alternative vacancy materialised. None did, and he was duly made redundant. His claim on the policy was rejected on the ground that he had known of the impending unemployment, but his complaint to the Insurance Ombudsman succeeded. It was held that he was justified in not treating the pre-inception letter as notice of redundancy. All it told him was that his employment on the particular project was likely to come to an end. In the past he had received such letters as a project neared its end, but this had always been followed by the finding of suitable alternative work. As the IOB Report observes, this was very much a borderline case, for the policyholder had at least been aware that there was a risk that he would shortly become unemployed, though it was by no means certain[3]. In another IOB case[4] the policyholder had a PPI policy under a loan which he subsequently refinanced. At that point a new policy was issued; on a literal construction of the policy this made the initial period (here 60 days) start to run again. The policyholder lost his job during that extended 60-day period. The Ombudsman held that the insurer was not entitled to reject the claim because the effect of this clause had not been properly brought to the policyholder's attention. It appears, however, that the clause would have been upheld if the policyholder had received proper notice of it.

1 IOB 11.12.
2 IOB 1993, para 7.12.
3 The same result would seem to follow if this case is considered from the point of view of the more general duty of disclosure – the policyholder would again be able to argue that his knowledge was merely of what had always previously been the position, namely that he worked on a contract basis and there was no certainty that a further contract would be forthcoming.
4 IOB 23.32.

Other reasons for dismissal

43.13 It is usual to exclude liability in the event of the policyholder being dismissed for misconduct, or voluntarily resigning or taking voluntary redundancy. In one IOB case[1] the policyholder argued that her resignation had not been voluntary, having been forced upon her by family circumstances. This argument was rejected, since the policy made no provision for this situation. In addition, the Ombudsman observed that, as is normal in PPI policies, the cover required the policyholder to become 'unemployed', a term which is defined as meaning that the policyholder is registered as unemployed and is actively seeking work. The policyholder could not meet this requirement either, since the same circumstances which caused her to give up work would prevent her from resuming it[2].

In another IOB case[3] there was an exclusion for any period of unemployment which resulted from 'You tendering your resignation for whatever reason'.

The insured was employed as a financial adviser, but resigned after four months. His ex-employer confirmed that if he had not resigned he would have been sacked. The Ombudsman held that the resulting claim was not caught by the exclusion: the case was properly to be regarded as one of constructive dismissal rather than of resignation. As the policy covered unemployment resulting from dismissal (so long as it was not brought on by wilful misconduct) the claim succeeded. A more extreme application of the same principle occurred in a case[4] where the policyholder lost his job when he was sent to prison. On his release he was unable to find employment and submitted a claim under the PPI policy. In this case the policy did not even exclude unemployment caused by the policyholder's own wilful act; even if it had contained such a clause, the Ombudsman observed that there was no proper evidence of a causal connection between the crime for which the policyholder had been imprisoned and his unemployment after his release[5].

[1] IOB 5.13.
[2] See also IOB 11.16.
[3] IOB 9.11.
[4] IOB 11.13.
[5] It may be doubted whether this is entirely convincing. It is surely common knowledge that those released from a term of imprisonment often have difficulty finding employment, whatever the offence.

Seeking work

43.14 Some policies require the policyholder to be registered for work and actively seeking work in order to be able to make a claim. In one IOB case[1] the policyholder was pregnant when made redundant. At the time of the claim she was in receipt of statutory maternity pay and was therefore unable to register for work. The Ombudsman held that her claim at that time could not succeed. The proper solution was for her entitlement to claim to begin when her maternity pay ceased and she was again able to register for work. In a more recent case[2], it was held that a woman who was on maternity leave following the birth of her child was not 'actually working at her business'.

[1] IOB 15.6.
[2] Ombudsmans News (April 2001, 04/03).

Problems of self-employment

43.15 Most PPI policies are expressed to provide cover if the policyholder becomes unemployed, and it is usual to impose a pre-condition that the policyholder must be in employment at inception. This gives rise to obvious difficulties where the policyholder is self-employed. Perhaps the first point to be made here is that it is unnecessary to examine carefully whether the policyholder is properly regarded as employed or self-employed. The distinction between an employee, working under a contract of service, and an independent contractor, working under a contract for services[1], is well known, but is not always easy to apply. In one IOB case[2] the Ombudsman was able to persuade an insurer that the policyholder was to all intents and purposes under the direction of the contractor for whom he worked and should therefore be treated as being an employee, despite the fact that he had gone through the formalities to be classed as an independent contractor for tax and National Insurance purposes. It is of course true that a person can have a different employment status for different purposes, but this policyholder appears to have been somewhat fortunate. It is commonly accepted that the tax authorities are reluctant to accept the independent status of workers, and it is a little difficult to believe that a person who was accepted by them as being an independent contractor should properly be treated as an employee.

At the same time it may be said that the case raises a very common and fundamental problem in dealing with those who are not employees. So long as policies continue to be written as they presently are, the fact is that they will be unsuitable for the self-employed, notwithstanding that this group may have at least as much need as the employed to protect themselves against the risk of being unable to repay loans. This problem also has attracted the attention of the Ombudsman. Given that such policies are unsuitable for the self-employed, it seems impossible to avoid the conclusion that the sale of them to the self-employed is an inevitable and obvious mis-sale. On this basis the Insurance Ombudsman has repeatedly held that, although claims on such policies from the self-employed cannot be accepted, the policyholder is entitled to set the sale aside and recover all his premiums with interest.

[1] See *Ready Mix Concrete (South-East) Ltd v Minister of Pensions* [1968] 2 QB 497, Mackenna J.
[2] IOB 9.13; see also IOB 11.2.

Requirement of continuous employment

43.16 PPI policies often have a requirement that at the inception of the policy the policyholder must have been in continuous employment for a certain period (commonly six months). The clause is intended to exclude those who regularly change employment and have frequent spells of unemployment. If the clause is interpreted literally, the result appears to be that a policyholder who does not meet this requirement at inception can never qualify for any cover even though he subsequently accrues enough continuous employment. The Insurance Ombudsman has held[1] that such a clause should be regarded merely as imposing a moratorium, so that although there is no cover at inception, cover does start to apply once the period of continuous employment has been completed[2]. In another IOB case[3] the continuous employment period required was 12 months. The policyholder left one job in July 1995, having been offered another. He then took a holiday until September 1995, when he started his new job. He lost his job in May 1996 and made a claim. The insurer relied upon the requirement of 12 months continuous employment as a ground for rejecting the claim, but the Ombudsman held that it was unreasonable for the insurer to behave in this way. The reasons for taking this view were that the policyholder had been offered the second job before leaving the first and that he had held the first job for about five years, implying that he was not a person who regularly moved from job to job. The only reason why he did not meet the strict policy requirement was that he had chosen to take an extended holiday in between the two jobs. This is an eminently sensible application of the power to make a fair and reasonable decision, but it could not be upheld by a court, given that the policy wording is clear and unambiguous.

[1] IOB 11.2.
[2] It may be observed that the logic of this, when coupled with the Ombudsman's approach to the selling of policies to those ineligible to benefit from them, would seem to be that the policyholder should be able to recover the premiums paid in the period before the period of continuous employment is completed. This point does not appear to have been taken in the cases discussed here.
[3] IOB 11.6.

Policies for the self-employed

43.17 More recently it has become somewhat more common to find PPI policies written to cater for the self-employed as well as for employees. In one of the first such cases to come before the Insurance Ombudsman[1] the policy provided that a self-employed policyholder could claim under the 'unemployment' section only if he became bankrupt. In the event it was not necessary for the Ombudsman to rule on this clause because the insurer agreed to treat the policyholder as employed because he had been working for a single employer for several years[2]. It is submitted that the strict wording of the clause would be unlikely to be upheld. Bankruptcy is still an event to which considerable stigma is attached, and it would surely be unreasonable to require a policyholder voluntarily to become bankrupt if it was clear that he had in fact ceased to work.

1 IOB 11.9.
2 See also the case cited above at para 43.15.

Age limits

43.18 PPI policies usually have an upper age limit for the cover, often the policyholder's 65th birthday. In one IOB case[1] where there was a clause of this type the insurer by oversight collected five premiums by direct debit after the policyholder's 65th birthday. It was held that this was inconsistent with the purported termination of the policy, and that the insurer should meet the claim for disability benefit. It seems unlikely that a court could have reached the same decision, given the automatic termination clause in the policy, which had been adequately brought to the policyholder's attention. Legally, the answer would seem to be that the policyholder would have been entitled only to the return of premiums, with interest, since the policy had automatically terminated and the extra premiums were paid under a mistake (whether the mistake was one of fact or of law would not seem to be relevant in the light of the decision in *Kleinwort Benson v Lincoln City Council*[2]). The decision must be regarded as a welcome example of the Ombudsman using his power to make a fair and reasonable decision even when this does not accord with the strict legal position.

1 IOB 11.1.
2 [1999] 2 AC 349, HL.

Duration of Payment

43.19 In one IOB case[1] the policy stated that benefit would be paid:

> 'until the period of disability ends or until a maximum of 60 months' benefit has been paid from the Inception Date of the Insurance, whichever occurs first'.

On a strict view of the wording this appeared to mean that there was no cover after the policy had been in force for five years, irrespective of when the claim was first made. The Ombudsman accepted the policyholder's argument that he was entitled to 60 months' benefit, whenever the claim was first made. It is submitted that a court would have come to the same conclusion – the wording is at best ambiguous, and this interpretation makes sense of the policy and achieves a just result.

1 IOB 11.10.

Transfer of cover

43.20 The practice of excluding pre-existing risks gives rise to obvious problems where cover is transferred from one insurer to another[1]: policyholders need to take care that they do not lose all entitlement when this happens. The problem is particularly acute when the transfer is not entirely voluntary. The policyholder in an IOB case[2] had mortgage protection through his mortgagee, a small building society. When the society was taken over by a larger society, the scheme was discontinued, but borrowers were offered the chance to transfer to the scheme operated by the acquiring society, subject to eligibility. Unfortunately, the policyholder was not eligible to transfer to the new scheme because he had been given notice of redundancy. At the same time he could not make a claim under the old scheme because the terms of that cover required him to be unemployed – it was not sufficient that he had been given notice of redundancy. Despite the unfortunate nature of the situation, the Ombudsman was unable to require the existing insurers to meet the claim, nor could he order a refund of premium, since the existing insurers had been on risk until cancellation and would have been liable to meet a valid claim made during that period. A different result was reached in another IOB case[3] where the policyholder had received notification from the lender that the cover had been transferred to a new insurer without any indication that the terms of the cover had changed. In fact there had been a change, which was a vital one from the policyholder's point of view because in the events which happened it took away his cover. The Ombudsman ruled that the lender had been under a duty to explain the new cover. In effect the lender, which was not a registered insurance broker, had sold the policy to the policyholder. The insurer was responsible under the (then) ABI Code for the activities of the lender and should meet the claim. The decision appears to err somewhat on the side of generosity towards the policyholder. In effect the lender had discontinued the old scheme and replaced it with a new one. Even if an explanation had been given, it would presumably not have been open to the policyholder to retain the old, wider cover.

[1] Cf the problems of PHI and medical expenses policies: Chapter 36 and 46 respectively.
[2] IOB 3.2.
[3] IOB 3.5.

Early repayment of loan

43.21 A borrower always has the right to pay off the loan at any time. If he does so, the question of the continuance of the policy may arise. In one IOB case[1] the policy provided that it could not be cancelled by either party. The Ombudsman refused to give effect to this clause, observing that the policy had been sold as an integral part of the loan. However, the loan had been repaid after only two of 120 instalments had been paid. In order to allow the insurer to recover its set-up costs, the Ombudsman ruled that the refund for early cancellation should be calculated as if the cover had been cancelled at the end of the first year.

[1] IOB 15.5.

Unsuitable policies

43.21 It must be clear from what has already been said in this Chapter that there is a certain incidence of the sale of PPI policies which are unsuitable in the sense that the policyholder is for one reason or another ineligible for benefit under them. This may be because of a pre-existing condition, or because of age, or because the policyholder is not in work (or regular work) at inception. The question arises, what is to be done in cases of this kind. Logically, there appear to be three possibilities. The first is to say that the policyholder has no remedy. The second is to require a refund of premiums, presumably with interest. The third is to require the insurer to admit the claim in whole or in part. The first solution is quite unacceptable. Where the policyholder is ineligible at the outset (and has no prospect of becoming eligible) then he has bought something which is worthless to him. It cannot be consistent with good faith or with any reasonable notion of good insurance practice that he should have no remedy at all. The second solution often provides a good halfway house. It has the merit of being logical – if the contract is to be regarded as improperly formed, then the usual legal remedy is to set it aside, and this involves restoring the parties to their pre-contractual position. The weakness of this approach is of course that the defect in formation is usually discovered only when a claim is made, by which time it is too late to give the policyholder the cover which he thought he had bought. However, it will often be the case that at the date of inception the policyholder simply could not have got the cover he wanted, so that no injustice is done by merely refunding the premiums. The third approach is in some ways attractive, but careful analysis and argument is needed to justify it. It is submitted that requiring the insurer to admit the claim can be justified if one of the following sets of circumstances can be established:

(1) the insurer[1] was aware of the policyholder's ineligibility and sold the policy regardless[2];
(2) the insurer has subsequently waived the ineligibility, as by leading the policyholder to believe that the claim would be paid[3];
(3) the insurer's documentation has failed to make the conditions of cover sufficiently clear to the policyholder, as in one IOB case[4], where the policyholder was a housewife and was thus ineligible because of a requirement that she be in 'employment' at inception.

[1] The knowledge of the insurer's agent can of course be imputed to the insurer for these purposes.
[2] IOB 15, leading article.
[3] See, for example, IOB 11.16.
[4] IOB 15.4.

Duties of intermediaries selling policies

43.22 In *Sumitomo Bank Ltd v Banque Bruxelles Lambert SA*[1] it was held that the agents of banks arranging loans owed no duty of care under the loan agreements but that they did owe duties as agent. Under the terms of the particular policies the obligation of disclosure was imposed upon the agent alone. A duty of care did arise between the bank and the agent regarding the agent's duties of disclosure under the terms of the policies.

[1] [1997] 1 Lloyd's Rep 487.

Policies for lender's benefit

43.23 Those who provide finance for the acquisition of consumer goods (motor cars are perhaps the most common example) may take out insurance to protect against the risk that the borrower may default. In *College Credit Ltd v National Guarantee Corpn Ltd*[1] the lender's agreement with the insurer to accept risks in respect of customers was subject to a maximum advance which the lender could make to any given customer. It was held that for the purpose of determining whether this limit had been exceeded, it was correct to ignore the additional cost of the premiums, which might be lent, but which were not insured.

1 [2004] 2 All ER (Comm) 409, Gross J.

The FSA's Concerns

43.24 In November 2005 the FSA issued an Update[1] on the subject of PPI, in which it highlighted serious concerns about this area of insurance practice. Although the FSA accepts that When properly structured, explained and sold, payment protection insurance can provide worthwhile cover for consumers against unexpected changes in their personal circumstances , it also called on firms to take urgent action to ensure that their selling practices for PPI are in line with regulatory requirements, following a programme of visits and mystery shopping that uncovered poor selling practices and a lack of proper compliance controls among a sample of firms. Among the problems uncovered were the following:

- there was a risk of inappropriate sales: around half of the firms failed to take reasonable steps to ensure that customers did not buy policies on which they could not claim or which provided only very limited cover;
- there were inadequate controls in place for non-advised sales: about half of the firms selling on a non-advised basis did not have adequate systems to stop their staff giving advice or were providing information that amounted to giving advice;
- advice on PPI was often likely to be poor: most firms did not have systems in place to assess suitability adequately;
- there was an over-reliance on product documentation given to the customer at the expense of explaining the policy to the customer orally: most firms selling by telephone did not give sufficient information on exclusions;
- the quality and timeliness of product and price disclosure by some firms selling single premium policies was poor;
- the level and structure of inducements and targets for sales staff could encourage mis-selling in some firms; and
- training and competence of sales staff was not adequate in around half of firms;
- compliance monitoring was variable and in some cases very poor.

Although by no means all firms suffered from all, or indeed any, of these problems, the FSA's research established that this is an area where an improvement in performance standards is urgently needed.

1 Available at http://www.fsa.gov.uk/Pages/Library/Communication/PR/2005/115.shtml

Chapter 44

Pension policies

Introduction

44.1 Pension policies are an area of immense importance at the present day. This results from the growth in personal pensions since their introduction in 1988, coupled with the increasing perception that the value of the State Retirement pension has declined, is declining and is likely to continue to decline.

Not all pension plans include life cover, and this Chapter will be limited to discussing those which are also insurance policies. This Chapter is therefore not in any way a full account of the law relating to pensions, for which reference should be made to more specialised texts[1].

To a certain extent the issues arising in relation to these policies are the same as those encountered in other forms of life policy, but some special points of difficulty are also found. It is also important to be aware that the regime for private pensions has fundamentally altered since 6 April 2006 as a result of legislative changes.

[1] See for example, *Tolley's Pensions Handbook* (2000, Tolley) and Frostick *Pensions Law in Plain English* (1999, Balladin).

The nature of money purchase pension schemes

44.2 This is the type of scheme which is invariably used in relation to personal pensions[1]. The policyholder contributes money to the scheme, either as a lump sum or by means of regular periodic payments. The contributions, less management charges and the cost of the life cover, are invested in managed funds of various kinds. The intention is that these funds will by good management grow over the period during which the policyholder is paying into them. At the encashment of the policy, the net value of the fund will be used to buy an annuity for the policyholder. The value of the annuity is dependent upon the combination of the value of the fund at the crucial time and the rates of annuity then available in the market.

[1] The alternative type of scheme, the defined benefits scheme, is not considered in the present work because it does not give rise to interesting issues of insurance law.

The selling of pension policies

44.3 Personal pensions were first introduced in 1988[1], and it is clear in retrospect that the claims made for them at that time were considerably exaggerated. The insurance industry saw them as a way of generating substantial new business, and, regrettably, this led to such policies being sold to a significant number of people for whom they were not suited. The obvious risk of money purchase schemes is that the underlying investment fund will not perform well, with the result that the value of the annuity will be reduced. The other major problem about money purchase schemes can only be understood by comparing them with their alternatives. Some people in employment will be eligible to join an employer's occupational scheme. These schemes have usually been defined benefits schemes, under which employees accrue an entitlement to a pension of a certain fraction of their final salary for every year's employment. The obvious benefit of these schemes is that the benefit is guaranteed, rather than being a matter of investment performance. The less obvious, but perhaps even more important, benefit is that in practice employers make substantial contributions to the fund in addition to those made by employees – it is common to find that the employer's contribution is of the order of three times as much as the employee's contribution. Few employers will make any payments at all to a private money purchase scheme. The inevitable consequence is that for most people who are eligible to join an employer's scheme, that scheme is likely to produce significantly greater benefits than a private money purchase scheme. Increasingly, however, employees will find that the option of joining a fully-funded defined benefits scheme is not available to them. The very high cost of funding these schemes has lead to a considerable decline in their availability in the period since the first edition of this book.

[1] ICTA 1988, Pt XIV, ss 590–658.

44.4 Another important change in relation to pension policies in the past five years has been the commpletion of the mis-selling review which was initiated as long ago as 1994, and which focused on the possible mis-selling of pension policies in the early years of the availability of personal pensions under ICTA 1988. It is not now necessary to repeat the details of that Review, which were dealt with in the first edition of this book.

FSAVCs

44.5 There is increasing interest among investors in supplementing their occupational pension provision by means of an Additional Voluntary Contributions ('AVC') Contract. Such contracts fall into two types. The simple AVC is an additional payment into the occupational scheme. Although it will not normally attract additional employer's contributions, it will enable further defined benefits to be built up, and there will be no commission charges to pay. The other type is the

Free-Standing AVC ('FSAVC'). The major advantages of this type are said to be portability, in that the FSAVC can be taken from one employment to another (which the simple AVC cannot) and privacy, in that the employer need not have any knowledge of what the employee is doing. These benefits are perfectly genuine, as far as they go, but they cannot entirely obscure the fact that the FSAVC is a money-purchase contract, with all the uncertainties and drawbacks to which such arrangements are subject (including the need to pay commission to the intermediary who arranges it). It follows that FSAVCs can very easily be mis-sold. An intermediary needs to give clear advice about what the investor is getting and about what the costs are. In cases where an in-house AVC is available, that fact must also be drawn to the investor's attention. Failure to comply with these requirements can render a sale non-compliant even where the product was suitable for the investor.

Stakeholder pensions

44.6 It would be pleasant to suppose that the lessons of pensions mis-selling in the past 15 years have been learned by the industry, so that there is no prospect of a further scandal when stakeholder pensions are finally introduced in the early years of the twenty-first century. Regrettably, such a supposition would also be somewhat nalfkve. The fundamental structural problems of the industry which contributed to the previous mis-selling are still largely in place, and it is submitted that the culture of the industry remains heavily geared to the idea of selling at almost any cost. Moreover, the low-cost structure of stakeholder pensions is such that those companies which opt to provide will be able to make a profit out of doing so only on the basis of a large volume of sales to offset the relatively high set-up costs. It may confidently be predicted that there will be mis-sales of stakeholder pensions, and that within the first decade of the twenty-first century there will have to be yet another exercise in cleaning up the mess made by the insurance and pensions industry.

The Future

44.7 A much more interesting and useful question at this point is what may be expected in future in relation to pension policies. The importance of pension planning will certainly not decline: if anything, it will increase. Money purchase schemes will take up a greater share of the market because of the reduction in the availability of defined benefit schemes. Whilst this is probably not good news for pensioners, one side effect will be a reduction in mis-selling issues. One of the major classes of mis-selling occurred where a person in a defined benefit scheme was wrongly advised that better returns were likely to be obtained under a money purchase scheme. There will inevitably be fewer such cases in future.

44.8 The latest reform of pensions law took effect on 6 April 2006. Its details are beyond the scope of the present work, but it may be noted that its intention is to make available a wider range of assets and legal structures for the purposes of pension planning, whilst at the same time restricting the total amount which high earners can put into their pension plans while still receiving tax relief. One effect of this is likely to be that pension policies ie pensions with life cover form a smaller part of the total pensions market, thereby reducing still further the importance of this topic in an insurance context.

Chapter 45

Legal expenses insurance

Introduction

45.1 Legal expenses insurance provides cover against the risk of incurring expense in pursuing or defending legal proceedings. The market has developed considerably in recent years as a result of the growth on conditional fee arrangements in civil litigation. Legal expenses insurance is found both in free-standing policies and as an adjunct to other policies, notably motor insurance policies, where it can provide valuable cover for the costs of recovering uninsured losses, which the insurer is often not prepared to take action to recover.

Where legal expenses insurance in sold in conjunction with a motor policy, the insurer of the legal expenses cover must not be the same party as provides the motor insurance[1]. This requirement is imposed in order to avoid the conflict of interest which can arise where an insurer provides both types of cover to the same policyholder and is therefore concerned on the one hand to defend the claim in its capacity as motor insurer but on the other hand to avoid the costs of the defence in its capacity as legal expenses insurer.

1 Insurance Companies Regulations 1994, SI 1994/1516, reg 5(1).

The cover

45.2 Legal expenses policies may cover only particular types of claim, as in the motor insurance example just given, or they may be more broadly drafted. Common features of the policies are that they cover both bringing and defending proceedings, that cover is limited to a specified amount and that the insurers, for obvious reasons, retain considerable discretion and control over the institution and continuation of proceedings.

An important issue in the operation of legal expenses policies is the making of the decision whether or not proceedings should be brought or defended. Insurers are naturally reluctant to become embroiled in hopeless proceedings, and policies therefore usually provide that cover is available only where it appears that the proceedings offer a reasonable prospect of success. The problem which then arises is that insurer and insured may disagree as to the merits of a particular case. The Insurance Ombudsman has consistently held[1] that the insurer must act reasonably in deciding whether there are reasonable prospects of success, but that the decision is ultimately an objective one. In the nature of things policyholders are somewhat inclined to see good prospects of success even where these do not in fact exist. There are a number of reported IOB decisions on this point. In the first[2] the complainant was a surgeon, who had a dispute with a hospital which had withdrawn a job offer to him after a dispute over the conditions of employment. He had two legal expenses policies, and both insurers initially accepted his claim, then withdrew cover on legal advice. He continued as a litigant in person and lost at first instance. He persuaded one of the insurers to fund the taking of advice on the prospects of an appeal. When this advice was unfavourable that insurer again withdrew cover. Not surprisingly, the Ombudsman rejected the complaint. A similar result followed in the next case[3] where the policyholders were seeking a remedy against a builder whose work for them was allegedly defective. The defendant made an offer of settlement. When the policyholders rejected it, the insurers withdrew cover. The Ombudsman held that it was perfectly reasonable for the insurers to accept the advice of the policyholders' solicitors to the effect that this offer was the best the policyholders could reasonably expect.

In considering the question of reasonable prospects of success, it is important to have careful regard to the policy wording. In the next IOB case to be considered[4] the incidence of the burden of proof proved to be decisive[5]. The policyholder was able to prove the existence of personal injury, but the insurer would not provide cover until he also supplied evidence that the proposed proceedings would have had a reasonable chance of success. On the particular policy wording the Ombudsman held that this was the wrong approach – it was for the insurer to show that there were no reasonable prospects of success, rather than *vice versa*. An interesting consequence of this is that the insurer would have been liable to fund the enquiries necessary to establish properly whether there was a reasonable chance of success[6]. It should be noted that this case appears to depend very much upon the unusual wording of the policy; legal expenses policies are generally drafted so that the policyholder bears the burden of establishing a reasonable chance of success.

1 See eg IOB 4.14, 5.11, 13.23.
2 IOB 16.5.
3 IOB 16.6.
4 IOB 16.6.
5 As to this point see further Chapter 10.
6 On the evidence before the Ombudsman it appeared that the insurer could have discharged the burden of showing that there was no reasonable prospect of success.

Choice of solicitors

45.3 Policies commonly provide that it is for the insured on the first instance to choose the solicitors who will represent him, though this choice often has to be submitted to the insurers for approval (no doubt this helps to ensure, among other things, that the insured does not choose an inappropriate or unduly expensive firm). If the insured does not make any choice, the insurers will usually be prepared to nominate a firm to act for him, and in these circumstances he will probably be required to accept that choice, unless he has good grounds to show that it is manifestly unreasonable[1]. An inquiry into the reasonableness of an insurer's decision about this point should not be seen as being the same as a decision on the merits of the claim: the question is the rather more limited one whether there are grounds on which the insurer could reasonably reach its conclusion. Although this is obviously not an administrative law question, it is perhaps not fanciful to suggest that the insurer's decision is unlikely to be challengeable unless it can be shown to be so unreasonable that no reasonable insurer, giving the matter proper consideration, could have come to that decision[2].

A subsequent request by the insured to change his solicitors should normally be accepted unless it can be seen to be unreasonable. The Insurance ombudsman has held that insurers acted wrongly in refusing to accept such a request unless the insured paid all legal costs incurred to date[3]. However, even where insurers act improperly in such a case, any claim against them must depend upon showing that the insured has actually been prejudiced. In the nature of things this is likely to be difficult, since the insured will need to demonstrate that different solicitors would have done things differently and that this would have led to a more favourable outcome. This is inevitably speculative.

1 IOB 13.19.
2 Cf *Associated Provincial Picture Houses Ltd v Wednesbury Corpn* [1947] 2 All ER 680, CA.
3 IOB 13.19: the reason for requesting transfer in that case was that the insured was moving to a different part of the country.

Timing of claim

45.4 Policies may be drafted on the basis of claims incurred or claims reported. It is obviously important to advert carefully to the difference. In one IOB case[1] there was a specific exclusion for:

> 'Legal proceedings which arise from … agreements for … provision of services … not made during the Period of insurance'.

The policy commenced in April 1995, and, early in 1996, it was discovered that there was likely to be a claim in respect of work defectively carried out in 1994. The policy required that the event giving rise to the claim must occur within the period of insurance, but the Ombudsman held that this was ambiguous – it could refer either to the defective work or the damage which resulted from the defective work and which gave rise to the claim. For this reason the insured's complaint was upheld.

In another IOB case[2] the policy required that the date of occurrence be within the period of insurance. 'Date of occurrence' was defined as:

> 'The date on which the event or series of events which may lead to a claim first occurred'.

The insured was diagnosed as suffering from asbestos damage in the form of pleural plaques. The diagnosis took place during the period of cover, but the insured sought to sue his former employer on the basis that he had been exposed to asbestos during his employment at various times between 1949 and 1968. This time the Ombudsman rejected the complaint. It was clear that the diagnosis was not an event which led to the claim – it merely confirmed a position which had existed for some time previously. The case is thus distinguishable from that mentioned in above on the basis that the event leading to the claim had happened much earlier. At the same time it may be suggested that the presence of the word 'first' in the second policy could be regarded as crucial. Had that word been found in the policy dealing with the defective work, it would have been open to argue that the series of events 'first' occurred in 1994, when the work was defectively done: everything which happened after that was merely a follow-on from it.

[1] IOB 13.21.
[2] IOB 16.4.

Increases in limit of indemnity

45.5 From time to time insurers increase the limit of indemnity under legal expenses policies. An IOB case[1] shows the dangers which arise in communicating this increase to insureds. The insurer stated that the increase was to apply to 'new and existing business' without explaining what this meant. It seems likely that it was intended to apply it to renewals of existing policies as well as to those insureds who had not previously held such a policy with the company. The insured's situation was that at the time of the notification his costs on an existing claim were below the old limit, but by the end of the case they had risen to a figure somewhere between the old limit and the new limit. The Ombudsman held that the notification was ambiguous, with the result that it was not reasonable to apply the old limit to costs incurred after the notification took effect. From a strict legal point of view it may be noted that the report of the case gives no indication that the incurring of extra expense could in any way be said to have been done in reliance on this notification. On the other hand, the question may be viewed as a simple one of the construction of the terms of the new policy, and it was no doubt possible to say that the interpretation chosen by the Ombudsman was a possible one.

[1] IOB 16.3.

Geographical limits of cover

45.6 Policies sometimes restrict cover to the UK (and the definition of what is included in the term 'United Kingdom' may vary from one policy to another). In one IOB case[1] the claimant was employed in Singapore and was injured in an accident at work. He decided to sue for damages for personal injuries and sought indemnity for the cost of issuing proceedings in the UK. The insurer rejected the claim on the ground that cover was restricted to events which occurred within the

UK (defined in this policy as extending to the Isle of Man and the Channel Islands). The wording of the clause was clearly defective, for it did not specify whether the events to which it referred were the events which gave rise to the claim, the incurring of the expenses or the proceedings for which indemnity was sought. This ambiguity naturally had to be resolved in favour of the policyholder, whose complaint to the Ombudsman therefore succeeded.

1 IOB 16.2.

Expert helplines

45.7 Some legal expenses policies offer the policyholder the benefit of advice over the telephone. This can give rise to difficulties where policyholders are not satisfied with the nature or the quality of the advice which they receive. In the nature of things it is difficult for insurers to provide a telephone helpline whose staff are genuinely competent to give off-the-cuff expert advice about every conceivable legal problem. The Insurance Ombudsman had to consider a case[1] where the policy (not a true legal expenses policy, but a policy where the helpline provision was an add-on) stated: 'We will give you advice over the telephone on a personal legal problem'.

The policyholder rang the helpline with a complex question about the interpretation of certain provisions of the Banking Acts in relation to investment bonds. He alleged that the answer he had received was inadequate, and he sought indemnity for the cost of obtaining Counsel's opinion. The Ombudsman held that the policyholder was entitled to expect that he would get suitably expert advice from someone with a detailed knowledge of banking law. This view rested partly on the promotional literature for the policy, which included the ambitious promise of 'Expert advice on any personal legal problem'. The Ombudsman accepted that the insurers could not employ experts in every field of law[2], but held that the proper course was for the matter to be referred to an outside firm of solicitors[3] with appropriate expertise, before giving oral advice to the policyholder.

1 IOB 16.8.
2 A fact which demonstrates the unwise character of the promise in the promotional literature.
3 It is quite unclear why solicitors rather than counsel were the appropriate point of reference.

After-the-event policies

45.8 A trend of recent years has been the growth of after-the-event legal expenses policies. These policies work on the basis that a prospective policyholder consults a firm of solicitors about his case. If the solicitors think that he has a reasonable chance of success, they may apply to insurers for cover, or in some cases may be authorised to sell to the client, on behalf of the insurers, a legal expenses policy in return for a one-off premium. On the face of it this arrangement contravenes one of the first rules of insurance, namely that it is not possible to insure against risks which have already materialised[1]. In fact, what is happening in these cases is that the solicitors are taking the case on a conditional fee basis. If the case is lost, they will look to be indemnified by the insurers, whereas if it is won, they will look to recover their costs from the defendants. From the point of view of both the solicitors and the insurers the success of this scheme depends upon the accurate assessment of the likely outcomes of cases presented to them. So far as routine cases are concerned (and in practice this appears to mean principally RTA's, tripping and employers' liability cases) solicitors may well be able to make reasonably competent assessments and may be able to generate a sufficient volume of cases to allow any errors to be accommodated. More unusual cases may require bespoke policies with approval by the insurers on an individual basis, possibly after taking Counsel's advice. It is usual for insurers to provide cover only where they are satisfied that the prospects of success are at least 60%.

It may be said that what is being insured in these cases is not the risk that a legal dispute will arise, but rather the risk that an existing dispute will be lost when pursued through the courts. The increasing restrictions on the availability of civil legal aid have tended to make these policies increasingly valuable and popular. At the same time it must be remembered that these schemes will provide cover only up to a certain level of fees. Policyholders need to be vigilant to ensure that these levels are not exceeded, since they will remain responsible for any excess. In calculating the amount of cover required it is also important to make some estimate of the fees likely to be incurred by the other side, since a losing party must normally expect to pay most of the winner's legal costs.

[1] But consider, for example, the use of 'lost or not lost' policies in marine insurance: MIA 1906, s 6.

Chapter 46

Travel insurance

46.1 This Chapter covers policies intended to cover risks associated with travel. Such policies may be taken out in connection with holiday travel or with business travel.

Types of policy

46.2 Travel policies may be for a particular trip (often a holiday) or they may be policies which cover any travel during a specified period.

Risks covered

46.3 The risks covered by travel insurance policies commonly include the following:

(1) cancellation;
(2) delay in travel;
(3) repatriation for illness or other emergency;
(4) medical expenses;
(5) personal accident;
(6) death;
(7) loss of personal possessions.

The selling of travel policies

46.4 A major issue in relation to travel policies is the way in which they are sold. In practice the vast majority of such policies are sold by travel agents in conjunction with the selling of the holiday. These travel agents will not be registered insurance brokers, and many of the operatives doing the selling have little training in insurance and are not familiar with the terms of the policy. In the circumstances it is not surprising that neither they nor the holidaymakers (whose priorities at that stage naturally lie elsewhere) pay much attention to the terms of the policies and whether those terms are suitable for them. The GISC Code of Practice[1] stipulated that in such cases attention should be drawn to the main features of the cover before the contract was entered into. There appears to be no specific provision relating to travel policies in ICOB, though the general provisions of ICOB 5.4 concerning product disclosure might well have the same effect. However, it does not really do anything to alter the facts that there is no proposal form and that the policyholder is unlikely to read the cover in full when it arrives (if the insurance is a single policy effected for a group of holidaymakers, he may never even see it). This tends to lead to the phenomenon known as 'underwriting at claims stage', with consequent dissatisfaction for the policyholder. The practice is obviously unsatisfactory, and it is relevant to note the effects in this context of the SGIP. That statement provides[2] that insurers will ask clear questions about matters which they have commonly found to be material in the class of insurance in question. The Ombudsman has taken the view that where no proposal form is used insurers are not entitled to rely upon any form of non-disclosure, since the absence of a form effectively waives the duty of disclosure. The inevitable response of the industry to this has been to write policies which have significant and sometimes unexpected exclusions.

As far as is known, there is no case in the Law Reports dealing with a modern travel policy. All the cases considered in this Chapter are therefore decisions of the Insurance Ombudsman. Given that the policies dealt with here are almost all personal lines policies, there will be very few cases where any policyholder is likely to go to court. Thus, this is an area where for all practical purposes the Ombudsman is the only relevant authority.

The Ombudsman has said[3] that one of the first issues when considering the terms of a travel policy is whether the terms have been sufficiently brought to the attention of the policyholder. This will normally be done simply by providing a copy of the policy document. However, where the terms are unusual or particularly onerous, the Ombudsman is likely to follow the principles laid down by the court in *Interfoto Picture Library v Stiletto Visual Programmes*[4] and to require that the terms be brought expressly to the policyholder's attention. It may not be enough that the travel agent has advised the policyholder to read the policy carefully[5], but a clear list of exclusions in the policy will normally be enough[6]. Where it would not have been possible for the policyholder to obtain better terms because the policy is in common form or because his circumstances would have precluded him from obtaining such cover, the likelihood is that the Ombudsman will find in favour of the insurer.

[1] The GISC General Insurance Code replaced the ABI Code of Practice for Non-registered Intermediaries, but the disappearance of GISC under the implementation of the FSMA 2000 appears to leave no specific Code for intermediaries such as travel agents.
[2] Clause 1(f).
[3] IOB 6, leading article.
[4] [1988] 1 All ER 348. The case is about limitations on contractual liability, but not in an insurance context.
[5] IOB 17.19.
[6] IOB 23.38.

46.5 A recent development in the selling of travel policies is Internet sales. It is becoming more common to book holidays on-line, and this process often involves the purchase of insurance. In many cases there is little or no explanation of the cover offered, which is a clear breach of the Code. Moreover, the problem of pre-existing medical conditions is sometimes dealt with by selling a basic policy excluding cover for such conditions. Policyholders are thus invited to contact the insurer by telephone for more extensive cover. The resulting telephone conversations are not always properly recorded and disputes may arise as to what disclosure was made and what advice was given on behalf of the insurer.

Cancellation

46.6 The cover for holiday cancellation usually specifies that the cancellation must be for reasons beyond the policyholder's control. Thus, it does not cover what is sometimes referred to as 'mere disinclination to travel'. Of course it is not always easy to define what amounts to mere disinclination. In one IOB case[1] the policyholder suffered a panic attack when about to board the aircraft to leave for the holiday. The Ombudsman held that this was to be regarded as a medical condition, sufficient to justify not travelling, and as more than mere disinclination.

Provisions of this kind can be problematic when the policyholder appears to have made a choice not to travel but argues that in effect he had no choice. In one IOB case[2] the policyholder was a Deputy Chief Constable. After he had booked the holiday it was announced that his post was to be abolished. He cancelled the holiday in order to be able to attend two job interviews which were scheduled during the holiday period and which could not be rearranged. On the facts it was clear that at the time of booking the holiday he could not reasonably have known what was to happen. He was not in the situation of the person who has simply decided to change his job purely voluntarily. He had in effect been forced to cancel the holiday, and the cancellation cover should apply.

1 IOB 8.15.
2 IOB 5.9.

46.7 A more puzzling IOB case[1] involving a travel policy occurred where the tour operator collapsed before the holiday started. The policyholder was able to recover most of the cost of the holiday from the credit card company through which the holiday had been paid for, but he then sought a refund of premium. The insurer relied upon an exclusion for claims arising from the tour operator becoming insolvent. The Ombudsman held that this exclusion did not apply because the policyholder was not making a claim under the policy, but rather seeking a refund of premium. The Ombudsman relied further on a statement in the 1990 Annual Report to the effect that it is unfair in travel policies to have a clause providing that the premium is never refundable. The example given in that Report[2] was that of the tour operator collapsing before travel. Consequently the insurer was required to refund the premium, less administration expenses and a deduction for the cancellation cover. It has to be said that the logic of this decision is hard to fathom. Certainly the exclusion did not apply, for the reasons given, but why was it appropriate to have any refund of premium at all? Admittedly most of the cover became irrelevant when the tour operator collapsed, but the usual principle surely is that the premium is refundable only when the policyholder has received nothing for it (ie a total failure of consideration). Here he had certainly received some cancellation cover.

[1] IOB 14.21.
[2] Paragraph 2.4.

46.8 Another common exclusion from the cancellation cover is cancellation on the ground of 'anxiety and depression'. Presumably this was originally excluded because it was thought to be too readily open to abuse. The Ombudsman has taken the view that where anxiety or depression has been clinically diagnosed (and proper supporting medical evidence will obviously be required) that is to be treated in the same way as any other clinical illness and should be within the protection of the cancellation cover even when this exclusion is found within the policy. It is conceivable (though perhaps not very likely) that the court would come to the same view – it is, after all, a matter of construing the policy, and one approach would be to say that the terms anxiety and depression means anxiety and depression falling short of that which can be clinically diagnosed. A more plausible view would be that this is a decision reached under the fair and reasonable jurisdiction.

46.9 An alternative approach to restricting liability under the cancellation head (and sometimes under other heads as well) is to attempt to exclude liability if the loss arises from any pre-existing condition[1]. This is an exclusion of a kind which needs to be clearly drawn to the policyholder's attention when the contract is taken out; otherwise it is likely that the Ombudsman will not allow reliance on it. Even where adequate notice of the exclusion can be proved, careful construction of the wording used is essential. In one IOB case[2] the exclusion was for 'persons receiving treatment or on a waiting list for in-patient treatment in a hospital or nursing home … or claims where the insured's travel plans were or would have been against their doctor's advice'. Prior to taking out the policy the policyholder had sought doctor's advice for chest pains, but it was only after the policy was taken out that she became more seriously ill and was admitted to hospital, where angina was diagnosed. The vital point here was that at the time when the policy was taken out the policyholder was not within the wording of the exclusion. This was not, as worded, a blanket exclusion for all pre-existing conditions; rather it applied only to conditions of a relatively serious character and whose seriousness was already known. The point of general interest to be derived from the case is that the vital time for determining whether the exclusion applies is when the policy is taken out, not the intended date of travel[3].

[1] For further discussion of clauses of this kind in other contexts see Chapters 36 and 43.
[2] IOB 9.22.
[3] For another case where the selling of the policy had not complied with the GISC Code and the Ombudsman refused to allow reliance on a pre-existing condition clause, see IOB 23.36.

46.10 Exceptionally, the insurer may require to be notified in advance of all serious or chronic pre-existing illnesses of those on whom the policyholder's travel plans depend. Such information may be used as part of the underwriting process, or it may be used simply to control the claims experience by preventing the policyholder from later seeking to cancel on the basis of events affecting persons other than those named. In one IOB case[1] of this kind the policyholder omitted to give the name of her sister, who had been ill for some time. When the sister died, the policyholder cancelled the holiday. The insurer naturally relied upon the fact that the sister's illness had not been notified. The Ombudsman held that the sister was not a person on whom the policyholder's plans depended, in the sense of being entirely reliant upon, since the policyholder would not have been precluded from travelling merely by the sister's continuing illness. Although the decision may at first sight seem surprising, it is submitted that it is legally correct. For most policyholders there must be a significant range of people whose death would cause them to cancel the holiday, but whose illness would not be sufficient reason for cancellation. The request for details of illnesses suggests that the insurers were thinking only in terms of cancellation due to illness. The sister was not in this category, and her illness therefore did not require to be disclosed.

[1] IOB 17.22.

Delay in travel

46.11 Travel policies often provide compensation at a fixed rate if the policyholder's departure on holiday is delayed for more than a specified period (these periods seem to have become longer in recent years, no doubt as a response to the growing prevalence of delays in air travel). This part of the policy is probably best regarded as a contingency provision rather than an indemnity provision, since the cover is at a fixed rate, bearing only the loosest relationship to any expenses actually incurred.

Repatriation for illness or other emergency

46.12 This section of the cover is also sometimes referred to as 'curtailment'. One issue which can arise here concerns the reasonableness of the decision to return, as against, for example, staying abroad and receiving treatment there. In one IOB case[1] the policyholder, who was pregnant, became ill during a flight and showed signs of spontaneous abortion. Although the local hospital was able to stabilise her condition, she chose to return to the UK for further treatment. The insurer argued that this had not been medically necessary, and pointed out that, contrary to a policy condition, no authorisation had been obtained from the local helpline. The Ombudsman held that the policyholder had acted reasonably in the circumstances, given the limited nature of local medical facilities and that the insurer should not be allowed to rely upon the technical breach of condition. It was also held that the insurers must meet the travel costs of the policyholder's husband – a co-insured – who had returned with her.

Cover of this kind can be invoked because of a crisis situation arising at home as well as because of the illness of a member of the holiday party. Thus, for example, a holidaymaker who hears that a close relative back in the UK is critically ill or dead should be able to claim under the curtailment provision if he chooses to return to the UK.

[1] IOB 23.37.

Medical expenses

46.13 The medical expenses section of the policy is primarily relevant for overseas holidays, since medical costs in the UK will normally be met by the NHS. It is common for the policy to require immediate notification of any medical problem to a designated contact point (often a telephone number). This allows the insurer to assess the seriousness of the situation and to ensure that appropriate emergency assistance (including repatriation, if appropriate) is provided. One important reason for this is that it can help the insurer to minimise the overall cost of claims. In one IOB case[1] the policyholder fell ill before leaving the UK[2], and no notification to the designated emergency service was made. The insurer sought to deny liability on this ground, but the Ombudsman held that the clause was only intended to apply to illness arising abroad. In the present case the policyholder had been able to receive immediate medical attention at no cost to the insurer. Thus, the failure to notify had caused no prejudice to the insurer. Had the clause made the notification a condition precedent to liability, the position would perhaps have been more complicated, but even in that event it would have been open to the Ombudsman to find as a matter of construction that the clause did not apply to illness arising in the UK.

Where the emergency centre is to be notified, it is usual to provide also that the insurer will not be liable for expenses incurred without that centre's approval. This can be problematic where the matter is urgent, and the policyholder is unable to contact the centre or to get a proper response from it (situations which appear to occur a good deal more frequently than they should). Although it is strictly speaking a breach of the policy terms to incur expense without approval, it may well be possible to show that the expenses would inevitably have been authorised had the centre been contacted, so that the insurers are not prejudiced. Moreover, the Ombudsman has held[3] that policyholders should be able to recover in these circumstances, provided that they have acted reasonably in incurring the expenses. It might perhaps be added that insurers who require policyholders to contact an emergency centre ought to be prepared to accept some responsibility for ensuring that the centre in question is adequately staffed to respond when emergencies arise. At least some of the difficult cases in this area appear to arise because that requirement is not met.

1 IOB 9.23.
2 Apparently there was cover for illness arising after travel had started but while still in the UK.
3 IOB 15.13.

Personal accident

46.14 These provisions are effectively to be interpreted in the same way as other more traditional personal accident policies[1]. One IOB case is perhaps worthy of mention in the travel context[2]. The policyholder fell from a window and died from her injuries. There was a suspicion (never proved) that the cause might have been suicide. The policyholder had a history of mental illness and had spent some time as an in-patient. If the insurers had known of that history, they might well have refused cover, but as usual there had been no proposal form, so they were precluded from relying upon non-disclosure[3]. Attention therefore focused on whether it was sufficiently established that the death was caused by 'accident'. The deceased had never stated an intention to commit suicide and there was no suicide note, but there was evidence that she had been in a disturbed condition for some days before her death. The latter evidence was of course equivocal in the sense that it might be used to make a case for suicide, but it might also be used to make a case that the deceased quite probably did not know what she was doing immediately before she fell from the window and might therefore have been incapable of forming the intention to commit suicide. In these rather unhappy circumstances the Ombudsman held that the balance of evidence pointed to accident rather than suicide. It is suggested that two points of general interest may be derived from the case. The first is that the Ombudsman (and presumably also a court, should the point ever arise) will be reluctant to find that a deceased has committed suicide. The idea is naturally a distressing one for relatives, and clear evidence will be needed. The second is that sudden and unexpected death will normally be presumed to be accidental in the absence of evidence to the contrary. In another IOB case[4] the personal accident section excluded accident caused by the effects of alcohol. The policyholder fell to his death from a hotel balcony while alone and after drinking alcohol. The Ombudsman was unconvinced that the cause of death was associated with alcohol (it appeared that the policyholder might simply have fallen asleep) but held that in any event it was not reasonable to rely upon the clause in these circumstances.

1 Chapter 35.
2 IOB 7.6.
3 See above at para 46.4.
4 IOB 23.35.

46.15 Another common issue in relation to the accident section arises where policyholders either go on holidays of a somewhat adventurous nature, such as mountaineering, or, while on an otherwise peaceful holiday, are seized with a sudden desire to do something more adventurous and dangerous. Few policyholders in such cases bother to read their insurance policy before undertaking the activity. The two situations give rise to different problems, though in either case it may be found that the policy has exclusions for the activities in question. In the first case, if the activity is excluded specifically[1] or if it is alleged to come within a more generic exclusion for 'dangerous activities[2]' or some similar wording, the question will arise, how this policy came to be sold to this policyholder. Given the obvious unsuitability of the policy, it is likely to be argued that the intermediary is in breach of duty by the mere fact of the sale.

In the second case the answer is likely to depend upon whether the activity is expressly excluded or whether the insurer seeks to bring it within some more generic phrase. In the former event, the insurer is likely to succeed, since there will be no element of ambiguity. However, the latter event is probably the more frequently encountered. Here, the outcome must depend upon the exact wording used and on some assessment of the degree of risk to which the policyholder was exposed.

1 As in one IOB case handled by the author personally in 1991, where policyholders setting out on a motorcycling holiday were sold a policy whose personal accident section explicitly excluded cover for accidents arising from motorcycling: the insurers were not permitted to rely on the exclusion.
2 As in IOB 15.12.

Loss of personal possessions

46.16 These clauses mainly give rise to difficulties because of the circumstances in which personal possessions are lost. Insurers appear to have two main objections to paying out. The first is that there are some cases where the circumstances of the loss are such that it is very difficult to prove that any loss has taken place. A common example is that of the policyholder whose expensive watch or camera is allegedly dropped into the sea from a moving vessel. There is rarely any independent witness to this incident. Unsatisfactory as this state of affairs is, it is really no more than an example of a general problem of insurance, namely the case where the evidence of loss is sketchy and the nature of the alleged loss gives the policyholder an obvious incentive to submit fraudulent claims. Insurers can do little in these cases except demand detailed signed statements, coupled with some evidence of having owned the item in the first place[1]. This may well deter at least some fraudulent claimants.

The second difficulty occurs where insurers believe that the property has been exposed to unnecessary risk, for example by being left unattended in an exposed and vulnerable place. The treatment of this problem has changed in the past decade. At one time it was usual for insurers to rely upon reasonable care clauses. However, following the re-interpretation of such clauses which resulted from the decision of the Court of Appeal in *Sofi v Prudential Assurance Co Ltd*[2], insurers have realised that such clauses will only rarely be effective to protect them in these cases. The practice has therefore grown up of having a specific exclusion from personal possessions cover in any case where the property was 'left unattended' at the time of the loss. The Ombudsman's approach to such clauses generally is considered in Chapter 38, dealing with contents policies. A particular example of the problems of such clauses in a travel context comes from an IOB case[3] where the wording was similar in effect, though different in form. The policy covered loss of up to £300 cash if your own money is stolen whilst being carried on your person or left in a locked safety deposit box.

During a flight the policyholder was asked by a stewardess to place his leather jacket in an overhead locker. On disembarking he discovered that the jacket and its contents (including £150 cash) had been stolen. The Ombudsman held that in the circumstances it would not be fair for the insurer to rely on the fact that the money was not being carried on the policyholder's own person. An extremely prudent person who had read the policy would no doubt have removed the wallet before parting with the jacket, but this was perhaps an unreasonable expectation in the circumstances. Restrictive clauses of this kind are generally vulnerable to the Ombudsman's application of the spirit of UCTA 1977 to insurance policies[4]. Moreover, it must now be open to question whether these clauses in so blunt a form can survive the operation of the UTCCR 1999, which do directly apply to insurance policies[5].

In one IOB case[6] the policyholder suffered loss when his pre-paid vouchers for hotel accommodation were rejected by the hotel and he had to pay cash. The hotel chain never made good on its promise to reimburse the cost of the vouchers. He sought to claim under the personal possessions section, alleging that the vouchers (which were within the scope of cover) had been 'lost'. Inevitably, the Ombudsman held that the vouchers had not been lost – all that had happened that that they had suffered a depreciation in value.

[1] For a case where the Ombudsman upheld an insurer's refusal to pay a claim of this kind, see IOB 17.21.
[2] [1993] 2 Lloyd's Rep 559, CA. See Chapter 12.
[3] IOB 14.23.
[4] See Chapter 10.
[5] See Chapter 10.
[6] IOB 17.20.

'Accommodation'

46.17 The Insurance Ombudsman considered a case[1] in which a travel policy was effected to cover a trip to South Africa via Amsterdam. The policyholders were delayed in Amsterdam because one of their passports was stolen. The policy covered 'accommodation' in these circumstances, and the Insurance Ombudsman held that it was within the reasonable expectation of the insured that reasonable sustenance and the cost of luggage storage should fall within the concept of accommodation. It is not at all clear that this decision does anything more than give the policyholder his legal entitlement. Although the IOB Report presents the case in the context of a discussion of reasonable expectations, it is surely perfectly possible to argue that 'accommodation' is a somewhat ambiguous term, and that the ambiguity should be resolved in favour of the policyholder.

[1] IOB 14.20.

Sports equipment

46.18 Travel policies often make special provision for sports equipment, which may be the subject of its own clause or may be included within a broader definition of valuables. The Insurance Ombudsman has held[1] that for these purposes surfing is a leisure activity rather than a sport on the ground that it does not have to be pursued as a sport. The same is no doubt true of other activities, notably skiing, but it may be questioned whether the same rule would apply to skis.

[1] IOB 14.23.

The role of 'helplines'

46.19 Many travel insurers provide so-called 'helplines' which their insureds are asked to contact if a possible claim arises during the holiday. These helplines are of variable quality. They may give inappropriate advice about what to do, and in some cases they may fail to provide the assistance which they promise (or which insurers promise that they will give). The simple rule in these circumstances is that they are the agents of the insurer, who must accept responsibility for their actions accordingly.

Chapter 47

Fire insurance

47.1 Fire insurance is sometimes found as an aspect of other policies, notably buildings polices, but it is recognised as giving rise to some specific issues of its own, and is therefore treated separately here. This Chapter deals with insurance on property against the risk of fire, but not with insurance for liabilities to third parties caused by fire.

Risks covered

47.2 The first and fundamental question in discussing fire insurance must be to know what insurance law understands by the term 'fire'. The essential point is that there can be no fire without ignition[1]; great heat by itself will not suffice. Despite the age of this rule, and despite technological advance, it does not appear to have been overruled. It might, however, be thought that it was ripe for reconsideration.

However, the fire need not be unintentional nor uncontrolled, as appears from *Harris v Poland*[2], where the policyholder hid her jewellery in the fire grate for safe keeping. Later, having forgotten that she had hidden in there, she lit the fire, and the jewellery was destroyed. It was held that this was a loss by fire within the meaning of the policy.

1 *Austin v Drewe* (1815) 4 Camp 360.
2 [1941] 1 KB 462, Atkinson J.

Difficult issues

47.3 Fire insurance has been the occasion of some of the most difficult arguments about warranties in insurance law. The classic example is *Hales v Reliance Fire and Accident Insurance Corpn Ltd*[1], where it was held that a statement on the proposal form that no combustible materials were stored on the premises must be construed as a promissory warranty applying throughout the policy, even though the question was framed solely in the present tense. The decision may perhaps be explained by reference to the obvious importance of the information to the insurers, though it is interesting to contrast *Hair v Prudential Assurance*[2], where a similar clause was held to apply only to the situation at the time of the policy. To some extent it may be said that all these cases depend upon the precise wording of the questions, though it may also be observed that the latter case was a personal lines policy, whereas the former was a case of commercial insurance, where a stricter construction of the proposal form was perhaps appropriate. Nevertheless, it is hard to resist the view that *Hales* is a decision which is rather harsh on the policyholder – the question was at best ambiguous, and a more sympathetic approach would have been to invoke the *contra proferentem* doctrine.

[1] [1960] 2 Lloyd's Rep 391, Mocatta J.
[2] [1983] 2 Lloyd's Rep 667.

Insurance against negligently caused fire

47.4 In *Mark Rowlands Ltd v Berni Inns Ltd*[1] it was held that insurance against fire must include insurance against fire negligently caused by the insured. In principle this decision must be correct. Indeed, a fire policy will normally also provide cover against the risk of fire deliberately started by a stranger[2]. However, it is equally obvious that the cover cannot extend to fire deliberately started by the insured or his servants or agents, since this infringes the general principle of insurance law that no policy covers the wilfully wrong acts of the policyholder. However, a policy may stipulate precautions to be taken against fire. In commercial policies, where the nature of the insured activity makes fire an obvious risk, these precautions may include employing someone specifically to guard against the risk of fire[3].

[1] [1985] 3 All ER 473, CA.
[2] For this point in a marine context see *Kiriacoulis Lines SA v Compagnie d'Assurances Maritime Aeriennes et Terrestres* [2002] Lloyd's Rep IR 795, CA.
[3] *LEC (Liverpool Ltd) v Glover* [2001] Lloyd's Rep IR 315, CA.

Loss by fire

47.5 There is no onus on the assured to show that the fire was caused otherwise than by his own negligent act – *National Justice Compania Naviera SA v Prudential Assurance Co Ltd, The Ikarian Reefer*[1]. The burden of proof in this regard falls on the insurers.

[1] [1993] 2 Lloyd's Rep 68.

Warranties

47.6 It is common in commercial fire policies covering places of entertainment to include the so-called 'auditorium warranty', which requires the insured, after the close of business each day, to carry out a thorough examination of the premises for smouldering matches, tobacco etc, to empty ashtrays and remove the material from the premises[1].

[1] *Pangood Ltd v Barclay Brown & Co Ltd* [1999] Lloyd's Rep IR 405, CA.

Insurable interest

47.7 A contract of fire insurance requires an insurable interest in the subject matter of the insurance to support it. *Glengate-KG Properties Ltd v Norwich Union Fire Insurance Society Ltd*[1], the insured property developer had no insurable interest in the architects' plans and drawings destroyed in the fire in one of the developer's buildings, as the plans were the responsibility of the architects and therefore did not form part of the property of the insured building. Naturally this rule does not extend to fire policies on goods, since there is no requirement of insurable interest in goods policies[2].

1 [1996] 2 All ER 487, CA.
2 LAA 1774, s 4; see Chapter 4.

Interested parties

47.8 There are many cases in which two or more persons, such as mortgagor and mortgagee, each have an interest in the same property. *Colonial Mutual General Insurance Co Ltd v ANZ Banking Group (New Zealand) Ltd*[1]. Bailor and bailee of goods may also have simultaneous (though not co-extensive) interests in the same property[2].

Since it is the same property which is exposed to peril, a composite policy is sometimes taken out by two or more persons for their respective rights and interests. A company will effect policies which will ensure for the benefit of their contractors and subcontractors: *Stone Vickers Ltd v Appledore Ferguson Shipbuilders Ltd*[3]. However, it is a matter of construction whether in a particular case one party has intended the insurance to enure for the benefit of another. In particular, there is no general rule that a landlord who insured demised premises automatically does so on behalf of both himself and the tenant[4].

1 [1995] 3 All ER 987, PC.
2 *Hepburn v A Tomlinson (Hauliers) Ltd* [1966] AC 451, HL.
3 [1992] 2 Lloyd's Rep 578, CA.
4 *Lambert v Keymood Ltd* [1999] Lloyd's Rep IR 80, Laws J, commenting on and distinguishing *Mark Rowlands Ltd v Berni Inns Ltd* [1985] 3 All ER 473, CA.

Sum insured

47.9 A fire policy always specifies the sum insured, which merely represents the maximum sum for which the insurers accept liability. Unless the policy is a valued policy[1], the assured does not, in the event of a loss, become entitled to be paid the sum insured as a matter of course. What he is entitled to is a full indemnity within the limits of the policy[2]. Full indemnity does not entitle the insured to interim payments, or the reimbursement of personal loss such as the cost of borrowing to make interim payments, in the absence of express contractual provision: *Anderson v Commercial Union Assurance Co plc*[3].

1 In practice valued policies are almost never found outside the area of marine insurance, where they are more or less universal; see Chapter 40.

[2] See also *Bryant v Primary Industries Insurance Co* [1990] 2 NZLR 142, NZCA for the proposition that a fire policy is purely a policy of indemnity.
[3] 1998 SLT 826, Ct Sess, Second Division.

'Reinstatement'

47.10 'Reinstatement' means the restoration of property affected by a fire to the condition in which it was before the fire; in the case of a total loss by rebuilding the building or replacing the goods by their equivalent, as the case may be, and in the case of a partial loss by repairing the damage. *Beaumont v Humberts*[1], where a valuer's reinstatement value, which was based upon reconstruction in the same style and general shape, but redesigned in parts according to modern practice, was not negligent although it did not provide for an exact or nearly exact copy of the original house. The case illustrates the important practical point that in the case of property which is not more or less brand new it will often be impossible to restore the property to its pre-loss condition. The idea of reinstatement is to provide the insured with an appropriate substitute item, having due regard to the circumstances of the case. From this point of view it is no doubt unfortunate that the term 'reinstatement' continues to be used. If the insured is not willing to reinstate, then the insurers are under no duty to pay the reinstatement cost[2].

[1] [1990] 2 EGLR 166, CA.
[2] *Bryant v Primary Industries Insurance Co* [1990] 2 NZLR 142, NZCA.

Meaning of 'fire'

47.11 The Insurance Ombudsman has held[1] that damage to a carpet caused by cigarettes is fire damage under a household contents policy, since the cigarette must have been alight and was therefore necessarily a source of fire. In another IOB case[2] the policyholder has a motor policy which covered, inter alia, damage from fire. The evidence was that the policyholder had been unable to turn off the engine and that smoke had been coming from under the bonnet. However, it appeared that he had been able to disconnect the battery in time to avoid further damage. The engineer's report said that the damage to the wiring loom was caused by excessive electrical build up causing overheating of the wiring circuit and melting of the plastic coating of the wires. The only damage to the vehicle was caused by the melting of the wires, and the smoke, without actual combustion, did not amount to a fire in the sense in which that term is used in insurance law. The insurers' rejection of the claim was therefore upheld. Although this point arose in the context of a motor policy, it is thought that it is of general application to fire clauses in any type of policy.

[1] IOB 13.14.
[2] IOB 8.12.

Effect of fraud

47.12 In *Nsubaga v Commercial Union*[1] Thomas J said that in fire policies it is usual to have a stringent clause voiding the entire policy in the event of a fraudulent claim or other fraudulent behaviour. Such clauses are in principle valid, and in commercial policies can be effectively incorporated by reference (SGIP, cl 1) would require rather more explicit notification in a personal lines policy)[2]. This was a case where it was clear that an insured loss had happened, but the insured was found to have fraudulently overstated the claim in a number of respects. The fraud was held to be sufficient to justify the insurers in rejecting the claim entirely. As a matter of general principle, fraudulent claims are of course not payable anyway, either because the claim is unjustified or because the making of such a claim amounts to a breach of utmost good faith.

1 [1998] 2 Lloyd's Rep 684.

2 See also *Ins Co of The Channel Islands Ltd v McHugh* [1997] LRLR 94, Mance J.

Burden of proof

47.13 Where arson by the insured is alleged, the insurers bear the burden of proving it, and that proof must be to a very high standard[1].

The standard Lloyd's fire policy expresses the insured perils as:

> 'Fire and/or lightning; fire consequent upon explosion, wherever the explosion occurs; explosion consequent upon fire on the premises insured. Explosion of domestic boilers and/or of gas used for domestic purposes or for heating and/or lighting.'

The inclusion of explosion as one of the insured perils is of some significance. It may be noted that this policy covers explosion whether as a *cause* of fire or as a *result* of fire. However, explosion quite independent of any fire is not covered.

1 *S & M Carpets v Cornhill Insurance Co* [1982] 1 Lloyd's Rep 423, CA, where it was held, on the facts, that the defence had been established.

Alteration of risk

47.14 In the specific context of fire policies it may be noted that it is common to include an express clause in the policy requiring the policyholder to notify the insurers of subsequent changes in the risk. Such a clause, without more, appears to add little to the policy, for the insurers will not be prejudiced by a failure to notify. Consequently, the requirement is sometimes supplemented by a requirement to obtain the insurers' consent before allowing any change in the risk. It is interesting to observe that some of the most important cases on the general principles of alteration of risk, such as *Shaw* and *Hadenfayre* are in fact cases of fire policies. *Shaw* is particularly important because it shows that the law treats such clauses as applying only to permanent alterations, not just to temporary alterations. It is perhaps instructive to consider the relationship between these cases and cases such as *Hales v Reliance Fire*[1], which deal with questions on proposal forms about the presence of inflammable materials, in particular with the situation where such material is stored on the premises, but only for a short time. It is obviously necessary for insurers to be able to control the risks they accept, either by requiring disclosure of the possibility of such risks, or by requiring disclosure of the risks when they happen. *Shaw* makes the second option very difficult[2], and it is therefore understandable that *Hales* should make the first option possible. As a general proposition it may perhaps be said that insurers who wish to make the disclosure of additional risk a condition of recovering under the policy need to do so in express terms. Even then, it would be prudent for them to include some right of cancelling or adjusting the policy in the event of such disclosure. Without this it seems likely that they will not be able to rely upon the failure to disclose.

[1] See above at para 47.3.
[2] See also *Thompson v Equity Fire Insurance Co* [1910] AC 592; and *Dobson v Sotheby* (1827) 1 Mood & M 90.

Acceptance of liability

47.15 Where the insurer wrongly fails to accept liability for a claim on a fire policy, the insured has no claim in respect of consequential damage caused by his inability to operate his business pending payment of the claim. The only remedy is a claim for interest on the sum outstanding[1].

[1] *Sprung v Royal Insurance (UK) Ltd* [1999] Lloyd's Rep IR 111, CA.

Chapter 48

Employers' liability insurance

Introduction

48.1 The relevant statute is the EL(CI)A 1969[1], as amended. This Act requires employers to have cover against the risk of liability to employees incurred through the acts or omissions of their employees. At various places the Act authorises the making of regulations to supplement its provisions. The relevant regulations are the Employers' Liability (Compulsory Insurance) Regulations 1998 ('EL(CI)R 1998')[2].

1 In force since 1 January 1972: Employers' Liability (Compulsory Insurance) Act 1969 (Commencement) Order 1971, SI 1971/1116.
2 SI 1998/2573.

The cover

Section 1: The basic requirement

48.2 Every employer carrying on business in Great Britain[1] must maintain in force one or more approved policies of insurance against liability for bodily injury or disease sustained by his employees arising out of and in the course of their employment in Great Britain[2]. Where those employees are not ordinarily resident in Great Britain the Act nevertheless applies to them if in the course of their employment they are present in Great Britain for a continuous period of at least 14 days[3]. Once they leave Great Britain the Act will cease to apply to them, unless and until they return for a continuous period of at least 14 days. This seems to follow from the general rule that accidents happening and diseases contracted abroad are not within the scope of the Act at all. One oddity is that each time they return they will not be covered by the Act until they have stayed for at least 14 days. On the other hand if they were to come to Great Britain regularly, the point might be reached where they were considered ordinarily resident, so that the Act would apply to them as soon as they set foot in Great Britain.

The requirement of insurance does not extend to covering disease contracted outside Great Britain, except in relation to offshore installations, to which the Act has been extended by the Offshore Installations (Application of the Employers' Liability (Compulsory Insurance) Act 1969) Regulations 1975[4] and the Employers' Liability (Compulsory Insurance) (Offshore Installations) Regulations 1975[5].

At least two important questions of construction arise in relation to this provision. The first is what is meant by 'arising in and out of the course of employment'. As to this the leading authority is *Vandyke v Fender*[6]. The second relates to the place where the disease is 'contracted'. It is well known that an employee who is, for example, exposed over a lengthy period to harmful substances may not show any signs of the resulting disease for many years. Quite commonly, the employee is by then an ex-employee and may be living outside Great Britain. Although the Act gives no further guidance on the point and there appears to be no relevant case law, it is submitted that the purposes of the act will be most effectively achieved if the disease is regarded as contracted in the place where the employee is exposed to the harmful substances which cause it, even if the symptoms of the disease do not manifest themselves until later. The position is no doubt more difficult where the exposure happens partly in Great Britain and partly outside, but it is submitted that a court would be likely to hold that the provisions of the Act applied in any case where the exposure within Great Britain could be regarded as having made more than a minimal contribution to the disease. There is of course no comparable issue about the place where injury is suffered, since this will usually be fairly obvious.

The policy may be provided by any insurer authorised to carry on business in the UK[7]. Since the implementation of the Third Insurance Directives[8] into English law by making amendments to the ICA 1982, this will include an insurer in an EEA state which has gone through the procedure for becoming authorised to offer insurance in the UK[9].

1 Thus the Act does not extend to Northern Ireland.
2 In practice many employers' liability policies provide wider coverage than is strictly required by the statute.
3 1998 Regulations, reg 4.
4 SI 1975/1289.
5 SI 1975/1443.
6 [1970] 2 QB 292.
7 Section 1(3)(a).
8 Implemented by the Insurance Companies (Third Insurance Directives) Regulations 1994, SI 1994/1696: see Chapter 33.
9 See Chapter 32.

48.3 An approved policy is one not subject to any restrictions or exemptions which are forbidden by regulations. The purpose of this is to ensure that policies issued under the Act provide a sufficiently wide cover to afford effective protection to employees, since the aim of the Act is really to provide injured employees with a fund against which they can claim compensation.

Regulation 2 of the EL(CI)R 1998 prohibits the use in policies issued under the EL(CI)A 1969 of terms which prevent liability from arising or, as the case may be, cause that liability to cease:

> '(a) in the event of some specified thing being done or omitted to be done after the happening of the event giving rise to a claim under the policy;'

The most likely things for which an insurer might want to exclude liability here are admissions of liability and failure to notify the claim within a set period. The very wide wording of this provision appears to preclude insurers even from relying upon a clause requiring notification within a reasonable time:

> '(b) unless the policyholder takes reasonable care to protect his employees against the risk of bodily injury or disease in the course of their employment;'

It may be observed that at the present day a clause of this kind would be unlikely in any event to help the insurer very much, in view of developments since 1971 in the law's interpretation of 'reasonable care' clauses in insurance policies[1]:

> '(c) unless the policyholder complies with the requirements of any enactment for the protection of employees against the risk of bodily injury or disease in the course of their employment;'

A clause of this kind would be likely to deprive the apparent cover of most of its value, since probably the majority of cases where the employer incurs liability will involve some breach of the Factories Acts:

> '(d) unless the policyholder keeps specified records or provides the insurer with or makes available to him information therefrom.'

However, reg 2(3) goes on to say that these prohibitions do not prevent the inclusion in the policy of terms requiring the policyholder to pay to the insurer sums applied in making good the claims of employees (including associated costs and expenses) in respect of risks insured under such policies. Thus, the insurer cannot escape having to compensate the injured employee, but it is legitimate to require the policyholder to repay the insurer on the basis of any of the circumstances listed in reg 2(1).

Section 1(2) authorises regulations to set a minimum limit of insurance cover in an authorised policy. Regulation 3 of the EL(CI)R 1998 sets the minimum level of insurance cover at £5m for any one occurrence (not any individual employee's claim). This limit was set at its current level in 1999, having previously been £2m[2].

In the case of groups of companies it is sufficient for the parent company to have insurance covering liability to its own employees and those of any of its subsidiaries, the minimum level of cover remains at £2m for any one occurrence.

[1] See Chapter 12.
[2] EL(CI)R 1971, revoked by the 1998 Regulations.

Section 2: Employees

48.4 An 'employee' for the purposes of the Act is anyone who has entered into or works under a contract of service or apprenticeship with an employer. The nature of the work is irrelevant, as is the form in which the contract is expressed or recorded. This definition appears to leave a possible gap in the scope of statutory insurance cover, since it is possible for an employer to become liable to someone who is working under his temporary control but whose contract of employment is with someone else[1]. Although the position is far from clear, it is suggested that a possible answer to this point would be to say that the worker concerned must be considered to have a temporary, and no doubt purely oral, contract of employment with the person under whose control he is working. At the same time there is a well-established distinction in law between an employee, who works under a contract of service, and an independent contractor, who works under a contract for services[2]. The former is within the scope of the Act, whereas the latter is not. This creates a certain incentive for employers to arrange their relationships with those who work with and for them so as to divest themselves so far as possible of the requirement to insure.

However, it is not necessary for an employer to take out insurance in respect of employees who are blood relatives[3]. Nor is it necessary to insure in respect of employees who are not ordinarily resident in Great Britain, again subject to the special rules for offshore installations mentioned above.

[1] Annotation to EL(CI)A 1969 in *The Encyclopaedia of Insurance Law* (1983, Sweet and Maxwell).
[2] The leading case on the distinction is *Ready Mix Concrete (South-East) Ltd v Minister of Pensions* [1968] 2 QB 497. See also *Express & Echo Publications Ltd v Ernest Tanton* [1999] ICR 693, CA.
[3] Oddly, the Act as drafted does not appear to exempt the employer who employs his in-laws.

Section 3: Exemptions

48.5 This section provides exemptions from the Act for a number of bodies. These are metropolitan, county and district councils and bodies corporate established under statute for the undertaking under national ownership or control of any industry. Bodies in the latter of these categories are of course much less numerous than they were when the EL(CI)A 1969 was enacted. There is also an exemption for a company with only one employee where that employee owns at least 50% of the issued share capital (ie in effect a one-person company)[1].

[1] Employers' Liability (Compulsory Insurance) Regulations 1998, Sch 2 (employers exempted from insurance), para 15, as inserted by Employers' Liability (Compulsory Insurance) (Amendment) Regulations 2004, SI 2004/2882 with effect From 28 February 2005.

Section 4: Certificates of insurance

48.6 This section allows the making of regulations connected with certificates of insurance. The intention is to ensure that certificates of insurance under the Act are issued to employers as appropriate and are surrendered if they cease to be valid.

In addition, s 4(2) requires the employer to comply with any regulations relating to the display of copies of the certificate of insurance for the benefit of his employees and to produce a copy of the certificate on the demand of an inspector authorised by the Secretary of State for that purpose. The EL(CI)R 1998 expand on this section. Regulation 4 requires the insurer to issue to the employer, within 30 days of the commencement or renewal of the insurance, a certificate of insurance in the form and containing the information specified in the Schedule to the Regulations. That Schedule merely sets out the familiar form of Certificate of Insurance which can be seen displayed in places of employment, showing the names of the parties, the date when the policy is to expire and reciting that the policy complies with the requirements of the Act. Regulation 6 deals with the display of the Certificate of Insurance. An employer who has received a certificate under reg 5 is required to display it or a copy of it at each of his places of business where he employs any person whose claims may be the subject of indemnity under the policy of insurance to which the certificate relates. The copies must be places where they can readily be seen by the employees to whom they relate and must be in such form as can readily be read by them (presumably this relates to language and to the size of the type used). They must continue to be displayed until the end of the period to which they relate (or the cancellation of the policy) but must not be displayed thereafter.

Section 5: Consequences of failure to insure

48.7 An employer who does not take out the insurance required by the Act commits a criminal offence[1]. However, the failure does not of itself give rise to any civil liability, though of course any incident which should have been insured is likely to give rise to liability at common law and/or under the Factories Acts[2] or the Employers' Liability (Defective Equipment) Act 1969.

1 EL(CI)A 1969, s 1.
2 *Richardson v Pitt-Stanley* [1995] 1 All ER 460, CA.

Transfer of undertakings

48.8 In *Theresa Bernadone v Pall Mall Services Group And Haringey Health Care NHS Trust*[1] it was held that both an employer's tortious liability towards an employee and that employer's rights of indemnity under its employer's liability insurance policy were transferred to the transferee of an undertaking under the Transfer of Undertakings (Protection of Employment) Regulations 1981[2].

1 [1999] IRLR 617, Blofeld J.
2 SI 1981/1794.

Chapter 49

Reinsurance

The concept of reinsurance – definition

49.1 Reinsurance is the process by which an insurer ('the primary insurer'[1]) who has accepted a risk from an insured passes on some or all of that risk to another insurer ('the reinsurer'). The process of reinsurance is of considerable practical importance, since it allows primary insurers to spread the risks which they have accepted to a greater degree and thus contributes to the vital task of the insurance market in distributing risk in a sustainable and economically efficient way[2]. The process of reinsurance can be continued beyond the first level of reinsurance. A contract which reinsures a reinsured risk is known as a *contract of retrocession*, the reinsurer being referred to as the retrocessionaire and the reinsured as the retrocedant. The presence of multiple levels of reinsurance may cause serious practical complications, and may be confusing if, as sometimes happens, the same insurer appears at different levels of the reinsurance as may happen if the risk is not clearly presented, and the insurer does not realise that it is in effect reinsuring itself. However, this situation does not give rise to significant issues of legal principle, and for the most part this Chapter takes as its paradigm case the contract of reinsurance which reinsures the liability of a primary insurer. It is also fair to say that for the most part the contract of reinsurance is merely another example of a contract of insurance, though, as appears in this Chapter, reinsurance does present some special features which are worthy of note.

1 Also known as 'original insurer', 'direct insurer' or 'cedant'.
2 The process is sometimes rather cynically compared to the practice of laying-off bets, commonly used by bookmakers for exactly the same reasons. Excessive reinsurance, as in the LMX spiral in the London market, can be economically counterproductive.

The nature of reinsurance contracts

49.2 A reinsurance contract is an arrangement purely between the reinsured and the reinsurer. The primary insured has no contract with the reinsurer, who does not become a joint insurer of the primary liability.

It follows that the ordinary rules for the creation of insurance contracts apply in full force to the creation of the reinsurance contract. In particular the requirements of insurable interest apply, as does the doctrine of utmost good faith[1].

So far as insurable interest is concerned, it is important to remember that the risk which is insured under the contract of reinsurance is not the same as that which is covered by the primary insurance. Rather, the reinsurance is against the risk that the liability under the primary contract will arise. Thus, a reinsurer providing cover for motor risks does not need to be authorised as a motor insurer, since what he is providing is not motor insurance.

[1] It may be noted in passing that *Pan Atlantic Insurance Co Ltd v Pine Top Insurance Co Ltd*, the leading case on non-disclosure and good faith, is in fact a case of reinsurance.

Privity of contract

49.3 It also follows from the above that the primary insured is not in privity of contract with the reinsurer. This point is also of practical importance. The primary insured need not concern himself with whether the contract of reinsurance has been properly formed, since his rights are solely against the primary insurer. At the same time, if the primary insurer is insolvent, or if the contract of primary insurance is for any reason defective, then it is of no help to the primary insured to know that there is effective reinsurance in place, for that reinsurance cannot be called on by him, and will not be called on at all unless liability under the primary insurance contract is first established.

Cut-through clauses

49.4 In an effort to deal with the problems identified in the previous paragraph some insurance policies contain cut-through clauses. These have been defined[1] as:

> 'a provision in a contract of insurance which typically purports to afford protection to a policyholder against the insolvency of its insurer'.

This is achieved by providing that in this event the reinsurer will make payment direct to the policyholder. Two essential questions arise. The first is whether the clause is valid. If so, the second is whether this effectively turns the reinsurer into a primary insurer, who will therefore need appropriate regulatory approval.

So far as English law is concerned the first of these questions gives rise to formidable difficulties. These arise partly as a result of the doctrine of privity of contract and partly because of the provisions of the IA 1986. The former may possibly be solved by making insured, insurer and reinsurer all party to the same contract, which can be executed as a deed if there is perceived to be a residual problem of consideration. The latter is more difficult to circumvent. If the contract provides that the insurer is to hold reinsurance proceeds on trust for the insured, then this might be open to attack as a preference under the IA 1986, s 239. However, the same argument does not apply if the insured acquires direct contractual rights against the reinsurer, since this has no effect on the position of the insurer. The practical problem about this latter arrangement is that it requires the identity of the reinsurer(s) to be known at the time when the original contract is entered into, and this requirement cannot always be met. It is no doubt for this reason that the trust device is more commonly used. In any event a contract which gave the insured direct rights against the reinsurer probably would turn the reinsurer into a primary insurer, with inevitable regulatory consequences.

1 Braithwaite (1997) 95 BILA Journal 22. The value of this article in preparing the current account of the subject is gratefully acknowledged.

49.5 It can thus be seen that there are serious difficulties in setting up a cut-through clause as an arrangement taking effect from the start of the contract. However, it may be that in some cases the reinsurer will be prepared to make payments direct to a policyholder, provided that it has appropriate protection against the risk of being sued also by the insurer. It would presumably not be proper for the liquidator of the insolvent insurer to agree not to sue, but the same effect can perhaps be achieved more indirectly by requiring the policyholder, in return for direct payments from the reinsurer, to agree not to attempt to sue on the insurance policy. The indirect effect of this is to prevent the insurer from ever acquiring any claim under the contract of reinsurance. There is no net loss to the reinsurer, which pays the same amount as it would otherwise have done, though the payment is made to a different party. A scheme of this kind was considered by Lightman J in *McMahon & Smith v AGF Holdings (UK) Ltd*[1], where the question considered was whether the scheme involved any net loss to the insurer. It was held that it did not, precisely because of the netting off of the claims against the reinsurer with the claims by the insured. The question of a preference was not considered in this preliminary hearing. It is submitted that from the point of view of the policy of the IA 1986 there is no reason why this scheme should be considered to amount to a preference. The point about a preference is that a company, knowing that it is or is about to be insolvent, must not deliberately order its payment strategies so as to favour one creditor over another in the event of liquidation. This does not mean that nothing can ever be done which improves the position of one creditor. It is accepted, for example, that it is legitmate in these circumstances to respond to creditor pressure by paying in whole or in part an outstanding debt, notwithstanding that, self-evidently, this puts the paid creditor in a better position than it otherwise would have been in the event of liquidation. Although s 239 of the IA 1986 is not expressed in quite this way, the case law[2] appears to support the idea that the real question is whether the payment is to be regarded as improper. It is of course true that the s 239 test says nothing about comparing the position of the paid creditor with the position of unpaid creditors, but it seems that the courts tend to have that point in mind when considering whether a particular payment is a preference. The curious thing about the scheme here considered is that it appears to help the paid creditors without prejudicing other unpaid creditors, since it effectively transfers the claims of the paid creditors to a different debtor. It is true that they get paid in full, but the payment is from assets which would not have been available to the insurer unless those claims had first been paid.

1 [1997] LRLR 159.
2 See eg *Re Deaduck Ltd (in liquidation), Baker v Secretary of State for Trade and Industry* [2000] 1 BCLC 148; *Re Agriplant Services Ltd (in liquidation)* [1997] 2 BCLC 598; *Wills v Corfe Joinery Ltd (in liquidation)* [1998] 2 BCLC 75, [1997] BCC 511.

49.6 A further interesting question, which will no doubt have to be considered before long, is whether the C(RTP)A 1999 can have any effect on the answer to the problems of cut-through clauses. The intention of that Act is to allow third parties to sue and be sued on contracts, provided that the contract is clearly intended to benefit them and provided that they are expressly named in the policy as intended beneficiaries. It would be easy enough to draft cut-through clauses so that they complied with these formal requirements. What is less clear is whether such a clause could then survive the operation of the IA 1986 provisions. The C(RTP)A 1999 is understandably silent on this point, but it is submitted that in the even of any conflict the answer ought to be that the IA 1986 prevails. The C(RTP)A 1999 is intended merely to provide a mechanism for alleviating some of the well-established problems created by the doctrine of privity of contract. It is not intended to override such mandatory provisions as those contained in the Insolvency Act which seek to establish an equitable balance among the various interested parties in the event of insolvency.

Utmost good faith in reinsurance[1]

49.7 In *Kingscroft Insurance Co Ltd v Nissan Fire & Marine Insurance Co Ltd*[2] the claimants sought to recover various amounts allegedly due under two facility quota share treaties ('the treaties') made between the claimants as 'the reinsured', underwritten by their underwriting agent ('W'), and the defendant ('Nissan'). Nissan claimed to be entitled to avoid both treaties on the grounds of:

(i) misrepresentation and non-disclosure as to the involvement of certain reinsurers in the pool and the existence of the pool's excess of loss reinsurance programme; alternatively;
(ii) the repudiation of the treaties arising out of the failure of the claimants to retain for their own account 50% of the risks ceded under them, as provided for by each of the treaties.

The claimants were all companies which at one time or another were members of a pool for which W acted as underwriting agent. By 1976 the pool comprised two classes of members: stamp companies (ie those who issued policies and incurred liabilities direct to third parties) and whole account share quota reinsurers ('WAQS reinsurers'), who reinsured the business written by the pool. In 1975, W invited Nissan to participate in the treaties, which W had originally negotiated with another reinsurer in relation to the writing by W of reinsurance of US umbrella liability insurance. With effect from 1 April 1976, Nissan accepted a share on each of them. At the time the treaties were made, six of the claimants were not then members of the pool and of those six, five had yet to be incorporated. The issues arising in relation to the construction of the treaties (from which Nissan's allegations of non-disclosure, misrepresentation and repudiation flowed) were as follows:

(i) whether the companies which became members of the pool after the conclusion of the treaties became parties to them;
(ii) whether the claimants were entitled to enter into excess of loss reinsurance contracts in respect of their retained share of business ceded under the treaties;
(iii) whether the WAQS reinsurers who were members of the pool qualified as 'companies underwritten by W'; and

(iv) whether the claimants were entitled to cede business to other members of the pool, whether stamp companies or WAQS reinsurers, under WAQS reinsurance treaties.

The trial was as to liability only.

It was held, as to (i), it was clearly the intention of the parties that the term 'the reinsured' should mean those companies which were from time to time members of the pool: their exact identity or number was immaterial to Nissan, since in business terms the reinsured was W's pool, whose composition was immaterial provided that W remained responsible for its underwriting and management. As to (ii), Nissan's contention that the agreement to retain 50% of the risk amounted to an undertaking to retain that proportion without the benefit of any reinsurance cover whatsoever was unsustainable: the expert evidence as to the market was that any prudent insurer who was writing an account of this size would obtain excess of loss protection, and Nissan could not have believed otherwise. To construe the material words otherwise was to give them a meaning which was contrary to commercial good sense. As to (iii), the WAQS reinsurers were included in the expression 'companies underwritten by W', since Nissan's general knowledge of the market meant that it was to be taken as knowing that any particular pool was likely to include non-stamp companies as well as stamp companies, all of whom shared in the business written by the pool. It followed from the above that, in answer to (iv) above, cessions within the pool were permitted. Nissan's defence therefore failed.

[1] See also Chapter 5.
[2] [1999] Lloyd's Rep IR 603, Moore-Bick J.

When liability arises

49.8 The reinsurer's liability to the reassured arises, and the reassured's cause of action accrues, when the reassured's liability to the original assured is ascertained, irrespective of whether the reassured has discharged that liability: *Hill v Mercantile and General Reinsurance Co plc; Berry v Mercantile and General Reinsurance Co plc*[1] (a reinsurer is not liable unless the loss falls within the policy reinsured and also within the cover created by the reinsurance, in respect of which parties are free to agree on ways of proving that those requirements are satisfied).

[1] [1996] 1 WLR 1239, HL.

Types of reinsurance

49.9 A basic distinction in reinsurance is that between compulsory or 'obligatory' reinsurance and optional or facultative reinsurance. The distinction may be expressed in the following way.

In facultative reinsurance the primary insurer approaches the reinsurer to seek cover for a particular risk or set of risks. The contract is then negotiated in much the same way as any other insurance contract. This kind of insurance gives rise to few special problems – it might almost be said that it is simply an application of the same principles as are relevant in primary insurance contracts.

In compulsory reinsurance the agreement made between the primary insurer and the reinsurer is that the reinsurer will accept, to the extent agreed, all the risks written by the primary insurer. In compulsory reinsurance, properly so-called, the reinsurance is automatic on both sides, that is to say that as soon as the primary risk is written, it is automatically added to the class of risks reinsured without the need for further action by either party. Agreements for compulsory (or 'obligatory') reinsurance are commonly referred to as 'treaties'. The advantages of this system are that it provides certainty and relative ease and cheapness of administration. From the point of view of the reinsurer the potential disadvantage of this arrangement is that he must accept the primary insurer's judgment of which risks should be accepted.

49.10 A third type of reinsurance is that which is, rather confusingly, called 'facultative/obligatory reinsurance'. In this type of insurance the primary insurer is entitled to choose which risks he will reinsure, but the reinsurer is obliged to accept those risks which the primary insurer chooses to pass on to him. From the point of view of the reinsurer this arrangement is less satisfactory than ordinary obligatory reinsurance, since it is possible for the primary insurer to cherry-pick the risks he will retain, while passing on the business of less good quality to the reinsurer. To some extent this problem can no doubt be countered by setting an appropriate premium. It should also be borne in mind that in such arrangements the reinsured is under only a limited duty of good faith in choosing which risks are to be ceded[1]. This type of reinsurance remains of some practical value in allowing insurers to redistribute, in whole or in part, risks which are exceptionally large by reference to the business which they normally transact, but which for commercial reasons they do not wish to decline entirely.

[1] See for example *Aneco Reinsurance Underwriting Ltd (In Liquidation) v Johnson & Higgins Ltd* [2000] Lloyd's Rep IR 12, CA, Cresswell J, where it was assumed that the reinsurer was simply compelled to accept whatever risks the insurer chose to cede. A slightly different aspect of the same principle appears in *Kingscroft v Nissan Fire & Marine* [1999] Lloyd's Rep IR 603, Moore-Bick J, where it was held that even under a quota share treaty there was no need to disclose that part of the portion of the risk retained by the primary insurer was protected by a separate excess of loss policy.

Treaty reinsurance – some practical issues

49.11 Reinsurance treaties may be further subdivided into two types, namely quota share and surplus. The simpler version is quota share, in which a proportion of the risks written by the primary insurer are automatically ceded to the reinsurer. Thus, in effect the reinsured reinsures a specified percentage of a given book of business. Different portions of the risk may of course be reinsured in different places, and it is usual for the primary insurer to retain at least some part of the risk for himself. In surplus reinsurance, by contrast, the arrangement is that the insurer retains in full the risk up to a certain amount (expressed either by relation to individual risks or in relation to the total of risks of a certain class) with the reinsurer accepting the surplus of risk over and above that retention.

49.12 In all the examples of treaty reinsurance so far considered, the arrangement has been for the cession of a proportion of the risk, and it is for this reason that this type of reinsurance is referred to as 'proportional'. A further type of reinsurance is that referred to as 'non-proportional'. This is usually found as a form of last-resort reinsurance, the most common examples being excess of loss and stop loss. Excess of loss provides cover against losses incurred on particular primary policies over and above a specified amount. The amount in question is usually fairly high, for the primary insurer will wish to keep a reasonable amount of the business for himself. It is usual to construct excess of loss cover in a series of horizontal layers. A consequence of this is that the premium for the higher layers is less than that for the lower layers, since there is less likelihood that the higher layers will be reached. It is a feature of excess of loss reinsurance that it covers claims arising from a single event or occurrence[1]. Some of the difficulties which may arise from this class of insurance are illustrated by *Brown v GIO Insurance Ltd*[2], where the Court of Appeal had to decide whether to uphold a provision in a contract of reinsurance which provided that 'The reassured shall be the sole judge as to what constitutes each and every loss and/or one event' where the contract provided for an excess and a limit of liability to be calculated on the basis of 'each and every loss and/or series of losses arising out of one event.'

Reference was made to the case of *The Glacier Bay*[3] in which the court examined the principles dealing with one party to a contract having a decision making power and with the court's attitude to contractual terms which could be argued to be ousting the court's jurisdiction.

It was held that the clause in this case did not fall clearly within any of the situations described in the *Glacier Bay* case as being ones where the court would be reluctant to enforce terms. It was accepted that in this case the point to be decided was one of mixed fact and construction and was very much for the expertise of a market man. The reassured could therefore make the decision. As to whether the decision could be challenged, it was held that it could be attacked if it was unreasonable but that in determining unreasonableness it would not be enough to show that on construction the court would take or had taken a different view. This may be regarded as a pragmatic view, intended to support the smooth functioning of the reinsurance market. The clause was no doubt inserted to simplify the administration of the treaty and, so far as possible, to ensure that there would no reason for any dispute to reach court. The interpretation adopted by the Court of Appeal effectively glosses the clause as meaning 'the reassured shall be the sole judge of these matters *as between the parties and subject to a residual right of appeal to the court in the case of wholly unreasonable behaviour by the reassured*', a solution which appears to preserve the honour of all parties (including the court) while also promoting the efficient administration of the treaty.

[1] For recent authority of the meaning of 'single occurrence' see *Mann v Lexington Insurance Co* [2000] 2 All ER (Comm) 163, Timothy Walker J.
[2] [1998] Lloyd's Rep IR 201, CA.
[3] [1995] 1 Lloyd's Rep 560 and [1996] 1 Lloyd's Rep 370, CA.

49.13 Another important case concerning excess of loss policies is *Denby v English and Scottish Maritime Insurance Co Ltd; Yasuda Fire and Marine Insur-*

ance Co of Europe Ltd v Lloyd's Underwriting Syndicate No 299[1] where the Court of Appeal has upheld the decision of the High Court and reversed a decision of Mr Justice Waller dated 14 June 1996.

The insurers insured firms of professionals on terms including an 'each and every loss' deductible and limit. The terms of the insurance provided that the insured had to show that each individual claim exceeded the excess or retention figure stipulated. If not, no claim could be made. If so, the recovery was then confined to the amount of the excess but subject to a per claim limit. There were other features of the insurance policies, notably that in all cases cover was subject to an overall limit, and in most cases it was subject to an aggregate retention which had to be exceeded before any claim could be made, which were features consistent with insurance on an aggregate basis.

The contracts of reinsurance provided:

> 'As regards liability incurred by the reinsured for losses on risks covering on an aggregate basis, if required by the reinsured, this reinsurance shall protect the reinsured excess of the amounts as provided for herein in the aggregate any one such aggregate loss up to the limit of indemnity as provided for herein in all any one such aggregate loss.'

It was held that the question of whether the original insurance was covered by the reinsurance policy required consideration of the terms of the original policies. It was held that notwithstanding some of the provisions in the underlying contracts of insurance being those typically identified with aggregate policies, they were nevertheless not aggregate policies but, rather, the antithesis of that – they were on an each and every claim basis. It was held that it was not open to the reinsured to add together causally unconnected claims which it had paid under such underlying policies and to present them to the reinsurer as one loss.

It was therefore held that payments made under the underlying policies were not recoverable from the reinsurers.

Stop loss insurance, by contrast, covers aggregate losses incurred on particular types or classes of policy, ie the total losses from that class of insurance in the period of insurance. Again, the insurer's retention is likely to be fixed at a fairly high level.

[1] [1998] Lloyd's Rep IR 343, CA.

The extent of the reinsurer's liability

49.14 Because reinsurance is effected as a series of discrete contracts, important practical issues arise about trying to ensure that the insurer is able to pass on to the reinsurer all (or the appropriate part) of the liabilities which he is seeking to reinsure. In this context a number of phrases are commonly found in reinsurance treaties, which require some consideration because they give rise to certain problems.

'To pay as may be paid thereon'

49.15 This is one of the earliest phrases used for the purpose of aligning liabilities between primary insurance and reinsurance. Although the position is by no means free from doubt it is suggested that the following propositions may be regarded as reasonably settled.

First, the clause allows the primary insurer to recover whatever he has paid under the policy, up to the policy limit, but not beyond[1]. Secondly, the reinsurer's liability arises once the primary insurer is liable – it is not necessary that the primary insurer shall actually have paid[2]. Where the primary insurer makes an *ex gratia* payment to his insured, this clause does not require the reinsurer to pay on the reinsurance policy. It might fairly be thought that this conclusion goes somewhat against the wording of the clause, but two important points need to be made. The first is that there is here a fundamental policy decision to be made about the extent to which the primary insurer is to be allowed to make decisions which prejudice the interests of the reinsurer. In those cases where liability is clear, no serious issue arises, for it is always obvious that the claim must be paid, and there is no real opportunity for the insurer to mistreat the reinsurer. The position is otherwise where liability is at best doubtful, for here an insurer who has reinsured all or most of the risk might be tempted to admit liability rather too readily, safe in the knowledge that the ultimate loss will fall on someone else. On the other hand, market practice accepts that there are cases where it is commercially appropriate to pay (at least in part) a doubtful claim, and it might well be suggested that the problem of excessive generosity on the part of the insurer could adequately be dealt with by the use of a general duty of good faith as between reinsurer and reinsured. Be that as it may, the second major point to be made here is that there is authority amounting to a settled doctrine to the effect that the reinsurer is not liable to any greater extent than the legal liability of the primary insurer[3].

1 *Uzielli v Boston Marine Insurance Co* (1884) 15 QBD 11, CA.

2 *Re Eddystone Marine Insurance Co* [1892] 2 Ch 423. The clause is therefore not properly to be compared with the 'pay and be paid' clauses commonly found in the rules of P & I clubs, the unfortunate effects of which are considered in Chapter 29.

3 The earliest important authority is *Chippendale v Holt* (1895) 65 LJQB 104, Mathew J; the leading authority may be said to be *Merchants' Marine Insurance Co Ltd v Liverpool Marine and General Insurance Co Ltd* (1928) 31 Ll L Rep 45, where the Court of Appeal confirmed the principle stated in *Chippendale.*

Follow the settlements

49.16 An alternative form of wording used in reinsurance policies requires the reinsurer to 'pay as may be paid thereon and to follow their settlements'. The question therefore is whether the addition of the phrase 'follow their settlements' allows the insurer to hold the reinsurer liable for settlements which may not be strictly in accordance with legal liability. In *Excess Insurance Co Ltd v Mathews*[1] Branson J held that this formulation allowed recovery where there was legal liability but the insurer had entered into a settlement as to quantum, and said *obiter* that the clause would also be effective to impose liability in those cases where the primary insurer entered into a settlement despite being under no legal liability. It is submitted that this was a sensible pragmatic decision. The rule in *Chippendale*, though no doubt hallowed by some degree of antiquity, is probably not a particularly useful one from the point of view of the insurance market, and it seems that the addition of the reference to following the settlements was intended to produce a different result. It would have been unfortunate if the courts had felt compelled to hold that it had failed in this objective.

In *Insurance Co of Africa v Scor (UK) Reinsurance Co Ltd*[2] it was held that the effect of a 'follow the settlements' clause is that the reinsurers must follow and honour any settlement entered into by the ceding company unless the reinsurers can show lack of good faith or collusion or failure on the part of the ceding company to take all proper and businesslike steps to have the amount of the loss fairly and carefully ascertained. This approach may fairly be regarded as a development of the approach of Branson J in *Excess Liability*. It is also another example of the court attempting to strike some reasonable balance between the interests of the insurer and those of the reinsurer. It is noticeable that the formulation adopted imposes on the reinsurer quite a heavy burden in seeking to challenge the legitimacy (and thus the binding nature) of any settlement entered into by the insurer.

In *Assicurazioni Generali SpA v CGU International Insurance plc*[3] the Court of Appeal reiterated the rule that clauses of this kind bind the reinsurers to all settlements except without prejudice and ex gratia settlements so long as the basis on which the claim was settled fell within the risks covered by the policy and the reinsured had acted honestly and in a businesslike fashio in making the settlement. This applied both in relation to the acceptance of liability and the determination of the amount of the claim[4].

[1] (1925) 31 Com Cas 43.
[2] [1985] 1 Lloyd's Rep 312, CA.
[3] [2004] Lloyd's Rep IR 457, CA.
[4] Other cases considered here included *Hill v Mercantile and General Reisurance Co plc* [1996] 1 WLR 1239 (see also para 49.8); *Re London County Commerical Reinsurance Office Ltd* [1922] 2 Ch 67; *Toomey v Eagle Star Insurance Co Ltd* [1994] 1 Lloyd's Rep 516; *Western Assurance Co of Toronto v Poole* [1903] 1 KB 376.

Establishing the insurer's liability

49.17 In *Commercial Union Assurance Co plc v NRG Victory Reinsurance Ltd; Skandia International Insurance Corpn v NRG Victory Reinsurance Ltd*[1] – the insurers sought summary judgment against the reinsurers.

It was common ground between the parties that to recover under the reinsurance policy the insurers had to establish that they were liable under the underlying insurance policy. The question to be determined was whether they had done so.

The insured had commenced proceedings in Texas but these had been settled. There was uncontested evidence before the court that if the proceedings had continued the insured would have been successful. It is not clear from the report why no contrary evidence was submitted by the reinsurers or what weight this would have been given.

The judge accepted that as the underlying insurance policy did not contain an exclusive jurisdiction clause it was reasonable to assume that the insured shipowner would proceed in whatever jurisdiction was most favourable to him. He held that this meant that one had to consider liability in that jurisdiction and not simply whether the insurer would be held liable by an English judge in the Commercial Court.

It was therefore held that the insurers had proved the loss in the same way as the insured had proved the loss against them – they had proved the amount of the insured's liability in the court of competent jurisdiction where they were properly sued. Accordingly they were awarded summary judgment. This judgment was subsequently reversed by the Court of Appeal[2]. The insurers of the cargo on board the *Exxon Valdez* had entered into settlements with the cargo owners after proceedings were commenced in Texas. The insurers then sought to recover under their contracts of reinsurance. The insurers succeeded at first instance in obtaining summary judgment against the reinsurers on the grounds that they would have succeeded if a judgment, rather than a settlement, had been obtained in Texas and that the evidence of the insurers' Texan lawyer, to the effect that the cargo owners' action would have succeeded if pursued, was not controverted.

The Court of Appeal has taken a different approach. It distinguished two situations:

(1) where a judgment is obtained in a foreign jurisdiction – in which case the judgment will be binding as to the reinsured's original liability unless–
  (a) in the eyes of the English court the overseas court was not of competent jurisdiction;
  (b) the judgment was in breach of an exclusive jurisdiction clause or other similar provision excluding proceedings before that court;
  (c) the reinsured did not take all proper defences or (d) the judgment was not manifestly perverse;

(2) Where a settlement is reached of the foreign proceedings – in which case the reinsured must show that it was legally liable to the original assured unless the reinsurance contract contained an effective 'follow the settlements' provision.

In this case it was held that the evidence was such that under English law the reinsurers would have an arguable defence that the insurers were not liable to the cargo owners and so the orders for summary judgment would be set aside.

[1] [1998] 1 Lloyd's Rep 80.
[2] [1998] 2 Lloyd's Rep 600.

Claims co-operation clauses

49.18 Many reinsurances contain provisions requiring the reinsured to notify reinsurers promptly of any event likely to give rise to a claim, to co-operate with reinsurers in the investigation of such clauses and not to admit liability without reinsurers' agreement. Such clauses are likely to be conditions precedent to liability under the follow the settlements clause, but a breach of the claims co-operation clause will not necessarily debar the reinsured from claiming on the policy – the effect will merely be that the reinsured has to prove as a matter of fact that the los sis covered by the policy, rather than being able to rely on the follow the settlements clause[1]. However, a clause worded in this way is not breached if there is a settlement without admission of liability[2]. Moreover, a term will be implied to the effect that reinsurers must not unreasonably withhold consent to settlements or admission of liability[3].

1 *Eagle Star Insurance Co Ltd v Cresswell* [2004] EWCA Civ 602, [2004] Lloyd's Rep IR 537, Morrison J.
2 *Gan Insurance Co Ltd v Tai Ping Insurance Co Ltd* [2001] Lloyd's Rep IR 291, Longmore J.
3 See n 2 above.

Arbitration clauses

49.19 Arbitration clauses are commonly found in commercial policies. An interesting case in the context of reinsurance is *Trygg Hansa Insurance Co Ltd v Equitas Ltd*[1], where the court considered the effect of s 6 of the AA 1996 on the incorporation of arbitration clauses into reinsurance contracts. Section 6 provides:

> 'a document containing an arbitration clause constitutes an arbitration agreement if the reference is such as to make that clause part of the agreement'.

There were arbitration clauses in the underlying insurance policies which the reinsurers argued were incorporated in the reinsurance policy by the provision 'to follow the same terms exclusions conditions … as the policy of the primary insurers'.

It was held that s 6 allowed the court to consider the previous authorities on the incorporation of arbitration clauses. The court concluded that there were no special circumstances which indicated an intention to incorporate the arbitration provisions of the direct policies in the reinsurance. The general rule of construction is that generally expressed words of incorporation have the effect of incorporating only terms relating to the subject matter of the contract unless circumstances prevailing when the contract was made show that it was the parties' intention to adopt an ancillary term. As the question of incorporation of terms is one which frequently arises the decision is worthy of attention. As a general point it may be observed that the application of the doctrine of privity of contract will usually mean that an arbitration clause in a primary insurance contract will not be incorporated into a reinsurance contract. In theory this outcome could be prevented either by the operation of the AA 1996 or by means of the C(RTP)A 1999, but it is suggested that in practice this will very rarely happen.

1 [1998] 2 Lloyd's Rep 439.

Timing of loss

49.20 In *Municipal Mutual Insurance Ltd v Sea Insurance Co Ltd*[1] the main question considered by the Court of Appeal was the relevance of the time at which a loss occurred for the purposes of determining the reinsurers' liability.

The case arose out of the delivery of two large machines into the care of the Port of Sunderland. Although the owners intended the machines to be sold, there were delays and they remained at the port for several years. During this time the machines were massively damaged by vandals and their more valuable components were stolen. The best evidence indicated that the damage occurred between March 1987 and September 1988. This led to a claim against the port authority which settled for nearly £3.2m.

The claimant insured the port authority for sums that it became liable to pay for loss or damage to property owned by third parties. The limit of indemnity was £5m for any claim or claims 'arising out of any one occurrence ...or attributable to one source or original cause.' The policy was continuous and there was therefore no need to determine exactly when the loss was sustained The claimant therefore paid the settlement with the owners of the machines and sought to recover from its reinsurers, of whom the leader was the defendant.

The reinsurance contracts were on the same terms as the underlying insurance except they were not continuous, but were renewed annually. Over the period of the damage a total of 12 reinsurers were involved. The cover was for £2.5m in excess of £500,000 in the 1986 and 1987 underwriting years and £3.5m in excess of £1.5m for the 1998 year. The claimant notified the reinsurers of the claim and asked them to agree a method of apportionment.

The Court of Appeal was asked to consider two issues:

(1) **Whether the claimant had any claim at all against the reinsurers**
Although the claimant could not show that any single act of vandalism or theft caused a loss greater than the policy excess, the court applied the analysis of a loss attributable to a single 'originating cause' set out in the judgment of Lord Mustill in *Axa Reinsurance (UK) plc v Field*[2] in which it was said that this phrase has a wide meaning and is chosen to open up the widest possible search for a unifying factor for the losses which it is sought to aggregate. In this case it was held that it was clear than the unifying factor was the failure of the port authority to have an adequate system to protect goods in its care.

(2) **Whether there was sufficient evidence that the loss occurred during the period of the reinsurance**
The Court of Appeal relied upon the *AXA Re* decision referred to above to overturn the judgment at first instance and held that there is no presumption that even facultative reinsurance is back to back. The reinsurance in this case was not continuous and this was an important difference between it and the underlying insurance. The reinsured had to do more than establish that some material loss or damage occurred during the time the reinsurance protection for a particular year was in place. The reinsured had to prove on the balance of probabilities the amount of a loss sustained during the year in question. It was held that there was no evidence that the loss occurring during the first and third years was greater than the deductibles. As to the second year, although it was far from conclusive what loss had been suffered the Court of Appeal was willing to quantify the loss taking into account the balance of probabilities and so some recovery was made.

[1] [1998] Lloyd's Rep IR 421, CA.
[2] [1996] 2 Lloyd's Rep 233, HL.

Reinsurers and the London market letter of credit scheme

49.21 In *Ludgate Insurance Co v Citibank NA*[1] the claimant's claims arose out of a dispute between the parties which followed the collapse of certain companies trading in the London insurance market in the early 1990s. The claimant contended, in short, that the defendant was wrongly retaining too much by way of collateral deposits in support of Letters of Credit ('LOC') it had issued and that it had also wrongly debited interest charges to its account.

The claimant was a company which underwrote all its business through an underwriting pool, Weavers. At all material times, Weavers was engaged in underwriting casualty, liability and property insurance and reinsurance emanating mainly but not exclusively from the US. The defendant operated the London Market letter of credit scheme which was established to enable reinsurers in the London insurance market (and, subsequently, other European reinsurers) to conduct reinsurance business in the US. If a claim is made in the US, a non-domestic reinsurer must be told promptly of its share of the claim and is required to put up security for that amount. US insurance companies are prepared to pay reinsurance premiums annually in advance, but they require LOC to be opened in their favour to cover the portion of the premium still to be earned by the reinsurer in order that their balance sheets will not be negatively affected. The London Market scheme enabled participants to substitute LOC for cash advances for both these purposes.

Weavers was sometimes required to establish LOC on business accepted by it and arranged such LOC through the defendant. The LOC issued apparently did not break down the liability for the LOC between the various companies within the Weavers' pool. The defendant's security was that Weavers had to maintain deposit accounts with it. Subsequently the claimant and other principals sought to establish segregated collateral accounts so that their cash collateral could be held in accounts in their own names.

When the claimant's segregated accounts were opened it entered into an agreement with the defendant which provided, inter alia:

> '1 We [the claimant] refer to:
>
> (i) the sundry letters of agreement ("the Agreements") now or hereafter entered into by you [the defendant] with [Weavers] in respect inter alia of any [LOC] now or hereafter issued by any branch of [the defendant] on behalf of and for the account of [Weavers].
>
> (ii) the accounts with [the defendant] in our name now or hereafter established by us with [the defendant] for the purposes hereof ("the Accounts"); and
>
> (iii) the proposal that [the defendant] agrees to waive in part its requirement that [Weavers] maintains certain deposits with [the defendant] in connection with the Agreements on condition inter alia that we maintain certain deposits with [the defendant] which, taken together with the deposits

which [Weavers] continues to maintain with [the defendant] at least equal the amount required to be deposited by the terms of the Agreements.

2 We hereby offer to agree with you as follows:

(i) we shall maintain in the Accounts a deposit or deposits equal in aggregate amount to that portion of [the defendant's] actual or contingent liability under the LOC as is notified to [the defendant] by [Weavers] from time to time as attributable to our interest in the LOC and (a) we shall be deemed to have requested [the defendant] to assume such liability under the LOC for our sole account on the same terms and conditions *mutatis mutandis* as the Agreements and (b) we shall not be entitled to withdraw any monies from the Accounts that would result in a breach of the foregoing requirement, Provided Always that if Weavers fails to so notify [the defendant] or [the defendant] is in receipt of conflicting or ambiguous instructions from [Weavers] or otherwise it would appear to [the defendant] that the monies in the Accounts and in the accounts of [Weavers] held or established pursuant to the terms of the Agreements would not together equal 100% of [the defendant's] actual and contingent liabilities ... then [the defendant] shall be entitled to retain in the accounts such additional margin as it considers appropriate in all circumstances until a solution satisfactory to it is effected in respect thereof.'

The agreement therefore limited the claimant's obligation to maintain sums on deposit to sums equal to that part of the defendant's actual or contingent liability under the LOC as was notified to the defendant by Weavers from time to time as attributable to the claimant's interest in the credits. This obligation would terminate if one or other of what the judge at first instance described as the 'trigger events' occurred.

Weavers started to suffer financial difficulties and the defendant became concerned to see whether it was possible to achieve some apportioning as between the different principals – ie the various companies in the Weavers' pool. The defendant said that it had the right under the agreement to allocate drawings in such manner as it considered appropriate in its sole discretion. The claimant said that the circumstances in which such right could be exercised had not arisen under the terms of the agreement and that, if it had, the exercise was open to attack on the grounds of unreasonableness.

The Court of Appeal upheld the decision of the judge at first instance and rejected the claimant's appeal. It held that the circumstances in which the court would intervene in the exercise by a party to a contract of a contractual discretion given to it by another party were extremely limited. Provided the discretion was exercised honestly and in good faith for those purposes for which it was conferred and provided also that it was not capricious or arbitrary or so outrageous in its defiance of reason that it could properly be categorised as perverse the court would not intervene. In this case the defendant was allowed to retain in the segregated account of the claimant such additional margin as it considered appropriate in all the circumstances. In the absence of a satisfactory solution being found there appeared to be no grounds upon which the defendant could properly be faulted in a court of law for exercising its discretionary power in the way it had and the appeal would be dismissed.

[1] [1998] Lloyd's Rep IR 221, CA.

Foreign judgment

49.22 The court ought to treat as binding the judgment of a foreign court in respect of the reinsured's liability under the original insurance contract, provided:

(1) the foreign court was of competent jurisdiction;
(2) the judgment had not been given in breach of any exclusive jurisdiction clause;
(3) the reinsured had taken all proper defences; and
(4) the judgment was not manifestly perverse[1].

[1] *Commercial Union Assurance Co plc v NRG Victory Reinsurance Ltd; Skandia International Insurance Corpn v Same* [1998] 2 All ER 434, CA.

Reinsurance – whether it is a market custom to share costs and legal expenses pro rata with reinsurers

49.23 In *Baker v Black Sea and Baltic General Insurance Co Ltd*[1] the House of Lords referred back to the Commercial Court the question of whether it is a market custom to share costs and legal expenses pro rata with reinsurers[2]. Black Sea and Baltic subsequently went into liquidation and so this litigation has been stayed. This means that this question will not be resolved unless and until it comes up for determination in another dispute.

[1] [1998] 2 All ER 833, HL. Earlier authorities in this area include *Scottish Metropolitan Assurance Co Ltd v Groom* (1924) 20 Ll L Rep 44, CA; *Insurance Co of Africa v Scor (UK) Reinsurance Co Ltd* [1985] 1 Lloyd's Rep 312, CA; *British Dominions General Insurance Co Ltd v Duder* [1915] 2 KB 394, CA. Lord Lloyd commented at 834 that these cases were not easy to reconcile or to understand.
[2] On the implication of terms generally, see *Liverpool City Council v Irwin* [1977] AC 239 at 253 per Lord Wilberforce the court may imply terms if it is simply spelling out what the parties know and would, if asked, unhesitatingly agree to be part of the bargain.

Rights of inspection of the reinsured's documents

49.24 In *Société Anonyme D'Intermediaries Luxembourgeois v Farex GIE*[1] it was held that if a right of inspection is not expressed then 'English law gives [the reinsurer] no procedural means of inspection unless they are first able to raise a triable issue on the material otherwise available to them.'

In *Trinity Insurance Co Ltd v Overseas Union Insurance Ltd*[2] the reinsurer did not request an inspection of records until six years after payments under the treaties had been stopped and an application for summary judgment had been issued by the reinsured. The court refused the reinsurer's application for a stay to allow it time to inspect making it clear that the reinsurer's conduct was a significant reason for his decision – ie the lateness of its application.

In *Aetna Reinsurance Co (UK) Ltd v Central Reinsurance Corpn Ltd*[3] in similar circumstances, partial leave to defend was granted to the reinsurers. Of relevance was the fact that the reinsurers' conduct did not play such a decisive role and that they had first requested inspection prior to the delivery of the relevant account by the reinsured.

In *Pacific & General Insurance Co Ltd (in liquidation) v Baltica Insurance Co (UK) Ltd*[4] it was held that one of the main considerations in such cases is the circumstance in which the claim to inspect comes forward. If the reinsurer passes by his right to inspect until the last minute and only applies when summary judgment against him is imminent the court will be reluctant to do other than proceed to summary judgment, but where there is a timely request for inspection that is a different matter.

In *Iron Trades Mutual Insurance Co Ltd v Companhia de Seguros Imperio*[5] it was pointed out that a reinsurer who seeks inspection is thereby deemed to have affirmed the contract of reinsurance and therefore to have lost his right to avoid the contract.

In *Commercial Union-Assurance Co plc v Mander*[6] the reinsurer applied for disclosure of documents relating to the insurers' liability under the original contract of insurance. The insurer said that such documents were privileged and that they were unnecessary to dispose fairly of the action. It was held that the test of relevance is a wide one and includes documents which might lead to a train of enquiry. It is not restricted to documents which will be admissible in evidence. Documents relating to negotiations leading to a settlement of a dispute are likely to be relevant. Where a contract indicates a 'follow settlement' clause insurers and reinsurers do have a common interest in the defence and investigation of the claim. Notwithstanding this, to establish common interest and to override privilege the reinsurer has to show a common interest in the documents at the time when they were obtained.

1 [1995] LRLR 116.
2 [1996] LRLR 156.
3 [1996] LRLR 165.
4 [1996] LRLR 8.
5 [1991] 1 LRLR 213.
6 [1996] 2 Lloyd's Rep 640.

Chapter 50

Miscellaneous cases

50.1 This Chapter deals with a number of areas of insurance, most of which have generated relatively little case law. They are treated only in outline. For more detailed coverage the reader is referred to specialist texts in these areas.

Compulsory insurances

50.2 This first section deals with two statutes which impose requirements of compulsory insurance[1].

[1] Other relevant areas of compulsory insurance are motor insurance (Chapter 37) and employers' liability (Chapter 48).

Nuclear Installations Act 1965

50.3 This Act governs the conduct of nuclear installations generally, and the only section which is relevant for present purposes is s 19, which deals with insurance cover. The scheme of the Act is to allow the granting to appropriate persons of licences to run nuclear sites. Section 19 requires the holder of such a licence to make provision for sufficient funds to be available to ensure that any claims established against that licensee in his capacity as licensee of that site can be satisfied. This requirement is subject to a number of clarifications and qualifications. First, the provision which is made for these purposes does not absolutely have to take the form of insurance, since s 19 refers to the provision being made 'either by insurance or by some other means'. In practice it seems likely that insurance will be the method most commonly used. Secondly, the section provides a minimum level of cover, which is currently £5m in respect of each *severally* of the following periods:

(a) the current cover period, if any;
In principle the cover period means the period of the licensee's responsibility for the site[1], but s 19(4) allows the Secretary of State to vary this where he considers it proper to do so by reason of the gravity of any occurrence which has resulted or may result in claims against the licensee

in respect of that site. The variation takes the form of giving a direction that one cover period is to end at a specified time and be immediately succeeded by a new cover period. The effect of this, coupled with paragraphs (b) and (c) below, is that each of the cover periods is required to be protected by a separate valid means of cover which will provide the necessary £5m of indemnity,

(b) any cover period which ended less than ten years before the time in question;

(c) any earlier cover period in respect of which a claim remains to be disposed of, being a claim made–

  (i) within the relevant period within the meaning of s 16 of the Act (the period of ten years beginning on the date of the occurrence which gave rise to the claim or, where that occurrence was a continuing one, or was one of a succession of occurrences all attributable to a particular happening on a particular relevant site or to the carrying out from time to time on a particular relevant site of a particular operation, the date of the last event in the course of that occurrence or succession of occurrences to which the claim relates[2]).

  and

  (ii) in the case of a claim such as is mentioned in s 15(2) of the Act, also within the limitation period of 20 years provided by that subsection. Section 15(2) deals with claims in respect of injury or damage caused by an occurrence involving nuclear matter stolen from, or lost, jettisoned or abandoned by, the person whose breach of duty gave rise to the claim.

Paragraphs (b) and (c), taken together, create separate insurance requirements for any period of cover ending not more than ten years previously – even if no claim has yet been made in respect of it – and any earlier period in respect of which there is an outstanding claim.

Section 19(3) deals further with the situation where the cover arrangements are not to be made by means of insurance and the same licensee would be required to make provision under s 19 in respect of at least two other sites. In such a case the licensee is not required to provide cover for the full £5m at each of the sites. Instead, s 19(3) declares that it is sufficient if the funds available to meet claims at all the sites collectively are sufficient to meet claims at the two sites of that licensee where the requirement for cover is highest. The Secretary of State is, however, empowered to give a direction raising that amount of cover required in such a case to a level higher than that provided under s 19(3), so long as that amount remains lower than the total amount of cover as calculated under s 19(1).

Section 18 of the Act adds a residual provision under which claims which exceed the amount of required cover may be met out of Government funds up to a total of £300m.

[1] Section 19(2).
[2] Section 15(1).

Riding Establishments Act 1964 ('REA 1964')

50.4 This Act makes the keeping of a riding establishment subject to a licensing requirement[1], the process being administered by local authorities. The only part of this process which is of interest here is that s 1(4A) of the Act[2] requires that a licence to keep a riding establishment must be subject to various conditions, one of which[3] is that the licence holder shall hold a current insurance policy which insures him against liability for any injury sustained by those who hire a horse from him for riding and those who use a horse in the course of receiving from him, in return for payment, instruction in riding and arising out of the hire or use of a horse as aforesaid and which also insured such persons in respect of any liability which may be incurred by them in respect of injury to any person caused by, or arising out of, the hire or use of a horse as aforesaid.

It should be observed that in some respects this provision goes further than does, for example, the EL(CI)A 1969, for it requires insurance to be in place not only for injuries *to* riders, but also for injuries caused *by* riders. This is a valuable protection for those who hire horses from riding establishments and then ride them on the public road, for example.

The Act gives no further guidance as to the terms of the policy. It is submitted that from this point of view the section must be interpreted so as to give effect to the intention of the Act, which is that there should be effective liability cover in relation to accidents caused to or by riders. An acceptable policy must therefore be one which does not contain limitations on the scope of the cover such as would defeat that purpose.

Failure to insure is a minor regulatory offence under s 1(9) of the Act. It may be that it would also be a breach of statutory duty and thus a civil wrong[4]. The point is of some importance because of the possibility that a horse rider might incur liabilities to third parties. These ought to be covered by the insurance policy required under the Act, and if they are not so covered, then the rider would in the first instance presumably be liable. The existence of a right of recourse against the keeper of the riding establishment would then be of value to the rider. At first sight the argument is an attractive one, but an obvious difficulty is caused by the decision of the Court of Appeal in *Richardson v Pitt-Stanley*[5], which holds that this argument does not hold good in the context of the EL(CI)A 1969[6]. There is an obvious need for caution in reasoning from the one statute to the other, but it is submitted that an examination of the judgments in that case can provide some guidance on this point. Russell LJ pointed out in that case that the 1969 Act does not make the failure to have insurance unlawful and then separately provide for a criminal sanction – it merely declares it to be a criminal offence. He adds that in those cases where regulatory offences give rise to civil liability it is usual to find that the breach will give rise to personal injury[7] to the claimant, rather than mere economic loss. Both the EL(CI)A 1969 and the REA 1964 fail both these tests. The conclusion that breach of the insurance requirement does not give rise to a civil action is also consistent with the general principle stated by Lord Diplock in *Lonrho Ltd v Shell Petroleum Ltd*[8], which is that where an Act creates an obligation and enforces it in a particular manner, it is to be presumed that that performance cannot be enforced in any other manner. On the other hand, another reason given for the decision in *Richardson* was that it was unnecessary to make failure to insure a civil wrong, since anything giving rise to a liability which is required to be insured under the Act is likely also to be a breach of the Factories Acts. This argument does not apply at all in the context of riding establishments, for the circumstances in which a rider could become liable to third parties may well not involve any breach of duty on the part of the keeper of the establishment. It is therefore possible to make a plausible argument that the REA 1964 is distinguishable from the EL(CI)A 1969, so that failure to insure would fall within the limited category of regulatory offences which also give rise to civil liability.

1 Section 1(1).
2 As added by the REA 1970, s 2.
3 Section 1(4A)(d).
4 *Mozley and Whiteley's Law Dictionary* (12th edn, 2001, Butterworths).
5 [1995] 1 All ER 460.
6 As to which, see generally Chapter 43.
7 The Factories Acts being the obvious example.
8 [1981] 2 All ER 456 at 451.

Other insurances

All risks

50.5 Property may be insured against all risks. In this case the nature of the casualty causing the loss is immaterial; the policy covers the loss however caused. The onus of proving the loss lies upon the assured – *Sofi v Prudential Assurance Co Ltd*[1]. In practice, however, the term 'all risks' is misleading, since even in policies which go by this name there will always be exceptions (war risks being one of the most common). Once the loss is proved, the onus is on the insurer to show that it arises from some excluded cause.

1 [1993] 2 Lloyd's Rep 559, CA.

Meaning of 'including shortage in weight but subject to an excess of 1% of the whole shipment'

50.6 *Coven Spa v Hong Kong Chinese Insurance Co Ltd*[1] has considered the meaning of an 'all risks' wording in a policy of insurance which provided 'including shortage in weight but subject to an excess of 1% of the whole shipment.'

A claim was brought for shortage but on the facts the judge found that there had been no physical loss of cargo during the voyage. The cargo loaded had all been discharged – it was a classic paper loss.

The Court of Appeal held that the shortage in weight had to be a physical loss occurring during the insured adventure. It held that:

(1) the basic insurance covered loss or damage on an 'all risks' basis including shortage in *weight*. The use of that word did not support a conclusion that the shortage in weight cover was for non-physical loss;
(2) the policy could not have been intended to insure goods which were simply not there;
(3) it was not possible to have an insurable interest in goods which were not there;
(4) the insurance only attached when the goods left the warehouse.

The case means that a paper loss is not of itself enough to found a cargo claim on 'all risks' insurance, even with the inclusion of shortage in weight cover. However, it appears that if the right wording is used such losses can be covered.

1 [1999] Lloyd's Rep IR 565, CA.

Contractors 'all risks' policies

50.7 This somewhat specialised class of insurance deals with the risks incurred by building contractors in relation to their building projects.

There is a commonly-used form of policy wording, misleadingly referred to as a contractors 'all risks' policy. The expression is misleading since the policy does not in fact cover all the possible risks arising from the work carried on by contractors. This section discusses some issues arising from that policy.

Clause requiring notification of possible claim

50.8 In *Alfred McAlpine plc v BAI (Run-off) Ltd*[1] the policy contained a standard form clause requiring the assured to notify the insurers of any likely claim 'as soon as possible' but did not expressly make this a condition precedent, whereas other terms of the policy were expressly stated to be conditions precedent. The claimants were the statutory assignees of the policyholders, who had gone into liquidation. Colman J held that the clause was not a condition precedent. Failure to comply (an accident giving rise to the prospect of a claim was not notified for 16 months) was a breach of contract, but the insurer's remedies depended upon being able to show any loss arising from the failure. On the facts no loss could be discerned, so the insurers were unable to rely upon the breach. The idea that the failure to notify might also be a breach of the continuing duty of utmost good faith, was also raised. It was held that there had been no breach, even if it could be assumed that the duty applied to a statutory assignee of a policy.

1 [1998] 2 Lloyd's Rep 694, Colman J.

Condition 13 of the standard Lloyd's commercial industrial and contractors combined liability insurance

50.9 In *Layher Ltd v Lowe*[1] it was held that it had not been shown that a party to compromised litigation had been brought within the wording of condition 13 of the Standard Lloyd's Commercial Industrial and Contractors Combined Liability Insurance which required immediate notice of 'a happening of any occurrence likely to give rise to a claim.'. At the relevant time although it could be said that a claim against the party was possible, it could not be said to be likely.

1 [2000] Lloyd's Rep IR 510, CA.

50.10 Some CAR policies also purport to provide a degree of cover for sub-contractors, and in such cases it must be a matter of construction of the policy whether the sub-contractors have become co-assureds so that insurers exercising subrogation rights cannot proceed against them[1].

[1] *BP Exploration Operating Co Ltd v Kvaerner Oilfield Products Ltd* [2004] EWHC 999 (Comm), [2004] 2 All ER Comm 266, Colman J.

Employee risk insurances

Bankers and stockbrokers insurance

50.10A Certain forms of property, such as money and securities for money, are in practice expressly excepted from the protection of an ordinary burglary policy. However, bankers and stockbrokers who habitually deal with such forms of property require protection against their peculiar risks. To give them adequate protection the policy must not only cover the stealing of money and securities for money, it must extend beyond the risk of ordinary theft and cover losses occasioned by fraud. Consequently, there are special forms of insurance for protecting bankers and stockbrokers against the loss of money and securities[1]. A point of some general importance arose in *Deutsche Genossenshcaftsbank v Burnhope*[2], where the relevant clause of the policy covered theft 'committed by persons present on the premises of the Assured'. A client company of the bank defrauded it of some £9m when the chairman of the company sent a junior employee to the bank to take possession of some documents. The employee was not party to the fraud. The question was whether the company could be said to have been present on the premises through the presence of the junior employee. It was held that it could not. The policy had probably been intended to distinguish between theft by electronic means and theft at the premises of the bank by a 'real live person'. As the theft had not been committed by a person present at the bank, there could be no liability. In truth the decision is a somewhat unconvincing one, for it seems unlikely that those drafting the policy had had this distinction in mind, and it would have been perfectly possible to hold that the junior employee as a representative of the company made the company 'present'.

[1] *Deutsche Genossenschaftsbank v Burnhope* [1995] 4 All ER 717, HL.
[2] [1993] 2 Lloyd's Rep 518; [1995] 4 All ER 717, HL.

Comprehensive crime policy

50.11 In *New Hampshire Insurance Co v Phillips Electronics North America Corpn*[1] the Commercial Court considered what was covered by the words 'other property' in three separate comprehensive crime policies. The claims arose out of allegedly fraudulent activities.

[1] *Insurance and Reinsurance Newsletter* (October 1998).

Insurance for theft by employees[1]

50.12 In *Proudfoot plc v Federal Insurance Co*[2] it was held that an administrator of the payroll did not fall within the definition of employee within the policy which included any 'director or trustee of an insured while performing acts coming within the scope of the usual duties of an employee.' The contractor was not holding an office of the insured but was holding funds for the insured and the inclusion of 'trustee' in the policy was not sufficient to find an intention to extend the definition of employee to the contractor.

1 Sometimes referred to as 'employee fidelity policies'.
2 [1997] LRLR 659.

Insurances of intangible interests

Business interruption insurance

50.13 Business Interruption policies protect against the risk of economic loss arising from the interruption of business activity through extraneous event[1]. They are complementary to, but distinct from, those policies which protect against the risk of physical damage to the real or personal property of the business. Both types of risk may of course be covered by the same policy.

1 For a general account of this type of policy see David Claughton *Riley on Business Interruption Insurance* (7th edn, 1991, Sweet and Maxwell).

Quantum

50.14 A special feature of business interruption insurance is that by its nature the loss against which it insures is to some extent speculative – the intention is to indemnify the insured for the profit which he *would have* made if the interruption had not occurred. Two basic problems therefore arise when calculating the amount due under a valid claim. The first is to decide what the turnover of the insured would have been, whilst the second is to establish what element of that would have been profit. The former problem is commonly solved to a large extent by looking at the turnover of the business for the corresponding previous accounting period, though of course this can give no more than an approximate result, since the trend of a business at any given time may be either up or down. In the modern practice it is common to provide for a liquidated sum per day in order to avoid these difficulties of proof.

The second problem is more complex, since a reduction of x% in turnover is likely to lead to a reduction of more than x% in profit (this is because many of the overhead costs of the business will remain despite the fall in turnover, though obviously the variable costs will be reduced). Any method of calculating the level of indemnity must therefore distinguish with reasonable accuracy between overhead costs and variable costs.

Material damage and business interruption policy

50.15 In *Insurance Corpn of the Channel Islands Ltd v Royal Hotel Ltd*[1] it was alleged that the claim for business interruption was fraudulent. This claim was upheld on the facts, and it was held that the effect of this was to vitiate the entire claim[2].

1 [1998] Lloyd's Rep IR 151.
2 See also Chapter 19 for a discussion of the general question of fraudulent claims.

50.16 Business interruption insurance is particularly exposed to the risk that a failure on the insurers' part to pay promptly will cause the policyholder to suffer further consequential losses. However, such losses cannot be recovered under a policy of insurance[1].

1 *Normhurst Ltd v Donoch Ltd* [2005] Lloyd's Rep IR 27, Chambers J.

Pecuniary loss insurance

Insurance in respect of loss of rent

50.17 An ordinary policy on buildings may contain a rent clause protecting the assured from the pecuniary loss which he may sustain: (1) if he is a tenant, by reason of his continuing liability to pay rent after the destruction of, or damage to the buildings; or (2) if he is a landlord, by reason of the suspension of rent, pending reinstatement, where the tenancy agreement so provides. Under the normal rent clause no liability attaches to the insurers unless the premises become unoccupied, and the extent of their liability is governed by the length of the period for which they continue to be unoccupied[1].

1 *Glengate-KG Properties Ltd v Norwich Union Fire Insurance Society Ltd* [1996] 2 All ER 487, CA.

Liability insurances

Directors and officers insurance

50.18 Director and Officers policies are commonly effected by companies concerned at the risk that their directors will incur liability to the company or to others for the conduct of their duties. Such insurances are now allowed under the Companies Act 1985, s 310. However, where the policy is taken out by the director it will not cover the risk of deliberate wrongdoing by that director. Consequently, it is usually preferable for the policy to be taken in the name of the company.

Public liability policies

50.19 Public liability policies protect against the risk of incurring legal liability, usually tortious, to third parties. Although they can be found as self-standing policies, it is common to find public liability cover included as one element of a more broadly-based policies. In particular, household buildings and contents policies often offer such cover as an optional extension.

50.20 Where an insurer has a right as against the policyholder to avoid the contract, no communication to the third party claiming against the insured will be held to amount to affirmation, since affirmation has to be communicated to the policyholder[1].

[1] *Spriggs v Wessington Court School Ltd* [2004] EWHC 1432 (QB), [2005] Lloyd's Rep IR 474, Stanley Burnton J.

Liability insurance

Meaning of 'compensation'

50.21 Where a local authority insured itself against liability for compensation arising out of the actions of its employees, including police officers, 'compensation' in the insurance policy included exemplary damages[1]. Where the damages were firstly for wrongful arrest and secondly for alleged abuse of the claimants while in the care of the local authority. The insurers sought to argue that it was contrary to public policy for these damages to be covered by an insurance policy[2] but this was rejected, apparently on the basis that the liability of the authority was purely vicarious, so that the public policy arguments could not apply.

[1] *Lancashire County Council v Municipal Mutual Insurance Ltd* [1996] 3 All ER 545, CA.
[2] See, by way of analogy *Hardy v Motor Insurers' Bureau* [1964] 2 All ER 742, CA; *Gray v Barr* [1971] 2 All ER 949; and see the discussion of illegality generally in Chapter 20.

Meaning of 'single claim'

50.22 The policy may fix the maximum sum payable in respect of any accident or accidents arising out of the same occurrence. As to what constitutes a single claim see *Haydon v Lo & Lo (a Firm)*[1] (theft of money in tranches and shares in parcels). It was held in that case that where a series of thefts had been perpetrated, involving different acts of dishonesty, there was only one cause of action and therefore the thefts constituted a single rather than a multiple claim for the purposes of the professional indemnity policy. As such on the facts of the case the excess of loss insurers were liable to indemnify the firm for losses exceeding the limit of liability on their primary insurance policy.

[1] [1997] 1 WLR 198, PC.

Meaning of 'Accidental'

50.23 In a public liability policy which covered liability arising from 'accidental bodily injury' the word 'accidental' was defined as meaning 'sudden, unforeseen, fortuitous and identifiable'. An employee of the insured deliberately assaulted a member of the public, who suffered serious personal injury as a result. Wilkie J held[1] that the liability for these injuries were covered by the policy. The question of whether the injuries were 'accidental' had to be viewed from the perspective of the assured, rather than from the perspective of the victim.

[1] *Hawley v Luminar Leisure plc* [2005] Lloyd's Rep IR 275.

Requirement of legal liability

50.24 In *P & O Steam Navigation Co v Youell*[1] consideration was given to whether P & O's liability insurance extended to settlements of passenger claims where they had not demonstrated that they were legally liable to compensate the passengers under the standard conditions of carriage as they were not in breach of their contractual duties which was a requirement of recovery under the policy. It was held that all that was necessary was for P & O to show a liability in damages to the compensated passengers. If that existed the form and nature of the compromise designed to avoid or satisfy claims in respect of the liability should not be determinative of the question as to whether or not there were valid claims under the policy. The authorities showed that P & O agreed to provide relaxing and enjoyable holidays – they were under a legal liability in damages and the judge was justified in holding that, had the matter gone to trial, the court would not have been prepared to uphold the exclusionary effect of the conditions.

[1] [1997] 2 Lloyd's Rep 136.

Other miscellaneous cases

Commercial property insurance

50.25 In the present work commercial property insurance is treated separately from the insurance of domestic property because the issues which arise are somewhat different, and the law's approach is significantly different.

In *Lonsdale & Thompson Ltd v Black Arrow Group plc*[1] the first defendants were freehold owners of a warehouse which they had leased to the claimants for 25 years. The lease contained a standard form term requiring the landlords to insure for replacement cost and the tenants to pay insurance rent. The landlords later entered into a contract to sell the warehouse, subject to the lease. Between exchange and completion the warehouse burned down. This did not frustrate the contract for the sale of the warehouse (risk having passed on exchange of contracts) and the transaction proceeded to completion. The report of the case is silent on the question whether the purchaser had insured the warehouse as from completion. The tenants purported to require the insurers to reinstate, but the insurers declined liability on the ground that they had no further liability to their insured, who had parted with their beneficial interest in the property by the time of the fire. The insurers argued that the landlords had suffered no loss because they had received the purchase price in full. The question therefore was whether it was relevant that the tenants clearly had suffered loss. It was held that the measure of indemnity in these circumstances was not limited to the damage to the reversion. Although that might in some cases be the measure of indemnity, it is a matter of construction whether it is so in any given case. Here, the evident intention was to insure for the benefit of the tenants as well as for the benefit of the landlords (though it was accepted that the tenants were not co-insured). On the face of it the decision appears to conflict with the principles laid down in *Castellain v Preston*[2], a case with similar facts but which was decided the opposite way. The vital difference here appears to lie in the fact that the landlords had an obligation to the tenants to reinstate, a feature which was absent in *Castellain*. This allowed the judge to hold that the measure of the loss which was being indemnified was different in the two cases. Once the warehouse burned down, the landlords came under a contractual obligation to the tenants to bring about reinstatement, and this duty was not affected by the subsequent sale of the warehouse.

In *London Tobacco Co (Overseas) Ltd v DFDS Transport Ltd*[3] the third defendants were road hauliers and were the sub-contractors of the first and second defendants in respect of the carriage of the claimants' consignment of cigarettes. The third defendants employed the fourth defendant as their subcontractor.

The fourth defendant collected the consignment. He stopped at a motorway service station and by prior arrangement the lorry was driven away by others and the consignment stolen. It was never recovered.

Having been sued by the claimants and having claims made against them by the first and second defendants the third defendants sought to recover from their insurers. Theft by bogus sub-contractor was not insured and a sub-contractor was defined as:

> '… any person not being an employee to whom property is entrusted for reward by … the insured and of whose services the Insured makes use for the performance of the contract.'

It was held that the fact that the fourth defendant, at the time he made his contract with the third defendants, had already decided to steal the goods, did not prevent a legal contract coming into existence; it merely meant that the contract was voidable by the third defendants; the fourth defendant was properly described as a sub- contractor although he was dishonest and had no intention of performing the sub-contract; it did exist and the third defendants could sue the fourth defendant upon it; the goods were loaded onto a vehicle of a person who was a sub-contractor with the third defendants and were lost either at that time or subsequently while being carried on his vehicle; the third defendants were therefore entitled to recover.

1 [1993] Ch 361, [1993] 3 All ER 648, Jonathan Sumption QC.
2 (1883) 11 QBD 380, Chitty J and CA.
3 [1993] 2 Lloyd's Rep 306, Hobhouse J, [1994] 1 Lloyd's Rep 394, CA.

Material facts

50.26 In *Aldridge Estates Investments Co Ltd v McCarthy*[1] it was held that the presence of squatters and the fact that property was unoccupied were material circumstances which had to be disclosed to the insurers of the property. It is of course always a question of fact whether a particular fact was material.

1 [1996] EGCS 167.

Bailees' insurance

50.27 Property may be covered in transit. In such a case the loss must be sustained in the course of the transit described in the policy. *London Tobacco Co (Overseas) Ltd v DFDS Transport Ltd*[1].

In *Waters and Steel v Monarch Fire and Life Assurance Co*[2] the claimants were wharfingers who insured under a floating policy all goods held by them 'in trust'. A fire occurred, in which some of their customers' goods were destroyed. The insurers refused to pay out beyond the claimants' personal interest (which would have been very limited), alleging that a policy by the claimants to cover the customers' interests would be illegal. It was held that the claimants had sufficient interest to support the policy. To the extent that it covered the customers' interests in the goods the claimants were to be regarded as having acted as unauthorised agents for the customers. In accordance with the normal principles of agency it was open to the customers to ratify this arrangement, whereupon the claimants would hold the balance of the policy moneys in trust for the customers.

The decision is undeniably convenient, since the practice of bailees of insuring goods in their charge on a goods basis rather than a liability basis is a commercially useful one. It is perhaps unfortunate that the court should suggest that the policy moneys would be held 'in trust'. It must be assumed that this phrase is used somewhat loosely, since an agent who receives money on behalf of his principal owes a fiduciary duty in relation to that money but is not normally thought to stand in the relationship of trustee to his principal.

The principle underlying this decision has in effect been approved by the House of Lords in *Hepburn v A Tomlinson (Hauliers) Ltd*[3], where the claimants were carriers of goods, who had effected goods policies covering the risk of theft. A consignment of cigarettes was stolen in transit, and the House of Lords held that the carriers were entitled to recover the full value of the goods. It was said that they would hold the amount beyond their own interest on behalf of the true owners of the goods, who were not parties to the action.

1 [1993] 2 Lloyd's Rep 306.
2 (1856) 5 E & B 870, 119 ER 705, Ex Ch.
3 [1966] AC 451.

Guarantee policies

50.28 Guarantee polices are encountered almost solely in the commercial context[1]. The terms include various kinds of policy which purport to provide cover against the risk that a third party will default on its obligations. In a domestic context one of the most commonly encountered forms of guarantee policy is that under which the NHBC provides cover against the risk of certain defects in recently constructed properties.

In *Paddington Churches Housing Association v Technical & General Guarantee Co Ltd (1999)*[2] it was held that under a performance bond giving a guarantee of performance on a construction contract in JCT form there was no liability on the guarantor until the net damage had been established and ascertained. This was an interim application to amend the Statement of Claim and decide a preliminary point of law under RSC Order 14A concerning the terms of a performance bond. In 1994, the claimant, a housing association, was the employer under a JCT contract With Contractors Design, 1981 Edition incorporating amendments 1 to 6. The contractor was Woodward & Co (Finsbury) Ltd ('Woodward'), and the purpose was a housing association building development at Longford Street, London NW1. At the request of the claimant Woodward arranged for the defendant to provide a performance bond guaranteeing payment by the defendant to the claimant of the 'net established and ascertained damages sustained by' the claimant, up to a maximum of £160,000, in the event of default by Woodward. In February 1996, Woodward went into liquidation, and the claimant terminated Woodward's contract and entered into a new contract with another builder to complete the works for the sum of £1,492,406 or such other sum as would become due under the JCT contract. Practical completion of the second contract took place in January 1998, and the defects period expired in January 1999, but no steps had been taken to calculate the final sums due under that contract. The writ in this action was issued in August 1997, and claimed immediate payment in full of the sum of £160,000. It was held that the 'net established and ascertained damages' sustained by the claimant could not be ascertained until the final sums due to the second contractor had been ascertained in accordance with the provisions of cl 27 of the JCT contract, and the additional costs arising, if any, calculated accordingly.

Until those calculations were effected and the amount of the ascertained sum for damages given to the defendant, there was no liability on the defendant to make any payment to the claimant. Leave to amend was therefore refused, and the case was dismissed.

[1] But are not written at Lloyd's.
[2] [1999] BLR 244 Technology & Construction Court (HH Judge Bowsher QC).

Domestic guarantee policies

50.29 The Insurance Ombudsman has also had occasion to consider a number of issues arising in relation to guarantee policies. In one case[1] the purchaser of a dwelling found from a pre-survey report that there were various defects. He negotiated only a small reduction in the purchase price. After completing the purchase he had the defects remedied and sought indemnity from the insurer under the New Home Guarantee Policy. However, the policy had an exclusion in respect of claims submitted by anyone other than the original buyer of the house (which the policyholder clearly was not) in respect of damage or defects known or reasonably discoverable immediately prior to the transfer of interest. The intention of this clause was clearly that such defects should be identified as part of the sale process and should be reflected in the sale price. The Ombudsman upheld the company's repudiation of liability on the basis that the existence of this stipulation was likely to have come to light in the conveyancing process.

[1] IOB 8.1.

Home income plans ('HIPs')

50.30 These plans were commonly sold in the 1980s, but the problems which they have created have led to a reduction in their number in the 1990s. The essence of the scheme is that investors (who are usually elderly) are induced to raise capital for their old age by mortgaging their homes (which are often not subject to mortgage before this scheme is entered into). The mortgage proceeds are commonly invested in a combination of an annuity and one or more investment bonds. The annuity is of course guaranteed for life or for some reduced period, depending upon the terms of the arrangement. The value of the bonds is subject to market fluctuation, and the income taken collectively is expected to provide for the investor's financial needs, including any element of repayment of the mortgage. In practice the scheme is often designed on the basis that in fact very little of the mortgage will be repaid, or even that the mortgage interest will simply accumulate. It is then assumed that outstanding sums will be repaid from the sale of the property on the investor's death. It is this last feature which makes these products unsuitable for all save the elderly: to put the matter bluntly, the scheme is only really capable of being suitable if the investor's life expectancy is relatively limited, so that the annuity can be for a reasonable sum and the accrued mortgage debt can still be less than the value of the property by the time of the investor's death. Regrettably, though predictably, there are a number of cases in which these schemes are sold to those whose life expectancy is too great to justify the sale. There are also cases where investors proceed to show a fine contempt for the medical profession by living much longer than had been expected. In these circumstances the course of events can be distressing, for the mortgage debt may reach a level where it exceeds the value of the property. The mortgagee is then likely to protect itself by exercising its power of sale under the mortgage. Thus, an elderly investor is forced to sell his home and move to something smaller and cheaper. If the annuity is for a fixed term, this may be accompanied by a further reduction in the investor's income. Inevitably, many sales of HIPs prove on investigation to be mis-sales. Although the mortgage of the property cannot be set aside, the Ombudsman has the difficult task of calculating appropriate compensation, taking into account the fact that the complainant will have received some benefit from the annuity and from any income payments made on the bonds. The 1996–97 PIAOB Report contained some useful guidance on the approach to be taken in dealing with questions of calculation.

First, where capital realised under a HIP has been spent on an asset which has a residual value at the time of the assessment of the compensation, that residual value is to be deducted from the compensation. The PIAOB gives the purchase of a car or a home improvement as examples of assets with residual values. The argument does not apply if the thing purchased has no residual value (such as a holiday, for example).

Secondly, where the complainant had an existing repayment mortgage at the time of the mis-sale, which would have been paid off by the date of the assessment of compensation, but the saving arising from the fact that it was paid off early has been spent on ephemera, the usual practice is not to make any deduction from the compensation in respect of either the capital of the mortgage or the interest on it. Although this may appear to give an unfair advantage to those complainants who have been spendthrift over those who have been more prudent, it is submitted that it would be unduly harsh not to make this distinction. Moreover, there is no need to expend great sympathy on regulated firms who find themselves in this position entirely through the misconduct of their employees.

Livestock insurance

50.31 Livestock insurance is a relatively specialised market with a small number of product providers. It is encountered in both the commercial market and the domestic market, the latter in the form of insurance of domestic pets. The risks covered by livestock policies are varied. It is possible to obtain what is in effect a form of life assurance for animals, a set sum being payable on death, but it is also possible to obtain cover which is the equivalent of medical expenses insurance.

Slaughter without insurer's consent

50.32 It is common to require that an insured animal shall not be slaughtered without the insurer's consent. This clause is no doubt inserted to discourage policyholders from claiming for unnecessary slaughter. However, the term is rarely made a condition precedent of liability, and there will inevitably be cases where the insurer's consent is not sought, but where it is apparent that the slaughter was necessary (this view may be backed by the opinion of a vet). In such circumstances the strict legal position would seem to be that the loss is covered, and the Insurance Ombudsman has held[1] that insurers should not rely upon this exclusion in such cases. It may be supposed that this view would be maintained even if obtaining a vet's consent were expressed to be a condition precedent to liability.

A common provision in livestock policies is that slaughter will only be an insured peril if it occurs in the same period of insurance during which the illness arises which requires the slaughter. This can produce obvious anomalies where the illness arises at the very end of one period of insurance and slaughter happens very early in the next period of insurance. In one IOB case[2] the Ombudsman held that reliance upon this clause was incompatible with the spirit of UCTA 1977.

Issues of non-disclosure can also arise in livestock policies. Insurers are naturally concerned with the medical history of any animal being insured, but it appears[3] that proposal forms are not always sufficiently precise or detailed in the information for which they ask. Many livestock policies are personal lines policies, and insurers need to have firmly in mind the requirement to ask clear questions about those matters which are material.

1 IOB 4.13; contrast IOB 4.12 where the policyholder was unable to produce any proper evidence of the need for slaughter, and the complaint was rejected.
2 IOB 4.13.
3 See for example IOB 5.14.

Medical expenses insurance

50.33 Medical expenses insurance is a growing market within the UK. This may be seen as reflecting increased unease about the quality and availability of appropriate care under the NHS.

Medical expenses insurance is often written as long-term insurance business, though it can also be written on a short-term basis. Premiums are normally age-related, and in most cases there is no no claims discount.

Risks covered

50.34 Most policies cover advice, treatment and post-treatment care, though there are sometimes financial limits, either for a claims year as a whole or for specific heads within these categories.

Standard exclusions

50.35 It is common to exclude conditions which existed before the policy was taken out. Sometimes there are permanently excluded, in other cases the exclusion applies for one or two years after the inception of the policy.

The Insurance Ombudsman has had to consider issues arising in medical expenses policies on a number of occasions.

Moratorium clauses

50.36 It is usual for policies of this type to include a moratorium clause which excludes cover for pre-existing conditions for a specified period of time after the commencement of the policy. One consequence of this is that proposal forms do not normally ask for disclosure of medical history. Unfortunately, this leads some policyholders to believe that their medical history is not relevant, and problems then arise when a claim for treatment for a pre-existing condition is rejected. On the one hand it may be said that since all medical insurers use such clauses, a policyholder is not especially disadvantaged by the clause of any one insurer[1]. On the other hand at least some policyholders might not take out the policy at all if they understood the deferment clause properly. In one IOB case[2] an insurer was required to make a full refund of premiums where a policyholder had switched from one insurer to another and had then been caught by the deferment clause. This case may also be regarded as illustrating one particular consequence of deferment clauses, namely that a policyholder who has any existing condition will very rarely be well-advised to change insurers.

Moratorium clauses commonly apply also to conditions 'related' to any pre-existing conditions. Where a policyholder needed treatment within the deferment period for varicose eczema, the Insurance Ombudsman held[3] that this was a condition related to the varicose veins which he had suffered before the inception of the policy.

Another problem arising from moratorium clauses is that many of them continue to apply until a period (commonly two years) has elapsed since the inception of the policy during which the policyholder has not received treatment or advice for the condition in question. This can have unfortunate effects for a policyholder whose post-operation care includes regular check-ups to monitor his progress. If every such check-up is considered to amount to advice in relation to the condition, then it may be many years before the deferment period in relation to that condition expires. The Insurance Ombudsman has given guidance[4] on his approach to such cases. He looks at whether the check-up was purely cursory or whether it involved substantial tests, and at whether it was conducted at the request of the doctor or on the policyholder's own initiative. Where the doctor wants to conduct substantial tests, this is a strong pointer towards the conclusion that the process involves advice within the meaning of the moratorium clause. Although the Ombudsman says that these criteria are applied as part of the process of reaching a fair and reasonable decision, it is submitted that the term 'advice' in relation to policies of this kind is open to a certain amount of interpretation and that there is no reason why a court should not adopt a very similar approach should the occasion arise. It must of course be acknowledged that clauses of this kind do create an unfortunate incentive for policyholders to neglect to go for post-treatment check-ups so as to cause the deferment period to expire as soon as possible[5].

[1] Though this would presumably be different if one insurer had a longer deferment period than was normal in the industry.
[2] IOB 4.4.
[3] IOB 8.9.
[4] IOB 9, leading article.
[5] IOB 15.8.

Specialists

50.37 Policies commonly provide that treatment must be given by an appropriately qualified specialist; it may even be necessary for the specialist to be someone recognised by the insurers. The Ombudsman has been prepared to construe requirements of this kind strictly, especially where there is a prior authorisation procedure[1].

[1] IOB 23.26.

Acute and chronic illness

50.38 It may generally be said that medical expenses policies are intended to cover acute conditions, but not chronic conditions. The Ombudsman has been prepared to recognise this principle, but the result has not always been to favour insurers. In one case[1] the policyholder suffered from chronic deafness. She had used a conventional hearing aid for some years, but this was causing increasingly common ear infections. The insurers refused to pay for the fitting of a bone-anchored hearing aid which was likely to eliminate these problems. The Ombudsman upheld the complaint. The operation was not done to relieve the chronic deafness, but to relieve the acute infections, and this was covered under the policy.

[1] IOB 23.25.

Cosmetic treatment

50.39 This is another fairly standard exclusion. In one IOB case[1] the policyholder had had a mastectomy. Following this there was some reconstruction of the breast which had been operated on and some realignment of her other breast. The insurers declined to pay for these operations, contending that they were cosmetic, but the Ombudsman disagreed, holding that they were a necessary part of completing the treatment. The decision appears humane, but more generous than the law would allow. The exclusion referred to cosmetic treatment, whether or not for psychological purposes, and it is hard to see why the reconstruction or the realignment were medically necessary.

[1] IOB 23.21.

Pregnancy etc

50.40 Many medical expenses policies exclude cover for care associated with pregnancy and childbirth. It is also common to exclude cover for other fertility problems. In one IOB case[1] the policyholder had an operation to terminate an ectopic pregnancy. The insurers relied upon an exclusion for 'treatment arising directly or indirectly from pregnancy, termination of pregnancy or childbirth' but the Ombudsman rejected this defence. There is an agreement between the insurance industry and the Equal Opportunities Commission to the effect that exclusions relating to pregnancy will be narrowly construed as applying only to claims relating to normal pregnancy and childbirth. In its terms this agreement relates only to payment protection policies[2], but the Ombudsman concluded that the same principle should apply to medical expenses policies. Consequently, the exclusion was held not to apply to emergency treatment in a case such as this.

A more unusual IOB case occurred[3] where the policyholder had chronic Antiphospholid Antibody Syndrome which required treatment during pregnancy but not at other times. The policy covered 'treatment of a medical condition which was due to or occurred during pregnancy or childbirth' (though not the pregnancy or childbirth itself) but the insurers declined to pay for the treatment on the ground that the *condition* existed at all times, even though the *treatment* was required only during pregnancy. The Ombudsman upheld this refusal, taking the view that the policy was intended to cover acute conditions, but not chronic conditions[4].

[1] IOB 23.22.
[2] As to which see Chapter 43.
[3] IOB 23.23.
[4] See also 'Acute and chronic conditions' above.

Part I

Miscellaneous

Chapter 51

Conflict of laws

51.1 Although the general principles of the conflict of laws are well-settled, their application in the context of insurance law can give rise to particular problems. This Chapter proceeds on the basis of the standard division of conflict of laws issues into jurisdiction, choice of law and enforcement. However, insurance and reinsurance must be dealt with separately because the Rome Convention[1] on applicable law applies to the latter but not to the former. Most of the reported case law in this area concerns questions of jurisdiction, though there are more recent authorities dealing with choice of law.

[1] Implemented in English law by the C(AL)A 1990, s 2.

Jurisdiction

51.2 Given that the issues in an insurance case will normally be contractual, it is possible for the policy to make express provision for which court is to have jurisdiction over disputes, and it is usual to do so. In international disputes at the present day it is normally necessary to have regard to the principles laid down in the Brussels and Lugano Conventions in order to establish jurisdiction. The Brussels Convention applies between members of the EU, whereas the Lugano Convention applies to members of EFTA who are not also EU members. The common law principles continue to apply to cases where the foreign jurisdiction is neither an EU member nor an EFTA member. The rules are now collected together in Regulation 44/2001[3], which, as appears below, contains a number of important provisions aimed specifically at insurance.

[1] 2001 OJ L 12.

51.3 The general rule is that persons domiciled in a Member State shall, whatever their nationality, be sued in the courts of that Member State, and persons who are not nationals of the Member State in which they are domiciled shall be governed by the rules of jurisdiction applicable to nationals of that State[1]. Persons domiciled in a Member State may be sued in the courts of another Member State only by virtue of the rules set out in the following paragraphs. If the defendant is not domiciled in a Member State, the jurisdiction of the courts of each Member

State shall, subject to Articles 22 and 23, be determined by the law of that Member State[2]. As against such a defendant, any person domiciled in a Member State may, whatever his nationality, avail himself in that State of the rules of jurisdiction there in force[3].

1 Article 2.
2 Article 3.
3 Article 4.

Contract

51.4 A person domiciled in a Member State may, in another Member State, be sued in matters relating to a contract, in the courts for the place of performance of the obligation in question; for the purpose of this provision and unless otherwise agreed, the place of performance of the obligation in question shall be in the case of the provision of services, the place in a Member State where, under the contract, the services were provided or should have been provided[1].

1 Article 5.

51.5 A person domiciled in a Member State may also be sued:

(1) where he is one of a number of defendants, in the courts for the place where any one of them is domiciled, provided the claims are so closely connected that it is expedient to hear and determine them together to avoid the risk of irreconcilable judgments resulting from separate proceedings;
(2) as a third party in an action on a warranty or guarantee or in any other third party proceedings, in the court seised of the original proceedings, unless these were instituted solely with the object of removing him from the jurisdiction of the court which would be competent in his case;
(3) on a counter-claim arising from the same contract or facts on which the original claim was based, in the court in which the original claim is pending;
(4) in matters relating to a contract, if the action may be combined with an action against the same defendant in matters relating to rights in immovable property, in the court of the Member State in which the property is situated[1].

The identical provisions of Article 5 of the Lugano Convention were considered in *Agnew v Lansforakringbolagens AB*[2], where the House of Lords had to decide whether an action brought by reinsurers to cancel and avoid contracts of reinsurance on grounds of 'misrepresentation of and/or failure to disclose and/or non-disclosure of material facts' was a matter relating to a contract so as to fall within Article 5(1) and so as to oust the jurisdiction of Article 2 pursuant to which a defendant has to be sued in the country in which he is domiciled.

Having first held that reinsurance is within the scope of the Lugano Convention (as primary insurance is not) the House of Lords held by a bare majority that Article 5(1) did apply. Although the duty of utmost good faith arises under the general law, if it did not exist as a matter of general law the parties would no doubt include it as an express term. It would be invidious to draw fine distinctions between duties which arise under the general law and those which arise as express terms of the contract. Equally it would be invidious to distinguish between pre-contractual and post-contractual obligations of good faith. The sensible course would be to regard them all as arising under the contract and therefore within Article 5(1). An obligation which, if not fulfilled, gives rise to a right to set aside a contract, is properly described as an obligation under that contract[3].

[1] Article 6.
[2] [2000] Lloyd's Rep IR 317, HL.
[3] The position would be different if breach of the obligation made the contract void *ab initio*: see *Kleinwort Benson Ltd v Glasgow City Council* [1999] 1 AC 153, HL.

51.6 A similar point arose in *AIG Europe (UK) Ltd v Anonymous Greek Insurance Co of General Insurances*[1], where reinsurers sought a series of negative declarations relating to their liability to primary insurers. The claim was based on alleged breaches of loss control clauses and alleged failures to give proper notice of claims. The case was argued on the basis that the loss control provisions were to be performed in Greece, but that the notice provisions were to be performed in London[2]. This was therefore a case where there was more than one obligation. The Court of Appeal held that in such circumstances the proper approach to Article 5(1) was to decide which of the obligations was in fact the principal obligation[3]. This is a matter of fact and cannot be affected by the characterisation which either party chooses to put on the matter. On the facts it was held that the notice provisions were the principal obligations, with the result that the English court had jurisdiction.

[1] [2000] Lloyd's Rep IR 343, CA.
[2] It is these obligations which have to be considered rather than the obligation under the contract to provide indemnity, since the applicant is alleging that this latter obligation is no longer binding on him.
[3] See also *Shenavi v Kreischer* [1987] ECR 239, ECJ; *Union Transport plc v Continental Lines SA* [1992] 1 Lloyd's Rep 229, HL.

Special rules for insurance

51.7

(1) An insurer domiciled in a Member State may be sued:
  (a) in the courts of the Member State where he is domiciled, or
  (b) in another Member State, in the case of actions brought by the policyholder, the insured or a beneficiary, in the courts for the place where the plaintiff is domiciled,
  (c) if he is a co-insurer, in the courts of a Member State in which proceedings are brought against the leading insurer.
(2) An insurer who is not domiciled in a Member State but has a branch, agency or other establishment in one of the Member States shall, in disputes arising out of the operations of the branch, agency or establishment, be deemed to be domiciled in that Member State[1].

In dealing with all the provisions it is important to be aware that 'domicile' in private international law is not at all the same thing as residence[2]. Domicile may be briefly described as referring to a person's permanent home country. So far as companies are concerned, the domicile is likely to be the place of incorporation, even when the headquarters is elsewhere.

An insurer who is not domiciled in a Contracting State but has a branch, agency or other establishment in one of the Contracting States shall, in disputes arising out of the operations of the branch, agency or establishment, be deemed to be domiciled in that State[3]. The rule that the proper focus for the action depends upon the defendant's location, rather than on that of the claimant applies whenever the defendant is domiciled within a Contracting State, even if the claimant is not domiciled in a Contracting State[4]. However, this applies only to primary insurance. The purpose of the rule is to protect primary insureds who are normally the weaker party in the insurance contract. This consideration is irrelevant in the case of reinsurance, so the rule does not apply to reinsurance[5].

In *Fisher v Unione Italiana De Riassicurazione SpA*[6] the claimant was a Lloyd's syndicate which reinsured the defendant, an Italian reinsurance company, by way of a Lloyd's policy (the retrocession contract). The retrocession contract contained a warranty that the defendant would retain a proportion of the original risk. The claimant issued a writ seeking a declaration that it was not liable because of the defendant's breach of the retrocession contract in failing to retain any part of the risk. A writ was issued in England and served on the defendant in Rome at their registered office under RSC Order 11[7]. The defendant's domicile was in Italy. The defendant applied under RSC Order 12, r 8 to set aside the writ on the ground that the English court had no jurisdiction.

The question to be determined was what was the obligation in question – the obligation of the claimant to pay under the retrocession (in England) or the obligation of the defendant to comply with a warranted retention of risk (in Italy, being the defendant's principal place of business).

It was held that a retrocessionaire wishing to deny liability has to plead the basis for that denial. If the basis is the reinsured's breach of a contractual provision that provision is the obligation in question. In this case the obligation was the retention of risk warranty. It is then necessary to determine where that obligation was to have been performed. In this case that was Italy and so the English court had no jurisdiction.

1 Article 9.
2 A more detailed discussion of the distinction will be found in any major private international law textbook. The leading such work is Dicey and Morris *The Conflict of Laws* (13th edn, 1999; 14th edn due September 2006, Sweet & Maxwell). A more manageable guide is Morris *The Conflict of Laws*, (6th edn, 2005, Sweet & Maxwell).
3 Article 9.
4 *Universal General Insurance Co (UGIC) v Group Josi Reinsurance Co SA* [2001] Lloyd's Rep IR 483, ECJ where the claimant was domiciled in Canada.
5 See n 4 above.
6 [1999] Lloyd's Rep IR 215.
7 See below for more detailed treatment of this provision and its successor.

51.8 In respect of liability insurance or insurance of immovable property, the insurer may in addition be sued in the courts for the place where the harmful event occurred. The same applies if movable and immovable property are covered by the same insurance policy and both are adversely affected by the same contingency[1].

1 Article 10.

51.9

(1) In respect of liability insurance, the insurer may also, if the law of the court permits it, be joined in proceedings which the injured party has brought against the insured.

(2) Articles 8, 9 and 10 shall apply to actions brought by the injured party directly against the insurer, where such direct actions are permitted.

(3) If the law governing such direct actions provides that the policyholder or the insured may be joined as a party to the action, the same court shall have jurisdiction over them[1]. Without prejudice to this rule , an insurer may bring proceedings only in the courts of the Member State in which the defendant is domiciled, irrespective of whether he is the policyholder, the insured or a beneficiary.

In *Jordan Grand Prix Ltd v Baltic Insurance Group; Baltic Insurance Group v Jordan Grand Prix Ltd*[1] an insurance company from Lithuania, at that time a non-Contracting State, had proceedings brought against it in England by an English company. The question was whether the Lithuanian insurance company could add Irish parties to its counterclaim in those proceedings. It was held that (1) Article 11 applies to all insurers, wherever domiciled – ie it extends to insurers domiciled in non-Contracting States. However, the reference to 'counterclaim' in Article 11 covers only a counterclaim against the original claimant and does not extend to counterclaims against new parties. Accordingly the insurance company could not join the Irish parties to the proceedings in England.

In *New Hampshire Insurance Co v Strabag Bau AG*[2] the Court of Appeal considered the application of Article 11 and the meaning of the words 'matter relating to insurance' in s 3 of the Brussels Convention. The claimant insurers sought a declaration that they were entitled to avoid a commercial policy, and proceedings were begun in the English court, notwithstanding that the defendants were companies domiciled in Germany. Article 11 of the Brussels Convention provides:

> 'An Insurer may bring proceedings only in the Courts of the Contracting State in which the defendant is domiciled …'

At first sight this would seem decisive, but the insurers sought to rely upon Article 35 of the Accession Convention[3] under which the UK became a party to the Brussels Convention. It was held that Article 35 applied only where there was an express written choice of law by the parties and did not invite or import the application of tests of the kind appropriate to determine the proper law of the contract in the absence of an express choice of law clause. There was no such clause in the present case. The court also rejected an argument that this provision was intended to apply only where the insured was a private consumer. Instead it applies to all disputes under policies of insurance, no matter what their capacity.

The provisions of this Section shall not affect the right to bring a counter-claim in the court in which, in accordance with this Section, the original claim is pending.

1 [1999] 2 AC 127, HL.

2 [1992] 1 Lloyd's Rep 361, CA.

3 The Convention on the accession to the 1968 Convention and the 1971 Protocol of Denmark, the Republic of Ireland and the UK, signed at Luxembourg on 9 October 1978.

Derogating from the insurance rules

51.10 The special rules relating to jurisdiction in insurance matters may be departed from only by an agreement which meets the following criteria:

(1) it is entered into after the dispute has arisen; or
(2) it allows the policyholder, the insured or a beneficiary to bring proceedings in courts other than those indicated in this Section; or
(3) it is concluded between a policyholder and an insurer, both of whom are at the time of conclusion of the contract domiciled or habitually resident in the same Member State, and which has the effect of conferring jurisdiction on the courts of that State even if the harmful event were to occur abroad, provided that such an agreement is not contrary to the law of that State; or
(4) it is concluded with a policyholder who is not domiciled in a Member State, except in so far as the insurance is compulsory or relates to immovable property in a Member State; or
(5) it relates to a contract of insurance in so far as it covers one or more of the risks set out in Article 14, namely–

1 any loss of or damage to:

(a) seagoing ships, installations situated offshore or on the high seas, or aircraft, arising from perils which relate to their use for commercial purposes;

(b) goods in transit other than passengers' baggage where the transit consists of or includes carriage by such ships or aircraft;

2 any liability, other than for bodily injury to passengers or loss of or damage to their baggage:

(a) arising out of the use or operation of ships, installations or aircraft as referred to in point 1(a) in so far as, in respect of the latter, the law of the Member State in which such aircraft are registered does not prohibit agreements on jurisdiction regarding insurance of such risks;

(b) for loss or damage caused by goods in transit as described in point 1(b);

3 any financial loss connected with the use or operation of ships, installations or aircraft as referred to in point 1(a), in particular loss of freight or charter-hire;

4 any risk or interest connected with any of those referred to in points 1 to 3;

notwithstanding points 1 to 4, all 'large risks' as defined in Council Directive 73/239/EEC(7), as amended by Council Directives 88/357/EEC(8) and 90/618/EEC(9), as they may be amended[1].

[1] Articles 13 and 14.

Prorogation of jurisdiction

51.11

(1) If the parties, one or more of whom is domiciled in a Member State, have agreed that a court or the courts of a Member State are to have jurisdiction to settle any disputes which have arisen or which may arise in connection with a

particular legal relationship, that court or those courts shall have jurisdiction. Such jurisdiction shall be exclusive unless the parties have agreed otherwise. Such an agreement conferring jurisdiction shall be either:

(a) in writing or evidenced in writing; or

(b) in a form which accords with practices which the parties have established between themselves; or

(c) in international trade or commerce, in a form which accords with a usage of which the parties are or ought to have been aware and which in such trade or commerce is widely known to, and regularly observed by, parties to contracts of the type involved in the particular trade or commerce concerned.

The consensus must be clearly and precisely demonstrated[1].

(2) Any communication by electronic means which provides a durable record of the agreement shall be equivalent to 'writing'.

(3) Where such an agreement is concluded by parties, none of whom is domiciled in a Member State, the courts of other Member States shall have no jurisdiction over their disputes unless the court or courts chosen have declined jurisdiction.

(4) The court or courts of a Member State on which a trust instrument has conferred jurisdiction shall have exclusive jurisdiction in any proceedings brought against a settlor, trustee or beneficiary, if relations between these persons or their rights or obligations under the trust are involved.

(5) Agreements or provisions of a trust instrument conferring jurisdiction shall have no legal force if they are contrary to Articles 13, 17 or 21, or if the courts whose jurisdiction they purport to exclude have exclusive jurisdiction by virtue of Article 22[2].

[1] *Prifti v Musini Sociedad Anonima de Seguros y Reaseguros* [2004] Lloyd's Rep IR 528, Andrew Smith J. See also *Salotti v RUWA Polstereimaschinen GmbH* [1976] ECR 1831.
[2] Article 23.

51.12

(1) Where related actions are pending in the courts of different Member States, any court other than the court first seised may stay its proceedings[1].

(2) Where these actions are pending at first instance, any court other than the court first seised may also, on the application of one of the parties, decline jurisdiction if the court first seised has jurisdiction over the actions in question and its law permits the consolidation thereof.

(3) For the purposes of this Article, actions are deemed to be related where they are so closely connected that it is expedient to hear and determine them together to avoid the risk of irreconcilable judgments resulting from separate proceedings[2]. This form of words appears to resolve the difficulties arising under Article 21 of the Brussels Convention, which was considered by The ECJ in *Drouot Assurances SA v Consolidated Metallurgical Industries*[3]. This was a maritime insurance case, where proceedings had been instituted in the Netherlands, and further proceedings were subsequently begun in France. Article 21 requires a court to decline jurisdiction if it appears that proceedings involving the same party and the same cause of action are already proceeding in another Convention country. The complicating factor in the present case was that in the Netherlands proceedings the insurers were not expressed to be parties to the proceedings, because Dutch law does not permit them to be named as parties, even where the action is being brought

on their behalf and is in effect being conducted by them. No such rule exists in France. Consequently the parties to the two actions were, at least nominally, not the same. The question referred to the ECJ was whether in these circumstances Article 21 should apply. The court ruled that Article 21 must be construed in a purposive manner. Its purpose was to avoid parallel proceedings before the courts of two different states with the consequent risk of conflicting decisions. The question therefore was whether there was such an identity of interest between insured and insurer that a judgment against one would have the force of *res judicata* against the other. The example which the court offers of this phenomenon is the exercise of rights through the doctrine of subrogation, where the insurer is simply standing in the shoes of the insured. Here it is clear that Article 21 applies, whatever name is being used in the action. The position is otherwise where the interests of insured and insurer diverge to a significant extent. The complexity in the present case was that the insurers of the hull had at their own expense refloated a stranded ship so as to allow salvage of the cargo. In the Dutch action the cargo insurers sued the master of the vessel for negligence in allowing it to become stranded. The hull insurers could not be joined to this action. In the French action the hull insurers claimed general average contribution against the cargo insurers. Thus the hull insurers were acting not in their capacity as insurers, but in their capacity as participants in the refloating exercise, and there was therefore not identity of interest between insured and insurer, with the result that Article 21 did not apply.

[1] Article 28.
[2] Applied in *Prifti v Musini Sociedad Anonima de Seguros y Reaseguros* [2004] Lloyd's Rep IR 528, Andrew Smith J.
[3] [1999] LRLR 338, ECJ.

51.13 Section 51 of the SCA 1981 In *National Justice Compania Naviera SA v Prudential Life Assurance Co Ltd, sub nom 'The Ikarian Reefer (no 2)'*[1] a jurisdictional challenge was raised by a non-party to the action, who was domiciled in Greece, to an application by the defendant to make him personally liable pursuant to s 51 of the SCA 1981 for the balance of the unpaid costs of the action. The Court of Appeal found that the vessel had been deliberately run aground and then deliberately set on fire on the authority of her owners. Costs were awarded to the defendants and the outstanding claim was for over £2.6m. The defendants alleged that the non-party (C) instituted, controlled and financed a fraudulent claim in respect of the scuttling of his company's vessel. Personal service was effected on C in Greece. C disputed the jurisdiction of the English court on the grounds that he was a Greek domiciliary and the attempt to render him liable for the defendant's costs was a civil or commercial matter under Article 1 of the Brussels Convention 1968. He should therefore be sued in Greece (Article 2) and none of the special jurisdictions under Article 6 applied. Article 25 by expressly providing that a 'determination of costs' was a 'judgment' within the meaning of the Convention, emphasised that the application to make C liable for costs, was a matter within the scope of the Convention in respect of which suit would have to be brought against him in Greece.

If however, the application against C was to be viewed as merely ancillary to the owners' action, then it arose in 'matters relating to insurance' within art 7 so that art 11 applied and C would have to be sued in Greece. In any event C argued that no leave had been sought or granted to serve the summons on him out of the jurisdiction. The defendant argued that the application against C was merely an incident of the owners' action which was properly rooted in England where the defendant was incorporated and domiciled and that the defendant did not therefore have to show that jurisdiction for that application could be separately founded for the purposes of the Convention.

The claim for costs under s 51 could not be sustained as a separate cause of action divorced from the substantive action in which the costs had been incurred and therefore there could be no question of C being 'sued' for the costs within Article 2. Such suit required a list and a cause of action which was capable of being brought separately. The Convention simply did not apply. Alternatively, the defendant's application could be brought within the Convention under Article 6. The Court of Appeal held that s 51 of the SCA 1981 gave it a statutory discretion in respect of costs, which was given to the court purely for the purposes of the proceedings before it. If C was not amenable to the jurisdiction of the English court in respect of the defendant's application, then he would be amenable nowhere else and not in Greece where he was domiciled. Where a non-party is out of the jurisdiction, leave is necessary under RSC Order 11, r 9(4). It could not be assumed that the non-party was already before the court as the real party in the action, since that would be the issue in the summons. A sufficient case for leave for service out of the jurisdiction in the discretion of the court should be made good. Under the CPR 1998 this would be the standard situation: there must be permission to join the non-party (CPR 1998 19.3) and permission, where necessary, to serve the new party out of the jurisdiction. In such a case, the applicant would prima facie have to bring himself within RSC Order 11, r 1. However, it was not at all clear that such use of Order 11 was within the rationale of *Siskina (Cargo Owners) v Distos SA*[2] or *Mercedes Benz AG v Leiduck*[3]. Moreover, once judgment with costs had been given against the party served within the jurisdiction, it was unclear how any applicant could bring himself within RSC Order 11, r 4(1)(d), for there was no longer any issue, not even one regarding costs, for trial involving that party. Sub-rule r (1)(c) and r 4(1)(d) would not seem to work in the case of a successful defendant who sought to join a non-party for the purpose of costs. In the circumstances, the judge suggested that it must be implicit in the new rule or inherent in the court's jurisdiction that, for the purposes of costs, the court had power to give permission to serve out on being satisfied that an appropriate case for it had been made good. The Brussels Convention does not apply to a claim under s 51 of the SCA 1981 as such an application is incidental to the court's substantive jurisdiction over its own process, including that of determining liability for costs incurred in that process. Against the possibility that this conclusion was incorrect, the judge considered the possible application of Article 6 to the case. Neither Article 6(1) nor 6(3) would assist the defendant. Article 6(2) offered the best possible route to jurisdiction under the Convention for a s 51 claim against a non-party. However, he indicated this view without intending to decide the point. The defendant's s 51 claim was not a claim 'in matters relating to insurance' but a claim in relation to costs. In general, this consideration of the possible bases of jurisdiction under the Convention merely served to demonstrate that the Convention was not designed to deal with an incidental claim for costs arising under the statutory discretion of the court seized of the proceedings in question. Consequently, the court had jurisdiction over C and Title II of the Brussels Convention did not apply to the defendant's s 51 claim against him. The fact that the defendant had not sought leave or permission to serve out of the jurisdiction would not necessarily nullify the defendant's summons. Retrospective leave should be given.

1 [2000] Lloyd's Rep IR 230, Rix J.
2 [1979] AC 210.
3 [1996] AC 284, PC.

Non-European cases

51.14 Where the defendant is not domiciled in any European country, so that none of the Conventions already discussed apply, an action can be brought in the English court if the defendant has some presence within the jurisdiction, since it is then possible to serve the claim form upon him, an essential precondition to the maintaining of an action. In the case of an individual defendant, this means a physical presence – a claim form can be served on any defendant who is physically present within the jurisdiction, even if he is only passing through the country and had no permanent presence in it.

In the case of a company the position is more difficult, since a company cannot be physically present anywhere. The rules are as follows:

A company registered in England is regarded as present here, and service upon it can be effected at the registered office[1].

A foreign company (ie one not registered in England) which has a branch[2] here must register with the Registrar of Companies the names and addresses of all persons authorised to accept service on its behalf[3]. Any document (including a claim form or other legal process) connected with the carrying on of business at that branch may then validly be served upon any of those so named[4].

A foreign company which carries on business here without a branch must similarly file with the Registrar a list of those authorised to accept service on its behalf[5]. Process may validly be served on anyone so named, and there is no requirement that the process be associated with the carrying on of business at that place[6].

1 Companies Act 1985, s 725.
2 Within the meaning of the Eleventh Company Law Directive. See Cheshire and North *Private International Law* (13th edn, 1999, Butterworths), pp 289–291 for a discussion of the problems of the term 'branch' in this context.
3 Companies Act 1985, s 690A.
4 Companies Act 1985, s 694A(2).
5 Companies Act 1985, s 690B.
6 Companies Act 1985, s 691.

Service of proceedings outside England and Wales

51.15 Where it is desired to serve the claim form on the defendant outside the jurisdiction the matter is governed by CPR 1998, 6.17–6.31[1]. CPR 1998, 6.19 provides that this may be done without the permission of the court if every claim made in the claim form is one which the court would have jurisdiction to hear under the Brussels or Lugano Conventions, and no proceedings in relation to the matter are pending in any other Convention State and the defendant is domiciled in a Convention State. Effectively, if the matter is concerned only with Convention States and their domiciliaries, then it is automatic that proceedings can be served out of the jurisdiction.

Where these requirements are not satisfied (most commonly because the defendant is domiciled outside the Convention States) the permission of the court is required before service can be effected. CPR 1998, 6.20 deals with these cases and lists a number of cases where the court may give permission for such service. The present discussion concentrates on those which are likely to be important in an insurance law context:

- CPR 1998, 6.20(1) covers the case where a remedy is sought against a person who is domiciled within the jurisdiction.
- CPR 1998, 6.20(5) allows the court to give permission in a contract claim where the contract:
  - (a) was made within the jurisdiction;
  - (b) was made by or through an agent trading or residing within the jurisdiction;
  - (c) is governed by English law;
  - (d) contains a term to the effect that the court shall have jurisdiction to determine claims in respect of the contract.
- CPR 1998, 6.20(6) extends the power to give permission to the case where the breach of contract is alleged to have been committed within the jurisdiction.
- CPR 1998, 6.20(5) and (6) are clearly of great practical importance in insurance law, since there will be many cases of insurance contracts made with foreign insurers which nevertheless meet one or more of these requirements.
- CPR 1998, 6.20(7) applies where a claim is made for a declaration that no contract exists, but the contract, if found to exist, would fall within CPR 1998, 6.20(5).

[1] Formerly RSC Order 11, though the new rules have minor differences. A full discussion of these rules may be found in Volume 1 of *Civil Procedure* (2006, Sweet and Maxwell).

51.16 The Lugano Rules do not of themselves exclude the possibility that a court will decline to hear an action on the ground of *forum non conveniens*, ie that there is another jurisdiction which is more appropriate to the trial of the action. In *Ace Insurance SA-NV v Zurich Insurance Co*[1] a reinsurance contract included a clause waiving any objection to Texan jurisdiction. It was held that the court could take this into account when deciding whether to hear the case. The defendant was domiciled in Switzerland, but the Court of Appeal held that the result would be the same in the case of an English-domiciled defendant[2].

[1] [2001] 1 All ER Comm 802; see also *Re Harrods (Buenos Aires) Ltd* [1991] 4 All ER 334.

[2] At paras [30]–[44]. See also *American Specialty Lines Insurance Co v Abbott Laboratories* [2004] Lloyd's Rep IR 815, Cresswell J.

51.17 In *New Hampshire Insurance Co v Philips Electronics Corpn North America Ltd*[1] the Court of Appeal dealt with an unusual case of the commencement of apparently pre-emptive litigation by insurers. The policy in this case was an employees' fidelity policy, under which the insured had submitted claims relating to events alleged to have happened in Illinois. The policy required the insured to wait at least 90 days after submitting their proof of loss to the insurers before commencing proceedings. The insurers alleged that on the proper construction of the policies some of the alleged events did not fall within the scope of the policy. Because of the commercially sensitive nature of the alleged losses the policyholders were reluctant to begin legal proceedings, but at the end of the 90-day period the insurers began proceedings in the Commercial Court claiming declarations that the facts alleged, even if true, did not give rise to valid claims under the policies. The writ was served out of the jurisdiction, pursuant to RSC Order 11[2], but the policyholders sought to have the service set aside on the ground that the appropriate forum was Illinois. The Court of Appeal upheld the decision of Rix J that whilst Illinois would be the appropriate forum for resolving disputed issues of fact, England would be the appropriate forum for resolving disputed questions of law. Although a negative declaration is an unusual form of relief, which will be granted only where there are very good reasons for doing so[3], these reasons did exist in the present case because the insurers were treating these proceedings in the nature of a test case to resolve general issues about the scope of their standard-form wording for policies of this type. This effectively left them in the position of being the natural claimants. However, the court must be careful to satisfy itself that the proceedings were not merely an attempt to pre-empt litigation in another more appropriate forum. That requirement was also satisfied here; the policies were governed by English law, and the English court was an appropriate place to resolve the legal issues. It was also relevant that the answers given to the questions of law raised in these proceedings might well prove to be decisive of the whole claim, thus saving the considerable expense associated with a trial as to the disputed factual issues. It was therefore proper in the particular circumstances to proceed with the application for negative relief.

1 [1999] Lloyd's Rep IR 58, CA.
2 Which was then the relevant provision.
3 *Camilla Cotton Oil Co v Granadex SA and Tracomin SA* [1976] 2 Lloyd's Rep 10, HL; in the particular context of Ord 11; see also *Insurance Corpn of Ireland v Strombus International Insurance Co* [1985] 2 Lloyd's Rep 138, CA.

51.18 Although applications of this kind will not commonly be considered acceptable, it is clear that there may be cases where it will be appropriate for insurers to issue such proceedings. As it happens, the particular facts of this dispute also involved a foreign element, which somewhat complicates the position, but the principle is of general application.

In *Insurance Co 'Ingosstrakh' Ltd v Latvian Shipping Co*[1] a clause in the insurance contract provided that 'all disputed claims' between the insurer and the insured were to be litigated in Moscow. It was held that this constituted an exclusive Soviet jurisdiction clause in relation to all the common disputes between insurer and insured: the court therefore declined to entertain jurisdiction.

Langley J had held that that provision was limited to disputes in relation to insurance monies paid out by the insurer, whereas the action related to monies received by the Latvian Shipping Company from the third party. He further held that English law had been impliedly chosen as the system of law with which the contract had the closest connection having regard to the 'pivotal role' of the second claimant, a P & I club. It followed that RSC Order 11, r 1(1)(d) permitted the insurer to serve out. The Court of Appeal, reversing Langley J's decision, observed that there was no commercial logic to a clause which provided only for certain disputes to be dealt with in a particular way but made no provision in relation to other disputes[2]. In those circumstances, and given that neither party had any connection with England, leave to serve out was to be refused.

In *Gan Insurance Co Ltd and Eagle Star Insurance Co Ltd v Tai Ping Insurance Co Ltd*[3] the defendants were Taiwanese insurance companies who had underwritten a policy of insurance of a Taiwanese company responsible for the construction of a computer chip factory in Taiwan. Tai Ping obtained facultative reinsurance of its line from various reinsurers including Gan and Eagle Star. The other Taiwanese insurer obtained facultative reinsurance from eight separate reinsurers. A claim was made against the insurers. Tai Ping co-ordinated the handling of the claims on behalf of the insurers. The direct insurers purported to rescind on the grounds that the insured had breached certain provisions. The insured commenced proceedings and a settlement was reached. Subsequently the reinsurers commenced proceedings against the Taiwanese underwriters and sought leave to serve the writs in Taiwan.

The court had to consider whether England was the appropriate forum It was held that it clearly was: English law was the proper law of the contract; England was the natural and appropriate forum in which to deal with issues relating to avoidance and the alleged breach of the claims co-operation clauses because of the location of most of the witnesses and documents. It was held that Tai Ping would not be unduly prejudiced by having to join its Taiwanese brokers to the English proceedings as they were all familiar with English. The claim was for a declaration that the contract had been broken and was not a claim to enforce the contract. It was held that the agent had demonstrated that England was the most convenient forum in the interests of justice and of the parties. It made no difference that the claim was essentially one for negative declaratory relief.

1 14 July 1999, unreported, CA.
2 See also *Continental Bank NA v Aeakos Cia Naviera SA* [1994] 1 WLR 588.
3 [1999] Lloyd's Rep IR 229, CIA.

Choice of law

51.19 Again, the contractual context enables the use of express choice of law clauses, and these are commonly encountered. Because of this, there is relatively little case law.

The Rome Convention deals generally with issues of choice of law in a contractual context. However, attention is drawn to Article 1.3 and 1.4 of that Convention, which reads:

> '1.3. The rules of this Convention do not apply to contracts of insurance which cover risks situated in the territories of the Member States of the European Economic Community[1]. In order to determine whether a risk is situated in these territories the court shall apply its internal law.
> 1.4. The preceding paragraph does not apply to contracts of re-insurance.'

Thus, contracts of primary insurance are outside the Rome Convention, but reinsurance contracts are within it. In relation to primary insurance the position where the risk is situated within the EU is governed by the The Financial Services and Markets Act 2000 (Law Applicable to Contracts of Insurance) Regulations 2001[2] which provide as follows.

[1] Which should now be read as a reference to the EU. However, the Convention does apply to risks situated elsewhere, even if the contracting parties are domiciled in the EU.
[2] SI 2001/2635. The rules were formerly in Sch 3A to the Insurance Companies Act 1982.

Contracts of General Insurance

51.20 In relation to a contract of general insurance which covers risks situated in an EEA State the position is that if the policyholder resides in the EEA State in which the risk is situated, the applicable law is the law of that EEA State unless, if such a choice is permitted under the law of that EEA State, the parties to the contract choose the law of another country[1].

If the policyholder does not reside in the EEA State in which the risk is situated, the parties to the contract may choose as the applicable law either the law of the EEA State in which the risk is situated; or the law of the country in which the policyholder resides.

If the policyholder carries on a business (including a trade or profession) and the contract covers two or more risks relating to that business which are situated in different EEA States, the freedom of the parties to choose the applicable law conferred by this regulation extends to the law of any of those EEA States and of the country in which the policyholder resides.

If any of the EEA States referred to above grant greater freedom of choice of the applicable law, the parties to the contract may take advantage of that freedom. Moreover, if the risks covered by the contract are limited to events occurring in one EEA State other than the EEA State in which the risk is situated, the parties may choose the law of the former EEA State as the applicable law. If the risk covered by the contract is a large risk the parties may choose any law as the applicable law.

Where the foregoing rules allow the parties to the contract to choose the applicable law and if no choice has been made, or no choice has been made which satisfies the requirement set out in regulation 6(1), the applicable law is the law of the country, from amongst those considered in the relevant paragraph ('the relevant countries'), which is most closely connected with the contract[2]; however, where a severable part of the contract has a closer connection with another relevant country, the law applicable to that part is, by way of exception, the law of that relevant country, and the contract is rebuttably presumed to be most closely connected with the EEA State in which the risk is situated.

References to the EEA State where the risk covered by a contract of insurance is situated are to:

(a) if the contract relates to buildings or to buildings and their contents (in so far as the contents are covered by the same contract of insurance), the EEA State in which the property is situated;
(b) if the contract relates to vehicles of any type, the EEA State of registration;
(c) if the contract covers travel or holidays risks and has a duration of four months or less, the EEA State in which the policyholder entered into the contract;
(d) in any other case–
 (i) if the policyholder is an individual, the EEA State in which he resides on the date the contract is entered into;
 (ii) otherwise, the EEA State in which the establishment of the policyholder to which the contract relates is situated on that date.

References to the country in which a person resides are to:

(a) if he is an individual, the country in which he has his habitual residence;
(b) in any other case, the country in which he has his central administration.

Where an EEA State (including the United Kingdom) includes several territorial units, each of which has its own laws concerning contractual obligations, each unit is to be considered as a separate state for the purposes of identifying the applicable law under these Regulations.

Nothing in regulation 4 restricts the application of the mandatory rules of any part of the United Kingdom, irrespective of the applicable law of the contract. If the parties to the contract choose the applicable law under regulation 4 and if all the other elements relevant to the situation at the time when the parties make their choice are connected with one EEA State only, the application of the mandatory rules of that EEA State is not prejudiced.

Any choice made by the parties under regulation 4 must be expressed or demonstrated with reasonable certainty by the terms of the contract or the circumstances of the case. In *American Motorists Insurance Co v Cellstar Corporation*[3] the Claimant insurer, based in Texas, had negotiated insurance for its worldwide operations (which included but were by no means limited to EEA States) with insurers in Texas, and the policy used expressions which were found particularly in the law of Texas. Although there was no express choice of law, the Court of Appeal found that a choice of Texas law had been demonstrated with reasonable certainty. Alternatively, the Court would have held that Texas was the legal system with which the matter was most closely connected. In considering documents which purport to indicate a particular choice of law the court is likely to give more weight to documents specific to the particular risk than to general standard form conditions[4]:

(1) Subject to the preceding provisions of this Part, the 1990 Act is to be treated as applying to the contract for the purposes of determining the applicable law.
(2) In determining whether the mandatory rules of another EEA State should be applied in accordance with regulation 5(2) where the parties have chosen the law of a part of the United Kingdom as the applicable law, the 1990 Act is to be treated as applying to the contract.
(3) In determining what freedom of choice the parties have under the law of a part of the United Kingdom, the 1990 Act is to be treated as applying to the contract.

[1] Regulation 4.
[2] In *American Motorists Insurance Co v Cellstar Corpn* [2003] Lloyd's Rep IR 295, CA, Mance LJ suggested that this must leave the court free to select the country with which the contract would otherwise have had its closest connection. It is submitted that this observation is clearly correct, despite the somewhat inelegant drafting of the legislation.
[3] [2003] Lloyd's Rep IR 295, CA.
[4] *Evialis SA v SIAT* [2004] Lloyd's Rep IR 187, Andrew Smith J.

51.21 In the *Cellstar* case[1], and again in *Travelers Casualty and Surety Co of Europe Ltd v Sun Life Assurance Co of Canada (UK) Ltd*[2] it was emphasised that where a single policy covers risks in more than one country, the court is most unlikely to accept that the resulting litigation should be 'scissored-up' with different legal regimes applying to risks in each country. It is far more likely to hold that there is a single system of law applicable to the whole contract. This is self-evidently a sensible and desirable approach.

[1] [2003] Lloyd's Rep IR 295, CA; see previous paragraph.
[2] [2004] Lloyd's Rep IR 846, Jonathan Hirst QC.

Contracts of Long-Term Insurance

51.22 The position in relation to these is as follows where: (a) where the policyholder is an individual, he resides in an EEA State; (b) otherwise, the establishment of the policyholder to which the contract relates is situated in an EEA State. In such cases The applicable law is the law of the EEA State of the commitment unless, if such a choice is permitted under the law of that EEA State, the parties choose the law of another country. If the policyholder is an individual and resides in one EEA State but is a national or citizen of another, the parties to the contract may choose the law of the EEA State of which he is a national or citizen as the applicable law[1]. Nothing in regulation 8 affects the application of the mandatory rules of any part of the United Kingdom, irrespective of the applicable law of the contract and Subject to the preceding provisions mentioned in this paragraph, the 1990 Act is to be treated as applying to the contract for the purposes of determining the applicable law.) In determining what freedom of choice the parties have under the law of a part of the United Kingdom, the 1990 Act is to be treated as applying to the contract.

[1] Regulation 8.

Article 4 of the Rome Convention

51.23 This provides that in the absence of an express provision to the contrary a contract is governed by the law of the country with which it is most closely connected (effectively enacting the common law rule). Article 4(2) adds that there is a rebuttable presumption that this is the country where the party who is to perform the contract is situated (in a reinsurance contract this means the reinsurer[1]) The first issue therefore is whether there has been an express choice of law. In *Brotherton v Aseguadora Colseguros SA*[2] it was held that a mere reference in the quotation to 'Jurisdiction Clause as attached' when no such clause was in fact attached was insufficient to amount to an express choice of law.

[1] *Lincoln National Life Ins Co v Employers Reinsurance Corpn* [2002] Lloyd's Rep IR 853, Moore-Bick J. The rule was similarly applied in *Tryg Baltica International (UK) Ltd v Boston Compania de Seguros SA* [2005] Lloyd's Rep IR 40, Cooke J.
[2] [2002] Lloyd's Rep IR 848, David Steel J.

51.24 If there is no express choice, the court must form a view about which country has the closest connection with the policy. In *HIB Ltd v Guardian Insurance Co Inc*[1] the reinsured's agent who placed the reinsurance and the reinsurers were English companies but the reinsured was based in the US Virgin Islands. The question arose as to the governing law and appropriate forum. It was held that as the contract involved an English broker providing professional services in England to obtain reinsurance in England with an English company the contract was governed by English law. A similar approach was taken in *General Star International Indemnity Ltd v Stirling Cooke Brown Reinsurance Brokers Ltd*[2], where an anti-suit injunction was issued to restrain proceedings in New York which the judge regarded as a clear abuse of process on the basis that the case was clearly subject to English law. The same principle may be adopted where there is an arbitration agreement and one party seeks to avoid the effect of that by issuing in another jurisdcition[3].

[1] [1997] 1 Lloyd's Rep 412.
[2] [2003] Lloyd's Rep IR 719, Langley J.
[3] *Tonicstar Ltd v American Home Assurance Co* [2005] Lloyd's Rep IR 32, Morrison J.

Assignment

51.25 Where a policy to which the Rome Convention applies is assigned, the proper law of the policy will normally be the appropriate law for determining the validity of the assignment[1].

[1] Rome Convention, Art 12; and see *Rauffeusen Zentralank Osterreich AG v Five Star General Trading LLC* [2001] Lloyd's Rep IR 460, CA.

Non-European cases

51.26 In *Gan Insurance Co Ltd and Eagle Star Insurance Co Ltd v Tai Ping Insurance Co Ltd*[1] the facts of which were given above, a question as to the proper law of the contract also arose. It was held that in light of the placement of the reinsurance contracts in London with London market reinsurers and with regard to the terms of the slips which included standard London market wording there was an implied choice of English law 'demonstrated with reasonable certainty by the terms of the contract/the circumstances of the case' – ie the test under Article 3 of the Rome Convention was satisfied. It was also held that the reinsurance contracts had their closest connection with England. It was therefore held that the proper law of the contracts was English law.

[1] [1999] Lloyd's Rep IR 229.

Chapter 52

Lloyd's

52.1 The Lloyd's insurance market dates back to the eighteenth century, having developed from Lloyd's coffee house[1]. Over the past 300 years it has developed from a very small and informal arrangement into a major player on the world insurance scene, regulated now by a Private Act of Parliament. It merits separate treatment on three grounds. First, it has its own unique regulatory structure. Secondly, the way in which contracts are formed at Lloyd's differs from that in use elsewhere, and it is necessary to understand the Lloyd's system in order to deal with important issues about liability on Lloyd's policies. Thirdly, in recent years the Lloyd's market has undergone very substantial difficulties, leading to a major reconstruction.

[1] For a history of Lloyd's, including the background to some of the scandals of recent years see Geoffrey Hodgson *Lloyd's of London: A Reputation at Risk* (Revised edn, 1986 Penguin).

Regulatory structure

52.2 The regulatory structure of Lloyd's derives from the Lloyd's Act 1982, which is a private Act of Parliament. Lloyd's is governed by its Council, underwriters being organised in syndicates. The traditional principle of Lloyd's business has been that each underwriter writes business only for himself, there being no form of joint liability. Moreover, insurance is written by individual underwriters, not by the Corporation of Lloyds, which merely provides the facilities within which business is written. Before the reforms of the 1990s it had also always been fundamental to business at Lloyd's that every underwriter accepted unlimited liability for his share of the claims, but that principle has now been abandoned in favour of a degree of limited liability. The subject of the reform of Lloyd's is a large and contentious one, which cannot be examined in detail here. Fortunately, the changes made appear to have little impact on the way in which business is placed, nor on the issues of insurance contract law which arise in relation to Lloyd's.

The formation of contracts at Lloyd's

52.3 The syndicate system used by Lloyd's, coupled with the way in which business is conducted in the Room[1], gives rise to tricky technical issues about contractual formation.

The practice is as follows. A broker wishing to place insurance at Lloyd's writes on a slip of paper the major terms[2] of the proposed insurance. He then begins the task of taking the slip around the Room and offering it to underwriters (many of whom specialise in particulars types of insurance), whom he invites to subscribe a line on the slip. The line consists of the underwriter initialling the slip (also known as 'scratching the slip') to indicate willingness on behalf of his syndicate to accept a specified proportion of the risk. The broker continues in this way until the percentages subscribed for by the various underwriters amount (ideally) to at least 100% of the risk. Sometimes he will continue well beyond this point, with the result that the slip is oversubscribed. In this event the practice of the market[3] is that the proportion of the risk subscribed for by each signatory abate *pro rata*. This practice is referred to as 'signing down'. Some underwriters seek to exclude themselves from the effect of signing down by writing words such as 'not to sign for less than x%' next to their scratch An alternative situation is that the broker is unable to get the slip fully subscribed. In this event there is no converse practice of 'signing up' in order to achieve 100% subscription. Both situations give rise to some analytical difficulties. In the case of signing down the question is when the contract comes into existence. The normal understanding of the market is that the underwriter is bound as soon as he has subscribed the slip, but that may make it difficult to understand how his proportion of the risk can later be reduced. A similar problem arises where the slip is never fully subscribed. It is suggested that the answer to this may best be found in identifying a collateral contract between the underwriter and the broker who places the risk. In signing the slip the underwriter subscribes for the specified proportion of the risk, but subject to terms which make that agreement defeasible either in the event of signing down or in the event that the risk cannot be fully subscribed. In effect the underwriter authorises the broker to adjust the contract as necessary in order to conform to the customs of the market.

A number of other issues arising out of the particular practices of Lloyd's are considered below, though it is recognised that the coverage given here cannot be complete.

[1] Ie the marketplace where underwriters have the 'boxes' from which they conduct business. Originally this was a single room, but the modern equivalent extends over several floors of the Lloyd's Building in London.
[2] Often in practice all the intended express terms, but in abbreviated form.
[3] *General Reinsurance Corpn v Forsakringsaktiebolaget Fennia Patria* [1983] QB 856, CA.

Payment of premium

52.4 As between brokers and underwriters in the Lloyd's market premium and claims payments are normally accounted for on a net basis. Careful consideration of accounting entries may therefore be necessary in order to establish exactly which items have been credited as paid.

In *Figre Ltd v Colin John Mander and Johnson & Higgins Ltd*[1] the question arose whether a retrocession contract had been renounced or repudiated where no premium had been paid for six years. When the premium was tendered it was not accepted. Two types of premium were involved – the 'minimum and deposit' premium and the 'adjusted' premium. The retrocessionaires claimed that it was an implied term of the reassurance that the minimum premium would be paid within a reasonable time of the date of inception – pleaded as five months – and that there had therefore been a repudiatory breach of the contract and that it was an implied term of the reassurance that the adjustment premium would be paid within a reasonable time of the date when such premium was to be calculated and that, 11-and-a-half years now having expired since that time, there was a repudiatory breach of the reinsurance. They also argued that the obligation to pay premium by a particular time was an intermediate term and the late payment of the premiums were breaches going to the root of the contract and/or substantial failures in performance.

1 [1999] Lloyd's Rep IR 193.

52.5 The judgment includes a useful review of the relevant legal principles. It was held as follows:

(1) a failure to make payment on the fixed date amounts to a repudiatory breach of contract entitling the other party to terminate the contract in three cases:
  (a) where the parties have expressly stipulated in their contract that the time fixed for performance must be exactly complied with or that time is to be of the essence;
  (b) where the circumstances of the contract or the nature of the subject matter indicate that the fixed date must be exactly complied with; or
  (c) where time was not originally of the essence but one party has been guilty of undue delay and the other party gives a notice requiring the contract to be performed within a reasonable time.

(2) A renunciation of a contract occurs when one party by words or conduct evinces an intention not to perform or expressly declares that he is or will be unable to perform his obligations under the contract in some essential respect. A mere refusal or omission to do something which a party ought to do will not justify the other in repudiating the contract. There must be an absolute refusal to perform his side of the contract.

Reference was also made to the position in the context of failure to pay a sum of money under a reinsurance contract – as stated in *Fenton Insurance So Ltd v Gothaer Versicherungsbank VVAG*[1], namely that '*one could rarely, if ever, infer a repudiatory intention under a treaty of this kind by reason of non-payment of balances simpliciter (by way of distinction from a failure persisted in despite receipt of demands and/or protests).*'

The judge referred to the fact that the contract in question was one of high-layer excess of loss reinsurance in respect of US casualty business – the nature of the risk being that there may be no claims activity at all or there may be no claims activity for many years after the risk is written. There was no provision that reinsurers were not on risk until payment of the premium and no time was stipulated in the contract for the payment of premium, although it was common ground that the minimum and deposit premium should have been paid within a reasonable time of the date of the slip. The late tender of the minimum and deposit premium was due to administrative error and mistake – the reinsurers thought it had been paid. The failure to deal with the adjusted premium was due to administrative error, oversight and mistake. At no time after the underwriting did the retrocessionaire complain about the non payment of the minimum and deposit premium, or demand the premium or warn the reinsurers that if premium was not paid within a particular time the contract would be terminated. There was evidence before the court that at the material times delays in processing payment in the London market were not uncommon.

On the particular facts of the cases it was therefore held that:

(1) None of the cases where a failure to make payment on the fixed date amounts to a repudiatory breach of contract applied.
(2) The reinsurers did not renounce the contract there was no evincing of an intention not to perform.
(3) It was common ground that the obligation to pay premium was an intermediate term but on the facts this did not help the retrocessionaire who was liable under the contract of retrocession. The reinsurer had to account for adjusted premium and the minimum and deposit premium together with interest on the latter.

It is submitted that the decision in this case rests very much on the particular character of the business and on the practice of Lloyd's. Although the general principles stated here are no doubt of much broader application, it seems unlikely that in any non-Lloyd's context their application would have led to the same result on these facts – by any other standards the delays are surely inordinately long.

[1] [1991] 1 Lloyd's Rep 172.

Limitation and contribution in a Lloyd's context[1]

52.6 In *Henderson v Merrett Syndicates Ltd (No 2); Hallam-Eames v Merrett Syndicates Ltd (No 3); Hughes v Merrett Syndicates Ltd (No 2)*[2] questions of limitation under the Limitation Act 1980 and contribution under the Civil Liability (Contribution) Act 1978 were considered in the context of allegations that run off contracts were negligently written and that years of account were negligently closed by way of reinsurances to close. From a limitation point of view the case is important because it provides House of Lords authority for the proposition that professional duties owed in contract can simultaneously be owed between the same parties in tort. Thus, claimants may be able to take advantage of the Latent Damage Act 1986, which does not apply to contractual claims as well as being able to rely upon the rule that a cause of action in tort does not accrue until the claimant has suffered some recoverable loss as a result of the defendant's breach of duty[3], whereas in contract it accrues as soon as the breach occurs, even if the claimant would be unable to claim more than nominal damages[4].

So far as the negligence aspect of this case is concerned it was held that when considering the apportionment that it was necessary to take into account the commercial structure of Lloyd's, the duties of the parties in relation to reinsurances to close having regard to the agency and sub-agency agreements and audit engagements and the regulatory regime.

[1] For limitation of actions generally, see McGee *Limitation Periods* (4th edn, 2002, Sweet and Maxwell). Limitation in relation to insurance claims is discussed in Chapter 19 of the present work.
[2] [1997] LRLR 247.

[3] *Pirelli General Cable Works Ltd v Oscar Faber & Partners Ltd* [1983] 2 AC 1; *Nykredit Mortgage Bank plc v Edward Erdman Group Ltd (No 2)* [1998] 1 All ER 305, HL.
[4] *Gibbs v Guild* (1882) 9 QBD 59, CA.

Payment from central fund

52.7 In *Society of Lloyd's v Clementson*[1] at first instance the Society of Lloyd's was held entitled to be reimbursed by members in respect of payments made from the central fund to meet underwriting commitments of those members which they had failed to meet. The decision was reversed by the Court of Appeal[2] on the basis that the scheme was capable of having anti-competitive effects and was thus contrary to Article 81 (ex Article 85) of the TEU.

[1] (1994) Times, 11 January.
[2] [1995] 1 CMLR 693, CA.

Option to renew

52.8 In *Touche Ross & Co v Baker*[1] it was held that a clause giving the assured an option to renew insurance did not have to be exercised against all the underwriters or none of them, since the liability of an underwriting member was several not joint. This is simply an application to particular facts of the general principle that an underwriter who subscribes a slip does so on behalf of himself and the names on his Syndicate(s) but not on behalf of any of the subscribers of any other line on the slip.

[1] [1992] 2 Lloyd's Rep 207, HL.

Underwriting agents' duty of care

52.9 As to the duty of care owed by underwriting agents to names, see *Henderson v Merrett Syndicates Ltd1; Brown v KMR Services Ltd*[2] (duty of care in relation to high-risk syndicates). These cases form part of the ongoing litigation in which Lloyd's names have sought to establish the principle that agents owed than a duty when advising them which syndicates they should join. In essence their argument was upheld in the *Henderson* case, where it was also decided that the duty was tortious as well as contractual[3].

As to the settlement of claims in the Lloyd's litigation in chronological priority rather than on the principle of rateable allocation, see *Cox v Bankside Member's Agency*[4]. See also *Axa Reinsurance (UK) Ltd v Field*[5]. See also *Baker v Black Sea and Baltic General Insurance Co Ltd*[6] (liability for syndicate's costs of investigating, settling or defending claims). In that case it was argued by the Lloyd's syndicate that in the absence of an express clause in the reinsurance contract they, as a pro rata reinsurer were not liable to pay their share of the costs and expenses of investigating claims. The House of Lords held that it could not be said that the Equitas[7] treaty did not achieve business efficacy simply because its express terms resulted in the cedant bearing all of the costs of investigating, settling and defending claims. Their Lordships generally supported the view that there should not, in the absence of a trade practice or usage, be a term implied by law providing for recovery of such costs but rather than giving their own judgment on the facts of the matter referred it back to the Commercial Court for determination of outstanding factual questions.

1 [1994] 3 All ER 506, HL.
2 [1995] 4 All ER 598, CA.
3 This decision has had a major impact on Lloyd's, contributing significantly to the need for reconstruction. The details of the reconstruction process, however, lie beyond the scope of the present work.
4 [1995] 2 Lloyd's Rep 437, CA.
5 [1996] 3 All ER 517 HL.
6 [1998] 2 All ER 833, HL.
7 The corporate entity into which the general business insurance liabilities of Lloyd's Syndicates allocated to the 1992 and prior years of account have been reinsured.

52.10 In *P&B (Run-Off) Ltd v Woolley*[1] it was held that the agreement between a Name and his managing agent can be enforceable even though it is not in writing, so long as there is a written agreement between the member's agent and the managing agent. In this event an agreement between the Name and the managing agent is deemed to come into existence under Lloyds Byelaw 8, and that is sufficient to make the agreement enforceable.

1 [2001] 1 All ER (Comm) 1120, Andrew Smith J.

The disputes and the reconstruction

52.11 This is an enormous subject with many ramifications. Only the briefest of summaries will be attempted here. Through the late 1980s and throughout the 1990s Lloyd's has struggled with protracted litigation arising from very serious allegations of misconduct on the part of managing agents and others. A concise summary of the allegations would be that relatively unsophisticated Names are said to have been induced to join particular syndicates, which then had poor quality business loaded on to them, while better quality business was deliberately reserved for other syndicates. It is also said that agents and some Lloyd's brokers wrote primary insurance which was of poor quality and/or reinsurance business which was not justified at all for the sole purpose of boosting their commission earnings at the expense of these Names. It is fair to say that these allegations have been contested to a greater or lesser extent. At the same time there is no doubt that a number of Names have been financially ruined as a result of a series of very bad years on the syndicates of which they were members. The litigation is ongoing, but some decisions have already been given, and those Names who have sought to sue Lloyd's on the basis of a failure of the Lloyd's regulatory structure to deal with the activities of miscreants within the organisation have had some degree of success.

The fundamental problem to which this success has itself given rise is that any compensation obtained by Names for these breaches of duty has of necessity had to come from within Lloyd's. In so far as Lloyd's itself has been the defendant, it has had to fund the compensation from its own resources, whilst any managing agents successfully sued will have had errors and omissions insurance also placed within the Lloyd's market.

52.12 At some points in this sorry saga it has seemed that Lloyd's faced financial ruin and possible extinction. That danger appears to have been averted, at least for the time being, by the reconstruction of Lloyd's in a new form. Essentially all the old liabilities, which were borne by individual Names on the basis of unlimited personal liability, have been novated to the new Equitas scheme, under which there is limited personal liability. The transfer has not been accomplished painlessly, however. Some Names have continued to pursue their grievances against Lloyd's, though most of this litigation appears now to have come to an end. However, these appear to affect the position of particular individuals, rather than undermining the Equitas settlement as a whole. For the moment it appears that Lloyd's is back on something approaching an even keel, with a new structure, though it will of course be many years before the full financial consequences of the problems are worked out.

Appendices

CONTENTS
(references in bold are to page numbers)

Appendix 1: STATUTES

Appendix 2: STATUTORY INSTRUMENTS

Appendix 3: REGULATORY CODES

Appendix 1

Statutes

Life Assurance Act 1774

(1774 c 48)

1 No insurance to be made on lives, etc, by persons having no interest etc

From and after the passing of this Act no insurance shall be made by any person or persons, bodies politick or corporate, on the life or lives of any person or persons, or on any other event or events whatsoever, wherein the person or persons for whose use, benefit, or on whose account such policy or policies shall be made, shall have no interest, or by way of gaming or wagering; and that every assurance made contrary to the true intent and meaning hereof shall be null and void to all intents and purposes whatsoever.

2 No policies on lives without inserting the names of persons interested, etc

And … it shall not be lawful to make any policy or policies on the life or lives of any person or persons, or other event or events, without inserting in such policy or policies the person or persons name or names interested therein, or for whose use, benefit, or on whose account such policy is so made or underwrote.

3 How much may be recovered where the insured hath interest in lives

And … in all cases where the insured hath interest in such life or lives, event or events, no greater sum shall be recovered or received from the insurer or insurers than the amount of value of the interest of the insured in such life or lives, or other event or events.

4 Not to extend to insurances on ships, goods, etc

Provided, always, that nothing herein contained shall extend or be construed to extend to insurances bona fide made by any person or persons on ships, goods, or merchandises, but every such insurance shall be as valid and effectual in the law as if this Act had not been made.

Gaming Act 1845

(1845 c 109)

18 Contracts by way of gaming to be void, and wagers or sums deposited with stakeholders not to be recoverable at law – Saving for subscriptions for prizes

… All contracts or agreements, whether by parole or in writing, by way of gaming or wagering, shall be null and void; and … no suit shall be brought or maintained in any court of law and equity for recovering any sum of money or valuable thing alleged to be won upon any wager, or which shall have been deposited in the hands of any person to abide the event on which any wager shall have been made: Provided always, that this enactment shall not be deemed to apply to any subscription or contribution, or agreement to subscribe or contribute, for or towards any plate, prize, or sum of money to be awarded to the winner or winners of any lawful game, sport, pastime, or exercise.

Policies of Assurance Act 1867

(1867 c 144)

SCHEDULE

Section 5

I *A.B.*, of, *&c*, in consideration of, *&c*, do hereby assign unto *C.D.*, of, *&c*, his executors, administrators, and assigns, the (within) policy of assurance granted, *&c* (*here describe the policy*). In witness, *&c*.

Marine Insurance Act 1906

(1906 c 41)

Marine Insurance

1 Marine insurance defined

A contract of marine insurance is a contract whereby the insurer undertakes to indemnify the assured, in manner and to the extent thereby agreed, against marine losses, that is to say, the losses incident to marine adventure.

2 Mixed sea and land risks

(1) A contract of marine insurance may, by its express terms, or by usage of trade, be extended so as to protect the assured against losses on inland waters or on any land risk which may be incidental to any sea voyage.

(2) Where a ship in course of building, or the launch of a ship, or any adventure analogous to a marine adventure, is covered by a policy in the form of a

marine policy, the provisions of this Act, in so far as applicable, shall apply thereto; but, except as by this section provided, nothing in this Act shall alter or affect any rule of law applicable to any contract of insurance other than a contract of marine insurance as by this Act defined.

3 Marine adventure and maritime perils defined

(1) Subject to the provisions of this Act, every lawful marine adventure may be the subject of a contract of marine insurance.

(2) In particular there is a marine adventure where—
- (a) Any ship goods or other moveables are exposed to maritime perils. Such property is in this Act referred to as 'insurable property';
- (b) The earning or acquisition of any freight, passage money, commission, profit, or other pecuniary benefit, or the security for any advances, loan, or disbursements, is endangered by the exposure of insurable property to maritime perils;
- (c) Any liability to a third party may be incurred by the owner of, or other person interested in or responsible for, insurable property, by reason of maritime perils.

'Maritime perils' means the perils consequent on, or incidental to, the navigation of the sea, that is to say, perils of the seas, fire, war perils, pirates, rovers, thieves, captures, seisures, restraints, and detainments of princes and peoples, jettisons, barratry, and any other perils, either of the like kind or which may be designated by the policy.

Insurable Interest

4 Avoidance of wagering or gaming contracts

(1) Every contract of marine insurance by way of gaming or wagering is void.

(2) A contract of marine insurance is deemed to be a gaming or wagering contract—
- (a) Where the assured has not an insurable interest as defined by this Act, and the contract is entered into with no expectation of acquiring such an interest; or
- (b) Where the policy is made 'interest or no interest,' or 'without further proof of interest than the policy itself,' or 'without benefit of salvage to the insurer,' or subject to any other like term: Provided that, where there is no possibility of salvage, a policy may be effected without benefit of salvage to the insurer.

5 Insurable interest defined

(1) Subject to the provisions of this Act, every person has an insurable interest who is interested in a marine adventure.

(2) In particular a person is interested in a marine adventure where he stands in any legal or equitable relation to the adventure or to any insurable property at risk therein, in consequence of which he may benefit by the safety or due arrival of insurable property, or may be prejudiced by its loss, or damage thereto, or by the detention thereof, or may incur liability in respect thereof.

6 When interest must attach

(1) The assured must be interested in the subject-matter insured at the time of the loss though he need not be interested when the insurance is effected: Provided that where the subject-matter is insured 'lost or not lost,' the assured may recover although he may not have acquired his interest until after the loss, unless at the time of effecting the contract of insurance the assured was aware of the loss, and the insurer was not.

(2) Where the assured has no interest at the time of the loss, he cannot acquire interest by any act or election after he is aware of the loss.

7 Defeasible or contingent interest

(1) A defeasible interest is insurable, as also is a contingent interest.

(2) In particular, where the buyer of goods has insured them, he has an insurable interest, notwithstanding that he might, at his election, have rejected the goods, or have treated them as at the seller's risk, by reason of the latter's delay in making delivery or otherwise.

8 Partial interest

A partial interest of any nature is insurable.

9 Re-insurance

(1) The insurer under a contract of marine insurance has an insurable interest in his risk, and may re-insure in respect of it.

(2) Unless the policy otherwise provides, the original assured has no right or interest in respect of such re-insurance.

10 Bottomry

The lender of money on bottomry or respondentia has an insurable interest in respect of the loan.

11 Master's and seamen's wages

The master or any member of the crew of a ship has an insurable interest in respect of his wages.

12 Advance freight

In the case of advance freight, the person advancing the freight has an insurable interest, in so far as such freight is not repayable in case of loss.

13 Charges of insurance

The assured has an insurable interest in the charges of any insurance which he may effect.

14 Quantum of interest

(1) Where the subject-matter insured is mortgaged, the mortgagor has an insurable interest in the full value thereof, and the mortgagee has an insurable interest in respect of any sum due or to become due under the mortgage.

(2) A mortgagee, consignee, or other person having an interest in the subject-matter insured may insure on behalf and for the benefit of other persons interested as well as for his own benefit.

(3) The owner of insurable property has an insurable interest in respect of the full value thereof, notwithstanding that some third person may have agreed, or be liable, to indemnify him in case of loss.

15 Assignment of interest

Where the assured assigns or otherwise parts with his interest in the subject-matter insured, he does not thereby transfer to the assignee his rights under the contract of insurance, unless there be an express or implied agreement with the assignee to that effect. But the provisions of this section do not affect a transmission of interest by operation of law.

Insurable Value

16 Measure of insurable value

Subject to any express provision or valuation in the policy, the insurable value of the subject-matter insured must be ascertained as follows:—

(1) In insurance on ship, the insurable value is the value, at the commencement of the risk, of the ship, including her outfit, provisions and stores for the officers and crew, money advanced for seamen's wages, and other disbursements (if any) incurred to make the ship fit for the voyage or adventure contemplated by the policy, plus the charges of insurance upon the whole: The insurable value, in the case of a steamship, includes also the machinery, boilers, and coals and engine stores if owned by the assured, and, in the case of a ship engaged in a special trade, the ordinary fittings requisite for that trade:

(2) In insurance on freight, whether paid in advance or otherwise, the insurable value is the gross amount of the freight at the risk of the assured, plus the charges of insurance:

(3) In insurance on goods or merchandise, the insurable value is the prime cost of the property insured, plus the expenses of and incidental to shipping and the charges of insurance upon the whole:

(4) In insurance on any other subject-matter, the insurable value is the amount at the risk of the assured when the policy attaches, plus the charges of insurance.

Disclosure and Representations

17 Insurance is uberrimae fidei

A contract of marine insurance is a contract based upon the utmost good faith, and, if the utmost good faith be not observed by either party, the contract may be avoided by the other party.

18 Disclosure by assured

(1) Subject to the provisions of this section, the assured must disclose to the insurer, before the contract is concluded, every material circumstance which is known to the assured, and the assured is deemed to know every circumstance which, in the ordinary course of business, ought to be known by him. If the assured fails to make such disclosure, the insurer may avoid the contract.

(2) Every circumstance is material which would influence the judgment of a prudent insurer in fixing the premium, or determining whether he will take the risk.

(3) In the absence of inquiry the following circumstances need not be disclosed, namely:—
- (a) Any circumstance which diminishes the risk;
- (b) Any circumstance which is known or presumed to be known to the insurer. The insurer is presumed to know matters of common notoriety or knowledge, and matters which an insurer in the ordinary course of his business, as such, ought to know;
- (c) Any circumstance as to which information is waived by the insurer;
- (d) Any circumstance which it is superfluous to disclose by reason of any express or implied warranty.

(4) Whether any particular circumstance, which is not disclosed, be material or not is, in each case, a question of fact.

(5) The term 'circumstance' includes any communication made to, or information received by, the assured.

19 Disclosure by agent effecting insurance

Subject to the provisions of the preceding section as to circumstances which need not be disclosed, where an insurance is effected for the assured by an agent, the agent must disclose to the insurer—
- (a) Every material circumstance which is known to himself, and an agent to insure is deemed to know every circumstance which in the ordinary course of business ought to be known by, or to have been communicated to, him; and
- (b) Every material circumstance which the assured is bound to disclose, unless it come to his knowledge too late to communicate it to the agent.

20 Representations pending negotiation of contract

(1) Every material representation made by the assured or his agent to the insurer during the negotiations for the contract, and before the contract is concluded, must be true. If it be untrue the insurer may avoid the contract.

(2) A representation is material which would influence the judgment of a prudent insurer in fixing the premium, or determining whether he will take the risk.

(3) A representation may be either a representation as to a matter of fact, or as to a matter of expectation or belief.

(4) A representation as to matter of fact is true, if it be substantially correct, that is to say, if the difference between what is represented and what is actually correct would not be considered material by a prudent insurer.

(5) A representation as to a matter of expectation or belief is true if it be made in good faith.

(6) A representation may be withdrawn or corrected before the contract is concluded.

(7) Whether a particular representation be material or not is, in each case, a question of fact.

21 When contract is deemed to be concluded

A contract of marine insurance is deemed to be concluded when the proposal of the assured is accepted by the insurer, whether the policy be then issued or not; and, for the purpose of showing when the proposal was accepted, reference may be made to the slip or covering note or other customary memorandum of the contract, …

The Policy

22 Contract must be embodied in policy

Subject to the provisions of any statute, a contract of marine insurance is inadmissible in evidence unless it is embodied in a marine policy in accordance with this Act. The policy may be executed and issued either at the time when the contract is concluded, or afterwards.

23 What policy must specify

A marine policy must specify—

(1) The name of the assured, or of some person who effects the insurance on his behalf:

(2)–(5)..

24 Signature of insurer

(1) A marine policy must be signed by or on behalf of the insurer, provided that in the case of a corporation the corporate seal may be sufficient, but nothing in this section shall be construed as requiring the subscription of a corporation to be under seal.

(2) Where a policy is subscribed by or on behalf of two or more insurers, each subscription, unless the contrary be expressed, constitutes a distinct contract with the assured.

25 Voyage and time policies

(1) Where the contract is to insure the subject-matter 'at and from', or from one place to another or others, the policy is called a 'voyage policy', and where the contract is to insure the subject-matter for a definite period of time the policy is called a 'time policy'. A contract for both voyage and time may be included in the same policy.

(2) …

26 Designation of subject-matter

(1) The subject-matter insured must be designated in a marine policy with reasonable certainty.

(2) The nature and extent of the interest of the assured in the subject-matter insured need not be specified in the policy.

(3) Where the policy designates the subject-matter insured in general terms, it shall be construed to apply to the interest intended by the assured to be covered.

(4) In the application of this section regard shall be had to any usage regulating the designation of the subject-matter insured.

27 Valued policy

(1) A policy may be either valued or unvalued.

(2) A valued policy is a policy which specifies the agreed value of the subject-matter insured.

(3) Subject to the provisions of this Act, and in the absence of fraud, the value fixed by the policy is, as between the insurer and assured, conclusive of the insurable value of the subject intended to be insured, whether the loss be total or partial.

(4) Unless the policy otherwise provides, the value fixed by the policy is not conclusive for the purpose of determining whether there has been a constructive total loss.

28 Unvalued policy

An unvalued policy is a policy which does not specify the value of the subject-matter insured, but, subject to the limit of the sum insured, leaves the insurable value to be subsequently ascertained, in the manner herein-before specified.

29 Floating policy by ship or ships

(1) A floating policy is a policy which describes the insurance in general terms, and leaves the name of the ship or ships and other particulars to be defined by subsequent declaration.

(2) The subsequent declaration or declarations may be made by indorsement on the policy, or in other customary manner.

(3) Unless the policy otherwise provides, the declarations must be made in the order of dispatch or shipment. They must, in the case of goods, comprise all consignments within the terms of the policy, and the value of the goods or other property must be honestly stated, but an omission or erroneous declaration may be rectified even after loss or arrival, provided the omission or declaration was made in good faith.

(4) Unless the policy otherwise provides, where a declaration of value is not made until after notice of loss or arrival, the policy must be treated as an unvalued policy as regards the subject-matter of that declaration.

30 Construction of terms in policy

(1) A policy may be in the form in the First Schedule to this Act.

(2) Subject to the provisions of this Act, and unless the context of the policy otherwise requires, the terms and expressions mentioned in the First Schedule to this Act shall be construed as having the scope and meaning in that schedule assigned to them.

31 Premium to be arranged

(1) Where an insurance is effected at a premium to be arranged, and no arrangement is made, a reasonable premium is payable.

(2) Where an insurance is effected on the terms that an additional premium is to be arranged in a given event, and that event happens but no arrangement is made, then a reasonable additional premium is payable.

Double Insurance

32 Double insurance

(1) Where two or more policies are effected by or on behalf of the assured on the same adventure and interest or any part thereof, and the sums insured exceed the indemnity allowed by this Act, the assured is said to be over-insured by double insurance.

(2) Where the assured is over-insured by double insurance—
  (a) The assured, unless the policy otherwise provides, may claim payment from the insurers in such order as he may think fit, provided that he is not entitled to receive any sum in excess of the indemnity allowed by this Act;
  (b) Where the policy under which the assured claims is a valued policy, the assured must give credit as against the valuation for any sum received by him under any other policy without regard to the actual value of the subject-matter insured;
  (c) Where the policy under which the assured claims is an unvalued policy he must give credit, as against the full insurable value, for any sum received by him under any other policy;
  (d) Where the assured receives any sum in excess of the indemnity allowed by this Act, he is deemed to hold such sum in trust for the insurers, according to their right of contribution among themselves.

Warranties, etc

33 Nature of warranty

(1) A warranty, in the following sections relating to warranties, means a promissory warranty, that is to say, a warranty by which the assured

undertakes that some particular thing shall or shall not be done, or that some condition shall be fulfilled, or whereby he affirms or negatives the existence of a particular state of facts.

(2) A warranty may be express or implied.

(3) A warranty, as above defined, is a condition which must be exactly complied with, whether it be material to the risk or not. If it be not so complied with, then, subject to any express provision in the policy, the insurer is discharged from liability as from the date of the breach of warranty, but without prejudice to any liability incurred by him before that date.

34 When breach of warranty excused

(1) Non-compliance with a warranty is excused when, by reason of a change of circumstances, the warranty ceases to be applicable to the circumstances of the contract, or when compliance with the warranty is rendered unlawful by any subsequent law.

(2) Where a warranty is broken, the assured cannot avail himself of the defence that the breach has been remedied, and the warranty complied with, before loss.

(3) A breach of warranty may be waived by the insurer.

35 Express warranties

(1) An express warranty may be in any form of words from which the intention to warrant is to be inferred.

(2) An express warranty must be included in, or written upon, the policy, or must be contained in some document incorporated by reference into the policy.

(3) An express warranty does not exclude an implied warranty, unless it be inconsistent therewith.

36 Warranty of neutrality

(1) Where insurable property, whether ship or goods, is expressly warranted neutral, there is an implied condition that the property shall have a neutral character at the commencement of the risk, and that, so far as the assured can control the matter, its neutral character shall be preserved during the risk.

(2) Where a ship is expressly warranted 'neutral' there is also an implied condition that, so far as the assured can control the matter, she shall be properly documented, that is to say, that she shall carry the necessary papers to establish her neutrality, and that she shall not falsify or suppress her papers, or use simulated papers. If any loss occurs through breach of this condition, the insurer may avoid the contract.

37 No implied warranty of nationality

There is no implied warranty as to the nationality of a ship, or that her nationality shall not be changed during the risk.

38 Warranty of good safety

Where the subject-matter insured is warranted 'well' or 'in good safety' on a particular day, it is sufficient if it be safe at any time during that day.

39 Warranty of seaworthiness of ship

(1) In a voyage policy there is an implied warranty that at the commencement of the voyage the ship shall be seaworthy for the purpose of the particular adventure insured.

(2) Where the policy attaches while the ship is in port, there is also an implied warranty that she shall, at the commencement of the risk, be reasonably fit to encounter the ordinary perils of the port.

(3) Where the policy relates to a voyage which is performed in different stages, during which the ship requires different kinds of or further preparation or equipment, there is an implied warranty that at the commencement of each stage the ship is seaworthy in respect of such preparation or equipment for the purposes of that stage.

(4) A ship is deemed to be seaworthy when she is reasonably fit in all respects to encounter the ordinary perils of the seas of the adventure insured.

(5) In a time policy there is no implied warranty that the ship shall be seaworthy at any stage of the adventure, but where, with the privity of the assured, the ship is sent to sea in an unseaworthy state, the insurer is not liable for any loss attributable to unseaworthiness.

40 No implied warranty that goods are seaworthy

(1) In a policy on goods or other moveables there is no implied warranty that the goods or moveables are seaworthy.

(2) In a voyage policy on goods or other moveables there is an implied warranty that at the commencement of the voyage the ship is not only seaworthy as a ship, but also that she is reasonably fit to carry the goods or other moveables to the destination contemplated by the policy.

41 Warranty of legality

There is an implied warranty that the adventure insured is a lawful one, and that, so far as the assured can control the matter, the adventure shall be carried out in a lawful manner.

The Voyage

42 Implied condition as to commencement of risk

(1) Where the subject-matter is insured by a voyage policy 'at and from' or 'from' a particular place, it is not necessary that the ship should be at that place when the contract is concluded, but there is an implied condition that the adventure shall be commenced within a reasonable time, and that if the adventure be not so commenced the insurer may avoid the contract.

(2) The implied condition may be negatived by showing that the delay was caused by circumstances known to the insurer before the contract was concluded, or by showing that he waived the condition.

43 Alteration of port of departure

Where the place of departure is specified by the policy, and the ship instead of sailing from that place sails from any other place, the risk does not attach.

44 Sailing for different destination

Where the destination is specified in the policy, and the ship, instead of sailing for that destination, sails for any other destination, the risk does not attach.

45 Change of voyage

(1) Where, after the commencement of the risk, the destination of the ship is voluntarily changed from the destination contemplated by the policy, there is said to be a change of voyage.

(2) Unless the policy otherwise provides, where there is a change of voyage, the insurer is discharged from liability as from the time of change, that is to say, as from the time when the determination to change it is manifested; and it is immaterial that the ship may not in fact have left the course of voyage contemplated by the policy when the loss occurs.

46 Deviation

(1) Where a ship, without lawful excuse, deviates from the voyage contemplated by the policy, the insurer is discharged from liability as from the time of deviation, and it is immaterial that the ship may have regained her route before any loss occurs.

(2) There is a deviation from the voyage contemplated by the policy—
- (a) Where the course of the voyage is specifically designated by the policy, and that course is departed from; or
- (b) Where the course of the voyage is not specifically designated by the policy, but the usual and customary course is departed from.

(3) The intention to deviate is immaterial; there must be a deviation in fact to discharge the insurer from his liability under the contract.

47 Several ports of discharge

(1) Where several ports of discharge are specified by the policy, the ship may proceed to all or any of them, but, in the absence of any usage or sufficient cause to the contrary, she must proceed to them, or such of them as she goes to, in the order designated by the policy. If she does not there is a deviation.

(2) Where the policy is to 'ports of discharge', within a given area, which are not named, the ship must, in the absence of any usage or sufficient cause to the contrary, proceed to them, or such of them as she goes to, in their geographical order. If she does not there is a deviation.

48 Delay in voyage

In the case of a voyage policy, the adventure insured must be prosecuted throughout its course with reasonable dispatch, and, if without lawful excuse it is not so prosecuted, the insurer is discharged from liability as from the time when the delay became unreasonable.

49 Excuses for deviation or delay

(1) Deviation or delay in prosecuting the voyage contemplated by the policy is excused—
- (a) Where authorised by any special term in the policy; or
- (b) Where caused by circumstances beyond the control of the master and his employer; or
- (c) Where reasonably necessary in order to comply with an express or implied warranty; or
- (d) Where reasonably necessary for the safety of the ship or subject-matter insured; or
- (e) For the purpose of saving human life, or aiding a ship in distress where human life may be in danger; or
- (f) Where reasonably necessary for the purpose of obtaining medical or surgical aid for any person on board the ship; or
- (g) Where caused by the barratrous conduct of the master or crew, if barratry be one of the perils insured against.

(2) When the cause excusing the deviation or delay ceases to operate, the ship must resume her course, and prosecute her voyage, with reasonable dispatch.

Assignment of Policy

50 When and how policy is assignable

(1) A marine policy is assignable unless it contains terms expressly prohibiting assignment. It may be assigned either before or after loss.

(2) Where a marine policy has been assigned so as to pass the beneficial interest in such policy, the assignee of the policy is entitled to sue thereon in his own name; and the defendant is entitled to make any defence arising out of the contract which he would have been entitled to make if the action had been brought in the name of the person by or on behalf of whom the policy was effected.

(3) A marine policy may be assigned by indorsement thereon or in other customary manner.

51 Assured who has no interest cannot assign

Where the assured has parted with or lost his interest in the subject-matter insured, and has not, before or at the time of so doing, expressly or impliedly agreed to assign the policy, any subsequent assignment of the policy is inoperative: Provided that nothing in this section affects the assignment of a policy after loss.

The Premium

52 When premium payable

Unless otherwise agreed, the duty of the assured or his agent to pay the premium, and the duty of the insurer to issue the policy to the assured or his agent, are concurrent conditions, and the insurer is not bound to issue the policy until payment or tender of the premium.

53 Policy effected through broker

(1) Unless otherwise agreed, where a marine policy is effected on behalf of the assured by a broker, the broker is directly responsible to the insurer for the premium, and the insurer is directly responsible to the assured for the amount which may be payable in respect of losses, or in respect of returnable premium.

(2) Unless otherwise agreed, the broker has, as against the assured, a lien upon the policy for the amount of the premium and his charges in respect of effecting the policy; and, where he has dealt with the person who employs him as a principal, he has also a lien on the policy in respect of any balance on any insurance account which may be due to him from such person, unless when the debt was incurred he had reason to believe that such person was only an agent.

54 Effect of receipt on policy

Where a marine policy effected on behalf of the assured by a broker acknowledges the receipt of the premium, such acknowledgment is, in the absence of fraud, conclusive as between the insurer and the assured, but not as between the insurer and broker.

Loss and Abandonment

55 Included and excluded losses

(1) Subject to the provisions of this Act, and unless the policy otherwise provides, the insurer is liable for any loss proximately caused by a peril insured against, but, subject as aforesaid, he is not liable for any loss which is not proximately caused by a peril insured against.

(2) In particular,—
- (a) The insurer is not liable for any loss attributable to the wilful misconduct of the assured, but, unless the policy otherwise provides, he is liable for any loss proximately caused by a peril insured against, even though the loss would not have happened but for the misconduct or negligence of the master or crew;
- (b) Unless the policy otherwise provides, the insurer on ship or goods is not liable for any loss proximately caused by delay, although the delay be caused by a peril insured against;
- (c) Unless the policy otherwise provides, the insurer is not liable for ordinary wear and tear, ordinary leakage and breakage, inherent vice

or nature of the subject-matter insured, or for any loss proximately caused by rats or vermin, or for any injury to machinery not proximately caused by maritime perils.

56 Partial and total loss

(1) A loss may be either total or partial. Any loss other than a total loss, as herein-after defined, is a partial loss.

(2) A total loss may be either an actual total loss, or a constructive total loss.

(3) Unless a different intention appears from the terms of the policy, an insurance against total loss includes a constructive, as well as an actual, total loss.

(4) Where the assured brings an action for a total loss and the evidence proves only a partial loss, he may, unless the policy otherwise provides, recover for a partial loss.

(5) Where goods reach their destination in specie, but by reason of obliteration of marks, or otherwise, they are incapable of identification, the loss, if any, is partial, and not total.

57 Actual total loss

(1) Where the subject-matter insured is destroyed, or so damaged as to cease to be a thing of the kind insured, or where the assured is irretrievably deprived thereof, there is an actual total loss.

(2) In the case of an actual total loss no notice of abandonment need be given.

58 Missing ship

Where the ship concerned in the adventure is missing, and after the lapse of a reasonable time no news of her has been received, an actual total loss may be presumed.

59 Effect of transhipment, etc

Where, by a peril insured against, the voyage is interrupted at an intermediate port or place, under such circumstances as, apart from any special stipulation in the contract of affreightment, to justify the master in landing and re-shipping the goods or other moveables, or in transhipping them, and sending them on to their destination, the liability of the insurer continues, notwithstanding the landing or transhipment.

60 Constructive total loss defined

(1) Subject to any express provision in the policy, there is a constructive total loss where the subject-matter insured is reasonably abandoned on account of its actual total loss appearing to be unavoidable, or because it could not be preserved from actual total loss without an expenditure which would exceed its value when the expenditure had been incurred.

(2) In particular, there is a constructive total loss—

(i) Where the assured is deprived of the possession of his ship or goods by a peril insured against, and (*a*) it is unlikely that he can recover the ship or goods, as the case may be, or (*b*) the cost of recovering the ship or goods, as the case may be, would exceed their value when recovered; or

(ii) In the case of damage to a ship, where she is so damaged by a peril insured against that the cost of repairing the damage would exceed the value of the ship when repaired. In estimating the cost of repairs, no deduction is to be made in respect of general average contributions to those repairs payable by other interests, but account is to be taken of the expense of future salvage operations and of any future general average contributions to which the ship would be liable if repaired; or

(iii) In the case of damage to goods, where the cost of repairing the damage and forwarding the goods to their destination would exceed their value on arrival.

61 Effect of constructive total loss

Where there is a constructive total loss the assured may either treat the loss as a partial loss, or abandon the subject-matter insured to the insurer and treat the loss as if it were an actual total loss.

62 Notice of abandonment

(1) Subject to the provisions of this section, where the assured elects to abandon the subject-matter insured to the insurer, he must give notice of abandonment. If he fails to do so the loss can only be treated as a partial loss.

(2) Notice of abandonment may be given in writing, or by word of mouth, or partly in writing and partly by word of mouth, and may be given in terms which indicate the intention of the assured to abandon his insured interest in the subject-matter insured unconditionally to the insurer.

(3) Notice of abandonment must be given with reasonable diligence after the receipt of reliable information of the loss, but where the information is of a doubtful character the assured is entitled to a reasonable time to make inquiry.

(4) Where notice of abandonment is properly given, the rights of the assured are not prejudiced by the fact that the insurer refuses to accept the abandonment.

(5) The acceptance of an abandonment may be either express or implied from the conduct of the insurer. The mere silence of the insurer after notice is not an acceptance.

(6) Where a notice of abandonment is accepted the abandonment is irrevocable. The acceptance of the notice conclusively admits liability for the loss and the sufficiency of the notice.

(7) Notice of abandonment is unnecessary where, at the time when the assured receives information of the loss, there would be no possibility of benefit to the insurer if notice were given to him.

(8) Notice of abandonment may be waived by the insurer.

(9) Where an insurer has re-insured his risk, no notice of abandonment need be given by him.

63 Effect of abandonment

(1) Where there is a valid abandonment the insurer is entitled to take over the interest of the assured in whatever may remain of the subject-matter insured, and all proprietary rights incidental thereto.

(2) Upon the abandonment of a ship, the insurer thereof is entitled to any freight in course of being earned, and which is earned by her subsequent to the casualty causing the loss, less the expenses of earning it incurred after the casualty; and, where the ship is carrying the owner's goods, the insurer is entitled to a reasonable remuneration for the carriage of them subsequent to the casualty causing the loss.

Partial Losses (including Salvage and General Average and Particular Charges)

64 Particular average loss

(1) A particular average loss is a partial loss of the subject-matter insured, caused by a peril insured against, and which is not a general average loss.

(2) Expenses incurred by or on behalf of the assured for the safety or preservation of the subject-matter insured, other than general average and salvage charges, are called particular charges. Particular charges are not included in particular average.

65 Salvage charges

(1) Subject to any express provision in the policy, salvage charges incurred in preventing a loss by perils insured against may be recovered as a loss by those perils.

(2) 'Salvage charges' means the charges recoverable under maritime law by a salvor independently of contract. They do not include the expenses of services in the nature of salvage rendered by the assured or his agents, or any person employed for hire by them, for the purpose of averting a peril insured against. Such expenses, where properly incurred, may be recovered as particular charges or as a general average loss, according to the circumstances under which they were incurred.

66 General average loss

(1) A general average loss is a loss caused by or directly consequential on a general average act. It includes a general average expenditure as well as a general average sacrifice.

(2) There is a general average act where any extraordinary sacrifice or expenditure is voluntarily and reasonably made or incurred in time of peril for the purpose of preserving the property imperilled in the common adventure.

(3) Where there is a general average loss, the party on whom it falls is entitled, subject to the conditions imposed by maritime law, to a rateable contribution from the other parties interested, and such contribution is called a general average contribution.

(4) Subject to any express provision in the policy, where the assured has incurred a general average expenditure, he may recover from the insurer in respect of the proportion of the loss which falls upon him; and, in the case of a general average sacrifice, he may recover from the insurer in respect of the whole loss without having enforced his right of contribution from the other parties liable to contribute.

(5) Subject to any express provision in the policy, where the assured has paid, or is liable to pay, a general average contribution in respect of the subject insured, he may recover therefor from the insurer.

(6) In the absence of express stipulation, the insurer is not liable for any general average loss or contribution where the loss was not incurred for the purpose of avoiding, or in connexion with the avoidance of, a peril insured against.

(7) Where ship, freight, and cargo, or any two of those interests, are owned by the same assured, the liability of the insurer in respect of general average losses or contributions is to be determined as if those subjects were owned by different persons.

Measure of Indemnity

67 Extent of liability of insurer for loss

(1) The sum which the assured can recover in respect of a loss on a policy by which he is insured, in the case of an unvalued policy to the full extent of the insurable value, or, in the case of a valued policy to the full extent of the value fixed by the policy, is called the measure of indemnity.

(2) Where there is a loss recoverable under the policy, the insurer, or each insurer if there be more than one, is liable for such proportion of the measure of indemnity as the amount of his subscription bears to the value fixed by the policy in the case of a valued policy, or to the insurable value in the case of an unvalued policy.

68 Total loss

Subject to the provisions of this Act and to any express provision in the policy, where there is a total loss of the subject-matter insured,—

(1) If the policy be a valued policy, the measure of indemnity is the sum fixed by the policy:

(2) If the policy be an unvalued policy, the measure of indemnity is the insurable value of the subject-matter insured.

69 Partial loss of ship

Where a ship is damaged, but is not totally lost, the measure of indemnity, subject to any express provision in the policy, is as follows:—

(1) Where the ship has been repaired, the assured is entitled to the reasonable cost of the repairs, less the customary deductions, but not exceeding the sum insured in respect of any one casualty:

(2) Where the ship has been only partially repaired, the assured is entitled to the reasonable cost of such repairs, computed as above, and also to be indemnified for the reasonable depreciation, if any, arising from the unrepaired damage, provided that the aggregate amount shall not exceed the cost of repairing the whole damage, computed as above:

(3) Where the ship has not been repaired, and has not been sold in her damaged state during the risk, the assured is entitled to be indemnified for the reasonable depreciation arising from the unrepaired damage, but not exceeding the reasonable cost of repairing such damage, computed as above.

70 Partial loss of freight

Subject to any express provision in the policy, where there is a partial loss of freight, the measure of indemnity is such proportion of the sum fixed by the policy in the case of a valued policy, or of the insurable value in the case of an unvalued policy, as the proportion of freight lost by the assured bears to the whole freight at the risk of the assured under the policy.

71 Partial loss of goods, merchandise, etc

Where there is a partial loss of goods, merchandise, or other moveables, the measure of indemnity, subject to any express provision in the policy, is as follows:—

(1) Where part of the goods, merchandise or other moveables insured by a valued policy is totally lost, the measure of indemnity is such proportion of the sum fixed by the policy as the insurable value of the part lost bears to the insurable value of the whole, ascertained as in the case of an unvalued policy:

(2) Where part of the goods, merchandise, or other moveables insured by an unvalued policy is totally lost, the measure of indemnity is the insurable value of the part lost, ascertained as in case of total loss:

(3) Where the whole or any part of the goods or merchandise insured has been delivered damaged at its destination, the measure of indemnity is such proportion of the sum fixed by the policy in the case of a valued policy, or of the insurable value in the case of an unvalued policy, as the difference between the gross sound and damaged values at the place of arrival bears to the gross sound value:

(4) 'Gross value' means the wholesale price or, if there be no such price, the estimated value, with, in either case, freight, landing charges, and duty paid beforehand; provided that, in the case of goods or merchandise customarily sold in bond, the bonded price is deemed to be the gross value. 'Gross proceeds' means the actual price obtained at a sale where all charges on sale are paid by the sellers.

72 Apportionment of valuation

(1) Where different species of property are insured under a single valuation, the valuation must be apportioned over the different species in proportion to

their respective insurable values, as in the case of an unvalued policy. The insured value of any part of a species is such proportion of the total insured value of the same as the insurable value of the part bears to the insurable value of the whole, ascertained in both cases as provided by this Act.

(2) Where a valuation has to be apportioned, and particulars of the prime cost of each separate species, quality, or description of goods cannot be ascertained, the division of the valuation may be made over the net arrived sound values of the different species, qualities, or descriptions of goods.

73 General average contributions and salvage charges

(1) Subject to any express provision in the policy, where the assured has paid, or is liable for, any general average contribution, the measure of indemnity is the full amount of such contribution, if the subject-matter liable to contribution is insured for its full contributory value; but, if such subject-matter be not insured for its full contributory value, or if only part of it be insured, the indemnity payable by the insurer must be reduced in proportion to the under insurance, and where there has been a particular average loss which constitutes a deduction from the contributory value, and for which the insurer is liable, that amount must be deducted from the insured value in order to ascertain what the insurer is liable to contribute.

(2) Where the insurer is liable for salvage charges the extent of his liability must be determined on the like principle.

74 Liabilities to third parties

Where the assured has effected an insurance in express terms against any liability to a third party, the measure of indemnity, subject to any express provision in the policy, is the amount paid or payable by him to such third party in respect of such liability.

75 General provisions as to measure of indemnity

(1) Where there has been a loss in respect of any subject-matter not expressly provided for in the foregoing provisions of this Act, the measure of indemnity shall be ascertained, as nearly as may be, in accordance with those provisions, in so far as applicable to the particular case.

(2) Nothing in the provisions of this Act relating to the measure of indemnity shall affect the rules relating to double insurance, or prohibit the insurer from disproving interest wholly or in part, or from showing that at the time of the loss the whole or any part of the subject-matter insured was not at risk under the policy.

76 Particular average warranties

(1) Where the subject-matter insured is warranted free from particular average, the assured cannot recover for a loss of part, other than a loss incurred by a general average sacrifice unless the contract contained in the policy be apportionable; but, if the contract be apportionable, the assured may recover for a total loss of any apportionable part.

(2) Where the subject-matter insured is warranted free from particular average, either wholly or under a certain percentage, the insurer is nevertheless liable for salvage charges, and for particular charges and other expenses properly incurred pursuant to the provisions of the suing and labouring clause in order to avert a loss insured against.

(3) Unless the policy otherwise provides, where the subject-matter insured is warranted free from particular average under a specified percentage, a general average loss cannot be added to a particular average loss to make up the specified percentage.

(4) For the purpose of ascertaining whether the specified percentage has been reached, regard shall be had only to the actual loss suffered by the subject-matter insured. Particular charges and the expenses of and incidental to ascertaining and proving the loss must be excluded.

77 Successive losses

(1) Unless the policy otherwise provides, and subject to the provisions of this Act, the insurer is liable for successive losses, even though the total amount of such losses may exceed the sum insured.

(2) Where, under the same policy, a partial loss, which has not been repaired or otherwise made good, is followed by a total loss, the assured can only recover in respect of the total loss: Provided that nothing in this section shall affect the liability of the insurer under the suing and labouring clause.

78 Suing and labouring clause

(1) Where the policy contains a suing and labouring clause, the engagement thereby entered into is deemed to be supplementary to the contract of insurance, and the assured may recover from the insurer any expenses properly incurred pursuant to the clause, notwithstanding that the insurer may have paid for a total loss, or that the subject-matter may have been warranted free from particular average, either wholly or under a certain percentage.

(2) General average losses and contributions and salvage charges, as defined by this Act, are not recoverable under the suing and labouring clause.

(3) Expenses incurred for the purpose of averting or diminishing any loss not covered by the policy are not recoverable under the suing and labouring clause.

(4) It is the duty of the assured and his agents, in all cases, to take such measures as may be reasonable for the purpose of averting or minimising a loss.

Rights of Insurer on Payment

79 Right of subrogation

(1) Where the insurer pays for a total loss, either of the whole, or in the case of goods of any apportionable part, of the subject-matter insured, he thereupon becomes entitled to take over the interest of the assured in whatever may remain of the subject-matter so paid for, and he is thereby subrogated to all

the rights and remedies of the assured in and in respect of that subject-matter as from the time of the casualty causing the loss.

(2) Subject to the foregoing provisions, where the insurer pays for a partial loss, he acquires no title to the subject-matter insured, or such part of it as may remain, but he is thereupon subrogated to all rights and remedies of the assured in and in respect of the subject-matter insured as from the time of the casualty causing the loss, in so far as the assured has been indemnified, according to this Act, by such payment for the loss.

80 Right of contribution

(1) Where the assured is over-insured by double insurance, each insurer is bound, as between himself and the other insurers, to contribute rateably to the loss in proportion to the amount for which he is liable under his contract.

(2) If any insurer pays more than his proportion of the loss, he is entitled to maintain an action for contribution against the other insurers, and is entitled to the like remedies as a surety who has paid more than his proportion of the debt.

81 Effect of under insurance

Where the assured is insured for an amount less than the insurable value or, in the case of a valued policy, for an amount less than the policy valuation, he is deemed to be his own insurer in respect of the uninsured balance.

Return of Premium

82 Enforcement of return

Where the premium or a proportionate part thereof is, by this Act, declared to be returnable,—

(a) If already paid, it may be recovered by the assured from the insurer; and

(b) If unpaid, it may be retained by the assured or his agent.

83 Return by agreement

Where the policy contains a stipulation for the return of the premium, or a proportionate part thereof, on the happening of a certain event, and that event happens, the premium, or, as the case may be, the proportionate part thereof, is thereupon returnable to the assured.

84 Return for failure of consideration

(1) Where the consideration for the payment of the premium totally fails, and there has been no fraud or illegality on the part of the assured or his agents, the premium is thereupon returnable to the assured.

(2) Where the consideration for the payment of the premium is apportionable and there is a total failure of any apportionable part of the consideration, a proportionate part of the premium is, under the like conditions, thereupon returnable to the assured.

(3) In particular—

(a) Where the policy is void, or is avoided by the insurer as from the commencement of the risk, the premium is returnable, provided that there has been no fraud or illegality on the part of the assured; but if the risk is not apportionable, and has once attached, the premium is not returnable;

(b) Where the subject-matter insured, or part thereof, has never been imperilled, the premium, or, as the case may be, a proportionate part thereof, is returnable: Provided that where the subject-matter has been insured 'lost or not lost' and has arrived in safety at the time when the contract is concluded, the premium is not returnable unless, at such time, the insurer knew of the safe arrival.

(c) Where the assured has no insurable interest throughout the currency of the risk, the premium is returnable, provided that this rule does not apply to a policy effected by way of gaming or wagering;

(d) Where the assured has a defeasible interest which is terminated during the currency of the risk, the premium is not returnable;

(e) Where the assured has over-insured under an unvalued policy, a proportionate part of the premium is returnable;

(f) Subject to the foregoing provisions, where the assured has over-insured by double insurance, a proportionate part of the several premiums is returnable: Provided that, if the policies are effected at different times, and any earlier policy has at any time borne the entire risk, or if a claim has been paid on the policy in respect of the full sum insured thereby, no premium is returnable in respect of that policy, and when the double insurance is effected knowingly by the assured no premium is returnable.

Mutual Insurance

85 Modification of Act in case of mutual insurance

(1) Where two or more persons mutually agree to insure each other against marine losses there is said to be a mutual insurance.

(2) The provisions of this Act relating to the premium do not apply to mutual insurance, but a guarantee, or such other arrangement as may be agreed upon, may be substituted for the premium.

(3) The provisions of this Act, in so far as they may be modified by the agreement of the parties, may in the case of mutual insurance be modified by the terms of the policies issued by the association, or by the rules and regulations of the association.

(4) Subject to the exceptions mentioned in this section, the provisions of this Act apply to a mutual insurance.

Supplemental

86 Ratification by assured

Where a contract of marine insurance is in good faith effected by one person on behalf of another, the person on whose behalf it is effected may ratify the contract even after he is aware of a loss.

87 Implied obligations varied by agreement or usage

(1) Where any right, duty, or liability would arise under a contract of marine insurance by implication of law, it may be negatived or varied by express agreement, or by usage, if the usage be such as to bind both parties to the contract.

(2) The provisions of this section extend to any right, duty, or liability declared by this Act which may be lawfully modified by agreement.

88 Reasonable time, etc, a question of fact

Where by this Act any reference is made to reasonable time, reasonable premium, or reasonable diligence, the question what is reasonable is a question of fact.

89 Slip as evidence

Where there is a duly stamped policy, reference may be made, as heretofore, to the slip or covering note, in any legal proceeding.

90 Interpretation of terms

In this Act, unless the context or subject-matter otherwise requires,—

'Action' includes counter-claim and set off:

'Freight' includes the profit derivable by a shipowner from the employment of his ship to carry his own goods or moveables, as well as freight payable by a third party, but does not include passage money:

'Moveables' means any moveable tangible property, other than the ship, and includes money, valuable securities, and other documents:

'Policy' means a marine policy.

91 Savings

(1) Nothing in this Act, or in any repeal effected thereby, shall affect—
   (a) The provisions of the Stamp Act 1891, or any enactment for the time being in force relating to the revenue;
   (b) The provisions of the Companies Act 1862, or any enactment amending or substituted for the same;
   (c) The provisions of any statute not expressly repealed by this Act.

(2) The rules of the common law including the law merchant, save in so far as they are inconsistent with the express provisions of this Act, shall continue to apply to contracts of marine insurance.

92 …

[Repealed by the Statute Law Revision Act 1927.]

93 …

[Repealed by the Statute Law Revision Act 1927.]

94 Short title

This Act may be cited as the Marine Insurance Act 1906.

SCHEDULE 1

Section 30

FORM OF POLICY

BE IT KNOWN THAT … … … as well in … … … own name as for and in the name and names of all and every other person or persons to whom the same doth, may, or shall appertain, in part or in all doth make assurance and cause … … … and them, and every of them, to be insured lost or not lost, at and from … … …

Upon any kind of goods and merchandise, and also upon the body, tackle, apparel, ordnance, munition, artillery, boat, and other furniture, of and in the good ship or vessel called the … … … whereof is master under God, for this present voyage, … … … or whosoever else shall go for master in the said ship, or by whatsoever other name or names the said ship, or the master thereof, is or shall be named or called; beginning the adventure upon the said goods and merchandises from the loading thereof aboard the said ship.

upon the said ship, etc

and so shall continue and endure, during her abode there, upon the said ship, etc

And further, until the said ship, with all her ordnance, tackle, apparel, etc, and goods and merchandises whatsoever shall be arrived at … … …

upon the said ship, etc, until she hath moored at anchor twenty-four hours in good safety; and upon the goods and merchandises, until the same be there discharged and safely landed. And it shall be lawful for the said ship, etc, in this voyage to proceed and sail to and touch and stay at any ports or places whatsoever

without prejudice to this insurance. The said ship, etc, goods and merchandises, etc, for so much as concerns the assured by agreement between the assured and assurers in this policy, are and shall be valued at … … …

Touching the adventures and perils which we the assurers are contented to bear and do take upon us in this voyage: they are of the seas, men of war, fire, enemies, pirates, rovers, thieves, jettisons, letters of mart and countermart, surprisals, takings at sea, arrests, restraints, and detainments of all kings, princes, and people, of what nation, condition, or quality soever, barratry of the master and mariners, and of all other perils, losses, and misfortunes, that have or shall come to the hurt, detriment, or damage of the said goods and merchandises, and ship, etc, or any part thereof. And in case of any loss or misfortune it shall be lawful to the assured, their factors, servants and assigns, to sue, labour, and travel for, in and about the defence, safeguards, and recovery of the said goods and merchandises, and ship, etc, or any part thereof, without prejudice to this insurance; to the charges whereof we, the assurers, will contribute each one according to the rate and quantity of his sum herein assured. And it is especially declared and agreed that no acts of the insurer or insured in recovering, saving, or preserving the property insured shall be considered as a waiver, or acceptance of abandonment. And it is agreed by us, the insurers, that this writing or policy of assurance shall be of as much force and effect as the surest writing or policy of assurance heretofore made in Lombard Street, or in the Royal Exchange, or elsewhere in London. And so we, the assurers, are contented, and do hereby promise and bind ourselves, each one for his own part, our heirs, executors, and goods to the assured, their executors, administrators, and assigns, for the true performance of the premises, confessing ourselves paid the consideration due unto us for this assurance by the assured, at and after the rate of … … …

IN WITNESS whereof we, the assurers, have subscribed our names and sums assured in London.

N.B.—Corn, fish, salt, fruit, flour, and seed are warranted free from average, unless general, or the ship be stranded—sugar, tobacco, hemp, flax, hides and skins are warranted free from average, under five pounds per cent., and all other goods, also the ship and freight, are warranted free from average, under three pounds per cent. unless general, or the ship be stranded.

RULES FOR CONSTRUCTION OF POLICY

The following are the rules referred to by this Act for the construction of a policy in the above or other like form, where the context does not otherwise require:—

1 Where the subject-matter is insured 'lost or not lost,' and the loss has occurred before the contract is concluded, the risk attaches, unless at such time the assured was aware of the loss, and the insurer was not.

2 Where the subject-matter is insured 'from' a particular place, the risk does not attach until the ship starts on the voyage insured.

3

(a) Where a ship is insured 'at and from' a particular place, and she is at that place in good safety when the contract is concluded, the risk attaches immediately.

(b) If she be not at that place when the contract is concluded, the risk attaches as soon as she arrives there in good safety, and, unless the policy otherwise provides, it is immaterial that she is covered by another policy for a specified time after arrival.

(c) Where chartered freight is insured 'at and from' a particular place, and the ship is at that place in good safety when the contract is concluded the risk attaches immediately. If she be not there when the contract is concluded, the risk attaches as soon as she arrives there in good safety.

(d) Where freight, other than chartered freight, is payable without special conditions and is insured 'at and from' a particular place, the risk attaches pro rata as the goods or merchandise are shipped; provided that if there be cargo in readiness which belongs to the shipowner, or which some other person has contracted with him to ship, the risk attaches as soon as the ship is ready to receive such cargo.

4 Where goods or other moveables are insured 'from the loading thereof,' the risk does not attach until such goods or moveables are actually on board, and the insurer is not liable for them while in transit from the shore to ship.

5 Where the risk on goods or other moveables continues until they are 'safely landed,' they must be landed in the customary manner and within a reasonable time after arrival at the port of discharge, and if they are not so landed the risk ceases.

6 In the absence of any further license or usage, the liberty to touch and stay 'at any port or place whatsoever' does not authorise the ship to depart from the course of her voyage from the port of departure to the port of destination.

7 The term 'perils of the seas' refers only to fortuitous accidents or casualties of the seas. It does not include the ordinary action of the winds and waves.

8 The term 'pirates' includes passengers who mutiny and rioters who attack the ship from the shore.

9 The term 'thieves' does not cover clandestine theft or a theft committed by any one of the ship's company, whether crew or passengers.

10 The term 'arrests, etc, of kings, princes, and people' refers to political or executive acts, and does not include a loss caused by riot or by ordinary judicial process.

11 The term 'barratry' includes every wrongful act wilfully committed by the master or crew to the prejudice of the owner, or, as the case may be, the charterer.

12 The term 'all other perils' includes only perils similar in kind to the perils specifically mentioned in the policy.

13 The term 'average unless general' means a partial loss of the subject-matter insured other than a general average loss, and does not include 'particular charges.'

14 Where the ship has stranded, the insurer is liable for the excepted losses, although the loss is not attributable to the stranding, provided that when the stranding takes place the risk has attached and, if the policy be on goods, that the damaged goods are on board.

15 The term 'ship' includes the hull, materials and outfit, stores and provisions for the officers and crew, and, in the case of vessels engaged in a special trade, the ordinary fittings requisite for the trade, and also, in the case of a steamship, the machinery, boilers, and coals and engine stores, if owned by the assured.

16 The term 'freight' includes the profit derivable by a shipowner from the employment of his ship to carry his own goods or moveables, as well as freight payable by a third party, but does not include passage money.

17 The term 'goods' means goods in the nature of merchandise, and does not include personal effects or provisions and stores for use on board. In the absence of any usage to the contrary, deck cargo and living animals must be insured specifically, and not under the general denomination of goods.

Appendix 2

Statutory Instruments

Employers' Liability (Compulsory Insurance) Regulations 1998

SI 1998/2573
(as amended by SI 1999/1820 and SI 2000/253)

1 Citation, commencement and interpretation

(1) These Regulations may be cited as the Employers' Liability (Compulsory Insurance) Regulations 1998 and shall come into force on 1st January 1999.

(2) In these Regulations—
'the 1969 Act' means the Employers' Liability (Compulsory Insurance) Act 1969;
'associated structure' means, in relation to an offshore installation, a vessel, aircraft or hovercraft attendant on the installation or any floating structure used in connection with the installation;
'company' has the same meaning as in section 735 of the Companies Act 1985;
'inspector' means an inspector duly authorised by the Secretary of State under section 4(2)(b) of the 1969 Act;
'offshore installation' has the same meaning as in the Offshore Installations and Pipeline Works (Management and Administration) Regulations 1995;
'relevant employee' means an employee—
(a) who is ordinarily resident in the United Kingdom; or
(b) who, though not ordinarily resident in the United Kingdom, has been employed on or from an offshore installation or associated structure for a continuous period of not less than 7 days; or
(c) who, though not ordinarily resident in Great Britain, is present in Great Britain in the course of employment for a continuous period of not less than 14 days; and
'subsidiary' has the same meaning as in section 736 of the Companies Act 1985.

2 Prohibition of certain conditions in policies of insurance

(1) For the purposes of the 1969 Act, there is prohibited in any contract of insurance any condition which provides (in whatever terms) that no liability (either generally or in respect of a particular claim) shall arise under the policy, or that any such liability so arising shall cease, if—
(a) some specified thing is done or omitted to be done after the happening of the event giving rise to a claim under the policy;

(b) the policy holder does not take reasonable care to protect his employees against the risk of bodily injury or disease in the course of their employment;

(c) the policy holder fails to comply with the requirements of any enactment for the protection of employees against the risk of bodily injury or disease in the course of their employment; or

(d) the policy holder does not keep specified records or fails to provide the insurer with or make available to him information from such records.

(2) For the purposes of the 1969 Act there is also prohibited in a policy of insurance any condition which requires—

(a) a relevant employee to pay; or

(b) an insured employer to pay the relevant employee,

the first amount of any claim or any aggregation of claims.

(3) Paragraphs (1) and (2) above do not prohibit for the purposes of the 1969 Act a condition in a policy of insurance which requires the employer to pay or contribute any sum to the insurer in respect of the satisfaction of any claim made under the contract of insurance by a relevant employee or any costs and expenses incurred in relation to any such claim.

3 Limit of amount of compulsory insurance

(1) Subject to paragraph (2) below, the amount for which an employer is required by the 1969 Act to insure and maintain insurance in respect of relevant employees under one or more policies of insurance shall be, or shall in aggregate be not less than £5 million in respect of—

(a) a claim relating to any one or more of those employees arising out of any one occurrence; and

(b) any costs and expenses incurred in relation to any such claim.

(2) Where an employer is a company with one or more subsidiaries, the requirements of paragraph (1) above shall be taken to apply to that company with any subsidiaries together, as if they were a single employer.

4 Issue of certificates of insurance

(1) Every authorised insurer who enters into a contract of insurance with an employer in accordance with the 1969 Act shall issue the employer with a certificate of insurance in the form, and containing the particulars, set out in Schedule 1 to these Regulations.

(2) The certificate shall be issued by the insurer not later than thirty days after the date on which the insurance commences or is renewed.

(3) Where a contract of insurance for the purposes of the 1969 Act is entered into together with one or more other contracts of insurance which jointly provide insurance cover of no less than £5 million, the certificate shall specify both—

(a) the amount in excess of which insurance cover is provided by the policy; and

(b) the maximum amount of that cover.

(4) An employer shall retain each certificate issued to him under this regulation, or a copy of each such certificate, for a period of 40 years beginning on the date on which the insurance to which it relates commences or is renewed.

(5) Where the employer is a company, retaining in any eye readable form a copy of a certificate in any one of the ways authorised by sections 722 and 723 of the Companies Act 1985 shall count as keeping a copy of it for the purposes of paragraph (4) above.

(6) In any case where it is intended that a contract of insurance for the purposes of the 1969 Act is to be effective, not only in Great Britain, but also—
   (a) in Northern Ireland, the Isle of Man, the Island of Guernsey, the Island of Jersey or the Island of Alderney;
   (b) in any waters outside the United Kingdom to which the 1969 Act may have been applied by any enactment,

the form set out in Schedule 1 to these Regulations may be modified by a reference to the relevant law which is applicable and a statement that the policy to which it relates satisfies the requirements of that law.

5 Display and production of copies of certificates of insurance

(1) Subject to paragraph (4) below, an employer who has been issued with a certificate in accordance with regulation 4 above shall display one or more copies of it, in accordance with paragraphs (2) and (3) below, at each place of business at which he employs any relevant employee of the class or description to which such certificate relates.

(2) Any relevant certificate which is required to be displayed in accordance with paragraph (1) above, shall be displayed in such number and in such positions and be of such size and legibility that they may be easily seen and read by any relevant employees, and shall be reasonably protected from being defaced or damaged.

(3) Copies of a certificate which are required to be displayed in accordance with paragraph (1) above shall be kept on display until the date of expiry or earlier termination of the approved policy mentioned in the certificate.

(4) The requirements of paragraphs (1), (2) and (3) above do not apply where an employer employs a relevant employee on or from an offshore installation or associated structure, but in such a case the employer shall produce, at the request of that employee and within the period of ten days from such request, a copy of the certificate which relates to that employee.

6 Production of certificates of insurance to an Inspector

An employer who is required by a written notice issued by an inspector to do so shall produce or send to any person specified in the notice, at the address and within the time specified in the notice—
   (a) either the original or a copy of every certificate issued to him under regulation 4 above which relates to a period of insurance current at the date of issue of the notice;
   (b) either the original or a copy of every certificate issued to him under regulation 4 above and retained by him in accordance with regulation 4(4) above.

7 Inspection of policies of insurance

Where a certificate is required to be issued to an employer in accordance with regulation 4 above, the employer shall during the currency of the insurance permit the policy of insurance or a copy of it to be inspected by an inspector—

(a) at such reasonable time as the inspector may require;

(b) at such place of business of the employer (which, in the case of an employer who is a company, may include its registered office) as the inspector may require.

8 Production by inspectors of evidence of authority

Any inspector shall, if so required when visiting any premises for the purposes of the 1969 Act, produce to an employer or his agent some duly authenticated document showing that he is authorised by the Secretary of State under section 4(2)(b) of the 1969 Act.

9 Employers exempted from insurance

(1) The employers specified in Schedule 2 to these Regulations are exempted from the requirement of the 1969 Act to insure and maintain insurance.

(2) The exemption applies to all cases to which that requirement would otherwise apply, except that for the employers specified in paragraphs 1, 12, 13 and 14 it applies only so far as is mentioned in those paragraphs.

10 Revocations and transitional

(1) Subject to paragraphs (2) and (3) below, the instruments specified in column 1 of Schedule 3 to these Regulations are hereby revoked to the extent specified in column 3 of that Schedule.

(2) Subject to paragraphs (4) and (5) below, in the case of an insurance policy commenced before, and current at, 1st January 1999, regulations 2 to 6 of, and the Schedule to, the 1971 Regulations shall continue to apply, instead of regulations 2 to 6 of, and Schedule 1 to, these Regulations, until the expiry or renewal of the policy or until 1st January 2000, whichever is the earlier.

(3) The certificate required to be issued by regulation 4(1) of these Regulations in respect of insurance commenced or renewed on or after 1st January 1999 but before 1st April 1999 may, instead of being in the prescribed form, be in the form and contain the particulars specified in the Schedule to the 1971 Regulations.

(4) Every authorised insurer who has issued a certificate in the form, and containing the particulars, specified in the Schedule to the 1971 Regulations in respect of insurance current at 1st April 2000 shall replace it by that date with a certificate in the prescribed form and the replacement shall then be the relevant certificate for the purposes of regulation 5 of these Regulations.

(5) The certificates to which regulation 4(4) of these Regulations applies include any certificate of which a copy is required to be displayed or maintained by regulation 6(1) of the 1971 Regulations immediately before 1st January

1999, and any such certificate shall be treated for the purposes of regulation 6 of these Regulations as having been issued under regulation 4 of these Regulations.

(6) Regulation 7 of these Regulations applies where a certificate is required, in accordance with paragraph (2) above, to be issued in accordance with the 1971 Regulations as it applies where a certificate is required to be issued in accordance with regulation 4 of these Regulations.

(7) In this regulation—
'in the prescribed form' means in the form, and containing the particulars, required by regulation 4(1) and (3) of, and Schedule 1 to, these Regulations;
'the 1971 Regulations' means the Employers' Liability (Compulsory Insurance) General Regulations 1971 as in force on 31st December 1998, including those Regulations as applied by the Employers' Liability (Compulsory Insurance) (Offshore Installations) Regulations 1975.

SCHEDULE 1

Regulation 4

'CERTIFICATE OF EMPLOYERS' LIABILITY INSURANCE

(Where required by regulation 5 of the Employers' Liability (Compulsory Insurance) Regulations 1998 (the Regulations), one or more copies of this certificate must be displayed at each place of business at which the policy holder employs persons covered by the policy)

Policy No … … … … …

1 Name of policy holder.

2 Date of commencement of insurance policy.

3 Date of expiry of insurance policy.

We hereby certify that subject to paragraph 2:—

1 the policy to which this certificate relates satisfies the requirements of the relevant law applicable in [Great Britain]; and

2

(a) the minimum amount of cover provided by this policy is no less than £5 million; or

(b) (b) the cover provided under this policy relates to claims in excess of [£] but not exceeding [£].

Signed on behalf of: ……………… (Authorised Insurer)

……………… Signature

Notes

(a) Where the employer is a company to which regulation 3(2) of the Regulations applies, the certificate shall state in a prominent place, either that the policy covers the holding company and all its subsidiaries, or that the policy covers the holding company and all its subsidiaries except any specifically excluded by name, or that the policy covers the holding company and only the named subsidiaries.

(b) Specify applicable law as provided for in regulation 4(6) of the Regulations.

(c) See regulation 3(1) of the Regulations and delete whichever of paragraphs 2(a) or 2(b) does not apply. Where 2(b) is applicable, specify the amount of cover provided by the relevant policy.'

SCHEDULE 2
EMPLOYERS EXEMPTED FROM INSURANCE

Regulation 9

1 A person who for the time being holds a current certificate issued by a government department [or the Scottish Ministers] [or the National Assembly for Wales] stating that claims established against that person in respect of any liability to such employees of the kind mentioned in section 1(1) of the 1969 Act as are mentioned in the certificate will, to any extent to which they are incapable of being satisfied by that person, be satisfied out of money provided by Parliament [or, in the case of a certificate issued by the Scottish Ministers, out of the Scottish Consolidated Fund] [or, in the case of a certificate issued by the National Assembly for Wales, out of monies provided by that Assembly]; but only in respect of employees covered by the certificate.

2 The Government of any foreign state or Commonwealth country.

3 Any inter-governmental organisation which by virtue of any enactment is to be treated as a body corporate.

4 Any subsidiary of any such body as is mentioned in section 3(1)(b) of the 1969 Act (which exempts any body corporate established by or under any enactment for the carrying on of any industry or part of an industry, or of any undertaking, under national ownership or control) and any company of which two or more such bodies are members and which would, if those bodies were a single corporate body, be a subsidiary of that body corporate.

5 Any Passenger Transport Executive and any subsidiary thereof.

[6 Transport for London or any of its subsidiaries (within the meaning of the Greater London Authority Act 1999).]

7 The Commission for the New Towns.

8 The Qualifications and Curriculum Authority.

9 Any voluntary management committee of an approved bail or approved probation hostel within the meaning of the Probation Service Act 1993.

10 Any magistrates' courts committee established under the Justices of the Peace Act 1997.

11 Any probation committee established under the Probation Service Act 1993.

12 Any employer who is a member of a mutual insurance association of shipowners or of shipowners and others, in respect of any liability to an employee of the kind mentioned in section 1(1) of the 1969 Act against which the employer is insured for the time being with that association for an amount not less than that required by the 1969 Act and regulations under it, being an employer who holds a certificate issued by that association to the effect that he is so insured in relation to that employee.

13 Any licensee within the meaning of the Nuclear Installations Act 1965, in respect of any liability to pay compensation under that Act to any of his employees in respect of a breach of duty imposed on him by virtue of section 7 of that Act.

14 Any employer to the extent he is required to insure and maintain insurance by subsection (1) of section 1 of the 1969 Act against liability for bodily injury sustained by his employee when the employee is—
(i) carried in or upon a vehicle; or
(ii) entering or getting on to, or alighting from, a vehicle,

in the circumstances specified in that subsection and where that bodily injury is caused by or, arises out of, the use by the employer of a vehicle on a road; and the expression 'road', 'use' and 'vehicle' have the same meanings as in Part VI of the Road Traffic Act 1988.

[**15** Any employer which is a company that has only one employee and that employee also owns fifty per cent or more of the issued share capital in that company.]

SCHEDULE 3
REVOCATIONS OF INSTRUMENTS

Regulation 10

1 *Reference*	2 *Title*	3 *Extent of revocation*
SI 1971/1117	The Employers' Liability (Compulsory Insurance) General Regulations 1971	The whole Regulations
SI 1971/1933	The Employers' Liability (Compulsory Insurance) Exemption Regulations 1971	The whole Regulations
SI 1974/208	The Employers' Liability (Compulsory Insurance) (Amendment) Regulations 1974	The whole Regulations
SI 1975/194	The Employers' Liability (Compulsory Insurance) (Amendment) Regulations 1975	The whole Regulations
SI 1975/1443	The Employers' Liability (Compulsory Insurance) (Offshore Installations) Regulations 1975	The whole Regulations
SI 1981/1489	The Employers' Liability (Compulsory Insurance) (Amendment) Regulations 1981	The whole Regulations
SI 1992/3172	The Employers' Liability (Compulsory Insurance) Exemption (Amendment) Regulations 1992	The whole Regulations
SI 1994/520	The Employers' Liability (Compulsory Insurance) Exemption (Amendment) Regulations 1994	The whole Regulations

SI 1994/3301	The Employers' Liability (Compulsory Insurance) General (Amendment) Regulations 1994	The whole Regulations

Appendix 3

Regulatory Codes

Financial Services Authority

The Financial Services Authority is the competent authority under the European single market directives for banking, insurance, investments, listing and other financial services matters. Its powers are conferred primarily by the Financial Services and Markets Act 2000 (FSMA), which unified the previous sectoral arrangements and regulators.

The FSA has authorisation, enforcement, supervision and rule making functions in relation to firms. It has registration functions under the various legislation applicable to mutual societies and related functions under other legislation applicable to financial services and listing.

FSMA requires the FSA to pursue four objectives:

- 'maintaining market confidence in the financial system';
- 'promoting public understanding of the financial system, including awareness of the benefits and risks of different kinds of investment or other financial dealing';
- 'securing the appropriate degree of protection for consumers, while having regard to the degree of risk involved in different kinds of investment or transaction, the expertise and experience of consumers, the needs of consumers for advice and accurate information and the general principle that consumers should take responsibility for their decisions';
- 'reducing the extent to which it is possible for a regulated business to be used for a purpose connected with financial crime, such as money laundering, fraud and insider dealing'.

FSMA applies these objectives directly to the FSA's general rule-making and policy-making functions. In carrying out these functions FSMA requires the FSA to have regard to a number of matters, which we refer to as 'principles of good regulation'. These are:

- 'the need to use our resources in the most efficient and economic way';
- 'recognising the responsibilities of regulated firms' own management';
- 'the principle that the burdens and restrictions imposed by regulation should be proportionate to the benefits';
- 'the international character of financial services and the desirability of maintaining the UK's competitive position';
- 'the desirability of facilitating innovation';
- 'the desirability of facilitating competition';
- 'the need to minimise the adverse effects of regulation on competition'.

The FSA is a body corporate and is subject to generally applicable company and accounting law. FSMA gives specific responsibilities to the FSA's non-executive directors – such as reviewing the economic and efficient use of the FSA's resources and setting the pay of executive Board members. It also sets out a number of explicit standards that the FSA must meet in carrying out its duties – for example, time periods within which it must take certain decisions.

Non-FSMA Legislation

In addition to FSMA the FSA has regulatory powers under the:

- Building Societies Act 1986;
- Friendly Societies Acts (1974 and 1992); and
- Industrial and Provident Societies Act 1965.

The following are some of the more significant functions the FSA has under non-FSMA legislation:

Enterprise Act 2002

The FSA is designated as a consumer enforcer under the Act. This gives the FSA power to apply to the courts to stop traders infringing a wide range of consumer protection legislation where those infringements harm the collective interests of consumers.

Unfair Terms in Consumer Contracts Regulations 1999

The FSA may seek an injunction to prevent the use of a contract term drawn up for general use in a financial services contract that appears to the FSA to be unfair.

Distance Marketing Regulations 2004

The FSA is designated as the body responsible for considering and, if necessary, taking action against persons responsible for breaching specified contracts.

Electronic Money Directive

The FSA is responsible for regulating the issuing of e-money (money stored on an electronic device such as a chip card or computer memory). Electronic Commerce Directive: The FSA has a number of powers under the directive including the power to direct that an incoming provider may no longer carry on a specified incoming electronic commerce activity, or may only carry it on subject to specified requirements.

The Financial Services and Markets Act gives us four statutory objectives:

- market confidence: maintaining confidence in the financial system;
- public awareness: promoting public understanding of the financial system;
- consumer protection: securing the appropriate degree of protection for consumers; and
- the reduction of financial crime: reducing the extent to which it is possible for a business to be used for a purpose connected with financial crime.

These are supported by a set of principles of good regulation which we must have regard to when discharging our functions.

The objectives also:

- provide political and public accountability. Our annual report contains an assessment of the extent to which we have met these objectives. Scrutiny of the FSA by Parliamentary Committees may focus on how we achieve our objectives;
- govern the way we carry out our general functions, eg rule-making, giving advice and guidance, and determining our general policy and principles. So, for example, we are under a duty to show how the draft rules we publish relate to our statutory objectives; and
- assist in providing legal accountability. Where we interpret the objectives wrongly, or fail to consider them, we can be challenged in the courts by judicial review.

Principles of good regulation

In pursuing our functions under the Act, we are required to have regard to additional matters that we refer to as 'principles of good regulation'. These are:

Efficiency and economy

The need to use our resources in the most efficient and economic way:

> The non-executive committee of our Board is required, among other things, to oversee our allocation of resources and to report to the Treasury every year. The Treasury is able to commission value-for-money reviews of our operations. These are important controls over our efficiency and economy.

Role of management

The responsibilities of those who manage the affairs of authorised persons:

> A firm's senior management is responsible for its activities and for ensuring that its business complies with regulatory requirements. This principle is designed to guard against unnecessary intrusion by the regulator into firms' business and requires us to hold senior management responsible for risk management and controls within firms.

Accordingly, firms must take reasonable care to make it clear who has what responsibility and to ensure that the affairs of the firm can be adequately monitored and controlled.

Proportionality

The restrictions we impose on the industry must be proportionate to the benefits that are expected to result from those restrictions:

In making judgements in this area, we take into account the costs to firms and consumers. One of the main techniques we use is cost benefit analysis of proposed regulatory requirements. This approach is shown, in particular, in the different regulatory requirements we apply to wholesale and retail markets.

Innovation

The desirability of facilitating innovation in connection with regulated activities:

This involves, for example allowing scope for different means of compliance so as not to unduly restrict market participants from launching new financial products and services.

International character

The international character of financial services and markets and the desirability of maintaining the competitive position of the UK:

We take into account the international aspects of much financial business and the competitive position of the UK. This involves co-operating with overseas regulators, both to agree international standards and to monitor global firms and markets effectively.

Competition

The need to minimise the adverse effects on competition that may arise from our activities and the desirability of facilitating competition between the firms we regulate:

These two principles cover avoiding unnecessary regulatory barriers to entry or business expansion. Competition and innovation considerations play a key role in our cost-benefit analysis work. Under the Financial Services and Markets Act, the Treasury, the Office of Fair Trading and the Competition Commission all have a role to play in reviewing the impact of our rules and practices on competition.

Contact details

25 The North Colonnade,
Canary Wharf,
London E14 5HS
Tel from UK: 020 7066 1000
Tel from Overseas: +44 20 7066 1000
web: www.fsa.gov.uk

Motor Insurers' Bureau (Compensation of Victims of Uninsured Drivers)

13th August 1999

Text of an Agreement dated the 13th August 1999 between the Secretary of State for the Environment, Transport and the Regions and Motor Insurers' Bureau together with some notes on its scope and purpose

THIS AGREEMENT is made the thirteenth day of August 1999 between the SECRETARY OF STATE FOR THE SECRETARY OF STATE FOR THE ENVIRONMENT, TRANSPORT AND THE REGIONS (hereinafter referred to as 'the Secretary of State') and the MOTOR INSURERS' BUREAU, whose registered office is at 152 Silbury Boulevard, Milton Keynes MK9 1NB (hereinafter referred to as 'MIB') and is SUPPLEMENTAL to an Agreement (hereinafter called 'the Principal Agreement') made the 31st Day of December 1945 between the Minister of War Transport and the insurers transacting compulsory motor insurance business in Great Britain by or on behalf of whom the said Agreement was signed and in pursuance of paragraph 1 of which MIB was incorporated.

IT IS HEREBY AGREED AS FOLLOWS:

INTERPRETATION

General definitions

1. In this Agreement, unless the context otherwise requires, the following expressions have the following meanings–

'1988 Act' means the Road Traffic Act 1988;

'1988 Agreement' means the Agreement made on 21 December 1988 between the Secretary of State for Transport and MIB;

'bank holiday' means a day which is, or is to be observed as, a bank holiday under the Banking and Financial Dealings Act 1971;

'claimant' means a person who has commenced or who proposes to commence relevant proceedings and has made an application under this Agreement in respect thereof;

'contract of insurance' means a policy of insurance or a security covering a relevant liability;

'insurer' includes the giver of a security;

'MIB's obligation' means the obligation contained in clause 5;

'property' means any property whether real, heritable or personal;

'relevant liability' means a liability in respect of which a contract of insurance must be in force to comply with Part VI of the 1988 Act;

'relevant proceedings' means proceedings in respect of a relevant liability (and 'commencement', in relation to such proceedings means, in England and Wales, the date on which a Claim Form or other originating process is issued by a Court or, in Scotland, the date on which the originating process is served on the Defender);

'relevant sum' means a sum payable or remaining payable under an unsatisfied judgment, including -

(a) an amount payable or remaining payable in respect of interest on that sum, and

(b) either the whole of the costs (whether taxed or not) awarded by the Court as part of that judgment or, where the judgment includes an award in respect of a liability which is not a relevant liability, such proportion of those costs as the relevant liability bears to the total sum awarded under the judgment;

'specified excess' means £300 or such other sum as may from time to time be agreed in writing between the Secretary of State and MIB;

'unsatisfied judgment' means a judgment or order (by whatever name called) in respect of a relevant liability which has not been satisfied in full within seven days from the date upon which the claimant became entitled to enforce it.

Meaning of references

2.1 Save as otherwise herein provided, the Interpretation Act 1978 shall apply for the interpretation of this Agreement as it applies for the interpretation of an Act of Parliament.

2.2 Where, under this Agreement, something is required to be done–

(a) within a specified period after or from the happening of a particular event, the period begins on the day after the happening of that event;

(b) within or not less than a specified period before a particular event, the period ends on the day immediately before the happening of that event.

2.3 Where, apart from this paragraph, the period in question, being a period of seven days or less, would include a Saturday, Sunday or bank holiday or Christmas Day or Good Friday, that day shall be excluded.

2.4 Save where expressly otherwise provided, a reference in this Agreement to a numbered clause is a reference to the clause bearing that number in this Agreement and a reference to a numbered paragraph is a reference to a paragraph bearing that number in the clause in which the reference occurs.

2.5 In this Agreement–

(a) a reference (however framed) to the doing of any act or thing by or the happening of any event in relation to the claimant includes a reference to the doing of that act or thing by or the happening of that event In relation to a Solicitor or other person acting on his behalf, and

(b) a requirement to give notice to, or to serve documents upon, MIB or an insurer mentioned in clause 9(1)(a) shall be satisfied by the giving of the notice to, or the service of the documents upon, a Solicitor acting on its behalf in the manner provided for.

Claimants not of full age or capacity

3.1 Where, under and in accordance with this Agreement–

(a) any act or thing is done to or by a Solicitor or other person acting on behalf of a claimant,

(b) any decision is made by or in respect of a Solicitor or other person acting on behalf of a claimant, or

(c) any sum is paid to a Solicitor or other person acting on behalf of a claimant, then, whatever may be the age or other circumstances affecting the capacity of the claimant, that act, thing, decision or sum shall be treated as if it had been done to or by, or made in respect of or paid to a claimant of full age and capacity.

PRINCIPAL TERMS

Duration of Agreement

4.1 This Agreement shall come into force on 1st October 1999 in relation to accidents occurring on or after that date and, save as provided by clause 23, the 1988 Agreement shall cease and determine immediately before that date.

4.2 This Agreement may be determined by the Secretary of State or by MIB giving to the other not less than twelve months' notice in writing but without prejudice to its continued operation in respect of accidents occurring before the date of termination.

MIB's obligation to satisfy compensation claims

5.1 Subject to clauses 6 to 17, if a claimant has obtained against any person in a Court in Great Britain a judgment which is an unsatisfied judgment then MIB will pay the relevant sum to, or to the satisfaction of, the claimant or will cause the same to be so paid.

5.2 Paragraph (1) applies whether or not the person liable to satisfy the judgment is in fact covered by a contract of insurance and whatever may be the cause of his failure to satisfy the judgment.

EXCEPTIONS TO AGREEMENT

6.1 Clause 5 does not apply in the case of an application made in respect of a claim of any of the following descriptions (and, where part only of a claim satisfies such a description, clause S does not apply to that part)–

(a) a claim arising out of a relevant liability incurred by the user of a vehicle owned by or in the possession of the Crown, unless–

(i) responsibility for the existence of a contract of insurance under Part VI of the 1988 Act in relation to that vehicle had been undertaken by some other person (whether or not the person liable was in fact covered by a contract of insurance), or

(ii) the relevant liability was in fact covered by a contract of insurance;

(b) a claim arising out of the use of a vehicle which is not required to be covered by a contract of insurance by virtue of section 144 of the 1988 Act, unless the use is in fact covered by such a contract;

(c) a claim by, or for the benefit of, a person ('the beneficiary') other than the person suffering death, injury or other damage which is made either–

  - (i) in respect of a cause of action or a judgment which has been assigned to the beneficiary, or
  - (ii) pursuant to a right of subrogation or contractual or other right belonging to the beneficiary;
- (d) a claim in respect of damage to a motor vehicle or losses arising there from where, at the time when the damage to it was sustained -
  - (i) there was not in force in relation to the use of that vehicle such a contract of insurance as is required by Part VI of the 1988 Act, and
  - (ii) the claimant either knew or ought to have known that that was the case;
- (e) a claim which is made in respect of a relevant liability described in paragraph (2) by a claimant who, at the time of the use giving rise to the relevant liability was voluntarily allowing himself to be carried in the vehicle and, either before the commencement of his journey in the vehicle or after such commencement if he could reasonably be expected to have alighted from it, knew or ought to have known that–
  - (i) the vehicle had been stolen or unlawfully taken,
  - (ii) the vehicle was being used without there being in force in relation to its use such a contract of insurance as would comply with Part VI of the 1988 Act,
  - (iii) the vehicle was being used in the course or furtherance of a crime, or
  - (iv) the vehicle was being used as a means of escape from, or avoidance of, lawful apprehension.

6.2 The relevant liability referred to in paragraph (1)(e) is a liability incurred by the owner or registered keeper or a person using the vehicle in which the claimant was being carried.

6.3 The burden of proving that the claimant knew or ought to have known of any matter set out in paragraph (1)(e) shall be on MIB but, in the absence of evidence to the contrary, proof by MIB of any of the following matters shall be taken as proof of the claimant's knowledge of the matter set out in paragraph (1)(e)(ii)–

- (a) that the claimant was the owner or registered keeper of the vehicle or had caused or permitted its use;
- (b) that the claimant knew the vehicle was being used by a person who was below the minimum age at which he could be granted a licence authorising the driving of a vehicle of that class;
- (c) that the claimant knew that the person driving the vehicle was disqualified for holding or obtaining a driving licence;
- (d) that the claimant knew that the user of the vehicle was neither its owner nor registered keeper nor an employee of the owner or registered keeper nor the owner or registered keeper of any other vehicle.

6.4 Knowledge which the claimant has or ought to have for the purposes of paragraph (1)(e) includes knowledge of matters which he could reasonably be expected to have been aware of had he not been under the self-induced influence of drink or drugs.

6.5 For the purposes of this clause–

(a) a vehicle which has been unlawfully removed from the possession of the Crown shall be taken to continue in that possession whilst it is kept so removed,

(b) references to a person being carried in a vehicle include references to his being carried upon, entering, getting on to and alighting from the vehicle, and

(c) 'owner', in relation to a vehicle which is the subject of a hiring agreement or a hire-purchase agreement, means the person in possession of the vehicle under that agreement.

CONDITIONS PRECEDENT TO MIB'S OBLIGATION

Form of application

7.1 MIB shall incur no liability under MIB's obligation unless an application is made to the person specified in clause 9(1)–

(a) in such form,

(b) giving such information about the relevant proceedings and other matters relevant to this Agreement, and

(c) accompanied by such documents as MIB may reasonably require.

7.2 Where an application is signed by a person who is neither the claimant nor a Solicitor acting on his behalf MIB may refuse to accept the application (and shall incur no liability under MIB's obligation) until it is reasonably satisfied that, having regard to the status of the signatory and his relationship to the claimant, the claimant is fully aware of the contents and effect of the application but subject thereto MIB shall not refuse to accept such an application by reason only that it is signed by a person other than the claimant or his Solicitor.

Service of notices etc

8.1 Any notice required to be given or documents to be supplied to MIB pursuant to clauses 9 to 12 of this Agreement shall be sufficiently given or supplied only if sent by facsimile transmission or by Registered or Recorded Delivery post to MIB's registered office for the time being and delivery shall be proved by the production of a facsimile transmission report produced by the sender's facsimile machine or an appropriate postal receipt.

Notice of relevant proceedings

9.1 MIB shall incur no liability under MIB's obligation unless proper notice of the bringing of the relevant proceedings has been given by the claimant not later than fourteen days after the commencement of those proceedings–

(a) in the case of proceedings in respect of a relevant liability which is covered by a contract of insurance with an insurer whose identity can be ascertained, to that insurer;

(b) in any other case, to MIB.

9.2 In this clause 'proper notice' means, except in so far as any part of such information or any copy document or other thing has already been supplied under clause 7–

(a) notice in writing that proceedings have been commenced by Claim Form, Writ, or other means,

(b) a copy of the sealed Claim Form, Writ or other official document providing evidence of the commencement of the proceedings and, in Scotland, a statement of the means of service,

(c) a copy or details of any insurance policy providing benefits in the case of the death, bodily injury or damage to property to which the proceedings relate where the claimant is the insured party and the benefits are available to him,

(d) copies of all correspondence in the possession of the claimant or (as the case may be) his Solicitor or agent to or from the Defendant or the Defender or (as the case may be) his Solicitor, insurers or agent which is relevant to–

(i) the death, bodily in jury or damage for which the Defendant or Defender is alleged to be responsible, or

(ii) any contract of insurance which covers, or which may or has been alleged to cover, liability for such death, injury or damage the benefit of which is, or is claimed to be, available to Defendant or Defender,

(e) subject to paragraph (3), a copy of the Particulars of Claim whether or not indorsed on the Claim Form, Writ or other originating process, and whether or not served (in England and Wales) on any Defendant or (in Scotland) on any Defender, and

(f) a copy of all other documents which are required under the appropriate rules of procedure to be served on a Defendant or Defender with the Claim Form, Writ or other originating process or with the Particulars of Claim,

(g) such other information about the relevant proceedings as MIB may reasonably specify.

9.3 If, in the case of proceedings commenced in England or Wales, the Particulars of Claim (including any document required to be served therewith) has not yet been served with the Claim Form or other originating process paragraph (2)(e) shall be sufficiently complied with if a copy thereof is served on MIB not later than seven days after it is served on the Defendant.

Notice of service of proceedings

10.1 This clause applies where the relevant proceedings are commenced in England or Wales.

10.2 MIB shall incur no liability under MIB's obligation unless the claimant has, not later than the appropriate date, given notice in writing to the person specified in clause 9(1) of the date of service of the Claim Form or other originating process in the relevant proceedings.

10.3 In this clause, 'the appropriate date' means the day falling–

(a) seven days after–

(i) the date when the claimant receives notification from the Court that service of the Claim Form or other originating process has occurred,

(ii) the date when the claimant receives notification from the Defendant that service of the Claim Form or other originating process has occurred, or

(iii) the date of personal service, or

(b) fourteen days after the date when service is deemed to have occurred in accordance with the Civil Procedure Rules, whichever of those days occurs first.

Further information

11.1 MIB shall incur no liability under MIB's obligation unless the claimant has, not later than seven days after the occurrence of any of the following events, namely–

(a) the filing of a defence in the relevant proceedings,

(b) any amendment to the Particulars of Claim or any amendment of or addition to any schedule or other document required to be served therewith, and

(c) either–

(i) the setting down of the case for trial, or

(ii) where the court gives notice to the claimant of the trial date, the date when that notice is received, given notice in writing of the date of that event to the person specified in clause 9.1 and has, in the case of the filing of a defence or an amendment of the Particulars of Claim or any amendment of or addition to any schedule or other document required to be served therewith, supplied a copy thereof to that person.

11.2 MIB shall incur no liability under MIB's obligation unless the claimant furnishes to the person specified in clause 9.1 within a reasonable time after being required to do so such further information and documents in support of his claim as MIB may reasonably require notwithstanding that the claimant may have complied with clause 7.1.

Notice of intention to apply for judgment

12.1 MIB shall incur no liability under MIB's obligation unless the claimant has, after commencement of the relevant proceedings and not less than thirty-five days before the appropriate date, given notice in writing to the person specified in clause 9.1 of his intention to apply for or to sign judgment in the relevant proceedings.

12.2 In this clause, 'the appropriate date' means the date when the application for judgment is made or, as the case may be, the signing of judgment occurs.

Section 154 of the 1988 Act

13.1 MIB shall incur no liability under MIB's obligation unless the claimant has as soon as reasonably practicable–

(a) demanded the information and, where appropriate, the particulars specified in section 154(1) of the 1988 Act, and

(b) if the person of whom the demand is made fails to comply with the provisions of that subsection -

(i) made a formal complaint to a police officer in respect of such failure, and
(ii) used all reasonable endeavours to obtain the name and address of the registered keeper of the vehicle or, if so required by MIB, has authorised MIB to take such steps on his behalf.

Prosecution of proceedings

14.1 MIB shall incur no liability under MIB's obligation–
(a) unless the claimant has, if so required by MIB and having been granted a full indemnity by MIB as to costs, taken all reasonable steps to obtain judgment against every person who may be liable (including any person who may be vicariously liable) in respect of the injury or death or damage to property, or
(b) if the claimant, upon being requested to do so by MIB, refuses to consent to MIB being joined as a party to the relevant proceedings.

Assignment of judgment and undertakings

15.1 MIB shall incur no liability under MIB's obligation unless the claimant has–
(a) assigned to MIB or its nominee the unsatisfied judgment, whether or not that judgment includes an amount in respect of a liability other than a relevant liability, and any order for costs made in the relevant proceedings, and
(b) undertaken to repay to MIB any sum paid to him–
(i) by MIB in discharge of MIB's obligation if the judgment is subsequently set aside either as a whole or in respect of the part of the relevant liability to which that sum relates;
(ii) by any other person by way of compensation or benefit for the death, bodily injury or other damage to which the relevant proceedings relate, including a sum which would have been deductible under the provisions of clause 17 if it had been received before MIB was obliged to satisfy MIB's obligation.

LIMITATIONS ON MIB'S LIABILITY

Compensation for damage to property

16.1 Where a claim under this Agreement includes a claim in respect of damage to property, MIB's obligation in respect of that part of the relevant sum which is awarded for such damage and any losses arising therefrom (referred to in this clause as 'the property damage compensation') is limited in accordance with the following paragraphs.

16.2 Where the property damage compensation does not exceed the specified excess, MIB shall incur no liability.

16.3 Where the property damage compensation in respect of any one accident exceeds the specified excess but does not exceed £250,000, MIB shall incur liability less the specified excess.

16.4 Where the property damage compensation in respect of any one accident exceeds £250,000, MIB shall incur liability only in respect of the sum of £250,000 less the specified excess.

Compensation received from other sources

17.1 Where a claimant has received compensation from–

(a) the Policyholders Protection Board under the Policyholders Protection Act 1975, or

(b) an insurer under an insurance agreement or arrangement, or

(c) any other source, in respect of the death, bodily injury or other damage to which the relevant proceedings relate and such compensation has not been taken into account in the calculation of the relevant sum MIB may deduct from the relevant sum, in addition to any sum deductible under clause 16, an amount equal to that compensation.

MISCELLANEOUS

Notifications of decisions by MIB

18.1 Where a claimant–

(a) has made an application in accordance with clause 7, and

(b) has given to the person specified in clause 9.1 proper notice of the relevant proceedings in accordance with clause 9.2,

MIB shall–

(i) give a reasoned reply to any request made by the claimant relating to the payment of compensation in pursuance of MIB's obligation, and

(ii) as soon as reasonably practicable notify the claimant in writing of its decision regarding the payment of the relevant sum, together with the reasons for that decision.

Reference of disputes to the Secretary of State

19.1 In the event of any dispute as to the reasonableness of a requirement made by MIB for the supply of information or documentation or for the taking of any step by the claimant, it may be referred by the claimant or MIB to the Secretary of State whose decision shall be final.

19.2 Where a dispute is referred to the Secretary of State–

(a) MIB shall supply the Secretary of State and, if it has not already done so, the claimant with notice in writing of the requirement from which the dispute arises, together with the reasons for that requirement and such further information as MIB considers relevant, and

(b) where the dispute is referred by the claimant, the claimant shall supply the Secretary of State and, if he has not already done so, MIB with notice in writing of the grounds on which he disputes the reasonableness of the requirement.

Recoveries

20.1 Nothing in this Agreement shall prevent an insurer from providing by conditions in a contract of insurance that all sums paid by the insurer or by MIB by virtue of the Principal Agreement or this Agreement in or towards the discharge of the liability of the insured shall be recoverable by them or by MIB from the insured or from any other person.

Apportionment of damages, etc

21.1 Where an unsatisfied judgment which includes an amount in respect of a liability other than a relevant liability has been assigned to MIB or its nominee in pursuance of clause 15 MIB shall–

(a) apportion any sum it receives in satisfaction or partial satisfaction of the judgment according to the proportion which the damages awarded in respect of the relevant liability bear to the damages awarded in respect of the other liability, and

(b) account to the claimant in respect of the moneys received properly apportionable to the other liability.

21.2 Where the sum received includes an amount in respect of interest or an amount awarded under an order for costs, the interest or the amount received in pursuance of the order shall be dealt with in the manner provided in paragraph (1).

Agents

22.1 MIB may perform any of its obligations under this agreement by agents.

Transitional provisions

23.1 The 1988 Agreement shall continue in force in relation to claims arising out of accidents occurring before 1st October 1999 with the modifications contained in paragraph (2).

23.2 In relation to any claim made under the 1988 Agreement after this Agreement has come into force, the 1988 Agreement shall apply as if there were inserted after clause 6 thereof

'6A. Where any person in whose favour a judgment In respect of a relevant liability has been made has–

(a) made a claim under this Agreement, and

(b) satisfied the requirements specified in clause 5 hereof,

MIB shall, if requested to do so, give him a reasoned reply regarding the satisfaction of that claim'.

IN WITNESS whereof the Secretary of State has caused his Corporate Seal to be hereunto affixed and the Motor Insurers' Bureau has caused its Common Seal to be hereunto affixed the day and year first above written.

THE CORPORATE SEAL of the SECRETARY OF STATE FOR THE ENVIRONMENT, TRANSPORT AND THE REGIONS hereunto affixed is authenticated by:

Richard Jones
Authorised by the Secretary of State

THE COMMON SEAL of the MOTOR INSURERS' BUREAU was hereunto affixed in the presence of:

James Arthur Read
Roger Merer Jones
Directors of the Board of Management
Byford Louisy
Secretary

NOTES FOR THE GUIDANCE OF VICTIMS OF ROAD TRAFFIC ACCIDENTS

The following notes are for the guidance of anyone who may have a claim on the Motor Insurers' Bureau under this Agreement and their legal advisers. They are not part of the Agreement, their purpose being to deal in ordinary language with the situations which most readily occur. They are not in any way a substitute for reading and applying the terms of this or any other relevant Agreement.

At the request of the Secretary of State, these notes have been revised with effect from 15th April 2002 and in their revised form have been agreed and approved by MIB, the Law Society of England and Wales, the Law Society of Scotland, the Motor Accident Solicitors' Society and the Association of Personal Injury Lawyers. Any application made under the Agreement after this date (unless proceedings have already been issued) will be handled by MIB in accordance with these notes.

Where proceedings have been issued in Scotland, for the words 'Claimant' and 'Defendant' there shall be substituted in these Notes where appropriate the words 'Pursuer' and 'Defender' respectively.

Enquiries, requests for application forms and general correspondence In connection with the Agreement should be addressed to:

Motor Insurers Bureau
Linford Wood House
6–12 Capital Drive
MILTON KEYNES
MK14 6XT
Tel: 01908 830001
Fax: 01908 671681
DX: 142620 Milton Keynes

1. Introduction – MIB's role and application of the Agreement

1.1 The role of MIB under this Agreement is to provide a safety net for innocent victims of drivers who have been identified but are uninsured. MIB's funds for this purpose are obtained from levies charged upon insurers and so come from the premiums which are charged by those insurers to members of the public.

1.2 MIB has entered into a series of Agreements with the Secretary of State and his predecessors in office. Under each Agreement MIB undertakes obligations to pay defined compensation in specific circumstances. There are two sets of Agreements, one relating to victims of uninsured drivers (the

'Uninsured Drivers' Agreements) and the other concerned with victims of hit and run or otherwise untraceable drivers (the 'Untraced Drivers' Agreements). These Notes are addressed specifically to the procedures required to take advantage of the rights granted by the Uninsured Drivers Agreements. However, it is not always certain which of the Agreements applies. For guidance in such cases please see the note on Untraced Drivers at paragraph 11 below.

1.3 In order to determine which of the Uninsured Drivers Agreements is applicable to a particular victim's claim, regard must be had to the date of the relevant accident. This Agreement only applies in respect of claims arising on or after 1st October 1999. Claims arising earlier than that are covered by the following Agreements:

1.3.1 Claims arising in respect of an incident occurring between 1st July 1946 and 28th February 1971 are governed by the Agreement between the Minister of Transport and the Bureau dated 17th June 1946.

1.3.2 Claims arising in respect of an incident occurring between 1st March 1971 and 30th November 1972 are governed by the Agreement between the Secretary of State for the Environment and the Bureau dated 1st February 1971.

1.3.3 Claims arising in respect of an incident occurring between 1st December 1972 and 30th December 1988 are governed by the Agreement between the Secretary of State and the Bureau dated 22nd November 1972.

1.3.4 Claims arising in respect of an incident occurring between 31st December 1988 and 30th September 1999 are governed by the Agreement between the Secretary of State and the Bureau dated 21st December 1988.

2. MIB's obligation

2.1 MIB's basic obligation (see clause 5) is to satisfy judgments which fall within the terms of this Agreement and which, because the Defendant to the proceedings is not insured, are not satisfied.

2.2 This obligation is, however, not absolute. It is subject to certain exceptions where MIB has no liability (see clause 6), there are a number of preconditions which the claimant must comply with (see clauses 7 to 15) and there are some limitations on MIB's liability (see clauses 16 and 17).

2.3 Nothing in the Agreement is intended to vary the limitation rules applying to claimants not of full age or capacity. Limitation for personal injury remains 3 years from the date of full age or capacity.

2.4 MIB does not have to wait for a judgment to be given; it can become party to the proceedings or negotiate and settle the claim if it wishes to do so.

3. Claims which MIB is not obliged to satisfy

MIB is not liable under the Agreement in the case of the following types of claim.

3.1 A claim made in respect of an unsatisfied judgment which does not concern a liability against which Part VI of the Road Traffic Act 1988 requires a vehicle user to insure (see section 145 of the Act). An example would be a case where the accident did not occur in a place specified in the Act. See the definitions of 'unsatisfied judgment' and 'relevant liability' in clause 1.

3.2 A claim in respect of loss or damage caused by the use of a vehicle owned by or in the possession of the Crown (that is the Civil Service, the armed forces and so on) to which Part VI does not apply. If the responsibility for motor insurance has been undertaken by someone else or the vehicle is in fact insured, this exception does not apply. See clause 6(1)(a).

3.3 A claim made against any person who is not required to insure by virtue of section 144 of the Road Traffic Act 1988. See clause 6(1)(b).

3.4 A claim (commonly called subrogated) made in the name of a person suffering damage or injury but which is in fact wholly or partly for the benefit of another who has indemnified, or is liable to indemnify that person. See clause 6(1)(c).

It is not the intention of this Clause to exclude claims for the gratuitous provision of care, travel expenses by family members or friends, or miscellaneous expenses incurred on behalf of the Claimant, where the claimant is entitled to include such claims in his claim for damages.

3.5 A claim in respect of damage to a motor vehicle or losses arising from such damage where the use of the damaged vehicle was itself not covered by a contract of insurance as required by law. See clause 6(1)(d).

3.6 A claim made by a passenger in a vehicle where the loss or damage has been caused by the user of that vehicle if:-
 3.6.1 the use of the vehicle was not covered by a contract of insurance; and
 3.6.2 the claimant knew or could be taken to have known that the vehicle was being used without insurance, had been stolen or unlawfully taken or was being used in connection with crime.

See clause 6(1)(e), (2), (3) and (4).

For an interpretation of 'knew or ought to have known' refer to the House of Lords judgment in *White v White* of 1st March 2001.

3.7 A claim in respect of property damage amounting to £300 or less, £300 being the 'specified excess'. See clause 16(2).

3.8 Where the claim is for property damage, the first £300 of the loss and so much of it as exceeds £250,000. See clause 16(3) and (4).

4. Procedure after the accident and before proceedings

4.1 The claimant must take reasonable steps to establish whether there is in fact any insurance covering the use of the vehicle which caused the injury or damage. First, a claimant has statutory rights under section 154 of the Road Traffic Act 1988 to obtain relevant particulars which he must take steps to exercise even if that involves incurring expense and MIB will insist that he does so. See clause 13(a).

MIB accept that if the MIB application form is sufficiently completed and signed by the Claimant, the Claimant will have complied with this Clause of the Agreement.

4.2 Other steps will include the following:

4.2.1 The exchange of names, addresses and insurance particulars between those involved either at the scene of the accident or afterwards.

4.2.2 Corresponding with the owner or driver of the vehicle or his representatives. He will be obliged under the terms of his motor policy to inform his insurers and a letter of claim addressed to him will commonly be passed to the insurers who may reply on his behalf. See clause 9(2)(d).

4.2.3 Where only the vehicle's number is known, enquiry of the Driver and Vehicle Licensing Agency at Swansea SA99 1BP as to the registered keeper of the vehicle is desirable so that through him the identity of the owner or driver can be established or confirmed.

4.2.4 Enquiries of the police (see clause 13(b) and Note 4.1 above).

4.3 If enquiries show that there is an insurer who is obliged to accept and does accept the obligation to handle the claim against the user of the vehicle concerned, even though the relevant liability may not be covered by the policy in question, then the claim should be pursued with such insurer.

4.4 If, however, enquiries disclose that there is no insurance covering the use of the vehicle concerned or if the insurer cannot be identified or the insurer asserts that it is under no obligation to handle the claim or if for any other reason it is clear that the insurer will not satisfy any judgment, the claim should be directed to MIB itself.

5. When proceedings are commenced or contemplated

5.1 As explained above, MIB does not have to wait for a judgment to be obtained before intervening. Claimants may apply to MIB before the commencement of proceedings. MIB will respond to any claim which complies with clause 7 and must give a reasoned reply to any request for compensation in respect of the claim (see clause 18) although normally a request for compensation will not be met until MIB is satisfied that it is properly based. Interim compensation payments are dealt with at paragraph 8 below.

Application Forms are available from MIB's office or their website: www.mib.org.uk.

Where a claim is made by the Claimant in person, who has not received legal advice, then if the claim is first made within 14 days prior to expiry of the limitation period, MIB will require the completed application form within the 21 days after the issue of proceedings.

5.2 It is important that wherever possible claims should be made using MIB's application form, fully completed and accompanied by documents supporting the claim, as soon as possible to avoid unnecessary delays. See clause 7(1). Copies of the form can be obtained on request made by post, telephone, fax or the DX or on personal application to MIB's offices.

5.3 The claimant must give MIB notice in writing that he has commenced legal proceedings. The notice, the completed application form (if appropriate) and all necessary documents must be received by MIB no later than 14 days after the date of commencement of proceedings. See clause 9(1) and (2)(a). The date of commencement is determined in accordance with the definitions of 'relevant proceedings' and 'commencement' given in clause 1.

When it is decided to commence legal proceedings, MIB should be joined as a defendent (unless there is good reason not to do so). Once MIB is a defendant, the Court will advise the relevant events direct and clauses 9(3),11 and 12 will no longer apply.

The form of words set out below should be used for the joinder of MIB as second defendant:

1. The Second Defendant is a Company limited by guarantee under the Companies Act. Pursuant to an Agreement with the Secretary of State for the Environment Transport and the Regions dated 13th August 1999, the Second Defendant provides compensation in certain circumstances to persons suffering injury or damage as a result of the negligence of uninsured motorists.
2. The Claimant has used all reasonable endeavours to ascertain the liability of an insurer for the First Defendant and at the time of the commencement of these proceedings verily believes that the First Defendant is not insured.
3. The Claimant accepts that only if a final judgment is obtained against the First Defendant (which judgment is not satisfied in full within seven days from the date upon which the Claimant became entitled to enforce it) can the Second Defendant be required to satisfy the judgement and then only if the terms and conditions set out in the Agreement are satisfied. Until that time, any liability of the Second Defendant is only contingent.
4. To avoid the Second Defendant having later to apply to join itself to this action (which the Claimant must consent to in any event, pursuant to Clause 14(b) of the Agreement) the Claimant seeks to include the Second Defendant from the outset recognising fully the Second Defendant's position as reflected in 3 above and the rights of the Second Defendant fully to participate in the action to protect its position as a separate party to the action.
5. With the above in mind, the Claimant seeks a declaration of the Second Defendant's contingent liability to satisfy the claimant's judgment against the First Defendant.

5.4 This notice must have with it the following:

5.4.1 a copy of the document originating the proceedings, usually in England and Wales a Claim Form and in Scotland a Sheriff Court Writ or Court of Session Summons (see clause 9(2)(b));

5.4.2 normally the Particulars of Claim endorsed on or served with the Claim Form or Writ (see clause 9(2)(e), although this document may be served later in accordance with clause 9(3) if that applies);

5.4.3 in any case the documents required by the relevant rules of procedure (see clause 9(2)(f).

Provided that the documents referred to above are forwarded to MIB, it is not necessary to enclose the Response Pack or the Notice of Issue.

5.5 In addition, other items as mentioned in clause 9(2), eg correspondence with the Defendant (or Defender) or his representatives, need to be supplied where appropriate.

5.6 It is for the claimant to satisfy himself that the notice has in fact been received by MIB. However, where the Claimant proves that service by DX, First Class Post, Personal Service or any other form of service allowed by the Civil Procedure Rules, was effected, MIB will accept that such notice has been served in the same circumstances in which a party to litigation would be obliged to accept that he had been validly served by such means.

5.7 It should be noted that when MIB has been given notice of a claim, it may elect to require the claimant to bring proceedings and attempt to secure a judgment against the party whom MIB alleges to be wholly or partly responsible for the loss or damage or who may be contracted to indemnify the claimant. In such a case MIB must indemnify the claimant against the costs of such proceedings. Subject to that, however, MIB's obligation to satisfy the judgment in the action will only arise if the claimant commences the proceedings and takes all reasonable steps to obtain a judgment. See clause 14(a).

6. Service of proceedings

6.1 If proceedings are commenced in England or Wales the claimant must inform MIB of the date of service (see clause 10(1) and (2)).

6.2 If service of the Claim Form is effected by the Court, notice should be given within 7 days from the earliest of the dates listed in clause 10(3)(a)(i) or (ii) or within 14 days from the date mentioned in clause 10(3)(b) (the date of deemed service under the court's rules of procedure). Claimants are advised to take steps to ensure that the court or the defendant's legal representatives inform them of the date of service as soon as possible. Although a longer period is allowed than in other cases, service may be deemed to have occurred without a Claimant knowing of it until some time afterwards.

6.3 Where proceedings are served personally, notice should be given 7 days from the date of personal service (clause 10(3)(a)(iii)).

6.4 However, by concession MIB will accept the notice referred to in note 6.1 above if it is received by MIB within 14 days from the dates referred to in notes 6.2 and 6.3.

6.5 In Scotland, proceedings are commenced at the date of service (see clause 1) so notice should already have been given under clause 9 and clause 10 does not apply there.

7. After service and before judgment

See Note 5.3 above.

7.1 Notice of the filing of a defence, of an amendment to the Statement or Particulars of Claim, and the setting down of the case for trial should be given not later than 7 days after the occurrence of such events and a copy of the document must be supplied (clause 11(1)).

7.2 However, by concession MIB will accept the notice referred to in note 7.1 above if it is received by MIB within 14 days after the proven date on which it was received by the claimant

7.3 MIB may request further information and documents to support the claim where it is not satisfied that the documents supplied with the application form are sufficient to enable it to assess its liability under the Agreement (see clause 11(2)).

7.4 If the claimant intends to sign or apply for judgment he must give MIB notice of the fact before doing so. This notice must be given at least 35 days before the application is to be made or the date when judgment is to be signed (see clause 12).

The 35 days notice does not apply where the court enters judgment of its own motion.

7.5 At no time must the claimant oppose MIB if it wishes to be joined as a party to proceedings and he must if requested consent to any application by MIB to be joined. Conflicts may arise between a Defendant and MIB which require MIB to become a Defendant or, in Scotland, a party Minuter if a defence is to be filed on its behalf (see clause 14(b)).

8. Interim payments

In substantial cases, the claimant may wish to apply for an interim payment. MIB will consider such applications on a voluntary basis but otherwise the claimant has the right to apply to the court for an interim payment order which, if granted, will be met by MIB.

9. After judgment

9.1 MIB's basic obligation normally arises if a judgment is not satisfied within 7 days after the claimant has become entitled to enforce it (see clause 1). However, that judgment may in certain circumstances be set aside and with it MIB's obligation to satisfy it. Sometimes MIB wishes to apply to set aside a judgment either wholly or partially. If MIB decides not to satisfy a judgment it will notify the claimant as soon as possible. Where a judgment is subsequently set aside, MIB will require the claimant to repay any sum previously paid by MIB to discharge its obligation under the Agreement (see clause 15(b)).

9.2 MIB is not obliged to satisfy a judgment unless the claimant has in return assigned the benefit to MIB or its nominee (see clause 15(a)). If such assignment is effected and if the subject matter of the judgment includes claims in respect of which MIB is not obliged to meet any judgment and if MIB effects any recovery on the judgment, the sum recovered will be divided between MIB and the claimant in proportion to the liabilities which were and which were not covered by MIB's obligation (see clause 21).

10. Permissible deductions from payments by MIB

10.1 Claims for loss and damage for which the claimant has been compensated or indemnified, e.g. under a contract of insurance or under the Policyholders Protection Act 1975, and which has not been taken into account in the judgment, may be deducted from the sum paid in settlement of MIB's obligation (see clause 17).

10.2 If there is a likelihood that the claimant will receive payment from such a source after the judgment has been satisfied by MIB, MIB will require him to undertake to repay any sum which duplicates the compensation assessed by the court (see clause 15(b)).

11. Untraced drivers

11.1 Where the owner or driver of a vehicle cannot be identified application may be made to MIB under the relevant Untraced Drivers Agreement. This provides, subject to specified conditions, for the payment of compensation for personal injury. It does not provide for compensation in respect of damage to property.

11.2 In those cases where it is unclear whether the owner or driver of a vehicle has been correctly identified it is sensible for the claimant to register a claim under both this Agreement and the Untraced Drivers Agreement following which MIB will advise which Agreement will, in its view, apply in the circumstances of the particular case.

The Untraced Drivers' Agreement Department of Transport Motor Insurers' Bureau (Compensation of Victims of Untraced Drivers)

14th February 2003

THIS AGREEMENT is made the seventh day of February 2003 between the SECRETARY OF STATE FOR TRANSPORT (hereinafter referred to as 'the Secretary of State') and the MOTOR INSURERS' BUREAU, whose registered office is at Linford Wood House 6–12 Capital Drive Linford Wood Milton Keynes MK14 6XT (hereinafter referred to as 'MIB').

IT IS HEREBY AGREED AS FOLLOWS:

INTERPRETATION

1. General interpretation

(1) In this Agreement, unless the context otherwise requires, the following expressions have the following meanings–

'1988 Act' means the Road Traffic Act 1988;

'1996 Agreement' means the Agreement made on 14 June 1996 between the Secretary of State for Transport and MIB providing for the compensation of victims of untraced drivers;

'1999 Agreement' means the Agreement dated 13th August 1999 made between the Secretary of State for the Environment, Transport and the Regions and MIB providing for the compensation of victims of uninsured drivers;

'applicant' means the person who has applied for compensation in respect of a death, bodily injury or damage to property (or the person on whose behalf such an application has been made) and 'application' means an application made by or on behalf of an applicant;

'arbitrator', where the arbitration takes place under Scottish law, includes an arbiter;

'award' means the aggregate of the sums which MIB is obliged to pay under this Agreement;

'bank holiday' means a day which is, or is to be observed as, a bank holiday under the Banking and Financial Dealings Act 1971;

'judgment' means, in relation to a court in Scotland, a court decree;

'property' means any property whether (in England and Wales) real or personal, or (in Scotland) heritable or moveable;

'relevant proceedings' means civil proceedings brought by the applicant (whether or not pursuant to a requirement made under this Agreement) against a person other than the unidentified person in respect of an event described in clause 4(1);

'specified excess' means £300 or such other sum as may from time to time be agreed in writing between the Secretary of State and MIB;

'unidentified person' means a person who is, or appears to be, wholly or partly liable in respect of the death, injury or damage to property to which an application relates and who cannot be identified.

(2) Save as otherwise herein provided, the Interpretation Act 1978 shall apply for the interpretation of this Agreement as it applies for the interpretation of an Act of Parliament.

(3) Where, under this Agreement, something is required to be done within a specified period after a date or the happening of a particular event, the period begins on the day after the happening of that event.

(4) Where, apart from this paragraph, the period in question, being a period of 7 days or less, would include a Saturday, Sunday, bank holiday, Christmas Day or Good Friday, that day shall be excluded.

(5) Save where expressly otherwise provided, a reference in this Agreement to a numbered clause is a reference to the clause bearing that number in this Agreement and a reference to a numbered paragraph is a reference to a paragraph bearing that number in the clause or schedule in which the reference occurs.

(6) In this Agreement–
   (a) a reference (however framed) to the doing of any act or thing by or the happening of any event in relation to the applicant includes a reference to the doing of that act or thing by or the happening of that event in relation to a Solicitor or other person acting on his behalf, and
   (b) a requirement to give notice or send documents to MIB shall, where MIB has appointed a Solicitor to act on its behalf in relation to the application, be satisfied by the giving of the notice or the sending of the documents, in the manner herein provided for, to that Solicitor.

2. Applicants' representatives

Where, under and in accordance with this Agreement–
   (a) any notice or other document is given to or by a Solicitor or other person acting on behalf of an applicant,
   (b) any act or thing is done by or in respect of such Solicitor or other person,
   (c) any decision is made by or in respect of such Solicitor or other person, or
   (d) any payment is made to such Solicitor or other person,

then, whatever may be the age or other circumstances affecting the capacity of the applicant, that act, thing, decision or payment shall be treated as if it had been done to or by, or made to or in respect of an applicant of full age and capacity.

APPLICATION OF AGREEMENT

3. Duration of Agreement

(1) This Agreement shall come into force on 14 February 2003.

(2) This Agreement may be determined by the Secretary of State or by MIB giving to the other not less than twelve months notice in writing to that effect.

(3) Notwithstanding the giving of notice of determination under paragraph (2) this Agreement shall continue to operate in respect of any application made in respect of death, bodily injury or damage to property arising from an event occurring on or before the date of termination specified in the notice.

4. Scope of Agreement

(1) Save as provided in clause 5, this Agreement applies where–
- (a) the death of, or bodily injury to, a person or damage to any property of a person has been caused by, or arisen out of, the use of a motor vehicle on a road or other public place in Great Britain, and
- (b) the event giving rise to the death, bodily injury or damage to property occurred on or after fourteenth day February 2003, and
- (c) the death, bodily injury or damage to property occurred in circumstances giving rise to liability of a kind which is required to be covered by a policy of insurance or a security under Part VI of the 1988 Act, and
- (d) it is not possible for the applicant–
  - (i) to identify the person who is, or appears to be, liable in respect of the death, injury or damage, or
  - (ii) (where more than one person is or appears to be liable) to identify any one or more of those persons, and
- (e) the applicant has made an application in writing to MIB for the payment of an award in respect of such death, bodily injury or damage to property (and in a case where they are applicable the requirements of paragraph (2) are satisfied), and
- (f) the conditions specified in paragraph (3), or such of those conditions as are relevant to the application, are satisfied.

(2) Where an application is signed by a person who is neither the applicant nor a Solicitor acting on behalf of the applicant MIB may refuse to accept the application (and shall incur no liability under this Agreement) until it is reasonably satisfied that, having regard to the status of the signatory and his relationship with the applicant, the applicant is fully aware of the content and effect of the application but subject thereto MIB shall not refuse to accept an application by reason only of the fact that it is signed by a person other than the applicant or his Solicitor.

(3) The conditions referred to in paragraph (1)(f) are that–
- (a) except in a case to which sub-paragraph (b) applies, the application must have been made not later than–
  - (i) three years after the date of the event which is the subject of the application in the case of a claim for compensation for death or bodily injury (whether or not damage to property has also arisen from the same event), or
  - (ii) nine months after the date of that event in the case of a claim for compensation for damage to property (whether or not death or bodily injury has also arisen from the same event);
- (b) in a case where the applicant could not reasonably have been expected to have become aware of the existence of bodily injury or damage to property, the application must have been made as soon as practicable after he did become (or ought reasonably to have become) aware of it and in any case not later than–

(i) fifteen years after the date of the event which is the subject of the application in the case of a claim for compensation for death or bodily injury (whether or not damage to property has also arisen from the same event), or

(ii) two years after the date of that event in the case of a claim for compensation for damage to property (whether or not death or bodily injury has also arisen from the same event);

(c) the applicant, or a person acting on the applicant's behalf, must have reported that event to the police–

(i) in the case of an event from which there has arisen a death or bodily injury alone, not later than 14 days after its occurrence, and

(ii) in the case of an event from which there has arisen property damage (whether or not a death or bodily injury has also arisen from it), not later than 5 days after its occurrence, but where that is not reasonably possible the event must have been reported as soon as reasonably possible;

(d) the applicant must produce satisfactory evidence of having made the report required under sub-paragraph (c) in the form of an acknowledgement from the relevant force showing the crime or incident number under which that force has recorded the matter;

(e) after making, or authorising the making of, a report to the police the applicant must have co-operated with the police in any investigation they have made into the event.

(4) Where both death or bodily injury and damage to property have arisen from a single event nothing contained in this clause shall require an applicant to make an application in respect of the death or bodily injury on the same occasion as an application in respect of the damage to property and where two applications are made in respect of one event the provisions of this Agreement shall apply separately to each of them.

5. Exclusions from Agreement

(1) This Agreement does not apply where an application is made in any of the following circumstances (so that where an application is made partly in such circumstances and partly in other circumstances, it applies only to the part made in those other circumstances)–

(a) where the applicant makes no claim for compensation in respect of death or bodily injury and the damage to property in respect of which compensation is claimed has been caused by, or has arisen out of, the use of an unidentified vehicle;

(b) where the death, bodily injury or damage to property in respect of which the application is made has been caused by or has arisen out of the use of a motor vehicle which at the time of the event giving rise to such death, injury or damage was owned by or in the possession of the Crown, unless at that time some other person had undertaken responsibility for bringing into existence a policy of insurance or security satisfying the requirements of the 1988 Act;

(c) where, at the time of the event in respect of which the application is made the person suffering death, injury or damage to property was voluntarily allowing himself to be carried in the responsible vehicle and before the commencement of his journey in the vehicle (or after such commencement if he could reasonably be expected to have alighted from the vehicle) he knew or ought to have known that the vehicle–

(i) had been stolen or unlawfully taken, or

(ii) was being used without there being in force in relation to its use a contract of insurance or security which complied with the 1988 Act; or

(iii) was being used in the course or furtherance of crime; or

(iv) was being used as a means of escape from or avoidance of lawful apprehension;

(d) where the death, bodily injury or damage to property was caused by, or in the course of, an act of terrorism;

(e) where property damaged as a result of the event giving rise to the application is insured against such damage and the applicant has recovered the full amount of his loss from the insurer on or before the date of the application (but without prejudice to the application of the Agreement in the case of any other claim for compensation made in respect of the same event);

(f) where a claim is made for compensation in respect of damage to a motor vehicle (or losses arising therefrom) and, at the time when the damage to it was sustained–

(i) there was not in force in relation to the use of that vehicle such a contract of insurance as is required by Part VI of the 1988 Act, and

(ii) the person suffering damage to property either knew or ought to have known that was the case (but without prejudice to the application of the Agreement in the case of any other claim for compensation made in respect of the same event);

(g) where the application is made neither by a person suffering injury or property damage nor by the personal representative of such a person nor by a dependant claiming in respect of the death of another person but is made in any of the following circumstances, namely–

(i) where a cause of action or a judgment has been assigned to the applicant, or

(ii) where the applicant is acting pursuant to a right of subrogation or a similar contractual or other right belonging to him.

(2) The burden of proving that the person suffering death, injury or damage to property knew or ought to have known of any matter set out in paragraph (1)(c) shall be on MIB but, in the absence of evidence to the contrary, proof by MIB of any of the following matters shall be taken as proof of his knowledge of the matter set out in paragraph (1)(c)(ii)–

(a) that he was the owner or registered keeper of the vehicle or had caused or permitted its use;

(b) that he knew the vehicle was being used by a person who was below the minimum age at which he could be granted a licence authorising the driving of a vehicle of that class;

(c) that he knew that the person driving the vehicle was disqualified for holding or obtaining a driving licence;

(d) that he knew that the user of the vehicle was neither its owner nor registered keeper nor an employee of the owner or registered keeper nor the owner or registered keeper of any other vehicle.

(3) Where–
(a) the application includes a claim for compensation both in respect of death or bodily injury and also in respect of damage to property, and
(b) the death or injury and the property damage has been caused by, or has arisen out of, the use of an unidentified vehicle,

the Agreement does not apply to the claim for compensation in respect of the damage to property.

(4) For the purposes of paragraphs (1) and (2)–
(a) references to a person being carried in a vehicle include references to his being carried in or upon, or entering or getting on to or alighting from the vehicle;
(b) knowledge which a person has or ought to have for the purposes of sub-paragraph (c) includes knowledge of matters which he could reasonably be expected to have been aware of had he not been under the self-induced influence of drink or drugs;
(c) 'crime' does not include the commission of an offence under the Traffic Acts, except an offence under section 143 (use of a motor vehicle on a road without there being in force a policy of insurance), and 'Traffic Acts' means the Road Traffic Regulation Act 1984, the Road Traffic Act 1988 and the Road Traffic Offenders Act 1988;
(d) 'responsible vehicle' means the vehicle the use of which caused (or through the use of which there arose) the death, bodily injury or damage to property which is the subject of the application;
(e) 'terrorism' has the meaning given in section 1 of the Terrorism Act 2000;
(f) 'dependant' has the same meaning as in section 1(3) of the Fatal Accidents Act 1976.

6. Limitation on application of Agreement

(1) This clause applies where an applicant receives compensation or other payment in respect of the death, bodily injury or damage to property otherwise than in the circumstances described in clause 5(1)(e) from any of the following persons–
(a) an insurer or under an insurance policy (other than a life assurance policy) or arrangement between the applicant or his employer and the insurer, or
(b) a person who has given a security pursuant to the requirements of 1988 Act under an agreement between the applicant and the security giver, or
(c) any other source other than a person who is an identified person for the purposes of clauses 13 to 15 or an insurer of, or a person who has given a security on behalf of, such a person.

(2) Where the compensation or other payment received is equal to or greater than the amount which MIB would otherwise be liable to pay under the provisions of clauses 8 and 9 MIB shall have no liability under those

provisions (to the intent that this Agreement shall immediately cease to apply except to the extent that the applicant is entitled to a contribution to his legal costs under clause 10).

(3) Where the compensation or other payment received is less than the amount which MIB would otherwise be liable to pay under the provisions of clauses 8 and 9 MIB's liability under those provisions shall be reduced by an amount equal to that compensation or payment.

PRINCIPAL TERMS AND CONDITIONS

7. MIB's obligation to investigate claims and determine amount of award

(1) MIB shall, at its own cost, take all reasonable steps to investigate the claim made in the application and–
 (a) if it is satisfied after conducting a preliminary investigation that the case is not one to which this Agreement applies and the application should be rejected, it shall inform the applicant accordingly and (subject to the following provisions of this Agreement) need take no further action, or
 (b) in any other case, it shall conduct a full investigation and shall as soon as reasonably practicable having regard to the availability of evidence make a report on the applicant's claim.

(2) Subject to the following paragraphs of this clause, MIB shall, on the basis of the report and, where applicable, any relevant proceedings–
 (a) reach a decision as to whether it must make an award to the applicant in respect of the death, bodily injury or damage to property, and
 (b) where it decides to make an award, determine the amount of that award.

(3) Where MIB reaches a decision that the Agreement applies and that it is able to calculate the whole amount of the award the report shall be treated as a full report and the award shall (subject to the following provisions of this Agreement) be treated as a full and final award.

(4) Where MIB reaches a decision that the Agreement applies and that it should make an award but further decides that it is not at that time able to calculate the final amount of the award (or a part thereof), it may designate the report as an interim report and where it does so–
 (a) it may, as soon as reasonably practicable, make one or more further interim reports, but
 (b) it must, as soon as reasonably practicable having regard to the availability of evidence, make a final report.

(5) Where it makes an interim or final report MIB shall, on the basis of that report and, where applicable, any relevant proceedings–
 (a) in the case of an interim report, determine the amount of any interim award it wishes to make, and
 (b) in the case of its final report, determine the whole amount of its award which shall (subject to the following provisions of this Agreement) be treated as a full and final award.

(6) MIB shall be under an obligation to make an award only if it is satisfied, on the balance of probabilities, that the death, bodily injury or damage to property was caused in such circumstances that the unidentified person would (had he been identified) have been held liable to pay damages to the applicant in respect of it.

(7) MIB shall determine the amount of its award in accordance with the provisions of clauses 8 to 10 and (in an appropriate case) clauses 12 to 14 but shall not thereby be under a duty to calculate the exact proportion of the award which represents compensation, interest or legal costs.

8. Compensation

(1) MIB shall include in its award to the applicant, by way of compensation for the death, bodily injury or damage to property, a sum equivalent to the amount which a court –
- (a) applying the law of England and Wales, in a case where the event giving rise to the death, injury or damage occurred in England or Wales, or
- (b) applying the law of Scotland, in a case where that event occurred in Scotland,

would have awarded to the applicant (where applying English law) as general and special damages or (where applying the law of Scotland) as solatium and patrimonial loss if the applicant had brought successful proceedings to enforce a claim for damages against the unidentified person.

(2) In calculating the sum payable under paragraph (1), MIB shall adopt the same method of calculation as the court would adopt in calculating damages but it shall be under no obligation to include in that calculation an amount in respect of loss of earnings suffered by the applicant to the extent that he has been paid wages or salary (or any sum in lieu of them) whether or not such payments were made subject to an agreement or undertaking on his part to repay the same in the event of his recovering damages for the loss of those earnings.

(3) Where an application includes a claim in respect of damage to property, MIB's liability in respect of that claim shall be limited in accordance with the following rules–
- (a) if the loss incurred by an applicant in respect of any one event giving rise to a claim does not exceed the specified excess, MIB shall incur no liability to that applicant in respect of that event;
- (b) if the aggregate of all losses incurred by both the applicant and other persons in respect of any one event giving rise to a claim ('the total loss') exceeds the specified excess but does not exceed £250,000–
  - (i) MIB's liability to an individual applicant shall be the amount of the claim less the specified excess, and
  - (ii) MIB's total liability to applicants in respect of claims arising from that event shall be the total loss less a sum equal to the specified excess multiplied by the number of applicants who have incurred loss through damage to property;
- (c) if the total loss exceeds £250,000–
  - (i) MIB's liability to an individual applicant shall not exceed the amount of the claim less the specified excess, and

(ii) MIB's total liability to applicants in respect of claims arising from that event shall be £250,000 less a sum equal to the specified excess multiplied by the number of applicants who have incurred loss due to property damage.

(4) MIB shall not be liable to pay compensation to an appropriate authority in respect of any loss incurred by that authority as a result of its failure to recover a charge for the recovery, storage or disposal of an abandoned vehicle under a power contained in the Refuse Disposal (Amenity) Act 1978 or Part VIII of the Road Traffic Regulation Act 1984 (and in this paragraph 'appropriate authority' has the meaning given in the Act under which the power to recover the charge was exercisable).

9. Interest

(1) MIB shall in an appropriate case also include in the award a sum representing interest on the compensation payable under clause 8 at a rate equal to that which a court–

(a) applying the law of England and Wales, in a case where the event giving rise to the death, bodily injury or damage to property occurred in England or Wales, or

(b) applying the law of Scotland, in a case where that event occurred in Scotland,

would have awarded to a successful applicant.

(2) MIB is not required by virtue of paragraph (1) to pay a sum representing interest in respect of the period before the date which is one month after the date on which MIB receives the police report (but, where MIB has failed to seek and obtain that report promptly after the date of the application, interest shall run from the date which falls one month after the date on which it would have received it had it acted promptly).

10. Contribution towards legal costs

(1) MIB shall, in a case where it has decided to make a compensation payment under clause 8, also include in the award a sum by way of contribution towards the cost of obtaining legal advice from a Solicitor, Barrister or Advocate in respect of–

(a) the making of an application under this Agreement;

(b) the correctness of a decision made by MIB under this Agreement; or

(c) the adequacy of an award (or a part thereof) offered by MIB under this Agreement

that sum to be determined in accordance with the Schedule to this Agreement.

(2) MIB shall not be under a duty to make a payment under paragraph (1) unless it is satisfied that the applicant did obtain legal advice in respect of any one or more of the matters specified in that paragraph.

11. Conditions precedent to MIB's obligations

(1) The applicant must–

(a) make his application in such form,

(b) provide in support of the application such statements and other information (whether in writing or orally at interview), and
(c) give such further assistance,

as may reasonably be required by MIB or by any person acting on MIB's behalf to enable an investigation to be carried out under clause 7 of this Agreement.

(2) The applicant must provide MIB with written authority to take all such steps as may be reasonably necessary in order to carry out a proper investigation of the claim.

(3) The applicant must, if MIB reasonably requires him to do so before reaching a decision under clause 7, provide MIB with a statutory declaration, made by him, setting out to the best of his knowledge and belief all the facts and circumstances upon which his application is based or such facts and circumstances in relation to the application as MIB may reasonably specify.

(4) The applicant must, if MIB reasonably requires him to do so before it reaches a decision or determination under clause 7 and subject to the following provisions of this clause–
(a) at MIB's option (and subject to paragraph (5)) either–
(i) bring proceedings against any person or persons who may, in addition or alternatively to the unidentified person, be liable to the applicant in respect of the death, bodily injury or damage to property (by virtue of having caused or contributed to that death, injury or damage, by being vicariously liable in respect of it or having failed to effect third party liability insurance in respect of the vehicle in question) and co-operate with MIB in taking such steps as are reasonably necessary to obtain judgment in those proceedings, or
(ii) authorise MIB to bring such proceedings and take such steps in the applicant's name;
(b) at MIB's expense, provide MIB with a transcript of any official shorthand or recorded note taken in those proceedings of any evidence given or judgment delivered therein;
(c) assign to MIB or to its nominee the benefit of any judgment obtained by him (whether or not obtained in proceedings brought under sub-paragraph (a) above) in respect of the death, bodily injury or damage to property upon such terms as will secure that MIB or its nominee will be accountable to the applicant for any amount by which the aggregate of all sums recovered by MIB or its nominee under the judgment (after deducting all reasonable expenses incurred in effecting recovery) exceeds the award made by MIB under this Agreement in respect of that death, injury or damage;
(d) undertake to assign to MIB the right to any sum which is or may be due from an insurer, security giver or other person by way of compensation for, or benefit in respect of, the death, bodily injury or damage to property and which would (if payment had been made before the date of the award) have excluded or limited MIB's liability under the provisions of clause 6.

(5) If, pursuant to paragraph (4)(a), MIB requires the applicant to bring proceedings or take steps against any person or persons (or to authorise MIB to bring such proceedings or take such steps in his name) MIB shall

indemnify the applicant against all costs and expenses reasonably incurred by him in complying with that requirement.

(6) Where the applicant, without having been required to do so by MIB, has commenced proceedings against any person described in paragraph (4)(a) –
  (a) the applicant shall as soon as reasonably possible notify MIB of such proceedings and provide MIB with such further information about them as MIB may reasonably require, and
  (b) the applicant's obligations in paragraph (4)(a) to (c) shall apply in respect of such proceedings as if they had been brought at MIB's request.

JOINT AND SEVERAL LIABILITY

12. Joint and several liability: interpretation

In clauses 13 to 15–

'identified person' includes an identified employer or principal of a person who is himself unidentified;

'original judgment' means a judgment obtained against an identified person at first instance in relevant proceedings;

'three month period' means the period of three months specified in clause 13(3); and

'unidentified person's liability' means–
  (a) the amount of the contribution which (if not otherwise apparent) would, on the balance of probabilities, have been be recoverable from the unidentified person in an action brought –
    (i) in England and Wales, under the Civil Liability (Contribution) Act 1978, or
    (ii) in Scotland, under the Law Reform (Miscellaneous Provisions) (Scotland) Act 1940, by an identified person who had been held liable in full in an earlier action brought by the applicant, and
  (b) where a court has awarded the applicant interest or costs in addition to damages, an appropriate proportion of that interest or those costs.

13. MIB's liability where wrongdoer is identified

(1) This clause applies where the death, bodily injury or damage to property in respect of which the application is made is caused, or appears on the balance of probabilities to have been caused–
  (a) partly by an unidentified person and partly by an identified person, or
  (b) partly by an unidentified person and partly by another unidentified person whose employer or principal is identified,

in circumstances making (or appearing to make) the identified person liable, or vicariously liable, to the applicant in respect of the death, injury or damage.

(2) Where this clause applies, MIB's liability under this Agreement shall not exceed the unidentified person's liability and the following provisions shall apply to determine MIB's liability in specific cases.

(3) Where the applicant has obtained a judgment in relevant proceedings in respect of the death, injury or damage which has not been satisfied in full by or on behalf of the identified person within the period of three months after the date on which the applicant became entitled to enforce it–
- (a) if that judgment is wholly unsatisfied within the three month period MIB shall make an award equal to the unidentified person's liability;
- (b) if the judgment is satisfied in part only within the three month period, MIB shall make an award equal to–
  - (i) the unsatisfied part, if it does not exceed the unidentified person's liability; and
  - (ii) the unidentified person's liability, if the unsatisfied part exceeds the unidentified person's liability.

(4) A judgment given in any relevant proceedings against an identified person shall be conclusive as to any issue determined in those proceedings which is relevant to the determination of MIB's liability under this Agreement.

(5) Where the applicant has not obtained (or been required by MIB to obtain) a judgment in respect of the death, injury or damage against the identified person but has received an agreed payment from the identified person in respect of the death, bodily injury or damage to property, that payment shall be treated for the purposes of this Agreement as a full settlement of the applicant's claim and MIB shall be under no liability under this Agreement in respect thereof.

(6) Where the applicant has not obtained (or been required by MIB to obtain) a judgment in respect of the death, injury or damage against the identified person nor received any payment by way of compensation in respect thereof from the identified person MIB shall make an award equal to the unidentified person's liability.

14. Appeals by identified persons

(1) This clause applies where an appeal against, or other proceeding to set aside, the original judgment is commenced within the three month period.

(2) If, as a result of the appeal or other proceeding–
- (a) the applicant ceases to be entitled to receive any payment in respect of the death, bodily injury or damage to property from any identified person, clause 13 shall apply as if he had neither obtained nor been required by MIB to obtain a judgment against that person;
- (b) the applicant becomes entitled to recover an amount different from that which he was entitled to recover under the original judgment the provisions of clause 13(3) shall apply, but as if for each of the references therein to the original judgment there were substituted a reference to the judgment in that appeal or other proceeding;
- (c) the applicant remains entitled to enforce the original judgment the provisions of clause 13(3) shall apply, but as if for each of the references therein to the three month period there were substituted a reference to the period of three months after the date on which the appeal or other proceeding was disposed of.

(3) Where the judgment in the appeal or other proceeding is itself the subject of a further appeal or similar proceeding the provisions of this clause shall

apply in relation to that further appeal or proceeding in the same manner as they apply in relation to the first appeal or proceeding.

(4) Nothing in this clause shall oblige MIB to make a payment to the applicant until the appeal or other proceeding has been determined.

15. Compensation recovered under Uninsured Drivers Agreements

(1) Where, in a case to which clause 13 applies, judgment in the relevant proceedings is given against an identified person in circumstances which render MIB liable to satisfy that judgment under any of the Uninsured Drivers Agreements, MIB shall not be under any liability under this Agreement in respect of the event to which the relevant proceedings relate.

(2) In this clause 'Uninsured Drivers Agreements' means–
- (a) the Agreement dated 21st December 1988 made between the Secretary of State for Transport and MIB providing for the compensation of victims of uninsured drivers,
- (b) the 1999 Agreement, and
- (c) any agreement made between the Secretary of State and MIB (or their respective successors) which supersedes (whether immediately or otherwise) the 1999 Agreement.

NOTIFICATION OF DECISION AND PAYMENT OF AWARD

16. Notification of decision

MIB shall give the applicant notice of a decision or determination under clause 7 in writing and when so doing shall provide him–
- (a) if the application is rejected because a preliminary investigation has disclosed that it is not one made in a case to which this Agreement applies, with a statement to that effect;
- (b) if the application has been fully investigated, with a statement setting out–
  - (i) all the evidence obtained during the investigation, and
  - (ii) MIB's findings of fact from that evidence which are relevant to the decision;
- (c) if it has decided to make an interim award on the basis of an interim report under clause 7(4), with a copy of the report and a statement of the amount of the interim award;
- (d) if it has decided to make a full report under clause 7(3) or a final report under clause 7(4)(b), with a copy of the report and a statement of the amount of the full and final award;
- (e) in a case to which clause 13 applies, with a statement setting out the way in which the amount of the award has been computed under the provisions of that clause; and
- (f) in every case, with a statement of its reasons for making the decision or determination.

17. Acceptance of decision and payment of award

(1) Subject to the following paragraphs of this clause, if MIB gives notice to the applicant that it has decided to make an award to him, it shall pay him that award–

(a) in the case of an interim award made pursuant to clause 7(5)(a), as soon as reasonably practicable after the making of the interim report to which the award relates;

(b) in the case of a full and final award made pursuant to clause 7(3) or (5)(b)–

(i) where the applicant notifies MIB in writing that he accepts the offer of the award unconditionally, not later than 14 days after the date on which MIB receives that acceptance, or

(ii) where the applicant does not notify MIB of his acceptance in accordance with sub-paragraph (a) but the period during which he may give notice of an appeal under clause 19 has expired without such notice being given, not later than 14 days after the date of expiry of that period,

and that payment shall discharge MIB from all liability under this Agreement in respect of the death, bodily injury or damage to property for which the award is made.

(2) MIB may, upon notifying an applicant of its decision to make an award, offer to pay the award in instalments in accordance with a structure described in the decision letter (the 'structured settlement') and if the applicant notifies MIB in writing of his acceptance of the offer–

(a) the first instalment of the payment under the structured settlement shall be made not later than 14 days after the date on which MIB receives that acceptance, and

(b) subsequent payments shall be made in accordance with the agreed structure.

(3) Where an applicant has suffered bodily injury and believes either that there is a risk that he will develop a disease or condition other than that in respect of which he has made a claim or that a disease or condition in respect of which he has made a claim will deteriorate, he may–

(a) by notice given in his application, or

(b) by notice in writing received by MIB before the date on which MIB issues notification of its full or (as the case may be) final report under clause 16,

state that he wishes MIB to make a provisional award and if he does so paragraphs (4) and (5) shall apply.

(4) The applicant must specify in the notice given under paragraph (3)–

(a) each disease and each type of deterioration which he believes may occur, and

(b) the period during or within which he believes it may occur.

(5) Where MIB receives a notice under paragraph (3) it shall, not later than 14 days after the date of such receipt (or within such longer period as the applicant may agree)–

(a) accept the notice and confirm that any award it makes (other than an interim award made pursuant to clause 7(5)(a)) is to be treated as a provisional award, or

(b) reject the notice and inform the applicant that it is not willing to make a provisional award.

(6) Where MIB has notified the applicant that it accepts the notice, an award which would otherwise be treated a full or final award under this Agreement shall be treated as a provisional award only and the applicant may make a supplementary application under this Agreement but–
(a) only in respect of a disease or a type of deterioration of his condition specified in his notice, and
(b) not later than the expiration of the period specified in his notice.

(7) Where MIB has notified the applicant that it rejects the notice, subject to any decision to the contrary made by an arbitrator, no award which MIB makes shall be treated as a provisional award.

APPEALS AGAINST MIB'S DECISION

18. Right of appeal

Where an applicant is not willing to accept–
(a) a decision or determination made by MIB under clause 7 or a part thereof, or
(b) a proposal for a structured settlement or a rejection of the applicant's request for a provisional award under clause 17,

he may give notice (a 'notice of appeal') that he wishes to submit the matter to arbitration in accordance with the provisions of clauses 19 to 25.

19. Notice of appeal

(1) A notice of appeal shall be given in writing to MIB at any time before the expiration of a period of 6 weeks from–
(a) the date on which the applicant receives notice of MIB's decision under clause 16;
(b) where he disputes a notification given under clause 17(5)(b), the date when such notification is given;
(c) in any other case, the date on which he is given notification of the decision, determination or requirement.

(2) The notice of appeal–
(a) shall state the grounds on which the appeal is made,
(b) shall contain the applicant's observations on MIB's decision,
(c) may be accompanied by such further evidence in support of the appeal as the applicant thinks fit, and
(d) shall contain an undertaking that (subject, in the case of an arbitration to be conducted England and Wales, to his rights under sections 67 and 68 of the Arbitration Act 1996) the applicant will abide by the decision of the arbitrator made under this Agreement.

20. Procedure following notice of appeal

(1) Not later than 7 days after receiving the notice of appeal MIB shall–

(a) apply to the Secretary of State for the appointment of a single arbitrator, or
(b) having notified the applicant of its intention to do so, cause an investigation to be made into any further evidence supplied by the applicant and report to the applicant upon that investigation and of any change in its decision which may result from it.

(2) Where the only ground stated in the notice of appeal is that the award is insufficient (including a ground contesting the degree of contributory negligence attributed to the applicant or, as the case may be, the person in respect of whose death the application is made), MIB may give notice to the applicant of its intention, if the appeal proceeds to arbitration, to ask the arbitrator to decide whether its award exceeds what a court would have awarded or whether the case is one in which it would make an award at all and shall in that notice set out such observations on that matter as MIB considers relevant to the arbitrator's decision.

(3) Where MIB has made a report under paragraph (1)(b) or given to the applicant notice under paragraph (2), the applicant may, not later than 6 weeks after the date on which the report or (as the case may be) the notice was given to him–
(a) notify MIB that he wishes to withdraw the appeal, or
(b) notify MIB that he wishes to continue with the appeal and send with that notification–
(i) any observations on the report made under paragraph (1)(b) which he wishes to have drawn to the attention of the arbitrator,
(ii) any observations on the contents of the notice given under paragraph (2), including any further evidence not previously made available to MIB and relevant to the matter, which he wishes to have drawn to the attention of the arbitrator.

(4) Where the applicant notifies MIB under paragraph (3)(b) of his wish to continue the appeal, or if the applicant fails within the specified period of 6 weeks to give notification of his wish either to withdraw or to continue with the appeal, MIB shall, not later than 7 days after receiving the notification or 7 days after the expiry of the said period (as the case may be)–
(a) apply to the Secretary of State for the appointment of an arbitrator, or
(b) having notified the applicant of its intention to do so, cause a further investigation to be made into the further evidence sent under paragraph (3)(b)(ii).

(5) Where MIB has caused an investigation to be made into any further evidence supplied by the applicant under paragraph (3)(b)(ii), it shall report to the applicant upon that investigation and of any change in a decision or determination made under clause 7 which may result from it and the applicant may, not later than 6 weeks after the date on which he receives the report–
(a) notify MIB that he wishes to withdraw the appeal, or
(b) notify MIB that he wishes to continue with the appeal.

(6) Where the applicant notifies MIB under paragraph (5)(b) of his wish to continue the appeal, or if the applicant fails within the specified period of 6 weeks to give notification of his wish either to withdraw or to continue with the appeal, MIB shall not later than 7 days after receiving the notification or

7 days after the expiry of the said period (as the case may be) apply to the Secretary of State for the appointment of an arbitrator.

(7) When applying to the Secretary of State for the appointment of an arbitrator MIB may send with the application such written observations as it wishes to make upon the applicant's notice of appeal but must at the same time send a copy of those observations to the applicant.

21. Appointment of arbitrator

(1) In the event of MIB neither applying to the Secretary of State for the appointment of an arbitrator in accordance with the provisions of clause 20 nor taking such further steps as it may at its discretion take in accordance with that clause, the applicant may apply to the Secretary of State for the appointment of an arbitrator.

(2) For the purposes of the Arbitration Act 1996 (where the arbitration is to be conducted in England and Wales) the arbitral proceedings are to be regarded as commencing on the date of the making of the application by the Secretary of State or the applicant (as the case may be).

(3) The Secretary of State shall, upon the making of an application for the appointment of an arbitrator to hear the appeal, appoint the first available member, by rotation, of a panel of Queen's Counsel appointed for the purpose of determining appeals under this Agreement (where the event giving rise to the death, bodily injury or damage to property occurred in England and Wales) by the Lord Chancellor or (where the event giving rise to the death, bodily injury or damage to property occurred in Scotland) by the Lord Advocate and shall forthwith notify the applicant and MIB of the appointment.

22. Arbitration procedure

(1) Upon receiving notification from the Secretary of State of the appointment of an arbitrator, MIB shall send to the arbitrator–
  (a) the notice of appeal,
  (b) (if appropriate) its request for a decision as to whether its award exceeds what a court would have awarded or whether the case is one in which it would make an award at all,
  (c) copies of–
    (i) the applicant's application,
    (ii) its decision; and
    (iii) all statements, declarations, notices, reports, observations and transcripts of evidence made or given under this Agreement by the applicant or MIB.

(2) The arbitrator may, if it appears to him to be necessary or expedient for the purpose of resolving any issue, ask MIB to make a further investigation and to submit a written report of its findings to him for his consideration and in such a case–
  (a) MIB shall undertake the investigation and send copies of the report to the arbitrator and the applicant,

(b) the applicant may, not later than 4 weeks after the date on which a copy of the report is received by him, submit written observations on it to the arbitrator and if he does so he shall send a copy of those observations to MIB.

(3) The arbitrator shall, after considering the written submissions referred to in paragraphs (1) and (2), send to the applicant and MIB a preliminary decision letter setting out the decision he proposes to make under clause 23 and his reasons for doing so.

(4) Not later than 28 days after the date of sending of the preliminary decision letter (or such later date as the applicant and MIB may agree) the applicant and MIB may, by written notification given to the arbitrator and copied to the other, either–

(a) accept the preliminary decision, or

(b) submit written observations upon the preliminary decision or the reasons or both, or

(c) request an oral hearing,

and if either of them should within that period fail to do any of those things (including a failure to provide the other person with a copy of his notification) he or it shall be treated as having accepted the decision.

(5) If the applicant submits new evidence with any written observations under paragraph (4)(b) MIB may at its discretion, but within 28 days or such longer period as the arbitrator may allow, do any of the following–

(a) make an investigation into that evidence,

(b) submit its own written observations on that evidence, and

(c) if it has not already done so, request an oral hearing,

and, except where an oral hearing has been requested, the arbitrator shall (in exercise of his powers under section 34 of the Arbitration Act 1996 if the arbitration is being conducted in England and Wales) determine whether, and if so how, such evidence shall be admitted and tested.

(6) If both the applicant and MIB accept the reasoned preliminary decision that decision shall be treated as his final decision for the purposes of clause 23 (so that clause 23(2) shall not then apply) but if either of them submits observations on that decision the arbitrator must take those observations into account before making a final decision.

(7) If the applicant or MIB requests an oral hearing, the arbitrator shall determine the appeal in that manner and in such a case–

(a) the hearing shall be held in public unless the applicant requests that it (or any part of it) be heard in private;

(b) the hearing shall take place at a location–

(i) in England or Wales, where the event giving rise to the death, bodily injury or damage to property occurred in England or Wales and the applicant is resident in England or Wales,

(ii) in Scotland, where the event giving rise to the death, bodily injury or damage to property occurred in Scotland and the applicant is resident in Scotland, or

(iii) in England, Wales or Scotland in any other case, which in the opinion of the arbitrator (after consultation with each of them) is convenient for both MIB and the applicant as well as for himself;

- (c) a party to the hearing may be represented by a lawyer or other person of that party's choosing;
- (d) a party to the hearing shall be entitled to address the arbitrator, to call witnesses and to put questions to those witnesses and any other person called as a witness.

23. Arbitrator's decision

(1) The arbitrator, having regard to the subject matter of the proceedings, may in an appropriate case–

- (a) determine whether or not the case is one to which this Agreement applies;
- (b) remit the application to MIB for a full investigation and a decision in accordance with the provisions of this Agreement;
- (c) determine whether MIB should make an award under this Agreement and if so what that award should be;
- (d) determine such other questions as have been referred to him as he thinks fit;
- (e) (subject to the provisions of paragraph (4) of this clause and clause 24) order that the costs of the proceedings shall be paid by one party or allocated between the parties in such proportions as he thinks fit;

and where the arbitrator makes a determination under sub-paragraph (a) that the case is one to which this Agreement applies, all the provisions of this Agreement shall apply as if the case were one to which clause 7(1)(b) applies.

(2) The arbitrator shall notify MIB and the applicant of his decision in writing.

(3) MIB shall pay to the applicant any amount which the arbitrator has decided shall be awarded to him, and that payment shall discharge MIB from all liability under this Agreement in respect of the death, bodily injury or damage to property in respect of which that decision is given.

(4) Where an oral hearing has taken place at the request of the applicant and the arbitrator is satisfied that it was unnecessary and that the matter could have been decided on the basis of the written submissions referred to in clause 22(1) and (2) he shall take that into account when making an order under paragraph (1)(e).

24. Payment of arbitrator's fee and costs of legal representation

(1) Subject to paragraph (2), MIB shall upon being notified of the decision of the arbitrator pay the arbitrator a fee approved by the Lord Chancellor or the Lord Advocate, as the case may be, after consultation with MIB.

(2) In a case where it appears to the arbitrator that, having regard to all the surrounding circumstances of the case, there were no reasonable grounds for making the appeal or bringing the question before him, the arbitrator may, in his discretion, order–

- (a) the applicant or,
- (b) where he considers it appropriate to do so, any Solicitor or other person acting on behalf of the applicant,

to reimburse MIB the fee it has paid to the arbitrator or any part thereof.

(3) Where, pursuant to paragraph (2), the arbitrator orders–
  (a) the applicant to reimburse MIB, MIB may deduct an amount equal to the fee from any amount which it pays to the applicant to discharge its liability under this Agreement;
  (b) a Solicitor or other person to reimburse MIB, MIB may deduct an amount equal to the fee from any amount which it pays to that Solicitor or other person to discharge its liability to the applicant under this Agreement.

(4) Where there is an oral hearing and the applicant secures an award of compensation greater than that previously offered, then (unless the arbitrator orders otherwise) MIB shall make a contribution of £500 per half day towards the cost incurred by the applicant in respect of representation by a Solicitor, Barrister or Advocate.

25. Applicants under a disability

(1) If in any case it appears to MIB that, by reason of the applicant being a minor or of any other circumstance affecting his capacity to manage his affairs, it would be in the applicant's interest that all or some part of the award should be administered for him by an appropriate representative, MIB may establish for that purpose a trust of the whole or part of the award (such trust to take effect for such period and under such provisions as appears to MIB to be appropriate in the circumstances of the case) or, as the case may be, initiate or cause any other person in initiate the proceedings necessary to have the award administered by an appropriate representative and otherwise cause any amount payable under the award to be paid to and administered by the appropriate representative.

(2) In this clause 'appropriate representative' means–
  (a) in England and Wales–
    (i) the Family Welfare Association, or a similar body or person, as trustee of the trust, or
    (ii) the Court of Protection; and
  (b) in Scotland–
    (i) a Judicial Factor, or
    (ii) a guardian under the Adults with Incapacity (Scotland) Act 2000, or
    (iii) (where the applicant is a child) the tutor or curator of the child or a person having parental responsibilities under the Children (Scotland) Act 1995.

ACCELERATED PROCEDURE

26. Instigation of accelerated procedure

(1) In any case where, after making a preliminary investigation under clause 7, MIB has decided that–
  (a) the case is one to which this Agreement applies, and
  (b) it is not one to which clause 13, applies,

MIB may notify the applicant of that decision and, instead of causing a full investigation and report to be made under clause 7, may make to the applicant an offer to settle his claim by payment of an award specified in the offer representing compensation assessed in accordance with clause 8 together, in an appropriate case, with interest thereon assessed in accordance with clause 9 and a contribution towards the cost of obtaining legal advice in respect of the making of the application.

(2) Where an offer is made under paragraph (1), MIB shall send to the applicant a statement setting out–
   (a) the relevant evidence it has collected disclosing the circumstances in which the death, bodily injury or damage to property occurred, and
   (b) its reasons for the assessment of the award.

27. Settlement by accelerated procedure

(1) The applicant shall not later than 6 weeks after he receives an offer under clause 26 notify MIB of his acceptance or rejection thereof.

(2) Where the applicant notifies MIB of his acceptance of the offer–
   (a) MIB shall not later than 14 days after receipt of the acceptance pay to the applicant the amount of the award, and
   (b) MIB shall be discharged from all liability under this Agreement in respect of the death, bodily injury or damage to property for which that payment is made.

(3) In the event of the applicant failing to accept the offer within the specified period, the application shall be treated as one to which clause 7(1)(b) applies.

MISCELLANEOUS

28. Referral of disputes to arbitrator

(1) Any dispute between the applicant and MIB concerning a decision, determination or requirement made by MIB under the terms of this Agreement, other than a dispute relating to MIB's decision for which provision is made by clause 18, shall be referred to and determined by an arbitrator.

(2) Where an applicant wishes to refer such a dispute to arbitration, he shall not later than 4 weeks after the decision, determination or requirement is communicated to him, give notice to MIB that he wishes the matter to be so resolved.

(3) For the purposes of the Arbitration Act 1996 (where the arbitration is to be conducted in England and Wales) the arbitral proceedings are to be regarded as commencing on the date of such application.

(4) Upon receipt of the applicant's notice MIB shall apply immediately to the Secretary of State for the appointment of an arbitrator and in the event of MIB failing to do so the applicant may make the application.

(5) The Secretary of State shall, upon receiving the application for the appointment of an arbitrator to hear the appeal, appoint the first available member,

by rotation, of a panel of Queen's Counsel appointed for the purpose of determining appeals under this Agreement (where the event giving rise to the death, bodily injury or damage to property occurred in England and Wales) by the Lord Chancellor or (where the event giving rise to the death, bodily injury or damage to property occurred in Scotland) by the Lord Advocate and shall forthwith notify the applicant and MIB of the appointment.

(6) The applicant and MIB shall, not later than 4 weeks after receiving notification of the appointment of the arbitrator, submit to him a written statement of their respective cases with supporting documentary evidence where available.

(7) Subject to paragraphs (8) to (10), the arbitrator shall decide the appeal on the documents submitted to him under paragraph (6) and no further evidence shall be produced to him.

(8) The applicant may, by notice in writing given to the arbitrator and MIB not later than the date on which he submits the statement of his case, ask the arbitrator to determine the appeal by means of an oral hearing and shall submit to the arbitrator and MIB a written statement, with supporting documentary evidence where appropriate, in support of that request.

(9) The arbitrator shall in such a case seek the view of MIB on the need for an oral hearing and MIB may submit to the arbitrator and the applicant a written statement, with supporting documentary evidence where appropriate, in support of its view.

(10) If, after considering those written submissions, the arbitrator decides that an oral hearing is necessary to determine the dispute–

(a) the hearing shall be held in public unless the applicant requests that it (or any part of it) be heard in private;

(b) the hearing shall take place at a location–

(i) in England or Wales, where the event giving rise to the death, bodily injury or damage to property occurred in England or Wales and the applicant is resident in England or Wales,

(ii) in Scotland, where the event giving rise to the death, bodily injury or damage to property occurred in Scotland and the applicant is resident in Scotland, or

(iii) in England, Wales or Scotland in any other case, which in the opinion of the arbitrator (after consultation with each of them) is convenient for both MIB and the applicant as well as for himself;

(c) a party to the hearing may be represented by a lawyer or other person of that party's choosing;

(d) a party to the hearing shall be entitled to address the arbitrator, to call witnesses and to put questions to those witnesses and any other person called as a witness.

(11) The arbitrator may, having regard to the subject matter of the proceedings and in an appropriate case, order that his fee or the costs of the proceedings (as determined according to clause 10(1)(b) of, and the Schedule to, this Agreement) or both his fee and those costs shall be paid by one party or allocated between the parties in such proportions as he thinks fit.

(12) Unless otherwise agreed, the decision, determination or requirement in respect of which notice is given under paragraph (2) shall stand unless reversed by the arbitrator.

29. Services of notices, etc, on MIB

Any notice required to be served on or any other notification or document required to be given or sent to MIB under the terms of this Agreement shall be sufficiently served or given sent by fax or by Registered or Recorded Delivery post to MIB's registered office and delivery shall be proved by the production of a fax report produced by the sender's fax machine or an appropriate postal receipt.

30. Agents

MIB may perform any of its obligations under this Agreement by agents.

31. Contracts (Rights of Third Parties) Act 1999

(1) For the purposes of the Contracts (Rights of Third Parties) Act 1999 the following provisions shall apply.

(2) This Agreement may be–
 (a) varied or rescinded without the consent of any person other than the parties hereto, and
 (b) determined under clause 3(2) without the consent of any such person.

(3) Save for the matters specified in paragraph (4), MIB shall not have available to it against an applicant any matter by way of counterclaim or set-off which would have been available to it if the applicant rather than the Secretary of State had been a party to this Agreement.

(4) The matters referred to in paragraph (3) are any counterclaim or set-off arising by virtue of the provisions of–
 (a) this Agreement;
 (b) the 1996 Agreement;
 (c) the 1999 Agreement;
 (d) either of the agreements which were respectively superseded by the 1996 Agreement and the 1999 Agreement.

(5) This agreement, being made for the purposes of Article 1(4) of Council Directive 84/5/EEC of 30th December 1983–
 (a) is intended to confer a benefit on an applicant but on no other person, and
 (b) to confer such benefit subject to the terms and conditions set out herein.

32. Enforcement against MIB

If MIB fail to pay compensation in accordance with the provisions of this agreement the applicant is entitled to enforce payment through the courts.

33. Transitional provisions

The 1996 Agreement shall cease to have effect after the 13 February 2003 but shall continue in force in relation to any claim arising out of an event occurring on or before that date.

IN WITNESS whereof the Secretary of State has caused his Corporate Seal to be hereunto affixed and the Motor Insurer's Bureau has caused its Common Seal to be hereunto affixed the day and year first above written.

SCHEDULE

MIB's Contribution Towards Applicant's Legal Costs

1. Subject to paragraph 4, MIB shall pay a contribution towards the applicant's costs of obtaining legal advice determined in accordance with paragraph 2,

2. That amount shall be the aggregate of–
   (a) the fee specified in column (2) of the table below in relation to the amount of the award specified in column (1) of that table,
   (b) the amount of value added tax charged on that fee,
   (c) where the applicant has opted for an oral hearing under clause and
   (d) reasonable disbursements.

TABLE

Amount of the award (1)	**Specified fee (2)**
Not exceeding £150,000	15% of the amount of the award, subject to a minimum of £500 and a maximum of £3000
Exceeding £150,000	2% of the amount of the award

3. For the purposes of paragraph 2–
   'amount of the award' means the aggregate of the sum awarded by way of compensation and interest under clauses 8 and 9, before deduction of any reimbursement due to be paid to the Secretary of State for Work and Pensions through the Compensation Recovery Unit (CRU) of his Department (or to any successor of that unit), but excluding the amount of any payment due in respect of benefits and hospital charges.
   'reasonable disbursements' means reasonable expenditure incurred on the applicant's behalf and agreed between the applicant and MIB before it is incurred (MIB's agreement not having been unreasonably withheld) but includes Counsel's fees only where the applicant is a minor or under a legal disability.

4. The foregoing provisions of this Schedule are without prejudice to MIB's liability under the provisions of this Agreement to pay the costs of arbitration proceedings or an arbitrator's fee.

THE CORPORATE SEAL of the Secretary of State FOR TRANSPORT hereunto affixed is authenticated by:
Richard Jones
Authorised by the Secretary of State

THE COMMON SEAL of the Motor Insurers' BUREAU was hereunto affixed in the presence of:

J.A. Read and R.D. Snook
Directors of the Board of Management
B Louisy
Secretary

Index

[all references are to paragraph number]